THE POLITICAL PLANS OF MEXICO

Thomas B. Davis
Professor Emeritus of Hunter College (CUNY)

Amado Ricon Virulegio
The College of Staten Island (CUNY)

UNIVERSITY
PRESS OF
AMERICA

Copyright © 1987 by

University Press of America,® Inc.

4720 Boston Way
Lanham, MD 20706

Library of Congress Cataloging-in-Publication Data

Davis, Thomas B. (Thomas Brabson), 1905-
The political plans of Mexico.

Includes bibliographical references and index.
1. Mexico—Politics and government—19th century.
2. Mexico—Politics and government—20th century.
3. Mexico—Constitutional history.   I. Ricon, Amado.
II. Title.
F1231.5.D38   1987   320.972   87-10568
ISBN 0-8191-6426-7 (alk. paper)

All University Press of America books are produced on acid-free
paper which exceeds the minimum standards set by the National
Historical Publication and Records Commission.

To The MEXICAN PEOPLE

whose national turmoil induced the Plans

whose political genius surpassed them.

TABLE OF CONTENTS

ACKNOWLEDGEMENTS

hen editors of a historical research program assume their
abors, they soon discover that they must engage the supportive
fforts of others, often persons uncounted and anonymous. To
he Staff of the vast New York Public Library we can only
ecord our thanks for their quiet competence in providing
aterials on call. The same can be said for the Library of
ongress. We are particularly indebted to its Photographic
ivision for prompt and competent deliveries which met every
eed and materially reduced the cost of our labors. The Yale
einicke Rare Book Staff proved models of intelligent
ccomodation. As every researcher knows, the Latin American
ollection at the University of Texas is nothing less than a
reasure trove in Mexican sources, and that Miss Nettie Lee
enson, its guide and administrator, embodies the very soul of
enerous counsel. For her understanding and helpfulness we are
ost thankful. We remain indebted to Mrs. Davis and Mrs.
icon, our respective wives, who were very supportive of our
ndeavour.

e are very grateful to our dear friend and colleague, Prof.
milio Conzalez Lopez for his unfailing encouragement. He
rought us together and perhaps we would never have made our
ay around often rocky shoals without his sure guidance.

o person has borne the burdensome labor of this collection
ore than our typist, Mrs. Liz Campanelli, on whom the task of
inal arrangement has fallen so squarely. Under the dexterity
f her nimble fingers the long manuscript began to shine. To
er and to all of the good people who met our every need, we
ow express our humble and hearty thanks.

. B. D.   New York, March 1987

. R. V.

PREFACE

The word "Plan" is used here to identify a public declaration issued in order to indicate principles or practices which should form the basis for a reform proposal in the national administration of the Mexican state. The multitude of Plans issued to promote various economic reforms or alterations of State government procedures are not considered in this collection. The Plans, as one might suppose, did not burst upon the public in a regular or conscious manner. Rather, national crises spawned the Plans: the War for Independence, the Constitutional crisis of 1823, the Church-State controversy of 1830-1835, two foreign wars in the next decade, the overthrow of the Santa Anna regime. Politically the nation stood united against the Maximilian intervention--there was no need to advance a Plan then--but the offerings r5tfgg ginning to proliferate when the Diaz Dictatorship settled upon the country and the well-spring of political dissent disappeared. With the overthrow of this administration Mexico again reaped an abundant harvest of Plans. After adoption of the Constitution in 1917, the response to subsequent Plans dwindled, and none have come forth since 1941. Apparently Plans have had their day in Mexico.

Originally the word "Plan" did not appear at the heading of documents advocating future public policy programs. Such words as Sentiments, Acts, Declarations, Decrees served as headlines, but ultimately Plan became the favorite designation. Also, the early format used in presenting a Plan varied somewhat, but within a remarkably short time the physical format became standardized. Typically the announcement would begin "Plan of . . ."--usually named for the village, city, or army post where the author was residing or stationed. After the title a justificatory paragraph (or more!) of Whereases [Considerandos] to explain the need of new men and ideas at the national level, usually there followed a listing of reform proposals. The Military largely held to a neat catalogue of points in orderly sequence and with a minimum of explanation, as if the principles would speak for themselves--as they often did.

Civilians, in rarer appeals to their own kind, found other terminology, and they were usually more verbose.

ix

Occasionally a lone civilian floated a Plan of his own, but without the support either of troops or of officialdom, his chances of success were nil. In 1841, a banner year for Plans, a concerned citizen published anonymously a whole Constitution of his own dreaming: a Plan, not with five or six points, perhaps, marching down a single sheet, but a thick pamphlet. This Plan, like so many other grassroot efforts in every country, was ignored and now it is a curiosity to be found only in remote libraries.

As the most casual reading of these Plans will indicate, precious few political, social, or economic ideas circulated in Mexico during the 19th century. At the margin of the 20th century new ideas lifted men to a larger perception, but not until the Liberal Party, safely based in St. Louis, Missouri, in 1906, issued a true political platform as its "Plan" did the yeast begin to work. Old stereotypes of Plans would never serve again. Not only did succeeding Plans change their pattern, they sharpened their language so that it would cut to the quick.

During the stagnant decade between the Texas War in 1836 and the war with the United States a decade later the Plans reveal little constructive thought. For all their protestations of progress, Mexico sat in darkness, never moving, wrapped in a serape of sheer incomprehension, stark, deserted by those from whom it might have expected leadership. Little showed that the Nation lived at all, save the spasmodic declarations that what was happening could never be.

The years served as a conveyor belt that drew many Plans to their appointed ends, where they were picked up by eager-handed citizens, then discarded when they read them, or else tried them in part and declared that there was no more to be done, nothing to be learned. Yet other Plans--rare beacons--shone down the years like safety lights and when, through various artifices, they were subverted their very shadows seemed to bring comfort.

And still the Plans rolled on--Plans from those who advanced a valid program, from those thoughtless persons who sought only acclaim, but especially from the Military which mistook the bayonet for the statesman's gavel. The more they demanded order the greater the confusion; turmoil but compounded the need for another Plan; today the Plans tumble out as from Mexico's attic--dusty reminders of another day. Once, it seemed, a nation cherished these things; now they are the curiosities of the nation's yesterdays.

We trail the Plans, rich in their mysteries, invitations to a world without doom, a path cluttered by the sure record of so many failures. Here are the Plans, both the logical and the unwarranted, the declaratory, the incomplete and the crude, all remarkably alike while posing as uniquely different. Some indicate intolerance and superstition, their fears groundless, their bases for action unproved. Still others, through some instinctive presentment, show a rule-of-thumb logic, an analytic foresight, a conclusive reasoning that moved Mexico out of the clutches of impending Fate and set the country, amidst the confusion, staring at a dream of Justice and Glory.

From the disorder we arrange the Plans in order--chronological order--since we are Historians and Time is dear to us. We are tempted to dust them off a bit, to straighten a twisted sentence, to clarify an uncertain reference, but to do so would play false with those departed champions of another generation. Rather, suspend Time; bring out the conceits of another age--never mind that they appear unused or neglected. From these gropings emerged a nation's life. Possibilities gave rise to patterns; the experiments confirmed national policy. On occasions the worry, the surfeit of Plans, became a sickness, a kind of flush fever, but once a national consensus had been confirmed, Mexicans could look upon the past ailment and its cure with a sort of pride.

The Plans form the mother-lode of Mexico's political resources, the quarries which activists mined in search of ideas which they could call their own. We, standing with the advantage of a one hundred year hindsight, judge these relics of dead issues, of political wreckage long since consigned to the great ocean of forgetfulness and silted over by the tides of national distraction. Each Plan its author had offered as a great light shining in the darkness, a sure guide for a lost and wandering nation, a glow that swelled or contracted as it attracted or lost adherents. Its lustre had made it seem alive of its own, and within its radiance its followers would be protected from the ancient chills of an unloved past. Now all the Plans are of yesterday, the last effusions poorer than the first.

As we contemporaries read the Plans in succession we may be struck with a certain angularity of expression, a certain stiffness of prose which does not arise wholly from a translator's infelicitous choice of words. Rather, we must remember that the authors of most of the Plans were soldiers generally of limited educational background who wrapped their proposals in trailing sentences long drawn out, but thanks to the agreement of gender and number, as the Spanish language requires, the sense is not wholly obscured. With a Division on their right and with a covey of lawyer-scribes discretely hidden on the left, the Generals advanced into the arena of political science. Posturing somewhat, occasionally striking a pose reminiscent of a mythical Napoleon, they clothed their best ideas with stiff garments of brocaded adjectives--tasteless ribands of justifications for their announced rebellion.

Their Plans reflect the overloaded prose of the barracks, the polite disguise of the officers' mess. Sometimes the Generals stumbled over their own rhetoric, and their cause became inextricably tangled with dependent clauses wandering in search of some logical subject or predicate. Occasionally it has seemed fair to let the clause struggle in the thicket which did so easily beset it; mercy for the English reader required, now and again, a period and a fresh beginning.

Certainly Mexicans of the last century and a half have divined the meaning of the Plans well enough. Those who would not or could not understand promptly lost their lives or their property--sometimes both. Ridiculous as some Plans sound to a later generation, pompous as they may be, unwise or grossly mistaken as some of them proved in practice, they defined the terms of life in Mexican public affairs. Misunderstanding or disobedience could bring a recalcitrant one before a firing squad of wobbly marksmanship. They played the game for real, and woe beside the man who minimized intent because it lay hidden behind grammatical underbrush.

A latter-day Translator may correct a grammatical expression or mercifully end a sentence, then supply an additional substantive for the ruling verb and thus flatter himself that he has thereby improved the whole. It may be that modern editorializing by translation has clarified an occasional point, but it

xii

is quite likely, too, that unwittingly he has tugged at a loose phrase and unraveled a line of thought. In this century or the last, in their own language or another, the emergent national saviours--even Generals--are entitled to stand on their own. They would expect no less, and such a respect their contemporaries extended to them.

When ideas move from one language to another, parallel words, even when supported by the comforting authority of bilingual dictionaries, often prove inadequate. Particularly annoying has been the inability of the English word "country" to convey the emotion of the Spanish language "patria". Mexicans visualize their nation in the feminine form so that "motherland" might be the most accurate translation. Since this term sounds stilted to English-language users, we have settled on "fatherland". The word "pais" first appeared in a Plan of 1911; thereafter it was used more frequently. Such a word may suffice for postal clerks and passport operatives, but to the heart only "La Patria" speaks, and it is to that pulsating target that the Planners aimed their emotional appeals. In later years other alternative terms for "La Patria" crept into use: The Nation, The Republic, or (more impersonally) The Constitutional Order. Late, too, was the capitalization of the word "Plan."

The Spanish words, junta and conveniente, seem to carry meanings all their own; at least, they appear in associations which suggest various English equivalents. The English language "convenient" more often confuses than clarifies. Affirmatively conveniente carries the positive concept of useful, good, or suitable, therefore fit for the occasion. If one thinks in terms of the day and the hour, that which is conveniente may be judged timely, opportune, or even expedient. If a proposal faces the ultimate negative--no es conveniente--the whole range of possible rejections become involved. Indeed, a project may be banished into oblivion for reasons as obvious as a shrug of the shoulders--just because. In this collection the word has been translated as seemed most convenient!

The word junta carries a varied set of associations. Sometimes it seems that a revolutionary gathering may be called a "junta;" again junta appears to have designated a committee meeting quite innocent of rebellious intent. Often Plans used the

xiii

word to apply to what was clearly a permanent governmental commission. At times a Junta seems designed to serve as an <u>ad hoc</u> committee which must report to a higher body. Alternatively, it seems to have been a body called into existence in order to advise the Executive, but since the Executive himself appointed the members, clearly it would offer its creator the advice which he most wanted to hear. In such a situation the Junta shared executive responsibilities and provided to a hesitant Executive a whipping boy when he was called upon to make an unpopular decision. Also, a Plan may call upon the Junta appointed by a departing Congress to govern is its stead, and once the crises has passed to name the next Executive. The national Junta would then fade away as the lonely Leader named an advisory council-his Junta-to advise <u>him</u>.

Behind the shadow of the Presidential chair lurks the Junta, sometimes master of all, again the servant of a few--short-lived, easily revived, impermanent, yet perpetual in Mexican political strategy, a convenience, even a consolation in time of trouble. The presence of a Junta often meant that trouble had disestablished the stable. The vote of a Junta could call men to a new way of thinking. A call for a Junta could signify that the existing administration was ready to surrender; a Junta able to voice the true national yearning could mean that peace was almost at hand. It served as a sort of political monkey wrench, a spanner adjustable to many expedients, a convenient instrument, often used, sometimes abused, but always ready to be tried again.

Almost all Plans carry an Introduction which justifies the issuance of the document itself. Across the decades the Introductions grew longer and more detailed. They began, as most petitions for public attention do, with the declaration, "Whereas..."; in Spanish, "<u>Considerando</u>...". Within these <u>Considerandos</u> we find laid out before us the presumed tribulations of the Republic, its hitherto ignored injustices, its unsolved problems, a restless populace, an Army rampant, an Administration dormant, and across the national shield a bar sinister of illegitimacy. To read the <u>Considerandos</u> is to encounter a bilious national record. Authors of each new Plan protest that they can abide this miserable record no longer, and with scarcely concealed gusto they offer long-deferred fulfillment to their equally long-suffering fellow citizens.

If we skip the Considerandos, which the demands of time and space in a later age require, we read in the proposals of a Plan quite another account-of a future so real that almost it can be tasted. Reach no longer exceeds the grasp; honesty can be secured on order; qualified men of good intentions will balance the budget; promises guarantee that public servants shall be both hard working and competent. The Army will relinquish control once the People have expressed the national will freely and truly; but--here the customary note--soldiers are to be treated in a manner worthy of a representative Democracy, for with the Army Independence was won!

In short, the Articles of Reform in the Plans no more truthfully project the Mexican future than do the Considerandos fairly reflect the past, troubled though it may have been. But the Articles of a Plan are more meaningful than the Considerandos because they are the proposals which, in one part or another, may become the program of the future. These are the proposals to cure national ills; the Considerandos elaborate, often at unconscionable length, upon a dead past yet unburied. Only one thing the Plans insist upon--the Past is not to be resurrected. This collection of the national political Plans of Mexico has largely ignored the backward-looking Considerandos, and has reproduced the Articles of the Plans in toto.

One Plan invites another; one suggestion prompts another. We must take the authors at their word--they aspired to promote the public good. Sometimes the cause of dissatisfaction was represented by a 'broadside', a throwaway leaflet, a flyer. Usually these declarations pretended to speak for or in the name of all Mexicans and carried screamer headlines MEXICANS ALERT! ATTENTION!! but if the issue were a single one that appealed to an obviously narrow group, it could be ignored as having the validity of a New Year s Resolution--a firm commitment to reform after a tremendous hangover. Having declared their intentions, the followers felt free to act as necessity might require.

Indeed, Plans occasionally amounted to little more than a transient declaration, but to be considered worthy of the name they were supposed to be serious in purpose and national in scope. Plans revealed the authors' dreams; they wrote with the hope of guiding the country into other paths and in the process would convert the old into the new. We follow the Plans, infinite, as inexhaustible as Man's search for glory. Each author shows a separate self, but in their totality they reveal a truth about Mexico; a conviction that a Person and a Cause can save the nation.

Often Mexico has stood in need of saviours. Thoughtful men, competent men, have hated the endless disorder which daily reminded them of the country at its worst. Of course no single Plan saved Mexico. Generally the authors thought of themselves as guides towards a future of Peace and Happiness, but in their declarations they did no more than make the Past a pattern for the Future. They could not know that the Future would differ from anything that the Nation had ever known.

When reading only the political Plans that, in a disjointed way, led to the constitutions, one finds nothing inherently interesting in the exercise; the texts hold together by grace of the calendar and without an explanation or a protagonist. One gets a shock almost as if he should see the X-ray photograph of his fiancee--a skeleton, inert and ugly, and in the skull the face of death--nothing of the charm of face or figure, the grace and lilt that holds the lover's heart. Any who know Mexico must find in the Plans alone the incontrovertible evidence of greed and power run amuck, something like those cavorting Death figures which Mexicans of the 19th century found at once so amusing and so sad. These Plans, we may insist, are not the "real" Mexico that we know. Yet they are! The X-ray does not lie. We are staring at a starker reality than we commonly see. If this prospect seems ugly to us, it is because we have not seen before this part of the body politic stripped of artifice. The X-ray is not meant to show beauty--it reveals old fractures now healed, bone chips, floating discs, darkened areas as well as clear bone--all marks of the hazards of life, and proof of present health in spite of past afflictions.

CHAPTER I
The Early Plans

In order to understand Mexican political Plans we must turn to their beginnings, for they arose out of the politics of stagnation. The idea of a political Plan boasts a paternity unassailably honorable--it grew out of the Revolution for Independence. As open rebellion against Spanish officials began, Mexican patriots found themselves crowded out of the cities and they were, therefore, denied access to the normal communication channels of the day. Faced with the necessity of spreading their propaganda which, as a later generation would say, was designed "to win the hearts and minds of the people," these early revolutionaries composed relatively concise declarations of their aims and of the issues confronting them. These items they reduced to a document, usually no more than a single sheet, which could be struck off on the portable printing presses which they rolled about on ox carts. Couriers distributed the sheets in those areas which might receive them, and as new issues arose another revolutionary declaration would follow.

These early revolutionary broadcasts concerned themselves with practical programs which would forward their cause rather than with political sophistry which might justify rebellion against long-established government. In October and November, 1810, Jose Maria Ansorena and Father Hidalgo broadcast their intention (which exceeded their present power) to abolish slavery. If supported by adherents which this declaration might bring, they hoped to issue subsequent decrees which would publicize the operation of a future administration to be staffed by native Mexicans, not by immigrant Spaniards.

Not the least of the provisions in these decrees were the specified punishments to be inflicted upon those individuals who refused to abide by the Decree as issued. And finally, the revolutionary rank of the signer secured the validity of the Decree. Ansorena drafted his decree, he said, "in punctual compliance with the sage and the pious dispositions of His Excellency Captain-General Sr. Don Miguel de Hidalgo y Costilla." Personal authority has always fueled the driving force behind the political Plan.

1

While these early military declarations with
their rudimentary schemes to gain adherents and to
finance a war amounted to no more than arbitrary
decrees, the word "Plan" kept appearing in first one
text and then another. In August, 1811, Ignacio Lopez
Rayon began to think of political structure for the
new State-to-be. He prepared a rough draft--as
lawyers will--of legal principles and practices to be
incorporated into the future national charter, and he
forwarded his conclusions to the second leader of the
movement, Fr. Morelos. Then Rayon issued a call for a
tribunal "to arrange a plan of operation in all our
America, and to dictate all suitable provisions for a
good political and economic order."

Lacking a national assembly so early in their
revolutionary movement, the Mexican leaders,
presuming to speak for their cause, struck off
suggested political guidelines--in a word, Plans.
Rayon, in 1812, drew up the "Elements of a
Constitution," and in 1813 Father Morelos listed
twenty-three points for a constitution. These
documents amounted to official and conscious drafts
of national political objectives by an element
outside the acting administration: PLANS.

From another quarter, in March, 1812, Dr. Jose
Maria Cos issued a Manifesto which advanced at length
a justification of the revolution against the Spanish
Crown. The next generation of Liberators would call
this portion of the declaration"Considerandos", which
in English would be translated as "Whereases." Then
the Doctor advanced two programs, one based upon a
peaceful settlement with the mother country, while
the other outlined in specific terms the alternative
of war. One list he labeled "Plan of Peace" and the
other a "Plan of War.(1)

Finally and explosively came the Plan of Iguala.
By title and intent the "Plan" as a political
instrument was born, stepping--Minerva-like--from the
head of Augustin Iturbide. Mexican acceptance of his
Plan forced Spain to join in the Treaty of Cordoba
(August, 1821), a document which embraced both the
military terms for cessation of hostilities and a
draft of a political framework for the new government.

---

(1) See the full text in Jose Maria Luis Mora, Mexico
y sus revoluciones, III, 191-193. (Edicion y prologo
de Augustin Yanez, Mexico, 1965)

Like other documents to follow, it served at once as a Treaty and as a political Plan. Within a few years the word "Plan" was accepted generally, and if some aspirant for public support chose other terminology--an Edict, an Act, or a Declaration--the public ignored the title. He had, they said, issued a Plan.

But General Santa Anna, ever alert to subversion, was standing in the wings. Soon he was broadcasting a Plan to overthrow the recently installed Emperor Iturbide, and thereafter he used the idea of a Plan to advance narrow, partisan positions. Early on he whetted his hortatory talents to a fine edge with Plans; he set the style, and with casual use of Rousseau's vocabulary his touch was sure for a long quarter-century. Not for him a simple declaration, a short proviso. Words flared from his pen; his Plans smoked of revenge upon opponents while, privately, he fanned little protests into general conflagrations.

Born with the touch of a master, the General assumed the idea of a Plan as if it were his own invention, and he used it for his special purposes. Initially he felt that the word 'Plan' did not convey an adequate connotation to the average citizen. When he used it in his Plan of Vera Cruz (December, 1822), he added the sub-title, "Suggestions for integrating the Nation," but thereafter the term carried its own meaning and none mastered its uses better than General Santa Anna himself.

From first to last the General showered his promises. He know how to offer carrot and stick simultaneously: "Future grades and promotions shall be kept open for Congress on triumph of the Cause, while those who knowingly oppose shall be suspended from employment". Militia and civilian volunteers were to share the military privileges [fueros] while Congress would recognize and reward merit to be acquired in the coming struggle. Promises right...promises left... And money for the Cause?...That problem he passed over easily: it should come from the public Treasury! If that Great Cow could not provide, then Santa Anna suggested that good patriots might feel free to make loans which 'in time' would be repaid punctually. In the code language of that day, he meant forced loans might be levied against opponents. If doubters remained, Santa Anna reminded them, "Nothing is said of the public debt, as this point has already been declared by the Congress". Even then he provided for

3

the Army: all Treasury payments were to be frozen, save for the Military.

Santa Anna used the Plan as a public relations gimmick: he never failed to summon his fellow citizens to some fancied national rampart "for the salvation of the Fatherland". He chose as his favorite slogan for ending a Plan the words "God and Liberty." All his public declarations and appeals carry over-burdened sentiments as obvious as the watermark of the paper on which they were written. After the loss of a leg occasioned by a foolish act of bravado, he made broad references to "those of us who have shed blood in behalf of the Nation." No other author of a Plan could wave before the Nation a leg as well as a flag.

Into this political vacuum the Generals jumped with gusto. As citizens of the Republic who had specific ideas on national policy certainly they had a right to advocate their position within the acceptable framework and through the traditional channels which their society afforded. However, the Military, in the performance of its special duty, lived a life of its own, one bounded by the terms of Command and of Obedience. By the nature of their work officers rotated from post to post, often in distant parts of the country, and they could have few civilian confidants. Easily the politically minded Generals resorted to violence--bold, brazen, and bloody--in order to enforce their declarations. Because the confusion of the democratic process alarmed them, the Generals thought that they wanted law and order based upon command, but their barracks revolts and the battles pitched against Mexicans themselves produced as near anarchy as a Western nation has produced. Appeal after appeal... Mexico endured many now forgotten Military bids for national attention by making cautious and vague references to revision of an almost new constitution while they gathered their skimpy forces for yet another assault upon the regular processes of government.

The Planners--Military or civilian--seem to have had a profound faith in the power of a properly phrased Appeal-to-Arms. If they could but compose the right slogan men would flock to their cause. As the Church-State conflict of the early 1830's closed in, General Bravo (December, 1833) advanced what he labeled a "Plan of Conciliation:

4

"Do not be afraid of tyrants; they shall soon receive their just reward for their attempts against the Altar and the Nation. To Arms, honest and brave Military Men! To Arms, patriotic Men! And all of you Citizens, lovers of real freedom, enemies of disorders and confusion, come help us pull down the spectre of anarchy. I invite you to the great work of regeneration, of peace, of glory."

Conciliation? Musket-ball conciliation: the peace of the grave for our enemies; glory for the victors--us or them!

Authors of Plans, in their introductory paragraphs, frequently protested that they were "inspired solely and exclusively by the most intense desire of securing the peace of the State which is menaced at this very moment by all the horrors of civil war," and the promise implicit if not expressed, "if the Plan is adopted, general quiet in the Republic shall prevail."(2) If a price must be paid, the Military declared that its members were prepared. The Garrison of Perote (September, 1841), led by "the Generals, the Commanders, and the officers of operations," issued a short Plan which expressed a sincere desire to sacrifice themselves for their country, but they warned that they would not lay down arms until a constitutional order had been restored. As for the country, it could only rummage about. In 1841 the desolate citizens of Vera Cruz appealed to the "worthy Generals" to work for the good of the country as declared in their Plans. The Army could not be ignored.

The popularity of Plans waxed and waned. During the decade of the 1840's it appears as if the Generals left their frustrations etched into their alternate Plans. The list is long: General Arista, General Valencia, General Urrea, General Duran, General Santa Anna, and a dozen others, sometimes joining forces occasionally standing alone. General Paredes ran with the pack, yet as the tide of chaos rose about him, he proclaimed alone. He tossed off his Plans with abandon, ignoring both repetitions and conflicts of texts. Often he stood at the Nation's crossroads dreaming--who knows of what great adventure?--yet like some mute spirit he sank into the anonymity of failure after glimpsing fair Paradise.

---

(2) See the Plan of the Garrison of Jalisco, (October, 1852)

The Generals found it convenient to issue their official declarations from a military post, generally at the quarters of the commanding officer (3) he presiding until they had reached "a suitable accord." Occasionally the commander went to the additional trouble of securing the attendance of one or more non-commisioned officers who would represent, presumably, the opinion of rank and file. Basically, this procedure was not as arbitrary as it may appear, for at the frontiers so far removed from the Vera Cruz-Mexico City axis the Generals enjoyed the firmest institutional connection with the capital then existing and could be presumed to have the most recent and most reliable news from the political center. Inevitably a General became a person of political consequence, and communities remote from the center could do no more than hope to ally themselves with the dominant and winning personality. The General--if anybody--could offer guidance.

Endorsement of a Plan could be dangerous for a General and his staff if not for the signatories further down the line, and issuance of one's own Plan, unless well considered and prior support assured, could be fatal. Robert P. Letcher, United States respresentative in Mexico, writing to Daniel Webster, Secretary of State, January 17, 1831, calmly referred to "a promunciamento made in Guanajuato for the overthrow of the government. Fortunately the insurrection has been suppressed by the Government. Some half-dozen leaders have been shot, and many others will be shot."(4) The rise and fall of Plans was not a matter of fun and games.

Various States occasionally issued Plans, and their effectiveness depended upon the political importance of the State.

---

(3) See, for example, the Declaration of Campeche (November, 1829), the Plan of Jalapa (September, 1830); the Plan of Duran (June, 1833); the Plan of Zavaleta (December, 1832); the Proclamation of the Federation of San Luis Potosi (April, 1837); or the Declaration of the Garrison of Tamaulipas (September, 1841).

(4) Manning, W.R., Diplomatic Correspondence, Inter-American Affairs, 377.

The frontier State of Durango ventured a Plan of its own (September, 1841), but it could offer no new ideas, only vague generalities: "A call for an extraordinary congress which, through the wishes of the people, shall have ample facilities to reconstitute the Republic without being bound by laws or previous Plans of any sort, save that which best comports with the interests and well-being of the people." Are such effusions "Plans?" Not very good ones certainly, but Mexicans accepted them as valid Plans.(5)

Normally "the Government" did not issue a Plan: it had no need to do so. It controlled the administrative and legislative machinery and its record indicated its program; its leaders, with access to the press, were able to proclaim the merits of the latest legislative action. Typically the Plan was reserved for those outside the Administration, but there could be exceptions. The tenuous administration of Manual Gomez Pedraza, in its search for whatever support it could muster, prepared its own Plan (December, 1832), but such action the public properly interpreted as a sign of weakness.

A Plan was intended as a public announcement, a public commitment to certain policies, and so it was universally understood. The Plan of the Conspiracy of Deputy Gondra (November, 1830) made an exception to all the rules. President Guerrero let himself become involved in the deep plot, and surely the knowledge of his prior connivance in such violent procedures as those devised by Deputy Gondra accounted for his pitiless murder some time later.

The many Plans of the Santa Anna decades, so nearly identical in the ideas which they presented and in the procedures which they advocated, really supported each other, like broken soldiers trickling

---

(5) The authorities of the State of Vera Cruz met in Jalapa in order to revise their State government (20 August, 1846), but they found that first they had to take a position on national administrative questions. The resultant declaration dealt as much with national as with State matters. However, they titled their draft a Plan." The pronouncement of Oaxaca (February, 1847) dealt more with State than with national concerns, but three days after its issue it was being called "a Plan."

7

back from the battlefield of a lost war. After the bruising internal struggle of Centralists vs. Federalists and then to be followed by the Texas debacle, the Mexican nation was struck numb. In 1841 the dam burst, and by September of that year the flood crested--fifteen for the month, one every other day. During that dreadful month the Plans fluttered down from the mountain posts or surged up from the Hot Lands until they were accepted as natural phenomena. They fell with the impact of a tack hammer pounding on an anvil--a high pitched racket that held the attention of the nation for the minutes on end.

The Generals hoisted their Plans--oily petards that seemed to light hope and promise to the multitude in the streets. When these sputtering declarations smoked and died away, the authors sank into the shadows, subdued, but waiting for another crisis, another chance at the big prize--the Presidency. Those Plans, mostly froth and jetsam, contained very little of political merit. The Planners were but striking out blindly at events beyond their control when they demanded a constitutional leader or--even more--a new constitution. If not that, then amendments to the old one of 1824, or at least a valid election. Behind it all ranged a sickening quiet: lost territory in the north, an army demoralized by ignominious defeat, the President as Commander-in-Chief captured by the enemy, then released and living in exile, fearful of returning home lest his Mexican enemies assassinate him, and yet another war in the north clearly impending. If any man cherished a constructive idea, this was the time to advance it, and there was none beyond the traditional simplicities repeated over and over again.

Behind the Plans stood the Military and when they declared that their troops would support them "arms in hand," they could be dangerous. True, not every battle was mortal, but the ragged armies ravaged the countryside. Most Plans of whatever period offered inducements in a 'revolutionary' army, a force for Reconstruction, for Regeneration [any positive word would do] which might carry the supporters of a particular Plan to a victory that would reward the enlistees in terms of their early and well-publicized support.(6)

---

(6) The Plan of Zabaleta (December, 1832); General Urrea (July, 1840) offered inducements to men in active service, and he provided also that military pensioners who might support the opposing side were to be deprived of their payments.

The early Plan of Cuernavaca (January, 1824) offered specific advantages to accrue: "All Americans who may wish to fight under their flags [of the States] be they military or natives, shall be very welcome." Americans and military included whites born in Mexico; natives meant Indians. Also, the Plan offered special promotion awards to veterans of the War for Independence if they should enlist early: "The first who shall enlist [in the Army] or sound the call [grito] in favor of this system in any city which is opposed to the aims of this Plan shall be given preference in the ranking." Then followed a cautionary proviso for would-be time-servers:

"For this purpose and so that none can declare himself to have been overlooked, an arbitrary period of thirty days is given, a period of time which for a thousand good reasons has been considered sufficient for every American who desires the salvation of the Nation and who has the firmness and who considers Honor can take sides; but be warned that the expressed period of time will only refer to those living far away, because experience of past occasions has taught us the undignified way in which many carry on, as it is commonly said "in order to fall heavy." It is necessary that those who live near and want to take sides to do so with rapidity...."

Whether one "fell heavy" or floated gently could determine a person's political future, or even life itself. The Plan of Ecatzinco (February, 1834) promised the best Army posts to those who should support the Plan, and to those who could bring in 2,000 recruits the sponsors offered a commission as General-of-Division. Those career soldiers who might reject a Plan were assured that on its triumph they would be separated from the service.

Not only could individuals "fall heavy"--the Army as an institution could do so. Since any Plan required military support, the authors frankly bid for Army approval. General Rangel's Plan (June, 1845) promised "to restore the Army in all its splendor and privileges (fueros)" and to discharge all officers who did not support his cause. Planners seem to have strained themselves to devise an expression more enticing than the last yet say the same thing: "the existence of the Army is guaranteed and it is to be

9

provided for as is due a well-merited military class of a free people."(7)

The Plans of the 1840's: there is something unreal about them, like the rasping of cicadas in the chill of the morning. The Plans failed because the self-interest of the Planners eclipsed their regard for the national welfare. If the nation should be served, it must first serve them. Given such an opportunity for the expansion of the ego, the best as well as the worst found abundant occasion to ring the changes of patriotism. Santa Anna's grandiloquent Plans—numbered propositions, dangerous if accepted as Truth—served as a political screen to obscure reality: hide behind them and the country is yours. The proposals: amend the Constitution, summon an extraordinary Congress, install an interim President, revise the system of State representation, enforce religious conformity with a bayonet—false issues designed to avoid a nation's need. For a society coming into being it was all too much to grasp.

Perhaps Rousseau's writing fired certain Mexican imaginations, or it may be that Mexican aspirants for national attention most readily turned to the recent French experience for justification of revolution. At any rate the vocabulary of Rousseau and the terminology of the victorious French Revolution frequently appeared in the declarations of the first Mexican Planners. Those leaders fancied themselves real revolutionaries if they could but swing the proper words into the right sequences, but the paucity of their vocabulary shows how little they understood Rousseau and how ill-prepared the public to follow the posturing aspirants. Within a quarter-century after Independence the fad of French Revolutionary diction had faded away.

Thus, even the shortest of Plans and the most routine of provisos provide a revelation of Mexico that used to be, a Mexico dominated by military men of small minds who could not adjust themselves to a country growing great. They culled their slender resources of language to express the aspirations of the nation, but they could not imagine a society which differed from that which they had always known.

---

(7) Plan of General Sales (August, 1846); General Paredes in the Pronouncement of Guanajuato (June, 1848)

10

All the while that Generals hurled anathemas at each other the Government in its civil aspects had to proceed in some manner. Within the straitened economic and social order of Mexico not only the opinions but the operations of civil servants could be crucial to acceptance of a Plan. Therefore, Plans repeatedly promised that civil employees would be left inviolate regardless of their political opinions or actions.(8)

Not all Plans proved ill-timed or inadequate. In each generation Mexico has faced problems that appeared insoluble, and now and again a General proposed a single, direct solution to a crucial problem which, it seemed to him, could be achieved by a single stroke of arms if necessary. Today the Plans preserve the patriotic breathing of their authors, now long dead, who once sought to rule the country with a bullet-backed proviso that bounced off the national consciousness. Their authors saw the world in stark contrasts--patriots vs. traitors, them vs. us--dreamers of a heavenly state while living in an inferno. Forgive the citizen--even the soldier--for past sins and omissions, but forget not the sweets of power and the satisfaction of revenge! Optimistic Plans and radiant hopes covered fearful unease: fail this effort and all is lost.

In a sense, too, the Plans distort while they reflect. Mexicans did not reject one Plan and rush headlong to acclaim the next. A living had to be made, crops to be harvested, two devastating foreign wars to be fought on native soil. Then a decade later when a cruel civil war had almost sealed a Liberal victory, the losers countered with a foreign intervention.

With the Maximilian intrusion the issuance of Plans ceased and the Emperor took over. He, himself, had become the issue--a Plan incarnate. After him the victors began again--Plans once more, promises to win friends, threats aimed at all enemies, active or potential.

---

(8) Declaration of the State of Oaxaca (May, 1834); Plan of Ortiz (July, 1851). Even more generous was the still earlier Plan of Zerecero (November, 1828) which provided half-salary to two exiled Generals "as long as they remain in any place of America as designated by the government.

11

Porfirio Diaz came into power with a Plan of his own, and under his Dictatorship a counter-Plan amounted to a death sentence unless the luckless General could escape northward to the United States. Yet these new Plans, few though they were, sounded a new note. Today we follow the plans as weathered sign posts on an ancient road, and they tell us that Mexico went that-a-way!

CHAPTER II

The Plan as a Political Document

Mexicans invented the Plan as a political document and no other country, not Spain nor the rest of Latin America, has used the Plan as an instrument of government. When is a public declaration in Mexico a Plan? When the Mexicans call it a Plan! It is their invention; they have used it to shape public policy, and they should know. If a political declaration is not specifically named 'a Plan', then in terms of this collection to be counted as a Plan it must 1) refer to political issues and structures; 2) its declarations must be couched in terms of the nation; and 3) it must proclaim issues of general concern.

The word "Plan" as used in the Mexican experience may follow its literal and basic meaning and be an outline or plan which some individual advances as a proposed political program. However, legislative bodies, state and national, have issued proposals for public administration, and these are Plans. Treaties such as that of Cordoba may outline future political institutions calculated to shape the nation: as such they should be added to the list. A Manifesto in Mexico, more generally has been a call for extra legal action on a specific issue rather than a long range administrative proposal.

Only rarely has the Manifesto assumed the role of a Plan. Typically it prescribed a return to the presumed virtues of an earlier day or it enjoined an observance of some hitherto ignored 'fundamental law,' but the "Plan" advanced a program of reform in a broad governmental area and it sought wide public support. Its sponsor occasionally renounced any possible benefits for himself. He offered to lead the new march for Justice to its merited triumph, and then he would retire, so he said, happy in the thought that he had served his country worthily. It was, presumably, as clear to him as to his countrymen that in order to effectuate the new developments, a victor in a national reform program would become the most obvious choice for President of the country.

Occasionally a Plan may seem terribly short of ideas; frequently, at heart, it is no more than endorsements of a Plan declared earlier and emanating from a large military cantonment. At one time and place each declaration served some Mexicans as a political guide. There is scarcely a Plan for which someone has not died: behind the printer's ink lies blood, the life-force of men who were convinced that by supporting a particular Plan they were serving their country with their ultimate sacrifice. It is not a matter of drawing academic distinctions but of evaluating purposes.

On occasion it appears that any man who thought politically had a Plan of sorts. An anonymous Salvadoran submitted a Plan in mockery; its publication in the rudimentary press became a matter of quiet smiles. The Military, with its ready force, seems to have thought in terms of Plans. There should be a representative republic, so they declared, but they had no memories of popular government. The Generals, so generous with their protestations, were like children playing at the edge of a cliff.

Once a Cuban who had chosen to take part in the Mexican struggle against Maximilian and had gained a General's commission for his efforts became fatally enmeshed in the politico-military conflict in his adopted country. As the French forces began their retreat, General Cabos, from the frontier city of Matamoros took aim at the still new and largely untested Constitution of 1857. In the shattering conflict that followed his forces disintegrated. He fled the field, took refuge in a nearby house and at a table began to record his sworn purposes--in a Plan, no less. He advocated restoring the former system of an emergency committee to establish a provisional government. He continued, "Only sums are to be withdrawn from the public treasury..." and here the Plan ends, for his pursuers pounced upon him. Iqnoring his text, they shoved him outside to his execution. His fragmentary Plan survives, as incoherent as his life--broken, isolated, out of time and place. It is a prayer that posterity might understand and forgive. Issuing a Plan could become almost a knee-jerk reaction, but much more dangerous. A Plan might become a Last Will and Testament.(9)

Some of the Plans are trivial renditions or unabashed examples of plagiarism for the signers were innocent either of monetary gain or of evil intent. Other Plans radiated a sense of dormant power, and those who opposed them did so at their peril.

---

(9) Plan of General Cabos, (November, 11, 1863)

The Plans smell of barracks, of stuffed uniforms long since moldy. Almost we can hear the rattle of arms; almost we can make out epaulettes too wide for the shoulders that sustained them.

The Plans are jealous of Time. They come as crisis-laden documents: hurry, hurry before an impending disaster breaks. They set specific date schedules in the land of Manana for the calling of a Council of Government, for its designation of a person to exercise the Supreme Power, for a convention with sovereign powers, for a free vote to ratify an undrafted constitution. The Plans are flecked with their demands for action "counting from this day,"... "The President shall act"..."The Congress shall meet"..."Within six months the Council shall present a constitution..."

Most of the Plans are formal bits of strained eloquence with controlled references to injustices and irregularities which the authors promise to remedy forthwith. And then the one-two punch: a promise of reward to supporters while those who should oppose the New Order of things were to be branded as traitors and enemies of their beloved Fatherland. Up from Vera Cruz, down from the Bahio the Plans streaked through the political wind tunnel to Mexico City--rather, to "Mexico" as local usage had it. The national capital <u>was</u> Mexico--everyone knew that in his bones. Without "Mexico" the Plans would come to nothing: with the Capital both power and glory would be theirs.

The decade between the foreign wars--Texas and American--were rootless years of indolent melancholy, and the Plans, long and short, of that time cast shadowy reminders of what might have been. As one reads them in succession the impression of their sameness grows, and the stereotyped justifications--the <u>Considerandos</u>--the unfamiliar names and places plus the remoteness of Time itself all tend to blur differences. Even the contemporaries themselves ignored distinctions. Occasionally economic and political issues mentioned in one Plan were omitted or appended in another as the pleasure of a commanding officer dictated. The Proceedings of the Citizens of Vera Cruz (September, 1841) seemed related to economic issues, but on being circulated

15

elsewhereit came to include political declarations as well.(10)

September, 1841, marked the height of Mexico's flood tide when every other day a Plan appeared, but the reading matter was much the same. The needless crowded the superfluous. During this disjointed period the Plans appear as nothing more than a host of political rejects which littered the landscape, verbal effusions which seeped out of the national consciousness. Seeking distinctions without differences, they passed as leonine wonders, but really were no more than a rush of effervescence, streams of bubbling ambition filtering through the cracks a General's ego.

For a long time the old Plans kept coming back as new. Then, suddenly out of the most routine of protests against the most traditional of Dictatorships came an original idea--a lily emerging from the trash pile: "Art. 6: The provisional Executive shall name a secretary of state...who shall be entitled "Minister of Interior Development [Fomento], and his responsibilities shall be to concern himself with all that relates to the development of the country, (11) and thereafter the Plan lists the interests involved in that development. The idea rested in limbo for a decade--until the Plan of April 22, 1853, revived the issue under the Dictatorship of the aged Santa Anna. It promised to create a new Cabinet post with a Minister of Fomento whose duty should be to promote industry, commerce, mining, transportation, and agriculture. National planning had come to Mexico!

Somewhat as North Americans seek some social or political reform by "passing a law" or by securing an amendment to their Constitution, so hopeful Mexicans have composed their Plans. Any time, any place served for drafting and declaring a Plan, although obviously some places would be more advantageous than others. Eligio Ortiz was imprisoned for some fault, but at a changing of the prison guard he and two others escaped. In the cell he inadvertently left a draft of his Plan (July, 1851) which some considerate guard

---

(10) See the Declaration of the Garrison and People of Tamaulipas (September, 1841), or of Peinoso of the same month, which adopted practically identical wording.

(11) The Citizens of Vera Cruz, (September, 11, 1841)

16

rescued and passed to a prowling newspaper reporter who secured its publication and thus duly recorded it in the annals of the country while securing for its author a fleeting immortality.

All the early Plans, generous as they were in their perpetual hopes for national regeneration, expressed the fervid nature of Mexicans, their style and artifice. Over them towered General Santa Anna, an active adventurer, practiced in the private nature of hypocrisy who bestrode the nation, sponsoring revolt for thrills, provoking thrills for misplaced patriotism. On occasions he scarcely bothered with a Plan in order to signal his intention to resume control of governmental operations: the revolt said it all.

CHAPTER III
The Early Planners

The Planners were drawn by the rambling disorder of national life where a scrap of knowledge passed for wisdom and bathos could attract a multitude. The Plans warned softly of anarchy while the Generals, looking back over their shoulders, headed into dark alleys of national consciousness where they might make a clumsy try for national favor. Today it appears that the freedom of Mexico menaced their sense of security. Little men, they did not realize that the country, a great curved horn which could not vanish into nothingness, was too big for them.

Mexico lived under a burden of surplus Generals, men who knew how to be Dictators but thought that they wanted to be constitutional Presidents. The conflict of impossibilities forced them to strut and to swagger, alternately to threaten to kill or to offer amnesty to former opponents whom they now professed to see as citizens who would have preferred another path toward full Democracy. Their Plans proposed dozens of miniature administrations to be staffed by hopelessly inadequate Presidents, each Plan repeating with monotonous regularity the alluring prospect of peace and prosperity. In the end the conflict exhausted the victors and they subsided, forced into contentment with accumulations of incidental loot and an assured pension.

Across the yellowed pages of now ancient newspapers, from the musty leaves of books long unopened flick the ghosts of ideas that men once entertained. Men thought that they were real, and called all those who denied them false to the Fatherland and the enemies of Independence. Once upon a time these black letters imprinted on paper now browned with age represented Truth or Falsehood, life or death: the victors collected, the losers--as always--paid.

Very quickly the Plans developed a terminology of their own. The early revolutionaries-turned patriots called their forces "the liberating Army," and with the defeat of Spain the rising Presidential aspirant, General Santa Anna, appropriated this appealing title for a new army which he dedicated to the overthrow of the self-crowned monarch, Iturbide.

Succeeding Presidents always had to be alert to the rise of a "liberating army," and then, somewhat later, to an "Army of Regeneration."

Indeed, Santa Anna himself introduced this word into his Plan of Casa Mata, and thereafter Mexico endured a plethora of Regenerators. Because the word grew hackneyed and since creative imagination scarcely circulated, the Planners by 1846 felt it necessary to add true and genuine in the hope of gaining enlistments for the genuine and truly Regenerative Army.

After the first flush of Independence Mexicans faced the turbulence of political and social readjustment. This situation they called 'anarchy' and early on the Planners began to talk of "avoiding anarchy" as a political aim which would be achieved by naming an individual variously designated as a Supreme Director, as Supreme Executive, or Director in charge of the Executive Office, and some even suggested the title of Dictator,. Declaring that "to care for the health of the nation is the first duty of all citizens," General Barragan offered to promote "such an interesting and sacred position by unifying public opinion--a glorious end in itself." These just wishes, so he said, were increased in him when he found himself proclaimed commander of three provinces.(12)

Among these early Planners stood General Antonio Lopez de Santa Anna, the most vocal of them all, a towering wreck of a man, barnacled, rotten at the core, a man who chose opportune moments to change his principles, and he ended by developing a proficiency for failure. But jealousy and suspicion among his fellow officers and a well-founded distrust by civilians diminished the Military clique, and in the end the civilian segment, supported--ultimately--by a rational element of the Military brought an end to the roundelay.

---

(12) Declaration of the Village of Celaya, (July, 1823)

19

Some of the military Planners, having no facts to constrain them, proclaimed without hindrance but Santa Anna never forgot where power lay. Simultaneously with his early Plan of Casa Mata he issued a declaration to the Army under the title "Minutes of Casa Mata." These Minutes amount to a Plan of his own, and they outline the role of the Army in the coming struggle to overthrow Iturbide.

The Army would become the essential tool in dozens of later revolts and Santa Anna but led the way. Those officers, commanders, and soldiers who chose not to support his Plan and movement would have full liberty to resign, to surrender rank, seniority and privileges, to move their residence to any place they might deem most convenient--a threat stated as an offer. Refusal to support the Plan, he declared, would indicate that soldiers "were not willing to sacrifice themselves for the cause of the country." Subordinate officers, therefore, faced the choice of supporting their commander's programs or of abandoning their careers and accepting the slur of cowardice. A man of pride could not think of accepting such an imputation, and within the thin economic strata of Mexico the surrender of one's career could prove catastrophic. Upon those who should accept his bid Santa Anna showered abundant promises: traditional security to civil servants, to the Army and the to Church; and besides, additional rewards in proportion to zeal evidenced in his behalf. Many subsequent Plans by a host of imitators sought to use the same form of psychological intimidation or enticement.

From first to last the Planners consistently radiated the theme of martial rewards for soldiers who would support the current appeal, a logical bid for the institution which could break the Administration. "The Army is to be taken care of as is befitting this noble institution" they promise. The liberal Plan of Ayutla repeated the pledge "to attend to whatever this noble institution may demand." Even to the end--the penultimate Plan--the Manifesto of General Netro (May, 1938) understood how to attract the Military: he promised to grant without quibbling the following terms, 1) Officers who support the San Luis Potosi secession will be promoted one grade; 2) soldiers are to receive 25% increase in pay, besides two pesos per day; 3) all men in uniform are to receive an increase of 25% and special bonuses for unhealthy assignments;

4) a special medal is to be awarded every man in this movement.

No shadow of doubt darkened the texts as the Planners composed their appeals. Occasionally they described the fate awaiting the country if one or another of their Plans with their intimations of salvation were not adopted--as if they had glimpsed the hellish abyss awaiting their native land if it should reject their particular solutions. But Mexico dwarfed the men: it was forever.

Reading the accumulation of Plans, piled high, causes the years to merge into a haze of charge and counter-charge, all made with the most polite reference. Opponents accused of rankest ineptitude are named with full titles and accorded public respect. Santa Anna, a stickler for punctillio, never forgot his manners. Once he accused publicly his former colleague, Anastasio Bustamante, of ineptitude, of official abuse, of governing despotically, of violating the constitutional order, and he promised to bring the offender to justice before the law, but in the Pronouncement of Perote (September, 1841) he titled him "His Excellency the Sr. General Don Anastasio Bustamante." A decade and a half later the sworn enemies of Santa Anna accorded him the same public respect. He had led the nation into slavery and depression, so they said, by using arbitrary and despotic powers; their condemnation grew lengthy and violent, but they referred to him as "His Excellency, the General." (Plan of Texca (March, 1835) Throughout the years this official decorum continued: the Mexican sense of the fitness of things.

Scarcely had the Constitution of 1824 been adopted and its text circulated before demands were regularly circulated to revise the document, and the overwhelming majority of the Planners for the next quarter-century included this proviso in their texts. What particular revisions should be made they preferred not to say: by avoiding specific proposals they could assume a righteous pose of desiring only the good of the whole country. Therefore, many of the Plans read so nearly alike that they testify not to surging patriotism but to ideological sterility. In their grandiloquence the Plans sounded as if they were for all Eternity; the Planners passed as an interlude in the nation's life.

21

These ambitious men knew only that they wanted the Presidency and with a bit of luck and the aid of troops available to them they intended to have it. A surprising number of them made it—for days or weeks as acting or interim Presidents, as the person in charge of Executive Power, or as commander of the occupying forces in the national capital. Their Plans varied only in the means whereby they would be confirmed for a more permanent residence in the National Palace. Usually they declared that with military victory they would convoke a constituent assembly. Immediately this new, extraordinary body should limit itself to one assignment—to revise the Constitution of 1824.

However, the provisos continued. A smaller body, chosen by the Military or by men appointed by them, would meet at the national capital and there would vote for the person who should serve as President pro tem. If this select body should choose the presiding military victor of the revolution, it would surprise no one, least of all the victorious general. After the new constitution had been drafted, the declaration said, another ballot would choose the permanent President. It would be no less logical for the permanent President to be none other than the recently elected President Pro tem who had so providentially saved the country from anarchy. Now and again the Plans varied in detail, but the principles of action remained the same. It was simply a matter of how long a string the Planners wished to pull.

Climbing to the top of the military ladder and on to national renown required not so much professional competence as political acumen. If an officer's faction lost in an outburst of opposition, he could expect to retain his military rating. If his group should win, then the commanding officers received adequate promotion, and they, in turn, extended their favors down through the ranks of their subordinates. If a line officer were so fortunate as to serve under a commander who chose the victorious side in no more than three or four successive revolutions, promotions could follow each other with dizzying rapidity, and the lucky individual could dream of a near day when he, in his turn, could 'pronounce', could summon his staff and request a vote of approval, and with Victory beckoning he might hope to become a person of importance himself.

22

Of course, in such a situation and in such a society, an officer could not possibly avoid 'politics' while devoting himself to his profession no more than a swimmer could ignore the current when crossing a river. However, if with the best of intentions, one took no active part in Mexican politics and devoted himself to military competence, he lost nothing positive by reason of his professional fidelity; he simply lost step with comrades of his age and rank. If an ambitious one should join efforts in a revolution with a declared Plan and the revolt should fail, normally he would have lost nothing vital. Rank and seniority would still be his, but he might expect assignments to remote or unhealthy areas.

For the politically minded to advance a Plan often meant an irreversible turn in his public career, a turn which sometimes led to personal advancement, sometimes to ignominy and occasionally to death. Therefore, the prudent person sought allies who might endorse his Plan even as it was being issued. With equal foresight one scoured his wits for an ennobling phrase, for a resounding expression which would characterize those companions who might support the new cause. "Restore" often appeared, for it suggested that things had been better in some past decade, and restoration could be considered only the mildest form of rebellion. When a revolutionary Plan named its forces "The Regenerating Army of the Mexican Republic" and proclaimed as its Commander-in-Chief one entitled "His Excellency General of Division and Well Merited of the Fatherland" rhetoric could do no more for the cause,(13) and its author might hope that this newest of Plans had smothered memory of its predecessors.

Friends and associates who endorsed a particular Plan would prepare a public as well as private statement to this effect. This action they called "giving an adhesion," and within a short time a Planner could judge the probable effect of his Plan by the number and character of 'adhesions' which he was receiving. Indeed, some of the shorter Plans amount to no more than an "adhesion" to an earlier and more comprehensive document plus an additional suggestion or two.

The freedom, the ease, and the willingness of the various Planners to declare all who opposed their

---

(13) See the Revolutionary Plan of October 8, 1849.

particular Plan as traitors to the Nation sounds presumptuous to the modern ear. Without the slightest hesitation authors and promoters of a Plan would state that all those who did not support their declaration at once and who refused to submit to its levies were to be branded as traitors, enemies of the people, enemies of Independence and of national unity. They were threatened with loss of their lives or confiscation of their possessions.(14)

The Planners generally labeled their cause "National" and therefore felt justified in characterizing their opponents as guilty of the crime of lesa Patria. It had proved an easy step to go from lesa Majestad to lesa Patria: a king had declared the first; a General could proclaim the second. With some irony the Manifesto of March, 1812, remarked that in truth resistance to Spain did not constitute lesa Majestad, for the royal officials could not function; at most, opposition should be labeled lesa gachupines. The crime of 'lesa' this or that would be flourished thereafter, most commonly as lesa Nacion, as the various Generals, declaring that they spoke for the Nation, sought to intimidate their opponents

---

(14) See the Plan of Cuernavaca, 1824, Article 28. Gregorio Melendez (November, 1850) was vague on specific details but clear on intent: "Those who are opposed to this Plan shall be punished by the commander of his section." But he promised to restore rank and active assignments to all Army personnel previously discharged. For good measure he added, "All individuals who, on this occasion, give their services to bring about this Plan shall be recompensed in due time."
Anastasio Zerecero called for the exile of certain persons, then concluded, "Any of the expatriated who shall return to the territory of the Republic within the time stated in Art. 2 shall be considered a traitor." The Plan of the Amphitrionic League (1835) called for the death of President Santa Anna and all the ministers who had assisted him under the Plan of Cuernavaca (1834). See also the Plan of the Conspiracy of Deputy Gondra (1830); also the Plan of Gregorio Melendez (November, 1850); the Second Plan of Blancarte (September, 1852); the Revisions of the Plan of Hospicio, (November, 1852); the Plan of the Declaration of Mexico (1854); the Plan of Nuevo Utrecho (1875); the Plan of Tuxtepec, (1876).

24

by charging them with this most terrible of political crimes. Indeed the Declaration of Independence had set the tone and Generals but followed the precedent. Thus at one extreme Death or at the other Bankruptcy yawned for the unwary of the unlucky who ignored or neglected giving an 'adhesion' as the occasion required.

However, declarations of amnesty or of toleration varied with the declarers themselves and their enforcement depended upon perceived shifts in public support. Deputy Zerecero first made the declaration which later became so common:"No one shall be molested or harmed for public opinions which he may have manifested by word or writing, or by actions until the publication of this law [to swear allegiance to the Constitution of 1824]." Plans and public declarations of the 1830's frequently express opposition to the reform program of the time and they remind the Administration that attempts to suppress opposition should not be blemished by personal vengeance. The Plan of Hospicio (October, 1852) repeated promises to permit refugee State administrators to return to the City and to enjoy their homes in peace, but a revision of the Plan in Tamaulipas called for an Assembly under the Plan "to expedite a judicious and thorough law of amnesty for all political crimes." Obviously all those brave declarations of no retribution for past political opinions had come to nothing.

The Plan of Ecatzinco (February, 1834) offered a way out of the morass. "No one shall be disturbed for past political actions or opinions, but all who oppose this Plan his life shall irremissibly be taken." It declared further that property owners who refuse to lend necessary help shall be treated as enemies of the State.

The Planners never established a stable balance between forgiveness and punishment for political errors. The Plan of the Congress (September, 1841) concluded by setting a chronological limit to its offer for "an absolute amnesty for all political crimes which have occurred since the 1st of August last until the date of the publication of this decree." The usual offer had been forgiveness of all political crimes "since Independence" or "since 1824."(15)

---

(15) See Colonel Escalada's Plan of May, 1833. General Duran (June, 1833) while willing to pardon

25

political offenses, came out strong for law and order. See the Declaration of Oaxaca (1834); the Plan of Texca (1835) provided amnesty for all political offenders since Independence, save for Santa Anna and his ministers. The Pronouncement of Toluca (1835) promised to protect the uncommitted: "Only those opposed to this Pronouncement shall be turned out of office," and as one might suppose, Nicolas Bravo's Plan of Conciliation promised a general amnesty for all political crimes, but the quality of his mercy was not to be too greatly strained: offenders must desist--he did not ask repudiation--from supporting all prior political commitments. General Urrea's Plan (July, 1840) presumably offered amnesty, and his opponents had reason to be wary: "All political mistakes since Independence are to be forgotten and no person is to be persecuted for so-called [sic] crimes of opinion." The Plan of the Factions (July, 1840) carried the usual proviso that no person should be punished for his political opinions and those now imprisoned were to be released. Notably, it made no exceptions. See also the Plan of the Garrison of Jalisco (October, 1852).

The Plan of the Factions (July, 1840) carried the usual proviso that no person should be punished for his political opinions and those then imprisoned should be released. It made no exceptions.

But exceptions, like forgiveness, require the best of human nature when the best is rarely on display. The Declaration of the Garrison of Mexico City (December, 1842) pledged to prevent Mexicans from being molested for their political conduct up to the present time.

26

Besides the stick--the carrot: authors of the various Plans, Pronouncements, and Declarations did not forget to offer enticements. For their adhesions they promised to military supporters various benefits--no transfer to the unfavorable posts, or they guaranteed employment for all commanders [jefes], officers, and troops, both National Guard and Regulars. Commissions would be granted to "qualified persons" who would not oppose the future Constitution: presumed military competence linked to political principle.(16)

General Urrea's Plan (July, 1840) recognized the Army as the enforcing arm of any agreement. Article I provided that "the troops of each Army shall withdraw to occupy positions outside the capital" and the final Article thoughtfully provided: "in order that the first Article shall take effect, the Government shall provide the funds and other necessities to each and all the forces." By 1846 the following article, with but the slightest changes, had become traditional, "The existence of the Army is guaranteed, it being treated as befits a military class of a free people."(17)

---

(16) See the Plan of Echegaray (December, 1858) or the Definitively Regenerative Plan (1855). The Pact of 1853 called for a general amnesty, but offered a curious proviso, "One shall not allege as merit that he served the cause of revolution, nor shall it be a disqualification that he opposed it."

(17) Plan of Regeneration (May, 1846)

In the abstract all Mexicans wanted to find a way out of the persistent political and civil turmoil of the early republican years. They approved of such general declarations as "No individual shall be molested for his political opinions" or "All that has passed in previous revolutions shall be entirely forgotten and no person shall be persecuted for them." But then came the exceptions which would sweep away certain specific enemies: "Only those who directly or indirectly opposed the general will as developed in this Plan shall be punished in accordance with the laws." Everything would be correct when the Revolution Triumphant had passed a law to provide punishment for its opponents. The formula: Legalism equals Justice. The necessity of frequent repetition of this sort of declaration bears mute testimony to its steady violation.

Magnanimous gestures toward those who from earlier days found themselves on the wrong side of the political fence were accompanied by a warning to adherents both within and without the movement. For the enlisted personnel, "Once sworn in the ranks of the Army, any person absent without leave for one week will be considered a deserter, shall lose his citizenship, shall be looked upon as guilty of treason to the Nation [lesa Patria], will be prosecuted, and once caught shall be executed by a firing squad within six hours." Deserting officers were assigned to a somewhat slower death, an unfavorable and often fatal posting to the hot lands. Those involved in the Declaration of Campeche (November, 1829) sought to protect themselves by inserting the Article, "The individuals embraced in this pronouncement cannot be moved from this station until the form of government for which they have declared shall have been settled." One did not lightly enlist in the forces of the most recent Plan.(18)

---

(18) See also the Plan of Potosi (1823), or the Declaration of Vera Cruz (July, 1832) when Santa Anna charged his opponents with "invoking sacred names in order to invest themselves with power, quenching their vengeance by making Mexican blood run in torrents in the fields and on the scaffolds, and systematizing the harshest and worst tyranny." Also, the Declaration of the Garrison of San Luis Potosi (December, 1845); the Plan of Regeneration (1846).

28

While promising condign punishment for opponents of a Plan, its supporters sought to strengthen their position by declaring that they were committed unto death itself "with weapons in our hands." Sometimes the wording varied, but the meaning was clear. General Santa Anna's Plans frequently concluded with a promise that became a standard expression for so many imitators, "[the forces] will not loose weapons from their hands without first seeing accomplished the aforementioned Articles." And so down the years Plans echoed the sanguinary refrain, "Death to the opponents of the Plan" and "We resolve to declare ourselves publicly and to sustain with arms in hand the following Articles..."(19)

Civilian officials within the Departments of government who disagreed with a Plan temporarily triumphant generally suffered a less drastic fate: they were called upon to resign forthwith. In a society with a narrow economic base, loss of one's government position could bring disaster upon a whole family. Such threats could inspire fear—and silence—if not loyalty. Since so many Plans were offered and since they covered both sides of the political scene, every man faced condemnation by one side or the other. Common sense had to prevail, and it became customary to offer pardon to civilian employees of the Administration for perceived political offenses. The Plan of Ecatzinco (1834) thoughtfully provided that officials to be exiled might take one-third of their wealth in gold or silver with them.

However, with the passing of years the penalty for rejection of a Plan became something less than traitorous to the nation. General Zapata's Plan of Ayala (1911) bridged the ancient gap by declaring, "Opponents of the Plan who take arms in hand shall be judged as traitors to the cause, especially those who once supported the Plan of San Luis Potosi." He limited retribution to those who opposed "with arms in hand," and to early converts to the revolution who, if they had not abandoned the movement had deserted his leadership. Such people he characterized

---

(19) The Revolutionary Plan (October, 1849); General Inclan in the Plan of Lerna (April, 1832); or the Manifesto of Colonel Hernandez Netro (May, 1938)

as "landowners, fancy politicians, and political hacks" and these unworthies faced the loss of two-thirds of their property. The General's vocabulary proved more violent than the specific punishments to be dealt out. After the Revolution of 1910 showers of death did not rain upon officials and administrators who had failed to support a Plan--they were merely repudiated. This left-handed disposition became the standard and logical proviso.

. . . .

Within a remarkably short time an Adhesion became the traditional method of declaring support for a public polity as favored by a military personage of somewhat more than local importance. Nearby communities and ultimately any larger cities in the general area tended to give endorsement at the strategic moment "in order to avoid the effusion of blood of its citizens" as well as to declare themselves "desirous of making a contribution to ending the evils which afflict the Republic no less than to follow the praiseworthy conduct of the capital city," and therewith it freely and of its own accord endorsed the Plan of this or that General whose forces lay not too far away.(20)

The Generals, Santa Anna included, never offered public criticism of the Judicial branch. Rather, they rendered verbal tribute to its faithful discharge of public duties; they testified to its importance, nor did they offer to clear the bench for a more complaisant personnel. One reason for this judicial immunity may be that the Mexican courts followed the results of successive revolutions as carefully as the United States Supreme Court is presumed to follow the election returns.

As for the civilian politicians, the Generals seem to have regarded them as day laborers who maintained the national machinery while they, the skilled craftsmen, answered calls for emergency repairs or construction. Political graft the Military understood and forgave--the modest loot of little men. Between the Military and the Politician there developed a gulf that until the appearance of Porfirio Diaz no man really bridged.

---

(20) For example, see the Pronouncements of Cutzamala and of Temoaya, (October, 1832), in El Fanal, November 11, 1832.

The Generals, hardened in their disdain, never
bothered to correct this public dichotomy, and when,
in the course of rotation, the civilians came into
power, they wisely forbore to inquire into the
devious practices and many perquisites to which the
Army had easily accustomed itself. When it seemed
necessary, and that was often--both of them pilfered
from the national Treasury.

Naturally it is sometimes difficult for a later
generation to distinguish between a barracks revolt
against some perceived injustice to the Military
class and a Plan of governmental reform seriously
considered. General Montana (December, 1826) sought
to arouse the nation to the presence of Freemasonry;
Gregorio Melendez (November, 1830) promised to
abolish the interstate customs houses. To be precise
one had to remain small, but Santa Anna's ability to
say all things to all men stood him in good stead as
he repeatedly issued his Plans from the capital
fortress of Perote. (21)

One gets the impression that for Santa Anna the
present Plan, the next, and the next was a means of
killing some vagary within himself, of quieting a
fever that he never lost. A man of brilliant parts,
he was recognized as such by his contemporaries even
while he teased them into being something less than
they intended to be. His repeated retirements and
exiles, his farewells and his trumpeted returns were
as sure as the flight of birds. A master of
flim-flam, he seems never to have rejected political
principle deliberately--he simply laughed it off
while gathering into his hands the reins of power.
But he finally misjudged his nation: while in exile
he ended his political life by offering to assist the
intrusive Emperor Maximilian.

Across the generations the Generals, military
politicians, were young men, mostly, whose lives
corresponded with the years of constant war within or
out. In either case they fought on their own land and
so stayed at home. Among themselves they were rebels
who practiced miniature wars and were content with
small rewards. Really these little soldiers--

---

(21) The Declaration of the Garrison of Vera Cruz
(January, 1831), or his half-Plan, half-Pronouncment
of September 9, 1841. Santa Anna was behind the Plan
of Quintinar, the Plan of Jalapa, that of Zerecero,
the Plan of Arista, and a host of others; that is, he
was the beneficiary of all of them.

<u>militarojes</u>--had no stomach for a definitive victory. Their short, repetitious Plans of Mexico's first half-century served as political pistols which a General could level at his opponent and annihilate him completely. Alternately the Generals beat Mexican ears with threats of Doomsday or offers of sweet hopes for happier days. But always there remained the thundering terror of the descent of troops, unbridled, let loose on the cities, a terror that struck nameless dread and drained the reservoirs of courage.

The Plans testify to the Generals' ambidextrous skill in holding their military associates in thrall for the big push with one hand and with the other to hoist their flaunting ambition to the top of the nearest and tallest flagpole. They never failed to assure wavering followers of the civilian and the military of rewards to be theirs if the Plan then batting the breezes in place of the national flag should receive their support. But the authors of all these early Plans were pulverized by the wasting wars. Tempted by Time, they gave all for the great Day when they, too, even <u>they</u>, might sit in the Presidential chair. Command of Army units as the only organized, effective societal grouping in Mexico gave them arbitrary power over the country. They responded to the opportunity for aggrandizement and made it a way of life. This was their Apple of Eden, the source of their capacity for harm. For the Planners failure became addictive; it drugged their senses if not their sensibilities.

Again, civilians of national renown might collaborate with some General on a Plan, but their efforts, marked by compromises, often echoed too much of committee reports, and the Republic turned away from their joint efforts, as Urrea and Gomez Farias learned. Paredes chose to go alone. As commander of the vital military post in the national capital, he found himself in an ideal position to evaluate the rising flood of Plans from back of Beyond, and he chose to denigrate them with successive Plans of his own, but not all with his name attached.(22)

---

(22) Apparently General Paredes was over-eager or else his secretarial staff became confused, for on January 3, 1846, he issued a "Plan of Mexico [City]: that was identical with the two Plans, one of them in his own name, issued earlier.

Rather the garrison under his command issued Acts, Pronouncements, or Declarations, all of them subject to revision or cancellation as Time and Opposition might indicate. Calderon de la Barca, who lived in Mexico during the greatest wave of Plans while her husband was serving as Spanish minister in that country, described the situation:

"This revolution is like a game of chess, in which kings, castles, knights and bishops are making different moves, while the pawns are looking on or taking no part whatever." To understand the state of the board, it is necessary to explain the position of the four principal pieces: Santa Anna, Bustamante, Paredes, and Valencia.

"The first move was made by Paredes, who published his plan, and pronounced on the eighth of August at Guadalajara. About the same time, Don Francisco Morphy, a Spanish broker who had gone to Manga de Clavo, was sent to Guadalajara and had conference with Paredes, the result of which was that the plan of that general was withdrawn, and it was supposed that he and Santa Anna had formed a combination. Shortly after, the Censor de Vera Cruz, a newspaper entirely devoted to Santa Anna, pronounced in favor the plan of Paredes, and Santa Anna, with a few miserable troops and a handful of cavalry, arrived at Perote. Here he remains for the present, kept in check by the government [through] General Torrejon."(23)

The Plans tell us more about the Generals than about the evils which they promised to correct. Ah--those Generals--jumpy, electric-quick to sense an opportunity, their physical and social needs sandbagged by rank and the unquestioned perogatives of unchecked graft. They sought two goals: the Presidency, of course; from its political heights they might cast Jovian thunderbolts at the envious ones below. They might even assign dangerous colleagues to the Hot Lands, the dreaded coastal regions so often fatal to those bred to the temperate uplands. Or, failing the Presidency in spite of gile and political strategy, they might strive for the ultimate accolade even more prestigious than the Presidency itself--to cajole Congress into voting the title to surpass all else, the right to hear the sonorous ring of an (official introduction as one entered the governmental) salon--"Benemerito de la

(23) Me. Calderon de la Barca, Life in Mexico, (1966), p. 497.

Patria." [Well-deserving of the Fatherland.] This title won, whether in the Presidency or out, it comforted a General all his days, even on those untoward occasions when he might pass slow years in exile.

In the process of voting this most esteemed of titles, the Congress acted with coy reserve and apparently without following any precedent. It appears to have over-ruled the Law of Probability: a vote for this man or another, each hopeful for himself. Congressional favor swooping as it would, a General waited helplessly, his military progress and his gile of small account. That great exemplar of Benemerito, Santa Anna, suffered repeated defeats at arms; he lost control of Congress, and he spent years in repeated exiles. "Benemerito" guaranteed nothing, yet men cherished the word for its own sake.

In the sad, the dreary years of Santa Anna the commanding officers of sufficient prestige to lead a reform movement against the government may have been competent in their profession, but they were not skilled in political subtlety. Nothing could conceal their rabid desire for office even if it had to be won at the point of a bayonet, but from a position of political eminence they planned to reap unmentioned rewards. With a Plan they tested the political currents and with its reception they might guide their warped ambitions. If the Presidency should escape them, there might loom a military promotion. With a modicum of public notice a colonel might expect to bear up under the weight of a General's epaulettes, and all the officers who followed a successful General could expect a promotion—the Plans assumed as much even if it was not clearly stated.

The Plans frequently read alike! Of course they do. The Generals did not possess minds fertile with new ideas. Besides, having drafted a Plan and in search of endorsements, they would send it to other near-by commanders. These worthies, in turn, would survey the text with a reasonably approving eye, call a meeting of their own staff and submit the document to the judgement of their subordinates. Out of this conference often came a ratification of the original Plan, but with a modification of three or four procedural points.

This textual alteration sometimes caused the declaration to be titled separately as a "Plan." Occasionally, as if to legitimize the variant off-spring, the introductory Considerandos would acknowledge the paternity, but--acknowledged or not--the resemblance was more than skin deep: it was bred in the bone.

The Plans challenged a General's literary skills, and many of them bear mute testimony of a close copy of another Plan recently declared. Also unspecified promises with vague and uncertain references often crept into the text.(24) Graciously their fellow officers understood what they had meant to say, and that served well enough.

---

(24) See, for example, the revisions of the Plan of Hospicio as attempted by Colonel Casanova after he had won Tempico for a surging revolution; or the Plan of General Salas (August, 1846) for its casual attitudes.

CHAPTER IV
The Plans and the Mexican Union

During the course of their struggle for Independence Mexicans did not greatly concern themselves about the precise nature of their future political union, but with final defeat of the Spanish forces in 1821 the machinery of self-government demanded attention. One of the earliest official documents, the Acta Constitutiva of 1824, affirmed the dilemma: "All sovereignty resides basically and essentially in the Nation," yet Article VI added, "Its integral parts are independent states, free and sovereign in that which touches their internal administration and government." Subsequently various Plans have justified calls for secession because they felt that the central Administration was violating state sovereignty.(25)

The early Plan of Cuernavaca (1824), Article Six, concluded, "The government of all the States shall be that of a Popular Representative Federated Republic."(26)

The Plan of Codallos (1830) lamented the lack of zeal "to maintain the integrity of the Federation as involved in the interesting areas of California, of beautiful Texas, and in the peninsula of Yucatan," and it called for dispatch of regular army units to those restless areas. For a generation the Plans echoed the phraseology of such as that of Zavaleta (1832) when it promised "to maintain in all its integrity and purity the system of popular, representative, federal government."

Under Spanish administration the political subdivisions were called "provinces." For a brief period the term 'provinces' and 'states' were used interchangeably. Finally the term 'States' was accepted for regular usage. The Constituent Act of Federation (1824) used both.

---

(25) See, for example, the Proclamation of San Luis, Potosi (April, 1837)

(26) The Agreement of the Free State of Jalisco (June, 1823) stated that "all the towns of the province [sic] favored in a clear and decisive manner a representative, federal government."

36

After the brief interlude of a native monarchial experiment, the concept of a popular representative federated administration was extended to the national congress which, on matters of general concern, should speak for all. Many Plans repeated as in a chorus that the nation was one and indivisible, yet they regularly referred to their political association as a "Federation." While alluding to "the Nation" and only slightly less frequently to "the Republic", it seems that they were thinking of "the Union" as an umbrella term for states associated in a federated compact.

Time and time again a Plan rested its justification upon the clear, unabashed sovereignty of a State: the State could reclaim its sovereignty and withdraw from the Union for certain and good reasons until such and such conditions should be met. In 1832 the State of Zacatecas declared, "The governor of the State shall proceed with its foreign policy in conformity with this decree, and in order to maintain its position it may raise up to 6,000 men of the civil militia and underwrite all expenses judged necessary." Whether the word "foreign" embraced the remaining Mexican states or referred to the countries across the sea is not clear.

The Decree of the States of Jalisco (February, 1836) very specifically declared that the State was seceding from the Mexican union and that it would not return to it nor associate with any other State which might accept the reactionary Plan of Uraga and of Hara y Tamariz. Indeed, the State declared its readiness to establish a pact of alliance with other States which, from its firm tone, should take precedence over the national union itself. Intermittently the call for States' Rights in a form so extreme as to suggest an impending secession has echoed across the country.

While the cause of States Rights has never suffered a definitive defeat as in the United States, it has never lost its marginal appeal either. When the State of Sonora sent its adhesion to the Revolutionary Plan of Arispe in December, 1837, it included an additional communication to the President which began, "The State of Sonora declares that it never renounced nor intended to renounce the preogatives of Sovereignty which it granted to the Nation in the Acta Constitutiva of 1824."(27) As the term was bandied about in Mexico, a political 'secession' meant no more than repudiation of the

---

(27) Antonio G. Rivera, La revolucion en Sonora, 32.

governing administration. When the action included a threat of defense of the State with weapons in hand, clearly the matter had become serious. Either a compromise had to be devised or the dissidents had to be suppressed by force of arms.

The idea of refusal to cooperate with the national administration under the banner of secession has sprouted in Mexico's political garden like a weed. In 1848 a priest, Father Jarauta, issued a short Plan of his own. After disavowing the national administration, he called upon the States to resume their sovereignty. However, he was not considering a permanent secession of any sort, for his next proviso summoned the seceding States to agree on some method of replacing the central administration which he hoped to overturn. General Blancarte, in his Plan of 1852, said that he issued his call from "the free and sovereign State of Jalisco." Article I read, "As of this day the State of Jalisco returns to the constitutional order from which the publication of Decree No. 135 had separated it." Article II continued, "As a consequence, it repudiates the existing national administration..." Unfortunately for Blancarte, he could not balance the issue of state governmental authority without defining the role of the national organization, and it is this difficulty which has frustrated all succeeding Mexican Staterighters. Only in the realm of theorists who delight in spinning legal fantasies have the Mexican states ever been sovereign.

Although never fully developed, the idea of State Sovereignty never died. The Plan of Zacatoaxtla (December, 1855) declared that if the national administration should not be put to rights, "division of the Republic and secession of some of the States will result." This event, the Planners frequently declared, would "bring about the ruin of the Republic and its national existence".(28)

The idea of a fully sovereign and free State within the Mexican union continued to remain a threat, a declaration of dissatisfaction to be broadcast by dissidents. The Plan of Nayarit (January, 1873) referred to "the Mexican Confederation" rather than to a Union or a Nation, and a few years later the Revolutionary Plan of Garza (September, 1891) gave a general endorsement to the idea of 'state sovereignty' as a means of expressing opposition to the centralized administration of Porfirio Diaz.

---

(28) The Plan of the Garrison of Jalisco (October, 1852), "The Mexican nation is one and indivisible." So also the Plan of Hospicio (October, 1852), which is a copy of that of Jalisco. The Pact of February 6, 1853, endorsed the nationalist position of the Plan of Jalisco.

The Plan of Arroyo Zarco (February, 1853) called for a national government for the good of all the Republic. The Basis for Administration of the Republic (April, 1853) declared State assemblies in recess. The Plan of the Declaration of Mexico [City] circa March, 1854) assumed that all State endorsements would declare that "The Nation is and always shall remain one, separate, indivisible, and independent." The Plan of Zacapaoaxtla (December, 1855) warned against "the continuation of anarchy, of terrible disorder, or division of the Republic, and of possible secession of some of the States." The Plan of Echeagaray (December, 1858) sought the organization of a national government without restrictions and with widest liberty--an implicit repudiation of States rights.

This long dormant concept blossomed during the Revolution (1910-1917) and "the Federation" often assumed the mystic role of "the Nation." The Plan of Santa Rosa (February, 1912) issued its call in the name of "the Federation." The Manifesto of General Gorostieta (October, 1918) referred to "the Federation of the States." Colonel Hernandez Netro in 1938 published his Manifesto on behalf of General Saturnino Cedillo, the local caudillo. It went the full route and declared the secession of the State of San Luis Potosi, and as a free and sovereign entity the Plan abrogated its national representation in the Mexican Union. Then, lest it appear too drastic, the Manifesto promised that "The present legal movement shall have as its faithful standard the exact observance of the General Constitution of the Republic." Presumably the secessionists were referring to the charter of 1917. How these two ideas could be combined is not clear, but crystal clear was the declaration that under the guise of state sovereignty the revolutionary movement would collect taxes and appropriate all sums found in town treasuries. Also, it would "accept loans either voluntary or forced." Such action would have amounted to effective secession.

Such actions reveal sure signs of political desperation. Sometimes a State or a combination of States have issued a Plan on the assumption that sponsorship by a large political segment would give the Plan greater public acceptance, but there is objective evidence that it did.(29)

---

(29) See the National Notice: State of San Luis Potosi (March, 1830), or the Plan of the Departments (October, 1841)

The State-sponsored Plans read like those issued by individuals on their own responsibility: they proclaimed eloquent aims for the Nation, but they advanced no political solution to the problems then harassing Mexico.

Among Mexicans the voice of Liberalism and Reform has most often been heard through the call for a relatively decentralized republican federation, but during most of the operative years centralization of effective national power remained a fact of life. This issue was most vigorously contested in the decades of 1830 and 1840 and 1850, the era of Santa Anna's greatest power and influence.(30)

---

(30) The Pronouncement of Toluca (1835) called for a 'centralized republic' with separation of powers, and Santa Anna to continue as President and Protector of the Nation. Also the Declaration of Campeche, November, 1829, stood for Federalism; the Plan of Quintanar, December, 1829, for Federalism; the Plan of Zeracero, February, 1830, for Federalism; the Plan of Codallos, March, 1830, for Federalism; the Plan of Jalapa, December, 1829, for Federalism; the Plan of Jalapa, September, 1830, for Federalism; the Declaration of the Garrison of Vera Cruz, January, 1832, for federalism; the Plan of the Government, December, 1832, for Federalism; the Plan of Zabaleta, December, 1832, for Federalism; the Plan of Colonel Escalada, May, 1833, for Centralism; the Plan of General Duran, June 1833, for Centralism; the Plan of General Arista, June, 1833, for Centralism; the Second Plan of General Duran, July, 1833, for Centralism; the Plan of the Allied States, July, 1833, for Centralism; the Plan of the Allied States, July, 1833, for Federalism. The Plan of Ecatzinco, February, 1834, promised to bring about pacification and stable conditions, to assure union, liberty, justice and equality of rights through a monarchy moderated by a constitution. The political games with "Liberalism" and "Centralism" as trump cards continued for a full generation.

Politically the numbing defeat of Mexico in the Texas War discredited the Centralist cause which Santa Anna was leading, while the State of San Luis Potosi most actively promoted demands for a type of states-rights, federalist administration, but Mexico continued so disoriented that Plans calling for one or another type of government tumbled out in obvious confusion. General Salas, in his second Decree for the Restoration of the Federal System (August, 1846) declared in favor of the Constitution of 1824 with its decentralized organization until something better could be devised. Legal definitions escaped him. The General would have done better to limit himself to a broad declaration, for the details of his so-called reorganization would have authorized the most extreme centralization.

All this agitation came to nothing. The Declaration of Jalapa (August, 1846) from the heart of Santa Anna country, called upon their intermittent President to stop considering ideas for constitutional reform and to take charge as an operative Dictator, because, said the Jalapenos, the Federation as established under the Constitution of 1824 had been destroyed.

Outbreak of war with the United States in 1846 did not result in a cementing of the bond between the Mexican States and the central government. Rather, the Oaxaca Declaration of February, 1847, revealed the fragile condition of national unity. It referred to "reconciling constitutional principles and those of justice with the circumstances of this particular State with the urgent necessities of the general government of the North." Almost Mexico City represented an alien administration.

Declarations by other states reveal the same attitude. In 1837 the City of San Luis Potosi, about as far north of the national capital as Oaxaca to the south, issued a Proclamation aimed at reorganizing the Mexican Union. Article II declared, "As soon as they find themselves free from the oppression in which they are held by the present administration, the confederated States shall reorganize themselves in every possible way in accord with their own constitution and particular laws."

In order to meet the oppression of Mexicans by Mexicans, Article III continued, "As of Today the Free State of San Luis Potosi enters into full exercise of its Independence and sovereignty in all that relates to its internal administration, and it disowns the general powers which exist today in the Nation." If put into operation, such action would have meant operative secession. In periods of crisis the central government was perceived as an uncaring or even a hostile entity.

Out of the mists of defeat in the war with the United States emerged Santa Anna, who should have been discredited forever, and by devoting his considerable political talents to the cause of Centralism, he rode the issue once more into the Presidency and transformed that office into a dictatorship. With Santa Anna overthrown, Federalism returned under the Plan of Ayutla, but the intervention of Maximilian under French protection interrupted its program. Monarchy represented the ultimate in centralization, but once that form of government had been ousted the struggling Federalists seemed about to resume their program. Then the country lapsed into the long dictatorship of Porfirio Diaz.

Still Federalism as a name and as a cause persisted. After proclaiming the indissoluble union of the Mexican Republic, Madero, in his Plan of San Luis Potosi, spoke of "the Federation" of Mexico. De la Huerta's Plan of 1923 referred to "the Federation" in the same breath with "the Union" and in 1929 the Plan of Vasconcelos characterized the Mexican Union as "a Federation." In the very last Mexican Plan (1940) the followers of General Almazan endorsed "the Federation" which they declared that the Congress of the United States of Mexico had accepted.

Almost to the end sponsors of action to secure reform have justified their Plans on the basis of secession--a sovereign State may secede from the Union at its own pleasure. As one reads further, a proud State, ever watchful for the liberties of all Mexicans, calls upon others to join its revolt and to declare that with triumph crowning their efforts all the States must adhere to the program of the victors. Although a State may claim the right to revolt, it does not contemplate living in single blessedness, nor in victory does it propose to permit equally sovereign states to walk a solitary path. Nothing the equivalent of an organized Southern Confederacy in the United States has ever harassed Mexico. Without political roots save in the hearts of the dissatisfied, state sovereignty has remained a stunted shrub of an idea.

The Constitution of 1917 presents a modern version of Federalism, but control of policies emanates from Mexico City. Post-Revolutionary Plans, beating the drum of Federalism, declare that Federalism means Confederation, while those in power continue to control through an operative Centralism, regardless of their own protestations. Those out of power seek it by appealing to Federalized localism: Principles and Practices forever at odds.

The Federation... The Confederation... the idea still sleeps within the Mexican political psyche. The very last Plan attempted to rally dissenters within the Administration by labeling the Mexican Union a Federation even while declaring utter fidelity to the Constitution of 1917 and to the concept of Democracy in Mexico where liberty, order and social justice should reign.

CHAPTER V
The Plans and the Constitution

Concurrently with the outbreak of their revolution against Spain, Mexicans promised each other that with the success of their movement there should be a Constitution, a marvelous document designed to embrace all public and private good, a document which might serve as a guiding light for all future governing officials. The agency to be authorized to produce this great charter would be a "Constituent Congress," a body to be summoned on call of a recognized leader, its members to be composed of sensible, competent men of proven merit who would meet as the call for the Congress might specify. In June, 1823, the State of Jalisco issued such a call. Within a year Mexico had its Constitution, but almost immediately those dissatisfied with that document demanded another Congress, this one to be "truly constituent," which would draft another constitution. This routine, to be embodied in so many future Plans, became the standard of those agitating for almost any kind of reform. Such Plans, Initiatives, or Act [Resolutions] carry the bloodstains of brave, devoted, but often defeated men. They indicate, too, the path of thwarted patriotism and of crushed ego. (31)

If the Plans are a fair guide, the Mexican people--at least those who were politically aware--early lost faith in the Constitution of 1824 as their rallying point, and they moved from revision and suggested amendments to demands for a new document. Usually the Plans specified that an "Extraordinary Body should, through dilatory tactics, keep itself in session for some imagined benefit to its members, its duties of revision often were circumscribed carefully, and it would be ordered to complete its task within a specific time.(32)

---

(31) See the National Notice of San Luis Potosi (March, 1830); the Project for the Political Reorganization of the Republic (December, 1832); the Declaration of the Citizens of Coatepec (September, 1841).

(32) See the Plan of Paredes (August, 1841); the Plan of Zacatecas (September, 1841).

Any Plan that entertained even a slight hope of adoption needed the support of the Army. Therefore, officers who had command of troops at the ready and with access to the Federal treasury commonly issued or sponsored Plans. The Project for Political Reorganization (December, 1832) with its hope of extensive revisions of the Constitution of 1824 does not once mention the Army--an error of judgment on the part of too trusting civilians.

Out of the political confusion of the Centralist-Federalist conflict of the 1830's General Barragan drifted into power. Needing a Plan and having no particular ideas on the matter, he plagarized the Proposal for Reorganization of the Republic, abridged it, and issued his personalized version as an Edict. Three months later he ordered a puppet Congress to re-issue his Edict as a declaration of Constitutional Bases (December, 1835). A man with no ideas could do no more.

Sometimes a State rather than an individual would sponsor a Plan, publish it in the primitive newspapers of the day, then seek the approval and assistance of other States.(33) Potentially, a combination of States could create a political crisis, but an alliance of States never held together for the long haul. The Plan of the Congress (September, 1841) called for "the Executive Power to be placed in the person or persons whom it is judged suitable," and in the meantime the current President would continue governing the Republic in company with those who had received the accolade "Well-deserving of the Fatherland,"--namely Nicolas Bravo and Antonio Lopez de Santa Anna, as well as the Generals in active service.

Occasionally a civilian found an opportunity to present a Plan of his own. He would introduce his proposal as a bill into the Legislature, but invariably the Plan was too long, too long to be read at a sitting, unless the sitting itself were too long! Such a bill, "The Plan for the Political Constitution of the Mexican Nation" (October, 1841)

---

(33) See the Plan of the Allied States (July, 1833); Declaration of the State of Oaxaca (May, 1834); the Proclamation of San Luis Potosi (April, 1837); that of the State of Zacatecas (September, 1841); the National Appeal of the State of Jalisco (December, 1857); the Plan of the Departments (October, 1841).

enters into the specifics of congressional representation, of election, of legislative powers, both state and national, of ratings for those promoting the general welfare, another for those winning national honors; it laid out qualifications for judges and drew lines of jurisdiction. The Plan provided for a National Institute to promote educational programs as devised by the legislative branch and as supported by provincial institutes. All in all, it testified to a thoughtful and informed authorship, but it reached beyond the comprehension of the literate public. The Generals kept the common touch.

Civilian Plans stated aims and aspirations, but they omitted any discussion of how these aims were to be achieved. In reply to Santa Anna's Plan of Tacubaya (September, 1841) the civilians stated, "A popular, representative, federal system and the Constitution of 1824 shall be established immediately." How this and other ends were to be achieved they did not say--merely, "The national shall proceed..."(34)

The robust citizens of Coatepec (September, 1841) appealed first to the patriotic impulses of the Military:

"The people and the Nation appeal to the Generals who today are issuing pronouncements against the tyranny of the factions that they do not return the sword to the scabbard until they have succeeded in seeing all Mexicans reestablished in the full enjoyment of their rights."

Then they offered a patriotic justification: "We have proclaimed the following Plan, one which we believe necessary to save the Republic from imminent risk of losing its independence and liberty." No doubt many authors of Plans were moved by the sincerest conviction that they possessed some formula which would certainly save the Nation. The ache which the anonymous civilian who issued his extended Plan felt for his contry "broke through language and escaped."

---

(34) See the Plan of the Seminary (October, 1841), composed while the Capital was under fire.

"It is a difficult enterprise to give
laws that will organize any nation in
the world, and much more difficult for
one like ours where the negative
principles are plentiful, where the
most sordid interests germinate,
fermenting anti-social passions and
where the monster of discord dominates."

And then gently, "Mexico has passed through all the
graduations of the political scale, but not in the
prudent, gradual manner that insures the best
results..."(35)

In the general confusion of national
irregularities the usual Plan embraced one or more of
the following points: 1) A national executive
committee of Junta shall meet within a designated
time span after the victory of the revolutionary
movement; 2) Each State shall choose two
representatives to serve in the impending national
Junta; 3) The Junta, in turn, shall name a Supreme
Director [sometimes he would be called "Supreme
Executive" and occasionally the Plan would require
the Junta to name three men who would serve jointly
as the "Supreme Executive Power"]: 4) The Executive
Power being installed, it should then issue a call
for the States, sometimes designated as Departments,
to name men--usually two--of known capacity and of
some financial competence, to serve in an
extraordinary Congress whose sole duty should be to
draft another Constitution. 5) With the Constitution
drafted and a call for elections issued by the
Executive Power, the work of the Extraordinary
Congress was done, and it would be ordered to
disband. 6) The newly elected Congress then should
assemble at a specified date. [Under some Plans this
Body might include members who had served in the
Extraordinary Congress; others specifically
prohibited it.]

---

(35) A Projected Constitution for the Mexican People
(October, 1841). See also the civilian drafts of
constitutions and of reorganization in 1835.

7) The Provisional Executive Power whether composed or one or more persons, would render an accounting to the newly regularized constitutional Congress.(36)

Frequently the Plans sought to set up a specific time schedule--so many days after occupation of the Capital for elections by the States, so many days after victory for appointment of temporary Executives; a specific time for the installation of permanent officers. Some Plans even declared a time limit for a Congress to write a new Constitution. Apparently the authors believed that with a proper Plan they could achieve an easy and sure constitutional reform.

Planners usually chose the most obvious way to secure reform--to promise a clean sweep; all Executive and Legislative personnel should cease forthwith to exercise their functions. The Judiciary, often unmentioned, they left unscathed and its personnel served as a reservoir from which to draw presumably unbiased and honest persons for other governmental functions. Indeed, the Chief Justice (often called the President) of the Supreme Court was to be required by the Plan of the Restorers (February, 1847) to appoint pro tem officials who would replace regular civil servants and to set the date for national alections. Sometimes a Plan resorted to direct action and named the interim President (or Supreme Director) who would, in turn, name the permanent President of the Nation.

Inevitably the Army, as the only organized, central group with national recognition had great influence, in the drafting of Plans. Its importance increased in periods of personal dominance such as that of General Santa Anna, or in time or crisis as the war with the United States. In 1845 General Paredes became infected with the Presidential fever which he contracted while serving as commandant of the Garrison of Mexico City. First, Paredes prepared

---

(36) See, for example, the Declaration of the Citizens of Coatepec (September, 1841, of Vera Cruz (September, 1841), or the Plan of the Congress (September, 1841).

the text of a Plan and distributed it to his staff. These officers dutifully and unanimously endorsed it as "The Declaration of the Army" (December, 1843), as if this unit represented the total of the armed forces. Then the General issued the identical text in his own name and forwarded it to presumably friendly colleagues throughout the command area, and they, after reading the text and with few or no changes, could endorse the Plan under the name of a nearby town. With endorsements from San Luis Potosi, Vera Cruz, and a few stations in between the General felt prepared to make a bid with force of arms for the Presidency.(37)

Such stereotyped Plans represented the most traditional thinking. They protested the acts of the current Administration and ordered that as of the date of issue all officials save the Judiciary should cease functioning, because on triumph of their revolution all acts after the issue date of the Plan would be declared null and void. As for the positive program favored by Paredes and cooperating Generals, they remained open-minded and, one suspects, vacant-minded on the matter. Their Plans promised "to summon an Extraordinary Congress with ample powers to constitute the Nation without any restrictions whatsoever in their magnificent functions." Such Plans, of no real significance then, mean less today—the signatures amounts to no more than a greasy thumb-print on the arm of the Presidential chair.(38)

---

(37) See the Plans of San Luis Potosi and Vera Cruz (December, 1845); the Declaration of the Army (January, 1846); Propositions of General Paredes (January, 1846).

(38) See almost any of the Plans of the 1850's: the Revised Plans of Ayutla (March, 1854), Plan Demagogico (April, 1854), Plan of the Garrison of Mexico City (August, 1855), Plan of Toliman (December, 1855), the Definitively Regenerative Plan (December, 1855); the National Appeal from Jalisco (December, 1857); the Plan of Echeagaray (December, 1858).

After General Blancarte had paid the ultimate price--death before a firing squad for expressing his dissatisfaction in two Plans--General Uraga assumed the dangerous task of advancing his program. He circulated Blancarte's Second Plan with subsequent revisions; he conferred with fellow Generals, and they followed his urging by composing parallel Plans of their own. (39)

However, Mexico had entered the dark shadow of anarchy from which no Plan, without military force, could rescue her. For a time various Generals offered the outworn ideas of the previous decade, but they were out of touch with the political thinking represented in the Plan of Ayutla (March, 1854). Once and for all General Santa Anna and the misfortunes which he represented had to be got rid of--a process requiring military force to be applied systematically and with purpose. When such a traditional Plan as that of Toliman (December, 1855) or that of Ayotla (December, 1857) or that of Echeagaray (December, 1858) appeared, Mexicans could realize how much progress the nation had made. The Military had run out of ideas. Time itself had ground down the cutting edge of the old Plans and civilians--such men as Benito Juarez--assumed national leadership.

After having heard calls for an Extraordinary, or, as it was sometimes labeled, a Constituent Congress, for a generation, Mexico finally won its Constitution of 1857. No sooner done than the Capital read of a Plan to revise the Constitution so as to include the outmoded ideas of the Santa Anna Era. But the weary nation had enough of demands for a revision of a constitution, even of the new one. (Plan of Echeagaray, December, 1858). Thereafter the monotonous calls to redraft the national charter eased a bit. The lines, both political and military, were redrawn as the country plunged into the bitter War of the Reform which served as a prelude to the Maximilian intervention. All political thinking ceased during these times of trial and during the period of political shakedown which followed. By 1870 came Plans with a broader appeal, Plans with their emphasis on social and economic reforms: demands for more schools, a restructuring of the

---

(39) See the Plan of October 20, 1852 and the Pact of February 6, 1853, and the Plan of Arroyo Zarco, February 4, 1853.

tax program, promotion of foreign trade while protecting home industry,(40) all reforms to be accomplished under the Constitution of 1857.

President Diaz introduced himself officially as a Presidential candidate with his initial Plan of La Noria (November, 1871) and with a follow-up Plan of Tuxtepec (January, 1876). His Plans vary only slightly, and they show but little evidence of political thinking. The aspiring candidate called not for a new Constitution, but for a political reform: No Re-election. The great President, Benito Juarez, had run afoul of that Mexican ailment, continuismo, and would not retire from office nor release his control of the effective political levers of power soon enough to satisfy the ambitious General. As a neglected Out who wanted so desperately to be In, Diaz appealed for reconstruction of the Constitution--not a new one--by a convention to be composed of men "of crystal-clear honor," and he promised that they would work "with loyalty, and they will support with understanding the truly national necessities." More than that the General who was to govern Mexico for the next thirty-five years did not say. (41) He, in turn, was ousted in 1910 by the cry which he had once raised so effectively: NO RE-ELECTION.

The Revolution of 1910-1917, beginning as a revolt against the aging Diaz, ended with the drafting of a new constitution. No one planned the sequence; the Revolution simply developed a logic of its own. The man who first led the movement against Diaz and who became the Revolution's first President, Francisco I. Madero, mentioned no constitutional issues in his Plan of San Luis Potosi.

---

(40) See the Liberating Plan (January, 1873); the Plan of the Progressive Republican Party (1872-1876).

(41) General Garza, a throw-back to the old days, issued his Revolutionary Plan in 1891. He promised that first he would organize a "Constitutional Army," and thereafter he would call for a constitutional convention which should amend the 1857 Constitution in various important ways. The nation had wearied of such routine appeals from the Military and President-General Diaz was alert. General Garza subsided into nothingness.

This Socio-Political Plan of March, 1911, declared the Constitution of 1857 to be the law of the land. The Popular Evolutionist Party, in its Program and Bases (June, 1911) offered the idea, "The government of a Nation by a Nation is embodied not only the President of the Republic, but in the Legislative Body, and in the Legislative and Executive Authorities of the States." It advanced no further into the political thicket. The author of the Plan of Texcoco (August, 1911) considered "constitutional order" to be at an end. he and his staff would assume the legislative and executive powers of "the Federation," but he made no reference to drafting a new Constitution.

General Reyes, in his Plan (November, 1911) promised "a revision of the Stamp Law, the moderation of all classes of taxes, and to initiate [his program] in a constitutional form and in order to support it he would re-establish a Free Zone along the whole northern frontier of the Republic." Clearly he felt that what he called his Revolutionary Plan would observe the recognized processes laid down in the Constitution of 1857. Having served so long under President Diaz, he could do no less.

Even the radical Revolutionaries did not question the adequacy of the Constitution itself. Rather, they protested the social inequities wrought by evil men. The fabled Emiliano Zapata in his Plan of Ayala (November, 1911) only appealed for Justice, Restitution and Reform, but not a new constitution. His later and extensive "amendments" of May, 1913, made no mention of any issue save repudiation of Huerta and Orozco. Reforms under the Plan of Santa Rosa (February, 1912) called for decentralization of military forces: "The States shall have their own militias and the Federation shall not be able to command these forces unless their respective Executives solicit them in accord with prior agreement with the local legislatures," but the Plan proposed no constitutional change.

General Orozco's wide-ranging Plan of the Empacadora (March, 1912) condemned certain practices as "unconstitutional;" he promised the election of what he considered a "constitutional President," and no administration would be recognized, he said, until it had "accepted the Revolution." Beyond that he did not go.

It appears that General Carranza fancied the term "constitutional." He issued his brief Plan of the Hacienda of Guadalupe (March, 1913) on his authority as "Constitutional" Governor of the State or Coahuila. His forces he repeatedly labeled "the Constitutional Army," but nothing in his first draft of in later re-drafts of his Plan makes the slightest reference to a new federal Constitution. A new constitution as a political issue began to win attention when officers of the Carranza forces met in Torreon (July, 1914) and promised that on triumph of their movement the Army should elect from its ranks delegates to a convention which would formulate a program for the newly elected officials to follow. This idea of a convention led, ultimately, to the drafting of a new constitution, but such a step was not declared publicly in 1913. Indeed, it may not have been considered even then as a possibility, nor was the public at large to be consulted in any event.

Carranza's ideas expanded as the prospects of victory increased, and so did his Plan, now labeled "Additions to the Plan of Guadalupe (December, 1914). As First Chief of the Revolution vested with Executive Power he promised to draft legislation which would guarantee a long list of reforms which the Revolution had promised, but apparently he saw these changes as no more than statutory provisions within the range of the Constitution of 1857.

General Zapata, not to be outdone, signed an extended "Program of Political Social Reforms of the Revolution (April, 1915) in which he summarized the specific aims of the Revolution and promised their fulfillment. He listed them in categories and at length. Among the political reforms he proposed abolition of the Senate and adoption of the parliamentary form of government, but he did not ask for the drafting of a new constitution. Apparently he and his Staff felt that all their many-faceted reforms could be acheived by amending the existing national charter.

Finally, the prospect of a new constitution was explicitly stated when General Carranza issued "A Decree Revising Certain Articles of the Plan of Guadalupe." (September, 1916) The Constitutionalist cause having triumphed and Town Councils having been installed, so he said, he ordered general election of delegates to a <u>constituent</u> <u>Congress</u>, an echo of a call almost as old as the nation itself. At very long last a Plan issued as a declaration of victory had publicly voiced an idea that had been developing in the public consciousness. The following year a constituent Congress drafted the Constitution of 1917--one that in many ways proved contrary to Carranza's wishes. On the question of a new Constitution the Plans had not been enough: they had followed--not led--public opinion.

The Plans so often had voiced the ecstacy of good men who mistook their dreams for reality; they prompted their causes with extravagant claims, their tongues running wild, often to their own hurt. To this day we cannot tell surely how much they really believed, how much expressed a temporary enthusiasm. Often another world which seemed wholly real existed within the mind of those championing a cause greater than they understood. Yet some restraint, some check on the thinking of the Planners made them hold back when they faced the necessity of redrafting a national charter. They could propose reforms, general or specific; they would paste amendments over the text of a constitutional paragraph; they preferred to accuse the Past rather than challenge the Future. Ultimately Victory itself pushed believers and pretenders together, and after seven years of civil strife Mexico won a new Constitution.

A Plan at issue, no less than a child at its christening, needs a good name. Emperor Iturbide, first to name a Plan, wisely chose a correct title--the Plan of Iguala, a short and pronounceable name, a name identified with a city commanding the royal highway between Mexico City and Acapulco and hence a place of note. A place name in the title of a Plan implies a response to a local demand, a voice calling for a leader, for one who has graciously answered the cry and has responded in terms of the Plan which he has signed, presumably, in the city and at the behest of its citizens.

Successful aspirants to revolutionary leadership learned not to give their own names to a Plan; a signature appended at the end of the document sufficed. In June, 1833, General Arista avoided a display of personal vanity by naming his Plan for the town of issue, but, sadly, he chose a place with a unfamiliar name--Huejotzinco. A month later he joined with another General in presenting an alternate Plan, and this time--alas--he was shouldered aside. His second effort was lost under a personal title - the Second Plan of Duran - and neither the name in the title nor the signatures at the end exerted magic appeal. Two generations later (1911) General Bernardo Reyes, probably the most distinguished commander of the Diaz regime, named a Plan for himself. Within military circles his name may have carried weight, but the egotistical gesture of one so clearly identified with the Diaz Administration won no public support. After General Reyes, in an exhibition of bravado, was killed, his Plan drifted into archival oblivion. From the beginning of Plans the wisdom of choosing the right name for one's effort has been clear, but many have ignored that obvious lesson.

Initially General Santa Anna popularized the idea of political Plans which, with their chants for independence, sovereignty, constituent congresses and revisions of an existing constitution, became the litany of Mexico. The General born shrewd but not wise, knew how to use this appeal in order to win an unsophisticated audience. He never named a Plan for himself. Endowed with a motherwisdom beyond his deserts, he chose place names for his Plans and so did his more perceptive imitators and successors. Supremely egotistical, they hid behind geography--a place--preferably one with a short name or one within the scope of the Spanish language, and ideally, they named their Plan for a city whose support they deemed crucial.

The name must be readily pronounceable: Atzcapotzalco would never do. No person ever issued a "Plan of Coatzalcoalcos", and if a commanding officer found himself ready to sign the text of a Plan while encamped near the town of Zacacapoaxtla, he would be well advised to hold his pen. In the 19th century one did not identify politically with the Indian population. No matter its political merits or its pious introduction, the Plan of Santa Maria Zoquizoquipan (December, 1853) was destined to have a poor reception.

Besides the merit of an attractive and pronounceable name, the city for which the Plan was to be named should indicate that the General enjoyed the support of a significant area. Consider the Plan of Arroyo Zarco (February, 1853)--what great idea ever originated in a creek? Nor could the "Pact of February 6, 1853"--a faceless thing, identifiable only by the calendar--long remain memorable. Mexico City itself would have been ideal, save that those controlling the national capital had no need to issue a Plan: they already controlled the levers of power. At most, the commanders of the garrison of Perote just outside the city could issue a Decree or a Pronouncement, but rarely did the citizens of the capital gather to endorse such repeated barracks protests against some perceived maladministration. They regarded the complaints as endemic.

Amidst the variables one sure rule applied: a Plan must be named for a place or a person associated with Mexico itself. If one were closely pursued by enemies and crowded into the United States, the example of Porfirio Diaz on his second effort should be helpful. With his first Plan--that of La Noria--firmly in hand, he stepped across the border to the nearest Mexican town and there, for a second time, he issued it under a new name--the Plan of Tuxtepec--then discretely withdrew to the United States. Since the Plan seemed to lack both fervor and friends, a third effort was in order. Diaz responded with the "Plan of Tuxtepec revised in

Palo Blanco." By that time the public presumably had forgotten the original draft.

Francisco I. Madero developed the Diaz example. In spite of close pursuit by the Diaz secret service, he escaped across the river to San Antonio, Texas, and from there he sent word to confederates in San Luis Potosi to release from that city the Plan which he and they had previously drafted there. Vasconcelos understood the rule: he issued his Plan in a border city, then fled to the United States. The titled Plan must be authentically Mexican!

Occasionally authors have tried a descriptive name. Early on they declared "The Sentiments of the Nation" or "Organic Bases;" later a "Plan of Conciliation" or "The Project of Pacification," and once the businesslike "Proposals for Reorganization of the Republic." To some the "Plan of Restorers" sounded inadequate, and so its followers gave it an alternative title which, when translated carries a double meaning: "The Saving Plan" if one prefers the banking concept, or the "Plan of Salvation" if the religious theme seems applicable.

Enemies might seize upon the Plan and give it an unfavorable label, as the "Demagogic Plan," but ready supporters could be alert and call the Plan "Regenerative." If that title were not enough, they could be emphatic--the "Definitively Regenerative Plan," for who could object to definitive regeneration? If the Public should not respond immediately to something so ennobling, then an ambitious General could always resort to 'Liberty'--the Liberating Plan. The State of Jalisco issued a "National Appeal" and thereby demonstrated a modicum of originality. If none of these terms seemed to voice the popular discontent, then one could drop back to the obvious--the Revolutionary Plan--or perhaps it would be best to let the project exert its own appeal: call it the "Plan of Santa Rosa" and see what would come of it.

But some people were not willing to let 'well enough' alone. Consider the fate of the Plan of Agua Prieta (April, 1920), a simple, unpretentious name, easy to write, to pronounce, and even to remember. Yet the adherents felt that something more was needed, and once started on developing a sub-title the lawyers on the committee could not be restrained.

An "Organic Plan:" good, there had not been an organic Plan in a generation, but an organic Plan of what? And here legalism overwhelmed common sense:"The Movemment for the Replevin of Democracy and Law."(42)

In Spanish the subtitle stands forth in all its glory: "Plan Organico del Movimiento Revindicador de la Democracia y de la Ley," but Mexicans use the polysyllabic revindicacion as seldom as English-speaking persons discuss the merits of "replevin." Common usage has joined with common sense: the documents remains the Plan of Agua Prieta. The knack, the art, or even the wisdom of naming a Plan to catch public fancy had ended along with the idea of the political Plan itself.

. . .

Plans were christened even before the Nation itself assumed an official name of its own. In strict fact, it was the Plans which named the Nation, or rather, took their choice of names, for that territory which today we call Mexico had no common denominator. Given the isolation forced upon its sections by the beetling mountains, the populace lived by talking to themselves, by reading their own local press, and then collecting their dreams which, they felt, could be rolled into one great National Experience.

The early Revolutionaries, determined to overthrow History, wanted to reject all official associations with the mother country: they would assume a new name for the country yet to be. Clearly Spain had not recreated itself overseas: the title of "New Spain" would never do. The great curved entity would always be--indeed, always had been-something different, but old habits and official titles die hard.

The various early Plans used the Spanish terminology of "New Spain," but it proved awkward to refer to "Old Spain"--always in terms of deprecation, and thus to visualize their new "Patria" as no more than a child of a careless parent. Rather, the early Plans began to proclaims

---

(42) The Dictionary defines Replevin as "regaining possession of..."

the glories of "genuine freedom" for Northern American. Since these early Liberators seemed self-consciously aware of a country further to the north which had established prior claim for "North America" as a part of its official title, their initial proclamations of Independence would declare the total independence of Northern America from any country "wherever they may be," while Mexico in those early Plans referred to Mexico City, the capital of "Northern America." Mexicans used the term "American" to designate their own native-born countrymen in order to distinguish themselves from European-born--to separate the New World from the Old.

The first revolutionary decree, that of Ansorena in 1810 abolishing slavery, referred to benefits accruing to "the American nation." Father Hidalgo's decree of the same year called the natives of Mexico "Americans," although later paragraphs made special reference to Indians as distinct from Americans. A call for the first national assembly in 1811 was issued in the name of the Supreme American Junta which would speak on behalf of "our Nation." The declaration of Dr. Cos in 1812 bore the title "A Manifesto from the American Nation to the Europeans who Inhabit the Continent," and he repeatedly used America as the name of the country. Rayon, in his Elements of a Constitution, named the country "America," and its residents as "the American People;" and Morelos, in expressing "The Sentiments of the Nation" (September, 1813) spoke of "an America free and independent of Spain."(43) The opening sentence of the Declaration of the Absolute Independence of New Spain begins, "The Congress of Anahuac legitimately installed in the City of Chilpancingo of Northern America..." and thus managed to incorporate two names for the new nation, neither of them "Mexico."

General indifference to the official name of the country continued. The Plan of Iguala (February, 1821) in its lengthy title referred to "The Governmental Junta of Northern America" for the "Mexican Empire."

---

(43) Morelos' Twenty-three Points for the Constitution" (November, 1813) again used the term America for the whole country.

Later sections of the document considered the possibility of a European prince coming "to Mexico," the first official reference to the country which took that name. The Treaty of Cordoba (August, 1821) stated that New Spain should henceforth be recognized as "the Mexican Empire," and the Court should be established in Mexico--that is, Mexico City. This common usage for the capital city continues even today.

The Constitutional Bases (February, 1822) referred to the Second Mexican Congress, the Mexican nation, and the Mexican Empire. In November of that same year Iturbide established the Organic Bases of the Constitutional Junta without being more specific than to assure the Republic that it was all for "the Empire," all done at "the Imperial Palace of Mexico," and he probably meant the capital city, not the nation.

In 1822 Guadalupe Victoria and Santa Anna joined in the issuance of the first type of revolutionary Plan that became traditional--a rallying call and a promise of rewards for all supporters--without once mentioning the name of the Nation. Presumably everyone should have understood, but apparently not enough did, for these two aspirants made another joint effort in February, 1823, and this time they became specific: "The America of North is absolutely independent of any other power..." By June 1823, Santa Anna launched himself on his political career with his own Plan of San Luis Potosi in which he promised that his army should be styled "Protector of Mexican Freedom," but otherwise he did not name the nation which was to benefit from his effusive dedication.

The Plan for a Political Constitution (1823) spoke of "the Mexican Nation" but declared that it was composed of all provinces of Anahuac or New Spain. The Agreement of the Free State of Jalisco (June, 1823) referred to "the great nation of Anahuac." The term "the Free States of Northern America" appeared twice in the bayonet-spiked Plan of Cuernavaca (January, 1824), but its third Article referred to "all the Natives of Anahuac and the resident Spaniards of the said States." Occasionally "Anahuac" had appeared as a possible name for the new nation, but the Aztec term was never popular outside the Mexico City area. "Northern American" could not appear distinctive enough for the country a-borning, and gradually the favorite term "the Mexican Nation" and "Mexico" as a political designation for the whole country came into use.

The citizens of Jalisco, being dissatisfied with national developments, declared in June 1823, that they were free and sovereign; they called upon other States to join them in that sovereignty, then to send delegates to a "general constituent Mexican congress which must establish the great nation of Anahuac." Mexican is the adjective which describes the people, and they sought to name the national Anahuac. However, the Constituent Act of Federation (January, 1824) rejected the original Indian name for the Valley of the capital and reverted to the increasingly common title "The Mexican Nation" while naming the place of issue as "Mexico."(44)

Later Plans found it unnecessary to use the term "Mexico" and were content to refer to "the Nation" or to "the Republic." In 1828 certain Generals were being exiled by the Sr. Deputy Anastasio Zerecero. He declared that they might receive half their salary as major generals as long as they remained in any place of America as designated by the government: America still meant Mexico. Not until the Plan of Quintanar (December, 1829) did a Plan use the term "Mexico" for the whole nation, "...in the capital of Mexico..." (44)

---

(44) Examples of the varied terminology:
American Nation (Hidalgo, 1810)
Supreme American Nation (Decree of Rayon, August, 1811)
America (Rayon, Elements of a Constitution, 1812)
New Spain (Declaration of Independence, 1813)
America (Morelos, Opinion of the Nation, 1813)
Northern America (Plan of Iguala, 1812) and its citizens to be called "Americans."
New Spain (Treaty of Cordoba, 1821)
Mexican Empire and Mexican Nation (Constitutional Bases, 1822)
Northern American, and America of the North (Plan of Casa Mata, 1823)
Mexican Nation (Plan for a Political Constitution, 1823)
Free States of Northern America, and also Anahuac (Plan of Cuernavaca, 1824)
Mexican Nation (Constituent Act, 1824)
The United Mexican States (Plan of Government, 1832)

For years thereafter "the nation" and "the Republic" sufficed. Those who read the Plans understood, because the Plans, while choosing names for themselves had named the Nation.

CHAPTER VII

Plans: Their Uses and Abuses

While the word "Plan" clearly proved the most popular label attached to Mexican offerings for the public good, occasionally titles other than "Plan" served for news releases. "Declaration" provided the next most popular title. "Agreement" suggested calm in the midst of public strife. At times the neutral words "Provisions" or "Projects" appeared as synonyms for "Plan," but no document so labeled aroused popular response: neutrality meant little to activists. The Plan, under whatever title, depended upon the drive, the appeal, the drawing power of a single individual.

Sometimes the difference between a Plan and a military accord between contesting Generals grows dim. When neither side felt sure of victory and a truce had to be arranged, they might agree to submit their terms to the next session of Congress. Certainly both sides would use all influence there to protect their adherents from punishment or loss of government employment; or, if retirement were to be forced upon certain individuals, then with adequate pension. Sometimes these truces might state a common agreement on certain political issues presumably harassing the nation and thus they could proclaim their separate documents as a Plan, but if the weight of their accord were to do no more than to balance a touchy military situation, then it seems exaggerated to dignify incidental political expression about future agreements with the term "Plan."(45)

Since a Plan sought support on whatever occasion, it needed a winning slogan with which the Declarer could sign off, a battle cry which might attract adherents who, presumably would be willing to die for the cause, some watchword that would give the movement the appeal of a noble purpose. Planners tried their considerable best. In the early day of the Republic, religious expression served as a rallying cry, because these slogans would not be questioned critically and they offered an air of sanctity for which one might die willingly. Who _____

(45) See, for example, the accord of General Valentin Canalizo, Santa Anna, Anastasio Bustamante, and others, October 6, 1841, in Anastasio Bustamante, El Gabinete Mexicano, II, 211.

st the call of

God and the Constitution
or
God and Liberty
or
God and the Law?(46)

Or one might inspire his armed supporters with the title "Army of Regeneration," a cleansing term with religious overtones. Again, if one were no more than a patriotic layman, the old rallying cry of Long live...(Viva) or Down with...(Muera) might serve. On such occasions the Generals could offer

Long Live the Republic
or
Long Live the Army
or
Long Live Peace and Order

but precede it with a prayer, "May the God of the Armies Protect our Cause!" During the strife of the 1830's Plans often closed with the aspiration: Religion and Privileges (fueros). The citizens of Coatepec chose the double appeal "God and Freedom" (September, 1841), but soon thereafter the religious guise went out of fashion. However, it could be revived on any pretext. The Plan of Nuevo Utrecho (March, 1875) a generation later stood for "God and Order," but excepting the Cristero revolt of the 1930's no other Plan has attempted to use Religion as its rallying cry. Instead, "Liberty" became the incontestable word. Any appeal that included this word invited a favorable reception in Mexico, and the slogan "God and Liberty" would elevate the cause beyond all criticism. There have been enough "Liberating Armies" to flatten somewhat the rugged terrain of Mexico, and the nation has reaped a bounteous harvest of "Liberators."

Since across the years "Liberty" as a political term proved more useful than religious appeals politicians have secularized the call to arms. As far back as 1837 the City of San Luis Potosi had

(46) Plan of the Factions (July, 1840); Pronouncement of Perote (September, 1841); Residents of Coatepec (September, 1841); Plan of Restoration of the Federal System (August, 1846). "God and Liberty" seems to have been the most popular slogan."

opposed the centralizing trend under Santa Anna with its political expression "Federation or Death," and thereafter the Mexican citizen was invited to die for a noble and self-sacrificing ideal, such as Freedom and Regeneration (Revolutionary Plan, March, 1875). Manuel Lozada, in 1873, names his forces "The Mexican Army of Populist Regeneration," a title which gave a moral, even a religious ring to the cause. Many Plans reveal a touching faith in some future "constitutional law," a solution which their authors expected men to fight for, to die for Plans which blandly declare that "on these matters a constitutional law shall decide."

After mid-century the Plans settled down to the politics of this world: "The Constitution of 1857 and No Reelection" (Plan of Sinaloa (November, 1876). The Revolutionary Plan of General Garza (September, 1871) resorted to slogans as if, in themselves, they would provide a force. Garza chose two doublets:

The Constitution of 1857 and National Integrity
and
Free Suffrage and No Reelection

This latter slogan Madero chose for his own movement in 1910. The Liberal Party, led by the Magon brothers in 1906, stood for "Reform, Freedom, Justice;" while the Socio-Political Plan (March, 1911) offered to its potential followers a real choice among the old slogans of years gone by:

The Constitution of 1857
The Free Vote
No Reelection

Zapata chose four noble words for his Plan of Ayala (November, 1911); Reform, Liberty, Justice, Law. His second Reform Plan greatly altered the text of the first, but he repeated these four 'picture' words. The Plan of Santa Rosa (February, 1912) voiced only two worthy aims: Land and Justice.

"Justice" as a slogan was tossed about rather carelessly during the Revolutionary period. Felix Diaz, in his Plan of October, 1912, declared his aim: "impose Peace through Justice," but by the time he issued his second Plan (February, 1916), he realized that he needed another slogan, and being--as always--short of ideas, he could do no better than copy that of Zapata: Peace and Justice, and he ignored his own previous aim of imposing any sort of Order through any means. Perhaps *imposition* smacked too much of the Diaz Dictatorship.

The Plan of Milpa Alta (August, 1919) did not equivocate: Effective Distribution of Land or Death. The slogan--as much threat as offer--would be meaningless unless a person were seeking land; and if a person had, through any means acquired a stretch of land which he intended to keep, triumph of such a Plan could amount to a real menace.

The Cristero Revolt of the Calles Administration, in its desperate effort to gain support from any quarter, tested the appeal of titles as well as of slogans. General Gorostieta named his guerilla forces "The National Guard," while smothering his General Staff under a title which amounted to a slogan: "The Directive Committee of the National Defense League for Religious Liberty," and this Body, he declared should be recognized as "the Supreme Authority of the Liberating Movement." However, his rallying cry varied according to the intensities of the moment. He tested "Down with [Muera] Bad Government" which recalled the battle cry of Independence. Its sentiments appeared valid and it carried traditions of ancient victory, but with the lapse of a century the call had become overladen with the dust of years past. The Cristeros were hunting for a slogan vague enough to sound moral and universal, yet contemporary in its appeal. For a time "God, Fatherland, and Liberty" served, but as the cause grew desperate the emphasis reverted to the strictly religious "Long Live [Viva] the Virgin of Guadalupe," and ultimately its distinctive cry, "Long Live Christ the King."

All other post-Revolutionary slogans appealed to secular values. The Plan of Agua Prieta could do no better than revive the former Madero slogan, "Effective Suffrage, No Reelection" presumably as a reminder that those leading the victorious Revolution had violated their own pledges. By March, 1929, the secular-minded opponents of the Calles Administration lapsed into the specific: their slogan in the Plan of Hermosillo turned uniquely personal--"Down with the domination of Plutarco Elias Calles." Perhaps they discovered that not enough people were outraged at President Calles personally, and therefore they included an alternative battle-cry, "Down with Imposition", a vague cry of protest. Colonel Hernandez Netro, in 1938, in his Manifesto reached the end of the line: his ingenuity could do no better than juggle the Time-proof aspirations of a hundred years ago--"Constitution, Justice, and Law."

The Almazanistas in 1940 abandoned entirely the idea of a unifying or identifying slogan. Rather, they permeated their whole Plan with generalized cliches of "Christian civilization," "Corporal and spiritual liberty," "Free determination of the national will," and "defense of Democracy." Where other Plans had dutifully ended with a prescribed slogan, the Almazanistas were content to promise an administration of liberty, order, and social justice. No official slogans for them, but their cliches served the same purpose.

. . . .

When reading the Plans, one after another, we endure stretches of sheerest monotony at the seemingly endless protestations of utter patriotism, of preferences for a promised republic-to-be which should be at once popular and representative. Alas, the Generals, the soldiers, the citizens assembled at the behest of the Military--none of them, either those summoning or those summoned--were political scientists. The 'popular will' shrank to their will; Rousseau's vocabulary and Montesquieu's practices they freely mixed with their conception of "a truly liberal government." Sometimes one is privately offended at their blatant plagarism, but Mexican political gruel was served rather thin in those wan days, and the Generals, dipping into the pot with the same spoon, came up with identical porridge. The Military--the Generals, the Commanders, and the officers--were not nearly as revolutionary as they thought or as their Plans declared. They merely proclaimed in rolling phrases what they hoped the majority of Mexicans were taking for granted at any particular time.

Then, suddenly the reader is pulled up short--a new idea has emerged from the verbal effluvium! The citizens of some city have urged not a General's right to Executive Power, but have asked for a wise man to guide economic development. To be sure the request is stated in wildly ecstatic terms--they want an impossibly wise man, a good man, a considerate and understanding person who could supply answers to the country's every need...and at no cost to the national Treasury. Yet underneath the wrappings of the dream lay a core of reality. Not immediately but slowly, insistently the idea spread as successive Plans, caging a bit, copying more than a little, publicized the new idea, and with successive burmishing by still other copyists the whole design emerges.

In these Plans of the 19th century no word echoed no consistently as "reestablish." It seemed to harken back to an earlier time of an unspecified date, a time when political and social institutions were deemed secure, when Generals were remembered as content to defend the Nation, and when unspecified Presidents administered civil affairs in an even-handed way. Of course Mexico never experienced such an idyllic existence. It had never known freedom from overly ambitious military men; its institutions of public life had never been secure, but in the trauma following defeat first in Texas and later with a conquering armies twice occupying the national capital, by comparison the earlier days seemed free of wrenching issues, when national sentiment would have it that Generals had put things to right because they owed a debt to the Nation.

In strict truth, so many Generals had dreamed of marching to fame and glory behind a mythical Plan of golden words that drafting such a document came as easily as a reflex action. Egotistical though the Generals may have been, brutal their age and rough their methods, yet each dreamed of a country at peace and in some mystical way "democratic," its citizens prosperous, State legislatures in agreement and himself--any General--its head and chief. Given the right Plan and an apt slogan, it might all be done!

Mexicans became sufficiently familiar with the idea of Plans that they were able to file successive issues into categories. When Diaz issued his Plan of La Noria, it was immediately compared with another Plan which some other hopeful General had issued. In 1872 Diaz complained that a spurious "Revised Plan of La Noria" was circulating. He denied that having issued any such document, and to his supporters he sent assurances that he would never have considered himself authorized to suggest revisions without the agreement of his friends and associates. The signature was personal, the agreement joint.

Sometimes a General might be dragged into a Plan inadvertently, even without knowing that others had named him as sponsor of some presumably immortal declaration. Justo Benitez notified the unsuspecting Diaz that an editor, Zarco, had just published in his newspaper a stupid paragraph baptized with the outworn name of "Plan Revolucionario" which was circulating clandestinely and which called for a Triumvirate to share the Executive Power--one of these to be Diaz. Zarco had thoughtfully excluded himself from the charmed Triarchy after naming his unsuspecting friends as monitors for Trouble.(47) Even a General could not be too careful about the company he kept.

While one individual traditionally issued Plans upon his own responsibility and named the document for the place where he proclaimed it, practices varied from time to time. For example, those men bent upon promising some great "regeneration" occasionally exchanged rough drafts of ideas on governing principles and practices involved in the formation of new governmental department. These notes circulated among a restricted group and they served, no doubt, to convert wavering officials to the impending revolution. A common text being agreed upon, the ranking officer among the plotters issued his Plan as a call to arms, a rebellion against an established authority, a new system to replace the old. Therefore, its prose needed to be direct and emphatic, its pronouncements without equivocation. Its effectiveness stood in direct proportion to the trust placed in the individual author.

Inevitably the Plan promoted "personalism", the bane of Mexican public life. The personal Plan tended to be shorter than the product of civilian committees. To a later generation the principles espoused often seem terribly small and unworthy of national attention. The political opinions of General Blancarte and a baker's dozen more are lost to a later generation, and only their blatant personal ambitions stand clear. General Santa Anna, the supreme egotist, developed a variant procedure: after his initial effort under the Plan of Casa Mata, he persuaded fellow officers to issue Plans which would call upon him to lead the movement and then he could graciously answer the appeal of his countrymen.

---

(47) _Archivo de Porfirio Diaz_, Justo Benitez to Diaz, February, 1869.

All such maneuvering did not pass unnoticed in state and national capitals. On occasion versions of the impending Plan would reach certain Congressional leaders and they, in defense, would draft counter-declarations which were calculated to solidify support for the Administration. But these efforts, while, in effect, "Plans" were not so labeled. Rather, they would be given a more general title such as "Constitutional Bases" or some such term. These outlines of basic national structure differed from the individual Plan in that they sought to inform and to consolidate, to quiet, not to inflame. Also, they tended to be longer than the simplistic declarations adopted in· concert by the Military; they were defensive in nature, and their issuance indicated a brewing revolt. Therefore, the congressional and state declarations came late and required close reading in a country where neither talents nor time were held in strict regard.

Across the years the Generals learned by trial and error that Plans had best be short. Carranza understood this, and his sketchy Plan of the Hacienda of Guadalupe (March, 1913) scarcely touched Mexican realities. The Plan emphatically repudiated General Huerta as a murderer of President Madero and it called all Mexicans to resist his administrators and subordinates. This appeal proved popular and enlistments swelled the Carranza armies. Thereafter, as basic issues began to loom out of the smoke of conflict, he amended his Plan and republished it in order to incorporate additional and popular accretions. As supporters "adhered" Carranza and his Constitutional Movement could feel both virtuous and effective, a happy combination in any country where men would swear to support a cause, rifle in hand. In the meantime Carranza dropped the word _Hacienda_ from the title and the "Plan of Guadalupe"--a totally satisfactory name in Mexico--became the Plan which led to Revolutionary victory. Only historians now recall its modest origin.

Even before General Carranza had forged a reality within his own order of things, General Orozco had already drifted out of touch with Mexican thinking. Late--too late in Mexican political life--Orozco issued his Plan of the Empacadora [the Cotton Gin] (March, 1912). Brevity never cramped the unhappy General's style. Indeed, a staff of indignant persons straight out of the Cave of Adullam must have conferred.

A battery of secretaries would have been needed to record the long, vivid, and repetitious protests which introduced the reader to the tangled state of the Mexican revolution in 1912 as portrayed by the Orozco contingent. Only a devoted follower would have made the effort to read such a Plan.

General Zapata followed more nearly the example of Carranza. His first Plan, short and limited in outlook, proclaimed Orozco as leader of his movement, but his amended Plan repudiated the General as a turncoat. To later Plans Zapata—or rather, his accumulated staff—added a series of wide-ranging issues so that the final Plan, save for the signature at the bottom, bore small relation to that under which Zapata began his revolutionary career.

Few men failed to recognize the political advantages of Plans properly drafted. They issued all their protestations in the name of high-sounding principles and of national well-being. Signatures of endorsers sometimes followed the text so closely that they obscured the sponsor's name. One thing stands clear: the Mexican Plan related solely to domestic affairs. Scarcely ever did it mention issues of foreign policy. As reflected in the Plans, the world beyond Mexico did not exist. Once the Plan of Regeneration (May, 1846) proclaimed General Santa Anna as the strongest support of the nation "in spite of European politics." Mexico's troubles in that year did not involve Europe. One wonders what the Planner had in mind—if anything. And then in the very last Plan (September, 1940) we find one disdainful reference to the "Totalitarian Triumvirate" [Hitler, Mussolini, and Stalin] coupled with a rousing condemnation of national planning boards. So little did foreign affairs touch Mexican politics.

As one protagonist or another advocated his latest idea, the national will in relation to domestic affairs emerged. We see the process time and time again in the Mexican experience and we are reminded that the Plans but lead a drummers' parade, and that behind them march a nation. With the support of no more than an incipient political party behind him in 1910 Francisco I. Madero brought down the Porfirian Dictatorship with his Plan of San Luis Potosi. Such is the power of the right Plan.

A Plan might be issued anonymously, of course, but its chances of survival were not great. Unsponsored orphans--possibly illegitimate--have never been considered valid risks in politics any more than in any other Good Society. Mexican Plans became a heap of declarations made, fought for, died for, and now mostly forgotten. They covered the range of national life--from the primitive days when the nation was struggling for existence to a time when Mexico stood mature among the powers of Earth. The Plans with their pet slogans have passed and are not: they glory has passed they by. They are nothing? Nothing more than a nation's irregular pulse, yet these alterations mark the rhythm of a nation's life. The Plans tell us what the future was.

CHAPTER VIII
Plans and The Special Issues
a. The Church and the Plans

When one examines the Plans for content, no
subject looms larger through the Mexican night than
the relations of State and Church. Beginning with
the War for Independence the Planners considered the
Roman Catholic Church an enemy of their incipient
State which would supplant the colony of Old Spain.
The Motherland had been generous with the Church. It
had granted land titles, had financed missionary
programs, and its armed forces had protected many
mission stations from Indian attacks. Tax exemptions
and personal privileges, called fueros, gave the
Church and its ministers a preferred position in the
colonial society of New Spain. A new State brought
into being by rebels who appeared to take the recent
French Revolution as their model might very well
menace the prerogatives of institutionalized
religion. Therefore the Church hierarchy withheld
support of the Independence movement; rebels found
their cause branded as offensive to good consciences
and their soldiers were denied religious
ministrations.

In defense the new leaders issued assurances of
religious regularity while protesting deep concern
for Church welfare. At the same time they repeatedly
warned the Church to keep to its proper role--that
of a comforter of distressed souls--otherwise it
would be exposed to ridicule and mockery. The
revolutionaries declared that their profound respect
for the religious mission of the Church required
that they assume this posture. (48)

These assurances proving unconvincing to the
hierarchy, more positive declarations very quickly
followed. Spokesmen for the revolutionary movement
issued pledges of unfailing loyalty to the Catholic
religion, Apostolic and Roman [it became customary
to state the matter in this official way]; they
declared that they accepted the dogma of the Church,
that they would defend its discipline, and after
emerging victorious they would permit no toleration

---

(48) Manifesto of Dr. Cos, (March, 1812)

or secret exercise of any other.(49)

After Independence the Victors proved as good as their word. The Plan of Iguala (February, 1821) specifically recognized the Church; it opposed the existence of any other sect lest any mixture might dilute its apostolic purity, and--moving from the sacred to the secular--recognized the civil and proprietary privileges [fueros] which had been assigned to the Church through the centuries.(50)

Recognition of the Church also led to positive acts--to protect its worthy ministers, and to encourage propagation of the faith. The new State appeared ready to assume the traditional role of Spain, the Motherland--that of "patron." However, subtle differences began to appear: the Constitutional Bases (February, 1822), while "recognizing the Church to the exclusion of any other," did not promise to root out the private practice of other faiths or sects. Later Plans followed this pattern.(51)

---

(49) See Rayon's draft of Elements of Constitution (1812); Morelos' Sentiments of the Nation (September, 1813); Declaration of Independence (November, 1813); Opinion of the Nation (November, 1813)

(50) Constitutional Bases, Second Mexican Congress, (February, 1822); Plan of Vera Cruz, (December, 1822); Plan of Casa Mata, (February, 1823); Plan of the Political Constitution of the Mexican Nation, (May, 1823); Plan of Potosi, (June, 1823); Plan of Cuernavaca, (January, 1824).

(51) Plan of Cuernavaca (January, 1824); Declaration of Vera Cruz (June, 1834); Plan of Puebla (May, 1834); Pronouncement of Toluca (May, 1835); Proposals for the Reorganization of the Republic, (September, 1835) stated that non-Roman Catholics were to be permitted to remain in the country and presumably could practice privately their own religious faith so long as they respected the official religion and laws of the country. So also the Edict of the Government of the District (October, 1835) and the Constitutional Bases (December, 1835); the Plan of Huejotzingo, (December, 1842)

Despite all the protestations of loyalty, it became clear that there would be no room for the Inquisition in Mexico, no institutionally sponsored prying into private religious observance.

The early Plans offered no hint of the turmoil to come. General Santa Anna's Plan of Vera Cruz (December, 1822) made the routine promise to support the secular as well as the regular clergy in all their special privileges. So also the Plan of Casa Mata: its first proviso having made brief reference to the issue, moved on, but Santa Anna's "Minutes of Casa Mata" did not refer to any religious issues which might have been discussed at the meeting. The Plan for the Political Constitution of the Mexican Nation (1823) lists as the first duty of citizenship "to profess the Catholic Religion, Apostolic and Roman, as the only one for the State," but in its detailed outline of a National Institute for education and culture the Church and its ministers were not mentioned.

This initially uncontested issue as well as other multitudinous subjects involved in establishing a frame of government absorbed public attention during the first administration after Independence. In the next two administrative terms the political issues--the actions of Congress, contested elections, and the role of the Army in the State--kept the nation at fever heat and religious questions subsided into the background. However, in 1832-1833 the Liberal majority in the Congress initiated a program of religious administrative reform which aroused the Church-oriented Conservatives. Then fell upon the public a veritable shower of Plans which declared that the State should positively support the Roman Catholic Church rather than guarantee its existence. It seemed that no Plan could hope to win a significant following if it did not deal vigorously with this influential segment of Mexican national life. Even the Army found itself Church-oriented. The Plan of Colonel Escalada (May, 1833) first pledged "to sustain at all costs the holy Religion of Jesus Christ, the statutes and the privileges of the clergy, and the Army, they being threatened by the intrusive authorities." Thereafter promises to defend the privileges both of the Church and the Army were repeated as a litany. (52)

Then zealotry--no more than faith turned wrong side out--took over. The Plan of Ecatzinco (February 1834) also called "the Plan of the Priests," while promising a restoration of all Church programs, called for deportation of all foreigners --with certain exceptions--unless they could prove that they were practicing Roman Catholics. The Plan continued by specifying additional taxes which would be devoted to increasing the splendor of public worship and to easing the financial strain of priests. This being done, current taxes for masses and provisions for pomp at funerals could be abated.

Dying for one's country has for so long carried pious overtones so closely akin to martyrdom for one's faith that the Army soon became embroiled in the public controversy. Since its special privileges were often coupled with those of the Church, the two institutions ran in tandem, and in ill-matched team they made of it. Under the terms of the Plan of Puebla (May, 1834) the Army pledged itself to protect the Church from any changes, but asked, in return, for an end "to a torrent of ecclesiastical innovations," otherwise unspecified, and then, somewhat ambiguously, the Plan promised that if that were done, the Army would cease its agitation.

Thereafter Church practices--always referred to in the most general terms--were paired with whatever Conservative program suited the sponsor of the Plan. In effect, Church leaders let their institution become the victim of whatever Conservative group or personality happened to promise most firmly the maintenance of the old order of things. Support of the Church program became the first step up the ladder to national acceptance and even to the Presidency. Santa Anna, a man of supple loyalties, quickly deserted the Liberal side and identified himself with the cause of Centralism and the Church. He called these bifurcated issues "the national

---

(52) See also: Plan of Cuernavaca (January, 1824); Plan of Duran (June, 1833); Plan of General Arista (June, 1833); Second Plan of Duran (July, 1833); Plan of Puebla (May, 1834); Plan of Vera Cruz (June, 1834); Plan of General Rangel (June, 1845).

freedom." Under his sponsorship the Declaration of Oaxaca (May, 1834) protested that it wished only to be freed from irreligion. While offering no specific program, the good citizens of Oaxaca devised a precise balance of three presumably equal components: they offered the slogan "Long Live the Federation, Religion, and Santa Anna."

The City of Vera Cruz would not be outdone. As the very source of Santa Anna's political power it could not suffer another city to outrank it in zeal for whatever cause the General might proclaim. Therefore, its City Council (June, 1834) duly recorded its opposition to the Liberal reform of the Church privileges, and declared that officials who enforced them were unworthy of public trust. Other Plans, announced here and there, indicated continued support for the most popular man in Mexico. The Declaration of Cuernavaca (May, 1834), more a remonstrance against the program of Liberalism than a real Plan, also called upon Santa Anna--ever ready to heed such appeals--to assume leadership of the Conservative forces and to rid the State of its unworthy servants.

Indeed, the Plans had declared approval of all Roman Catholic interests so regularly that only by indirection can we ascertain the existence of other religious groupings within the country. A number of defeated Liberals, forced into exile in New Orleans, were accused of having organized an "Amphitrionic Junta" and in September, 1835, of having issued a declaration of freedom of worship for Mexico. Their presumed Plan opposed any official relationship with the Vatican, and, according to the released text some of the Church buildings they proposed to assign as synagogues, or else to turn them over "to other cults." Even more: they would order into exile all Church officials who, with good reason, were suspected of having opposed the Liberal religious reform program which embraced nationalization of all Church real estate and buildings, its valuables, and silver, while surplus sacred vessels used in religious services were to be distributed to needy congregations. Thus the Church would have become a Department of the Administration and as such would be subject to supervision by laymen. Finally, "it would be permitted for private individuals to continue with Catholicism as long as they do not disturb public order or make converts."

This Plan, so diametrically contrary to Mexican tradition, was publicized by the League opponents, and it may well be that, with the lines of political distinction drawn so tightly, the Conservatives did try to circulate a counterfeit Plan as bad propaganda for the other side--a kind of political "dirty trick."

But the Plan of Olarte (December, 1836), quite detailed and with many specific proposals, indicates a latent dissatisfaction with many parochial practices, especially in matters of finance. This Plan sought to regulate the price which the Church might charge legally for special rites observed for private consolation--the basic ones should be free of charge--and all collections from the pious were to be audited by the Town Council. Also, the resident priest would be required to perform the public rites if he were in town and not ill. In addition, the Plan sought to regulate diocesan charges and expenses. State endowments were to cover the basic costs of Church maintenance and operation, but not collections from the parishes. Therefore, the State should audit Church expenses and it would determine a fair proportion to be assessed against the parishes. Clearly the Plan indicates resentment against Church assessments for its religious ministrations. Its call for a public audit indicated that the author presumed that the local priest was reporting parish collections dishonestly, and that some of the priests were so lazy that they required a special declaration to remind them of their duties. No other Plan directly supported General Olarte, and with this reform suggestion he disappeared into the mists of History.

But not the General's basic reform program. Even as the Church-State controversy reached its public apex, successive Plans issued by laymen--and quite anonymously--proposed constitutional revisions: 1)that one duty of the State should be to maintain public worship and 2) that the President, joined by two counsellors, should consider or approve pontifical bulls. Probably the most striking item about this and subsequent Plans is that they attempt to dispose of the issue in so summary a fashion. Even Gomez Farias, who had introduced the controversial reform program of 1832, was content to conclude the matter in his Plan of July, 1840: "The Catholic, Apostolic, and Roman Religion shall be protected by wise and just laws." Since for a decade Conservatives had been well aware of what he considered 'wise and just,' the attempt to gloss over the differences failed utterly.

In September, 1835, a "Concerned Citizen" circulated anonymously a proposed draft of a Constitution. Its interest, in the midst of public religious controversy, dealt almost exclusively with problems of political operation. The document would have authorized the Legislative Branch to "protect and maintain public worship" while the President, joined by two counsellors, should approve the pontifical bulls". Beyond that...nothing. Perhaps the brief reference indicates that a fair segment of the population did not feel as deeply committed to the Church issue as national headlines would indicate.

Even the Conservative opposition concluded with an obvious generality. General Valencia's Plan (September, 1841) declared "null and void from now on all that may be contrary to the holy religion which we profess." The citizens of Vera Cruz, in September, 1841, elaborated upon his declaration: "The Provisional Executive should declare null and void all that may be contrary to Religion, Independence, and individual guarantees, and to all that which characterizes a truly liberal government."

However, fifteen years of Independence, of controversy, and of military guarantees had left their mark. Another civilian draft of a proposed constitution in 1841 began with the religious proviso that had become traditional: "The religion of the Nation is Catholic, Apostolic, and Roman," but then it swerved wildly, "The tolerance of any other shall be sanctioned at the places that public convenience should require and according to the judgment of the authorities and in the manner that shall be dealt with later." The declaration of tolerance as a public necessity testifies to the loosening of the ties which the Roman Catholic Church earlier had fastened upon the public mind.

During the next decade, as occasioned by the war with the United States, the Plans reflected a change of emphasis on the religious issues. The nation stood in desperate need of money during that conflict, and the Church, as possessor of liquid assets, became the object of repeated attempts to lay hands upon its treasury. Those supporting the efforts of the government had no reason to issue a Plan; the opposition found itself crowded into a corner. Public need was obvious and great; reluctance of the Church to part with its funds was no less evident. The Pronouncement of Oaxaca (February, 1847) attempted to split the difference--it would permit Church contributions "to support the just war against the United States of the North" but it opposed national legislation which violated the immunities of the Church. Therefore, its Legislature refused to enforce within the State those Federal laws which permitted appropriation of Church property. The Pronouncement authorized the military commander of the State to modify various terms of the Plan as exigencies of war might require "save in relation to the essence of the Federal system, the Catholic religion, and the immunities of the Church." A second Pronouncement relieved the military commander of responsibility for guiding events: the State Legislature should determine the disposition of Church property and would establish public polity. Doubtless the luckless commander welcomed the legislation affecting his State, but the problem for the nation remained.

The Plan of the Restorers (February, 1847) faced the issue of appropriation of Church property directly and declared without equivocation, "None of the decrees relative to the occupation of the property of the Dead Hands shall go into effect." General Paredes, bidding for Church support, published a Plan in June, 1848, which promised, "The property of the honorable clergy shall be strictly protected."

With the end of the war the crisis lapsed, only to arise again with the onset of the War of the Reform. Eligio Ortiz (July, 1851) again promised in general terms "to protect the property of the clergy," but the Definitively Regenerative Plan (December, 1855) reverted to the language of twenty years earlier, "[The religion of Mexico] is and shall remain Catholic, Apostolic, and Roman without tolerance of any other," and the clergy, it promised, should enjoy its traditional privileges. On the critical question of Church and State Mexico seemed to be getting nowhere fast.

Not until 1854 did Mexico have a presumably organized political party separate from the influence of a dominant individual. In April of that year the Program of the Pure Republican Party appeared anonymously and without personal sponsorship. The Program dealt almost exclusively with Church matters. It recognized "The necessity of Catholic worship and agreed that its ritual ought to be the national rite in our country," while proposing elimination of Church political power, the establishment of fees for religious services by the State, and the authorization of taxes upon the clergy.

With the outbreak of the War of the Reform, a religiously oriented conflict which the purest of Republican parties could not have survived, the issue was contested on the battlefield. For four years Mexico suffered the horror of a wasting civil war. If any such war can be won, the Liberals emerged victorious, and their Laws of the Reform defined the place of the Church in Mexican society.

Although the Liberal Party won this extended conflict, it could not put into operation its full Church-State program because the Conservative forces promptly sought for and secured foreign intervention. European forces, under the nominal leadership of Maximilian, landed in Vera Cruz and pressed their way to the capital. Maximilian assumed that he would have the support of the Church, which he did have in a nominal way, but it proved of small use on the battlefield. Meanwhile his opponents centered their resistance on the issue of the establishment of an intrusive Monarchy and his use of alien troops. Once the Monarchists had been defeated, the authors of successive Plans were content, generally, to leave the details of Church-State relations to civilian settlements.

The Plan of Nuevo Utrecho (March, 1875) sounded like something out of the remote past when it began by repudiating the new Constitution of 1857, then proposing an intricate process for naming an interim President who should promote the peace and prosperity of the country. In so doing one of his duties would be "to respect the Catholic religion" and to grant it necessary liberties, to maintain harmony with it, and to name a commission to negotiate a Concordat with the Vatican. However, Porfirio Diaz, on gaining the Presidency, managed to do all these things without resorting to a Concordat, and the Church as a public issue faded from public consciousness.

．．．．．．．

So well did the new President steer his way through this quagmire that when the revolution against his Administration erupted thirty-five years later, religious issues formed no part of the initial protest. However, the Church had an interest in the outcome of the revolution and ultimately it did become involved. The Church whose name and interests figured so largely and so frequently in earlier Plans was seldom--and then only obliquely--mentioned in the revolutionary Plans of 1910-1917. During the period the Church came to be considered in alliance with the enemy of the Revolution, the "scientific" politicians and the big landholders. Yet, considering later hostility expressed toward the Roman Catholic Church, amazingly few Revolutionary Plans mentioned the institution.

Inevitably the issue grew. The Pact of Torreon (July, 1914), one of several "revisions" of the Plan of Guadalupe, declared that the Revolution represented "a struggle which emanates from a praetorianism, from a plutocracy, and from the clergy." Therewith the Military Staff pledged the Constitutionalist Army to "admonish, to punish, and to demand the proper responsibilities of the members of the Roman Catholic clergy who both materially and intellectually have aided the usurper, Victoriano Huerta." So easily did the officers pledge the revolutionary cause to a religious contest that continued for years.

In 1916 Felix Diaz tried another tack: he promised religious freedom to all faiths and services. However, with rising hostilities toward the Church and in the face of demands to control it and to strip it of property, this policy of neutrality was considered favorable to the Church. Indeed, the first Plan of Felix Diaz made no mention of religious issues at all. Thereafter, all Plans of whatever Revolutionary group abandoned any declaration concerning the Church or the public issues which had settled about that institution.

With the cause of the Revolution triumphant the new Constitution of 1917 defined a restricted role for the Church within the State. However a constitutional proviso and a revolutionary administration could not solve so easily this basic issue. Beneath the surface of public proclamations the religious issue slowly came to a boil. During the Calles Administration the Cristero Movement, as its name would indicate, made religion its motivating force. Its Manifesto of October, 1928, called for a restoration of the Constitution of 1857 without the laws of the Reform--in effect, a return to the outmoded Constitution of 1824. A Directive Committee of the National Defense League of Religious Liberty would name a Civilian Leader who would be recognized as Military Commander, and he, in turn, should recognize the Directive Committee as the Supreme Authority of the Liberating Movement. Lengthy titles ornamented with a plethora of capital letters formed a literary arch for the concluding multiple slogan:

Long Live Christ the King
Long Live the Virgin of Guadalupe
Death to Bad Government

"Death to [Down with] Bad Government" had been one of the slogans of the early movements under Father Hidalgo. The Plans had come full circle.

The very last Plan, that of the Almazanistas (September, 1940) veered from direct references to institutionalized religious concepts, but it took refuge behind a bulwark of broad, highly moral pretensions. It opposed "forcing the mind of the child and young people into the mold of Marxist Communism," and it called for "the moral unity of the family." While invoking the hallowed name of Father Hidalgo, this last effort cried havoc against an Administration which would admit to Mexico "political and social outcasts, the troublesome agents of foreign government." According to the 'code language' of the day, this meant that the dissenters were opposed to the policy of the Cardinas Administration in admitting Spanish Republican refugees from the wrath of the Franco Dictatorship. Such a policy, challenged the Almazanistas, would amount to a cowardly renunciation of Democracy, "a failure to

84

preserve Christian civilization as represented in our families, our homes, our corporal and spiritual liberty, and all that which ennobles and dignifies the human being and leaves it free to determine popular will." And then, throwing all to the winds, the Almazanistas looked not to the Church to establish their moral security, but to the democratic institutions of Mexico. Thus ringed about, they said, "Mexico could never yield to appeasement or be guilty of the cowardly renunciation of Democracy."

But all in vain. Their protestation of lost social and domestic bliss, of human nobility and dignity, echoed through a countryside now out of touch with Plans and Planners, even of those proclaiming the most noble sentiments. It had become useless in Mexico for dissident Planners to call upon the Church or upon any institutionalized religious entity in an effort to preserve what they conceived to be the deepest moral imperatives of Western society. So far as the Planners were concerned, within a secularized society the Church and the State had parted company. As for the Church, across the years loud-mouthed military support had proved to the smallest of its blessing if not the greatest burden that it had been called upon to bear.

Institutionally the Plans never offered more than vain protestations about issues that they could in no wise solve. The cause of Religion had been poorly served; the Nation suffered repeated turmoil in the name of religion, and in the end the authors of Plans even avoided religious vocabulary while affirming public morality. Their offerings—the Plans—had fallen under that ancient judgment: weighed in the balance and found wanting.

b. Monarchy and the Plans

After signing the Treaty of Cordoba with the Spanish Minister O'Donoju, Mexicans concluded that they had done with Spain and--hopefully --with Monarchy, but conversion of the royal colony into a viable Republic did not come so easily. Spanish troops remained in the fortress of Vera Cruz, and the ideal of a Monarchy kept floating before over-heated imaginations. Iturbide tried to establish a Mexican Monarchy and thereby earned the dissent of his countrymen, and especially that of Santa Anna, no mean antagonist. In one of the earliest Plans--that of Potosi (June, 1828)--Santa Anna blasted supporters of Monarchy as "hare-brained leaders." He branded as scarcely less misguided those who advocated a centralized republic, as persons who worked for private aims. Not so Santa Anna: he declared that he was heeding the cries of the majority who wanted a federal [decentralized] republic, and he worshiped as sacred the opinion of the people--so he said. Five years later he proclaimed himself a dedicated Centralist.

The image of Monarchy with an ideal King, beneficent wise, and just, kept drifting before certain Mexican eyes. Monarchists, high-minded as well as soft-headed, seemed to feel that only they could bring order to Mexico and that they owed a debt to the country to do so. Mexico's disorder offended them; lawlessness they felt an anomaly; a King or a Royal Person could issue an order to cease and desist and it would be done. Their fixation tethered their attention to ambiguous schemes, but their determination could never counterbalance the openness of Mexican life.

Now and again public mention of Monarchy appeared in odd or informal ways: the charge laid against the authors of the Second Plan of Duran (July, 1833). On June 1st of that year the General thought that he had cleared himself of the accusation by declaring that he favored installation of a Supreme Dictator who should govern "without tyranny." But five weeks later he had undergone another change of opinion, and with General Arista he signed a new and different Plan--one issued in the form of a letter to General Santa Anna. They repudiated the established Federal Republic and called for the "re-establishment of the empire of peace" and the installation of any form of government which would be deemed suitable. Promptly the opposition press accused the Generals of advocating Monarchy for Mexico, and for good measure identified a prominent citizen, Gutierrez Estrada, as a supporter of a scheme to import a European monarch. Although never definitely confirmed, the charge probably carried a modicum of truth, for this individual led the royalist promotion of the Maximilian intervention twenty years later. Plans specifically rejecting Monarchy kept the idea alive in the Mexican mind.(53)

Monarchy had to endure its full share of lunatic fringe advocates, and among these were proposals to establish an Indian monarchy for Mexico. The Plan of Ecatzinco (February, 1834), sometimes called the Plan of the Priests, would have installed an Indian descendant of Montezuma to rule the tempestuous descendents of the conquerors, but the idea was laughed out of existence.

Occasionally incidental proponents such as Haro y Tamariz advanced a Plan advocating Monarchy. This individual added the thoughtful note that if no candidate were available for the coronation chair, he would accept the nomination. The Mexican public ignored the offer so blandly made. However, the Plan of Zoquizoquipan, disregarding inconvenient details, went to the heart of the matter and proclaimed General Santa Anna as Emperor of Mexico (December, 1853), but the wily General-President, presumably remembering the fate of Iturbide, let the nomination pass from him. Behind these declarations Monarchists were testing public sentiment, poking the political brambles, then looking about to see if they were being observed.

Mexican Plans were suspended during the French occupation under Maximilian, because every patriotic citizen knew what his country expected of him. The foreign Monarchy, with ideas of its own, had no taste for the previous Mexican declarations. The home-grown Plans had burst spontaneously out of the open society of the New World and the Emperor and his entourage could never understand the importance of the plain fact. What mattered to Royalists a Plan

---

(53) The Plan of Regeneration (May, 1846); Plan of General Salas (August, 1846); the Definitively Regenerative Plan (December, 1855).

of this or that place...of Guadalajara...or of
Jalapa? Plans of a General Valencia or of a General
Rangel amounted to nothing...Plans by nobodies.
European Monarchy would regenerate the country!

Maximilian, the intended Emperor, on the advice
of his future Court, appointed what he declared to
be an Assembly of Notables--all Mexicans and some of
they by no means notable. This body delivered a
commission report which amounted to a Plan.
Spontaneity ill adapts itself to Monarchy; planning
by remote control promotes the gentlest form of
revolution. Restorers of Monarchy faced several
difficulties: first, the new Constitution of 1857,
so obviously Federalist and republic that by no
stretch of the imagination could it serve Royalist
purposes, and besides, the Constitution had already
generated loyalties of its own. Second, supporters
of the Maximilian intervention had to offer
Imperialism as if it were nothing more than another
Mexican alternative: they had to broadcast a Plan!

The Provisional Plan of Government: a document
drafted by Mexicans who had savored other Plans and
the taste had lingered. Monarchy would be sweetened
to the Mexican palate and Mexican teeth would not be
set on edge. First, a Declaration: the French
General commanding the intervention forces
proclaimed on order of Maximilian the creation of an
"Executive Power" as a branch of government. Three
Mexicans were to staff it, and then to assume
nominal direction of Mexican affairs. An Assembly of
Notables, to be appointed by this Executive Power,
would determine the ultimate form of government
while accepting guidance from the Royal Power. This
Assembly would be authorized to consider only an
agenda presented by the Executive Power should enjoy
the privilege of an absolute veto. When the Assembly
of Notables should have proclaimed the definitive
form of Government, then the Committee of Three in
the Executive Power would fade away and the Emperor
could be duly proclaimed.

With the support of the French Army all these
groups behaved properly. The Assembly of Notables
proclaimed its Plan, "the definitive form of
government to be adopted in Mexico" and it outdid
all previous Plans by offering thirty pages of
justification...of "Considerandos."

Then with but one page more of evaluation it offered the presumed throne to a foreign prince. Resistance to these schemes show how little support the Royalists ever enjoyed in Mexico and how vainly they dreamed. With defeat they felt that they had lost much, not merely the small support which they had in the beginning.

Monarchy in Mexico ended so miserably. Its effective forces were defeated finally at Queretaro, and the Emperor himself was executed on the Hill of the Bells nearby, but he, like so many still in the land of the living, sought to shape events after his death. He issued a unique document--a Post-Mortem Plan which is called his "Abdication," a Plan designed to take effect after his death. Mercifully he allowed himself and the reader no more than two paragraphs of Considerandos; then he named as Regents those who might govern the country until a Congress as provided in the Mexican Constitution should convene. Nothing could have been more completely ignored: an illegitimate monarch could confer no shadow of legitimacy on any sort of successor. After the Maximilian Affair no Plan ever suggested a return to Monarchy as a solution of Mexican problems.

The cause had been reduced to a romantic gesture, to laments whispered into friendly ears, a salute to obscure supporters who had gone on before, a proposition that had caught men between their dreams and their common sense. The tradition of Monarchy in Mexico died a violent and ugly death.

c.Texas and the war with the
United States in the Plans

When one considers the vast territory which
Mexico lost to the United States within a decade,
the Plans carry few and remarkably brief references
to this devastating national dismemberment. Yet a
careful reading of the Plans indicates that later
developments did not strike Mexico totally without
warning. Apparently the Planners sensed something of
the dark future which might be in store for their
country. In the Plan of Jalapa (December, 1829) the
Reserve Army "ratified its oath to maintain the
federal pact respecting the sovereignty of the
States and preservation of their integrity." This
devious resolution may refer more to a declaration
of the political relationship of the States and
opposition to the noncooperation of various
individual States rather than to loss of specific
territory on the frontier, but authors of the Plan
seem to have sensed, too, the rising trouble to the
north. Repeated calls for "territorial integrity"
indicate fears of secession, and probably not only
that of the Texas territory.

However, dispatch of troops to the ultimate
national boundaries did not solve the more delicate
issues of political adjustment. Within a year
military service in Texas had become sufficiently
unpopular that the State of San Luis Potosi (March,
1830) asked revocation of the order to send its own
civil militia to such a remote area. At the same
time the State served a "National Notice." Article
VI indicated that the State of San Luis Potosi
wished to ignore the issue of patrolling any part of
distant Texas because it suffered an abundance of
problems within its own borders. The State, within
the very heartland of Mexico, posted notice of its
intention to secede. It sought to postpone any
question involving the remote frontier; local
interest had transcended a growing national crisis.

Regardless of his own zeal a provincial
commander could not really reverse such
thinking--but he could try! The Second Plan of Duran
(July, 1833) paid tribute to the Army as the
guarantor of Independence and Freedom, and concluded
with the bellicose aspiration, "In case of a Spanish
invasion or of any other foreign country, may the
veterans be the first to present themselves to
punish such reckless boldness." Spain, still

holding the fort at Vera Cruz, continued to be the favorite enemy of independent Mexico, but the General's reference to "any other country" showed that he was considering all possibilities.

Within official circles, however, a certain unease about the northern frontier continued. The introduction to the Plan of Codallos (March, 1830) protested that "no energetic measures have been taken to maintain the integrity of the Federation as involved in the interesting areas of California and the fertile lands of beautiful Texas and in the Peninsula of Yucatan." The peninsula, deemed neither interesting nor beautiful, Codallos dismissed without benefit of a glowing adjective. Article VI called for dispatch of a part of the standing army to the frontiers of the Republic in order to "maintain its integrity." Clearly, these frontier departments had been identified as areas of unrest where national authority had not been forcefully expressed. There the Army might serve a useful purpose and the dispatch of troops to remote areas was calculated to relieve Mexico City of the constant threat of military intervention. Thereafter--nothing but silence on the issue of the northern provinces.

The Nation let matters drift, so that when the issues did erupt, they had grown so intertwined with the Centralist-Federalist controversy that a national consensus proved impossible. Instead of settling problems of national administration in a rational manner each party preferred to charge the other with something it conveniently labeled "treason." Thereafter the victor in the political shoving match could cause the leaders of the opposition to seek safety outside the country. By 1835 General Santa Anna had led the Centralists to an initial victory and had set his opponents on the run in order to escape his vengeance.

Just at this juncture the Mexican press mysteriously found available a particularly convenient document with which it could discredit even further the relatively liberal Federalists. According to this revelation, certain exiled Federalists in New Orleans had issued a declaration called the Amphyctionic Plan (September, 1835) which supported the Texas secession, as it was then labeled, in order to express their opposition to

President Santa Anna and his entourage. According to
the text of this Plan, the exiles favored supplying
the people of Texas with "weapons, money, or
recruits—anything that they may need in order to
defend themselves, and to hold the attention of the
Mexican government."

While sentiments in support of States
dissatisfied enough to threaten an imminent
secession normally amounted to no more than standard
political fare for Mexico, the Amphyctionic Plan
developed a more positive program. It called for "a
union and close alliance with the Northern United
States, especially with the citizens of Louisiana
who are to have free entry into Texas as brothers."
A union and close alliance does not necessarily
imply annexation to the United States, but in the
light of later developments, the Mexican public
certainly presumed that it did. In reply the exiles
who might have been involved protested the
Amphyctionic Plan as a spurious document issued by
their political enemies in order to blacken the name
of Federalism. Thereafter the exiles, on returning
from their involuntary sojourn abroad, observed a
great silence on the issues of the North—a silence
no more profound than that of their opponents.

Popular attention in Mexico had turned to other
issues—those of domestic politics. Mexicans grouped
themselves into two loosely organized political
segments, Centralists and Federalists, which
alternately advanced candidates for the Presidency
or busily undermined an incumbent with political
anathemas. The Declaration of Toluca (May, 1835)
almost evaded the growing crisis on the northern
frontier. It bravely called for "the independence of
the nation in its present territorial
integrity"—the gentlest of reference to the Texas
issue. If the Planners recognized California as a
separate issue, their declarations do not reveal it.
General reference to "northern frontiers," which
embodied perhaps one third of the nation, served to
screen the issue from critical examination. A
seventeen page proposed revision of the Mexican
constitution (September, 1835) carried not one word
about the problem of the northern territories.

The Plans, headline proposals for the good of
the country, totally failed to inform the citizens
of the critical situation facing the nation. Not
until after military defeat in Texas did General
Olarte issue his Pronouncement of Papantla
(November, 1836). In an extravaganza of purple prose
he called upon the nation's citizens to enlist in
the Army and to redeem the loss of Texas; otherwise,
he promised, the war would continue indefinitely.
All that was required--so ran the Plan--was that the
central administration, which he judged fully
responsible for the mess in Texas, should reform
itself, abolish anarchy, enlist 200,000 Mexicans,
and Texas would be re-integrated into Mexico. Thus,
he promised, "The ambitious intentions of the
Cabinet of Washington and the stale intrigues of
Madrid would be contained." How Madrid became
involved he did not say. Since the Spanish garrison
was still quartered at the fortress in the Vera Cruz
harbor, he may have found it easy to conjure up the
image of an aggressive or revengeful Spain. Today
such charges of "stale intrigues" are considered
figments of an overblown imagination.

However, immediately after the numbing loss of
Texas in 1836 the Proclamation of the Federation of
San Luis (April, 1837) had a great deal to say about
the situation. Ministers in the cabinet, it
declared, had permitted the country to be
dismembered "due to the irregularity with which the
war had been waged against the Texas rebels." The
nation had raised taxes in order to supply the Army;
widow benefits had been voted, yet all, it
protested, had been wasted--all under the
administration of the "old bosses." Therefore, the
State of San Luis Potosi chose to secede. After this
satisfyingly clear and strong condemnation of the
administration, the State, despite its resolution,
remained in the Union.

As revealed in subsequent Plans, disintegration
of the Mexican armies in Texas, capture of their
President and Commander-in-Chief, and his flight
into exile all occasioned remarkably little protest
or demand for governmental reform. The Plans knew
Texas no more, and, as the shower of Plans in the
early 1840's indicate, Mexican attention turned to
the immediate problems of a domestic administration
paralyzed by total defeat.

The impotent government of Mexico never recognized the secession of Texas nor could it accept the boundaries which that State had laid out for itself. Rather, it chose to consider Texas in a perpetual rebellion which the government had not been able to repress. When the United States in 1845 accepted Texas into its Union, the northern Republic logically supported all prior Texas territorial claims. Since both sides displayed equal intransigence, hostilities resumed quickly and inevitably.

With the onset of war Mexican leadership sought to roll all issues involving the northern frontiers into one--recovery of lost territory. General Rangel's Plan (June, 1845) required a Presidential Executive Committee to be chosen from among those who would not have approved a Texas Treaty. He would have organized a National Guard with two-fold duties: to preserve public order and to re-enforce units which might be sent to Texas. Then he turned to a practical matter: the troops must be paid punctually, a thing which, he declared, had not been done up to that time. The curious Salvadoran Plan (August, 1845) promised that a new constitution would be decreed, but should not take effect "until the war with Texas and the United States or with any other country shall have ended."

Indeed, the Plans indicate that in this national emergency Mexicans did not know what more to do. The Plan of Regeneration (May, 1846) referred to "the question which now involves Texas and North America being so vital to the Republic" and promised to allocate one-fourth of the national budget to this problem. "The Army of the North shall receive this sum in order to conduct the war which so deeply involves the national honor."

"Regeneration" also required that a congress should establish a Republic (sic) "and clearly explain all matters relative to the question of Texas and other frontier departments"---a muted reference, presumably to New Mexico, California and perhaps to Yucatan. No one, declared the Plan, possessed better qualifications to lead the Nation in this restorative process than General Santa Anna, notwithstanding the errors which had marked his career. The Plan of Jalapa (August, 1846) ignored the wider call for regeneration. Its sponsors would be satisfied with a military victory "in a war being

94

unjustly waged by the United States and under General Benemerito Santa Anna it should continue until he had "secured a complete triumph over the United States" or until that power had sued for peace "in an honorable way."

If vague generalities laden with patriotic garlands could win public acclaim, then General Salas felt that he could draft the necessary expressions as well as any. Only his signature distinguishes the Salas Plan from others of that sad period. (August, 1846) He called upon the Congress and the faithful to gather and "to decree whatever the national honor may require." This Plan, the sponsor declared, would bring genuine regeneration, and, apparently in order to make the endorsement easier for this potential supporters, he issued the text with a blank space at the top so that when a city or populated place had endorsed the Plan, its name could be added easily. Thus the endorsers could pledge themselves to secure an election under the terms of the Constitution of 1824, and to constitute a nation "by adopting any form of government save monarchy." That being done, General Salas felt that the nation would be prepared to wage war with the United States and to settle the question of Texas.

Within the same month the Garrison of Vera Cruz issued a simplistic Plan that would sidestep all critical issues: Congress should settle the questions involved in the war with the United States, and all Mexicans would be obligated to obey the decisions of that body. The garrison nominated as national leader in this crisis the enduring General Santa Anna, "he having given (despite his errors) the firmest support to public liberties and to the security of the public domain."

Even Santa Anna's most ardent supporters could not ignore his many mistakes; they could compensate for them only by overstating his possible merits. Thus it became the style to insert into the Plans an endorsement of General Santa Anna as the national leader. The Plan of the Restorers (February, 1847) named him as interim President under the terms of the Constitution of 1824 which he had subverted during the Centralist administration of the previous decade. But regardless of all that, the interim President would be empowered to wage war against the United States--and then, so casually--"all other matters shall be carried out according to the

Constitution and the laws in force."

General Santa Anna, waiting in the wings, heard and heeded the call of his militant countrymen. He returned from exile to assume the leadership of his nation, and never was a country more ineptly served. The war, but not the agony, ended under his obviously ineffective administration both as President and as Commander-in-Chief in the war against the United States. Thereafter, the Plans, never specific about the issues of Texas or the United States, simply ceased mentioning the subject. The Plan of Eligio Ortiz (July, 1851) paid homage to the dreadful past by calling for a repudiation of the Treaty of Guadalupe Hidalgo with the United States. With that gesture the problems of the north and of Senior Ortiz as well, appear no more in the political Plans of Mexico.

d. Spaniards and the Plans

Every war in progress defines its enemies, but some definitions are more precise than others. In the Mexican War for Independence Spain, the ruling, the imperialist power, would surely be the Enemy...but Spaniards...? Individual Spaniards living in Mexico and--perhaps supporting the cause of Independence --what of them...or of inoffensive Spaniards who asked only to be let alone?

The initial Decree of 1810 which began by abolishing slavery concluded with an order requiring all foreigners to leave the Province of Morelia at once, a proviso that theoretically would have cut a wide swath, but probably it was aimed only at Spaniards. This Draconian measure either proved impractical or unpopular. Too many Spaniards ranked too high within the select group which controlled entrance into the ranks of colonial administration for the hostile declarations to become effective, or as private citizens the assistance of certain Spaniards greatly eased the burden of revolution. The logic of hostility and the practical advantage of cooperation contradicted each other. Therefore, in an about-face, Dr. Cos, early in 1812, made a bid for Spaniards without distinction to remain in Mexico and to aid in the building of a new nation; he even urged that they promote the war effort. However, he concluded by promising that if they should wish to leave the country, they might have perfect liberty to depart and to proceed to any destination they might wish--obviously to Spain, the presumed oppressor.

Revolutionary ambivalence toward Spaniards continued. Rayon's Elements of a Constitution of that same year required "any foreigner" to secure a letter of naturalization, but all "Europeans" should "vacate their positions in government, regardless of whatever class they may be." A position in the future Administration already loomed as a prize worth winning, and the patriots repeated the restriction regularly in the early decrees which served as Plans for the budding State. (54)

---

(54) Morelos' Sentiments of the Nation (September, 1813) provided that "only Americans shall have [government] employment, and only useful foreigners free from all suspicion" shall be admitted into the country.

By the end of hostilities over a decade later the reservoir of hatred had run dry and prospects of a compromise emerged. The Plan of Iguala (February, 1822) promised to leave occupants of government positions undisturbed. The only test, the Plan boasted, would be that of merit. Easing the path of possible transgressors continued. The Plan of Vera Cruz (December, 1822) signed by Santa Anna and Guadalupe Victoria, promised equality of all persons, including "foreigners who may obtain a letter of citizenship." As a sign that wartime hostilities had waned, the Plan agreed to accept all foreigners who did not oppose the Plan.

However, Spain itself continued to obstruct the process of reconciliation. The Mexican War for Independence did not reach its end with a definitive military victory such as that of the North Americans at Yorktown, nor were hostilities followed reasonably soon thereafter by a treaty of peace with the mother country. Rather, after being driven from the mainland, Spanish forces hunkered down in the fortress at San Juan de Ullos at the entrance to the port of Vera Cruz where, on royal order, they maintained a symbolic blockade. Because their mere presence offered no practical barrier to commercial activity, Mexicans left the garrison undisturbed. There it persisted as a reminder of the war that had been. For over a decade foreign troops so close at hand served as a convenient symbol when desperate politicians beat the drums of patriotism as they sought to rally citizens to one cause or another.

After the death of Ferdinand VII in 1836, fifteen years after Mexican victory, Spanish troops vacated the fortress. By doing nothing they had succeeded in perpetuating in Mexico the concept of Spaniards as public enemies. Occasionally later Plans reflected fear of (if not hatred of) Spaniards by proposing that discriminations be laid against them. These subsequent Plans reflected that segment of public opinion which labeled Spaniards as an active menace to the State, and their authors hoped that occasional expressions of open hostility towards Spaniards would gain a measure of popular support for almost any Mexican Declaration.

For example, the Plan of Cuernavaca (January, 1824), while trying to be all things to all persons, alternately stretched and snapped the bonds of brotherhood: "All natives of Anahuac [an alternate name for 'Mexico' then in use] and resident Spaniards of the said States, of whatever class they may be, are citizens and brothers of each other." Yet the Plan would have denied Spaniards public employment, a seat in the national Congress, or a role in provincial administration. At the same time the Plan recognized their past services and offered to grant a pension according to individual merit and fitness, a qualification which would have to be proved before the proper investigatory body. Indeed, this early Plan promised Spaniards respect and protection, but it warned that at the slightest sign of disloyalty they were to be disarmed [this proviso three years after the Treaty of Cordoba], charged with treason, and their property confiscated upon conviction before a military court. The Plan spoke of "natural rights" in the distribution of employment in the public sector: jobs were to be given to native Mexicans and to be denied to Spaniards "because it is convenient for their own safety." Clearly the Native Sons were prepared to scramble for prized government positions even while proclaiming universal brotherhood. Fraternity had its practical limits.

Then, repeating the promise of Dr. Cos, Spaniards, after having been ousted from government service, might remain in Mexico or leave as suited their personal convenience. But--forget Brotherhood here--those who chose to live in Mexico would be required to surrender all weapons, and any person found hiding weapons would be charged with treason and if found guilty should receive the death sentence. A cloud of general suspicion continued. The Propositions of an Ad Hoc Committee (April, 1824) called for the expulsion of all suspicious foreigners and those who had surrendered and turned

in arms but who had not sworn to support the cause
of Independence were to be suspected of treasonable
designs. The word "treason" flashed about rather
easily in those contentious days and the accused
faced either death or confiscation of property at
the whim of the armed supporters of any dominant
political grouping.

Spaniards faced an ambivalent society. Once the
conflict of Independence had ended, Mexicans seemed
ready to offer acceptance, but on other occasions
they gave abundant proof that they had learned to
hate the Motherland. General Santa Anna, ever ready
to press a public cause to the limit, issued the
brief Plan of Perote (September, 1828) which, while
declaring opposition to the election of Gomez Farias
as President, pronounced with greater fervor against
Spaniards: "The resident Spaniards in the Republic
being the origin of all our wrongs, it is demanded
of the Chambers of the Union a law for their total
expulsion." He secured the law, but enforcement
lapsed. His Plan of Jalapa (September, 1830) again
raised the spectre of a Spanish menace: "Expulsion
of Spaniards is to be strictly enforced, and they
are to be placed under guard until arrangements for
their disembarkation are completed."

Such ferocity amounted to nothing. As the burst
of Plans in the decade of the 1830's indicate,
Mexican public interest centered around issues wider
than harrassment of Spaniards for whatever they may
have done during the era of the War for
Independence. Yet latent hatreds, like old sores,
emerged now and again. The Plan of Ecatzinco
(February, 1834) promised its adherents that upon
victory all debts to foreigners--that is to say, to
Spaniards--would be repudiated and that Spaniards,
this time specifically named, would be expelled
within ninety days.

There the matter rested: the Spanish population
continued steadily uneasy and not a little fearful
lest a wave of vindictive patriotism should
overwhelm it, never knowing when Spaniards would be
charged with responsibility for any or all of
Mexico's insoluble problems. But contention over
Church and State issues, defeat in the Texas War and
in the War with the United States provided easier
targets of public wrath. Almost, Spaniards were
forgotten and forgiven. The Definitively

Regenerative Plan (December, 1855), so backward in many respects, promised to protect all inhabitants of Mexico in the exercise of their civil rights, and Mexicans understood that to include Spaniards. "All persons," it promised, "Mexicans by adoption [that is, naturalized] are to be received as full citizens with rights to employment and public positions without any distinctions whatsoever." The Plan ran ahead of its time; the stigma of a foreign blood taint remained. As late as 1910 Jose Limantour was ruled ineligible to succeed Porfirio Diaz to the Presidency because his father had not been a native Mexican.

The wildest blast against Spaniards came not from some declaration during the heat of the struggle for Independence but in the contemporary post-Revolutionary period a hundred years later. The single-issue declaration, the Plan of El Veladero (May, 1926) testifies to a lingering Mexican hatred of Spaniards, long after Spanish attempts to re-occupy ports lost in the Independence hostilities, two generations after Spanish participation in the Maximilian affair.

Within the memory of living persons Spain had not been a national enemy, yet the declaration stands: El Veladero declares that Spaniards are to be sent into exile, their property to be confiscated by the State, to be sold and the proceeds to be distributed to the poor. The Plan goes further: all legal authorities who might refuse to sign the necessary papers which would be required in the enforcement of these measures should be punished as criminals and judged guilty of high treason against the Fatherland. Like punishment should be visited upon any official who might thereafter permit Spaniards to enter the country.

This weird Plan of El Veladero began by repudiating "from now to eternity" Article 13 of the ancient Plan of Iguala, issued in 1812: "The persons of whatever citizenship and their properties will be respected and protected by the government." Surely this is the last time that the first Plan of Independence will be the object of public protest. El Veladero presumed that a civil war with its death and destruction would result from its war on Spaniards but its authors faced that grim possibility with fortitude as they forwarded their

101

appeal "to country peasants, to the National Army, and to foreign nations." With this flourish the authors and their cause sank into the Mexican mist of Has-Beens.

But spirits of old prejudices lingered long after possible offenders had been given a decent and proper burial. In 1939 with the defeat of the Spanish Republic many of its supporters fled the victorious Franco Dictatorship and in Mexico met a generous reception from the Cardenas Administration. Certain reactionary individuals led by General Almazan, once a Madero revolutionary himself, rebelled at the availability of Mexican society to such liberal-minded persons. In what was to be Mexico's last Plan they recorded their cry: "The land of our forefathers and of our children is turned into an international dumping ground and is attracting and receiving the political and social outcasts, the troublesome agents of foreign governments." Still there had been progress of a sort: 1) very few Mexicans responded to their cry, and 2) while they could protest a polity and a practice, the time had passed when persons of small renown could brand Spaniards publicly.

Not since these post-Revolutionary blasts have Planners seen fit to turn upon Spaniards as fit objects of their wrath. They found that Mexicans had no room in their hearts for such unadorned hatred. Mexicans had acquired another system of values which no longer included the outworn calls to the barricades: the cause had become a parody of patriotism. An end must come to all things.

e. Freemasonry and the Plans

Throughout Mexican history enmities have developed over the place of Freemasonry in Mexican society, yet the Plans scarcely mention the subject. The issue lives underground and its importance may be appreciated only in terms of Mexican life, not by public declarations. The Plans scarcely acknowledge its existence.

Freemasonry as a public phenomenon arose early--during the first administration after Independence, when the American Minister, Joel R. Poinsett, not only introduced one branch of the Order into Mexico, but he promoted Freemasonry as a political factor. Inevitably, he aroused such resentment by his irregular activity that the Administration asked him to leave the country.(55)

In response to this unpleasant episode, General Montano, otherwise unknown to history, in one of the earliest Plans (December, 1826) demanded the dismissal of the American Minister and the adoption of adequate provisos which might avoid such a situation in the future: "The Supreme Government shall draft a law for the Central Congress of Unity for the extermination in the Republic of all kinds of secret meetings, whatever may be their origin." The Plan sounds off on this special issue, but beyond that...nothing. Montano's Plan, being so limited, aroused no general response, and with the departure of Poinsett the aggravation subsided, but the problem remained.

Within the councils of government the role of Freemasonry in the national administration continued to arouse intense controversy. The final draft of the Plan of the Conspiracy of Deputy Gondra (November, 1830), while lashing out at all opponents, promised to discharge all civil servants who should voluntarily continue serving in the existing administration. An earlier draft of 1827 had stated specifically: "None of the employees who belong to have belonged to the Scottish Rite

---

(55) Joel .R. Poinsett discovered that Scottish Rite Freemasonry had but recently been introduced into Mexico. In an excess of zeal he sponsored a companion Rite, that of York. Thereafter an unfortunate and unhealthy rivalry developed between the two branches of the Order. See also Thomas B. Davis, Aspects of Freemasonry in Modern Mexico, (New York, 1975).

103

without having been initiated into the York Rite before this pronouncement shall remain."(56)

Apparently, in those days the ties of fraternal regard were loose indeed; and quite obviously, too, membership in the Order enhanced one's advancement in the various branches of public employment.

In the midst of the Liberal-Centralist controversy of the 1830's over the role of the Roman Catholic Church in State affairs, Freemasonry became associated with the Liberal Party. The Centralist declaration of Cuernavaca (May, 1834) protested the Liberal program under Gomez Farias, and it called upon General Santa Anna to assume control of the government and, presumably, to abolish the recent laws passed to reform Church administration; also, it asked the banning of the Masonic Order. Whereas General Montano had been content to call for an end to 'secret meetings' of all sorts, the Declaration of Cuernavaca specifically named Freemasonry as the object of its abomination.

Thereafter both Centralists, the Liberals, as well as the Freemasons were content to let the Order remain in Mexico's darkest closet of political skeletons. The Plans made no further reference to the matter, but on the operating level of practically the issue has continued to vex Mexican public life.

---

(56) Among Freemasons of English tradition and usage it is obligatory to enter Freemasonry be receiving three initial degrees according to the York Rite, and thereafter the candidate may choose whether he would prefer additional advanced degrees according to either York or Scottish Rite ritual. Scottish Rite Masonry, coming to Mexico by way of France and Spain, had not followed this practice: it had conferred its own first three degrees. Obviously Deputy Gondra's advisers where drawn from vigorous supporters of the York Rite.

f. Indians and the Plans

Because they controlled the political process, the conquering white men assumed the prerogative of issuing Plans, and in these documents they evidenced small concern for Indians. The native peoples, living within the traditional environment, were deemed unworthy of official notice. They grubbed; they carted; they could be drafted into any Army that happened to be billeted in the vicinity of Indian villages and as enlisted personnel they could be forced to fight for any cause---convenient people for the drudge occupations of any social group. The earliest Independence Plans mentioned Indians casually and thereafter so far as specific reference indicates, they were forgotten for decades. Indeed, the Planners foreswore the very name "Indian." A hostile reference in a Plan carried the term "savages" or "barbarians;" the neutral reference rested content with "the indigenous natives"--a term which included those Indians living peacefully in villages and performing chores for Europeans. As late as 1875 the "final solution" of the Indian race wars of Yucatan included a program of white colonization which would eliminate or assimilate Indians.(57)

Plans of the Independence period appealed to Indians for support by offering specific benefits upon the establishment of the new State. The Decree Abolishing Slavery (October, 1810) called for an end to the tax on the processors of maguey by "indigenous natives," and it set precise limits on the excise taxes to be laid against their distilled aguardiente. Father Hidalgo's parallel decree abolishing slavery (November, 1810) also promised abolition of forced labor from Indians. The Plan of Iguala (February, 1821) recognized the right of the Indian, along with all native-born Mexicans, to any employment "according to his merits and virtues."

---

(57) Plan of the Garrison of Jalisco (October, 1852); Basis for the Administration of the Republic (April, 1853); Progressive Republican Party Program (1872-1876).

105

After 1835 those Plans which refer to citizenship stated that all persons born in the national domain were to be counted as citizens and were to be judged on the basis of their individual qualifications. That much the Plans conceded the Indian.(58) However, insertion of a literacy requirement eliminated most tribal Indians from any prospect of civic employment.

Rather, it proved easier to keep the Indian as the object of romantic imagination, and as such he appeared from time to time in the Plans. When the Liberal-Centralist turmoil of the 1830's threatened to tear the State apart, two priests, more worried than practical, advanced the curious Plan of Ecatzinco (February, 1834). They declared Mexican attempts at domestic government a failure, and in its place they proposed a monarchy, the first public mention of monarchy since the fall of the Iturbide experiment. Presumably the priests believed that the fault with that initial effort lay with the person, not the system. Therefore, they proposed that an Emperor--not white, but an Indian--should sit on the Mexican throne, and that no person could be more legitimate than a descendent of Moctezuma himself. They would, they said, find twelve unmarried (the text of the Plan specifies that they should be celibate) Indians who were undoubtedly descended from the last Aztec monarch; they would be ordered to draw by lot, the winner to be declared Emperor. After marrying a white woman of unspecified lineage, the lucky monarch should then promise to support the Centralist program.(59)

The Plan continued: In the lower ranks of State and municipal government Indians should be represented equally with whites, but within their own

---

(58) Definitively Regenerative Plan (December, 1855); the Plan of Urrea and Gomez Farias (July, 1840); a Projected Constitution, Anonymous, (October, 1841).

(59) Somewhere in the drafting process of their document the priests forgot one detail of their initial proposal. Article VIII stipulated that if the choice for the Emperor should fall upon a white, he must then marry an Indian, but they did not require that this woman should be an undoubted descendent of Moctezuma.

areas the Indians were to elect their governing officials as they had done "before the constitutional system." Furthermore, they provided that the national congress, when assembled, should include Indians. On political matters the priests did not say more, but on Church issues they sounded surprisingly liberal: "All ecclesiastical positions as well as those of a subordinate rank shall be distributed equally among the Indians and the more suitable casts." Presumably this last proviso embraced those with a Negroid trace.

In the dark days of civil turmoil that resulted in the loss of the Texas territory, the Plan of the Priests, as it was called, served as a source of amused comment. Out of the defeat of this war and subsequent disasters arose again the fantasy of a mythical Indian--an idealized Indian princess-no less-who surely existed somewhere out in the bush. Some worthy person, white and single, should find her, marry her, and then rule Mexico thereafter, his own legitimacy being sealed by the union--Indians and whites united within the mystic bonds of matrimony. Thus the Definitively Regenerative Plan (December, 1855) in Mexico's most crucial year of trial offered this dreamy solution to a nation's problems.

As for Indians who lived beyond the grasp of white society, they were considered wild and barbarous. If Indians resisted white incursions, then the district was said to have suffered invasions of savages, and some of the Plans provided on that account for State exemption from certain taxes due to the Federal government.(60) Thus the roving desert Indian, caught between the frontier closing in from the United States on the north and from Mexico in the south had small choice: the ruling societies of both countries considered him a menace. Santa Anna's Bases for the Administration of the Republic (April, 1853) referred to "defense of the districts against the wild tribes." Generally the Plans of the nineteenth century classified Indians as hostile aliens who must be totally eliminated.

---

(60) Plan of Hospicio (October, 1852); the Second Plan of Blancarte (September, 1852); also parallel provisions in the Plan of the Garrison of Jalisco (October 1852); Basis for the Administration of the Republic (April, 1853).

Not until the Revolution of 1910-1917 did Indians gain favorable mention in the Plans of the ruling, white class. The Program of the Liberal Party (July, 1906), while embracing many social reform programs, made but passing reference to Indians. The indigenous race, it declared, needed protection; therefore, all land confiscated from agents of the Diaz Dictatorship should be given to Mayas, Yaquis, or other tribes whose land had been despoiled or else such lands should be sold in order to amortize the national debt. National debts being what they are, the tribes enjoyed small prospects of receiving significant awards under such a proviso.

The concept of Indians as wards of, rather than enemies of, the State persisted. Perhaps this paternalistic category indicated an improvement over earlier attitudes. Thereafter, it became an acceptable public gesture for a Plan to make some reference to "the indigenous races," although the great landmark Plans of the Revolutionary era ignored Indians completely. Madero's Plan of San Luis Potosi (October, 1910) totally overlooked Indian problems. Zapata, who drew such wide support from the Indian segment of the population in his Plan of Ayala, offered nothing specifically for Indians. Orozco's wide-ranging Plan of the Empacadora does not mention Indians; Carranza's Plan of Guadalupe, its Modifications, Additions, or Revisions, all failed to mention Indian interests or concerns.

The Indian, now so much a part of the contemporary Mexican psyche, won recognition only gradually, and even then solely in the Plans of minor Revolutionary figures. Point VIII of the Socio-Political Plan (March, 1911) promised that "the indigenous race shall be protected in every sense of the word, promoting thus by every means its dignity and prosperity." The Program and Basis of the Popular Evolutionist Party (June, 1911) offered something more specific, "diffusion in all classes, especially in the indigenous race, of rudimentary education, which shall consist of instruction in the Spanish language, or reading and writing;"--in other words, turn them in to brown White Men. The Plan of Santa Rosa (February, 1912) went even further: it would reserve specific public funds for Indian education. Also, each State should retain twenty percent of its federal tax collections for "The Twenty Percent Indian Education Fund," but the proviso gave no indication of what the education should consist.

The first Plan of Felix Diaz ignored all such matters. He recognized no social ills; instead he challenged old soldiers to rally to his name and to his family. Few volunteers responded to his invitation. His second Plan (February, 1914), presumably on advice of counsellors, displayed a wider appeal. He made two references to "indigenous people" and proposed agricultural reforms from which they might benefit--rights to land, roads, ejidos, irrigation, agricultural schools, experiment stations. He even declared his support for return of expropriated land during the Diaz Administration to Indian villages, but this devolution should be accomplished only after due trials and regular court decisions. Rather casually he added the promise, "Wider education for the popular classes." He may have thought that Indians might be included within that classification, but "the popular classes" failed to rally to the Diaz standard.

Even those Revolutionary leaders who were considered especially radical drafted their Plans in general terms: they hoped to be all things to all people. Not until his Second Plan (April, 1916) did Zapata, in his longer and more detailed declaration, reveal a modicum of public interest in Indians as a particular people. Indeed, his promised programs, in their general scope, showed no more generosity than that of Felix Diaz in <u>his</u> last pronouncement. The difference lay in the fact that Zapata was believed and the son of the Dictator was not! Perception is also politics, and the "indigenous people" remained Indians and followed leaders of their own choosing while the whites compounded Plans to confound their opponents.

CHAPTER IX
Plans During the Last Half-Century

With the onset of the Diaz Regime provisions of
the various Plans showed that a new era had spawned
different interests. Political manipulations had
pervaded the pre-Diaz Plans--Centralist or
Federalist constitutions, the role of Church and
State, special congresses, operation of the
Executive Power, continued special privileges for
the Army and the Church. But after the national
purging of the Maximilian affair economic
considerations and corporate grants dominated the
promised age of Justice and Equity.

The new Administration showed itself anxious to
encourage public corporate activity such as the
railroad and the telegraph. Even during the last
pre-Diaz period mention of railroads began to appear
more frequently in the Plans: railroads were
recognized as factors in public well-being. And the
newspapers: in the long Santa Anna twilight
newspapers and the press were not recognized as
institutions of public concern, but by 1875 Thomas
Jefferson himself could not have defended the Press
and its freedom more roundly than did Iglesias. The
following year President-to-be Diaz in his Plan
demanded that high officials announce their
adherence to his party by issuing a statement to the
Press--a private assurance would never do. Also,
each 'adhesion' when announced publicly served to
advertise the Plan. The Press had become a clear and
obvious factor in the political life of Mexico.

General Diaz issued his Plan of La Noria in 1871
and redrafted it a year later for a second and
successful drive for the Presidency. The changes
amounted to little in themselves, but in terms of
the Plans of the Santa Anna period the new
generation of Plans had undergone a metamorphosis.
Diaz appealed for support with a surfeit of
patriotic phrases: "Lovers of the Constitution and
of free election..." "...the principles of earlier
days"... "the noble and patriotic sentiments of
dignity and justice"... "Strict observance of the
Constitution will be the real guarantee of peace."
Yet he called for a convention to draft a program of
constitutional reconstruction "without any pretense
of completeness nor through any desire to impose
[reform] as preconceived resolutions, and protesting
that from here on I shall accept without reservation

or any reserve the decisions of the convention." In the meantime he claimed the solid ground: he stood for the Constitution of 1857 and free elections.

In 1871 the budding Dictator held forth like a Populist, "We will fight, then, for the cause of the People and the People shall be the only judge of its victory," and then in terms as modern as yesterday's headlines, "Less government and more freedom." Nor could he resist the worn phrase from Rousseau, "The general welfare of the inhabitants of the republic..." But the Military would not be forgotten while urging the cause of the People: All the Military who supported the latest revision (1876) were to be granted full recognition of rank, tenure, and decorations.

Among the Generals Diaz did not stand alone in appealing for respect of civil liberties. The Liberating Plan of General Lasada (1873) declared that he favored freedom of the press "provided its productions promote progress and morality," and publishers would be "sternly prohibited from occupying themselves with offensive publications ..without having sufficient justification." The General promised that the slightest failure in this matter would be duly punished. Since Lasada's campaign collapsed promptly and he was heard of no more, the editors were spared argumentative sessions regarding sufficiency of justification.

A civilian, Iglesias showed himself a more serious candidate in 1876. His Plan of Salamanca carried a five-page introduction and lengthy explanatory paragraphs setting forth his points rather than the customary enumerated listing. Besides stressing the need for good and efficient administration (as every aspirant was bound to do) he also raised issues which the Military had ignored: free elections, human rights, freedom of the Press, independence of the Judiciary, sovereignty of the State, more public education, economic revival, and extensive public works. Generals of the Santa Anna era never talked of such things. Public awareness had expanded, as General Rocha discovered when, in March, 1875, he issued his dreary "Revolutionary Plan" that represented a reversion to an earlier generation.

President Lerdo de Tejada (1872-1876) sought to organize a modern political party [the Republican Party] and to have it issue a platform—in effect, a Plan—which would express the wider social interests of a new age: promotion of private business by withdrawal of the government from construction and other projects, free trade and free enterprise, protection of property and an end to brigandage, a law and order appeal. The budding Party also remembered to favor economy in government, reduction of the government payroll, and, of course, total fulfillment of the Constitution.

But Porfirio Diaz won the election of 1876—his personal popularity overcame all—and the new President sponsored a long period of economic growth with all factors of public life centered in an administration under his personal control. Some fifteen years later, General Garza, from his hide-away in the United States dared issue a "Revolutionary Plan" in 1891. Against the union of Diaz agents and United States marshalls his effort came to nothing. Indeed, his Plan scarcely justified the term "revolutionary;" rebellious would have been better. In the tone of the Santa Anna years, it called for a constitutional convention which should revise the Constitution so as to minimize the election of military heroes and to prohibit re-election to the Presidency. Also, he called for amendments to repeal the dreaded 'Fugitive Laws' under which Diaz had so notoriously eliminated his opposition. As regards the new order of things, Garza favored clear provisions for State sovereignty, promotion of economic development (which the incumbent President Diaz was accomplishing at a great rate), and finally the General raised an issue to become popular twenty years later—the distributions of public lands. Garza's planned revolt failed almost at its beginning, and his announced reforms, both great and small, remained unrealized and forgotten save by gathering clusters of refugee dreamers.

Years of Independence had wrought a sort of romantic glaze on the Mexican image of long ago, but as the decades spun out, Mexico came to be perceived as a colonial dependency of the Republic of the North, and Diaz the Iron-fisted Dictator declared a lackey of foreign capitalists. By the end of the century a groundswell of unrest had begun, and in spite of all Diaz's efforts he was never able to contain fully the mixed bag of exalted reformers. Ultimately, in July, 1906, a subterranean Liberal Party issued its Plan which we recognize today as a genuine political Platform. It had a further advantage: since it received endorsement of an organized political party, a rare thing in pre-Revolutionary Mexico, it was divorced from the personal domination of an ambitious or disgruntled General.

The "Program of the Liberal Party" ignored all other Plans. It disdained the little, with inconsequential appeals to an individual, or to a class such as the Army or the Church. Rather, it faced Mexican problems as if they were those of a modern State, not of a primitive fiefdom. The product of the Liberal analysis stands as a tribute to honest and clear thinking, and it set the tone for the impending struggle. Scarcely an issue which developed later in seven years of civil war fails to appear here as a proposition calling for consideration. Uniquely, too, its text frankly declared that it was issued from the United States. No other Plan had dared to admit that it had first seen the light of day in the Colossus of the North.

After 1906 all reformers wanted action. In anticipation of the coming national election 1910 still another group from 'respectable families' issued their Plan, the "Platform of the Anti-electionist Party" in April, 1910. Clearly the Upper Class group had read the Anarchist Magon material of 1906, but they toned down the ringing charges, shortened the text considerably, and referred to the social and economic problems in the most general fashion. Near the end of their Platform they reverted to full tradition and promised "to improve the Army so that it could better discharge its high duty," and they called for universal military training. The nation remained unmoved: the lightening had not struck.

The election of 1910 registered the customary victory for the Diaz Administration, but it brought no easing of pressure. Suddenly everything broke wide open as with the dropping of a ripe melon. Francisco I. Madero issued his Plan of San Luis Potosi, and Mexico would never be the same again. Not for seven years and after a great flurry of conflicting Plans did the nation again find the constitutional adhesive that would bind the parts together again.

Considered objectively, the Plan of San Luis Potosi (October, 1910) sounded like those ancient Plans of the pre-Diaz period. It centered upon politics and processes, a repudiation of men in power, a challenge to those executing the laws, a repudiation of _continuismo_, that dread political ailment that had so often afflicted Mexican leaders. In 1871 Diaz had thought that he favored "No Re-election" but by 1910 the new revolutionaries, chanting that motto over and over again, ran him out. Madero asked for a provisional President who would be responsible to a future Congress, punishment for all who resisted the Plan, reward for those who should accept it, and he made an encouraging offer to the Military who might fight for the cause. The Plan concluded with a peroration that beat the drums of patriotism in a manner worthy of long-departed Santa Anna and ended with a confession of frustrated political pique. Madero justified his cause by quoting Diaz of the early days. All in all, the Plan, framed within the traditional limits of an earlier day, seemed a small thing with which to start a revolution. Madero proved himself a great man with little understanding.

The generation that fought the Revolution endured the agony of seeing the country, grown sullen, being torn apart. Mexico, it appeared, desired the rest of the world only as a resource for explosives useful for blasting its own people to Kingdom Come. Then came the Plans, showers of Plans, from every man or group which had an idea that it thought would save the country. Early on—General Caborca. The General labeled his Plan (April, 1911) "Revolutionary" because he had quickly endorsed the Plan of San Luis Potosi. And then the Plan of Texcoco (August, 1911) —a throwback to the days of Santa Anna, a barracks revolt based on no other idea than repudiation of the government in power. Save for the fact that its sponsors were in revolt, nothing justified the boast, "this revolutionary Plan." General Bernardo Reyes (November, 1911) could do no better. He accepted the political slogans of the Madero movement while opposing its administration. He sounded an uncertain note about alienation of land, promised to honor expenses incurred in support of his "Revolution," and after the manner of the century past he cast his Plan

114

to the political winds. Other Plans endorsed the
Maderista revolt or responded to the revolutionary
ferment in general (Plan of Paracuaro, April, 1913).

Five States and the Federal District itself
(March, 1911) advanced their "Socio-Political Plan,"
much broader in scope than Madero's concept of
Mexico's greatest need. After three paragraphs of
introductory Considerandos, which had become
obligatory, the Plan turned to the new impulses of
social reform first publicized a half-decade earlier
by the Liberal Party. That Party, alas, had been
made obsolete by the spattering of the Revolution.

So soon the dam burst: social reform became all
the rage. A whirlwind of eloquent Considerandos and
a commanding list of Mexico's ailments, new
political parties with really new names, such as The
Program and Bases of the Popular Evolutionist Party
(June, 1911) ballooned into existence. Although now
forgotten, Plans from such parties as these reveal
the impulses behind the Mexican Revolution. Even
those who were disillusioned by Madero's ineffective
leadership--such as General Orozco--were ready to
endorse a wide range of economic and social reforms
and to condemn the Dictatorship "of the single
individual who can convert himself into an
Executioner." So quickly had the reputation for the
much-praised Dictator declined!

Felix Diaz, heir to the family leadership felt
that even yet there must be some power in The Name.
Two years after the outbreak of revolution he issued
a call for the Old Army to join him in an overthrow
of the Present Administration [he avoided calling
Madero by name] and thereafter, he promised, Mexico
could have a new and really honest election,
"nothing like the cruel joke of false elections such
as the last fraudulent one." Then he turned backward
to quote an old speech which he had given in 1908 on
Discipline as the supreme good of the Fatherland.

It must have been with some disillusionment that
Felix Diaz learned of the small numbers attracted to
the bearer of The Name as he sought to capitalize
upon the presumed popularity of his father's
administration. He tried again in 1916 but on that
venture he made not a single reference to his
family. Somewhat instructed by four years of civil
war, he offered a wider program the second time
around, but not wide enough.

He reflected a conservative, property-oriented mind that remained out of touch with the great movement of the nation. He promised that all reforms under the new Diaz would be regularized: a comprehensive redistribution of land, both public and private, but only after a report of a federal commission; the same procedure would be followed in adjusting water rights for the dry areas. Lands already confiscated should be returned; there should be no intervention in rural property without a country order. His attention centered on valid titles, on legal contracts and authorized concessions. With the collapse of his Plan the conservative element in Mexican society no longer tried to ride the revolutionary whirlwind.

With Madero the Dictatorship had ended, but the Revolution had stalled. Zapata voiced demands for reform. His Plan of Ayala (November, 1911) as first issued, began in the traditional style: Considerandos which justified the revolt against the Diaz regime (which by that time had already ended) and a repudiation of its authority and its acts. Positively--it endorsed the Madero Plan of San Luis Potosi; it named Orozco as military leader of the South. And that was all! The revolutionary impact of the Plan rested upon the additions which Zapata and his legal staff kept adding during the course of the fighting. The real Zapata, the revolutionary leader from the hills, added (April, 1916) such provisos as "opponents of this Plan who take arms in hand hall be judged as traitors to the cause, especially those who once supported the Plan of San Luis Pososi." Indeed, the first amendments to the primitive Plan of Ayala (May, 1913) carry no advance ideas at all. They merely add the name of General Orozco to the lengthening list of those whom the Revolution repudiated. In this second document Zapata stepped forward and proclaimed himself the legitimate leader of the Revolution.

Now the advisory staff of legalists and sociologists come into their own. The rural leader signed their proclamations, voiced their demands for a cure for Mexico's ills. Land distribution had been a 'sleeper' issue heretofore. The Zapata signature made it big: expropriation under various guises, rural banks to extend credit to the new owners, agricultural experiment stations, equalization of land taxes, practical education for farm children, abolition of poll taxes so that all might vote.

Beside the demands for improvement of life for rural folk, Zapata endorsed measures of concern to urban dwellers and to factory workers: the equivalent of a mechanics lien law, railroad legislation to prevent preferential rates, closer regulation of foreign corporations, revision of mining and oil regulations, land expropriation for public utilities. Zapata had been ushered into the modern world; these issues lay far beyond the experience either of the leader or of the men fighting under him. Surely he felt more nearly 'at home' as he concluded his Additions with the century-old promise that he and his men would support their current effusion "with arms in hand", yet they sounded a relatively new note in Mexican politics, "We are partisans for principle, not of man." Zapata's revolution had overreached him, and another hand had composed the latest document. One is reminded of the ancient Biblical account: "The voice is the voice of Jacob, but the hands are the hands of Esau."

The amended and generously re-drafted Plan of Ayala suffered yet another turn of fate--the Revised Plan of Ayala at Milpa Alta (August, 1919). Veterans of the Zapata stand-off in the South issued it and except for the title it bore no resemblance to any Plan of Ayala. The Revolution had closed, not opened, their minds.

Rather, the revolutionary reconstruction of Mexico began with the Plan of the Hacienda of Guadalupe by General Venustiano Carranza (March, 1913). Its short text covered no more than one page, double spaced, of a modern typewriter. It contained no vivid phrases, no compelling slogans. The General announced his repudiation of Venustiano Huerta and of any official who might recognize his government. In a bid to spread revolt Carranza offered to recognize as legitimate Governor the first person who should wrest a State from Huerta and assume control. As for Carranza, he declared himself interim President until elections could be held.

Thereafter the Plan grew with repeated editions, additions, and endorsements. Carranza himself endorsed each new issue of the re-named Plan of Guadalupe, but he made no attempt to hide its origin or development as a Staff production. Indeed, one

117

"Modification" of the Plan was drafted by an aide in San Antonio and forwarded to Carranza for approval.

The General's staff officers, as they stated in their Pact of Torreon (July, 1914) endorsed what had become known as the Plan of Guadalupe, yet they added significant amendments: a call for a convention which should draft a new constitution for the country, and a self-denying ordinance which declared that no commander of the Constitutionalist forces should stand for election to the future Presidency. Also the Staff openly recognized that some working agreement must be made with the Roman Catholic Church.

With so many elements endorsing his original Plan and then declaring amendments to it, Carranza found himself obliged to issue the "Additions to the Plan of Guadalupe." Since he did not mention the two major issues which his officers had declared at Torreon, they must have felt quietly repudiated, but ultimately they were vindicated. Their "additions" rather than the original Plan of Guadalupe represented the Revolutionary program. In time Carranza did summon a convention which drafted the Constitution of 1917. At long last the contested social issues first proclaimed in the Platform of 1906 were to receive constitutional recognition.

The Constituent Congress duly met on call of Carranza and completed its draft of the Constitution of 1917 which embodied every thrust of the Revolution. But the very next Plan, that of Milpa Alta in 1919 began by stating in Article I "The political Constitution of 1857 is declared in effect..." This after almost a century of Administration under two constitutions! The Plan called for a restoration of land occupied during the Revolution, indemnification for losses which the original owner may have sustained, and a judicial determination of awards. However the Plan promised, "The assignment of property into lots or parcels of land will be free to those who take up arms in order to defend this Plan..." The hoodwink of Justice could be tilted ever so slightly.

Very quickly the new Constitution of 1917 became the Palladium of the People and Planners proclaimed a revolution in its behalf, not against it. The concept of "the Revolutionist as Constitutionalist" charmed the Planners as they called for rebellion against negligent officeholders who were ignoring the new charter. The Revolution itself had appropriated all the stirring slogans, all the appealing programs: the Plans were bled white. There was nothing left to say except "I could do it better." Vain all appeals to Democracy, to honesty (promised) in office or to honest elections to be held after a victory on the battlefield. So also visions of Liberty...of Land...stale warmed-overs from a former and richer feast. Therefore, the calls for action became more general--simply outrage at 'bad government,' wild charges without citation. A later generation can only guess at what affront occasioned the eruption, but they proved to be small volcanos without great lava overflow.

Most of the later Plans, with their frequent use of political cliches, show that the struggle to frame an acceptable constitution had drained the reservoirs of public thought. "Sovereignty of the people" they wore to a frazzle; so also "Sovereignty of the Free State of..." They made frequent reference to "brave men" but women are addressed only as "free," bravery being a quality not attributed to them; but the pre-Diaz Plans had ignored women as an entity. Even "National sovereignty" won a tepid response; "integration" or "re-integration" of one facet or another of public life was promised. "Democratic institutions" apparently never had a more promising prospect that at the hands of the eager deliverers. The new Constitution would be safe with those who would "keep and cause to be kept" that great document.

Scarcely had the Revolutionary struggles been transferred to legislative halls before the victorious revolutionary Generals felt that something was slipping from their grasp, that Carranza was not rewarding them according to their deserts. Therefore, the future President Calles and his allies issued the Plan of Agua Prieta (April, 1920) with the sub-title, "The Organic Plan of the Movement for Recovery of Democracy and Law." Since the Carranza forces had been known as "the Constitutionalists," the rebels, with an obvious lack of originality assumed the title of "the Liberal Constitutional Army." Clearly the Army officers were staging a barracks rebellion, a cuartelazo, which carried no ideas at all save that those who felt themselves Out desperately wanted In.

Carranza, unable to suppress the revolt of his former subordinates, met his end while a fugitive in the backwoods. The victors then nominated themselves and called for free elections: not surprisingly they were elected. Resort to arms is a contagious thing: by 1923 General Adolfo de la Huerta had become disillusioned with the vain conduct of the victorious group. He seceded and issued his Plan under the title "Revolutionary Manifesto," but without a slogan!

This revolution against the Revolution promised to fulfill the terms of the new Constitution—its provisions on labor and its agrarian program. There should be really effective suffrage, even for women who had been "duly registered and were being educated to the discharge of communal duties"—whatever these may have been. There should be more practical forms of education with less of bookishness. The Plan logically repudiates all authorities who do not support it, but whether they were to be subjected to the death penalty which the Manifesto would have abolished is not clear.

Clearly the Revolutionary facade of national unity had begun to crumble. Not only from some atavistic recess of the most reactionary citizenry, but also from some of the most loyal supporters did protests begin to arise. Vasconcelos, the educator of the Revolution, next became disgusted with what he regarded as neglected social programs, small educational effort, and gross political irregularities. He accepted a nomination for the Presidency, but when he lost heavily (and predictably), he issued his Plan (December, 1926)—a condemnation of the Calles Administration for its "dictatorship without decency, without honor." He promised, of course, to install an honest government, but beyond these generalizations the Plan said nothing. Apparently he expected Mexico to rise to defend his own indignation—and it did not. He seems never to have forgiven his countrymen for the slight to his ego.

The revolutionary habit persisted. General Gorostieta (October, 1928) "issued from the glorious region of Los Altos," a Manifesto that could not be ignored, and later it circulated surreptitiously in Mexico City. The document carried a plethora of slogans, some political, others religious, which adherents could adopt at their pleasure.

Only in the most general terms did this newest Planner reveal the central issue of his revolt, the place of institutionalized religion within the Mexican State. The movement adopted the popular slogan "Long Live Christ the King," and its adherents acquired the title of "Cristeros," but nowhere does the formal expression appear in the Manifesto. The Plan repudiated the still new Constitution by declaring for the Constitution of 1857, but without the Laws of Reform which had sought to define the role of Religion within the State. For all practical purposes therefore, the Movement was supporting the Constitution of 1824 with the addition of a "Catholic Memorial", a petition drafted by Mexican prelates and presented to the Congress in 1928.

The program of the Cristero Movement voiced no general ideas of national concern save that of a fair distribution of ejidal lands. Rural property was to be redistributed "for the common good, but in a just and equitable manner and with prior indemnification." Its stated aim was "to make property available to the greatest number." As for the urban folk, the Movement promised to recognize labor unions and to support their aims "provided they be fair." What limitations might be placed upon these subjective judgements the Manifesto did not say. Another Zapata just out of the hills might very well have drafted its terms.

The political possibilities of the Cristero Plan had begun to wear thin when some unreflective officers issued the Plan of Hermosillo (March, 1929). It reads like a throw-back to the days of Santa Anna when Generals, confident of military support, would bid for the Presidency without the least shadow of justification save a desire for office. Its provisions: all current administrative officers who do not support the movement are to be repudiated, their acts to be declared void. The Movement, when triumphant, shall fill all vacant posts, issue all decrees on issues deemed vital to the country, and the Armed Forces shall be reorganized. It concludes with a diatribe against President Calles--"the bungling man,"..."This dreadful man" who directs "the shabby structure of imposition politics," who has stained the soil of the Fatherland "with the purple blood of all liberties" "after having guided the daggers that were responsible for the infamous assassination of General Alvaro Obregon and thus inundated the Fatherland with a black surge of an

121

uncertain future." The Plan should stand for all time as the literary model of a barracks revolt.

After a decade and equally within the parameters of the ancient practices appeared the Plan in support of the Saturnino Cedillo revolt, a protest movement based in the politically important State of San Luis Potosi, the site of so many earlier Plans of protest. In the name of "States Rights" the Governor issued his declaration of secession from the Mexican Union as administered by President Cardenas because that official had "interfered with the faithful observances of the Constitution of the Mexican Republic." Rather, the Free and Sovereign State, having abrogated completely its national representation declared that it stood for something called "legitimate Institutions." Then, by force of arms if necessary, it would defend "the exact fulfillment and observance of the General Constitution of the Republic." Like so many earlier Plans, this one sought to dominate the national administration while standing apart from it.

The Plan followed every conventional procedure. It awarded the armed forces a resounding title; its slogan sounded noble enough to attract volunteers; as was so commonly done, it characterized the opponents as traitors who would "stand thereby exposed by such circumstances to corresponding sanctions." [Let the opponents figure that one out.] It declared "the Commander-in-Chief of the movement authorized to seize funds, public or private, as he might deem necessary, and on triumph of the movement restitution would be made to those who could present a receipt. The Military should receive the traditional goodies: promotion of one rank for all officers who might joint the Movement, a 25% increase in pay for all ranks, and private soldiers were to enjoy two pesos per day in addition. Finally, a point so dear to the Military heart, a special Service Medal would be awarded to all who should actively support the Cause. The Plan had everything and achieved nothing.

The authors of Mexico's last Plan, the Plan of the Almazanistas (September, 1940) tried a different tack: their Plan would be composed in the language of modern times. General Almazan, the real leader of the revolt against the Cardenas Administration, would not be mentioned by name; a "Substitute Constitutional President, General Hector F. Lopez should sign the Plan. It would be addressed to the whole nation and not be identified with a particular State or area; it should proclaim support of the Constitution of 1917 and accuse those in authority of violating it in spirit and in deed. The Plan would proclaim "that national sovereignty resides essentially in the people," and it promised "to defend and reintegrate Democracy in Mexico." Finally, "if calamity of a fratricidal war should occur, those at fault will not be those we represent...but those who ignore the sovereignty of the people." Against Mexican disinterest the Plan never had a chance.

Even as the Plan as an implement for revolution waned, a new element to be tested for public acceptance appeared. All previous Plans had centered upon Mexican issues and personalities: the Almazanistas would justify overthrow of the Administration on its inadequate response to the world crisis of the 1930 decade and the issues that brought on World War II. Its authors made hostile references to "tripartite Totalitarianism," to Hitler, Stalin, and to Mussolini [Japan and Emperor Hirohito were spared], but Marxist Communism and Six-year Plans as a menace to the nation received their heaviest condemnation. These alien influences revived the vocabulary of "exploitation" and "oppression" and permitted the introduction of a new idea, "the republic of the proletariat." Marx received as careless a reference as had Rousseau so many Plans ago.

As always, the authors of a Plan favored Liberty, but these latter day Planners deemed a more precise description necessary--"a spiritual and material Liberty," for the Almazanistas tritely charged, Liberty was "in chains," and they summoned Rousseau's "popular will" to "ennoble and dignify the human being" as it defended democratic institutions in Mexico. This last Plan specialized in positive picture-words such as "the venerable state of Father Hidalgo, "the union of all Mexicans..." "Christian civilization...", "defense of our families...", "the banner of Democracy" or "the union of Democracy in the Americas..."; and it promised that upon victory of the Cause "standards of living shall rise and liberty, order and social justice shall reign."

These defenders of a new order of things charged the administration of President Cardenas, who was not

123

named, with an equal number of unfavorable propaganda terms: illegal despotism, persecution and political assassination, forcing the minds of the child and young people into the mold of Communism, attacking the inviolability of conscience and the moral unity of the family.

To avoid such unhappy prospects the Almazanistas offered no specific program of reform; they preferred the easy generality. They would raise the standard of Liberty, preserve Christian civilization, defend corporate and spiritual liberties and all that which ennobles and dignified the human being. They exhorted every Mexican to do everything in his power to block electoral fraud, and they promised that "ultimately all sacrifices and self-denial shall be accompanied by the understanding of all democratic people. But the touch was gone, the issues too vague. Their Plan reads like an essay of political comments worthy of a newspaper editorial, and who would want to die for that? Certainly few Mexicans chose martyrdom for their cause.

The essence of a Plan had rested in its personalism--its personal endorsement if not its authorship--and it is missing here. The Plan had become a committee report or a political campaign document with correct references to hallowed concepts. After a century and a quarter the Plan had turned planless. The Plan, the deathless declaration, had subsided into a sigh for olden times.

The Mexican Plans, no matter which side they may have supported, show that Victory has favored armed might. In its domestic conflict nothing else had served: there was no substitute for force. But now the Plan had suffered the fate of that strong man of ancient days, "And Samson wished not that his strength had gone from him."

And so, apparently, the Plans have come to an end. Mexico has not seen one in forty years. Never before has it known such a lapse. Perhaps there will be no more, and Mexico will abandon its unique political procedure. As the sparse post-Revolutionary Plans show, Mexicans have lost the knack or do not feel the need. When wrenched out of the life that gave them being, the glamour vanished. Some of the Plans are old now--a century and a half--others less than a third that age, but once upon a time each of them marked the path of fame and fortune for some, or of eclipse and death for others. The sources of Mexico's national life once coursed through its Plans.

First we read the Plans as obvious, separate documents, but considered in the light of the emerging nation they take on a meaning of their own. Then our concept of the Nation is forever changed; once the Plans cease we look around us and the Nation has transformed itself. Glass and glitter dominate the age-old capital streets: the very air smells of traffic; pedestrians worm their way around tangled knots of people. A startled memory rejects the Present and longs for the musty odor of volumes long shelved in ancient libraries. We who have read the Plans--we have a private knowledge of a Past which insulates us against the present sense of the possible.

The Plans began when those who were politically alert believed in The Great Leader. From afar they were acquainted with the Great Washington whose mythical fame they accepted without question. Then, before their eyes drifted the vision of Napoleon--a man of their generation, a fabulous General of many victories, of enemies fleeing pell-mell, of decrees signed with an imperious flourish of the pen. Glory and power beckoned to the Individual Triumphant. Absence of organized political parties left a vacuum of power, and the commanding Personality, Plan in hand, could rush in to claim the Presidency at will. Many willed to do it, but inability frequently cancelled desire. Across the years of the Planners Mexico endured a flood of mediocrity; its national life seldom produced enough of superiority. Yet somehow the yarns of unrelated Plans weave together the dismembered circumstances that form the warp of the nation's history.

Dr. Thomas Davis

TEXT OF THE MEXICAN POLITICAL PLANS

DECREE OF DON JOSE MARIA ANSORENA ABOLISHING SLAVERY, PAYMENT OF TRIBUTE AND OTHER TAXES

19 October, 1810

In punctual compliance with the sage and pious dispositions of His Excellency, Sr. Captain-General of the American Nation, Dr. Don Miguel de Hidalgo y Costilla, to whom the Undersigned should render the most expressive thanks for such singular Benefits, I notify all Owners of Slaves that as soon as this Superior Order reaches you to place them at liberty, granting them the necessary Documents of Identification with the accustomed entries so that they may be able to buy and to sell, to appear before a Law Court, to grant Testaments, Codicils, and to execute all else that is transacted and accomplished by Free People, and if the said Slave Owners should not do so, they will suffer irremissibly both Capital Punishment and the confiscation of all their belongings. Under the same Decree it is equally imposed that in the future no slaves shall be bought nor sold, and neither the court clerks nor the public notaries shall extend these sorts of contracts under the penalty of being suspended from office or the confiscation of all their belongings as it is not required by Humanity nor dictated by Mercy. It is also the pious feeling of His Excellency that there be abolished forever the payment of tribute for all degrees of casts, be they what they may, so that no Judge nor Collector shall demand this payment and neither shall it be required of the poor who previously satisfied this payment, as the purpose of His Excellency Sr. Captain-General is to Benefit the American Nation as far as he possibly can. By the same token I notify all the Customs Administrators, office receivers, and Border Posts that the indigenous natives shall not pay nor shall be demanded of them licenses for the scrapings of Magueys nor for the fruit of Pulques as what the destitute People earn with their work barely enables them to pay for their board and subsistence and that of their families; neither will they charge for the Sugar Cane liquor [aguardiente de cana] more than one peso per barrel for those which are sent from the

Factories to the Capital, and this only for once, so
that having the barrels to go from one area to
another nothing else should be demanded, because with
the first peso being collected the tax is considered
satisfied. Consequently this order must be passed to
the Customs of this city so that they may immediately
communicate the same to the office receivers and
border posts in their charge for their due
information. All the people are warned that if all
plunder is not stopped and if they do not remain
quiet they will be hanged immediately, for which four
gallows are prepared in the main Square. I also warn
all foreigners that they leave this City at once, and
if they should not do so they will be arrested and
sent by the Cordillera to the Army.

So that this Order shall reach everyone and that
none allege that he is ignorant of the same, I
command it to be published by proclamation.

(Signed) Jose Maria Ansorena

Published in Valladolid,

Morelia.

Hernandez y Davalos, Coleccion de documentos, II,
169-170.

* * * * *

DECREE OF SR. DON MIGUEL HIDALGO Y COSTILLA
ABOLISHING SLAVERY

29 November, 1810

From the happy moment that the brave American
nation took arms to cast off the yoke which during
the space of three centuries oppressed the nation,
one of its main objectives was to eliminate as many
taxes an possible; but in the urgent and critical
circumstances of the times the complete abolition of
taxation cannot be managed. The new government being
generous without losing sight of the high ideals
which voice the prosperity of Americans, it hopes

128

that they may begin to enjoy such rest and relaxation to the degree that the urgency of the nation permits by means of the following declarations which are to observed as an inviolable law.

THAT the selling of men being against the cry of Nature, all laws of slavery are abolished, not only in the traffic and commerce made with them, but also that relative to the purchase; therefore, in accordance with the recent plan of the new government, they can acquire [property] for themselves as free people in the same manner as observed by other classes of the Republic; consequently in accordance with the declaration made the owners, be they American or European, must give [their slaves] their liberty within the course of ten days under pain of death which will be applied to them if this Article is not observed.

THAT no individuals of the races under the former legislation who carried with then the stigma of this vile traffic through the same requirement of payment of tribute which was demanded of them shall not pay it in the future, they being exempted from this imposition so hateful to the free citizen.

THAT some compensation to this latter class being necessary for the unavoidable costs of war and other indispensable levies for the defense and integrity of the nation, the freedmen will make a contribution of two and a half percent tax on the produce of land and three percent shall come from land of Europeans, and the laws which established a tax of six percent are hereby abolished.

THAT the purposes of welfare and magnanimity being known, attention is turned to the relief of litigants, hereby granting to them in perpetuity the favor that in all their business, dispatches, writs, documents, and other judicial and extra-judicial operations they may use ordinary paper, hereby abolishing all the laws, government orders and royal orders which establish the use of stamped paper.

THAT every citizen is allowed to manufacture

gunpowder without demanding of him any license, nor [a license] for the components from which it is made; it being understood positively that the government must have preference in sales which are made for the expenses of the troops; furthermore, wine and other prohibited drinks shall have free licensing, granting to all the faculty of making and selling it, but paying the dues established in New Galicia.

THAT in equal manner monopolies on all kind of dyes shall be abolished; also other levies of properties, community funds, and all kinds of labor which is demanded of the Indians.

LASTLY, the protection and encouragement of planting, development, and harvest of tobacco being beneficial, it is granted to farmers and others who wish to dedicate themselves to such an important branch of agriculture the right to sow, to traffic and to trade in the same, it being understood that those who undertake with efficiency and determination this type of harvest will be made believers in the benefaction of the government.

In order that this [Decree] may be known to all, and its due accomplishment, I command that it be published by proclamation in this Capital and other cities, villages and conquered places, and that there be sent a sufficient number of these edicts to the courts, judges, and to other people to whom it may concern, for their information.

(Signature)

Hernandez y Davalos, Coleccion de documentos, II, 243-44.

* * * * *

DECREE OF SR. HIDALGO DECLARING LIBERTY OF SLAVES

6 December, 1810

From the happy moment that the brave American nation took to arms to cast off the yoke that for the space of nearly three centuries had oppressed it one of its principle objectives was to abolish the many taxes with which it was unable to advance its well being; but since in the critical circumstances of the day it has not been possible to draft adequate provisos for that purpose, for the necessity of reales that the government (1) has for the costs of the war, attention is given just now to providing a remedy for the most urgent matter through the following declarations:

1st. That all slaveholders are to give liberty to their slaves within the space of ten days, under pain of death, [a penalty] which shall apply for transgression of this article.

2nd. That the payment of tribute taxes shall cease hereinafter in respect to the races that were paying it and all payment that was being demanded of the Indians.

3rd. That in all judicial affairs, documents, writings, and proceedings use shall be made of ordinary paper, the use of stamped paper being hereby abolished.

That anyone who may be providing instruction in the use of powder shall continue to manufacture it without any other proviso save that of offering the government a priority in sales for use of its armies; and all the separate components of which [powder] is composed shall likewise be free [of regulation].

In order that this notice may reach everyone and be duly obeyed, I order that it shall be published as an edict in this capital and the other cities, towns, and conquered places, and an adequate number of copies shall be dispatched to the courts, judges, and other persons who may be responsible for this information

---

(1) Fr. Hidalgo used the word 'reino.' He did not use his ecclesiastical title.

and observance of it.

Given in the City of   Signed
Guadalajara

                     Miguel Hidalgo y Costilla
                       Generalisimo of America
                     Lic. Ignacio Rayon, Sec.

Hernandez Y Davalos, Coleccion de Documentos, II, 256. no. 152.

* * * * *

DECREE ESTABLISHING THE FIRST NATIONAL JUNTA

21 August, 1811

Sr. Don Fernando Seventh and in his Royal name the Supreme American national Junta was installed for the conservation of its Rights of Defense of the Holy Religion and the indemnification and liberty of our oppressed Nation.

The lack of a Supreme Chief in whom the confidence of the Nation could be deposited and who could be obeyed by all was going to precipitate us into most dreadful anarchy, disorder, confusion, and despotism; and it's necessary consequences were the bitter fruits which we were beginning to taste after eleven months of work and hardships for the benefit of the Nation. To repair such great damage and to carry out the ideas adopted by our Government and first representatives of the Nation, it has been considered an absolute necessity to establish a tribunal which is to be recognized as supreme and whom all will obey; to arrange a plan of operations in all our America, and to dictate all the suitable provisions for good political and economical order. In fact, in a meeting [junta] of Generals held the 19th of August of the current year, it was agreed at its first meeting for the installation of a supreme American National Junta to be composed for the time being of three persons and to keep two vacancies to be occupied when the occasion should arise for an equal number of distinguished [benemerito] persons. It was also agreed at the second meeting that the election should fall to their Excellencies Srs. Licenciado D. Ignacio Rayon, Minister of the Nation, Dr. Don Jose Sixto Berdusco, and Lieutenant-General D. Jose Maria Liceaga.

132

In order that it may be known to all and its decrees, orders, and dispositions be punctually and firmly obeyed, it is published by proclamation which will be affixed according to custom in the usual places for its observance and due fulfillment. [The event] should be solemnized with demonstrations of the most joyous sort--an establishment which makes us hope to see very soon both the freedom of our Nation and the prospect of seeing its opponents punished in direct proportion to their disobedience.

Given at our National Palace, (Signed)

                                    Lic. Ignacio Rayon
The Villa of Zitaquaro.

Hernandez y Davalos, Coleccion de documentos, III, 300.

* * * * *

ELEMENTS OF A CONSTITUTION
by
Ignacio Lopez Rayon

1812

1. The Catholic Religion will be the only one without toleration of any other.

2. Its Minister as of now will be and will continue to be endowed as they have been up to this time.

3. The dogma will be sustained through the vigilance of the Tribunal of the faith whose rules conforming to the sound spirit of discipline will place its members far from the influence of the constituted authorities and of the excesses of despotism.

4. America is free and independent of every other nation.

5. Sovereignty springs directly from the people; it resides in the person of Senor Don Fernando VII and its practice in the supreme National American Congress.

6. No other rights to this sovereignty can be considered, no matter how incontestable it may appear, when it may be prejudicial to the independence and happiness of the Nation.

7. The Supreme Congress shall consist of five members named by authority of the Provinces; but for now it will stand at the number of three members who exist by virtue of the irrevocable communication of authority which they hold and in fulfilllment of the pact celebrated in convention assembled by the Nation on the 21st of August, 1811.

8. The authority of each representative shall last for five years; the senior member shall be President, and the junior one shall serve as Secretary in confidential matters or those which concern all the Nation.

9. All of [the representatives] ought not to be elected in one year, but successively one each year, the senior member surrendering his authority as the junior member comes on.

10. Until the capital of the Kingdom can be secured the present [members] cannot be substituted for others.

11. The term of the representatives will be counted as beginning with the glorious moment when we take possession of Mexico [City].

12. The persons of the representatives will be inviolable during their term of service; a charge can be laid against them only in event of high treason, and only with the confidential knowledge of the current representatives and of those who have so served.

13. The [private] circumstances, the income and the other conditions of representatives who may now or have been in office shall be reserved for the particular drafting of the constitution by the Junta, and certainly remaining also as an irrevocable point

the absolute choice of the Provinces.

14. There shall be a Council of State for such cases as declaration of war or drafting [terms] of peace, to which those [officers] of Brigadier or above must agree, and the Supreme Junta ought not to be able to pass judgment without these requirements.

15. Also, there must be a Supreme Junta to reach an agreement with the Council in the event of there being extraordinary expenses, or being obliged to pledge the property of the nation or when considering increases which are related to the common cause of the Nation, yet they ought to take into consideration beforehand the opinion expressed by the representatives.

16. The offices of Grace and Justice, War and Treasury, and their respective Tribunals will be systematized according to knowledge of the circumstances.

17. There shall be a National Protector named by the representatives.

18. The drafting and repeal of laws and whatever business may be of interest to the Nation ought to be proposed in public sessions through the National Protector before the Supreme Congress in the presence of the representatives who will give assent or dissent, yet reserving decision to the Supreme Junta by a plurality of votes.

19. All foreign residents who favor the liberty and independence of the Nation will be received under the protection of the Laws.

20. Any foreigner who wishes to enjoy the benefits of American citizenship should request a letter of naturalization from the Supreme Junta which will be granted with the agreement of the respective Town Council and the vote of the National Protector, but only [native] Patriots shall secure [government] employment, nor shall any privilege or letter of nationalization prevail in this matter.

21. Although the three Powers, Legislative, Executive, and Judicial, may be the attributes of sovereignty, the Legislative is inerrant, and never can it be over-ruled.

22. No employee whose honorarium arises from public funds or which raises the person involved above the class in which he lived or may give him greater distinction than his equals may be designated as enjoying a benevolence, but with rigorous justice [for work done].

23. Representatives will be named every three years by the respective Town Councils, and these [persons] ought to consist of the most honorable persons and in proportion not only from the Capitals, but also from the towns and the District.

24. Slavery is forever proscribed.

25. To anyone born after the happy independence of our Nation no barriers will be placed against him save personal defects, nor can their lineage be held against them; the same situation shall prevail for those who have attained the rank of Captain or higher or may be accredited with some extraordinary service for the Fatherland.

26. Our ports will be free to all foreign nations, with those limitations which may assure the purity of dogma.

27. Any person who may have committed perjury against the Nation, without prejudice to any penalty which may be applied to him, is declared infamous and his goods the property of the nation.

28. The positions held by Europeans are declared vacant, regardless of whatever class they may be, and likewise [the positions] of those who have in any public way have without doubt been influential in sustaining the cause of our enemies.

29. There shall be complete freedom of the press on subjects purely scientific or political, provided

that the latter [subjects] serve to enlighten and not to condemn established legislation.

30. Examinations for artisans are to be completely abolished, and they will be judged on the basis of their performance.

31. Every one will be respected in his own home as if it were a sacred asylum, and the celebrated Corpus hayeas (sic) of England will be administered with amplifications and restrictions which circumstances may require.

32. Torture as a barbarism is proscribed without a contrary opinion even being admitted for discussion.

33. The days of the 16th of September on which our blessed independence was proclaimed, the 29th of September and the 31st of July, birthdays of our Generals Hidalgo and Allende, and the 12th of December, sacred to our most gracious protectoress, Our Lady of Guadalupe, will be solemnized as the most important of our Nation.

34. Four military orders will be established, and they will be that of Our Lady of Guadalupe, that of Hidalgo, of the Eagle, and of Allende, the Magistrates being eligible for them as other very meritorious citizens who may be considered worthy of this honor.

35. There shall be in the Nation four grand Crosses pertaining to the said Orders.

36. There shall be four Captain-Generals in the Nation.

37. In the event of war officers of Brigadier and above and the Council of War of the Supreme National Congress shall nominate which of the four Generals should be Generalisimo for executive and interrelated situations--an investiture which may not confer promotion nor increase in salary once the war shall have been concluded, and the rank [of Generalisimo] can be removed in the same way that it was constituted.

38. The three present members of the Junta shall be Captain-Generals even when they are no longer serving because this rank ought no to be considered inherent in the position of representative and leaving to circumstances the nomination of the fourth American. Here are the fundamental principles on which the great work of our happiness is to be shaped--it is to be based upon liberty and independence, and our sacrifices, although great, are as nothing in comparison with the future happiness which is offered to us all for the last portion of our lives, and a transcendental [happiness] for our descendents.

The American people, forgotten by some, pitied by others, and disdained by the majority will yet appear with the splendor and dignity which it deserves for the gallantry with which it has broken the chains of despotism; cowardice and idleness will be the sole charges which may disgrace the citizen, and the temple of honor will open its door equally to merit and virtue; a holy emulation will exalt our brothers and indeed we shall have the sweet satisfaction of saying to them, "We have aided and guided you; we have made abundance substitute for scarcity, liberty for slavery, and happiness for misery. And so Thanks be to the God of all destinies who has deigned to look with compassion upon his people."

Licenciado Rayon

Felipe Tena Ramirez, Leyes fundamentales de Mexico, 1808-1967, 24-27.

* * * * *

A MANIFESTO FROM THE AMERICAN NATION TO THE EUROPEAN WHO INHABIT THIS CONTINENT

16 March, 1812

After a lengthy justification of the Mexican cause against Spain, Dr. Cos offered the following two plans:

Plan of Peace

I. Sovereignty resides in the mass of the people.

II. Spain and America are integral parts of the monarchy subject to the King, but equal as to each other and without dependence or subordination of one in respect to another.

III. Faithful America has a better right to convoke a Cortes and to call for representatives from the few patriots of Spain, which is infected with unfaithfulness, than Spain has to summon from the Americas deputies through whom we would never be adequately represented.

IV. The Sovereign being absent, the inhabitants of the Peninsula have no right to appropriate for themselves the supreme power and to represent the Royal Person in these dominions.

V. All authority proceeding from this basis is null.

VI. To conspire against this [authority] the American nation is doing no more than exercising its right.

VII. Far from this [action] being a crime of lesa majestad (in case it should be anything it would be lesa gachupines) it is a service worthy of recognition by the King and an outburst of patriotism which His Majesty would approve if he were present.

VIII. After what was occurred on the Peninsula and on this continent since the overthrow of the throne the American nation as its creditor is a guarantee for its security, and it can do nothing less than put into execution the right which it has of safeguarding these dominions for their sovereign by themselves, and without the intervention of Europeans.

From such incontestable principles the following just claims [may be deduced]

I. That the Europeans resign command of the armed forces to a National Congress [which shall be] independent of Spain but representative of Ferdinand VII and which shall guarantee his rights in these dominions.

II. That Europeans remain classed as citizens, living under the protection of the laws, without being prejudiced in their persons, families, or lands.

III. That the Europeans presently employed remain with their honors, rights [fueros] and privileges, with some share in the income of their appointments, but without control of them.

IV. That independence being declared and sanctioned, each party--one and all--shall cast into oblivion all offenses and past events, and taking for this purpose the most active steps; and all the inhabitants of this land, both natives and Europeans, shall constitute without distinction a nation of American citizens, vassals of Ferdinand VII, devoted to promoting the public welfare.

V. That in this event America will be able to assist the few Spaniards committed to sustaining the war in Spain with the assessments which the National Congress may impose in testimony of its fraternal feeling with the Peninsula, and of [the fact that] both desire the same end.

VI. That the Europeans who spontaneously desire to leave the Kingdom may secure a passport for any place most convenient to them, but in this case the employees may not receive in advance the portion of the income which has been assigned to them.

Plan of War

The Indubitable Principles upon which It is Founded.

140

I. That the war between Europeans and American ought not to be more cruel than between foreign nations.

II. That the warring parties recognize Ferdinand VII. The Americans have given the most evident proofs of this, swearing to it and proclaiming it everywhere, carrying his portrait as an emblem, invoking his name in their credentials and legal measures, and by stamping [his name] on its coins and specie. Upon this supposition rests the enthusiasm of all, and upon this path the party of the revolution has always traveled.

III. The inviolable rights of people and of war between infidel nations and barbarians ought to be no less between us who profess the same faith, are subjects of the same sovereign and [are governed by] the same laws.

IV. To act through hatred, rancor, or personal vengeance is contrary to Christian morality.

V. Supposing that the sword is to decide and not the force of reason and prudence through treaties and agreements drafted upon the basis of natural equality, the struggle ought to be continued in such a way as to be less opposed to a humanity too harrassed to cease being the object of our tender compassion.

From here certain just claims are logically deduced:

I. That prisoners may not be treated as criminals of lesa majestad.

II. That no one shall be sentenced to death nor sentenced for this cause, but all shall be held as hostage awaiting an exchange.

III. That they shall not be restrained with shackles nor prisons, but these being a mere precaution, they shall be left loose in a place where they do not prejudice the party where they were captured.

141

IV. That each person shall be treated according to his class and rank.

V. That the articles of war not permitting the effusion of blood save in actual combat, one concludes from this that no one is to be killed nor hostile action be taken against those who flee or who give up their arms once they have been made prisoners by the conqueror.

VI. That it being against the same law, and that of natural law as well, to enter into settlements with fire and sword, or to assign every fifth or tenth person of the town to have his throat cut and among whom are mixed both the guilty and the innocent, nobody is to dare under the severest penalties to commit this horrible act which so deeply offends both a Christian nation and good laws.

VII. That the inhabitants of undefended towns through which the armies of both sides pass indiscriminately shall not be abused.

VIII. That at this time when the whole world is disillusioned concerning the real causes of the war and the artifice of tying this cause to that of religion as was pretended at the beginning no longer has standing, let the ecclesiastical state abstain from prostituting its ministry with declarations, suggestions, and any other means; [let it] contain itself within the limits of its superintendents.

And the ecclesiastical tribunals shall not intrude their arms, forbidden [to them] in matters purely for the State, that does not belong to them, because otherwise they lower their regard, as experience has shown, and they expose their decrees and censures to mockery, derision, and ridicule of the public which, in the mass, is anxiously awaiting the triumph of the motherland.

It being understood that in this case we will not be responsible for the results on the part of people enthused for their nation, although for our part we protest from now on and forever our respect and

profound veneration of its [the church's] character
and jurisdiction in things suitable to its ministry.

IX. That this being a business of the greatest
importance that concerns each and all the inhabitants
of this land without distinction, let this Manifesto
be published through the medium of the periodicals of
the capital of the kingdom in order that the people,
composed of Americans and Europeans, informed of that
which most interests them, may indicate their will,
and what ought to be the norm of our operations.

X. That in case none of the Plans proposed be
admitted, reprisals will be rigorously watched.

Behold here, our brothers and friends, the
religious and political propositions founded on the
principles of natural equality which we make, [for we
are] aghast at the evils which afflict the nation. In
one hand we present the olive branch and in the other
the sword. . . . . .

                                        Jose Maria Cos

Jose Maria Luis Mora, Mexico y sus revoluciones,
(Mexico, 1965), III, 190-194

* * * * *

THE SENTIMENTS OF THE NATION
of
Twenty-three points issued by Morelos for the
Constitution

                                14 September, 1813

Sentiments of the Nation

1. That America is free and independent of Spain and
of any other Nation, Government, or Monarchy, and
thus being sanctioned, gives the reasons to the world.

2. That the Catholic Religion may be the only one,
without tolerance of any other.

143

3. That all its ministers shall be supported by all, and only from tythes and the "first fruit" [offering], and the people shall not have to pay for any more perquisites than those of their devotion and [free will] offering.

4. That the dogma be sustained by the hierarchy of the Church who are the Pope, the Bishops, the Curates because every plant which God did not plant should be pulled up: omnis plantatis quam no plantabit Pater meus Celestis cradicabitur. Matt. Chap. XV. [Every plant which my heavenly Father hath not planted shall be rooted out.]

5. Sovereignty springs immediately from the People, who wish to vest it in its representatives, dividing its powers between the Legislative, Executive, and the Judiciary, the Provinces electing their representatives, and these [electing] the rest, who should be men of wisdom and probity.

6. [In text from which this copy was made--1881-there was no article with this number.]

7. That the representatives shall serve for four years, turn about, the oldest [in service] leaving in order that newly elected persons should take their place.

8. That the allotment for the representatives should be competent sustanance not excessive and for the present shall not be more than eight thousand pesos.

9. That only Americans shall obtain [government] employment.

10. That foreigners shall not be admitted [to the country] if they are not artisans competent to instruct and are free from all suspicion.

11. That the fatherland will not be free nor ours while the government is not reformed, overthrowing the tyrannical and substituting the liberal and casting out from our soil the Spaniard who has testified so much against our Nation.

12. That since a good law is superior to every man, those which our Congress may dictate ought to be such as to compel constancy and patriotism, so as to moderate both opulence and indigence.

13. That the general laws apply to all without exception of privileged persons, and that the latter should enjoy [privilege] only in the exercise of their ministry.

14. That in order to issue a law it should be discussed in the Congress and passed by a plurality of votes.

15. Slavery should be prescribed forever and the same [should apply] for castes, all being equal and the sole distinction among Americans should be that of vice or virtue.

16. That our Ports should be open to all friendly foreign nations, but in order that the latter do not become involved in the kingdom more than friends ought, there should be only certain Ports designated for this matter, and prohibiting the disembarcation at the other ports and requiring a tax rate of 10% or some other tax on their merchandise.

17. That each person shall keep his property and be honored in his house as if it were a sacred refuge, with penalties being set for violators.

18. That the new legislation will not admit torture.

19. That in [the new legislation] by constitutional law there shall be established in all the towns the celebration of the 12th of December dedicated to the Most Holy Mary of Guadalupe, and charging all the towns to observe this monthly devotion.

20. That no foreign troops or those of any other kingdom shall set foot on our soil and if it should be in aid, then they will not be where the Supreme Junta [is located].

21. That no expeditions shall be made outside the

limits of the kingdom, especially overseas, but expeditions to propogate the faith to our brothers by land are not of this class.

22. That the infinite number of taxes, pechos [an ancient tax], impositions which are particularly oppressive, shall be done away with, and each individual shall be singled out for five percent of his income, or some other equally light charge which does not oppress too much, as the alcabala [a sales tax], the estanco [a monopoly tax], the tributo [a tax] and others, because with this small contribution and with good handling of property confiscated from the enemy, it will be possible to ease the burden of the war and pay the salaries of [government] employees.

23. That likewise the 16th of September shall be solemnized every year as the anniversary on which the voice of independence was first sounded and our holy liberty commenced, for it was on that day that the lips of the Nation were opened in order to reclaim its rights and the sword was seized in order to be heard, remembering always the merit of that great hero, Senor Don Miguel Hidalgo, and his comrade, Don Ignacio Allende.

Chilpancingo, September 14, 1813.

Jose Maria Morelos

Felipe Tena Ramirez, Leyes fundamentales de Mexico, 1808-1967, 29-31.

* * * * *

ACT OF THE CONGRESS OF CHILPANCINGO, DECLARING THE INDEPENDENCE OF NORTHERN AMERICA

6 November, 1813

A Declaration of the absolute independence of New Spain effected in Chilpancingo by the rebel Congress.

A Solemn Act of the Declaration of Independence of Northern America

146

The Congress of Anahuac legitimately installed in the City of Chilpancingo of Northern America by its Provinces solemnly declares in the presence of God, the moderator and arbiter of empires and the author of societies, who gives and takes away in accordance with the inscrutable designs of His providence: THAT through the present circumstances in Europe it has recovered the exercise of its usurped sovereignty and it dissolves dependence upon the Spanish Throne and by this same concept it shall remain forever broken; THAT it is the arbiter qualified to establish the laws which it considers most conducive to domestic happiness, to wage war and peace, to establish alliances with the Monarchs and republics of the old continent; also to celebrate agreements with the Roman Pope for the regime of the Catholic Church, Apostolic and Roman; and to send ambassadors and consuls; THAT is does not profess nor recognize any other Religion but the Catholic one, and it will not allow nor tolerate either the public use nor the secret practices of any other; THAT it will protect [the Church] with all its power and will watch over the purity of its faith and of its dogmas and the conservation of its regular bodies; THAT it declares guilty of high treason all who oppose directly or indirectly the independence [of the Nation] either by protecting the European oppressors by word or act, or in writing, or else by refusing to contribute to the expenses, subsidies and dues to continue the war until its independence may be recognized by the foreign nations; AND reserving to its Congress the right to present [to foreign nations] by means of a written ministerial note a manifesto of its complaints and the justice of this resolution-already recognized by Europe itself-which will circulate through all foreign ministerial cabinets.

(Signatures)

Given at the National Palace, Chilpancingo

Hernandez y Davalos, Coleccion de documentos, I, 887.

* * * * *

THE OPINION OF THE NATION
or
TWENTY-THREE POINTS DECLARED BY MORELOS FOR THE CONSTITUTION

21 November, 1813

The Sentiment of the Nation

1st. THAT America is free and independent of Spain and of any other Nation, Government, or Monarchy, and let it be so sanctioned, giving the reasons to all the world.

2nd. THAT the Catholic Religion is the only one, without tolerance of any other.

3rd. THAT all its Ministers should be supported by all, and only Tythes and First Fruits [are mandatory], and the People shall not have to pay any other religious assessments save those of its devotion and offerings.

4th. THAT the Dogma shall be sustained by the Hierarchy of the Church, who are the Pope, the Bishops, and the Priests, because all plants that God did not plant must be torn out: "omnis plantatis quam nom plantabit Pater meus Celestis Cradicabitur." (Matt. Ch. XV)

5th. THAT Sovereignty springs directly from the People who want to deposit it with their representatives, dividing its powers into legislative, executive and judicial, the Provinces electing their representatives and the latter must be learned men of probity.

6th. [In the original from which this copy was taken [in 1881] the article of this number does not exist.]

7th. THAT the representatives will serve for four years, taking turns, the senior in service leaving to be replaced by the newly elected.

8th. The salary of the representatives will be an

148

adequate emolument and not excessive, and for the time being will not exceed six thousand pesos.

9th. THAT only Americans shall be employed.

10th. THAT no foreigners may be admitted [into the country] except craftsmen who are able to teach, and they shall be free of all suspicion.

11th. THAT the Nation will not be completely free and our own while we do not reform the Government, crushing the tyranical and substituting the liberal and expelling from our land the Spanish enemy who has so often declared itself opposed to this Nation.

12th. THAT as a good Law is Superior to any man, those passed by our Congress must be such that enforce steadiness and patriotism, moderate both opulence and poverty, and increase the daily wage of the poor in order that their customs may be improved; and may cast out ignorance, plunder and thievery.

13th. THAT the general Laws embrace everyone without exception of privileged Groups, and that these be only with regard to the practice of their official service.

14th. THAT to issue a law it must be discussed first in Congress and then decided by a majority vote.

15th. THAT slavery be outlawed forever and so also any distinction of races, all being equal, and only vice and virtue will distinguish one American from another.

16th. THAT our Ports shall be open to all foreign and friendly nations, but that these shall not become established within the Kingdom no matter how friendly they may be, and there shall be only designated Ports for this purpose, prohibiting landing in all the others and fixing ten percent or other tax against its merchandise.

17th. THAT the property of everyone be protected and respected in his home as a sacred preserve and establishing punishments for violators.

18th. THAT in the new Legislation torture will not be admitted.

19th. THAT in [new legislation] there shall be established by Constitutional law the celebration of every twelfth of December dedicated to the Patroness of our liberty, the Sacred Mary of Guadalupe, in every town and obligating the people for the monthly devotion.

20th. THAT the foreign troops or of another Kingdom do not set foot upon our land, and if by chance to help us, they shall not serve on the Supreme Junta.

21st. THAT no expeditions are to be made outside beyond the limits of the Kingdom, especially those overseas, but [expeditions] to propagate the faith to our brothers by land are not of this class.

22nd. THAT the infinite number of tributes, taxes, and impositions which burden us be taken off, and to specify for each individual a tax of five percent of his income, or other such light tax, that does not oppress so much, such as sales taxes, state monopoly, the tribute and others, because with this small contribution and good administration of the properties confiscated from the enemy the heavy cost of the war and salaries of [government] employees can be covered.

23rd. THAT the 16th of September of every year also be solemnized as the Anniversary day in which the voice of Independence arose in a loud voice and our Sacred liberty began, because on that day the lips of the Nation opened to reclaim its rights and grasped the sword to be heard, remembering always the merit of the great Hero, Sr. don Miguel Hidalgo and his Comrade, D. Ignacio Allende.

Chilpancingo.   (Signed)

                                       Jose Maria Morelos

Hernandez y Davalos, Coleccion de documentos, VI, 215-216.

* * * * *

PLAN OF IGUALA

A PLAN OF INDICATIONS FOR THE GOVERNMENT WHICH SHOULD BE INSTALLED PROVISIONALLY, WITH THE OBJECT OF MAKING SECURE OUR SACRED RELIGION AND ESTABLISHING THE INDEPENDENCE OF THE MEXICAN EMPIRE, AND IT SHALL HAVE THE NAME OF GOVERNMENTAL JUNTA OF NORTHERN AMERICA, PROPOSED BY COL. D. AGUSTIN DE ITURBIDE TO HIS EXCELLENCY VICEROY OF NEW SPAIN, COUNT OF VENADITO.

24 February, 1821

[After an impassioned appeal for popular support for this Plan which had been endorsed by his Army, Iturbide presented the following:]

1. The religion of New Spain is and will be the Catholic, Apostolic, Roman, without tolerating any other.

2. New Spain is independent of the old one and of any other power, even of our continent.

3. Its government will be a moderate monarchy in conformity with a particular constitution and adaptable for the kingdom.

4. Its Emperor will be D. Ferdinand VII, and he not presenting himself personally in Mexico within the time the Cortes will determine to give him his oath, in his place will be called His Most Serene Infante D. Carlos, Sr. D. Francisco de Paula, the Archduke Carlos, or other person of the reigning house who is deemed suitable by the Congress.

5. Until the Cortes shall meet, there shall be a Junta whose object will be to secure such a meeting and to see that the Plan is fulfilled in all its provisions.

6. The said Junta, which will be designated as Governmental, must be composed of the members mentioned in the official letter to His Excellency the Viceroy.

151

7. Until Sr. D. Ferdinand VII, presents himself in Mexico and takes his oath, the Junta will govern in the name of His Majesty in virtue of the oath of fidelity which he has given to the nation; nevertheless all orders which he may give will be suspended pending the taking of the oath.

8. If Sr. D. Ferdinand VII should not deign to come to Mexico and until it is resolved which Emperor is to be crowned, the Junta or the Regency will govern in the name of the Nation.

9. This government will be supported by the Army of the "Three Guarantees" which will be mentioned later.

10. The Cortes will determine the continuation of the Junta or whether it should be replaced by a Regency until the person who is to be crowned arrives.

11. The Cortes will immediately establish the Constitution of the Mexican Empire.

12. All the inhabitants of New Spain, without any distinction as Europeans, Africans, or Indians, are citizens of this Monarchy with the right to any employment in accordance with his merits and virtues.

13. The persons of whatever citizenship and their properties will be respected and protected by the government.

14. The secular and regular Clergy will be preserved in all their special rights [fueros] and privileges.

15. The Junta will take care that all branches of the State shall remain without any alteration, and all political employees, ecclesiastics, civilians, and military [shall remain] in the same station in which they are found today. Only those will be removed who indicate that they do not want to accept this Plan, substituting them with those who are more greatly distinguished in virtue and merits.

16. A protecting army will be formed, which will be named that of the "Three Guarantees," for under its

protection it will undertake: first, the conservation of the Catholic religion, Apostolic and Roman, cooperating by every means in its power, so that there will not be any mixture with any other sect, and that it may attack in due course enemies who might damage it; second, Independence under the aforesaid system; third, close union of Americans and Europeans; because guaranteeing bases so fundamental to the happiness of New Spain and before consenting to the violation of the same [the Army] will sacrifice itself by giving its life from the first [in rank] to the last man.

17. The troops of the Army will observe the greatest discipline, obeying to the last letter all ordinances, and the commanders and officers will continue as they are today; i.e., in their respective ranks with option to accept vacant positions which may be vacated by those who do not want to continue under its banner or for any other reason, and preference will be given to those who may be chosen for necessity or convenience.

18. The troops of the said Army will be considered of the line.

19. The same will happen for those who immediately take up this Plan. Those who do not defer, those from the prior system of independence who will join immediately the said army and the peasants who want to enlist will be considered as troops of the national militia, and the nature of all [arrangements] for the interior and exterior security of the kingdom will be dictated by the Cortes.

20. The employees [of the State] will be considered according to their real merit, by virtue of reports received from their respective superiors and provisionally in the name of the nation.

21. Until the Cortes is established all crimes will be prosecuted in conformity with the Spanish Constitution [of 1812].

22. As for the crime of conspiracy against independence, [offenders] will be sent to prison

without taking any further steps until the Cortes may decide the penalty for this the greatest of crimes, except for lese divine Majesty.

23. A look-out will be maintained for those who encourage disunion and are reputed to be conspirators against independence.

24. Since the Cortes to be installed will have to be constituted, it is necessary that the Deputies receive sufficient powers for this purpose; and to further this aim still more, it is of great importance that the electors know that their representatives have to be for the Congress of Mexico and not that of Madrid.

Therefore, the junta will prescribe fair regulations for the elections and will fix the necessary time for them and for the opening of the Congress. As the elections cannot take place in March, the limit will be stretched as far as possible.

Iguala.   (Signed)

24 February, 1821.   Agustin de Iturbide

Castillon, J.A., Mexico: Informes y manifiestos, 1821-1904, I, 495-496. Ward, History of Mexico (1826) in the Appendix gives what purports to be a translation of the Plan of Iguala. However, it varies so greatly from the accepted Spanish text that one concludes that variant drafts circuited in contemporary Mexico.

* * * * *

TREATY OF CORDOBA

24 August, 1821

New Spain having proclaimed its independence of the Old and having an army to sustain this proclamation and the provinces of the kingdom having approved of it, and the capital in which the legitimate authority had been removed being besieged,

and since there remained only for the European
government in the fortified cities of Vera Cruz and
Acapulco, which are ungarrisoned and without means of
resistance to a well-directed siege which would last
some time; and there arrived at the first mentioned
port Lieutenant-General D. Juan O-Donoju with the
character and representing the Captain-General and
superior political chief of this kingdom, appointed
by His Sacred Majesty who, anxious to avoid the
misfortunes which grieve all the people in
alterations of this kind, and trying to reconcile the
interests of both Spains, invited to a meeting the
first chief of the Imperial Army, D. Agustin de
Iturbide, in which was to be discussed the great
transaction of Independence, unfastening without
breaking the relationship which united both
continents. The meeting was realized at the Village
of Cordoba on the 24th of August, 1821, and with the
representation of Spain by the former and that of the
Mexican Empire by the latter. After having conferred
in detail on what was more convenient for one nation
and the other, considering the present state of
affairs and the latest happenings, they agreed to the
following articles which they signed in duplicate to
give them all the solidity which these documents are
capable of, each keeping an original for better
security and validity.

1. This America will be recognized as a sovereign and
independent nation and will henceforth be called the
"Mexican Empire."

2. The government of the Empire shall be a moderate,
constitutional monarchy.

3. D. Ferdinand VII, Catholic King of Spain, will be
the first to be called to reign over the Mexican
Empire (prior to the oath as designated in Art. 4 of
the Plan) and in event of his renunciation his
brother the Most Serence Sr. Infante D. Carlos, and
in event of his non-acceptance or resignation the
Most Serence Sr. Infante D. Francisco de Paula; and
in case of his non-acceptance or resignation, the
Most Serene Sr. D. Carlos Luis, Infante of Spain,
previously heir of Etruria, today Luca, and in event
of his non-acceptance or resignation, the one whom

the Cortes of the Empire may designate.

4. The Emperor shall establish his Court in Mexico [City] which will be the Capital of the Empire.

5. Two commissioners will be appointed by his Excellency Sr. O-Donoju, who will go to the Court of Spain to put in the Royal Hands of Ferdinance VII a copy of this treaty and the exposition which will be attached thereto, so that it may serve His Majesty as an antecedent while the Cortes offers him the Crown with all formalities and guarantees what a matter of such importance warrants, and it implores His Majesty that in the matter of Article no. 3 he will kindly notify the Most Serene Infantes named in the same articles in the order named therein, interposing his benign influence that the person to come to this Empire may be one of the individuals from his august House, since the prosperity of both nations is involved, and on account of the satisfaction which Mexicans will enjoy in adding this relationship to the others of friendship with which they will be able to join the Spanish people.

6. In accordance with the spirit of the Plan of Iguala, immediately there will be appointed a Junta composed of the leading men of the Empire who are known for their virtues, their fortunes, their representation, their destinies, and ideas, who are designated by force of general opinion, whose number may be quite considerable in order that the meeting of such cultured persons will assure success in their decisions which will be emanations from the authority and faculties which are granted to them as per the following articles.

7. The Junta dealt with in the previous Article will be called the Governmental Provisional Junta.

8. Lieutenant-General D. Juan O-Donoju will be a member of the Government Provisional Junta in consideration of the suitability that a person of his kind should take an active and immediate part in the government, and that it is indispensable to omit some of those who were mentioned in the said Plan in conformity with the spirit of the same.

9. The Governmental Provisional Junta will have a president whom it, itself, shall name, and whose election will fall on one of the persons belonging to it or outside of it, but who must win the absolute majority of votes; if in the first balloting one should not be elected, a second vote shall take place between the two candidates who obtained the most votes.

10. The first step of the Governmental Provisional Junta will be to issue a manifesto to the public on its installation and will give the reasons which brought them together, along with other explanations which they may consider convenient for the enlightenment of the people regarding their interests and modes of procedure in the election of deputies for the Cortes, of which more will be said later.

11. The Governmental Provisional Junta will name at once the election of a President, a Regency to be composed of three persons from the Junta or outside of it, in whom the executive power will rest and who will govern in the name of the monarch untïl he clasps the scepter of the Empire.

12. Once the Provisional Junta of Government has been installed, it will administer provisionally in accordance with the laws in force in all that does not oppose the Plan of Iguala, and while the Cortes may be drafting the Constitution of the State.

13. The Regency, immediately after being appointed, will proceed to summon the Cortes in accordance with the method determnined by the Provisional Government Junta, which is in accordance with Article no. 24 of the said Plan.

14. The executive power shall reside in the Regency, the legislative [power] in the Cortes, but as some time will have to pass before they meet, and so that both will not have overlapping authority, the Junta shall exercise the legislative power; first, for the cases which may occur which cannot wait for the meeting of the Cortes and then proceed in conjunction with the Regency; second, to serve the Regency as an

auxiliary and consultant body in its deliberations.

15. Every person who belongs to a society, the system of government being altered or the country passing over to the hands of another Prince, remains in the state of natural liberty to go with his fortune wherever he may deem it convenient, without any other law whatsoever to deprive him of this freedom, unless he may have contracted a debt with that society against which he perpetuated some crime, or in some other method known to politicians. In this case there are Europeans domiciled in New Spain, and Americans living in the Peninsula; therefore they will be free to remain by adopting this or that nation as a Fatherland, or to request a passport which cannot be denied, to leave the Empire in the time allotted, bringing their families and taking their properties; but on leaving with the latter they shall pay the export duties then established or those to be established by those authorized to do it.

16. The aforementioned alternative shall not be in force with respect to public employees or military personnel who are notoriously opposed to Mexican independence; necessarily these will leave this Empire within the time prescribed by the Regency and will take their belongings and pay their taxes as mentioned in the previous article.

17. The occupation of the capital by the troops of the Peninsula being an obstacle to the realization of this Treaty, it is indispensable that they be vanguished; but as their commanding officer of the Imperial Army, joined his sentiments to those of the Mexican nation, does not wish to obtain it by force for which they have enough resources; nevertheless, considering the bravery and steadfastness of the said Peninsular troops and due to lack of means and expedients wherewith to maintain themselves against the system adopted by the whole nation, D. Juan O-Donoju himself offers to use his authority over the said troops to effect their

departure without the shedding of blood and through an honorable capitulation.

Villa of Cordoba.   (Signatures)

                              Agustin de Iturbide

                              Juan O-Donoju

Alaman, Lucas, Historia de Mejico, V, 24-27, as copied from the Imperial Gazette of Tuesday, 23 October, 1821.

* * * * *

CONSTITUTIONAL BASES: SECOND MEXICAN CONGRESS

24 February, 1822

The Deputies who compose this Congress and who represent the Mexican nation are declared legitimately constituted and that national sovereignty resides in them.

THEREFORE, they declare that:

The Catholic religion, Roman, and Apostolic shall be the only one for the State, to the exclusion of any other.

It adopts for its government a conservative constitutional monarchy with the title The Mexican Empire.

The sovereign Congress calls to the throne of the Empire, in accord with the general will, the persons designated in the Treaty of Cordoba.

It not being suitable that the Legislative, Executive, and the Judicial power should remain united, the Congress declares that the exercise of the Legislative Power upon the persons who presently compose the Regency, and the Judiciary upon the courts that now exist or shall be named in the future, and each and all of these bodies being responsible to the nation for the period of their administration in accord with the laws.

The sovereign Congress declares the equality of civil rights of all free inhabitants of the Empire whatever may be their origin in the four quarters of the earth.

In order for the Regency to enter into the exercise of its functions, it shall take the following oath:

Do you recognize the sovereignty of the Mexican nation as represented by the deputies who have been named for this Constituent Congress.? --Yes; I so recognize them.

Do you swear to obey the decrees, laws, and ordinances which it may establish in accord with the purpose for which it was convened? And will you cause them to be observed and executed? [Will you] preserve the independence, liberty, and integrity of the nation, the Catholic religion, Roman, and Apostolic without tolerance of any other, and promote in all things the good of the Empire? --Yes; I so swear.

If you so act, may God assist you; and if not, may action be taken against you.

The Regency will then be recognized.

Tena Ramirez, Felipe, Leyes fundamentales de Mexico, 1808-1967, 124.

* * * * *

ORGANIC BASES OF THE CONSTITUTIONAL NATIONAL JUNTA

2 November, 1822

1. [The National Junta] shall have the initiative to

160

draft a Constitution which will be formed for the Empire and consequently the plan or project which seems more proper and convenient according to circumstances will be agreed upon in order to consolidate the form of Government proclaimed and established in accord with the adopted bases, ratified and sworn to by all the Nation.

2. The corresponding organic law which will determine the manner in which the Constitution itself should be discussed, decreed and sanctioned will accompany the draft of the Constitution and so will satisfy the interesting purpose of avoiding the objections and reasoning of the legislative and executive power on this point, for which it will proceed in accordance with the latter [power].

3. Even though in the draft of the Constitution will be included everything concerning the representatives system, it will be the special objective of the Junta to order the call for immediate national repre - sentation, establishing the regulations which may be most fair and adaptable to the circumstances of the Empire and the manner in which its government was proclaimed, established and sworn; placing themselves for this purpose in agreement with the Government itself, and in accord with which in an identical case, the Governemental Provisional Junta attested, in fulfillment of the corresponding articles of the Plan of Iguala and the Treaty of Cordoba; and whatever in this manner should be ordered by the summons will be absolutely observed (for this one time) excepting that which is adopted or rectified in the Constitution and in accordance with the light of experience.

4. In the shortest possible time the [Governmental Provisional Junta] will proceed to organize a plan for Public Finance, so that there may be the necessary funds for its handling of the national expenses and cover the present considerable deficit; placing itself in agreement with the Executive Power.

5. The Junta will conserve for national representation the exercise of the Legislative Power

in all those cases which in their opinion cannot be
reserved, so that it will have authority and
consequences that the Constitution must strive for,
and will so propose as urgent to the Executive Power.

6. For the discussion of the draft of the
Constitution, for the convocation, for the
regulations and other laws, the speakers from the
Administration will be admitted.

7. As its first business the Junta will draft for its
domestic administration a regulation which may be
fitting to give the plan order and facility to all
its operations and to determine the just limits of
the inviolability of the deputies, circumscribing it
exactly to what is needed for the free exercise of
its functions.

8. It will publish a manifesto to the Nation, thus
inspiring the confidence that it can offer by the
zeal and resolution of the great duties involved in
its commission.

9. The Junta shall have a President, two
Vice-Presidents, and four Secretaries.

10. For this time and until the formation and
adoption of the regulation in which it will be kept
in mind the convenience of the perpetuity of these
offices, for the uniform dispatch of the objectives
of their respective functions, sets of three
candidates shall be proposed for me [Iturbide] for
the election of the persons who will fulfill them,

11. The treatment of the Junta toward the President
as His Excellency and the spokesman of His Lordship
will be impersonal.

12. Alternates may be elected for Vice-Presidents and
Secretaries.

13. If there should be some acts of the dissolved
Congress which may not have been recorded nor
authorized, the Junta will put right this defect by
an agreement in relation to what had been resolved by

the Congress itself and it will communicate its resolution to the Government in order that it may make whatever observations and arguments that the interests of the public sector may require.

14. If there should be found in the [documents] of the Secretary of the Congress extraneous matters not brought to the knowledge of the Legislative Power, the Junta will order them to be returned to the concerned parties so that they may file them where they belong.

15. The person commissioned to receive the papers from the Secretary of the dissolved Congress will deliver them to the Secretaries of the Junta with their index and with the corresponding inventory.

Imperial Palace of Mexico,   (Rubric of Iturbide)
the Second Year of Independence

Castillo Negrete, Mexico en el siglo XIX, XIII, 493-495. Felipe Tena Ramirez, in his compilation Leyes Fundamentales de Mexico, 1808-1967, presents the Bases Organicas as a part of the Reglamento Provisional Politico del Imperio Mexicano.

* * * * *

PLAN OF VERA CRUZ

6 December, 1822

First. The union will be maintained with all the Europeans and Foreigners residents in this country and who are not opposed to our system of real freedom.

Second. Those born in this land, the Spaniards and foreigners living in it, and the foreigners who should obtain from the Congress a letter of citizenship according to law are citizens without any distinction.

Third. Citizens shall enjoy their respective rights in accord with our particular constitution, founded on the principles of equality, property and freedom in accord with our laws which will be explained in detail, respecting, above all, their persons and properties, which are those most in danger during times of political convulsion.

Fourth. The secular and regular clergy shall be maintained in all their special privileges [fueros].

Fifth. Transient foreigners will have a generous welcome by the government which will protect their persons and properties. The Congress will indicate the necessary requirements, so that they may live in the country.

Sixth. The branches of State [administration] will remain without any variations, and all the political employees, civilians and military men will be kept in their jobs and places of employment, except those who would oppose the present system, for these, with a statement of cause, will be suspended until the resolution of Congress.

Seventh. Free and open commerce will be permitted as well as other traffic of business in the interior, and no one shall be molested in travels and transactions.

Eighth. The employments, ranks and honors of any kind that they may be which from the present call [grito] for genuine freedom of the nation which henceforth, should Iturbide grant it, shall not be recognized unless the nation wishes to approve them, because they naturally will not serve the purpose of general usefulness, but that of compromising the persons on whom they are conferred in order in this way to increase his faction as Novella did on another occasion.

Ninth. In civil and criminal cases judges shall proceed according to the Spanish Constitution [of 1812], laws and decrees still in force, issued until the hasty extinction of the Congress in everything that is contrary to the genuine freedom of the nation.

Tenth. In cases of conspiracy against the real

freedom of the nation the people will be safeguarded, leaving it to the disposition of the sovereign Congress to dictate in due course the penalty which must be applied to them, as one of the greatest of crimes.

Eleventh. Political authorities, both civilians and military men, are especially charged that they be on the alert for the emissaries and kind of individuals who with their machinations attempt to corrupt the healthy opinions of the people with respect to real freedom, assuring [the people] in such a case that once verified the judges will proceed to a complete investigation; and if from it there should result criminals of the crime of lese Nation action will be taken in conformity with that explained in the aforementioned declaration.

Twelfth. Consequently no person can, pretending diversity of opinions or distinction of parties, take the life of anyone. Any authority of judge, be he who he may, will be held as a criminal of murder in cold blood and judged in like manner by the laws; also being useless any pretext or excuse that the execution was ordered by a superior authority, for he who gives the order and the one who executes it will be considered as such, except expressly in an action of war.

Thirteenth. When with obstinacy the well-founded cries of the people are scorned, and when they are divested of their most sacred rights by means of force, not having any fruit of their just claims other than to double the means of the oppressor to continue oppressing them, without the slightest hope of remedy, then they are left with no other recourse than to repel force by force. This is the painful situation in which we find outselves.

Fourteenth. Consequently, a liberating army will be created, and it will be composed of the units already formed which adhere to the system of real freedom. These troops shall observe the greatest discipline and will be considered of the line. All their commanders [jefes] and officers will be maintained in the grades and employments which they have to date, with preference to those on the roster and to others who shall obtain merits by their new services, and there shall be respect for those who remain neutral; the Congress shall determine their grades and promotions, but as for those who would knowingly oppose, they will be suspended from their employments until [Congress] itself should decide this point.

Fifteenth. The companies of national militia and the civilians who should enter to serve with them, joining the army, will be considered as provincials and will enjoy the privileges [_fueros_] of the military in conformity to Ordinance, without prejudice for favorable declarations which the Congress should make afterward with respect to these units, as well as for some of their individuals in particular, in accordance with the merits which they may have required.

Sixteenth. Those who have joined [the Army] since the Cry of Iguala up to today shall be remembered, without forgetting their good services in the first revolution; considering as very special those who will do so again to restore to the nation its rights which at present are abused.

Seventeenth. For the provision of all kinds of employments, everything will be considered according to the merits, talents, and public virtues of those to whom they must be given, the Congress fixing the necessary regulations for this effect; but until it meets only those jobs which are of absolute necessity or of convenience can be given and these provisionally.

Eighteenth. If some commanders and the rest of their troops, disregarding their honor and becoming deaf and insensible to the outcries of their own conscience and of the land in which they were born should try to fight and to destroy their own brothers who sustain their dearest rights, it may be necessary (although with much regret) to use arms [against them], and may the war decide what neither justice nor the most sacred ties, nor the sweetest love for the nation, nor even nature itself can attain; we, as for our part, behaving with the greatest moderation, always observing the rules of war and of people, with the firm protest before God and men that we shall save as far as possible the slightest drop of blood, blood that will eternally cry "Northern America".

Nineteenth. The troops of the liberating army shall be supported from recognized branches of the Public Treasury, and when good patriots shall spontaneously make some loans with such an object, they shall be in time repaid by the nation with all punctuality. Nothing is said of the public debt, as this point has already been declared by the Congress.

Twentieth. The Treasury officials and administrators of said branches, without an express order and approval of the respective chief in each province and approval by the system of freedom, shall not release any sums whatsoever, and they will only be able to do so in the case of an extreme urgency, for the precise purpose of relief of our troops, but even in this case they shall secure as promptly as possible the document or written evidence prescribed and without such requirement it shall not be credited.

Twenty-first. The depositions published by don Antonio Lopez de Santa Anna shall be observed in our glorious call [grito] of freedom of the second day of this month, which were consulted by their Excellency the Provincial Deputation, and which are exactly as follows:

> THAT the Three Guarantees which were published in Iguala shall be inviolably observed, and the troops will sustain them with the greatest efficiency, it being considered a crime of lese Nation against any who should attempt to violate any one of them. Another [deposition] is that an armistice shall be arranged with the General commander of Ulloa in order that between this and that point hostilities shall not break out and a prudent and honorable harmony be maintained, in accordance with the agreement between the commander and the commission which for this

167

purpose will be delegated by Its Excellency the Municipal Body; trying, of course, that with the approval of the high government immediately two commissions shall be appointed who are to go to Spain to combine its delivery with reciprocal commercial treaties which may have to be established with advantage for both hemispheres.

AND finally, immediately and on an interim basis the freedom of maritime transactions from the Peninsula for the free importation of goods and the extraction of fruits and wealth, without any other dues than those to be designated in the tariff sanctioned by the Mexican Cortes shall be re-established, and likewise the freedom of every individual to enter or leave the country without any obstacle with all their belongings, be what they may be.

Twenty-second. And lastly, in reference to all that which is specified in the present Plan, it to be understood as without affecting the higher authority of the sovereign Congress, both recognized and free, which may effect appropriate variations in accordance with the nature of the matters which are referred to therein, for we are very far from initiating the abuses and arbitrary conduct of those who have wanted to claim that their private opinion represents national sovereignty.

Long live the nation!

Long live the sovereign free Congress!
Guadalupe Victoria

Long live the real freedom of the nation, without admitting nor ever recognizing the orders given by don Agustin Iturbide.

(Signed) Antonio Lopez de Santa
Anna Guadalupe Victoria

Vicente Riva Palacio, <u>Mexico a traves de los siglos</u>, IV, 86-87. Another draft of the Plan with but minor variations is found in J. M. Bocanegra, <u>Memorias</u>, 187-191.

* * * * *

PLAN OF CASA MATA
or

1 February, 1823

INDICATIONS TO RESTORE TO THE NATION ITS NATURAL AND
INALIENABLE RIGHTS AND TRUE FREEDOM

A Plan to restore to the Nation all that of which
it had been stripped by D. Agustin de Iturbide; this
measure being so absolutely necessary that without it
it is totally impossible that Northern America should
enjoy in the coming years a solid and permanent peace.

* * * * * * * *

1. The Catholic Religion, Apostolic and Roman, will
be the only one for the State, without tolerating any
other.

2. The America of the North is absolutely independent
of any other power, be it what it may.

3. It, of itself, is sovereign and the exercise of
this sovereignty resides solely in its national
representation which is the Sovereign Mexican
Congress.

4. It is free and furthermore with its present
emancipation it is now in a natural state.

5. As independent, sovereign, free, and in its
natural state, it enjoys an absolute right to
constitute itself in accordance with what appears may
be most suitable for its happiness, by means of the
sovereign Constitituent Congress.

6. To the above [Body] it is the right, uniquely and
positively, after examining the votes of the
provinces and after hearing the learned men and
public writers, and finally, after mature
consideration to declare the form of its government,
to appoint the first civil servants and to dictate
its fundamental laws, without any one person being
able to do so, whatever may be his rank because the

169

will of one individual or of many, without it being expressly and legitimately authorized for this purpose by the people, can never be called the voice of the nation.

7. It is as if the Constituent Congress had not declared anything, since it had to act with violence and without freedom.

8. In accordance to what has been said, it is evident that D. Agustin de Iturbide, having violated the Congress scandalously within its very walls, perfidiously played false to his solemn oaths and availing himself of force and intrigue, as is publicly and notoriously known, to get himself proclaimed Emperor, all without consulting the general will of the people. Such a proclamation for any point of view is void, without any value or effect, and particularly for an act of such importance on which was going to depend the future of America; there was no Congress, for the majority of the deputies were absent.

9. Therefore, he must not be recognized as Emperor, nor should his commands be obeyed in any way whatsoever. Rather, for such criminal acts those committed since August 26th to this day, and above all the scandalous and criminal dissolution of the Sovereign Congress and the later ones that he will continue committing, he shall have to answer to the nation, which in due course will arraign him with the corresponding charges in accord with the laws, [charges] which will also reach those who join him, who continue usurping the rights of the people, who cry out under a yoke heavier than the one prior to this iniquitous government.

10. In compliance with the aforementioned article, universal justice calls out vigorously, [so also] the honor and the public vindication of Northern America, highly offended by a man under the guise of a liberator, has been outraged without the pretended allegation of inviolability being worth considering, for supposing this the formal, solemn and free declaration of the form of government by the

constituent Sovereign Congress, and furthermore also the solemn, formal and free election of the person to whom it was due; and lastly, because it being a measure provisionally adopted, even though the said Congress had sanctioned the first and second, it could have derrogated or restricted the article of the Spanish Constitution which concedes it.

11. Neither would it have served as an allegation that the said proclamation was strengthened because of the later facts; for example with the emission of orders which up to date have been issued under the name of the pretended Emperor, because the circulation of these does not give sufficient color of legitimacy to some acts intrinsically void and groundless, just as it does not and cannot grant this long possession, nor does it label it with its true meaning: long usurpation of the rights of the people.

12. In free countries without a Congress, which is the gathering of everybody, or at least, of the greater majority of the deputies appointed precisely by the provinces in a legal manner, there is no national representation, nor a legislative body, and without either Constitution or laws there is no obligation for its fullfillment due to the absence of a genuine source [of authority] from whence it should emanate.

13. With the dissolution of the Congress the nation finds itself in a total orphanage and without its first constituted legitimate authority, because he who is de facto as the head of it, has the substantial defect of invalidity, as declared in the prior articles, which makes it totally null, for it has no other laws than those of ambition, caprice, and passions; and as a consequence we find ourselves in complete anarchy.

14. In order to avoid the continuation of the fatal results of this latter situation, it will be our principal duty to try to re-unite by all humanly possible means, all the deputies until we shall have formed the Sovereign Mexican Congress, which is the real voice of the Nation, and only it maintenance

will be able to save us from actual shipwreck.

15. With sufficient number of deputies gathered at
the place of their choice in order to form a
congress, and being in absolute freedom, they will
then notify the provinces in order to inspire in them
that confidence in the government which they do not
have at present. Also, they will make [the provinces]
understand the defects and non-validity of the
resolutions dictated in Mexico [City], which not
having any other origin than abuse and force, do not
obligate their compliance; likewise it will rest with
them to dictate the measures, instructions, and
opportune providences to continue with the enterprise
until the people have given the last touch to the
great work of our political regeneration with which
[the Congress] is entrusted.

16. The Congress being free and located in the place
of its choice, it will proceed to appoint a Junta or
a Regency to be composed of individuals whom it deems
worthy and in whom the executive power will be
entrusted. Such a government will be the only
legitimate one, and the one which the provinces,
authorities and the inhabitants of this America will
recognize as such provisionally, until the permanent
Constitution of the State is proclaimed, and [the
Congress] shall delegate likewise the supreme
judicial power in accordance with the circumstances,
because it must remain separate.

17. In order that the Congress can begin to sanction
the first bases of the permanent Constitution of the
State, it is necessary not to lose sight of what is
indicated in the sixth article, which must be done in
full session of the Congress, as it is so demanded by
justice, public policy, and the tranquility of
America; because unfailingly depending on these first
steps is nothing less than our happiness forever or
else everlasting unhappiness. It must be done with
all solemnity, circumspection, judgement and
pre-vision which a matter of such gravity demands,
avoiding in this way even the slightest shade of

complaint from the provinces.

(Signed)

Antonio Lopez de Santa Anna

Guadalupe Victoria

J. M. Bocanegra, Memorias, I, 184-187.

* * * * *

MINUTES OF CASA MATA

1 February, 1823

The Major Generals, Commander of separate corps and officers of Headquarters, and one for each grade of the Army gathered at the quarters of the Commander-in-Chief to confer on the capture of Vera Cruz, and [to discuss] the dangers which menace the Nation due to lack of a national representation, the only bulwark which sustains civil freedom. After having amply discussed matters regarding its happiness, in accord with the general will, it was agreed on this day the following:

Art. 1. It being undeniable that sovereignty resides exclusively in the nation, the Congress shall be installed as promptly as possible.

Art. 2. The convocation of the new Cortes shall be made as per the bases prescribed for the first [congress].

Art. 3. Regarding the deputies who formed the suppressed congress, there were some who due to their liberal ideas and firmness of character achieved the appreciation of the people; but at the same time others did not duly correespond to the trust placed in them. The Provinces shall have the free right to re-elect the former and to substitute the latter with others more suitable for the fulfillment of their arduous obligations.

Art. 4. As soon as the representatives of the nation have gathered together they shall establish their residence in the city or town which they may deem most convenient for beginning their sessions.

Art. 5. The corps which compose this army and those who hereafter adhere to this Plan shall confirm the solemn oath to sustain at all costs the national representation and all its fundamental decisions.

Art. 6. The commanders, officers and troops who are not willing to sacrifice themselves for the good of the country may move to any place they may deem it most convenient.

Art. 7. A commission shall be appointed which will proceed with copies of these minutes to the capital of the Empire and place the same in the hands of his Majesty the Emperor.

Art. 8. Another commission with another copy shall depart for the city of Vera Cruz to propose to the governor and city council of said city what has been agreed upon by the army to see whether they adhere to it or not.

Art. 9. Another commission shall go to the chiefs of the subordinate corps of this army which are besieging El Puente and the villages.

Art. 10. In the meantime the supreme government, aware of what has been agreed upon by the army, answers that the provincial deputation of this province shall be the one which shall decide on administrative matters if the said resolution be in accord with their opinion.

Art. 11. The army will never make any [criminal] attack against the person of the Emperor because it considers the matter decided by the national representation. He may locate in the villages or wherever circumstances should determine, and [the army] will not disband on any pretext whatsoever until it is so decided by the Sovereign Congress, being attentive to who will support it in their deliberations.

General Headquarters
Casa Mata
(Signatures of the Military

Suarez y Navarro, Historia de Mexico, 28. The version given in Riva Palacio, Mexico a traves de los siglos, IV, 88-89, omits Article 7.

* * * * *

PLAN OF("Fulano") (1)

1823?

Army

1st. It shall be called Imperial.

2nd. It shall be composed of all those who may wish
to adhere to this plan, save those officers from the
rank of Colonel and above who have surrendered, nor
any of the five principal so-called liberators.

3rd. The commanding officer shall be _____.

4th. The ranks and the second command categories shall
be given by the said First Commander _____ on
an interim basis.

5th. The purpose of the Army shall be to indemnify Don
Augustin the First for the slander that has dishonored
him, to restore him to the Throne in his particular
case, or to support him within America eminently and
decorously as is due his great merit, and always at the
head of the Army and of the government.

---

(1) An early Plan, in manuscript form, designed to
support the return of Iturbide as Emperor. Library,
University of Texas, Nettie Lee Benson Latin American
Collection. This Plan, quite short and incomplete, is
signed by the anonymous figure of Spanish culture, Don
Fulano.

6th. The Army shall defend property [rights] and shall
be scrupulous in the rights of all.

Government

1st. Its form shall be that of an Emperor, with a presiding Junta to be composed of the Bishops of America, either personally or through proxy; six principal commanders of the Imperial Army, a deputy from each Province and twelve persons to be named by the Army either from within or outside it, as it may choose.

2nd. Whether he remains "The Right Ilustrious Mexican" the Emperor shall be called that, and in fact he only will be that in the event of having it, and if not he shall have this title with some addition that may indicate calling him this because it had been legitimate, although with the head of the government separate he shall also have immediately the designation that may be established.

3rd. The Government shall try for union and will ask for the protection of the Holy Alliance.

4th. The present Congress shall govern on an interim basis through those citizens who may choose it, provided that they be none of those [presently governing], nor those who may reject this plan because the latter may not have any position at all.

Religion

1st. The Religion shall be only the true Catholic, Apostolic and Roman, without tolerating any other.

2nd. The Administration of the Church shall never be touched by any other than the Roman Pontiff, and the particular churches by their bishops, except under title of protection or as patron the Government should take some part.

3rd. The Bishops shall govern their Dioceses as they feel that they ought, while the successor of St. Peter decides according to his pleasure.

4th. The properties of the Church shall never be taken by force under any pretext whatever, without pontificial permission for it in advance. Spain disgraced itself through contrary principles.

Legislation

1st. It shall be that which appears suitable to the Junta yet to be formed.

2nd. It shall not be the Spanish Constitution.

3rd. It shall not permit freedom of the press as has done up to now.

4th. It shall be totally conforming to the Canons.

5th. In military matters it shall determine the Emperor and the Interim First Commander.

6th. In everything it shall follow moderation and virtuous mediocrity rather than opulence and dangerous arrogance.

Fulano

* * * * *

PLAN FOR RESTORING THE LIBERTY OF THE MEXICAN NATION
AND FOR MAINTAINING INDEPENDENCE (1)

1823

1st. An army under the designation Restorer is to be created, to be composed of all the Forces which wish to join it voluntarily. It will be subdivided into as many sections as there may be Provinces which may

---

(1) This Plan exists in two drafts: a preliminary one which the author heavily revised. The second, which is given above, is relatively unmarred and is more complete. The penmanship on both copies appears to be that of a practiced scribe who wrote with a fine quill and in a great hurry. This royalist Plan is unsigned and presumably was never published. Manuscript, Library, University of Texas.

adopt this plan. Each section shall be commanded by the General or Commander [Jefe] who may be placed at its head, without dependence of one section on the other, and all shall obey the Government as a common center in everything that may not be contrary to the execution of this plan whose liberal fulfillment shall be its only purpose.

2nd. This Army shall protect the Nation so that in full and absolute liberty it may elect such representatives as it wishes, from whatever class they may be so that in conformity with the general will they may establish the form of government most suitable for the conservation of religion, Catholic, Apostolic, and Roman, the exclusion of every sect, and of the Independence and Union, and of a just and reasonable liberty.

3rd. It being indispensable that the Congress which now ceases, neither the Provincial Deputies nor much less the Army which was called the liberator shall have the authority to constitute the State nor to annul or to ratify anything that the Nation had adopted. The declaration of the form of Government that is to constitute the Nation shall be reserved to the future Congress.

4th. In consequence, and besides having to have a provincial government that may execute this plan and avoid anarchy, there shall be established at the same time that there is declared in the Capital of Mexico a Regency which shall govern in the name of S. D. Augustin Iturbide the First, who, until a Congress, legitimately elected and authorized decides to the contrary, is in fact our Constitutional Emperor. By virtue of which authority it shall establish a commission to call him on behalf of the Nation to come and occupy the Throne in case it shall be a Monarchial Government. But if it should be another of those well known in politics, he shall always have the primacy that is fitting among fellow citizens, with the august title of Liberator.

5th. The Regency of which the preceding article speaks shall be composed of a General, an ecclesiastic, and an individual of any of the other classes of state, who will be designated by the General who shall support this plan in the Court and who shall reach an agreement as soon as possible with all or the major part of the Generals of the Provinces which may adhere to this pronouncement.

6th. The Government which was in existence the first of the previous March shall be reestablished only in so far as may be absolutely necessary in order to conserve the unity of the Nation, avoiding anarchy; that is to say in the four Secretaries of Office, who shall be composed of the same persons who were serving then, or those whom the Regency may wish to name if someone may wish to resign or does not consider the Regency itself that may exist as convenient.

7th. In an arduous or urgent situation when the Regency may need to consult, it shall form a Junta composed of an individual from each Province, elected by the same Regency, nor shall this Junta have more authority than that of expressing its opinion, and the Regency shall be free to follow it or not, since it alone is to be responsible to the future Congress.

8th. Thus, because some of the said Deputies of the Congress that ended can be useful for the Junta, and because the new [Congress] may consider, perhaps, that it is fair to examine the conduct of the others, they shall all remain in the Capital until the new Congress is to be installed.

9th. The Regency, without losing a moment of time, shall occupy itself in drafting a Code for election of Deputies of the Sovereign constituent Congress, in which it shall endeavor to provide that the People can attend the primary election, subdividing them into sections of a hundred or at most of two hundred persons.

10th. The Regency shall not be able to impose any impediment or condition for the election of Deputies because all Mexicans who have reached eighteen years and do not have any physical impediment for serving are eligible for it. The number of Deputies is already established at one for every ninety thousand souls, and their qualifications are to remain at the judgment and prudence of the electors, who shall be very careful to distribute the responsibility among all classes of the State, nor will it be forgotten that the Deputies who have composed the first Congress are barred politically from entering the second, in which, after the reinstallation their decisions and conduct are to be reviewed.

11th. The free States of Jalisco, Zacatecas, Oaxaca and others that had their provincial Congress shall not be subject to the provincial Government of Mexico, but they shall conduct their elections for the General Congress under the form which the Regency prescribed.

12th. The present Congress shall cease its functions, and likewise the Supreme executive power.

13th. No one shall be persecuted for opinions, nor shall any action be taken against any citizen; rather their persons and property shall be respected. He who may stain the sword outside armed action or as a defender of citizens shall be punished with the full force of the law.

14th. The Government shall take all provisions that it may judge necessary in order that no one may interfere with the execution of this plan, and it shall be necessary to proceed to the arrest and solitary imprisonment of all persons who may oppose it, an indictment on prior information having been given, or with other sufficient data, but no sentence shall be executed until the new Congress shall decide.

15th. All those who may adhere to this plan from Sergeant through to Second Corporal and soldier shall be taken care of according to their merits, seniority and services, evaluating as very relevant actions that were taken in the period of our struggle, and giving the same consideration to those civilians who may join.

16th. There shall be an unlimited freedom of the press in regard to the form of government, hoping that the sages will enlighten the Nation on so interesting a subject.

17th. To the Reverend Bishops and other Prelates is entrusted the preaching of obedience to the newly constituted authorities, both the secular and the regular clergy keeping their same special privileges [fueros] and ministry.

18th. The Restoring Army takes under its special protection the person and interests of the Spaniards who have declared openly and have performed services in behalf of our independence and liberty; but in reference to our notoriously irreconcilable enemies, whether known or suspected, the Government shall take again the most efficient means for a remedy, yet in all things fair and in line with the security, tranquility, and well-being of the Nation.

19th. Whoever may favor or assist directly or indirectly the enemies of the common good and true liberty that is based on the punctual execution of this plan shall be treated as criminals and traitors.(2)

(Unsigned)

---

(2) A separate section in a preliminary draft is carried as a marginal in the second draft, but was omitted from the final text. It reads as follows: "The Senores Victoria, Bravo and Guerrero shall certainly have a share in a Cause so just and in a Plan so liberal, but if they should not choose it, they shall retire to their homes with full salaries which they shall enjoy."

* * * * *

TWO DECREES

CHANGE FROM THE MONARCHICAL FORM OF GOVERNMENT
TO THAT OF THE REPUBLICAN

31 March, 1823

The constituent sovereign Mexican Congress, in its session of the 29th inst. has issued the following decree:

1st. It is declared that the Congress finds itself reunited with a majority of one hundred and three deputies and in full and absolute freedom to deliberate; and therefore in a condition to continue its sessions.

2nd. That the executive power of Mexico existing up to now has ceased to exist since the 19th of March of last year.

3rd. That both resolutions be passed on to the supreme executive power which is appointed, so that in due course it may communicate the same to whom it may concern.

* * * * * * * *

The constituent sovereign Mexican Congress in its session of the 30th, inst. has declared the following:

1st. The executive government will be provisionally exercised by a body with the name of Supreme Executive Power.

2nd. It will be composed of three members who will alternate the Presidency once a month in the sequence of their appointment.

3rd. The Supreme Executive Power shall be addressed as "His Highness", and that of its members as "His Excellency" only in official answers.

4th. These shall not be able to be elected from among the members of Congress.

5th. This body will be guided by the last regulation that was presented to the Congress for its approval for the previous Regency, except that in connection with the General-in-Chief and while another is drafted in accordance with the circumstances at the time.

Gamboa, Leyes y constituciones de Mexico, 297-298.

* * * * *

PLAN OF THE POLITICAL CONSTITUTION OF THE
MEXICAN NATION

16 May, 1823

The Congress of deputies elected by the Mexican nation, recognizing that no man has rights above another if that man has not himself given it; that no nation has a right above another nation if that [nation] has not granted it; that the Mexican [nation] is, as a consequence, independent of the Spanish [nation] as well as of all others, and being so, it has the authority to constitute a government which may better assure the general welfare, and so declares the following bases of the political constitution.

1. The Mexican nation is the society of all the provinces of Anahuac or New Spain which forms a political unit.

The citizens who compose [the nation] have rights and are subject to duties.

Their rights are: 1) That of Liberty which is to think, speak, write and print, and to do all that which does not transgress the rights of another; 2) That of equality which is to be governed by the same law without other distinctions than those established by the law itself; 3) That of property which is to say the right to spend, to give, to sell, to save, to export whatever may be one's own without any other restrictions than those designated by law; 4) That of having no law other than that which was passed by a congress composed of their representatives.

Their duties are: 1) To profess the Catholic religion, apostolic and Roman, as the only one of the State; 2) to respect legitimately established authorities; 3) not to offend their fellow man; 4) to cooperate for the general good of the nation.

The rights of citizens are the elements which form those of the nation. The power of the latter is the sum of the powers of the former.

The sovereignty of the nation, one, inalienable, and imprescriptable, can exercise its rights in various ways, and from this diversity results the differing forms of government.

[The form of government] of the Mexican nation is republican, representative, and federal.

The nation exercises its rights through the following: 1) by citizens who elect representatives of the legislative body, 2) through the legislative body which passes the laws, 3) by the executive who causes the citizens to abide by them [the laws], through the judges who apply [the laws] in civil and criminal cases, and through the senators who cause the primary functionaries [of government] to respect [the laws].

2. Citizens are to elect individuals of the legislative body or the national Congress of the Senate, of the provincial congresses and of the Town Councils.

Election will not be direct at the present time. It will be by means of electors as the law may prescribe.

The bases are: for the legislative body one individual for each 60,000 souls. For the Senate three individuals proposed for each electoral junta of the province.

For the provincial congresses thirteen in the provinces of less than 100,000 souls, fifteen in those of more than 100,000, seventeen in those of more than a million.

For the town councils an alcalde, two regidores, and one syndic in towns of less than 1,000 souls; two alcaldes, six regidores, and two syndics in those of more than 16,000; three alcaldes, ten regidores, and two syndics in those of more than 24,000; four alcaldes, twelve regidores, and two syndics in those of more than 40,000; four alcaldes, fourteen regidores, and two syndics in those of more than 60,000.

3. The legislative body or national congress is composed of deputies who will be held inviolable for their opinions. It shall be installed and dissolved on the precise day which the Constitution designates: it shall debate and resolve in the form which it [the Constitution] prescribes: upon the initiatives of its members or of the senators it shall prescribe the laws and general decrees which the national welfare requires; it shall revise those [laws] by a plurality or repeal them by a two-thirds [majority] of votes: it shall discuss again those which the Senate may oppose and not ratify nor repeal them except with the agreement of two-thirds of those voting: it shall decree the ordinances of the army, navy, and the constitutional militia: it shall set the boundaries of provinces and districts after taking into account the composition of the territory and the population: it shall name the individual members of the Executive Body every four years: it shall decide whether there is a basis for shaping a charge against the secretaries of the State and the magistrates of the supreme tribunal of justice: it shall determine the forces for sea and land, shall fix the costs of national administration, shall set the tax rate for each province, approve the treaties of alliance and commerce, lay out the general plan of education, protect the national institute and name the professors who should staff it; it will distribute supreme authority in the separate provinces so that the provinces should achieve as much of an equality as possible and that no one may accumulate the basis for undue power; it shall establish two gradual promotion scales, one of interest for the general welfare and the other for honors and distinctions so that the executive body may reward merit in a suitable manner; it shall create a tribunal composed of individuals from its own body to judge the deputies of the provincial congresses in those precise cases which a clear and well-considered law shall determine; it shall limit itself to the functions which the constitution assigns to it.

4. The executive body shall be composed of three individuals. It will reside in the place designated by the legislative [body]. [The Executive Body] shall, within fifteen days present to the legislative body the inconvenience which a law would produce; it will distribute the laws that are presented to it and shall cause them to be executed without modifying or interpreting them; it shall name and remove secretaries of State, name all judges and magistrates, the civil employees of the nation, and the ambassadors, consuls, or public ministers on nomination by the Senate; it shall provide the public employees and those of the Treasury on nomination of the provincial congresses and the military [personnel] on its own motion without consultation or nomination; it shall grant, in accordance with the law, those honors or distinctions which the law specifies; it shall order the investment of national funds as the law may stipulate; it shall present to the legislative body each year through the respective secretaries a detailed account of the income and the expenses of the nation; it is to dispose of the armed force as the good of the nation may require; it will declare war and make peace after prior consultation with the Senate and in conformity with its wishes and will give an account to Congress afterward: it will direct diplomatic and commercial relations with the approval of the Senate; it shall make clear at the opening of each legislature the state of the nation; it shall keep within its assigned powers and in no event shall it exercise legislative or judicial functions.

5. There shall be a provincial congress and a prefect in each one of the provinces in which the national Congress may divide the State.

The Congress will be composed of the individuals stipulated in the second article and will be presided over by their own membership rotating according to the order of their election.

[The Congress] shall name for the Senate two from a list of three persons made from each electoral junta of the province; it shall propose three men for political employment and an equal number for the Treasury of the province; it will name the commander of the national guard [in the province]; protect the provincial institute and appoint the professors who should staff it. [Its further duties shall be] to communicate the laws and decrees which the Congress may agree upon and the executive body may issue, to approve or revise the decisions which the town councils are to prepare to meet the needs of the towns, to fix the costs of provincial administration, to determine the plan of government of the province and the system of contributions necessary to meet the tax rate that it should have in meeting the national expenses and the total for all the provinces; to present both to the legislative body for its knowledge; it may not impose export nor import taxes without the prior approval of the national congress; it may make those regulations and approve the provisions which the government of the provinces requires; to inform the senate of infractions of the constitution, and [notify] the executive body of neglect or misconduct of function- aries [of the government].

The prefect shall execute or cause to be executed the laws and the decrees which the provincial congress may communicate to him as well as the plan of administration and the system of taxation drafted by it; he shall be responsible in case of non-compliance, and responsibility shall be required of him in the manner which the law prescribes.

6. Enlightenment is the basis of every individual or social good. In order to spread it and to advance it, all citizens ought to set up private educational establishments.

Besides those which citizens may form, there shall be public institutes--a central one in a place designated by the legislative body and a regional one in each province. The national [institute] shall be composed of professors named by the legislative body and trained in the four classes of physical sciences, exact, moral, and political. It shall carefully promote the general plan of education drafted by the legislative body: it shall make the precise rules and instructions for fulfillment [of the educational program]; it shall circulate to the provincial institutes the laws and decrees relative to public instruction which the executive body shall duly communicate to it. It will determine the teaching methods and will vary these according to the development in learning; it shall make the precise rules and instructions for fulfillment [of the educational program]; it shall circulate to the provincial institutes the laws and decrees relative to public instruction which the executive body may communicate to it. It will determine the teaching methods and will vary these according to the develop- ment in learning; it shall protect the establishments which the arts and sciences may form; it shall open correspondence with the academies of the most enlightened nations in order to collect information relative to the most useful discoveries and to disseminate the information to the institutes of each province. It shall arrange for tests or experiments that may be of most interest for the welfare of the nation. It shall present to the legislative body annually four reports relative to the four classes of science and shall indicate their backwardness or progress and the most useful means for their establishment.

The provincial institutes shall take care to promote the fulfillment of the educational programs in their respective provinces. They shall promote the education of the citizens and each year they shall send to the national institute four reports on the state of public instruction and suitable measures taken for its progress.

7. Individuals of the Mexican nation ought not to be judged by any commission. They ought to be judged by judges duly appointed by law. They have the right to challenge those of whom they may be suspicious; they have the right to demand an accounting of those who may delay the dispatch of their cases, of those who do not sustain them as the law may require, and they also have the right to compose their differences through arbiters or arbitrators.

With the civil and criminal codes simplified, civilization advanced and the morality of the people improved, juries will be established in civil and criminal [cases].

In the meantime there shall be in each town alcaldes as provided in Article two; in each political sub-division a judge with professional training [juez de letras]; in each province two magistrates, and the place which congress may designate a supreme court of justice.

The alcalde and two resident citizens, each named by the differing parties, shall exercise the functions of conciliators in civil cases.

The professionally trained judge [juez de letras] shall try cases in the first instance, and he shall render judgment on his own responsibility in all criminal and civil cases in which there may be an appeal.

189

The civil [cases] which may not be determined by law, will be decided by him and two colleagues which he shall name, choosing one from a list of three which will be furnished by each of the contesting parties. In criminal cases in which there may be the imposition of a penalty, it shall not be executed without the approval of the magistrate and colleagues.

The second instance in civil and criminal cases must be substantiated by the magistrate of the province, and sentenced by him and two colleagues whom he will choose from the lists that the two opposing parties in civil cases may propose, and in criminal cases from a list offered by the criminal or his defender, and the assignee [syndic] of the town council.

There shall be no third instance if the sentence of the second shall confirm that of the first, but if there shall be in a contrary situation, then it will be decided by the magistrate who will be residing in the province and by two colleagues named as in the prior cases.

The supreme tribunal of justice composed of seven magistrates will be familiar with the reasons of nullity against sentences given in the last instance and of the criminal charges against the magistrates of the province; it will pass upon the competence of the latter; it shall promote the most prompt administration of justice and will pass judgment upon those judges and magistrates who may delay cases or who do not support [the cases] in accord with the law or who may give sentences against the express statute.

8. The senate will be composed of individuals elected by the provincial congresses on nomination of the electoral juntas of the province. [The senate] must reside in the place where the national congress may designate; it must be zealous to preserve the

constitutional system; to propose to the legislative body bills which it may judge necessary to achieve that object; to refer to that body the laws which may be contrary to the constitution, or may not have been discussed or agreed to in the form which the constitution provides; it may pass judgment upon individuals of the executive body, upon the deputies of the legislative, upon magistrates of the supreme tribunal of justice, and upon the secretaries of State in those precise cases which a clear and well thought out law may designate. [The senate] may convoke an extraordinary congress in those cases which the constitution prescribes; it may arrange for the constitutional militia, giving to its commanders orders adequate for particular cases, which the constitution will designate.

(Signed)

Lorenzo de Zavala,

Doctor Mier and Others

Felipe Tena Ramirez, Leyes fundamentales de Mexico, 1808-1967, 147-152.

* * * * *

PLAN OF POTOSI

5 June, 1823

Art. 1. An army shall be formed as soon as possible, which will be called the protector of Mexican Freedom.

Art. 2. Its duty shall be to sustain inviolably the Catholic religion, Apostolic and Roman; to guarantee and protect its worthy ministers, propagators of the faith in Jesus Christ; and it shall observe exactly

the other two guarantees pledged in the Plan of
Iguala; it shall respect the property, security, and
equality of every citizen, and maintain order and
public tranquility.

Art. 3. This same army will request the activation of
a new summons for a new Congress which will be
affected in complete freedom and without any
restrictions whatsoever, so that in accordance with
the ample powers and instructions that the provinces
shall lend to their respective representatives, we
may obtain the realization of the constitution of the
State.

Art. 4. It will be the obligation of this same armed
force to sustain and guarantee to the provinces that
by their spontaneous will they may pronounce
themselves for a federal republic, due to the fact
that they are free to be able to do it, provided that
it be done in order and by general will of the
people. Therefore they shall proceed in the manner
most conducive to their prosperity.

Art. 5. While those newly called to the Congress may
be meeting to constitute the nation the provinces who
want to be independent may be governed by their
provincial deputations.

Art. 6. The army will be placed where it is more
convenient for its objective, but without intervening
whatsoever in any hostile operation; it will only be
permitted as its natural right to repel force by
force, in case it should be attacked or some one
should dare to assault the sacred freedom of the
people.

Art. 7. The present sovereign congress and the
temporary supreme government will be officially
presented with copies of this Plan and will request
it to kindly refrain from dictating orders which have
the tendency to oppress those who for their own
benefit wish to provide for themselves according to

what has been said, nor should they oppose this army which has no other aim nor any other purpose in its resolution than to contribute to the complete happiness of its own citizens, and to avoid the disasters which might be caused by those who oppose our liberty.

Art. 8. As long as there is an armed force directed toward Guadalajara or toward any other point which wishes to be free, the commanding officer shall be presented with a copy of this Plan, making him responsible before God and man for the wrongs which may arise if he persists in his purpose.

Art. 9. Likewise copies of this Plan shall be remitted to all the provinces of the nation.

Art. 10. They shall be considered as criminals for violating liberty as those who, heedless of the voice of justice, should attempt to harass the free people and in due course shall be judged by the respective authorities.

Art. 11. The army shall be pleased to give this new testimony of its liberal ideas, and will sustain at all costs all that is contained in these articles.

Art. 12. The units which shall compose the army will march to their provinces as soon as the nation is constituted according to the will of the people; recommending in general all those individuals who for their services have merited the reward which the nation grants to her worthy [benemeritos] sons.

Art. 13. The individuals who, forgetful of what they owe to their country should work against the ideas of this Plan, either with weapons or with seduction, a case will be formulated and they shall be judged as attempting the crime of lese Nation.

Art. 14. The [public] employees of all classes who may be included in the previous article shall be separated from their employments by the respective provincial deputations after a prior corresponding indictment.

* * * * * * * *

Patriots, look at my purpose! I wish to liberate you from new disasters. This I offer you. I know that there are wild-eyed leaders who will hope that we may be governed by the hateful monarchical system. Others for private aims desire a centralized republic, unheeding the cries of the majority of the provinces which want to constitute themselves under a federal form. I, who worship as sacred the opinion of the people, and who want them to constitute themselves with all liberty as they find themselves in their natural state, I have decided to help them against those who would attempt to impose a new yoke: I shall not loose the weapons from my hand until I have seen my nation freely constituted, and out of imminent danger that at present menaces it from all sides.

(Signed)

Antonio Lopez de Santa Anna

J. M. Bocanegra, Memorias, I, 256-258.

* * * * *

THE AGREEMENT OF THE FREE STATE OF JALISCO

16 June, 1823

In the city of Guadalajara on the 16th of June, an extraordinary session of the provincial deputation of this capital being in session, . . . the undersigned Director-Secretary said: That the will of all the towns of the province for the system of a representative federal government is manifested in the most clear and decisive manner; that the deputation has adopted the same feelings, and must be

in accordance with the will of the towns which it has
the honor of representing; and as a result of this,
and of what has been agreed by this same corporation
in its session declares that the occasion has arisen
to effect the much expected decree, to establish this
province as a Federal Sovereign State with the others
of the great Mexican Nation, under the name of the
Free State of Jalisco, and that for this purpose
there be published and circulated the outline and
plan of the government which are as follows:

[Then follows a Plan for the Government of
the State, On the same day was issued the following:]

Art. 1. The deputies who are appointed in this
State for the general constituent Mexican Congress
must establish the great nation of Anahuac, under the
system of a federal republic, in accordance with its
uniform and general will.

Art. 2. Consequently, they must proceed at once
to arrange the bases of the general federation of the
Mexican States and to establish a general
constitution for all of them, and for this purpose
only may they exercise the powers which are granted
to them.

Art. 3. The indicated bases of Federation and the
general constitution of the federated States shall
not be published as a law unless they have been
ratified by the provincial congresses of the State
themselves.

Art. 4. As in the system of federal government,
every federated State cannot have more than one vote
in the general congress; therefore in order to avoid
useless expenses to the State, only three regular
deputies will be elected to it, and the same number
of alternates for the general constituent Mexican
Congress.

Art. 5. The powers of these deputies shall be
revocable according to the judgment of the provincial
congress, on the terms which shall be determined once
it has been installed.

Art. 6. On the day following the election of the deputies for the general constituent Mexican Congress, the persons will be appointed who are to form a part of the constituent provisional congress of this State, which should be fifteen official delegates and five alternates.

[Six more articles outline the organization of the State assembly.]

J. M. Bocanagra, Memorias, I, 259 and 266.

* * * * *

DECLARATION OF THE VILLAGE OF CELAYA

1 July, 1823

To look for the health of the nation is the first duty of all citizens. The only way to obtain such a glorious end is to unify public opinion. Such has been the aim of Citizen Brigadier Miguel Barragan who has always kept them in sight. These just wishes have increased in him as he found himself proclaimed Commander of Valladolid, Queretaro and Guanajuato, both by all the free citizens who comprise these provinces and as appointed by the supreme executive power.

To give, therefore, completeness to such an interesting and sacred position, he thought it indispensable to summon the leaders of these provinces and the generals at present in San Luis Potosi for a conference in this city, which, with those invited, was realized in the afternoon of the present day. The following came to his residence for this purpose: the citizens Brigadier Luis Cortazar, general commander of Queretaro; colonel Pedro Otero of Guanajuato; colonel Jose Maria del Toro with ample powers-of-attorney from general Antonio Lopez de Santa Anna; and having the same Col. Barragan from Brigadier Jose Armijo. The General made clear at once the object of meeting, and after a long, sustained, and scrupulous discussion, in which the citizen Colonel Jose Maria Marquez was appointed secretary of this meeting, the following articles were agreed to:

196

1st. It being an absolute necessity to avoid anarchy and to recognize a central point of unity, this [point] must be the Supreme Executive Power; both because of there being embodied in it the legitimacy of its nomination as well as for being composed of the most trustworthy individuals of all the nation, and because of well-known and publicized virtues. On account of these powerful reasons to withdraw obedience has never even been considered.

2nd. The troops of said gathered commanders obligate themselves to sustain at all costs the general opinion of the province in which they find themselves, as explained by their commissions already made for this purpose.

3rd. This resolution will be made known to the commissioners for the provinces of Valladolid, San Luis Potosi, Guanajuato and Queretaro so that, meeting as soon as possible, they may manifest with complete freedom what may be the opinion of their constituents.

4th. This Junta recognizes likewise as General-in-Chief of all troops residing in the aforementioned provinces the citizen Brigadier Miguel Barragan.

With which this act was concluded and signed as written evidence.

(Military signatures follow)

J. M. Bocanegra, Memorias, I, 268-269.

* * * * *

PLAN DE CUERNAVACA

16 January, 1824

The Plan or indications which the Citizens Brigadier General Francisco Hernandez and Colonels Antonio Aldama, Luis Pinzon, and Guadalupe Palafox address with the highest respect to the Supreme Sovereign Mexican Congress and Supreme Governing

Power with the just purpose of realizing the true Independence and Liberty of the States of Northern America, taking into consideration the very critical circumstances and serious risks which menace our Nation, lest it drag again the chains which for three hundred years have subjugated it.

1st. The Religion of the Free States of Northern America is and shall always be the Catholic, Roman and Apostolic, with the exclusion of any other, according to the declaration of the Sovereign Congress.

2nd. The States mentioned shall be entirely and absolutely independent of all foreign nations.

3rd. All the natives of Anahuac and resident Spaniards of the said States, be what class they may be, are citizens and brothers of each other, for which reason they will never be able to separate from the alliance, considering that they will at last see themselves definitely free from any other Power, because as long as they do go by the aforementioned system they will never be able to constitute themselves, even if they want to, such less find themselves safe from the apparent Liberty which they enjoy up to now, because their conflicts will not allow them to get it.

4th. Said States will never allow, under any pretext whatsoever, that its government and [public] employments be menaced nor obtained by any kind of Spaniards, because they definitely belong to the native sons of their land, therefore by a natural right and also because it is convenient for their own safety.

5th. There never will be admitted for any reason or pretext an Emperor or Viceroy to govern us, unless the government falls on a single individual with another name or title which he may be given.

6th. The Government of all the States shall be that of a Popular Representative Federated Republic, in accordance with the Declaration of the Sovereign

Congress.

7th. So that it may with all frankness continue in its session of established order, it is an absolute necessity that the present Sovereign Congress order all members who are not Americans to leave that august assembly, replacing them in the best manner. For the said effect we submit ourselves to their disposition, which we shall sustain until we have shed our last drop of blood with the army which we command, vowing the same for the Supreme Executive Power so long as it is in accord with our Sovereign dispositions.

8th. The persons and property of every citizen shall be respected and protected, doing likewise with that of every Spaniard, as long as he does not contravene directly or indirectly that which is agreed to in this Plan.

9th. The departments of the States and other offices shall remain in force and effect without any other alteration than of those political employees, civilians and military men occupied by Spaniards and those who are opposed to the Nation shall be provided for provisionally as soon as possible by Americans of real merit and virtues who will be carefully chosen.

10th. The Spaniards who shall have to leave their places which must be filled by Americans shall be granted a pension which the government will assign, according to their merit and fitness which they have proved to have up to now for the Nation to settle their just claim.

11th. Every Spaniard who does not agree with the present Plan has the liberty of living wherever he may please outside the States and also of remaining as long as they are welcome, but with the understanding that if he who chooses to stay is observed showing the slightest sign of treason to the Nation, once verified, he shall be punished by the death penalty and his properties shall be confiscated for the benefit of the States.

12th. Justice will be administered in accordance with the decrees given and to be given by the Sovereign Congress.

13th. If the Nation should be invaded by foreign forces, the Army shall be increased to the number considered necessary to guarantee its Independence and Liberty, and it will be called from now on The Army of the Mexican Union, taking under its protection the Catholic, Apostolic and Roman, Religion, sacrificing itself completely to maintain it and the National Representation, and to maintain systematized the government of the States.

14th. All Americans who may wish to enlist under their flags, be they military men or natives, shall be very welcome and by their good conduct, devotion and fidelity will be treated with the respect which they deserve, but preceded by the oath to keep faith in the manner which will be explained later.

15th. Those so-called "Insurgents" who since the year 1810 have sacrificed themselves for the Nation and who can present legal proof of having served the country with the aim of promoting its well-being shall be assisted to get located and they will be given the same ranks which the Nation gave them at that time so long as they duly present themselves to sustain the just cause of the present plan, because, if otherwise they will lose the right to present a claim because of having been judged unworthy.

16th. At the moment that the announced Plan is published we shall begin to organize the Army in every way with the force that it has at present and so on until completing the necessary number; consequently the first who shall enlist in it or sound the Cry in favor of this system in any city which is opposed to the aims shall be given preference in their ranking. For this purpose and so that none can declare himself to have been overlooked, an arbitrary period of thirty days is given, a period of time which for a thousand good reasons has been considered sufficient for every American who desires the salvation of the Nation and who has the firmness and who considers honor can take sides; but he warned that the expressed period of time will only refer to those living far away, because experience of past occasions has taught us the undignified way in which many carry on, as it is commonly said "In order to fall heavy" it is necessary that those who live near and want to take sides do so with rapidity because, on the other hand, they will not be able to claim the incontestable right which others may win on account of their forehandedness and effective presentment [before the enlistment officer], but let them weigh motives so strong that they may appear as clear as the light of day.

17th. The Army shall completely organize itself with all rapidity possible as the present critical circumstances so demand it and if by chance there should be formed a Regiment and the commanders and officers would be needed, they will be chosen from those who have distinguished themselves by merit, aptitude, and service.

18th. The Commanders [jefes] and officers will take care with the most exact scrupulousness that their subordinates perform to the letter with the established military procedures for the Army which the Sovereign Congress legislates for that purpose.

19th. [Public] employments will be given in the name of the Nation as may be judged necessary, submitting them to the approval of the Sovereign Congress.

20th. Every citizen who may present himself to take sides and cannot be placed in the Army shall be employed in other branches without affecting the individuals of those branches who are in the promotion list, in accordance with their merit and aptitude.

21st. The persons below shall be considered for very distinguished service and given preference in their placement at the same instant that they can be appointed: 1st. Those who are in favor of this plan. 2nd. Who assist in throwing out some armed force of the cities which oppose it. 3rd. Who denounce any conspiracy or attack which the enemy should attempt against the Army that maintains the just rights of the Nation. 4th. Who help the troops, wherever they may be, to provide for its maintenance, in case they should need it.

22nd. There shall be a Fidelity Committee [Junta] composed of nine individuals of total probity and with the following authority: 1st. To take an oath from all military men or individuals of any kind they may be, who may present themselves to take sides with the Army, because without this requisite none shall be able to take arms. 2nd. To make a report of their previous Offices and Services. 3rd. To give a written evidence on the day an individual presents himself. 4th. To carry in the Books of the Government, which for this effect they must have the same which remains stated in the previous articles, the signature of the person presented, who for the requirement will present himself with his written evidence to one of the Chiefs who command the Army, so that he may be able to give him the certificate of his enlistment where it belongs and his assignment.

23rd. Those who cannot take their oath in the mentioned Junta due to legal inconveniences will do so in their Division or towns, the Commanders being requested that all should be done, although provisionally, in the order expressed in the prior article, so that when the Junta requests the information that they may need, it can be sent promptly and no one whom it wishes to represent will be harmed.

24th. Every military man, whatever rank he may be, who having sworn to keep fidelity and has taken up arms and then should retire from his corps without permission from him who should grant it, will be considered as a deserter after eight days have passed, and by the same token, he shall lose the right of citizenship and shall be unworthy of American society; moreover his desertion should be looked upon as treason to the Nation; he will be prosecuted and once caught will be shot to death within six hours.

25th. The Fidelity Committee will take the oath referred to in Article no. 22 in the following order and manner: Do you swear before God and the Nation to shed to your last drop of blood to maintain the Catholic, Apostolic and Roman Religion, to sustain the national representation by obeying its orders and those of the established government? I so swear. Do you swear to oppose firmly, giving your life first, that no Nation may govern us, no matter under what flattering promise the situation may offer of a good Government? I so swear. Do you swear that you will not break any of the Articles which are included in the present plan and be faithful to the Nation under the established bases, under the penalty that if you should break your promise, which is considered as very sacred, you shall be punished with all vigor as stated in the previous article? I so swear. You will be told, "If you should do so, God will reward you, and the great and generous Nation, without forgetting your hardships, will reward your merits."

26th. The individuals who comprise the Army which sustain the present cause shall not harm any of their fellow beings, except when they may be obliged by force to do so, refusing the just ideas which they may be offered, and furthermore when it is expected that the Sovereignty of the Nation should warrant it, because this is the only means with which the complete security and peace of its inhabitants can be obtained.

27th. Three days after the announcement of this Plan, all Spaniards without distinction of classes or person, shall present such weapons that they may have, be they what they may, otherwise [the weapons] will be picked up, and in case anyone should hide them or resist delivering them, they will be considered as traitors of the Nation and punished in accordance with Article No. 11.

28th. Any American, no matter who he may be, who should make an attack against the Nation, helping directly or indirectly on projects opposed to this plan shall suffer the death penalty.

29th. No American will attempt a criminal act against the persons and properties of the Spaniards, because even though they be wronged by one of them, they should present their complaint before the competent authority, under penalty that to him who should proceed otherwise punishments will be applied in accordance with the law.

30th. In order to proceed in everything with the most mature agreement, and to obtain the success and welfare which they want, never on any account whatsoever or on any pretext, whatever it may be, shall any of the four leaders who drafted the present Plan determine anything whatsoever by themselves but, rather, in common agreement and conforming in everything and with everyone involved, because otherwise everything without this essential requirement will be null and without value and effect. Anyone who should deviate from this pact will be responsible to the charges which the Nation may place [against him].

31st. Since the purpose is not to go against any of the Sovereign dispositions of the Congress, and if, obeying them blindly these just measures will be remitted immediately with due respect, and we point out that if we have resolved to put them into practice with weapons in our hands, it is not with the object of imposing [these measures] and much less with the aim of dictating laws, because this [authority] belongs exclusively to their sovereignty, but to make them know that they have a support in them and with the unanimous opinion for the legitimate security; and that the Spaniards be removed from all knowledge, direct or indirect, in matters of the Nation as it belongs to all the sons of this land, who are the only owners of this part of the Northern world.

(Signatures follow)

General Headquarters,
Town of Cuernavaca.
The first year of absolute liberty.

Manuscript, Doc. #3768, Library, University of Texas.

* * * * *

CONSTITUENT ACT OF THE FEDERATION

31 January, 1824

Art. 1. The Mexican nation is composed of the provinces embraced within the territory hitherto called that of New Spain, in which was included the captaincy-general of Yucatan and the commandancy-generals of the internal provinces of the East and the West.

Art. 2. The Mexican nation is forever free and independent of Spain and of any other power, and it is not nor can it be the patrimony of any family or person.

Art. 3. Sovereignty resides basically and essentially in the nation, and for this reason to this [entity] belongs the right to adopt and to establish through the agency of its representativees the form of government and the other fundamental laws that may seem most suitable for its preservation and greater prosperity, and for modifying or changing them as it may believe most convenient.

Art. 4. The religion of the Mexican nation is and shall be perpetually Catholic, Apostolic, and Roman. The State protects it with wise and just laws and prohibits the exercise of any other whatever.

Art. 5. The nation adopts for its form of government a representative, popular, federal republic.

Art. 6. Its integral parts are independent states, free and sovereign in that which touches their internal administration and government, as is detailed in this Act and in the general Constitution.

Art. 7. The States of the Federation are, as of now, the following: Guanajuato; the interior of the West, composed of the provinces of Sonora and Sinaloa; the interior of the East, composed of the provinces of Coahuila, Nuevo Leon and Texas; the interior of the North composed of the provinces of Chihuahua, Durango and New Mexico; that of Mexico; that of Michoacan; that of Oajaca; that of Puebla of the Angels; that of

Quetero; that of San Luis Potosi; that of Nuevo
Santander, which shall be called Tamaulipas; that of
Tabasco; that of Tlaxcala; that of Vera Cruz; that of
Jalisco; that of Yucatan; that of Zacatecas. The
Californias and the part of Colima (without the town
of Tonila, which will continue united to Jalisco)
shall be for now territories of the Federation,
subject directly to the supreme powers of the latter.
The territorial divisions and the towns which make up
the province of the isthmus of Guazacualco shall
return to the [provinces] to which they belonged
hitherto. The Laguna de Terminos shall belong to the
State of Yucatan.

Art. 8. Under the Constitution it shall be possible
to increase the number of states embraced within the
prior article and to modify them as it is deemed more
suitable to the happiness of the towns.

Division of Powers

Art. 9. The supreme powers of the nation are, for
their execution, divided into legislative, executive,
and judicial; and never shall two or more of these be
united in one corporation or person, nor shall the
legislative power be lodged in one individual.

Legislative Power

Art. 10. The legislative power of the Federation
shall reside in a chamber of deputies and a senate,
and they shall compose the general congress.

Art. 11. The individuals of the chamber of deputies
and of the senate shall be named by the citizens of
the States in the manner which the Constitution
provides.

Art. 12. The basis for naming the representatives of
the chamber of deputies shall be that of population.
Each State shall name two senators, as the Constitution prescribes.

Art. 13. The issuance of laws and decrees pertains

exclusively to the general Congress:

I. To sustain national independence and to provide for the conservation and security of the nation in its foreign relations.

II. To keep peace and public order in the interior of the Federation, and to promote its enlightenment and general prosperity.

III. To maintain the independence of the States among themselves.

IV. To protect and to guide the liberty of the press in all the Federation.

V. To keep the federal union of the States; to set up definitive boundaries, and to settle their differences.

VI. To sustain a proportional equality of obligations and rights which States have before the law.

VII. To admit new states or territories to the federal union, incorporating them into the nation.

VIII. To fix each year the general expenses of the nation, in view of the budgets which the executive power shall present to it.

IX. To establish the taxes necessary to cover the general expenses of the Republic; to determine the investment [of funds], and to give an account of it to the executive power.

X. To arrange for commerce with foreign nations, and between the different States of the Federation, and the Indian tribes.

XI. To contract debts on the credit of the Republic and to designate guarantees to cover them.

XII. To ratify the public debt of the nation and to indicate the means of consolidating it.

XIII. To declare war on the basis of data which the executive power may present to it.

XIV. To grant privateering patents, and to declare valid or invalid the seizures by land or sea.

XV. To designate and to organize the armed forces of land and sea and to set the quota of each State.

XVI. To organize, arm, and to discipline the militia of the States, leaving to each of them the naming of the respective officers and the authority to drill it according to the discipline prescribed by the national congress.

XVIII. To approve treaties of peace, alliance, and friendship, of federation, of armed neutrality and of whatever other sort may be celebrated by the executive authority.

XIX. To equip every type of harbor.

Art. 14. In the Constitution other general and special and economic powers of the Congress of the Federation will be designated as well as the method of implementing them, and also the prerogatives of this body and of its individual [members].

Executive Power

Art. 15. The supreme executive power shall be lodged by the Constitution in the individual or individuals whom the latter shall indicate. They shall be residents and natives of any of the States or territories of the nation.

Art. 16. The powers [of the executive branch], besides those that shall be established in the Constitution, are the following:

I. To place in execution the laws designed to consolidate the integrity of the Federation and to sustain its independence from without and its union and liberty within.

II. To nominate and to remove freely official secretaries of state.

III. To be responsible for the collection and to determine the distribution of the general tax funds in accord with the laws.

IV. To name the employees of the general offices of the Treasury, according to the Constitution and the laws.

V. To declare war after a decree of approval of the Congress; and this [body] not being in session, as the Constitution shall designate.

VI. To command the permanent forces of land and sea and of the active militia for defense abroad and for domestic security of the Federation.

VII. To command the local militia for the same purposes; although to use it outside the respective States it shall obtain prior consent of the general Congress which shall judge the force necessary.

VIII. To name the employees of the army, of the active and armed militia in accord with the ordinances, laws in effect, and as the Constitution may provide.

IX. To give retirements, to grant leaves, and to set the pensions of the military in accord with the laws as the previous attribution of authority indicates.

X. To name diplomatic envoys and consuls with the approval of the Senate, and while this body is being established, with the present Congress.

XI. To direct diplomatic negotiations, to celebrate treaties of peace, friendship, alliance, federation, truce, armed neutrality, commerce and others; but in order to approve or to deny its ratification to any of these the prior ratification of the general Congress should be secured.

XII. To take care that justice should be administered

promptly and fully by the general courts and that its decisions should be executed according to the law.

XIII. To publish, circulate, and to cause to be kept the general Constitution and the laws thereof; it being able for one time only to object to these [laws] within ten days whenever it may appear convenient to it and suspending its execution until a resolution of the general Congress.

XIV. To issue decrees and ordinances for the better fulfillment of the Constitution and the general laws.

XV. To suspend employees for as long as three months and to deprive them of half their salary for that time and for the employees of the Federation who may disobey the orders and decrees; and in such cases when it believes that a case should be made against such employees, it shall forward relevant material to the respective courts.

Art. 17. All the decrees and orders of the supreme executive power must be signed by the secretary of the branch [of government] to which the subject belongs, and without this requisite they shall not be obeyed.

Judicial Power

Art. 18. Every person who inhabits the territory of the Federation has the right to prompt, complete, and impartial justice; and for this purpose the Federation deposits the exercise of judicial power in a Supreme Court of Justice, and in the courts that shall be established in each State; it being left to the Constitution to determine the authority of the Supreme Court.

Art. 19. No person shall be tried in the states or territories of the Federation save under the laws passed and the courts established prior to the fact for which he may be judged. Therefore, all judgment by special commission and every retroactive law is forever prohibited.

Special Government of the States

Art. 20. The government of each State will be divided for its exercise into the three powers, legislative, executive, and judicial; and never shall it be possible to unite two or more of these into one corporation or person, nor the legislative [power] be deposited in one individual.

Art. 21. The legislative power of each State shall reside in a Congress composed of the number of individuals which their special Constitution shall determine; [they shall be] elected by popular vote and are removable in the time and manner which [the Constitutions] may provide.

Executive Power

Art. 22. The exercise of executive power in each State shall not be entrusted for more than an allotted time, which shall be set in their respective Constitutions.

Judicial Power

Art. 23. The judicial power of each State shall be exercised by the tribunals that its Constitution may provide.

General Provisions

Art. 24. The Constitutions of the States shall not be contrary to this [Constituent] Act, nor to that which the general Constitution of the latter.

Art. 25. Nevertheless the legislatures of the States shall be able to organize their domestic government provisionally, and while they are verifying it the laws in effect shall be observed.

Art. 26. No criminal of one State shall find asylum in another; rather, he shall be handed over to the authority which claims him.

Art. 27. No State, without the consent of the general

Congress, shall establish any tax or tonnage, nor shall it maintain troops or ships of war in time of peace.

Art. 28. No State, without the consent of the general Congress, shall impose taxes or duties on either imports or exports unless the law does not regulate how they ought to do it.

Art. 29. No State shall enter into a transaction or contract with another, or with any foreign power, nor engage in war, save in case of an actual invasion or in case of such immediate danger that admits of no delay.

Art. 30. The nation is obliged to protect through wise and just laws the rights of Man and of the citizen.

Art. 31. Every inhabitant of the Federation has freedom to write, print, and to publish his political ideas without the necessity of a permit, of revision, or approval prior to publication, under the restrictions and responsibility of the laws.

Art. 32. The Congress of each State shall submit annually to the general Federation a detailed and comprehensive report of the income and expenses of each treasury unit within its respective districts along with an account or the origins of both entries, of the branches of industry, agriculture, trade and manufacturing, indicating progress or decline, with the causes that produce it; of the new branches that can be established along with means to achieve it; and of their respective population.

Art. 33. All debts contracted before the adoption of this [Constituent] Act by the Federation, subject to their liquidation and classification according to the rules that the general Congress may establish, are recognized.

Art. 34. The general Constitution and this Act guarantee to the States of the Federation the form of government adopted in the present law; and each State is committed to sustain the federal union at all costs.

Art. 35. This Act may be changed only at the time and terms which the general Constitution prescribes.

Art. 36. The execution of this Act is committed under the strictest responsibility to the supreme executive power, who, after its publication, shall arrange for it in all points.

Mexico [City]

(Signed by members of the current Congress)

Tena Ramirez, Felipe, Leyes fundamentales de Mexico, 1808-1967, 154-159.

* * * * *

PROPOSITIONS OF AN AD HOC COMMITTEE

6 April, 1824

To advise on what should be done to secure public peace and order.(1)

1. The Administration shall rest on a person elected among the present members of the Supreme Executive Power by them themselves. The person on whom the election may fall shall be designated as Supreme Director of the Mexican Republic and his title of courtesy shall be that of "Excellency."

2. They shall also elect a Vice-Director in the case of physical or moral impossibility of the former, and the one nominated shall be able to command troops to whom the Supreme Director may entrust them.

3. The Supreme Director shall remain until he is

---

(1) The text is an amended and interlined copy of a committee report. The underlined portions were lined out in pencil.

213

constitutionally replaced and can only be removed in the cases provided in the order of February 28th, last.

4. Apart from the faculties consigned in the act and in the laws of the Supreme Executive Power, the Supreme Director shall have all that is necessary to carry out effectively the system of federation, in accordance with the same act; that of taking immediate command of troops; that of dividing the territory of the republic into military departments as he may judge necessary apart from the laws concerned; that of increasing, diminishing and re-ordering the army as it may be more convenient for it to fulfill its duties; that of suspending all types of employees of the federation, yet maintaining their rights; that of expelling from the territory of the Republic the foreigners who may be suspicious, numbering among these those who have surrendered and who have not sworn [to support] independence; that of arming and training the civilian militia; that of moving it; that of moving the Congress as may be most convenient; that of requesting supplements reimbursible with the loans for which it is authorized; and that of requesting aid from the armed forces of other countries up to six thousand men, in case of invasion by foreign troops. (2) [The Director has been empowered and shall be able to use the officers of the army who may be named as Governors of the States or as Deputies of their Congresses, and also. . .] (3)

5. He shall be able to confer military command to the Governors.

6. In compliance with the subordination which they owe to the Supreme Government as it aims for the domestic tranquility of the federation, the Governors of the States shall abide by the Director in that which may upset the tranquility of all the respective

---

(2) At the top of the page, apart from the text, "to issue privateer patents."

(3) Bracketed portions marked out in pencil.

States, about which they shall give a report on their own accord or in case that later the Director himself may require it.

7. Each State shall appoint as soon as possible by means of its Congress an individual within its walls or from outside [if he is not a deputy of the Congress], (4) who will come to form Council and whose opinions the Supreme Director will hear in the serious matters which he may deem convenient. The designated persons shall be provided with compen - station and travel allowances in accordance with the decrees passed for the Deputies by the general Con - gress.

8. This Council shall be formed as soon as seven of its members are present, and meanwhile the Director shall consult with the persons in whom he has the most confidence.

9. The general Congress shall limit itself to discussing the constitution, to systematizing of finances and public credit, reform of the regulations of the civilian militia [and the drafting of those laws which may be recommended or approved by three-quarters of the Deputies present in the session.](5)

10. [If some law should be passed which should transgress the authority of the Supreme Director, he shall be empowered to suspend it, giving notice to Congress.](6)

11. The Congresses of the States shall continue working on their constitutions, systems of finance, and other matters pertaining to their authority but in the areas which require their domestic government, they shall take care not to weaken those of the Supreme Director, who otherwise shall be able to suspend them.

---

(4) A marginal addition.
(5) Bracketed portion marked out in pencil.
(6) Ditto.

12. By this decree the decrees of the 26th and 27th of January referring to the extraordinary faculties conceded to the Government shall cease.

13. [After the constitution has been discussed, the Congress shall take this law into consideration in order to revoke or reform it.](7)

14. The new regulation for freedom of the press will be given as soon as possible.

(Signed) Espinosa
Ramos Arispe
Marin
Ibarra
Becerra
Gomez Anaya
Mora
Garcia

---

(7) The whole point was underlined in pencil.

The printed and amended text is found in the New York Public Library. HTC p.v. 47, #7

* * * * *

PLAN DE MONTANO

23 December, 1826

1st. The supreme Government shall draft a law for the general Congress of Unity for the extermination in the republic of all kinds of secret meetings be that what they may be called or their origin.

2nd. The supreme Government will totally reorganize the secretaries of its office, giving said positions to men of known worthiness, virtue, and merits.

3rd. The President shall issue without loss of time the necessary passport for the emissary to the Mexican republic of the United States of the North.

4th. He shall see that the Federal Constitution and the laws in force are exactly and religiously enforced.

(Signed) J. Manuel Montano
Otumba.

H.W. Ward, History of Mexico, II, 565 and Suarez y Navarro, Historia de Mexico, 90.

* * * * *

PLAN OF RINCON

31 July, 1827

The Garrison of Vera Cruz, on disavowing the authority of General Barragan, drafted the following Plan and issued it publicly on July 31, 1827. Its articles were as follows:

Art. 1. [The garrison of Vera Cruz] repudiates all dictation which does not emanate from the high authority of the Federation, because those of this station entertain quite contrary sentiments.

Art. 2. His Excellency the Sr. Commander will be informed of the attitude in which we now find ourselves and the reasons which now motivate us.

Art. 3. Our position will be on the defensive until we receive orders from the same high authority to whom we submit ourselves.

217

Art. 4. As a sign of our respectful recognition of the supreme authority of the Federation and of the institutions indicated in the constitutional charter, the troops will take the oath before the flags of their respective unit.

Art. 5. Lives and property will be respected, and our stipulations will be faithfully fulfilled.

Moved by the patriotic sentiments of good Mexicans, it has reached the point where we present ourselves, arms in hand, to sustain the duty which the law, the general welfare of the republic, and our just liberty imposes upon us.

(Signed) Jose Rincon
Vera Cruz.

Suarez y Navarro, Historia de Mexico, 87. General Ampudia's brigade accepted this Plan with modifications.

* * * * *

PLAN OF PEROTE

16 September 1828

The Plan is preceded by a long and vivid account of the troubles which have harrassed the country. It concludes as follows:

The People have signified their intentions. Their opinion has not been respected; and now, wearied with the plotting of its detestable domestic enemies, the Nation raises its voice along with that of the Army, to the august sanctuary of the laws and to the Supreme Executive of the country and demands a remedy for impending evils, which may be found in the following Plan:

1st. The people and the Army will annul the elections made in favor of th Minister of War D. Manuel Gomez Pedraza, who by no means is admitted either as President or Vice-President of the Republic because

218

he is declared an enemy of our federal institutions.

2nd. The resident Spaniards in the Republic being the origin of all our wrongs, it is demanded of the Chambers of the Union a law for their total expulsion.

3rd. In order that peace and the federal system which happily rules us may be strengthened it is necessary that His Excellency, the national hero General D. Vicente Guerrero be elected as President of the Republic.

4th. That the legislatures which have thwarted the vote of the people proceed immediately to new elections in conformity with the vote of its members, saving the nation in this way from a civil war which threatens it.

5th. The liberating army intends that no Mexican blood may be shed in the present uprising, unless it may be compromised in its defense. The forces which sustain the right of the people profess obedience to the general constitution of the United States of Mexico and to His Excellency the President of the Republic and to the national hero [benemerito de la Patria] D. Guadalupe Victoria and shall not loose their weapons from their hands without first seeing accomplished the aforementioned articles which it has sworn to maintain.

(Signed) Antonio Lopez de Santa Anna

General Headquarters of the Liberating Army in Perote.

Castillo Negrete, Mexico en el siglo XIX, XVII, 269. A translation of Santa Anna's full address which precedes the Plan may be found in H. W. Ward, History of Mexico, II, 582-586.

* * * * *

DECLARATION OF CAMPECHE

6 November, 1829

Gathered at the quarters of the Commander of the corps, the officers of the garrison, of the navy, and employees of the Federation, after having been called to order, the first named said: That the commanders of the permanent battalions Nos. 6 and 13, artillery and 2nd active of infantry had declared to him that the insurrection proclamation [pronunciamiento] which they had issued in behalf of the type of the central government for the welfare of independence and security of the nation, constantly menaced as it has been by the dangerous system and is harrassed under the federal system, due to the disorganization in which the army and national finance find themselves is due to the imminent risk which has been seen in the recent invasion of the host of the Spaniards; and due to the general discontent with which its most dear sons see it march towards disaster and noticing also the weakening of the tremendous elements which should carry it to the peak of its greatness, they wished that the junta, publicly manifesting its feelings would occupy itself with establishing the bases which must be organized and carry out the said pronouncement. As a consequence of all this, after a detailed discussion, it was unanimously agreed by vote to declare the following articles:

1st. The corps of this garrison having declared, as they have done, for the central government, the Junta is for the proposition, stating as essential the maintenance of independence at all costs, as the object of most importance for all Mexicans.

2nd. The authority of the current President of the Republic is recognized in everything that does not oppose this pronouncement, and providing that that which is adopted be for the welfare of the nation.

3rd. The present general congress is declared summoned in order to convene another one which will arrange the form of a central republican government, establishing as its basis the unity of political and military command, in those entities which are at present designated as States.

4th. That as a consequence of the previous article, the general in command shall naturally have the command of both as well as everything related to the branches of finance, of the Federation, as well as those of the State.

5th. The functions of the congress, senate, and governor of the State are declared recessed because they are found in contradiction with the ideas of this pronouncement.

6th. The courts of all kinds will be maintained in the discharge of their duties, only demanding of them the oath to adopt the newly established system.

7th. It is granted to the general commander or to his successor, in case the former should not accept, the faculties of provisionally arranging interim government of the towns in a way which more nearly conforms to the general welfare.

8th. The individuals comprised in this pronouncement may not be transferred from this city until the form of government which they have called for has been settled.

9th. All the [civil] employees shall be required to take an oath to maintain and preserve [this pronouncement] at all costs, and he who should not do so will cease in the exercise of his functions. The military units which have verified it promise not to put down their arms until after having obtained the object which they have proposed to carry out.

With which this act was concluded and signed by the members of the junta, agreeing to remit a copy to the general commander of this State in order that he may answer immediately whether he shall adopt it, and whether he adheres to this resistance movement, remitting another copy at the first opportunity to His Excellency the President of the Republic for the same purpose.

(Signatures) follow

J. M. Bocanegra, Memorias, II, 103-104; also Suarez y Navarro, Historia de Mexico, 170. Also El Astro Moreliano, Supplement 23 November, 1829

* * * * *

221

PLAN DE ZERECERO*

30 November, 1828.

D. Anastasio Zerecero, advised by Zavala, presented the following propositions:

1st. Pardon from the sentence of capital punishment is granted to the Vice-President of the Republic, D. Nicolas Bravo, and to General D. Miguel Barragan, as well as to all those who took up arms against the government to support the Plan called that of Montano.

2nd. Within thirty days those persons mentioned in the aforementioned article shall leave the territory of the Republic for a period of ten years, and they shall remain under guard until the instant of embarkation.

3rd. The generals Bravo and Barragan shall be succored annually with half the salary which major generals should enjoy as long as they remain in any place of America designated by the government.

4th. Any of the expatriated who should return to the territory of the Republic within the period of time stated in Article No. 2 will be considered as a traitor.

(Signed) Sr. D. Anastasio Zerecero

---

* Sometimes the name is spelled "Cerrecero."

Jose Maria Tornel y Mendivil, Breve resena historica de la nacion Mexicana, 246.

* * * * *

PLAN OF JALAPA

4 December, 1829

The Reserve Army owes to its honor and the respect which it deserves [to offer] an explanation of these facts that [the citizens] may be persuaded of the calm and circumspection with which it has proceeded in all its operations and that out of respect for the sacred purpose of reintegrating its fellow patriots into the enjoyment of the rights which the fundamental laws give them it has been decided to adopt the Plan which includes the following articles:

1st. The Army ratifies the solemn oath it has made to maintain the federal pact, respecting the sovereignty of the states and preserving their indissoluble unity.

2nd. The Army promises that it will not put down its weapons until it sees the constitutional order re-estabished with the exact observance of the fundamental laws.

3rd. For this purpose its first vote given in the exercise of its right of petition is that the Supreme Executive Power yield the extraordinary faculties with which it is invested, requesting that it immediately issue a summons for the prompt meeting of the august Chambers (Congress) in order that these may deal with the great wrongs of the nation and their rapid remedy, as the council of the government consulted it; hearing at the same time the petitions Mexicans may see fit to direct them regarding the reformations which must be established in order that the republic, free of abuses in the administration in all its branches, can promote its felicity and enhancement.

4th. The second vote of the Army is that those officers against whom the general opinion has pronounced itself may be removed.

5th. The Army, on manifesting its fervent hopes for

the rapid remedy of the wrongs which afflict the republic, far from pretending to emerge as legislator, professes the most blind obedience to the supreme powers and recognizes all the legitimate authorities constituted in the civil, ecclesiastic, and military order, in all that which does not oppose the federal constitution.

6th. The Army promises that it will try to preserve at all costs the public tranquility, protecting the social guarantees and persecuting all evil doers for the greater security of the roads and towns through which they travel.

In order to carry out this Plan we have agreed:

I. That copies of this [Plan] be remitted with a courteous official letter to the supreme general government, to the honorable legislators, to their Excellencies the Governors of the States, and to the general commanders and other military chiefs, and to the ecclesiastic prelates.

II. That an invitation be sent by means of a commission to the illustrious victors of Juchi and Tampico, to the citizen: Generals Bustamente and Santa Anna, so that placing themselves at the head of the revolutionary army and of all the Mexicans who adhere to this plan, without distinction of times and parties, they may lead them in their operations as soon as possible, the quicker to obtain their stated objectives.

III. In case, by no means expected, that the above mentioned generals should refuse such a laudable wish, the one of highest rank among the revolutionary chiefs shall take command. Likewise, all our military brothers of the garrison of Campeche will be invited so that abjuring their pronouncement they may unite with the present one and contribute to the re-establishment of the reign of laws in force, from the infraction of which proceed the general evils of the Republic and the great miseries which afflict the Mexican Army.

(Drafted by the Staff of General Anastasio Bustamente)

Suarez y Navarro, Historia de Mexico, 173-173, and Lorenzo de Zavala, Ensayos historicos, 305-306; Bocanegra, I. M. Memorias, II, 54-56; El Astro Moreliano, Supplement, 14 December, 1829.

* * * * *

PLAN OF QUINTANAR (1)

23 December, 1829

In the capital of Mexico on the 23rd of December 1829 the commanders and officers who undersign assembled and resolved: That their oaths as citizens and as soldiers of their native land call upon them to save it.

That the Army of Reserve has solemnly promised to uphold the system of a popular representative federal government as adopted by the nation in its fundamental laws, and consequently to uphold the constitutional order which has been altered by the scandalous transgression of these very laws. That this is also the will of the states and of the people of this capital, and that if they should remain silent a civil war would result from an opinion not pronounced.

That the national Congress is not now in session, it having agreed to close its extraordinary sessions on the 16th instant, which decree should have been acted upon by the Executive and not returned with comments, as [such action] is prohibited in Article No. 73 of the federal Constitution, and that by virtue of the same the Senate was placed in recess at

(1) General Luis Quintanar was the first signatory. This document is sometimes called the "Decree of the Great Mexico or the Re-establishment of the Constitution and the Laws."

once. That neither did the Congress exist when the deputies were appointed to exercise the executive power. Therefore, the appointment of Sr. Jose Maria Bocanegra is null and also because the designation fell upon a representative.

That even if it were legal, Sr. Bocanegra could not exercise the executive power because he had taken his oath before the assembled Chambers in accordance with Article no. 101 of the Constitution.

That this solemnity of law was dispensed with by the Executive [Power] by virtue of its extraordinary faculties which it had received from the said Chambers, and of which he had sworn not to make use, and so passing over in this manner the legislative power and the Constitution itself. That notwithstanding that oath, made only to deceive the people, he continued exercising the all-inclusive faculties in order to create sycophants and to lavish employments.

That the General who exercised the executive power left this city to place himself at the head of a division against the Army of Reserve, thereby provoking the civil war for a personal interest; and that due to the invalidity of the appointment and the exercise thereof by Sr. Bocanegra the nation finds itself without a legitimate and constitutional government to rule it.

That from one moment to another this acephalous situation threatens tremendous ruptures and disturbances which compromise security and public order.

Everything being carefully considered and with the best and purest desires for the public good, it was unanimously agreed:

1st. To adopt the plan for the re-establishment of constitutional order and the free exercise of the sovereignty of the States which the Army of Reserve proclaimed at the City of Jalapa on the 4th instant, renewing consequently the oath to maintain the federal Constitution and the existing laws.

2nd. To present its wishes to the Council of Government so that, listening to the voice of the people and in the exercise of its functions with which it is empowered by the Constitution, the president of the Supreme Court of Justice may issue a call to take care of the supreme executive power by appointing two persons who must associate with him, in accordance with Article 97.

3rd. To respect and protect all the legitimately constituted authorities in their free exercise of their attributed powers.

4th. That the garrison of this Capital, without participating in any administrative act, but maintaining at all costs order and public tranquility and opposing the entry of any force which might come to prevent the present announcement, will remain assembled until the arrival of the Army of Reserve.

5th. That this act be circulated to the honorable legislators and governors of the States.

(Signed)

General Luis Quintanar
and others

_____

Lorenzo de Zavala, Ensayos historicos, 305-308; Riva Palacio, Mexico a traves de los siglos, IV, 224, n.; Suarez y Navarro, Historia de Mexico, 180, n-181,n; El Astro Moreliano, 28 December, 1929

* * * * *

PLAN OF AYACAPIXTLA

27 December, 1829.

The generals, commanders, and officers undersigned and who belong to the federal army of operations being met in a council of war on this date, and bearing in mind:

227

THAT as subordinates of the supreme government of the nation they have marched this far in obedience to orders of their superiors:

THAT [the supreme government] no longer exists as a consequence of the pronouncement of the capital of the nation:

THAT His Excellency Sr. D. Vicente Guerrero declared that he would separate himself from the Army, according to a notice given in a note of the 25th of the present month:

THAT the general opinion of the same army is in agreement with that of the reserve, and if this had not been manifest earlier, it was on account of blind obedience to the government.

THAT its silence any longer would lead to anarchy. They have agreed to the following:

Art. 1. To adhere to the Plan declared in Jalapa the fourth of the present month to support the Constitution and the laws.

Art. 2. To support the present government at all cost.

Art. 3. To recognize formally the government established in the capital of the federation.

Art. 4. That notice of this determination be given to His Excellency Sr. Vice-President D. Anastasio Bustamanate in order that he may dispose of this force as may be necessary.

Art. 5. That the General of Brigade D. Ignacio de Mora remains invested as General-in-Chief of this army.

(Signed) Ignacio de Mora
Gen. of Brigade Jose Velazquez.

V. Riva Palacio, Mexico a traves de los siglos, IV, 230.

* * * * *

PLAN OF DEPUTY D. ANASTASIO ZERECERO

24 February, 1830

[After a survey of recent developments, the Deputy continues:] Let us all proclaim federation; let us swear again the observances of the federal pact, and let this oath be as a sign of our reconciliation and our alliance. Let us forget mutually our errors; let us give ourselves a fraternal embrace [abrazo], and all united, let us strive for the welfare and solid happiness of the nation. Here are the objectives which comprise the propositions which I have the honor to present to the Chamber and to which I submit them for its deliberation.

1st. The Plan which was pronounced in Jalapa by the Army of Reserve on December 4th, 1829, is approved in accordance with the literal terms of its articles.

2nd. Consequently, in accordance with Articles 1 and 2, and 3 of the said Plan, the form of a popular representative federal government as adopted by the nation shall be maintained and preserved at all costs, thus sustaining scrupulously the Constitution sanctioned on the 4th of October, 1824.

3rd. The Legislatures of the States shall busy themselves immediately with initiation of amendments which they may deem suitable for the federal constitution, assembling for this purpose those who have not been brought together. The executive shall also make reforms in administration which it may deem convenient, issuing the laws or decrees which may be necessary for that purpose and shall urge informed persons to write on the subject of consitutional reform.

4th. In every State, district, and territory they shall solemnly swear again to support the federal Constitution of the year 1824.

5th. The executive of the Union shall impose the solemnity of the oath with respect to the District and the territories. In the State it will be regulated by the governors. The Army shall take the same solemn oath, every corps doing so before its own flags or banners.

6th. No one shall be molested nor harmed for the public opinions he may have manifested by word, by writing, or by actions until the publication of this law.

(Signed)

Anastasio Zerecero

J. M. Bocanegra, Memorias, II, 242-243.

* * * * *

PLAN OF CODALLOS

11 March, 1830

The undersigned Commanders and Officers, seeing that some military men, under the pretext of the Constitution, laws, and public opinion have converted themselves with impunity into transgressors against the sovereignty of the States, legitimately proclaimed in their honorable legislatures and Governors, without any other right than that of the bayonet, seeing the felony with which the good faith of the people has been deceived, that being zealous of the national pact celebrated in 1824 were deceived by the Plan of Jalapa, which seemed to guarantee said pact, but not having been carried out, have found out that when the authors cannot reach the end which they proposed under the auspicies of the Constitution and laws at the time it was proclaimed, they were violating these same laws, appealing to public opinion and establishing themselves as their own regulators, it being common knowledge that any bold man is able to seduce some troops accustomed to uprising, or with the part of the unwary people who are in favor of innovations that perhaps they do not understand, he overcomes the authorities, removes them from their positions and observes also that no energetic measure is taken to maintain the integrity of the federation as involved in the interesting [areas] of California and the fertile lands of beautiful Texas and in the peninsula of Yucatan. It is demonstrated that the present governors have a part in those events or at least that the fear of losing their prey is more important for their interests than national independence and the form of government adopted and freely sworn to by all the people; in fact, convinced that under this state of affairs the nation find itself at the critical moment of losing its political existence which so many and great sacrifices have cost the Mexicans, we have firmly resolved to sacrifice ourselves in favor of the Nation, sustaining at all costs the following Plan.

1st. The honorable legislatures of the States, their Governors and other public authorities who have been divested of their positions since the 4th of December last shall be immediately installed to their former places as existed on that date.

2nd. The august general Congress, in accordance with the Constitution, shall not concern itself with matters which have been dealt with or that may arise regarding the validity of the deputies and governors of the States, as these matters pertain to the previous administration, and it shall only see to it that the acts of these [bodies] do not oppose the general laws.

3rd. The general government shall with all energy lend all the help of its resources to the States, so that in due time the previous articles will be effected, and should they not do so, the responsible persons shall be judged as traitors to the system of the Federation.

4th In the same manner shall be judged all the public employees who should act against the Plan.

5th. The August Congress of the Union, as soon as it is free from the coercion under which it has passed laws and decrees against both their principles and the Constitution, shall decide regarding the person who legitimately should assume the Presidency; and if it should judge an absolute necessity for the welfare of the people, to effect a new presidential election, it may do so.

6th. As soon as the national sovereignty shall adopt this present Plan, part of the permanent army shall be destined to Yucatan, Texas, and the other frontiers of the Republic in order to maintain its integrity; and the other part shall withdraw from the capital to the points where the sovereign Congress deems convenient, so that its deliberations can be effected with absolute freedom.

7th. Until the corps of the Army are sufficiently far away in the opinion of the general Congress, it shall not deliberate on the person who should be the legitimate president or regarding the new elections.

8th. As soon as a Commander of the highest rank or of greater seniority than the undersigned presents himself, he being worthy of the trust of the troops supporting this pronouncement, he will be given command of the army.

9th. The army sustaining the sovereignty of the States will be named: the "Federal Mexican [Army]", which respects the authorities, the people and properties of the citizens, punishing severely those who rise up against it.

10th. If, as it is expected, the government of the Union adopts this Plan, the States shall form a coalition to sustain their sovereignty by establishing a provisional government until the federal system is established in all its purity.

11th. A copy of this Plan will be remitted to the august Chambers of the Union, to His Excellency the Vice-President, to the honorable legislatures of the States, to its worthy governors, to the general commanders of Division for approval and adherence.

(Signed)
Juan Jose Codallos
General   Headquarters,
Fortress of Santiago a Barrabas

Suarez y Navarro, Historia de Mexico, 207-208.
Riva Palacio, Mexico a traves de los siglos, IV,
238, n.

* * * * *

NATIONAL NOTICE: STATE OF SAN LUIS POTOSI

13 March, 1830

[A brief headline insists: "Not a pronouncement
of the State of San Luis Potosi." A lengthy
introduction (over two pages, double column) surveys
the continuing Mexican crisis, reports on the impact
of the declaration of Jalapa on December 4, 1829, and
then asks support for the following nine articles as
the basis for national action.]

Introduction: The State of San Luis [Potosi] asks
His Excellency the Vice-President of the Republic
that its territory not be occupied by other troops of
the Federation that those which inspire confidence
for its quiet and its sovereignty.

Art. 1. It asks all the Republic to express its wish
upon the necessity which there is [for reform] and
for the reforms of the constitution whereby one
person should be named by each legislature, and
designating one place for the meeting in the Villa de
Leon in order that this great commission should draft
the measures and that they should be passed to the
respective legislatures so that they can examine them
and adopt them by the right of initiative, provided
that they judge them [properly] framed.

Art. 2. The principal bases of the council [junta] of
commissioners of the States for the reforms of the
constitution shall be: that of simplifying the system

233

in such a way that complications between the Union
and its integral parts will be avoided; to assure
with firmer guarantees than exist today the
sovereignty of the States and their indissoluble
union; to declare in a precise way that the federal
powers cannot impose a contribution upon a citizen of
the States.

Art. 3. Also the Council of Commissioners shall
concern itself with presenting projects in order that
the Federal treasury may not exist in the present
disorder, in simplifying the system, in adopting the
many economies that the nation is calling for
without, through this measure, damaging the rights
and the fortune of private individuals.

Art. 4. In order to avoid disputes between parties
over whether the Legislative Chambers have the
freedom to act, and over whether the laws passed from
January of the current year to the present date were
forced out by violence from deputies intimidated by
force, they being unaccustomed to the rabble, it is
requested of the sovereign congress of the Union that
it move its residence and in some free spot there
deliberate upon this project without an appeal to
arms, no matter from what quarter they may come.

Art. 5. It is also asked of the sovereign congress
that it not take into consideration any subject until
it shall have moved its residence.

Art. 6. It is asked of His Excellency the
Vice-President that he remove the minister of
[foreign] relations and of war on account of the old
opinions of these men, against the present system of
government, they not having given evidence that they
have foresworn them; and on account of the measures,
direct and indirect, which they have transmitted in
order to disorganize the States, and to facilitate
the shift to centralism, and because they do not
merit the public confidence of federalists. It is
also requested that election of ministers should
devolve upon citizens who, in the years '23 and '24
publicly stated their opinions in favor of a federal
administration.

Art. 7. His Excellency the Vice-President is asked to revoke the order to send the civil militia of the State to Texas, because it is contrary to the authorization number 11 of Article 110 of the general constitution.

Art. 8. Protest is hereby made against every accord or proviso which may tend to weaken the foregoing requests while they have not been rejected by the majority of the legislatures and as they were found before the pronouncement of the Army of Reserve or through deliberation of the chambers, they being quite free and outside the District.

Art. 9. Let the above be printed and communicated with an official appeal to the Legislatures and the Governors of the State to urge them to accept [the provisions above], and with respectful memoranda let the above be sent to the Chambers as the sort of initiative that falls within its scope, and to His Excellency the Vice-President for his attention to that which concerns his [authority].

El Astro Moreliano, 25 March, 1830.

* * * * *

PLAN OF JALAPA

24 September, 1830

At the Mesa de Serrato on the 24th of September 1830: Gathered at the quarters of Brigadier General Don Juan Jose Codallos, General Commander of the Vanguard Division of the Mexican Federal Army, the leaders of the three sections which make up the said Division, a Captain, a Lieutenant, and a sub-lieutenant for each of them, and a Sergeant and a Corporal for these ranks: with the object of dealing as a Junta of War with matters pertaining to the welfare and prosperity of the Nation by placing her under the auspices of the Federal system in all its fullness. For such a great enterprise it was necessary to discuss and to agree upon the manner of removing some of the obstacles which made war unending and delayed the consolidation of the system of Government adopted by the free and express will of the Mexican Nation. It was agreed first to appoint a Secretary since the stated one from the Division was indisposed; therefore the appointment fell by unanimous vote on the Commissioner of War Capitan D. Nicolas Jalisco. The presiding General spoke in the following terms: Comrades-in-Arms--we are not factious as with impunity we are called by the Serviles, because those who are under that name are the ones who took up arms without principles or system. What a difference! We, yes, we have taken them up for the most just of causes, and our operations have as a basis a Plan of Salvation which adopted and sworn to shall always be as a model for others. Already you have seen [the Plan] and it is engraved in our hearts; but in order to recall it, you have it within view and it is with this object that I have summoned you to a Junta of War. Its articles are well thought out and guarantee our ends, but the circumstances have induced me to present some additional articles which will consolidate the future peace which we hope for. Look at them; examine them, and with the frankness of Republican Comrades each of you give your opinion. Then, being in agreement with the stated principles, I shall have the satisfaction of adding my own.

The preceding objectives which the Junta had to deal with being thus expressed, the project of additional articles to the Plan proclaimed by the Federal Army in Sirandaro on the 11th of March of the current year was read and placed for discussion, and after a long debate was approved by acclamation as follows:

1st. All employees and authorities who in the present circumstances may have become unworthy of the public trust are exempted from the situation foreseen in Article No. 10 of our Plan, thus protecting directly or indirectly the Plan of Jalapa.

2nd. No individual who may have been known as a Centralist shall obtain any employment in the

Republic, he being likewise excluded from any votes, active or passive, in elections.

3rd. All Commanders and officers will be separated from the military who, on being approached by any party of the Town, Capital, or countryside where they may be, do not join them, abandoning the ranks of the dissidents; they become included in this warning as soon as they take up arms against the federal Army, and have liberty to verify their joining within the peremptory period of twenty-four hours subsequent to both forces being advised.

4th. The leaders of the parties will suffer the same persecution, who, being cited to join, should defect from them without a just motive which prevents them, and those whose omission should give a margin for the loss of an action or by ruining a project ordered by the commanders of the Division.

5th. As soon as the Federated Army starts to occupy the Towns and States where there should be dissident forces the Commanders who occupy the said places will effect a punctual fulfillment of the laws of general expulsion of the Spaniards, guarding them while plans for their disembarcation from the Republic are completed.

6th. The Federal Army will not lay down their weapons until after having completed the total expulsion of the Spaniards and after having realized to the letter the articles of this Plan and the additions to it.

7th. These additions shall be communicated to the Chambers of the Union, to the Legislatures and Governments of the States, to constitutional City Councils, and to the General Commanders of the dissident troops.

8th. The same communication shall be sent to His Excellency, the President General and to the Commanders of the Mexican Federal Army for their due information and compliance.

The matter thus ended, this act was signed by the Commanders, officers, Sargeants, and Corporals chosen by their sections according to the general and special orders of yesterday, to which I testify.

(Signed)
Juan J. Codallos et al.

Original manuscript, #4735, Library, University of Texas.

* * * * *

PLAN OF THE CONSPIRACY OF THE DEPUTY GONDRA

1 November, 1830

The Junta in charge of directing the operations of the patriots in the glorious revolution whose object is to re-establish public affairs to the state which they were in the month of November 1829 have discussed and agreed to the following Plan, which must be observed by all the friends of the legitimacy of the residency, His Excellency Major-General D. Vicente Guerrero and of his government, which plan is revised and approved by the said Excellency.

1st. In every state of the Federation there shall be a Junta [or committee] composed of five individuals, which will communicate with that of Mexico [City]. These juntas will be called minors, and shall be subjected to those of Mexico, which will be denominated the major junta of approval [junta mayor de aprobaciones]. The individuals who compose them shall be appointed by the major junta [junta mayor], and they will be sent the regulations which must rule them.

2nd. The object of the minor juntas shall be of directing opinion in favor of the reaction, executing punctually and promptly in whatever the major junta shall order. They shall be to get acquainted with individuals and their opinions, appointing some more interested assistants in the towns who will put into practice what the major junta directs and will communicate with them.

3rd. No minor junta of a state shall communicate with that of another, and to avoid this communication the major junta shall not advise to any one about the others in any case whatsoever nor for any pretext whatsoever.

4th. The minor juntas shall observe the same conduct with their assistants whom they may appoint in the towns, being careful that they are not known among themselves and that the ones of the same town are not aware of the existence of their comrades, but that each one should believe himself to be the only one commissioned.

5th. This secret will make impracticable the discovery of individuals involved in case that our glorious revolution should be discovered.

6th. To each one of the persons appointed for the minor juntas and for the assistants of the same an oath shall be demanded of them of never divulging in any case whatsoever the people whom they may know, if they should be discovered by accident.

7th. The minor juntas shall not know who belongs to the major junta, and maintaining the same order, the assistants shall have no knowledge of the one who belong to the minor juntas.

8th. Every person of the major junta shall try to enlist three individuals, charging them to enlist others each one more, advising themselves mutually of having done so, but without naming who they are. The minor juntas will do the same.

9th. In no case whatsoever shall the names of those involved be investigated as it is enough to know their numbers. This precaution will always be maintained by the revolution so that in case of a denunciation very few shall be discovered, even if they break their oaths which will be demanded of them.

10th. The particular tasks of the major junta will be directed to taking over the capital of Mexico. In order to obtain it, it will avail itself of every means it believes necessary, no matter how costly they may be, and in exchange for whatever sacrifice.

11th. The people, in order to obligate themselves, need to feel and to see the benefit which they will obtain. The major junta, and in its case the minor ones, will allow and offer them the wealth and properties of some certain individuals, while trying, in some way to save [the possessions] of those who favor our just revolution.

12th. Once the capital of Mexico is taken the minor juntas shall be advised by special messengers so that they can put into effect their movement in the manner that will be indicated to them and to the governors of the states so that they can acknowledge and recognize whoever shall be placed in Mexico [City] again.

13th. His Excellency D. Vicente Guerrero shall be called immediately to occupy the Presidency.

14th. Until this gentleman can reach Mexico [City] the leadership of the government will be assumed by D. Jose Maria Bocanegra, as he is the person to whom His Excellency D. Vicente Guerrero had left in charge when he placed himself at the head of the army which was to sustain the rights of the people.(1)

15th. In case that D. Jose Maria Bocanegra should not

---

(1) An early draft read: "While the general legislature is coming together and deciding about matters relating to the Presidency and in accord with the wishes which the towns have indicated, command shall fall upon D. Guadalupe Victoria, the current president and general of Division."

want to take the leadership, it will be given to the first chief of the three who are to be at the head of the patriots for the taking of the capital.

16th. All acts directed against our glorious revolution after the capture of Mexico [City] will be considered as an action against the liberty of the country, and he who by any means should be opposed to the consummation of such an interesting enterprise shall be punished as a traitor.

17th. The congress shall meet immediately and will mainly occupy itself in re-establishing public affairs to the state they had in November 1829.

18th. Therefore, the legislatures of the states which may have suffered alteration or reformation shall be re-established to the same situation they were in on the above mentioned date.

19th. The [civilian] employees who find themselves discharged by the present government by virtue of retirement, resignation, or violent separation, shall be restored to their positions, and if those who have resigned should not want to return, they shall ratify their resignations, and in this case the administration shall provide for their replacement.

20th. None of the employees who voluntarily continue serving in the present government(2) shall stay in their positions. These will be replaced by individuals who have made some service in the present revolution.

21st. All the Commanders and officers of the army, both those in the permanent corps a well as the active ones who declared themselves in favor of the Plan of Jalapa, shall be retired with absolute

---

(2) An earlier draft of December 1827 read, "None of the employees who belong or have belonged to the Scottish Rite without having been initiated into the York Rite before this pronouncement shall remain."

furlough, effecting indictments of the principal
leaders so that the penalty may be applied in
accordance with the [military] ordinance.

22nd. The permanent and active corps shall be
dissolved; the commanders and officers who did not
rise up before Sr. Guerrero retreated to the south
shall enjoy the payment which by ordinance belongs to
them.

23rd. The corps of the civil militia shall compose
the Mexican army.

24th. These corps shall be divided into two classes:
one of which will be called the permanent civil
militia [milicia civica fija] which will not be able
to leave its town without a permit from the congress.
The other one will be called the civil militia of the
coasts [militia civica de las costas]; this militia
will be composed of the soldiers and sergeants who
today form the permanent and active corps, and never
under any pretext whatsoever (unless due to a sudden
invasion whose number cannot be resisted) can they be
in the interior towns nor in any other place further
away from the coast than seven leagues. The permanent
civil militia shall be composed wholly of citizens
whom the city councils should name and those not
appointed shall contribute with an amount in
proportion to their salaries.

25th. The Commanders and officers of these corps
shall be appointed from those in the present
revolution who have declared in favor of the
legitimacy of the presidency of Sr. Guerrero, and
whether they be of the permanent civilian militia or
of those of the coast they shall enjoy the salary
which the permanent [army] enjoys today.

. . . .

[The text of the Plan of this conspiracy was
published by opponents of the plan. Two paragraphs
warn that the plot may still be active.]

This Plan with a difference of some words in one

242

or another article was discussed and approved in the so-called Grand Lodge of the Mexican Nation on the 27th of July, 1818, to make war against the government in favor of the presidency of Sr. Guerrero, as long as another who is not this ex-general be elected. The same Plan with some alterations which have been indicated in some articles seem to guide us in their present purposes. This belief is based upon seeing how few of the conspirators were discovered or compromised in a revolution which must have been widespread. It is assumed that they act with impudence and it can be said with satisfaction.

We give this material to the public with two purposes: the first, so that the governors do not assume that there are few revolutionaries and be neglectful, satisfied with their disorganization and insignificant number. It may not be so and one being careless may bring upon the republic great misfortune; the second, so that the military men of the permanent army may know that since the year 1828 it was being schemed to destroy it and to condemn the soldiers and sargeants to live on the beaches, so to end their existence with the rigor of the unhealthy and mortal climates. The permanent army is the target against which the factions and friends of disorder are fighting. They hate it because it is composed of honest friends of law and order. Soldiers, do not let yourselves be deceived by those who think only of destroying you!

Broadside, New York Public Library

* * * * *

DECLARATION OF THE GARRISON OF VERA CRUZ

2 January, 1832

In the heroic city of Vera Cruz on the second of January, 1832, being gathered together the commanders and officers of this garrison and that of the fortress of Ullua, in the house of Colonel D. Pedro Landero, having been previously called by the general

commander D. Cirianco Vasquez, taking into
consideration the political situation of the
Republic, threatened by the most bloody revolution by
the notorious and repeated actions of the enemies of
our institutions and personal guarantees, and the sad
and dangerous alternative of the federation being
exposed to suffer the most ominous yoke or feel the
bad effects of the horrors of anarchy, and
particularly this City, justly alarmed by the
insidiousness of ambition, they agreed to the
following:

THAT the protection dispensed by the ministry is
constant, whether in their newspapers or in any other
obvious ways against the assaults committed against
the Constitution, [against] public guarantees or
individuals, and that very soon the ruin of the
system of the agents of the ministries will be
consummated as soon as this city falls to its
intrigues, as these things were unfortunately very
near and in that case the sacrifices of free Mexicans
would have been in vain;

THAT on the other hand the horrible revolution which
was being prepared in various States of the
Federation to which His Excellency General D. Antonio
Lopez de Santa Anna and other leaders of this
garrison were being invited would be so much more
terrible when it had penetrated throughout the
present administration which would certainly produce
the increase of evils instead of cutting or modifying
the ones we are against;

THAT it was evident that the ministry was hated and
that everywhere public opinion was voiced against
their management without obtaining anything but the
persistence of these officers in their errors and
injustices;

THAT it is also known that His Excellency the
Vice-President had manifested being firm in the midst
of these vicissitudes in favor of the system that
governs us, and that he had avoided many times the
progress of the passions of the ministry;

THAT if His Excellency had not removed his secretaries the state of isolation to which the ministerial maneuvers would have reduced him with respect to which he was led to believe that the party of the ministry was only one that the current administration counted upon, and if the secretaries were to be removed the Vice-President would have no support. Meanwhile the anarchists would involve the nation in the most disasterous disorder;

THAT to remedy such enormous and extraordinary evils this garrison should look for a means between the extremes, renewing its vows of maintaining at all costs the Constitution and the laws proclaimed in the Plan of Jalapa. The present Vice-President of whom it shall be requested energetically, in accordance with Article 4 of the said Plan, the removal of a ministry against which public opinion has pronounced itself and that it only inspires the distrust of the friends of the constitutional order and of the individual rights; and that finally, it was convenient that His Excellency the General Santa Anna be invited to place himself at the head of this garrison if he adopts these principles with which he would calm the jeopardy of the States and of all Mexicans, excited and angry because of seeing very near the fatal day in which they will be reduced to slavery or in which they will precipitated to the abyss of anarchy, but seeing the ministry replaced by men of prestige and righteousness, the calm of the spirits will be re-established as well as the trust of the people, the moral force in the government and the respect of the constitution and the laws, the only anchor which may save us from revolutions and consequent evils in the present year;

THAT the supreme magistrate of the Republic ought to be renewed in an epoch always full of agitations in all nations in which the public power is elected.

All being in unanimous agreement with all that declared by the commanders and officers who undersign herewith, and after explaining in detail the fundamentals of these principles, they declared the following:

1st. The garrison of Vera Cruz renews its vows made for the Plan of Jalapa, of maintaining at all costs their oaths for the observance of the federal constitution and the laws.

2nd. To request of His Excellency, the Vice-President, the dismissal of the ministry whom public opinion accuses of protecting Centralism and tolerators of all the attempts committed against the civil freedom and individual rights.

3rd. Two commanders of this garrison will be commissioned to present this resolution to His Excellency General D. Antonio Lopez de Santa Anna, and to implore His Excellency that, being in agreement with it, to please come to this city to take command of the troops.

4th. In this event the garrison will abstain from any course of action and from taking any further steps in this respect because His Excellency General Santa Anna should issue this declaration and any dispositions which he may deem convenient to His Excellency the Vice-President and to the other authorities of the Federation and of the States, issuing all other convenient providences so that the laudable wishes of those undersigned may be accomplished.

And having all expressed their conformity to the expressed article, the following were appointed to present them to His Excellency, General Santa Anna.

(Signed)

Ciriaco Vasquez, General commander of
the City, and others.

Suarez y Navarro, Historia de Mexico, 263-265, n.

* * * * *

PLAN DE LERMA

27 April, 1832

The proclamation of General Inclan, and the articles for which he pronounced are the following:

All the misfortunes which at present involve the Republic originate in the mistaken direction that in Jalapa was started as the national movement and was promoted by the Army in Reserve. There it was sworn with solemnity and universal happiness to re-establish the rule of the Constitution which had been destroyed by the events that overthrew the legal order of the election which fell on General Manuel G. Pedraza as first magistrate of the nation. Nobody thought that the administration which then existed on being destroyed the same vices of illegitimacy which had occasioned its ruin would continues, because at last the revolution could not justify itself against the government which then ruled the Republic, but was due to the lack of legal title with which it had been installed. Of course not even its aberrations in the exercise of power had been so serious that no other hope of remedy was left than the dangerous resort to use of weapons, nor can the destructive principle of all social order be admitted or that any fault of the governors authorizes its subjects to withdraw its obedience and resist them by force. The illegitimacy, therefore, with which General Guerrero achieved the Presidency of the Republic was the only reason which called for the proclamation of Jalapa; the justice of which was acknowledged by all the nation and confirmed by the general Congress. As a consequence of this, the legitimately elected President should have been called, and that it be declared admissible by the competent authority to proceed to new elections to return to the constitutional course from the point where it was lost. This was not, unfortunately, the conduct of the directors of the said movement in the exaltation of a triumph due to the simultaneous agreement of all the nation. They did nothing but substitute one nullity for another, and believing that with the prestige of power it would be easy to dazzle the sight of those who were nearer to observe.

They, themselves, elected themselves in a government hidden behind a General who wanted to lend his name to the working of a new usurpation with which it was not possible that the nation could conform. The disastrous war of the South was the first effect of the mistakes to which the proclaimers of Jalapa allowed themselves to be led. As General Guerrero, who had just been substituted, placed himself at the head of the dissidents, it was not difficult for the government to give to its enterprise an aspect of personality, as if it were only a matter of re-establishing a man whose fate should not have prevailed upon the opinion of all the nation. In support of this pretext a war was maintained for a long time; it would have continued if the most horrible treason that the world has ever known had not occurred; if it had not arisen to put an end to something more fatal than the war itself. The nation found that its dearest interests were compromised at the hands of a government which had showed itself a frank oppressor of all the principles of morality and decency. Public indignation was heard from everywhere until it broke out into a declared war which can only be concluded with the real observance of the constitution. If the leader of Vera Cruz is sincere in his protestations, he will agree to the necessity of making the government of the Republic legitimate, which is the only way of returning to the course of order; but if, as it is supposed by his enemies, that he only moves based on his personal aims, this is the best occasion to discover it, and the nation, anxious for peace and quiet, will gather its strength to frustrate his liberty-killing plans. The troops which I have the honor of commanding, being convinced of this truth, they have agreed to effect the following declarations:

1. The oath of obedience to the constitution and the general laws are ratified.

2. Consequently no other government is recognized as legitimate except that one which, in accordance with the constitution itself, was elected in 1828.

3. This determination shall be officially communicated to the present government of Mexico and

to General Santa Anna; and if there should be opposition on behalf of one or the other party, it shall be fought with weapons until the Republic is put in complete enjoyment of its rights.

4. As long as there is a common agreement on the terms that are arranged to carry into effect what is indicated in Article No. 2, this Division will maintain perfect neutrality, without helping any of the belligerent parties.

Lerna, State of Toluca.

(Signed)
Ignacio Inclan

Suarez y Navarro, Historia de Mexico, 284.

* * * * *

DECLARATION OF VERA CRUZ

5 July, 1832

In the heroic city of Vera Cruz, on the 5 of July 1832, gathered therein the commanders and officers of this garrison and that of the fortress of Ullua, in the house of Colonel Ciriaco Vasquez, with the object of determining their opinions on the methods which may be most suitable so that the verification of the re-establishment of the Constitution and laws may be secured. I refer on behalf of the said garrisons to the memorable day of January 2nd last, and in order that the peace of the Republic may be firmly established on solid and indestructible bases, they began to deal with this so interesting subject with the required thoroughness. It was unanimously agreed to re-establish the dominion of the Constitution and laws in a positive way, differing therefore from the one followed by the authors of the Plan of Jalapa, who, with the most unheard of perfidy, invoked only these sacred names in order to invest themselves with power, quench their vengance, making Mexican blood run in torrents in the field and on the scaffolds, and to systematize the hardest and worst tyranny. It is indispensable to legalize the Executive in accordance with the same principles which sustain these garrisons and other troops and towns which have adhered to their insurrection. They also agreed that this measure is all the more necessary and urgent because of the tyrannical and usurping power which is called government. It precipitates itself every day in further outrages against public freedom and individual guarantees. On this matter they bore in mind the criminal means which the referred usurping power adopted in order to answer the just petition of January 2nd, causing new losses in the fortunes, new shedding of blood, new mournings and tears in the families, and new evils of all kind in society, of greater or more fatal consequences than that experienced by the war of the south. It was also borne in mind that the bad faith and immorality of the same usurping power are more obvious every day, the proof of which is the apparent removal of the ministry which it held out only as a trap for the imbeciles and the unwary, because far from forming a ministry again with persons who deserve the public trust because of their aptitude and known love for independence and federal institutions, there remained one of the senior secretaries, and the other secretaries are filled by upper echelon officers so that by this manner the Machiavellian policy and the tortuous ways continue without any alteration and are systematized by these people. Finally, a summary was read of new assaults against the freedom of the press, of persecutions, of infamous intrigues and other reprehensible acts which are well known to the public, all committed by the usurping power of January 2nd up to date. And totally convinced of the reality of what has been expressed, they agreed to draw up a new declaration of their feelings in order that His Excellency General-in-Chief Antonio Lopez de Santa Anna may be so kind as to take it into consideration for the next conference which is to be held on the National Bridge with their Excellencies D. Guadalupe Victoria and Sebastian Camacho, and their feelings are contained in the following articles:

1st. The garrisons of Vera Cruz and those of Ulua,

reiterating the protest which they made on January 2nd of the present year, once more call for its faithful observance, and that its Articles Nos. 84 and 85 be carried out as soon as possible.

2nd. That consequently there be separated from the Executive Power the person who is exercising it now, and that those designated by the same Constitution in its Articles Nos. 97 and 98 should begin to function until such time as the legitimate president may take possession of office.

And in conclusion, having agreed that at once a committee of five individuals of this Junta be appointed to place in the hands of His Excellency the General-in-Chief a copy of the present document, and implore him at the same time not to consent that any of the preceding articles be changed in any way, not only because in its exact accomplishment is the whole community interested, but because they show in an unmistakable manner the purity of the intentions of His Excellency as well as all of his subordinates.

Signed by officers of the two garrisons

Suarez y Navarro, Historia de Mexico, 309-310

* * * * *

PLAN OF THE STATE OF ZACATECAS

10 July, 1832

The Secretary of the Congress of the Free State of Zacatecas, considering: First: that when the States adopted the Plan proclaimed in Jalapa by the Army in Reserve, it was under the impression that through it the constitutional order of the Republic would be re-established. Second: That far from re-establishing the constitutional order as he had promised in his pronouncement, General Bustamante occupied the chair of the Presidency unconstitu-tionally, and that to maintain himself in [the chair] the fundamental charter has been violated several times.

Third: That to obtain the removal of this ministry a civil war has been necessary, which has caused lamentable damages. Fourth: That the war cannot cease except by giving the government a general constitutional character, and that it cannot have until His Excellency Manuel Gomez Pedraza is recognized as its legitimate president, [the person] who obtained in September 1829 the absolute majority of the votes of the States, and who has been already called by General Santa Anna and many commanders and officers to take possession of this office. It is hereby decreed:

1st. The State of Zacatecas recognizes as constitutional President of the Republic His Excellency Manuel Gomez Pedraza.

2nd. This recognition will continue in effect even if the Chamber of Deputies of the general Congress does not attest the votes omitted by the legislatures of the States in the year 1828 since it is unquestionable that General Pedraza obtained the absolute majority of said votes and he had the constitutional requisites at the time of elections, and considering the present representatives of the nation without the necessary freedom to concern themselves with this matter.

3rd. The government of the State will proceed with its foreign relations in conformity with this decree, and to maintain its position it can raise up to six thousand men of the civil militia and underwrite all the expenses judged necessary. The government [of the State] will be informed and it will see to the publishing, printing and circulation [of the Plan], and that it be duly complied with.

Given in the Chamber of Sessions of the honorable Congress of Zacatecas.

(Signed)

Antonio Eugenia de Gordoa,
Deputy President

Suarez y Navarro, Historia de Mexico, 312.

* * * * *

DECLARATION OF THE LIBERATING ARMY

7 November, 1832

Declaration of the Commanders and Officers who compose the Eleventh Division of the Liberating Army.

In the City of Merida, seventh day of the month of November, 1832, being met in a council of war under the presiding officer, Senor Colonel Don Francisco de Paula Toro, the commanders and officers who undersign and compose the garrison of this plaza and those of the Eleventh Liberating Group of the command of the same pronounced [their political opinions] on the 4th day in the towns of Tenabo, Jecetchakean, and Calkini, convinced of the following considerations:

Art. 1. That the political posture in which the Mexican Republic finds itself and to which the undersigned have the honor to belong imperiously demands a frank demonstration of opinion and sentiments in order to cooperate to bring an end to evils so serious as to weigh down in a destructive way upon the great interests of the country.

Art. 2. That being familiar even to the last bit of evidence with what is the unheard-of cause of public turmoil that has filled the soul of the Nation: the Federal constitution not being completed nor laws that regularly form the soul of every regularly organized State.

Art. 3. That being convinced that the unanimous vote of the Yucatecans is definitely against the administration that governs the State without enjoying the least expression of opinion through the usurpation of their constitutional rights that has been done to them, they have decided to support and to pronounce [their opposition to the Administration] in the Articles that are expressed below:

1) His Excellency Senor General Don Manuel Gomez Pedraza is the legitimate president of the Mexican nation.

2) General Don Anastasio Bustamante is not the constitutional Vice-President of the Republic.

3) The civil employees of this State and those of the Treasury of the Federation who in November, 1829, accepted their appointments through nomination of the Supreme Government, will be recognized.

4) Likewise all the employees of the State who in the same time span were legitimately named to their positions will be recognized in the class of provisionals.

5) The said Sr. Colonel D. Francisco de Paula Toro is recognized as commanding General of the State; he will be entrusted with the execution of the present declaration, a copy of which shall be sent to His Excellency General of Division D. Antonio Lopez de Santa Anna and placing this garrision under his orders as a part of the Liberating Army. With this done, matters were concluded, and the above was signed as written evidence of the same.

> (Signed) Francisco de Paula Toro and
> fellow officers.

El Panel, extra edition, no. 13, 11 November, 1832.

* * * * *

PLAN OF THE GOVERNMENT (1)

9 December, 1832

A project for the solid and stable peace of the United Mexican States, for the re-establishment of a truly national and federal administration.

1st. There shall be an absolute cessation of all kinds of hostilities.

---

(1) Sometimes called the Project for Pacification. A text issued on 13 December was marred by many errors in Composition.

2nd. All acts of popular elections made to nominate representatives for the general Congress, legislatures of the States which occurred in the Mexican federation from the 1st of September, 1828, until the day of publication of this Plan are covered forever with the sovereign mantle of the nation, and consequently the legitimacy or illegitimacy will not be dealt with anymore.

3rd. The governors of the States and the political leaders [jefes politicos] of the territories who are functioning as of today are authorized to adopt whatever provisions that they may deem convenient in the use of their sovereignty and to truly nationalize the government so that the towns of their respective demarcations may proceed with all the electoral acts necessary to carry out completely a new election for representatives to their legislatures, territorial deputies and the general Congress, acting in all possible ways in accordance with what is prescribed in the federal constitution and the laws of the States, with the understanding that for this time only they will elect the total number of representatives, as a general renovation must be carried out so that the nation may unquestionably return to its federal regime, following thereafter the dispositions for ordinary situations.

4th. All the new legislatures must be installed and be in open sessions by the 15th of February, 1833, or before if possible, and all and each one will proceed on March 1st, next, to elect for this time two senators and two persons for President and for Vice-President, remitting the results of the election of these two persons to the Secretary of Public Relations, giving their credentials to the appointed senators, so that they and the deputies may be in the capital of the Federation on the 26th of March.

5th. On the 25th of the same month the Chambers of the Union will be installed; on the 26th, both Chambers shall open the documents of election for President, and shall proceed thereafter in accordance with the federal constitution so that the election may be sanctioned and published not later than on

March 30th.

6th. Counting from eight days before the preliminary elections until the last ones mentioned in the articles Nos. 3 and 4 may be accomplished, there shall be no military force which is paid out of the national budget in the capitals of the States and territories, neither shall commanding generals reside in the said capitals during those days.

7th. The decree of October 12th of the current year regarding extraordinary faculties is revoked as well as the fatal law of the 27th of September 1823.

8th. The citizen General Manuel Gomez Pedraza shall be recognized as the legitimate President of the Republic up to April 1st, at which time the functions of the supreme magistrate of the nation must terminate in accordance with the fundamental law.

9th. As soon as it is installed the future Congress shall initiate an amnesty or a Law of Oblivion for all that has occurred from February 1st, 1828 until this day; by the said amnesty all shall remain guaranteed in their legal rights which they currently possess, and for no event or happening of those past years can they be deprived of what they had before the issue of this decree, and while this amnesty is conceded everyone shall maintain the position which they enjoyed on that day without the least change.

10th. The citizen General-in-Chief of the Liberating Army, Antonio Lopez de Santa Anna, under the investiture and command of power with which he has been trusted by the States which have pronounced together with the citizen General Manuel Gomez Pedraza, by mutual accord propose the present project of peace and order, and they pledge their work of honor to execute it exactly, if it should be accepted.*

(Signed)

Puente de Mexico   Manuel Gomez Pedraza

                          Antonio Lopez de Santa Anna

Suarez y Navarro, Historia de Mexico, 359-360.

* An issue of the Plan four days later carried the additional proviso:

SINCE it may well happen that at the date of this Plan some States may find that they have two governors at the same time, the authority granted to these functionaries ought to be exercised by the magistrate who is recognized by the majority of the people of the State over which he presides.

* * * * *

PLAN OF ZAVALETA

23 December, 1832

Gathered in the hacienda of Zavaleta, the generals Antonio Gaona, Mariano Arista, and Colonel Lino Alcorta, commissioned on behalf of His Excellency General-in-Chief Anastasio Bustamante; and the generals Juan Pablo Anaya, Gabriel Valencia, and Ignacio Basadre on behalf of their Excellencies President of the United States of Mexico, Manuel Gomez Pedraza and General-in-Chief Antonio Lopez de Santa Anna, to come to a suitable agreement regarding the project proposed by the two last mentioned generals, on the 9th of the present month, to His Excellency General Anastasio Bustamante and to the generals, commanders, and officers of the division under his command. Their respective powers-of-attorney having been checked and found correct, and after having read the decree of the general Congress of the 8th instant, which neither approves nor disapproves the contents of the said project, and in compliance with the 6th Article of the armistice celebrated on the 11th instant between the belligerent division, and using the authority for modifying, reforming, adding or taking out what they judge convenient and useful for the welfare of the people, by virtue of the full powers with which they are invested and with mutual consent have agreed to the following articles:

1st. The army pledges, as proof of its good faith, to maintain in all its integrity and purity the system of popular representative federal republican government as is designated in the constituent act of the federal Constitution and that of the individual States.

2nd. To be protected forever beneath the sovereign mantle of the Nation are all the acts of popular elections designed for the appointment of representatives for the general Congress and the legislatures of the States as they have occurred in the Mexican Federation from September 1st, 1828, to the day of the publication of this Plan; and therefore their legitimacy or illegitimacy shall not be dealt with further.

3rd. In the use of their sovereignty and in order to nationalize the government the governors of the States and the political leaders [jefes Politicos] of the territories which are functioning as of today are authorized to adopt as many provisos as they may deem convenient in order that the towns of their respective demarcations may proceed to all the electoral acts necessary in order to verify completely a new election of representatives in their legislatures, territorial deputations, and general Congress, arranging everything as closely as possible to what is prescribed in the federal Constitution, the individual constitutions and laws of the States which are in force up to the date of this Plan, it being understood that for this time only they will elect in full the total number of representatives, since a general renovation must be effected in order that the Nation may unquestionably return to its federal regime, continuing henceforth in accordance with the dispositions for ordinary cases.

4th. All the legislatures should be installed and in open session by February 15, 1833, or before if possible, and each and every one shall proceed on March 1st next to elect for this time two senators, and two persons for the President and Vice-President, remitting the minutes of the election to the Secretary of Public Relations and shall grant their credentials to the two senators appointed so that they and the deputies may be in the city of the Federation on March 20th.

5th. On the 25th of the same month the legislative Houses of the Union shall be installed; on the 26th both Chambers shall meet in order to open the documents of the acts of election of President and Vice-President, and they will proceed with the rest in accordance with the federal Constitution, in order that the election may be sanctioned and published by March 30th at the latest.

6th. The citizen Manuel Gomez Pedraza shall be recognized as the legitimate President of the Republic up to the 1st of April, on which day the functions of the supreme magistrate of the nation must terminate, in accordance with the fundamental law.

7th. As it could happen that on the date of this Plan there may be some States in which two governors might be found, the attributions which Article 3 grants to those officers should be exercised by the magistrate who is recognized by the majority of the towns of the State over which he presides.

8th. The following initiatives for future national representation shall be effected through legal channels as soon as the legislative sessions are open:

1) That the general Congress shall sanction with its honorable authority this Plan by approving the necessity and the suitability of the extraordinary measures which have been adopted to save the nation from the dangerous crisis in which it finds itself, and in order to make legitimate the authorities

elected by the people, and in order to regularize constitutionally the general government in the forthcoming period of four years. 2) An amnesty for all that has occurred from September 1st, 1828, up to the present day. Under the said amnesty all those who have adopted this Plan or who may adopt it within the period pointed out in one of the following articles shall maintain the legal rights which they have today; and for no event whatsoever nor for any happening of those days can they be prejudiced in what they may have obtained before this Plan is published; and while the amnesty is granted those who are referred to in this article shall maintain the position in which they find themselves as of today without the slightest innovation. 3) [To amend] those [innovations] which the government may not judge convenient in order that the Army may be replaced in the organic law already decreed, and its necessities be provided for and everything directed so that the armed forces shall concur to insure independence, to strenghthen freedom and to see that the established regime is religiously observed. 4) The republishing of the decree of October 12th instant on the extra-ordinary authority of September 27th on conspirators submitted to the military jurisdiction, and that of the 14th and the 24th of April regarding desertion of officers.

9th. All employees and the grading of employment as granted by their Excellencies the General-in Chiefs of both belligerent forces will be subjected to the approval of competent authority.

10th. In the meantime under the amnesty which is granted as mentioned in the second part of the 8th Article, nobody shall be molested for the services rendered nor for opinions expressed during the revolution.

11th. All the individuals of the Army and employees of the Federation shall adopt the present plan of peace; any infringement of them shall be considered as an assault against the common welfare of the Nation; and both the general officers and private persons who, drawing a salary from the public budget,

should after four days move a distance of approx-
imately six leagues from their place of residence,
the forces which support the Plan may not join them,
and they shall be deprived of their employments in
accordance with the exception which we made to them
in Article 8.

12th. The retired and pensioned persons who should
not be considered competent to continue because they
have closed their careers shall be liable to the same
punishment if after four days have passed and they
should continue lending their services to the administration now existing in Mexico.

13th. His Excellency the President and their
Excellencies the Generals-in-Chief of both forces
shall circulate the present Plan to all the
authorities, be they civil or military, for their
exact compliance.

And as written evidence thereof, the generals and
the colonel mentioned above signed two copies of this
agreement and remitted them to the respective
Generals-in-Chief of both divisions for their
ratification.

(Signed)

Suarez y Navarro, Historia de Mexico, 362, n.

* * * * *

A PROJECT FOR THE POLITICAL REORGANIZATION OF
THE REPUBLIC

24 December, 1832

A project for the political reorganization of the
Republic which the constitutional legislature of
Zacatecas dispatches to the Honorable Congresses of
the United States of Mexico.

Art. 1. Each state of the Federation shall name two
commissioners.

Art. 2. The commissioners with which the prior Article deals shall meet at the place where His Excellency the President D. Manuel Gomez Pedraza resides and when those of at least three-fourths of the States have met, he shall convoke an extra-ordinary assembly to be composed of five deputies for each one of them, and elected popularly in accord with the laws that are in effect for these elections or according to those given by the respective authorities.

Art. 3. The day on which elections are to be held for deputies, the place and the day on which the assembly is to be held for deputies, the place and the day on which the assembly is to be installed, and the formula for the oath of office which its members are to take before commencing to exercise their functions shall be expressed in the call for a convocation. The assembly cannot be installed without the concurrence of at least three-quarters of its individuals.

Art. 4. The authority of the extraordinary assembly of representatives is:

First: To set, before anything else, the day when, in all the States, the elections for deputies and senators to the general Congress are to take place, as well as [elections] for President and Vice-President of the Republic.

Second: To count and to validate the vote which the President and the Vice-President may obtain, and to prescribe the formula of oath of office which these functionaries are to take. The validation should be reduced solely to examining to see whether those elected have or do not have the constitutional requisites.

Third: To make in the constitution the additions, suppressions, and modifications which experience and progress in understanding has shown to be necessary in order to consolidate the federal regime, to expedite its march and to make more effective the sovereignty, independence, and liberty of the States. In order to facilitate this with the legislatures

262

shall remit to the Assembly their initiatives on reforms within the time limit which it, itself, shall predetermine. The constitution being reformed as it may be, it shall be circulated to the States and those articles in it that are not accepted by an absolute majority of the legislatures shall not be considered sanctioned, and they shall not be published. Within four months after having been dispatched to the legislatures by the secretary of the Assembly, an authorized copy of the revised constitution as circulated by that secretary should be received with one of these two expressions placed by each Article: Accepted or Not Accepted.

Fourth: To frame a right of petition.

Fifth: To organize the Treasury of the Federation, and to set up rules for recognizing, liquidating, and classifying the public debt.

Sixth: To abolish the law of September 27th, 1823.

Art. 5. The Assembly should conclude its sessions within eight months, and if concluded within this period and if the votes of the legislatures on the revised constitution have not been received, [the Assembly] shall be recessed, and it shall not meet again save to compute the votes and to forward [the total] to the Administration so that it may be published as the approvals may indicate.

Art. 6. If, for any reason, the election of a President for April 1st shall not have been held or if the one elected shall not have been prompt to take possession of his office, the Assembly shall name three individuals who shall exercise the supreme power temporarily, and if the Assembly itself shall not have met, the body [junta] of commissioners shall make the nomination.

Art. 7. The body of commissioners shall cease in all its functions as soon as the Assembly is installed, and while the meeting of the later is being verified it shall serve as a consultive body to His Excellency the President D. Manuel Gomez Pedraza or to the three individuals in whom the supreme executive power may be temporarily placed, without the President or those who may take his place being obligated to consult it for opinions in all matters, nor to conform precisely to its judgment.

Art. 8. The Assembly shall not be able to concern itself with other subjects than those specified.

Art. 9. While the general constitution has not been revised according to Article 4, grant 3, everything compatable with this Plan remains in effect. Also, all that is in conformity with it--the general laws and the rules government debate, the Assembly being empowered in this latter instance to make additions or revisions.

(Signed)
Francisco Garcia
God and Liberty
Manuel G. Cosio
Citizen deputy secretaries

El Fanal, Vol. II, no. 22, 7 November, 1833.

* * * * *

PLAN OF COLONEL ESCALADA (1)

26 May, 1833

1st. This garrison pledges to sustain at all costs the holy Religion of Jesus Christ, the statutes and privileges [fueros] of the clergy and the Army, they being threatened by the intrusive authorities.

2nd. Consequently it proclaims as protector of this cause and as Supreme Chief of the Nation, the illustrious conqueror of the Spaniards, General D. Antonio Lopez de Santa Anna.

---

(1) General Gabriel Duran issued a practically identical Plan on June 1, 1833.

3rd. All acts of the intrusive governors, Amescua and Salgado, as well as the last elections held in this state are null.

4th. This [State] will be administered by a political leader [jefe politico] appointed by a Junta of the honest residents of this capital and shall last until the majority of the Nation should designate the bases of the political regeneration of the Republic.

5th. No persons shall be molested on account of political opinions which they may have had, and consequently they, their individual lives and their property shall be scrupulously respected.

(Signed)
Colonel Escalada

Mariano Arista, Resena historica, 80; V. Riva Palacio, Mexico a traves de los siglos, IV, 324.

* * * * *

PLAN OF GENERAL DURAN (1)

1 June, 1833

1st. This Division pledges to sustain the Catholic, Apostolic, and Roman Religion and the statutes and privileges [fueros] of the clergy and of the Army, which are threatened by the intrusive authorities.

2nd. It proclaims as protector of this cause and supreme magistrate of the Nation the illustrious conqueror of the Spaniards, General Antonio Lopez de Santa Anna.

3rd. All the acts emanating from the intrusive governor, Lorenzo Zavala, as well as the last elections held in the State are null.

(1) Except for an offer to soldiers to re-enlist, this plan is identical with that of Colonel Escalada.

4th. This [State] will be administered by its governor, His Excellency Sr. D. Melchor Muzquiz, and the council which existed when the former was overthrown and it shall continue until the political regeneration of the Nation [shall have been accomplished.]

5th. If, unfortunately, a bloody struggle should arise, the rights of war shall be maintained, and the commander or leader who infringes upon it or consents to its violation shall be treated as a murderer.

6th. The sargeants, corporals and retired or discharged soldiers who present themselves for service shall be received; they shall be paid for their previous time, as if they had just separated, continuing in their employments. The deserters who present themselves shall be pardoned and spared corporal punishment.

7th. The individuals of the local militia who should voluntarily present themselves shall be placed in the active class, if they should so wish.

8th. No person shall be molested on account of political opinions which they may have had, and consequently their personal security and their property shall be scrupulously respected.

S. Augustin Tialpan.   (Signed)
                               Gen. Gabriel Duran

Mariano Arista, Resena historica, 82.

* * * * *

PLAN OF GENERAL ARISTA (1)

8 June, 1833

In the city of Huejoingo, on the 8th of June, 1833, there being gathered all the Commanders and

---

(1) Also called "Plan of Huejocingo"

266

officers of the Protector Army of Religion and Privileges [fueros] at the quarters of its General-in-Chief D. Mariano Arista, in order to endorse the insurrection that the forces of which it is composed was verified at the entrance of Ameca on the 6th instant. The said General stated to the Junta the sad circumstances in which the Nation finds itself by virtue of which the general Congress had openly decided against Religion and the Army. Having heard the reasons which he expounded, the individuals declared their sentiments and supported them in the following manner:

The injustice with which the religion of our fathers has been attacked after the false philosophers assumed control of the destinies of the Mexican nation and to which they were not directed either by virtue nor merit but to act in accord with their masters, requires all Mexicans to rally to save the Nation in accord with the prescription of the sacred religion for which they must sacrifice themselves. How can it be denied that its ruin is intended when one cannot hear any other reasoning than those who want its extermination in the general Congress? A quick glance at the way this assembly proceeds will be enough to know the object of its aims and the facility with which it believed it could wrench from Mexicans the jewel which Providence destined for them, from whose hands they have received so many riches. Such great disrespectfulness for those unnatural people, who either do not recognize the riches or else their propensity towards evil leads them to disgrace.

The proofs of this assertion we practically have in wanting the decrease of belief, trying to introduce fatal tolerance which directed us to errors. To take away from the ecclesiastics their wealth, as it has been done, and denying obedience in all that which concerns the sacramental element to the Holy Father of the Church produces the consequences of facile speculation.

To whom shall we approach in such circumstances that do not admit of any other end than to decide whether to succumb or to lose the precious pearl that Providence has given to us? To the man of virtues, to him who at all times and in all ages has respected Religion and its ministers, who will examine the laws with respect that is required, to the Division General D. Antonio Lopez de Santa Anna, who likewise will see in the soldiers the men who gave [the Nation] Independence and to whom they have been favored with propositions to destroy them, stripping them of their possessions, denying them encouragement and preservation, and trying by every means to secure their ruin.

A fundamental law provides for the conservation of pure religion and without any mixture of any kind, and at the same time that it should be considered, it is being attacked and properties upon which it subsists and its services and its ministers depend are plundered and beliefs in false philosophy is promoted.

A State so dedicated requires a prompt remedy; and taking advantage of the anchor that can save us from such destructive shipwreck, there is no other recourse than to choose the soldier of fortune in order that he may call to their duty all those who scandalously drift away and to restrain them within the orbit of their obligations.

Ten years of a practical experience has made known the advantages of the system that, on examining its theory, it could be improved, but being opposed, as is demonstrated, to the customs, education, and circumstances of the Nation, that which should be the first has done nothing else but to open the door for its ruin. What is the advantage of the diversity of convulsions that there have been, is not the extermination of its best sons and servants? Has the Nation at any time been consolidated under the system it adopted? Let the politicians answer, and make the assertion if it is in conformity with the prevailing customs, a system for whom education and the knowledge of rights that man must know are prescribed.

On proclaiming itself the popular federal

representative the Mexican Army accomplished the resignation of its major privileges and submitted itself to the simple rights of the citizens. What has been the recompense of this incalculable action? Desires to destroy it, to annihilate it, confounding those men who gave Independence and Freedom. This ingratitude without end is not mentioned but for the principle that within reach of the whole nation may be included the sacrifices of those who have not hesitated to offer themselves for the common welfare. Guided by these circumstances and declaring that the interests of the nation and not reactions of parties that have so ruined the nation impels us to proceed in accordance with its duties. The good faith with which they proceed is the surest guarantee which they can present to their fellow patriots.

For such overwhelming reasons and impelled by noble principles, the Nation being overburdened as it now is by a future far from being flattering, it is agreed by the part of the Army in the meeting here to proclaim to the face of the Nation the following articles:

1st. The Army will protect and defend the religion of its forefathers, preserve it intact, and to the secular and regular clergy [it promises] all its privileges [fueros], preeminences, and properties which they have always enjoyed.

2nd. It proclaims as supreme dictator General Antonio Lopez de Santa Anna, so that he may remedy the evils which the nation suffers today, until he himself puts her in the enjoyment of its true happiness.

3rd. The Army shall preserve in full force the statutes [fueros] and possessions that it has been granted, its strength in time of peace and of war in conformity with the law, without it being diminished in any case, according to that indicated by law.

4th. The same Army vows to the Nation that it has no intention of establishing any kind of tyranny, that it will always sustain [the nation's] independence and freedom, whose benefits have been obtained with its blood.

5th. By no means shall individuals who are charged with crimes, with harm to the Nation, or for some reason find themselves being held before some tribunal be granted or receive protection.

Being thus in agreement, the oath which was verified with all the formalities was administered to the troops, it being signed by all the commanders and officers of the Army, as requested, and also by a sergeant, a corporal and a soldier per corps, in the aforesaid city of said day, month and year.

(Over a hundred signatures follow)

Earlier plans have carried a vigorous paragraph of introduction, but this Plan is the first to resort to such lengthy and generalized charges for justification.

J. M. Bocanegra, Memorias, II, 486-489.

* * * * *

SECOND PLAN OF DURAN

6 July, 1833

A letter which the rebel Generals Arista and Duran send from Puebla on July 6th, 1833, to His Excellency the President of the Republic, proposing a Plan of pacification by the establishment of a Borbon as Emperor of Mexico, annotated by a patriot.

. . . .

His Excellency Antonio Lopez de Santa Anna: General Headquarters in Puebla. Very Beloved General: None of us gave any message to Lieutenant Colonel N. Cespedes for you, and anything that on our part this officer has said to you is only a supposition; he came to us last night saying in your name that he wishes that we present him with propositions with the laudable object of seeing the civil war ended; we also wish it with all sincerity, and the most authentic proof that we can give is that by virtue of your invitation we proceed to declare in this private letter what are our aims and intentions.

Almost nine years of the most difficult experience are sufficient to convince us that the system of a federal republican government is not suitable for Mexicans; the majority of the nation, all the sensible part, and even those interested in the conservation of the same recognize that truth; but the latter refuse to confess it because they only pretend to sacrifice the general welfare of the associates on the altar of excessive ambition and of their unquenchable aspiration.

The idea of incriminating any of our fellow countrymen is very far from us. This measure is not necessary for this saving Plan because we have "pronounced" for it, and we shall continue sustaining it until we die; it remains sanctified by all those who do not close their ears to the voice of reason and justice: if by their action and words men are to be known, those who compose the present congress of the Union and the legislatures of the States have formed with their procedures a cumulative process by which the nation shall judge them. Which is the project, which is the law useful for Mexicans that has been published since April last up to date, and which does not in itself carry the stamp of the spirit of vengeance and of animosity which are directed to their authors? Sr. Gomez Farias in his dispositions has not behaved better; the wrongs were ever increasing; the persecutions so unjust as cruel did not cease; the governors conducted themselves in a way entirely contrary to the agreement in Zabaleta last December, and the Army which is the firm support of the nation, has risen up in mass, protesting the outrages done to [the nation] and trying to open for [the nation] the only road that at this time can quickly pacify her, and consequently re-establish her ruined credit and elevate her to the rank she should occupy among the other civilized countries of the world.

We do not consider ourselves infallible, but we believe that the articles which we will expound below cover fully the aim indicated: read them with thoughtful attention, seriously meditating the contents of each of them, and kindly tell us with frankness your opinion, discarding the modesty which characterizes you and which you must forget for the good of the nation for which so many have sacrificed themselves.

1st. In no case nor for any reason whatsoever shall it be pretended to effect any reformation of any kind, regarding the holy religion of Jesus Christ which we profess and which at all times shall be that of the Mexican nation.

2nd. There shall be recognized as supreme chief of the same nation under title of Dictator, His Excellency General Antonio Lopez de Santa Anna.

3rd. The Clergy and the Army shall keep without any restrictions whatsoever their privileges [fueros] and preferences which they have respectively enjoyed thus far in accord with the dispositions which were granted to them.

4th. All individuals who are in prison for their political opinions shall be set at liberty; those who have had to abandon their homes by virtue of the law of July 23rd last, or of any other which may have been dictated on the same subject may return to their homes and no one shall be persecuted except real criminals who shall be judged in accord with the laws and by impartial judges of probity and learning, appointed according to those laws.

5th. Since it is the permanent army which made the nation independent and free, it shall always be permitted to be the custodian of those precious treasures, and that in the case of a Spanish invasion or of any other foreign country may the veterans be the first to present themselves to punish such reckless boldness.

6th. The empire of peace being re-established because

every good man sighs for it and with the public
treasury and the Army organized in the best possible
manner, the Supreme Dictator shall summon a national
Convention that in the shortest possible period of
time shall give to the Mexican nation the form of
government which they may deem suitable, but it shall
not be that of a federal republic, for it has been
demonstrated that it only produces evils. [There
follow several long paragraphs which lament the sad
state of the Nation, protest the selflessness of the
Army, and appeal repeatedly to General Santa Anna to
accept leadership of this reform as sponsored by the
military.] The open letter continues:

We swear to you that we are not guided by any
factious spirit, that we only want the welfare of our
nation, and that we find ourselves convinced that we
shall only see it ruined if we let it continue as
heretofore; we shall die before succumbing, or the
war shall go on forever if you are deaf to the voices
of experience and of truth.

We believe that it will not be so because you are
docile of character, and because nobody exceeds you
in the love for the land in which you were born. The
nature of this letter and the rapidity with which we
do it does not permit us to explain our ideas any
further, although their background will not escape
your well-known understanding.

We wish you perfect health, and we remain your
most affectionate friends and obedient servants who
kiss your hand.

(Signed)

Gabriel Duran

Mariano Arista

Original circular, Library of the University of Texas.
HMT p.v.5, Doc. No. 495910.

* * * * *

PLAN OF THE ALLIED STATES

30 July, 1833

[The Plan that was proposed to be followed by Gomez Farias to overthrow Santa Anna was that of an alliance of various States. It was proposed by the Congress of Jalisco by the decree of October 17, 1833.]

1st. The allied States, in proportion to their population, shall draw up a contingent of the armed forces as due from each of them to form an army of the allied States of the West.

2nd. This army shall be composed exclusively of domestic troops to the number of ten thousand five hundred men of all arms, eight thousand infantry, two thousand horse, and five hundred artillery.

3rd. Each State shall maintain in active service the contingent of this force that will pertain to it; [each State] will place in campaign one-third and the rest will be the garrison of the State, and be destined to form the army of reserve of this campaign.

4th. The allied army shall be divided into as many sections as there are confederated States: each section shall bear the name of the State to which it belongs, and shall be commanded by a leader [jefe] who shall also bear the name of the State(1); another leader shall command the reserve in each State; the commanding general of the army shall be appointed by the general government out of a ticket of three which each State shall propose.

5th. Every section of the army of the campaign shall have its own treasury and the State to which it belongs shall take care that it is provided with funds.

_____

(1) The Generals would be known publicly as "Sr. Don. Zacatecas", "Sr. Don. Morelia" and so on.

6th. The general headquarters of the army shall be in Queretaro.

7th. The troops of the allied army shall be relieved in turn by halves, and they will not be able to be kept in campaign service more than a year; those who leave at present shall be relieved, one half after a year and the other after eighteen months. The service of garrison duty shall last two years; the relief of the second half of the troops who serve at least three years must be effected for this time only.

8th. The allied States shall not have either permanent or active troops; and the corps or soldiers of this class who pass over to the allied army shall be admitted into its employ and assigned to the civic corps, being required to swear before the officers, sergeants, and before one soldier per company of never aspiring to belong pemanently to the military service.

9th. The allied States obligate themselves, first: to regard all individuals of their respective sections that formed the campaign as their favorite sons, supplying according to their employment those who do not have by themselves any income, and [providing the things necessary so that they may spend their lives without misery in an honest occupation and be publicly beneficial. Second: to establish a military pension for the fathers, widows and orphans of those who may die during a campaign, and that by this cause they are left without any resource to subsist. Third: to recognize the sons of those who die during a campaign and to grant them a hoped-for protection. Fourth: to create a protective Junta of the defenders of freedom that, taking care of the efficacious compliance of the present article, does not have any other objective than to see that this duty of the Fatherland is carried out.

10th. The allied States pledge themselves to carry out and maintain what is agreed to by the majority of the committed States.

11th. The allied States shall propose in a reciprocal

manner the measures which they judge opportune to strengthen the union, and secure their objectives. Copies of all the laws, orders, and decrees which they agree upon their internal regime shall be sent to each other.

12th. Fifty thousand rifles shall be bought on the credit of the allied States and these shall be distributed among themselves in proportion to their population, taking into consideration on distributing the rifles what each one has at present. The States shall put at the disposal of His Excellency the Governor of Zacatecas, D. Francisco Garcia, the value of those [rifles] belonging to them, and the said Senor shall celebrate the contract, inviting contractors of this purpose who shall put [the rifles] in San Luis Potosi where the States will go for their contingent.

13th. The allied States shall reciprocally appoint a commissioner near the governments of the same who must remain in their commission until the plan of the coalition may be established.

14th. The Agreement that each State draws up, be it adopting this Plan in all its parts or modifying it, shall be sent officially to each on of them by the respective governor.

15th. Until the Plan of Coalition is approved by the allied States with all the careful attention which its purpose deserves, they shall abide by the one presented by His Excellency, Sr. Governor of Zacatecas in the simple terms adopted by the supreme government of the Union.

(Signed)

Guadalajara.

Santiago Guzman

This Plan is given as a part of the historical narrative of C. M. Bustamante, <u>Cuadro</u> <u>Historico</u>, IV, 302-304.

* * * * *

PLAN OF CONCILIATION*

2 December, 1833

1st. A national assembly will be established with the object of consolidating the running of the government and of settling domestic disputes.

2nd. In order to reconcile wherever possible the various interests, the social differences as well as the desires compromised in the present struggle, resort shall be made on this occasion to a decision by the casting of lots among four individuals from each State and territory who, gathered together at the place chosen for this purpose, shall form the national assembly.

3rd. This assembly shall be vested with a sovereign character during the time that it lasts, which shall be for ninety business days from its installation, and the members who compose it shall be inviolable while their legislative mission lasts.

4th. The four individuals drawn by lots from each State and territory will be composed of a military man whose rank will be from captain upwards, of a parish priest, of a practicing lawyer, and of a property owner whose real estate properties are valued at 25,000 pesos or more, but excluding from these four types of persons those who have an active part in the present revolution.

5th. The States shall assign to the members of the respective assembly the subsistence allowance which they deem suitable.

6th. To effect the said drawing in every State and territory there shall be drawn up list of all the residents living in it who belong to each one of the designated classifications and in each capital the drawing shall be done publicly.

---

* Also called the "Plan of Bravo."

7th. With respect to the time and place of the commission of the national assembly, the belligerent parties, accepting this Plan of conciliation, shall agree on the day and place; the formalities of its installation shall be arranged by the present general congress.

8th. Admitting the present Plan, the belligerent parties will immediately cease hostilities. The executive power will be delegated, during the time the national assembly lasts, on the President of the Supreme Court of Justice, and the present legislature will suspend its sessions.

9th. A general amnesty shall be promulgated for all the political crimes, returning their property to those from whom it was taken for these reasons.

10th. In the act of adherence to this Plan of conciliation those who have pronounced in favor of any other shall entirely desist from their previous commitments.

. . . .

Fellow Patriots: It is time to think seriously of saving the nation. Its ailments are many; we must attend to its relief; let us sincerely desist from so many egotistical pretentions which blind us and return to the path of justice and reason. It is time to put an end to willfulness, to audacity, and to the excesses of a government led astray into iniquitous paths. The time has come to demand a severe accounting of those persons who profane our institutions. Hear the voice of a veteran of freedom; take refuge under the flags of religion, of law and experience. Are you not tired of so many vexations, of so many tribulations? Follow the example of my comrades-in-arms in their decision and their patriotism. If they honor me with their confidence, spontaneously calling me to be the chief commander of their operations, should I therefore deserve less from you? Do not be afraid of the tyrants; they shall soon receive the just reward for their attempts against the altar and the nation. To Arms, honest and brave Military Men! To Arms, patriotic Men! And all of you citizens, lovers of real freedom, enemies of the disorder and of confusion, come to help us pull down the spectre of anarchy. I invite you to the great work of regeneration, of peace and of glory.

But, if led by healthy inspirations, our proud oppressors should try to cooperate in the re-establishment of peace in good faith and with guarantees, abjuring their leader, their criminal purposes, restraining the fury for the demagogues whom he shelters in his shadow, and clearly admitting the proposed conciliation, then I, my comrades, and everyone shall sheath our swords, and the nation, being pleased, shall proclaim a day of glory, which might perhaps erase so many pages of its history, stained with blood which was shed by blind ambition. And if, Oh, Misfortune!, their arrogant destiny makes them deaf to our fraternal invitation, may its murderous steel find in our breasts impenatrable walls which shelter our nation, or if the angry heavens have chosen it as an instrument of its justice, may it reign.....but over ruins and corpses. Glorious it will be to die martyrs at the same time for the faith in Jesus Christ and for the freedom of our nation!

(Signed)

Chichihualco.   Nicolas Bravo

J. M. Bocanegra, Memorias, II, 491-492; C. M. Bustamante, Cuadro historico, IV, 245-246.

* * * * *

PLAN OF ECATZINCO (1)

2 February, 1834

A Plan to bring about the pacification and stable tranquility of the Mexican nation and to assure a solid union, liberty, justice and equality of rights among her children.

1st. The Mexican nation adopts for its government a monarchy moderated by a constitution which shall be drafted for this purpose.

2nd. The summons to the constituent Congress shall be effected by the generals who support this Plan, and they, themselves, shall guarantee the legal freedom of elections.

3rd. The number of deputies in the constituent congress shall correspond to one out of every hundred thousand people of the population, and in the same number of Indians for those of the other classes.

4th. The constituent congress shall deal exclusively with the formation of the constitution of the monarchy, which should be concluded after six months of its installation, and with the manner of election of the Emperor and the creation of the Council of State, which ought to be done within the same period of time.

5th. The constituent Congress shall elect twelve young celibates at present living and born in Mexican territory from those who can prove without a doubt to be the most immediate descendants of the emperor Moctezuma, and from these one who Divine Providence destines for emperor will be chosen by lot.

6th. The one whom chance designates shall be immediately crowned by the Congress, giving his oath to maintain the Catholic, Apostolic, and Roman Religion in its integrity and purity as received from our ancestors, never allowing the public exercise of any other, and to maintain and cause to be maintained the constitution of the Empire; to preserve and sustain just freedom and equality before the law, and [to preserve] the integrity of the national territory.

7th. Within six months after his election the emperor should be married, if he be Indian with a white

---

(1) Also called "The Plan of the Priests." Sometimes the Plan is named for its co-signers.

280

woman, and if he may be white with a pure Indian.

8th. There will be a permanent state council composed of two persons elected by each province of which one shall be Indian and one of the other classes, [all] over forty years of age.

9th. Neither the constituent Congress nor the emperor nor the Council of State shall be able to change the articles of this Plan, which are not provisional.

10th. The commissions, positions, or employments of popular origin cease as of this moment, or else the nation does not recognize this Plan; but the branch of Justice shall continue temporarily in its present situation.

11th. In every capital of the provinces, which are called States, and those of the territories a temporary political leader [jefe politico] shall be appointed: in those of a district or a demarcation, a perfect; in those of party a sub-perfect; and in every town a policemen--the city councils ceasing to function.

12th. The Indians shall elect immediately and temporarily their Governor and republic in the towns in which they lived before the constitutional system and their assigned functions and authority shall be the same as before.

13th. The prefects and sub-prefects shall exercise the functions which the sub-delegates and lieutenants performed earlier.

14th. For the time being the national army shall be composed of sixty thousand men, and to provide for this many openings those who first adhere to this Plan, in accordance with their aptitude and fitness, will be considered favorably, along with preference to the individuals of the present permanent army and militias which shall adopt it.

15th. The individuals of the permanent army who, within three months at most, do not adhere to this

281

Plan shall have no right to an employment or promotion of any kind in case [the Plan] should triumph.

16th. Those who may be able to collect more than two thousand armed men for that reason alone shall have an appointment of General-of-Division, and when they enlist six [thousand men] they shall meet or name by proxy in order to choose their commanding officer [primer jefe].

17th. The respective dioceses shall arrange for the maintenance, increase, splendor, and expenses of public worship and of their ministers, so that for every thousand people there is a priest placed in the most convenient location to administer the sacraments to them.

18th. For the expenses of public worship they shall be assigned the income of the tithes which the same ministers shall collect from it as is regulated by the ecclesiastic authority, and it shall be paid with total integrity and parity for which the civil authority shall lend assistance and give the necessary support and shall supply from its fund any deficiency in case the taxes should not be enough for its object.

19th. As soon as the arrangement mentioned in the previous article is effected, the tariff for masses, functions, and pomp of the funerals, and the parochials assessments shall stop being paid.

20th. All the ecclesiastic positions as well as those of a subordinate rank shall be distributed equally among the Indians and the more suitable casts.

21st. The interior custom houses are abolished, and for the time being no other civic taxation shall be imposed except the following: Whoever earns one to four reales daily or should have some business, employment, commission or positions that should produce up to five hundred pesos per annum shall pay six reales per annum; those who by the same means should have an income coming to one thousand pesos

282

shall pay double; the owners of houses whose value exceeds twenty-five pesos shall pay in the same proportion as the foregoing; the owners of houses or income whose value exceeds one thousand pesos shall pay two for every thousand; the owners of rural properties shall pay annually four per thousand on the value of the land they may cultivate, and eight per thousand on the value of the land they do not cultivate. These assessments shall be collected faithfully by the governors and police agents who shall take five percent for expenses and recompense.

22nd. The maritime custom houses shall continue, and the goods introduced through them shall pay twenty percent more than what they are now paying.

23rd. The branches [for the sale of] stamped official paper, post office, lotteries, and other offices shall continue just as they are now.

24th. By this Plan the employments, ranks, condecorations, salaries, positions and pensions granted by the previous governments are recognized and approved; and those who may legally prove having been turned out shall be restored if it were possible or else they may be appropriately and duly indemnified, and the same for those who should be removed by this Plan; but those who do not accept the new positions which might be given to them shall have no rights whatsoever.

25th. All the civilian employments as well as ecclesiastical and military, shall be granted in the future equally to Indians and other classes.

26th. The national debt to foreigners is recognized as contracted up to this day; those contracted in the future shall not be recognized as contracted up to this day; those contracted in the future shall not be recognized nor paid, nor any other contract of any kind that may be celebrated with foreigners of Mexicans; but those contracted so far shall be faithfully carried out.

27th. All persons not born in Mexico shall leave the

country within three months, except the sons of
Mexicans, the diplomatic envoys, the ecclesiastics
approved by their respective dioceses, those who are
sixty years of age, wives of sons of Mexicans who own
real estate to the value of 40,000 pesos, those of
twenty-five years residence in the country and can
competently prove that they profess the Catholic,
Apostolic and Roman religion.

28th. Those who by virtue of the previous article
should have to leave Mexican territory shall not be
able to take out more than one-third of their wealth
in gold or in silver; but the rest may be in
clothing, goods or produce of the country.

29th. The foreign commerce is reduced to our ports
and in exchange of cloths, fruit, or goods except
silver and gold, that not even in bullion nor in
wrought form may be taken out of Mexican territory.

30th. Not even for exchange can cloth, fruit, or
goods be introduced which is manufactured or
produced, that there may be a sufficient quantity for
consumption.

31st. Individuals of other nations shall not pass
through our ports into the interior without an
express license from the government, which will be
able to give it to a person for a limited period of
time.

33rd. To all the towns who may not have sufficient
land or water in relation to their population shall
be given whatever is necessary of water and of land
1000 varas in every direction; and the various owners
from whom it was taken shall be indemnified.

34th. To the military who served in this enterprise
and after its success should request their
retirement, they shall be given an area of 50 varas
square in the town which they may choose, the
tillable land in which can be sowed half a fanega [of
grain], a pair of yoked bullocks, and besides these
one hundred reales in pesos and a medal of honor.

35th. In no way shall anyone be molested because of his prior actions or opinions; but whosoever should oppose the success of this enterprise, his life shall irremissibly be taken.

36th. The religious hospitals which were eliminated shall be re-established as soon as possible.

37th. The bodies of the faithful shall be buried in the places and in the manner practiced before the constitutional system.

38th. Every Mexican is authorized to promote and protect this enterprise by every means that his patriotism may dictate and as circumstances may provide; but the property owners who should refuse to lend the necessary help shall be treated as enemies of the national cause.

39th. For the time being the undersigned of this Plan will act as "First Leaders"; but once [the Plan] has been accepted in good faith, the leader will be an accredited general of the Army; he shall be recognized as commanding officer; meanwhile should the case arise, the provisions as stated in Article 16 shall be observed.

(Signed)
Ecatzinco,
Fr. Carlos Tepistoco Abad

Fr. Epigmenio de la Piedra

2 February, 1834

El Telegrafo, Mexico, 5 February, 1834;
J. M. Bocanegra, Memorias, II, 539-543.

* * * * *

PLAN OF PUEBLA

11 May, 1834

The oath which the garrison of Puebla makes to sustain unscathed, and without tolerating any other, the Catholic, Apostolic, and Roman Religion, as well as the form of government.

[The expositive section contains the fundamentals which serve to understand the articles and consist of the following: to pledge the simple truth of sustaining the objectives and aims of the Plan without protecting the deficits and errors; in which the reformations were attempted inopportunely and contrary to the will of the nation; and in fact, it endangered the existence of the form of government adopted by the Republic.]

1st. The artillery brigades on foot and on horseback, along with the first, second, twentieth and twenty-sixth battalions of the civil militia of this capital, solemnly ratify the oath which they have given to sustain unharmed and without any tolerance for any other the Catholic, Apostolic and Roman Religion that the nation and the State adopted Main Article Nos. 3 of their respective fundamental charters.

2nd. In the same manner they ratify [their oath] to preserve and defend at all costs the form of popular federated representative republican government, sanctioned also by the said in their Articles 4 of the general and 25 of the particular [state] code.

3rd. Consequently they shall resist any law, decree, proviso or order which tends to alter the dogma or the discipline of the Church as is conserved so far or to upset in any way whatsoever the system indicated of government.

4th. By these same principles they vow to respect, sustain and obey the supreme powers of the Federation and of the State in all its deliberations that do not oppose the bases of this Plan and the other legitimately constituted authorities.

5th. The corps which undersigns [this document] and the others who will adopt it in the State shall be

286

subject to the orders of His Excellency the Governor and General Commander D. Cosme Furlong to whom it shall be requested to effect by every means that he promote the common good on receiving his command, together with the other commissions which are his.

6th. Through the person of His Excellency he shall request from the august Chambers and legislature of the State a measure to end the torrent of ecclesiastic innovations which, under the name of reforms, are agitated in their midst under the assurance that as soon as [the reforms] are obtained the corps in insurrection shall cease their hostile and defensive attitude and shall give as many services as are demanded to maintain the proclaimed objectives, as it has done hitherto.

7th. As the said corps do not doubt from the uniformity of feelings that in this matter have animated the city councils, the authorities of the State and the rest of their civil militia, they shall be guided by the corresponding excitements, so extraordinarily violent, to support them in everything; and ordinary mail copies of this Plan shall be sent to all the other States of the Federation for their knowledge.

8th. The employees of the State, civilians as well as the military, of any position who do not adhere to this Plan, so just as is demonstrated in Articles No. 1 and 2, shall be removed from their employments and exiled from the State.

9th. The purpose that guides their combination being so righteous, without relation to personalities but only on the principles which are stated, the insurrection of Orizaba and Cordoba is not recognized, nor any other which tends to the same objectives, while the authorities who have been removed are not restored and the development which this Plan determines is not promoted.

10th. If this should not be so, the corps which undersign commit themselves in accord with what is offered in Article No. 6 to accomplish so far as they

287

are concerned the disposition of this honorable legislature relative to the restoration of peace in the State of Vera Cruz.

11th. The garrison of the capital and other points of the State in which it is necessary to maintain its place and internal tranquility now and at all times shall continue in force and exclusively by its civil militia, they being paid through its funds as has been done so far, as was so ordered by the supreme federal government through its circular of November 6th last.

12th. If the commanders of the permanent army and officers without command who find themselves at present in the State in this insurrection, and the other employees of the Federation do not support [this Plan] within twelve hours, they shall leave [the State] within twenty-four hours.

13th. This insurrection does not in any way restrict the freedom of the honorable legislature and of their Excellency the Council to effect their subsequent deliberations.

Puebla.   (Signatures of the Civil Militia follow)

J. M. Bocanegra, Memorias, II, 565-567.

* * * * *

DECLARATION OF THE STATE OF OAXACA

23 May, 1834

Long live the Federation, Religion, and General Santa Anna!

In the capital of the free State of Oaxaca, on 23 May, 1834, gathered in the convent of Santo Domingo the commanders and officers of the garrison and a multitude of citizens of the nation voluntarily, and taking into consideration the serious evils that weighed upon the Mexican nation and the danger it had of losing its religion and peace forever, they had to agree unanimously:

1st: To adopt the Plan that for support of the Catholic, Apostolic and Roman religion and of our Constitution was proclaimed in Puebla on the 11th instant.

2nd. To proclaim the heroic General Santa Anna for supporting our religion and national freedom.

3rd. To disown, as it is against the will of the people, all corporations, any commander, or any authority who opposes the present insurrection.

4th. To recognize and obey as chief of the insurrection in this capital Lieutenant Colonel Andres Laflor.

5th. To invite Brigadier General Antonio de Leon to make a parallel pronouncement and in case he does so to acknowledge him as superior leader of all those in insurrection in the State.

6th. To respect and protect the legitimately constituted authorities who may adopt this Plan.

7th. To make no assault by any means against the property, personal security and the political opinions of Mexicans.

8th. To announce respectfully and humbly to His Excellency the President of the Republic, placing ourselves at his honorable service, so that, as he has so many times freed us from despotism, he now may free us from irreligion.

9th. That this declaration may be circulated to the governors of the States and legislatures.

God, Federation, and Santa Anna.

Fuerte de Santo Domingo

Oaxaca, May 23, 1834.   (Signatures of the military)

J.M. Bocanegra, Memorias, II, 571–572.

* * * * *

PLAN OF THE DECLARATION OF CUERNAVACA

25 May, 1834

The Mexican Republic being submerged in the most terrible chaos and disorder and confusion which has subjected her to the violent measures with which the legislative bodies have filled her during this period of blood and tears, displaying the attempts of absolute dogmatism for destruction of the fundamental charter which has cost so many sacrifices, it is indispensable to manifest expressly the reality of the votes emitted by the people in order that an exact and positive remedy may be applied and that it may be sufficient to calm the evils and to destroy the existence of the Masonic lodges which produce the germ of internal divisions.

Considering also that the spirit of remonstrance is general and of one voice from every part of the Republic and that to express this concept to which the conduct of the legislatures give rise, it is not necessary to itemize facts that from their very nature have produced the general dislocation of all the social relationships, the Villa of Cuernavaca, inspired by the most righteous intentions and with the wish to establish a new era, placing a veil over the past happenings, freely and spontaneously manifests its wishes by means of the following articles:

1st. That its will is in open repugnance to the laws and decrees of proscription of persons; those that have been drafted on religious reforms; the tolerance of the Masonic sects and with all the other dispositions which transgress the limits prescribed in the general constitution and those of the individual States.

2nd. That it is in agreement with this same will and consent of the people that the general Congress as well as the individual legislatures not being able to function save by virtue of the powers which their respective constitutions prescribe, laws and provisions which they have dictated and falling notoriously out of that circle must be declared null, without any value or effect, as if they had emanated from a private individual.

3rd. That the people respectfully claim the protection of these just and legal bases of His Excellency the President of the Republic, Don Antonio Lopez de Santa Anna, as the only authority which today is in the position to dispense it.

4th. The people declare that the deputies who have taken part in the passing of the laws and decrees referred to have not been equal to their trust, and they hope that these persons as well as the other officials who have been obstinate in carrying on the resolutions of this nature may be removed from their positions and not intervene either in favor or against this declaration until the nation, represented anew, may be reorganized in accordance with the Constitution in the most suitable manner for its welfare.

5th. That for the support of the provisions which His Excellency the President may dictate in conformity with the ideas expressed, we offer the effective cooperation of the forces which you have here gathered together.

. . . .

These articles have been proclaimed by the people in mass and approved by the Junta for which purpose it has been approved by the City Council and by leading citizens of this City. Notification of which is immediately being sent to His Excellency, the First Magistrate of the Republic, so that this plan may product its effect through his better knowledge.

Cuernavaca.   (Signed)

His Excellency Ignacio Echeverria
Jose Mariano Campos, Ec.

El Telegrafo, 27, May 1834; also Bocanegra, II, 573-574.

The Plan Received wide and prompt endorsement and was sometimes called "The Plan Salvador" of Cuernavaca; also the "Grito Nacional" of Cuernavaca.

* * * * *

DECLARATION OF ITS EXCELLENCY THE CITY COUNCIL
OF VERA CRUZ

20 June, 1834

The nation being led from error to error to the border of the fearful precipice of anarchy, its political existence was in danger and its social ties, already weak and slack, almost broke when simultaneously the towns recognized their rights and, making an effort, public opinion developed in the most fearful manner and claimed the prompt remedy of such great evils.

The claims on religious matters arose in terrible laws which ended by arousing incensed feelings and one day, or if you want, a preoccupation arising from the most noble origin made believe that the governors did not work in agreement with the wishes of their constituents nor the constitutional charter.

The most profound horror of civil wars has restrained the vote of the City Council of Vera Cruz which is of all the people of Vera Cruz and of the whole nation, but it would become a criminal act if it kept silent when the Congress being dissolved, the council suspended and without authority to execute the laws, no more than a slight push would be necessary for anarchy to run loose with all its deplorable consequences. This City Council would never forgive itself for not having cooperated, it being able to do so, in avoiding [this situation] and the necessity to reestablish the constitutional course of the State. It is necessary to look into the future, but without being able to disregard the demands of the moment, in this way eliminating forever, if it be possible, the germ of matters and disputes which would end in a disasterous war.

Considering, therefore, the aforesaid: In order to show its patriotism and respect for law and the will of the people, this body agrees:

1st. The laws passed on religious matters being against the constitution are null: their effects shall cease, and the legislators who are responsible for them have become unworthy of public trust and shall cease in the discharge of their positions.

2nd. His Excellency the General-President, responsible for the strict observance of the laws, is their legal protector; the observance [of the laws] is demanded of him as well as the obligation of the Catholic religion, in accordance with the Constitution.

3rd. This City Council shall appoint a political chief of the Department of Vera Cruz who shall be responsible for public peace and finance, his appointment and his operations being subject to the approval of the government.

4th. In order to name the person who will fill the position the Junta created by Decree no. 263 shall meet in the capital of the State and shall reside in the same for the exercise of its authority.

5th. The appointed public chief by virtue of this declaration shall communicate this agreement to His Excellency the General-President, to the general Commander, to the authorities of the other towns of the State which we hope will join those of Vera Cruz so that all will work by mutual agreement for the establishment of constitutional order.

6th. The judicial and political authorities shall take care of public order: that public funds shall be collected and watched over, and that this step be not blemished by personal vengeance.

(Signatures of the City Council)

Castillo Negrete, Mexico en el siglo XIX, vol. 20, 59-62.

* * * * *

PLAN OF TEXCA

23 March, 1835

1st. General Antonio Lopez de Santa Anna is not recognized as having the right to exercise the government of the Republic as the President of the same when one cannot justify his having impeded the national [Congress] in the exercise of its functions before competent judges who might deliberate outside the influence of his army.

2nd. The authorities of the Federation shall reply as well as those of the States who may not yet have fulfilled the term allotted to their respective positions, and who would have been removed by virtue of mobs or motives supported in the Plan of Cuernavaca.

3rd. The governors and legislatures whose terms should have expired shall be responsible for governing their States; in the meantime citizens will be elected who, in accordance with their particular constitutions, are to replace them.

4th. As the States and Territories become free from the oppression of General Santa Anna and from the anti-constitutional government left organized in Mexico, elections shall be effected for deputies and senators for the general congress, while avoiding that they may be the result of efforts of factious groups.

5th. There shall be an absolute forgetfulness of all past events and nobody shall be charged for crimes committed as a consequence of political differences which have agitated the Republic since its independence to this current date.

6th. This amnesty does not include General Antonio

Lopez de Santa Anna who must be judged for havinç
prevented the general congress from exercising its
functions, nor [does it include] his ministers who
shall answer for the official communications
authorized by them against the constitution and laws.

7th. All civil and military employments which were
granted with tenure shall be given back as long as
the objective of the revolution in which they took
part was not of attacking the political independence
of the Republic and were cancelled on account of
differences of opinion.

8th. The corps of the army, retired officers, and
those without command shall be considered in all
their benefits, as justice demands and the usefulness
which their services provides to the nation.

9th. As the success of this Plan without any doubt
shall be based upon the Constitution and its
principles, and as upon its adoption depends the
establishment of a solid and permanent peace, the
services rendered in its favor shall be awarded, at
the same time that the responsibility shall be
demanded of all who, by any way, should act against
it.

(Signed)

Texca

J. Alvarez

Manuel Primo Tapia.

J. M. Bocanegra, Memorias, II, 631-632

* * * * *

PRONOUNCEMENT OF ORIZABA

19 May, 1835

First: The City of Orizaba desires that the federal
system by which the nation is governed be changed,
adopting another form of government more suitable to

its needs, demands, and customs, and that which will guarantee its independence, domestic peace, and the Catholic religion which we profess. Second: It desires also that His Excellency the General President D. Antonio Lopez de Santa Anna should please provide his official protection, as he has been urged, for the free and spontaneous emission of the wishes of the people in favor of a change in the system, and this being done, he should dictate whatever measures which may be conducive to the realization of their wishes. Third: A copy of this declaration shall be dispatched to the same His Excellency the Sr. President, to the interim President of the Republic and to His Excellency the Governor of the State to the effect that they deign to interpose their distinguished respects to whom it may concern in order that the patriotic desires of the inhabitants of Orizaba should be attended to.

(Signed by City officials)

The Capitular Room,

Town Council of Orizaba

J. M. Bocanegra, Memorias, II, 633.

* * * * *

PRONOUNCEMENT OF TOLUCA

29 May, 1835

1st. That their desires being in accord with those of the nation as manifested in an unmistakable manner, [the citizens of Toluca] wish that the form of government, as more convenient for its welfare, be that of a popular representative central republic.

2nd. That in the constitution that for this end has been established, there be included as essential basis such as: the Catholic, Apostolic, and Roman religion exclusively, the independence of the nation in its present territorial integrity, the separation of powers, and the legal freedom of the press.

3rd. That for the heroic sacrifice and noble feelings in favor of the freedom of the nation rendered so generously by the Illustrious and Meritorious General Antonio Lopez de Santa Anna he be continued to be recognized as President and Supreme Chief of the Nation and Protector of its votes freely expressed.

4th. That for the preservation of public order while the central constitution is adjusted the present authorities shall continue in their posts, subject to the administrative laws, whose object is the preservation of public peace and the maintenance of individual guarantees, being removed from their offices only those who manifest opposition to this Plan.

5th. That in order that the public peace may not be altered nor the free and spontaneous expression of the will of the people be coerced, the supreme government of the Republic is respectfully asked to issue such measures as it may judge convenient for that purpose.

6th. That in order to avoid any difficulty that may interfere with the prompt and effective resolutions for the success of this wonderful enterprise, their wishes are again duplicated through which in the Plan of Cuernavaca and the latest electoral actions the present representatives of the government were given authority to change even the form of government, if it should be justified, as today it is justified, by public demand and of common necessity, granting now the authority not given before that was necessary for the former [administration].

7th. Copies of this Plan and the prior expositions will be sent to the supreme powers of the nation and of the State so that each one to whom it may concern shall devise the most adequate measures for the complete realization of the [nation].

(Signed by the citizens of Toluca)

J. M. Bocanegra, Memorias, II, 634-635.

* * * * *

PLAN OF THE AMPHYCTIONIC JUNTA (1)

4 September, 1835

After a lengthy and detailed discussion which began at eight o'clock at night and terminated at one in the morning, a majority of more than two-thirds of the votes agreed to the following articles which for the confidential Plan:

1st. The chiefs and supreme directors of the enterprise for the return of the federal system and establishment of a government eminently free in Mexico shall be Don V. Gomez Farias, Don Juan Antonio Mejia, and Don Lorenzo Zavala.

2nd. The first as Vice-President and considered chief of the Republic due to the treason of Santa Anna; he shall give the orders and dispositions which are convenient, listening to the judgment of the other two when they can meet and when these have been marched to execution the rest shall follow in so far as possible the instructions of the first and can only deviate from them in urgent cases and as circumstances demand.

3rd. Sr. Mejia shall be General-in-Chief of the Federal army, composed for the time being of all those who can be enlisted in the State of Louisiana; afterwards of the civil militia which is to be created in all the States through which he passes until he arrives in Mexico [City].

4th. Sr. Zavala shall be director and chief of all the settlers of Texas to whom shall be given weapons, money, people, and anything that they may need to defend themselves and to hold the attention of the Mexican government there while Sr. Majia occupies the port of Tampico de Tamaulipas.

5th. The three supreme directors shall agree to the declared Plan under the bases of a federal system, and shall try to make it understood in a manner that attracts but does not compromise. With the exception of Santa Anna and the ministers who advised him and

(1) A Plan of the same nature, published anonymously, and showing signs of plagarism appeared again in 1854 under the title Plan Demagogico -- See El Universal, April 19, 1854; also Gaston Cantu, El pensamiento de la reaccion mexicana, 399-400.

helped him with the so-called Plan of Cuernavaca, who are to suffer capital punishment no matter what their later conduct may have been; as for the rest everything is to be forgotten and a complete amnesty for the past as an inexorable vigor for the future.

6th. The legislatures and governors existing in March 1834 are reinstated, with the exception of the people who do not inspire confidence and after Mexico [City] is captured things will return to the state they were in the said month, for which Sr. Gomez Farias shall get them started on the road and the deputies and senators shall be summoned with suitable advance notice.

7th. Once the Congress is installed and what is called the permanent army is disarmed and dispersed, Sr. Mejia in the name of and as General-in-chief of the Federal army shall make the following request to the Congress, vowing the most submissive obedience and without any threat, but certainly offering not to release arms from their hands until all the resolutions which may devolve are fulfilled.

First Petition: That the same general Congress declare itself, due to the extraordinary and urgent circumstances, legal and competently authorized to effect suitable reforms to the Constitution of the year 1824 without being able to touch the form of government, the independence of the nation, and absolute freedom of the press.

Second Petition: That all the bishops and ecclesiastics as well as the seculars of whom it is suspected with good reason to have gone against the reforms should leave the Republic immediately.

Third Petition: That all ecclesiastical councils cease, leaving a governor of the mitre and delivery to the government of all money and precious jewelry.

Fourth Petition: That all convents of priests and nuns be secularized and eliminated and their real estate and furniture, silver and jewels be put at the disposal of the government with the exception of the

ornaments and sacred vessels, which shall be
distributed among the poor churches. The buildings
and churches of the convents shall serve as
hospitals, charity houses, hospices, barracks, or
workshops, or some shall be sold for synagogues or
temples for other cults.

Fifth Petition: That it be declared that all Mexicans
are free to worship God as they wish; that all
communication between the government and Rome be cut
off, although it could be permitted for private
individuals who wish to continue with Catholicism as
long as they do not disturb public order and make
proselytes.

Sixth Petition: To distribute equally all lands and
all rural and urban properties, no matter under what
title they are possessed, as long as the owners are
left with at least one-third part, and all the rest
shall be given to the poor inhabitants, giving
preference to the army: to those individuals will be
given a sufficient portion of lands and houses as a
reward for their services.

Seventh Petition: That there must be a union and
close alliance with the Northern United States and
their citizens, especially those of Louisiana, who
are to be held as brothers; they are to be able to
pass without the necessity of a passport; they shall
only be charged one-third of the duties which are
charged to other nations; and great care must be
taken that a considerable number of English do not
enter the Republic, nor that [the British] Cabinet
should have any influence in Mexican matters.

New Orleans	(Signed) Valentin Gomez Farias
	Juan Antonio Fejia
7 September, 1835	and 37 other signatures

P. Mariano Cuevas, S. J., *Historia de la iglesia en
Mexico*, V. 232-235. The authenticity of this Plan has
been questioned frequently.

* * * * *

DRAFT OF A [PROPOSED] MEXICAN CONSTITUTION

17 September, 1835

FIRST SECTION:

Concerning Citizens, their Rights and Obligations

1st. The following are Mexican citizens; First, those born in the territory of the Republic. Second, those born abroad of Mexican parents who have not lost their rights after the declaration of independence. Third, foreigners who were residing in the Republic at the time of the publication of the Constituent Act, who accepted it, and swore to it. Fourth, foreigners who were residing or had resided in the Republic, and had obtained citizenship papers, who possessed a useful profession and who have acquired property.

2nd. No Mexican citizen can: First, be arrested nor judged save in conformity with this Constitution and the laws existing before his crime, and by the tribunals established earlier. Second, be tortured to demand from him some declaration, nor be subjected to penalties that are not those established by law, nor for a crime which is not personally his. Third, be deprived of the free use of his property, unless it is for public use and proceeding from a permit from the supreme judicial power, and the indemnity shall be paid in advance upon judgment by an expert in whose appointment the interested party is to take part. Fourth, lose the inviolability of his home and of his papers, except in cases foreseen expressly by the law, and by order of a judge or competent authority in writing, and the reason mentioned therein, which will be delivered to the citizen in order to complete acceptance of the judicial finding.

[Articles 3 and 4 are missing--apparently misnumbered]

5th. Every citizen in the exercise of his rights may: First, elect and be elected for official employments, the person possessing the qualities which the

301

constitutional law of elections may require. Second, publish his ideas in the press, subject to the rules and to the responsibility which the laws impose for false statements of the facts he may say and for the other abuses which may be committed. Third, request in writing, without force or tumult, alone or accompanied, to the authorities of his municipality or of his department, as he judges it convenient for his interests, or for that of the public.

6th. Any person who is not a citizen or a resident of the Republic shall not be able to acquire property in it without an express and titular license from the legislative power; and in order to enjoy any employment, income, or emolument of any kind from the national revenue the citizen must be in exercise of his rights: this does not deal with their suspension due to a case pending sentence.

7th. Rights of citizenship are lost forever and can be recovered only by express and titular dispensation by the Congress, requiring for this action two-thirds of the votes of both chambers, First: for treason against the Nation; Second, for attempt against the life of the Supreme Magistrate of the Republic who is in exercise of his office; Third, for treacherous murder of any man.

8th. The same rights of citizenship are lost and can be restored in the way that the laws may establish. First, to adopt another nationality, or to serve another government, or to receive from it some condecoration or income without a permit from the Executive Power. Second, for residing the greater part of a year out of the Republic without a license from the same Executive Power.

9th. The rights of the citizenship are suspended: First, for not being included in the census of the municipality in which he resides, or by refusing to fulfill the obligations that this Constitution demands. Second, for a pending criminal case for which an order of imprisonment has been issued. Third, for a temporary sentence of suspension imposed by law.

10th. All citizens are obligated: First, to subject themselves to the laws and regulations issued and published in accordance with the dispositions of this Constitution. Second, to contribute towards the expenses of the State to which he may belong in accordance with the laws dictated by the general Congress. Third, to take up arms for the common defense, for order and public security, they being summoned by legitimate authority and in accordance with the law. Fourth, to discharge the obligation of public appointment, not having a legitimate excuse as judged by the authority which is to evaluate it.

SECOND SECTION

ON THE GENERAL ORGANIZATION OF THE REPUBLIC

Art. 11th. The public authority is divided for its exercise into Legislative Power, Executive, and Judical Powers, and never can two of them join, nor can any of its authority fall on a single person, or corporation, except in the cases expressly foreseen in this Constitution.

12th. The Republic shall be divided by a constitutional law into departments which, excepting on the frontier, shall be less than a hundred nor more than two hundred and fifty thousand people. These departments shall be subdivided into municipalities, and they shall contain within themselves all the necessary resources for their administration and internal development, the administration of justice in civil and criminal cases; but the tribunals for the second and third Instance shall be situated at every two or at most at every four departments.

13th. In every department there shall be a departmental junta of nine deputies which shall be elected with four substitutes every two years by popular vote, which shall have the following authority: First, to appoint substitute deputies, which may be lacking in one or another election, due to death or exoneration, or by having entered to replace regularly elected deputies in the General Congress, or into the junta itself. Second, to effect the proposed elections and to give their sanction in the cases that by this Constitution it has the authority to act. Third, to inspect and direct the administration of the funds of the municipalities, properties and income that belong to the towns, i.e., destined for development or for use of them, and to appoint the employees who, according to the laws, should administer them. Fourth, to propose to the executive a group of three for the appointment of a Governor, and to the latter a ticket of three [terna] for the prefects. Fifth, to draw up the statistics of their department and to remit the same to the executive every year with their comments and requests of all that may be suitable for the welfare and progress of the country. Sixth, to draft the regulations and dispositions believed necessary to promote them and to see that they are carried out; to advise the Government on publishing them and without going against the Constitution or the laws and general dispositions. Seventh, to call attention in its report to the petitions which citizens may make and which it believes can be attended to by the Supreme Powers; to inform the Government at least once a year regarding the good or bad conduct of each one of its employees existing in its territory, including the Governor. Eighth, to inform the Supreme Judicial Power also every year on the conduct of judges and to propose the measures deemed opportune for the prosecution and quick punishment of delinquents.

14th. In every department there shall be a Governor appointed by the President who shall not serve more than four years in his position; in every municipality there shall be a Prefect appointed and not removable by the Governor. The powers of these officials as agents of the Supreme Power shall be those embraced within his authority and which shall be detailed by a law.

THIRD SECTION

CONCERNING THE LEGISLATIVE POWER

Art. 15. The Legislative Power shall be exercised by

304

two Chambers, one of Deputies and the other of Senators.

16th. The Chamber of Deputies shall be composed of a Deputy elected by each department, but [a department] should have more than 120 thousand people; they shall appoint one for every 80 thousand and another for the rest if it surpasses 40 thousand, and the same number of alternates as Deputies are elected.

17th. These elections shall be accomplished by popular vote according to constitutional law which will regulate them and will determine the qualifications which the electors must have as well as those who can be elected.

18th. This Chamber will be renewed by halves every two years, leaving in the first biennium the Deputies which the Chamber shall fix for this time, and thereafter those of greater seniority.

19th. The Chamber of Senators shall be composed of thirty-nine Senators elected by the departmental juntas among those nominated by a commission of three Senators, three individuals appointed for this purpose by the Supreme Executive, and three to be appointed by the Judicial Power.

20th. For this nomination the Governors of the departments shall remit lists of the individuals in their department who have besides that of having served the first political positions of the Republic, or in their respective career having fulfilled those which the same law shall designate with an income of not less than three thousand pesos or having a property that amounts to 40 thousand pesos.

21st. From these lists the Commission shall make up another which may contain three individuals for each seat which is to be filled, for those who must leave as well as for those who have been absent. The ones who are to leave [the Senate] may be re-elected even though they may not be nominated.

22nd. The departmental juntas shall elect the total

number of new Senators, each and all, in one day, and
once the count of the votes for the Senate has been
made, those who have a greater number of votes will
be considered elected and in case of a tie those whom
the Chamber decides.

23rd. This Chamber shall be renewed by thirds of its
numbers every four years, in order that it shall
arrange on meeting for the first time, and afterwards
those of greater seniority or those who have been
substituting for them.

24th. Only the general Congress shall have the
authority to pass general laws in the diverse fields
of public administration and those pertaining to
sustaining and defining the rights of the Nation and
of its citizens, and for the following points:

First: To protect and maintain public worship.

Second: To grant dispensations of law.

Third: To grant amnesties and pardons.

Fourth: To create and staff employments and to
determine the honors and pensions which those who are
serving are to enjoy on retiring.

Fifth: To decree taxes and to arrange for their
administration.

Sixth: To take charge of the national wealth and to
assure its good administration.

Seventh: To establish and maintain public credit, and
to contract debts on its behalf.

Eighth: To determine what the armed forces of land
and of sea, permanent and active, should be; and of
the latter class what annually should be in effective
service; arrange for the replacements of these
forces, and to approve the regulations for its
organization and discipline.

Ninth: To decree peace and war, and to approve

treaties and concordats.

25th. When the ordinary sessions of the Congress begin, the Executive shall present an account of what has been spent in the previous year from October to October, and of what the public income has produced, stating the differences that may be calculated in expenses and income in the current year, and attaching a list of the pensioners who may have died or have been appointed and of the new ones, if there be, stating the reason why they have obtained the pension, and another list of the employments that have been provided in the year, stating whether they were by creation or vacancy, and the cause of this.

26th. The Congress, in view of the data presented, preferentially shall decree the sum which it deems convenient and the taxes with which it must be covered, and the active force that besides the permanent [one] must be in service until not later than March next, after which time or other shorter that may be designated by the Congress, it is understood to be permitted to retire, unless its subsistence is not expressly extended ahead of time.

27th. In the annual address the Executive shall present to the Auditor of the Exchequer, which shall entirely depend on the Chamber of Deputies, the accounts of the previous year. In this office they shall be audited and once verified by the Inspecting Commission of the said Chamber, they shall be approved or not, in accordance with the result of the audit according to the reports or information which it deems suitable to take beforehand.

28th. Those responsible for the accounts shall answer to the respective tribunals, and if the Secretary of Finance is believed to be responsible for an infraction of the law, he shall be accused in the Chamber by the same commission. If in the annual address the accounts should not be presented, the Secretary of the Financial Office shall be suspended from the exercise of his office, and shall be responsible for the results. The Chamber of Deputies shall become a grand jury, provided that through any citizen an accusation may be presented against any of the Secretaries of State or a criminal case may be filed against the President or against either of his two counsellors or against the grand Justices to determine whether or not the accusation has any foundation.

29th. If by an absolute majority the accusation is believed to have a foundation, a commission of Deputies shall be appointed who shall take the matter up and support it in the Chamber of Senators, which shall pronounce the final sentence, absolving or sentencing the accused according to their judgment for the Welfare of the Nation. If the accusation should be criminal against the President or the Counsellors, or the grand Justices, it is the duty of [the Commission of Deputies] to sustain it in both Chambers.

30th. The members of the Chambers, the officials of their Secretaries and the departmental Deputies, from the day of their appointment, shall be judged from the first Instance by the tribunals which shall be formed according to the internal regulation of both Chambers, composed of individuals of the same: the Deputies shall judge the Senators and the latter [shall pass judgment upon] the Deputies.

31st. Only in the Chamber of Deputies can the laws for the Executive, for the supreme Judicial Power be initiated.

32nd. The Executive Power shall initiate above all what deems suitable, except on matters of taxes: its initiatives shall be formulated in the State Council.

33rd. The supreme Judicial Power shall be able to initiate in everything pertinent to the good administration of justice, amnesties, pardons, dispensations and clarifications of the law. Its initiatives shall be drafted by the Supreme Court of Justice.

34th. The Deputies can initiate that pertaining to taxes and in every other matter except the amnesties, pardons, and dispensations of law; but its initiatives shall be signed by at least seven, and shall pass on to a commission composed by the fourth part of the Chamber, which, taking turns, shall meet every day. This commission shall determine if it is or is not to give an account of the project to the Chamber; if agreed in the affirmative, it shall be read in the Chamber and shall be passed to the respective commission which shall determine and set its limits.

35th. The laws and decrees on taxes and on the permanence of the active troops in service can be initiated only by the commissions in charge of these branches even though there may not be seven individuals in them.

36th. In the initiatives that the supreme Executive and Judicial Powers may make, the Congress shall not make modifications, but will either admit or dismiss them in their entirety, but in that made by the Deputies the Chamber shall draft modifications and variations which it may judge convenient. If the Chamber of Deputies, proceeding in accordance with the regulations, should approve a bill, it shall pass it on to the Senate for its revision. This Chamber shall adopt it or not in its entirety, without being able to make any variation or amendment whatsoever.

37th. If the Senate does not agree to the bill, it shall return to the Chamber of Deputies, and it cannot be proposed again until half of the Chamber has been changed, and if then the project should still be insisted upon, the Senate shall not be able to reject it save by a two-thirds of those voting present; in that case it shall remain suspended as it was until the other half has been changed; and if then it should still be insisted upon by the initiating Chamber by a two-thirds vote of its members, it can no longer be rejected by the Senate and shall pass to the Executive.

38th. The Executive must publish the laws within fifteen working days of the session of the Congress; and if it shall not publish them and shall not advise the Chamber of the reason of their delay, expressing its compliance with the pending law, it is understood not to be sanctioned, and it shall not be able to be proposed again until half of the initiating Chamber has been changed, or insisted upon by a two-thirds vote and the Senate should by a majority vote approve, in which case the law shall be published.

39th. The laws on taxes and increase or decrease of the active militia does not require the sanction of the Executive and it shall be published as soon as it is issued by the Chambers; the same for the constituent and constitutional [laws] when the departmental juntas may sanction them.

40th. The corrections, variations, or additions to this Constitution or to the constitutional laws can only be initiated by one of the three supreme powers. The initiating power will pass its resolutions with its reasons to all the departmental juntas; each one separately shall answer within five days of receipt stating only if it is or not to be taken into consideration, and the majority of votes being affirmative, the Congress in the initiating Chamber can effect the variations which it deems convenient, and passing to the Chamber as a law, it shall send it for sanction to the juntas, which within five days of receipt each one shall answer in the affirmative or negative. In any event the one which should not answer it is understood to consent: the majority of votes shall prevail.

41st. When on account of physical or moral impediment of the President or of one of his Counsellors or of the grand Justices or by sentence pronounced against them in a criminal cause, they should not be able to continue in the exercise of their position, once the initiative has been made for this declaration, it will follow in the Congress the regular process of a law, and if it should pass as such, it shall be sent for sanction to the departmental juntas which shall give approval or not in the terms of the previous article.

42nd. The ordinary sessions of the Congress shall begin on the first of January and shall last one hundred working days. In that time the Congress may deal with all the matters of their concern, and the one hundred days being elapsed, the sessions will be closed and the Congress shall be able to meet by summons issued by the Executive for one or two specified matters in each session, or by summons of the tribunals of joint Chambers to determine on some accusation presented or to be presented, that they feel has some foundation; in which case the corresponding Chamber shall be summoned or, finally, a majority of the departmental juntas may issue a demand for a meeting of Congress to the said tribunal in order that it may take into consideration whatever business that [the tribunals] may present. The Congress being met in extraordinary sessions shall be able to consider every matter which may not need the sanction of the Executive.

FOURTH SECTION

CONCERNING THE EXECUTIVE POWER

Art. 43. The Executive Power shall be exercised by a President, and only to resolve by a majority of votes the resolutions which he must take on the points that this Constitution expresses shall it be associated with its two Counsellors.

44th. In every public or Government act the President himself shall serve alone as representative of the first magistrate of the Republic; his person shall be inviolable and can never be accused for any act of his administration except for personal connivance with crime of treason against the Nation; only then and in criminal cases can be judged by the Chambers in the form that the Secretaries of State [?? sic]; in civil suits he shall answer in the Supreme Court of Justice.

45th. Every four years on the first of January the President shall cease [exercise his office] and the first Counsellor will enter into the exercise of the office; the second shall remain as first, and in his place will enter the one who has been appointed by the departmental juntas, to whom will be proposed by each one of the powers a group of three individuals who will be Mexican by birth and in the exercise of their rights, nor shall they be ecclesiastics nor pledged by vote to any corporation. Everything [shall be arranged] in the manner and form according to the constitutional law of elections.

46th. Through death or temporary absence of the President or of one of his two Counsellors the Chamber of Deputies shall appoint a temporary one, and if the temporary absence should be indeterminate or for more than two months, groups of three persons shall be set up so that the departmental juntas shall choose the day to be arranged for the election for the one lacking, but in no case can the place of the others or the ticket of three be altered. Meanwhile the Chamber shall appoint a temporary one, the most senior actively engaged in the office of the Secretary shall occupy the place of the absentee.

47th. The President, without the agreement of his two Counsellors, shall exercise the following powers:

First: To watch over the observance and prompt execution of the laws; issue the orders and regulations that are conducive for this purpose and for good government, progress and welfare of the country, and resolve the request of private people on the governmental points which are not contentious.

Second: To arrest through his subaltern agents all delinquents, and people who create such persons, delivering them to their respective judge within twenty-four hours, together with their antecedents.

Third: To effect collection of taxes and to invest the public income in accordance with the law, watching over its accountancy and good management.

Fourth: To appoint all the employees to positions which are created by law; to grant them the honors, retirements and pensions that the statutes assign them; to fill the vacancies subject to the laws and regulations; and to concede the honors and prerogatives to the employees of his offices to those who, in his opinion, have worked well, even though the law of retirements does not grant them.

Fifth: To command the armed forces of land and sea that by decree of the Congress may be in active service.

Sixth. To suspend any employee of his employment up to three months whenever he believes he may deserve it.

Seventh. To grant letters of citizenship in accordance with the laws, and grant or refuse entry or permanent residence in the Republic to foreigners.

Eighth. To remove freely the Secretaries of State, diplomatic employees, General Commmanders, and special assignments.

Ninth. To cause to be obeyed and executed the sentences and dispositions of the Judicial Power for the punishment or arrest of delinquents.

48th. The president shall join with his two Counsellors to agree upon the resolutions on the following points:

First. To publish the laws, to approve orders and pontificial bulls.

Second. To direct the diplomatic relations of any kind, to draft and ratify treaties and agreements, but for its ratification it requires the approval of the Congress; likewise for the declaration of war or to make peace.

Third. To appoint Secretaries of State, Ministers for foreign Courts, Governors, General Commanders, Superior officers of the army and navy, from Lieutenant Colonel upwards.

Fourth. To initiate laws.

Fifth. To suspend, providing it is judged convenient, for two months the sessions of Congress, only in the legislative part, and for only once in a year, and to call, if necessary, all the alternates for them to incorporate themselves to the Chamber of Deputies until its immediate replacement of half of its members.

49th. The President is the Supreme Commander of the armed forces of sea and of land; but he cannot personally command it, not even part of it, neither he nor any of his Counsellors without the prior consent of the general Congress, requested by himself; and in this case his office shall be provided for on an interim basis by the Chamber of Deputies, and he shall be subject to the new Executive as any other General. He shall have no [right of] intervention in the Government, nor shall he command a greater force than that placed under his orders.

50th. For the dispatch of business the President shall have four Secretaries, one for internal affairs, another for external, another for finance and one for war who will also handle affairs related to the navy while the laws do not provide anything else, and no disposition of the President shall be legal or obeyed by any authority if it has not been issued through the corresponding Secretary of State who shall be responsible in his field for any commission against the laws, or for omission in its accomplishment, he having been charged at least once without effect by any citizen. The same rules shall be observed in the Judicial Power with respect to their Secretary of State.

51st. The President shall call to form a Council of State for as many as sixteen persons whom he many judge useful in all the branches of administration. He shall fix the regulations at will so that they shall serve him as advisers in the matters of their profession about which he may wish to consult. These advisers shall not be removable by the President, and they shall keep the jobs which they should have while they serve in the Council, and responsibility to which they are subject.

FIFTH SECTION

CONCERNING THE JUDICIAL POWER

Art. 52. The Supreme Judicial Power shall reside in a Council to be composed of three Grand Judges which shall be renewed by thirds every four years, the first to have been appointed leaving and the one who has lately been elected entering. This election shall be effected in the same terms as that of the Counsellor who is to be election to another a Judge should be lacking, he shall be replaced as in the Executive Power.

53rd. The Grand Judges in what is pertinent in the discharge of their authority shall be inviolable, except in case of treason, murder, and bribery, proved, for which crimes they shall be judged by the Chambers in the same manner as the Secretaries of State.

54th. To the Supreme Judicial Power belongs the following powers:

First. To see that all complaints and claims of the citizens be heard and judged in accordance with their rights by a competent judge.

Second. To see that all delinquents are judged, whatever his class may be, demand his prosecution, suspend him in the exercise of his employment, and to present charges against any judge or any authority who may be remiss in the arrest or prosecution of delinquents; or who may act against the laws or who does not comply with orders given to satisfy authority.

Third. To see that the sentences and other judicial decisions are executed promptly and punctually, and that the laws be observed with exactness.

Fourth. To propose to the Legislative Power the laws believed convenient for the better administration of justice, and for amnesties, pardons, and commutation of such penalties that it believes equitable, suspending execution [of sentences] until the matter is resolved.

Fifth. To staff all employments of the judicial branch, and of its Secretaries of State, being able to remove freely the Secretary, and to grant to these employees and to the Magistrates of the Supreme Court (for whose election it does not belong) the pensions to which they may have a right according to law.

Sixth: To resolve the questions of law which may occur in the tribunals, remitting immediately to the Congress all the antecedents so that in the future the law may be made clear.

55th. The Supreme Judicial Power shall not interfere with cases of a purely military nature, nor in those purely spiritual when they do not refer to corporal or civil punishment; in all the other pure or mixed cases that according to the laws should belong to civil, ordinary, and military jurisdictions, it has the Supreme Inspection, and the judges without suspending its course shall give them the information as extensive as is requested so that they may act in conformity with their authority.

56th. When the Executive Power should by some act exceed its powers or should break the Constitution, the Supreme Judicial Power, being requested by a Supreme Power or by the party prejudiced, shall declare if there has been an excess, and in this case the law or determination shall be suspended immediately. The same Power which had been exceeded will be able to declare the act null, but if it should not do so after ninety days the Supreme Judicial Power, being informed in writing and effecting the consultations which seem proper to it, shall definitely sentence and without appeal concerning the nullity or validity of the decision or the law in question; this decision shall be published by [the Supreme Judicial Power] and shall be obeyed without recourse by all the authorities, and anyone who does not comply with [the decision] shall be guilty of a crime.

57th. In each municipality there shall be established by a common law the justices of peace and the tribunals of the first Instance which are believed suitable in accordance with the locality and number of inhabitants; and to each two, or at most four departments a tribunal of second and third Instance shall be installed for civil and criminal matters.

58th. In the Capital of the Republic there shall be established and organized by a constitutional law a Supreme Court of Justice whose Magistrates shall be elected in the same manner as for Senators, and they shall judged in the same manner as these.

59th. The following shall be subject to the cognizance of this Supreme Court:

First. Civil and criminal cases of the Secretaries of State who may have been Presidents or Grand Judges, of the diplomatic Employees and Consuls of the Republic, of the Governors of the departments, of the Judges of the third Instance, and in the second and third, of the Judges of the first and second, of the civil cases of the Counsellors of the Grand Judges, and Presidents.

Second. The decision of competency among any judges or tribunals established or to be established.

Third. The lawsuits on appeals of efficacy, of nullity in the third Instance, and any other extraordinary situation which may be conceded or is conceded by the laws, and those businesses against which the Government or some department may have a lawsuit.

60th. The Supreme Judicial Power may appoint up to six lawyers established in the Capital, moveable at its will to serve as substitutes of the Magistrates of the Supreme Court, and that joined together with them may serve as counsellors for the drafting of propositions and in all cases in which it may be convenient to consult them.

* * * * * * * *

presented to the Commissions of the Congress of the
Nation.

J. M. Michelena

Original publication, New York Public Library.

* * * * *

PROPOSAL FOR REORGANIZATION OF THE REPUBLIC

23 September, 1835

Presented to the General Congress by the
Respective Commission.

The state of the Republic is really dangerous and
everybody knows how critical our situation is.
Parties which try to supplant each other and repair
their breakdown; nonconformists who hope to prosper
by the disorder; the ambitious and famished, who are
afraid to lose their positions and jobs and without
any merit or work have pinned their hopes on making a
living; timid Governors, because they considered
their authority very precarious and soon to change;
insolent Governors, because they believe the bonds of
the laws broken or untied; laws suspected of being
groundless, and for the same reason weak and without
force; States without governors or legislatures, they
having been totally lacking and others having their
prestige and morale undermined; a general Government
which is impeded to do good by laws which should not
exist and unable to work due to lack of laws which
should be given. Such is an imperfect picture of our
society and, even worse, the crisis in which it finds
itself. From this situation to an unbridled anarchy
is a very short distance. It is astonishing as to
politics, and to make us extremely religious, the
gratitude and recognition of the special providence
of our God, in spite of so many powerful causes we
have not fallen yet into that abyss, the most

318

unfathomable, the worst for societies.

The seriousness of the evil demands energetic remedies without delay in their application. The sacred duty of natural conservation compels the Congress of the nation to occupy itself day and night without resting in investigating the means to turn away from us both the evils experienced as well as those to be feared.

In this belief the commission of reorganization has not lost a moment in its discussions and its tasks, and it hurries to present its first or maiden efforts, despising the fear of censure for haste, never so unjust as in our critical circumstances.

The Commission considers two types of measures very urgent; one that comprises the restitution to local authorities their respectability or prestige which has or seems to have been lost, and to the laws that force which the perverse appear not to recognize; and the other that contains those (laws) which announce what should be in the future and dissipate in some unfounded fears and nourish in others just hopes, and let still others feel the real advantages, and take away from all of them the predisposition, the cause of uncertainty and weakness, which makes them apt to lend themselves unwittingly to the instigations of bad men, thus serving as ladders to reach for the dagger which later will be used to pierce their own hearts.

The Commission has hoped to obtain these very interesting aims. Its members have been busy since their appointment drafting bills. The first contains the measures which must be taken, step by step, in order to forestall evils, give a provisional organization to the parts of our society which they do not have, and to standardize all of them to remove them from danger. The second project contains the principal organic bases of the system which in its judgment is convenient to follow in the future. Today it presents the first of said projects; and a few hours later it will have the honor of presenting the second.

319

The Commission does not flatter itself that the ideas presented here will completely fill the objectives and satisfy the needs; but, it does expect, and this is one of the greatest advantages to which it aspires, that the circumspect discussion which its measures will experience in the congress will sweep away unknown difficulties and clarify an horizon which now is covered with clouds and threats. With this draft can be effected additions or opportune variations to the following articles.

Art. 1. The governors who at present exist in the states shall continue in office, even if they may have completed the time prefixed by the constitutions of [the States]; but their stay in office and the exercise of their authority shall be subject to the supreme government of the Nation.

Art. 2. The legislatures shall cease immediately in the exercise of their legislative functions; but before dissolving and joining those that are in recess they shall appoint a departmental junta, to be composed as of now of five individuals, chosen from their own number or outside of it, so that it will function as counsellor of the Governor; in the case of a vacancy of this office let them propose a ticket of three men [a terna] of whom one must be chosen, to the supreme general government, and while the latter appoints, the governmental functions shall be carried out by the first named among the laymen.

Art. 3. In the states where the legislature cannot meet the city council of the capital shall take its place, only for the act of electing five individuals of the departmental junta.

Art. 4. All the judges and tribunals of the states and the administration of justice shall subsist as of now, while the law to organize this branch is not issued, but the appeals of nullity and responsibility of the supreme tribunals that were terminating before this time in those same states shall be placed now before the Supreme Court of Justice of the Nation.

Art. 5. For the time being all the subordinate

employees of the states shall continue in office, but both they as well as the positions, the income, and the branches which they manage remain subordinate to and subject to the disposition of the supreme government of the nation through the respective governor.

Bench of the Commissions of the General Congress. September 24, 1835.

(Signed)

Tagle. Pacheco Leal. Cuevas. Ansorena. Valentin.

The undersigned Commission complies with the presentation it made to the Congress in its dictum of yesterday, presenting today the project of bases of reorganization. It has already indicated in the said dictum the aims it proposed at the beginning of this work and the suitability and even the necessity that it finds that the Congress, taking it into consideration, should settle the uncertainties which our citizens cherish, some in good and others in bad faith.

The Commission has respected, as it should, that which it believes to be the vote of the majority of the nation, but only up to the point in which it is in accordance with the true interests of the latter. Persuaded that all systems of government have their own particular inconveniences and their peculiar advantages, it has tried to avoid any extreme, to take from each one of them what offers a solid advantage, keeping out what is harmful. The Congress will see in the project an intermediate system and shall decide whether it is what a prudent policy demands.

The bases which we present are of cardinal importance and those which have been or can be grounds for uneasiness, and we have been careful to express them in terms, neither so general that the uncertainty ceases to exist, nor so detailed that they develop all the points of each one.

The Commission does not aspire anything else but success; to obtain it has hastened its deliberations; it has requested counsel from outside and it awaits the observations to be made about it in the discussion of the project which we now present.

1st. The Mexican nation, one, sovereign, and independent as it has been until now, does not profess nor protect any other religion than the Catholic, Apostolic, and Roman, nor does it tolerate the public exercise of any other.

2nd. To all transients, residents, and inhabitants of the Mexican territory, while they respect the religion and laws of the country the nation will protect them and will cause to be protected the rights which legitimately belong to them: the rights of people and the international rights which designate those belonging to foreigners; a constitutional law shall declare those points to the Mexican citizen.

3rd. The governmental system of the nation is republican; representative, popular.

4th. The exercise of the supreme national power shall continue to be divided into legislative, executive, and judicial, and shall not be able to be united under any pretext. A competent arbiter shall be established so that none of the three may be able to trespass the limits of their authority.

5th. The exercise of the legislative power shall reside in a congress of representatives of the nation, divided into two chambers; one of deputies and the other of senators, which will be popularly and periodically elected. The constitutional law shall establish the requisites which the electors and the elected ones, and everything relative to the essential organization of these two parts of the mentioned power, and to the scope of its authority.

6th. The exercise of the executive power shall reside in a president elected by the people, indirectly and periodically, Mexican by birth, which other circumstances as well as those of his election, his term of office, his powers, and the manner of exercising them, the constitutional law shall establish.

7th. The exercise of the judicial power shall reside in the tribunals and judges which the constitutional law shall establish. Its individuals shall have life-tenure. Their qualifications, their number, their residence, responsibility and manner of election shall be determined by the said law.

8th. The national territory shall be divided into departments, on the basis of population and location. Their number, extension, and subdivisions shall be detailed by a constitutional law.

9th. In each department there shall be a governor and a departmental junta. The latter shall be elected by the people in the manner and number that the law shall establish, and the former shall be periodically appointed by the supreme Executive Power, as proposed by the said junta.

10th. The executive power of each department shall reside in the governor, subject to the supreme Executive of the nation. The departmental juntas shall be the council of the governor; they shall be in charge of everything directed to the welfare and prosperity of the departments, and shall have economical-municipal, electoral and legislative authority, as the particular law will explain on its organization; being in all that refers to the exercise of those of the latter class, subject to and responsible to the general Congress of the nation.

11th. The functionaries of the said two powers in the departments and their subordinate agents must be born in Mexican territory or in some place which was a Spanish-American possession and today is an independent nation, and they shall also be natives or residents of the same departments. The constitutional law shall state the intervention which the general Executive and governors of departments are to have in the appointment of their [civil] employees.

12th. The judicial power shall be exercised to the last instance by tribunals and judges resident therein, appointed and confirmed by the high court of justice of the nation with intervention of the departmental juntas and those of the superior tribunals, in the terms and with the responsibilities which the constitutional law shall specify.

13th. The laws and regulations for the administration of justice in both civil and criminal [cases] shall be one and the same in all the nation, and likewise shall be those that shall establish the general tax regulations.

14th. A law shall systematize the public finance in all its branches: it shall establish the method of accounting, shall organize the tribunal for auditing of accounts, and shall arrange its jurisdiction in economic matters and determine the basis of legal appeals in this branch.

Room of Commissions of the national Congress.

Mexico [City], September 25th, 1835.

(Signed)

Tagle, Pacheco Leal. Ansorena.

Valentin. Cuevas.

Original pamphlet, New York Public Library. HCC p.v. 303.

* * * * *

EDICT OF THE GOVERNMENT OF THE DISTRICT

23 October, 1835

Citizen Jose Gomez de la Cortina, colonel of the Battalion of "Comercio" and governor of the District.

Through the Secretary of Public Relations has been communicated to me the following decree:

324

His Excellency temporary President of the Mexican Republic, to its inhabitants, let it be known: That the General Congress has decreed the following:

1st: The Mexican nation, one, sovereign, and independent as it has been up to now, does not profess nor protect any other religion than the Catholic, Apostolic and Roman, nor does it tolerate the exercise of any other.

2nd. To the transients, residents and inhabitants of the Mexican territory: while they respect the religion and the laws of the country, the nation will protect and will cause to be protected the rights that legitimately pertain to them: the rights of people and international [usage] which designate what are those of foreigners: a Constitutional law shall declare the particulars to the Mexican citizen.

3rd. The governmental system of the nation is that of Republican, Representative, and Popular.

4th. The exercise of the supreme national power shall continue to be divided into legislative, executive, and judicial which shall not be joined under any pretext or case whatsoever. There shall be established, furthermore, an efficient arbitrator so that none of the three can trespass the limits of its authority.

5th. The exercise of the legislative power shall reside in a Congress of representatives of the nation, divided into two chambers, one of deputies and the other of senators, who shall be popularly and periodically elected. A constitutional law shall establish the requisite that both the elected and the electors must have, the time, manner and form of elections, the term of the elected and everything relative to the essential organization of these two parts of the mentioned power, and to their scope of authority.

6th. The exercise of the judicial power shall reside in a supreme court of justice, and in the tribunals and the judges which the constitutional law will establish, their qualifications, their number and term, their location, responsibility and manner of election, the said law shall arrange before hand.

8th. The national territory shall be divided into departments on the basis of population, locality, and other pertinent circumstances: their number, extension, and subdivisions a constitutional shall detail.

9th. For the government of the departments there shall be a governor and departmental commissions [juntas]: the latter shall be elected by the people, the manner and the number that the law shall establish, and the former shall be periodically appointed by the supreme executive power upon nomination of the said commissions.

10th. The executive power of the departments shall reside in the governor, under the authority of the supreme executive of the nation. The departmental commissions shall be the council of the governor: they shall be charged with determining or promoting whatever may be conducive to the welfare and prosperity of the departments and shall have the economical-municipal authority, both electoral and legislative, that the specific law of its organization shall explain: being in that which relates to the exercise of the last class, subject to and responsible to the general Congress of the nation.

11th. The functionaries of the said two powers in the departments and their immediate agents must be Mexican citizens, natives or residents of the same departments. The constitutional law shall state the other qualifications and the intervention which the general executive and the governors of the departments will have in the appointment of their employees in them.

12th. The judicial power shall be exercised in the departments up to the last instance by tribunals and judges resident in them, appointed or confirmed by the high court of justice of the nation, with intervention of the supreme executive power, of the departmental commissions and of the superior tribunals in terms of and with the responsibilities which the constitutional law shall specify.

13th. The laws and regulations for the administration of justice in the civil and criminal areas shall be the same in all the nation, and likewise those laws that establish the general taxes shall be the same.

14th. A law shall systematize the public finance in all its branches; it shall establish the method of accounting; it shall organize the tribunal for reviewing accounts and shall arrange the economic and appellate jurisdiction in this branch.

(Signed)

Miguel Barragan.

Palace of the National Government.

V. Riva Palacio, Mexico a traves de los siglos, IV, 357, n.

* * * * *

CONSTITUTIONAL BASES

issued by the Constituent Congress,

December 15, 1835

The interim President of the Mexican Republic to its inhabitants: Know Ye, That the general congress had decreed the following:

Art. 1. The Mexican nation, one, sovereign, and independent as it has been until now, does not profess nor protect any other religion than the Catholic, Apostolic, and Roman nor does it tolerate the exercise of any other.

2nd. To all transients, residents, and inhabitants of the Mexican Territory, while they respect the religion and laws of the country, the nation will protect them and cause to be protected the rights which legitimately belong to them: the right of people and international law that are [the rights] of foreigners: a constitutional law will indicate the details to the Mexican citizen.

3rd. The governmental system of the nation is republican, representative, and popular.

4th. The exercise of supreme national power shall continue to be divided into legislative, executive, and judicial, and they are not to be united for any reason nor under any pretext. There shall be set up an arbiter competent to assure that none of the three should be able to trespass beyond its own established powers.

5th. The exercise of legislative power shall reside in a congress of representatives of the nation, divided into two chambers, one of deputies, the other of senators who will be popularly and periodically elected. The constitutional law shall establish the requirements for electors and those elected, the time, method and form of elections, the duration of the terms of those elected and all that relative to the essential organization of these two parts of the said power, and the range of its power.

6th. The exercise of executive power shall reside in a president [chosen] by indirect, popular, periodic election, a Mexican by birth whose other circumstances as well as his election, term, powers and mode of exercising them a constitutional law shall establish.

7th. The exercise of judicial power shall reside in a supreme court of justice and in the tribunals and justices which a constitutional law shall establish: their qualifications, their number, residence, responsibility, and mode of election--all the said law will predetermine.

8th. The national territory will be divided into Departments on the basis of population, location, and other relevant circumstances: their number, extent, and subdivisions a constitutional law shall detail.

9th. For the administration of the Departments there shall be governors and departmental commissions [juntas]: the latter shall be elected by popular vote in the manner and in the number which the law shall establish; the former shall be named periodically by the supreme executive power on nomination of the said commissions.

10th. The executive power of the Departments shall reside in the governor who shall be subject to the supreme executive of the nation. The departmental commissions [juntas] will be the governor's council; they will be entrusted with the responsibility of determining or promoting whatever may promote the well-being and prosperity of the Departments, and shall have economic-municipal powers, electoral and legislative, which will construe the particular law of its organization; it being subject to and responsible to the general congress of the nation in reference to its exercise of the laws of the latter class.

11th. The functionaries of the aforesaid two powers of the Departments and their immediate agents will necessarily be native Mexican citizens or residents of the same Departments. The constitutional law shall give the other qualifications and the role which the general executive and the governors of the Departments are to have in the appointment of employees [in the Departments].

12th. The judicial power shall be exercised in the Departments until the last instance by courts and by judges resident [in the Departments], but named and confirmed by the high court of justice of the nation, with the intervention of the supreme executive power, and of the departmental commissions and of the superior tribunals within the terms and with the responsibilities which the constitutional law shall specify.

13th. The laws and the regulations for the

administration of justice in civil and criminal
affairs shall be the same throughout the nation;
likewise with those laws which will establish the
general tax legislation.

14th. A law shall systematize the public treasury in
all its branches; it shall set up a system of
computation and accounting, shall organize a system
of auditing accounts, and shall arrange the economic
and legal jurisdiction in this branch [of the
service].

Ordered to be published by Miguel Barragan.

October 13, 1835.

Felipe Tena Ramirez, Leyes funadmentales de Mexico,
1808-1967, 202-204.

* * * * *

PRONOUNCEMENT OF PAPANTLA (1)

20 November, 1836

Mexican Federalists! I am standing at the foot of the
flag that is waving over the tops of Coyosquihuit,
the brave residents of the seashore. This was
impregnable to oppressors. Here the Lion of Spain
roared, was and could never do anything else than to
flee bathed in blood and covered with ignominy. Today
we meet to fight with the same efforts against a
cruel and blood thirsty government that, tearing
apart our federal constitution, seems that it would
have obtained its triumph if we were so vile that we
would not know how to grasp our swords against such
great injustices. We invoke freedom and federation:
for its re-establishment we fight under the concepts
of the Plan in fifteen articles that we have sworn to
support and about which you have heard.

Inhabitants of the coast! Come to increase the

---

(1) Also known as "The First Plan of Olarte".

330

ranks of the conquerors of your rights outraged behind a mask of a refined hypocrisy. To defend the people from tyranny is an eminently religious act. To work for the restoration of our laws is the truest patriotism. Fellow citizens, let us not aspire for libertinism, but let us not suffer the decay of servility that devours us. Here are revealed our best feelings.

The central government of Mexico which flagrantly established anarchy is responsible to the Nation for the blood that runs in Texas. The change of system of the government produced that schism; let us return to our duties and these will be sufficient to reintegrate ourselves to that vast and beautiful territory. The states, free and invested with the sovereignty that they lost, shall make themselves respected, and with the weapons of two hundred thousand nationals shall know how to contain the ambitious intentions of the cabinet of Washington and the stale intrigues of Madrid.

Take up your rifle and come to where the field of freedom and of honor is. I invoke your comrade-in-arms, the old republican, and your constant friend.

FEDERATION OR DEATH: let this be our motto.

(Signed)

Field of Coyosquihuit

Mariano Olarte

Original Broadside, New York Public Library.

* * * * *

PLAN OF PAPANTLA

20 November, 1836

1st. The Spaniards who have entered the territory of the Republic from September 27th, 1821 and thereafter shall leave the country, and all relations with the Cabinet of Madrid shall be cut off while the latter

331

does not openly and frankly recognize the political independence of the nation.

2nd. There shall be established a representative, popular, federal regime, proceeding immediately to the reform of the constitution of the year 1824 by a congress of representatives, elected as provided in the second section of the Third Title of the mentioned code, and that they may be fully authorized for the said object by their respective constituents.

3rd. The representatives of the territories, no matter what their population may be, shall have voice and vote in the congress stated in the previous article.

4th. Meanwhile the Congress being installed, the Republic shall govern without provisional executive power through three individuals elected by citizens most esteemed for their civic and moral virtues who reside in the Federal District.

5th. The chief who may occupy the capital of the Federation or the one who takes the lead with the proclamation of liberty is authorized, on being successful, to designate the citizens who should elect the executive power mentioned in the previous article; without this action the said chief may be nominated for that office.

6th. The congress cannot last more than eight months and its authority shall be limited only to appointing the three individuals for the executive of the Union as soon as it is installed, and to the reform of the constitution of the year 1824.

7th. In the new fundamental law that may be formed, besides marking clearly the division and the designation of the powers and strengthening solidly one's rights as a man and as a citizen; in order to protect them against all kind of abuse it shall designate with precision as principles: 1) that the civil legislation of the federation is to be the same for all inhabitants of the Republic; it should also be observed the same with respect to the states in that which relates to its internal administration; 2) that no person shall ever be forbidden the right to manufacture, possess and carry weapons.

8th. In the states which free themselves of oppression provisional governors shall be appointed in the form outlined in Article 5 of this Plan, and they shall function until the reforms of the general constitution have been concluded, and they find that the bases for the organization of the several states are established.

9th. The Juntas of citizens who may appoint the provisional governors in their states elect at the same time one individual for the council of government of the Union, who shall continue [in office] until the publication of the new fundamental law.

10th. The military, civil employees, and citizens who contribute to the liberty of the Republic shall obtain the awards which they deserve for their services; but the commanders of the divisions cannot remunerate them nor grant any promotions that is not done through a strict, graduated scale.

11th. Those who, without belonging to the Army, should commit themselves to take up arms for the present Plan shall enjoy during the time that their services should be necessary the salary corresponding to the grade they would be destined for as if they were veterans; and if they should become disabled in campaign, they, their wives and children shall have the right to a pecuniary allocation which corresponds in such cases to the individuals of the Army in accordance with the laws and regulations currently in force.

12th. The permanent army shall have the means of substinance, arranging it in such a way as to fill successfully the noble aims of its institution and to have the splendor that corresponds to the military class of a free country.

13th. The war shall continue energetically against

the settlers of Texas, provided that the form of government whose destruction gave rise to its division is reestablished and that they should not return to order and persist in rebeling in that part of the territory of the Republic.

14th. The civil employees, the military and anyone who, enjoying some pension drawn on a state treasury, should oppose in any way the reestablishment of the form of government, republican, popular, federal, and representative, shall lose by this same fact their positions or allocations, as unworthy of living at the expense of the people to whose oppression they contribute.

15th. For the support of this Plan the principles recognized by the civilized nations in the manner of waging war shall be observed; but if by misfortune some of the agents of tyranny should deviate from them, then the right of reprisal will be used.

(Signed)

Mariano Olarte

Original Broadside, New York Public Library.

* * * * *

THE SECOND PLAN OF OLARTE

20 December, 1836

[After two long paragraphs of vivid criticism of the current administration and of exclamatory appeals for support of his Plan, Colonel Olarte concluded:]

1st. A representative, popular, federal regime shall be reinstituted and maintained. The States shall continue to enjoy sovereignty in their internal administration.

2nd. A congress of deputies elected in accordance with the manner and form provided by the laws of elections shall be in charge of making the necessary and convenient reforms in the Constitution of 1824. The individuals who shall compose the said congress shall come with authority given by the people for this purpose.

3rd. While its installation is being effected, the national government shall be administered by three individuals.

4th. The Chief or Citizen who promotes this pronouncement from the Capital for the Federation is authorized to summon a commission of citizens known for their honesty, civil virtues, and love of freedom. This commission shall have as its only purpose to elect the three persons mentioned in the previous article; but the one who shall have led the insurrection cannot be appointed among them.

5th. The congress shall occupy itself only with the reforming of the constitution and in electing three persons who shall be in charge of the executive [power] of the Union until the elected magistrate shall take possession of it in accordance with the new constitutional order. The duration of the Congress shall be for six months, extendable up to eight months on their judgment, but by no means or under any pretext shall it pass this limit.

6th. The council of the two provisional governments mentioned in Articles No. 3 and 5 shall be the one that should have functioned from 1833 to 1836.

7th. In the revisions of the constitution individual guarantees shall be strengthened in the most solid manner. The division of the supreme powers shall be established, stating in an unmistakable manner its organization, their duties and their authority, and finally the circumstances, manner, and requisites with which they must be elected shall be clearly expressed.

8th. A new division of the territory shall be affected.

9th. The civil laws shall be the same for all

inhabitants of the Republic, and everyone shall be subject to them.

10th. The States, as they free themselves from oppression, shall organize their particular government binding themselves to the federal laws and to their respective constitutions until the revised federal constitution is promulgated.

11th. For the said purpose the person who in each state shall lead the movement in favor of this Plan and of liberty is authorized to appoint, once the Capital of the State has been occupied, a Junta of persons widely known as liberals and patriots who shall elect a citizen as the political chief who shall preserve public order and convoke new elections in conformity with the particular laws of the same State; the said official shall cease to function as soon as the Legislature shall have met and decreed whatever may be suitable.

12th. The military, the civil employees, and citizens who may protect this Plan effectively shall obtain awards which the first constitutional congress shall decree as proposed by the government without affecting the promotions by roster that entitle the first and second [grades]; but these promotions cannot be conferred by a General, a Leader [Jefe] or any other person, but by the officials to whom this authority belongs, according to the laws. Those who receive payments from the public Treasury shall keep the rights that the laws provide in this matter, as long as they preserve a strict neutrality with respect to this Plan.

13th. Those who although not belonging to the army should commit themselves to sustaining with arms in hand the present Plan shall enjoy during the time that their services are necessary the salary corresponding to the rank to which they would be destined, as if they were veterans; and if they should become disabled or die during the campaign, they, their wives, and their children shall have the right to financial remuneration that corresponds in such cases to the individuals of the army in accordance with the laws and regulations in force.

14th. The integrity of the territory of the Republic shall be sustained against any kind of pretensions or attempts to impair or lessen it.

15th. The existence of the army as it is and as a force which the purposes of its institution demand shall be guaranteed.

16th. No person shall be persecuted for his political opinions nor deported from the territory of the Republic; this can be done only with those who oppose this Plan.

17th. The interior Customs Houses of the Republic shall cease forever and only those of the ports authorized as recently as the year 1824 shall remain; likewise every law providing for a sales tax on the goods that circulate in the Republic, including foreign products that will only pay at the time that they are introduced under the terms that the government shall dictate will cease.

18th. It is forever forbidden to introduce into the Republic goods and fruit which may be made or produced in the country, as well as the goods which are and will be manufactured therein; it being the right of any citizen of the Republic to confiscate or to make free use of half of what is confiscated, without any other requisite than to present the confiscated goods to the nearest Judge to certify the confiscation; half of it will be for the confiscator and the other half for the Nation, of which the Judge will give a receipt certifying the fact, besides applying a fine of half the value of the confiscation to the one who introduced them, or else imprisonment.

19th. The value of the money shall be increased a certain percentage which will be determined by the government while the government declares that the new currency which it shall mint may be expressed thereon at double its value, and each person in the Republic shall present the capital that he may have in reales to the commission which the government may appoint. To each one of them they shall return half of their capital in the new currency which will represent the total value of what he turned in and the other half of the value shall go into the national Treasury. Subject to the penalties that the government shall impose on those who do not comply, the government shall dictate the necessary measures to prevent fraud.

20th. It is absolutely forbidden to take out of the country silver and gold which is not stamped and meet the requirements stated in the previous article or be subject to the confiscation as provided in Article 18.

21st. The parochial prerequisites such as baptisms, funerals, marriages and regular masses shall all be given without any stipend whatsoever; and only the masses of confraternity shall be paid, there being funds destined for this purpose, as well as for those people who request them to be said for devotion, or baptisms, funerals and marriages which are wanted to be done pompously, but the parish priest being in the town where the masses may occur must go to that place, and only in case of illness or something similar shall he be excused.

22nd. The tithes and offering of the First Fruits shall be scrupulously paid and collected by the priests with intervention of the Judges of the towns. Written statements shall be presented to the public mentioning therein what each one paid for the satisfaction of the interested parties. The resulting amounts shall be remitted to the Bishops and the receipts shall be signed by the Bishops and Governors of the States. From each collection the salaries of the priests will be paid. There shall be three kinds of parishes: the first shall get two hundred pesos, the second one hundred and fifty, and the third one hundred per month. They shall have vicarages endowed in proportion to the priests. The Bishops shall see that the priests comply and that the vicarages have their corresponding ministers and that they should not be lacking. The supreme Government shall endow the Bishops in proportion to their rank as well as to the other employees who work in the Bishop's Palaces, and all these salaries shall come out of the tithes.

23rd. The Canons shall cease in their functions and

in their place in order that the cathedrals do not lack the necessary services of worship the religious houses every month shall take turns to attend all the ceremonies of the canons, and to each priest who should attend shall be paid one peso daily. The resulting sum shall be delivered to their priests so that they may distribute it according to the constitutions of each order.

24th. The treasurer of the collection of tithes shall be under the supervision of the Bishops and the latter shall be in charge of the payments to the priests and other employees, giving an account to the Government of the balance, providing the Government demands it, requiring authorization in accordance with the government for the investment of the monies destined to the divine services in the churches of the cities as well as those of the towns of the diocesc which may have some necessity.

25th. In order to be free of any kind of fees, parochial as well as of a sales tax, all citizens of the Republic shall be subject to a common, equal fee, but according to classes: that is, according to their capacity to pay which shall be paid as fixed by the government, and the mayors of the towns shall present a written statement of each collection to the Treasury of the State, who with the receipt and the approval of the Governor shall pass it to the printers for its printing which once done shall be signed and returned to the towns to be exhibited to the people for their satisfaction. These [lists] must be made in duplicate: one for the people and the other for the files of the said Mayors. These equalizations shall be revised each year for the increase or decrease of the value of the assessments. Besides, any citizen may be able to go before the Judge to get a reduction of the fee on proof of the party of the decrease in value of this property.

26th. The Municipalities, according to their expense budget for which the government's approval has been obtained, shall take whatever steps may be necessary to cover the costs of the collection of the taxes, taking care that the collectors shall be trained. And if the allotment should not be enough, they shall apply to the government for an increase, so that in this way the youth may progress.

(Signed)

Issued at Papantla.

Col. Mariano Olarte

Manuel B. Trens, <u>Historia de Vera Cruz</u>, IV, 95-100.

* * * * *

PROCLAMATION OF THE FEDERATION OF SAN LUIS

14 April, 1837

"LONG LIVE THE FEDERATION!!" In the city of San Luis Potosi on the 14th of April, 1837, the seventeenth year of the independence and the first of the re-establishment of the Federation, gathered at the quarters of the 2nd Active Battalion, under the presiding direction of Lieutenant Colonel of the Army Ramon Garcia Ugarte, Officers, and fellow countrymen who undersign. Considering:

1). That the independence of the Nation, the most sacred object of Mexicans, finds itself threatened by different courses and most particularly by our old bosses who, under the pretext of treaties that do not have as bases the acknowledgement of Independence, try to lull the unwary in order to gain the necessary time and effect their depraved purposes.

2). That Mexican territory finds itself dismembered since two years ago by the irregularity with which the war has been made against the rebel Texans.

3). That to a great extent this has come from the slovenly way in which the present Minister has regarded the worthy Army of the North, reducing it to misery and this despite the fact that all the Republic has contributed to increase the national Treasury for just such a sacred objective.

4). That neither has this condition been produced by the national income, nor by that received from the multiple taxations with which they have burdened the people, nor the other infinite resources that never has the public income been sufficient to satiate the ambition of some of the tax contractors, protected as they are by well-known personalities.

5). That for this reason the unhappy widows of the soldiers of the Nation, the Worthy Permanent Army and all the employees cry in silence in misery and die of

341

hunger, those who, sacrificing their lives to the service of the Nation should receive their salaries from the National Treasury.

6). That for this reason the Mexican Nation finds itself in complete chaos due to the lack of laws that insure individual guarantees and national liberties: it has agreed to rise up and demand re-establishment of the Federal system, in accordance with the following articiles:

Second: As soon as they find themselves free from oppression in which they are held by the present administration the confederated States shall reorganize themselves in every way possible in accord with their own constitutions and particular laws.

Third: In consequence, as of today the Free State of San Luis Potosi enters into full exercise of its Independence and sovereignty in all that relates to its internal administration and it disowns the general powers existing today in the Nation.

Fourth: The States which may have declared also [against the central government] shall begin a relationship among themselves so that in common agreement they can appoint a temporary general Government which should exist until constitutional elections are verified.

Fifth: No individual shall be molested for his political opinions. All that has passed in the previous revolutions shall be entirely forgotten, and no person shall be persecuted for them. Only those who directly or indirectly, oppose the general, will as developed in this Plan shall be punished in accordance with the laws.

Sixth: All the individuals who constitute the Permanent Army are invited in the name of the Nation as well as all other Mexicans so that they may cooperate in the re-establishment of freedom.

Let this be our motto:

FEDERATION OR DEATH!!
(Signed)
Ramon G. Ugarte
and others

Manuel Muro, Historia de San Luis, 151, 153.

* * * * *

PLAN OF ARISPE

27 December, 1837

First: The Nation declares the system of Popular, Representative Federal administration to be valid and in full effect.

Second: The Nation recognizes the Citizen-President Anastasio Bustamante as Head of State without more restrictions in the exercise of Supreme Power than that which his Ministers may be responsible for before the First Constitutional Congress.

Third: This same President of the Republic shall convoke an Extra-Ordinary National Congress in which all the States may have an equal number of representatives for the purpose of revising within the stipulated space of six months the Constitution of 1824. This Assembly shall not be empowered to use its power for any other end, under the penalty of having all that it may do beyond this declared null.

Fourth: The States that may adopt and decide for this Plan shall organize their internal administration provisionally while the federal Constitution is being revised and promulgated.

Jose Urrea

Antonio G. Rivera, La revolucion en Sonora, (Mexico, 1969), 28-29.

* * * * *

PLAN OF THE FACTIONS

16 July, 1840

The conditions under which the factions offered to submit to the supreme government: Minister of War and Navy.

1). It not having been the intention of Citizen Jose Urrea and the forces under his command to attack in any way the person of the President of the Republic, General Don Anastasio Bustamante, this said person is restored to the exercise of his functions of office.

2). In the exercise of his authority as President of the Republic he shall cause the fire of the troops that presently are opposing those of Citizen Urrea to cease. The latter shall, for his part, do the same.

3). The aforesaid Senor President, organizing a ministry which deserves public confidence, obligates himself to reestablish in full force the Constitution of 1824, and then convoking a congress for the specific purpose of revising it.

4). Under these basic provisions peace and order shall be reestablished and no one shall be molested for his opinions that may have been manifested or for principles sustained, and those who find themselves prisoners for sake of their political opinions shall be set at liberty.

Minister of War and Navy: His Excellency the Senor President having declared to the General-in-Chief of the forces of the supreme government that operate on the bases under which they offer to lay down their arms, it has been resolved that it is not possible to guarantee to you more than life if within four hours counting from nine o'clock of this morning the forces are not placed at the disposition of the Supreme Government. In case this is not done, you will be responsible before God and men for the evils that may follow as a consequence of the hostilities that have already taken place.

At the order of His Excellency the Senor President I have the honor to communicate the same for you for your knowledge and for other purposes.

344

God and Liberty

(Signed)

D. Jose Urrea and
D. Valentin Gomez Farias

Boletin del Gobierno, 22 July, 1840

* * * * *

PLAN OF URREA AND GOMEZ FARIAS

19 July, 1840

First: The Constitution of 1824 shall govern while it is being revised by a congress composed of four deputies for each one of the States established therein, and one for each territory existing in May, 1834.

Second: Once redrafted the said Constitution of 1824 shall be submitted to the sanction of the legislatures of the states, and it shall not be considered as sanctioned except that it should have been approved or amended by an absolute majority of the said legislatures.

Third: In the revisions that should be made to the Constitution of 1824 the following bases shall be respected:

1) The Catholic, Apostolic, and Roman Religion shall be protected by wise and just laws.

2) The form of the respective government [shall be] popular and federal.

3) The division of powers.

4) The political freedom of the press without previous censorship for its printing nor for the circulation of printed matter.

5) The organization of the land and sea force shall make up the army of the Republic.

6) Equality of civil rights among all the inhabitants of the national territory, who are subject to the obligations of Mexicans, except the restrictions which the development of the navy of the country requires.

Fourth: For the realization of the previous articles, a provisional government shall be established in this capital whose functions shall be limited exclusively to the directing of foreign relations of the Republic and to stop the oppression of the States and territories, leaving them in perfect liberty to organize their internal administration.

Fifth: The provisional government mentioned in the previous article shall be entrusted to a Mexican who meets the requirements stated in the Constitution of 1824 and shall be elected immediately by the individuals of the military and justice courts and by the present deputies and senators who have been for the unlimited reforms of the Constitution of 1836.

Sixth: The Republic commits itself to return the ten percent increase on the consumption tax which has been paid until today; this [tax] shall no longer be charged in those places where they have pronounced [against the government] where only the laws and fiscal regulations until May 31, 1834, shall prevail.

Seventh: Eight months after the present revolution shall have succeeded the internal customs shall be abolished and from then on no contributions of any kind shall be charged or imposed on the internal circulation of goods, either nation or foreign.

Eighth: The military employments which may have been conceded until now [shall be guaranteed] as well as the civil ones given for life in accordance with the laws, as long as those who obtain them shall not oppose the political regeneration of the Republic which must be effected by the present Plan.

Ninth: The Army of the Republic shall be paid with the greatest punctuality, as well as the retired, widows and pensioners.

Tenth: All political mistakes which may have occurred since the independence of the Republic as effected until the present time shall be forgotten and no person shall be persecuted for the so-called crimes of opinion.

(Signed)

Valentin Gomez Farias,
General-in-Chief.

Jose Urrea, Major General.
(A multitude of signatures follow)

Castillo Negrete, Mexico en el siglo XIX, vol. 21, 172-174.

* * * * *

PROPOSITIONS OF JOSE URREA

23 July, 1840

Art. 1. The troops of each army shall withdraw to occupy positions outside the capital.

Art. 2. It is agreed by all the belligerent forces that the constitutional laws of the year '36 should be without force and effect.

Art. 3. A convention shall be summoned which shall give a new constitution based upon [the principles] laid down in the Constituent Act and shall come into effect immediately.

Art. 4. The elections of members of the commission shall be conducted in conformity with the laws under which the deputies to the constituent congress were elected.

Art 5. The present Excellency President shall form a provisional government, he being the leader, until the prior articles [of this Plan] shall begin to come into effect.

Art. 6. No person shall be molested for political opinions declared from the year 1821 to the present; consequently, their persons, employment, and proper-ties shall be respected, regardless of how much

they may have taken part in this or in past revolutions.

Art. 7. In order that the first article should take
effect, the government shall provide the funds and
other necessities to each and all the forces.

Signed by the commissioners
of Jose Urrea.

J.M. Bocanegra, <u>Memorias</u>, II, 832-833.

* * * * *

PLAN OF PAREDES

8 August, 1841

1st. A national extraordinary Congress shall be
summoned, elected on the widen basis, and fully
authorized to revise the Constitution, and solely
with the exclusive authority.

2nd. In the meantime the Supreme Conservative Power
shall vest executive power in a citizen whom it
trusts with extraordinary faculties, and he shall
account for his actions to the first constitutional
Congress.

3rd. For this purpose the present Congress, which
shall assemble for these actions only, shall initiate
and the Supreme Conservative Power shall declare the
incapacity of the present President of the Republic.
The former [the Congress], moved by the Supreme Court
of Justice, shall initiate it, and the Supreme
Conservative Power shall declare the will of the
Nation with respect to the person who shall take
charge of the Executive.(1)

4th. The latter shall designate the day of the
installation of the extraordinary Congress, the
manner of its election, and the period that it should
last in the discharge of its duties.

Guadalajara.

(1) A variant reading: "For this purpose the present
Congress which shall assemble for these actionly only
shall initiate and the Supreme Conservative Power

348

shall declare the will of the nation in respect to the person who is to enter into the exercise of executive [power]."--Castillo Negrete, Mexico en el siglo XIX, vol 21, 273.

V. Riva Palacio, Mexico a traves de los siglos, IV, 463. Also known as the Plan of Jalisco.

The Plan is also attributed to "The Garrison of Guadalajara." See J.M. Bocanegra, Memorias, II, 836, who uses the text of Riva Palacio. It is found also in C.M.Becanegra, El Gabinete Mexicano, II, 133-134.

* * * * *

DECLARATION OF THE CITY COUNCIL OF VERA CRUZ (1)

28 August, 1841

Art. 1. That the laws of the 26th of November and the 27th of December, 1839, which imposed an increase in the consumer goods be revoked.

Art. 2. That customs duties at the seaports be revised in a way that will promote the increase of imports from abroad and will remove the unjust impediments to trade.

Art. 3. That the present basis for attachments [of goods] be cancelled and another more just and rational be substituted.

Art. 4. That the abolition of interior custom houses be declared, with the payment of duties being collected at the ports of entry.

Art 5. That the law which established the monopoly of tobacco be revoked.

Art 6. That the law that established the personal tax be revised, establishing it upon a proportional and more just basis.

---

(1) This Declaration economic in nature, gave rise to others which included political provisos. See the Declaration of Tamaulipas. September 10, 1841.

7th. That the Municipality make known to the nation the wish of the residents of Vera Cruz as expressed in these articles, and by bringing them to the official of the principal authorities of the department, and by publicizing them through the medium of the press.

V. Riva Palacio, Mexico a traves de los siglos, IV, 464.

* * * * *

PLAN OF ZACATECAS

2 September, 1841

Here are the wishes of Zacatecas as expressed by its agency the constitutional council [junta] which it hopes will be recognized by the distinguished Camara, and in this confidence the following initiative is respectfully presented.

Art. 1. The present Congress will be declared "in session". Thus, very quickly a convocation of an extraordinary Congress with ample powers for reconstituting the nation as is most suitable for the liberty and well-being of the people can be expedited.

Art. 2. The basis of the convocation will equal representation of the departments; place and time for the meeting and the duration of the Congress to be determined. In order to be a Deputy [to the Congress] it will be sufficient to have reached one's 25th birthday and to be exercising the rights of citizenship.

Art. 3. On sending out the call for the convocation, a time will be set for the departmental councils [juntas] within which they are to choose two individuals in order to vest them with the supreme power of the nation. Those who secure the majority of the votes of these councils shall be considered elected; the counting of the votes will be by the extraordinary Congress.

Art. 4. In the time while this body is to meet the Supreme Court of Justice will name another individual who may take charge of the general government; this individual, meeting with the extraordinary Congress,

350

will continue exercising the executive power along with the two persons whom the departmental councils will have named, and the three will continue to exercise the same power until the constitutional government is established.

Art. 5. The departments, until being given the new constitution, will resume all the powers and faculties necessary for expediting their administration without disturbing the general expenditures of the Republic; and, in addition, they are to be subject to the dispositions which the first constitutional Congress may issue to the revision and approval of their acts.

(Signatures)

El Siglo XIX, 12 October, 1841

* * * * *

DECLARATION OF BUSTAMANTE

2 September, 1841

1st. That it was the will of the nation that no person should ever dominate it despotically, without being subject to the laws that it itself has given and may give in the future and without receiving precise authority by law.

2nd. That the supreme powers be not deprived, and much less violently and in a tumult, of the resources which the law establishes as necessary for social attentions.

3rd. That the government be not obliged to accept the hard alternative of overtaxing the national fruits and goods to the benefit of foreign fruits and goods, or else to lack the necessary means for those things which it is forced to attend to.

4th. That the supreme executive power deploy all the resources within its reach and use all the faculties necessary, even though they are not in the Constitution, providing that they are not contrary to the re-establishment of constitutional order and public peace.

351

5th. That as many reforms or measures as may be necessary or deemed convenient for the permanent remedy of public wrongs be discussed and decreed pacifically by the authorities and through constitutional channels, without the violence that armed forces produce.

6th. That it is understood that there is disapproval as from today of all and any results of a single way of acting.

7th. That the general Congress, when it judged it opportune, shall use paragraph 13, article 14 of the third constitutional law to grand amnesties.

(Signed)

Bustamante. Muzquiz.

Pena y Pena. Gomez Anaya.

Castillo Negrete, Mexico en el siglo XIX, vol. 21, 183; C.M. Bustamante, *El Gabinete Mexicano,* II, 139-140.

* * * * *

PLAN OF GENERAL VALENCIA

4 September, 1841

The capital being free, a junta of the people shall meet at once as in the ancient Roman Elections to designate the citizen who is going to exercise the Executive [Power] temporarily. The Executive shall immediately summon the Congress which is to be constituted for the nation, with such ample authority as necessary.

The provisional Executive shall arrange for the convocation under the same law that served for the calling of the constituent Congress that met in 1823.

The Congress, in order not to distract itself from the attentions of its sovereign mission, shall not deal with any other matter because all of its rules being annulled, it will be enough to have recourse to the principles of common rights that are called guarantees and that shall be inviolable. To help the Executive with their advices the same popular junta shall appoint another one of twenty-four citizens, native of all the Departments, which shall be replaced by those whom they designate as soon as it is possible for them to do so. The provisional Executive shall be responsible to the first constitutional Congress for all of his acts, declaring as null from now on all that may be contrary to the holy religion which we profess, to the independence that Hidalgo proclaimed and that Iturbide consummated, to the republican system which has the unanimous vote of the nation, to individual guarantees, and to everything that constitutes a liberal government in which are excluded despotism and the disorders of license. The judicial power shall be exercised with absolute independence in accordance with the laws, its functions being purely judicial.

International law shall be observed with foreign nations up to the very last iota, our pride consisting in absolute independence from every foreign power and in the faithful compliance with treaties. The nation shall observe decorum in all its transactions and the most rigid fidelity in all its promises.

(Signed)

General Gabriel Valencia

V. Riva Palacio, Mexico a traves de los siglos, IV, 467.

* * * * *

353

DECLARATION OF THE GARRISON OF SANTA ANNA DE TAMAULIPAS

4 September, 1841

Being met in special session [junta] the Commanders and officers of this garrigon heard read several documents which had been forwarded by His Excellency General D. Antonio Lopez de Santa Anna. [Then follows a survey of the Mexican situation.]

With this assurance, subject to judicious deliberation of this committee, it issues the declaration which follows:

Art. 1. The Garrison of Santa Anna de Tamaulipas adopts the first and second articles of the bases which the garrison of Guadalupe has proposed to the nation on August 8th of this year [1841].

Art. 2. Furthermore, it adopts the Third in these terms: The present Congress which will meet for this act alone, moved by the Supreme Court of Justice for reason of public advantage, will initiate and the Conservative Power will declare the will of the nation in respect to the person who is to enter into the exercise of the executive [office].

Art. 3. There were adopted wholly the declarations of the committee [junta] and the Government of the Department of Jalisco relative to the consumer tax, to the guidelines for commissions and for individual taxation; these dispositions being published in Guadalajara the 4th of August last.

Art. 4. This garrison is placed at the orders of His Excellency Sr. General D. Antonio Lopez de Santa Anna to whom will be sent forthwith an account of the present declaration.

Siglo Diez y Nueve, 12 October, 1841

* * * * *

8 September, 1841

I accuse Your Excellency and His Excellency the Sr. General Don Anastasio Bustamante of having infringed upon the Constitution in the articles which I have designated, and, in consequence I do not recognize the said General as commander [jefe] of the Army nor as President of the Republic, nor Your Excellency as a legitimate agent of the government for communications relative to the Ministry of War. All the blood which we have spilled in defense of the Republic, all that we are disposed to sacrifice all over again, and I can assure you that seven million citizens declare it to be the will of the Nation:

1st. That His Excellency General Anastasio Bustamante does not continue governing [the Republic] despotically, without being subject to the laws and much less at the head of troops.

2nd. That when it is verified that such a thing has occurred as a very punishable infraction of the Constitution and against that ordered by the supreme conservative power, he must remain in agreement with the minister who has authorized his actions, subject to the judgment established by the laws in order to make his responsibility effective.

3rd. That the supreme conservative power declare as from now on and hereafter the nullity of the acts of the president General-in-Chief as being contrary to the Constitution and the laws, indicating the course which must be given to the accusation.

4th. That the president General-in-Chief, instead of the use of force and ever more by force wants to decide the questions, as he has announced officially, is separated from the exercise of executive power, even when he pretends to return to the constitutional order; because of having violated it, he must be judged in accordance with the laws.

5th. That in the extraordinary crisis in which the Republic finds itself today on account of the ineptitude and the abuse of the president General-in-Chief and its present minister of War, another measure of salvation is not adopted: that the public sanction of the bases which His Excellency General D. Gabriel Valencia has proclaimed in his manifesto on the fourth instant.

6th. That in the twelve powers what were voted to the supreme executive power as he had done, for him to use any powers, even if they are expressed in the constitution, as the one he has already put into practice, governing despotically at the head of the troops with the title of President General-in-Chief.

7th. That amnesty be granted to all the inhabitants of the Republic regardless of whatever means that may have united in the spreading of their political ideas, it being understood that in the amnesty are included even those who may find themselves sentenced.

8th. And finally: That all Mexicans, giving themselves on this occasion an embrace [abrazo] of reconciliation before the God of Justice, forgetting entirely all the political principles which have given rise to our separation and the public wrongs which we all lament, shall consecrate ourselves sincerely to one single end: the salvation of the country.

God and Liberty.   (Signed)
At the Fortress
of Perote

                                      Antonio Lopez de
                                      Santa Anna
                                      Juan N. Almonte.

J.M. Bocanegra, Memorias, II, 837-838; Castillo Negrete, Mexico en el siglo XIX, vol. 21, 305-306; V. Riva Palacio, Mexico a traves de los siglos, IV, 466-467; C.M. Bustamante, El Gabinete Mexicano II, 154-155. The latter text is dated September 9th.

* * * * *

THE PROPOSAL OF DURANGO

9 September, 1841

The Department Council [Junta] does not consider it
urgent to concern itself with the change of persons
in the government of the nation. It hopes to see an
agreement in the wishes of the people on the organization of a provisional government while the Congress

Art 1. The present Congress is declared in session.

Art 2. Therefore, on October 1st it will immediately
issue a call for an extraordinary Congress which
through the wishes of the people [will have] ample
facilities to reconstitute the Republic without being
bound by laws or previous Plans of any sort, save
that which best comports with the interests and
well-being of the people.

Art. 3. The basis of the convocation will be: freedom
in elections, equal representation of the Departments, the place and duration of the Congress.

Art. 4. In the meantime until a new constitution is
issued the Departments will have all the facilities
sufficient to meet their necessities of their internal administration; however, with the proviso that
they shall be subject to the dispositions which the
revisions of the first constitutional congress may
dictate.

(Signatures)

El Siglo XIX, 13 October, 1841

* * * * *

DECLARATION OF THE GARRISON OF TAMAULIPAS

10 September, 1841

The undersigned being in the house of General
Francisco Vital Fernandez with the purpose of
agreeing on that which is most practical for freeing
Tamaulipas from the disorders which are the result of
the surprising anarchy with which it sees itself

357

menaced as a consequence of the opposition that the authorities of this State offer to supporting the Plan proclaimed in Vera Cruz, Jalisco, Mexico [City], and Tampico by the Bienmeritos Santa Anna, Paredes, Valencia, and Rivas. General Fernandez, mentioned above, said that the basis of salvation which was presented uniquely in the difficult circumstances to which it had been reduced by the discord which had prevailed in the nation lay in following His Excellency Sr. Gen. D. Antonio Lopez de Santa Anna, and in appealing for an extraordinary congress, freely elected without influence of political parties in order that it might construct a nation in accord with its interests. Further, he said that this [solution] was proposed in the Plan proclaimed Jalisco, Vera Cruz, Mexico [City], and Tamaulipas, and for that reason he was of the opinion that it ought to be supported; also that the reasons for repudiating the present government of Mexico were so well founded and so just that he was surprised that the nation had tolerated it even up to the present time.

[After additional remarks on Mexico's difficulties and its hope for redemption under General Santa Anna, the declaration concludes:]

And having taken into consideration all that had been said by General Fernandez, the meeting proceeded to the nomination of a president and a secretary, and it unanimously chose for the first post the General himself, and for the second, Don Ramon Rodriquez Cardenas. The Committee being thus organized, it agreed by a totally unanimous vote on the following articles:

Art. 1. The citizens of the capital [of Tamaulipas] support the Plan proclaimed in Guadalajara, Vera Cruz, and Tampico with this difference--that it repudiates absolutely the Conservative Power and the right of intervention which was granted to it in the said Plan; the present Congress should exercise the right.

Art. 2. The call for election of the latter will be

issued and the call will be in the same terms as that issued on June 27, 1823, which equalized representation in the constituent congress at the rate of three representatives for each Department.

Art. 3. The laws of November 26th of 1839 and of December 27th of the same year which imposed the tax on consumption are hereby annulled.

Art. 4. The import schedules at the maritime customs houses will be reformed in such a way as to promote an increase in imports from the exterior and will put a stop to barriers to trade.

Art 5. The present guidelines for attachment of property are now declared annulled, and others more fair and rational will be substituted.

Art 6. The abolition of interior custom houses is hereby declared, and the duties which are paid in them will be collected in the maritime customs.

Art 7. The law which established the monopoly of tobacco is annulled.

Art 8. Laws which impose personal taxation will be revised; the taxation will be established on a more equitable and proportional basis.

Art 9. The Committee [junta] in the most explicit and extensive way authorizes Sr. Don General Francisco Vital y Fernandez to use all possible methods of supporting the will of the people as [that will] is made evident in this act. It authorizes him to take all the measures which he deems necessary in favor of the issues which have been invoked.

And having achieved the purpose of the meeting, all the individuals who composed the Committee in Victoria, Tamaulipas, signed the declaration of September 16, 1841

[Signatures follow]

El Siglo XIX. 16th and 19th October, 1841.

* * * * *

DECLARATION OF THE RESIDENTS OF COATEPEC

11 September, 1841

After two paragraphs of explanation, the Residents declared: We have proclaimed the following Plan, one which we believe necessary to save the Republic from the imminent risk of losing its independence and liberty.

Art. 1. National representation will continue in the Junta chosen by the people.

Art. 2. The principal purpose of this Junta will be first, to designate the citizen who by his well known virtues and heroic services to the Republic is worthy of the confidence to exercise temporarily the executive power. Second, to name a committee [junta] of twenty-four citizens, natives of all the Departments, which will serve as an advisory board to the provisional executive. These said citizens will be replaced by the Departments themselves as soon as they enjoy absolute freedom.

Art. 3. The provisional executive will immediately draft the call for a new national representation by prescribing the most just rules adaptable to the circumstances of the Republic and taking into consideration those which were established in the law which convoked the constituent Congress of 1823.

Art. 4. The powers of the new national assembly will be as wide as are necessary in order to constitute a nation in the manner most suitable to its future well-being.

Art. 5. The provisional executive will be responsible to the first constitutional Congress for all his actions, principally for those which he exercises in order to reestablish public peace and order, declaring void from this time thenceforth all that which may be contrary to religion, to independence, to individual guarantees and to all that which characterizes a truly liberal government.

Art. 6. Likewise whatever acts that General D. Anastasio Bustamante is exercising are declared null from the moment that with the express violation of his powers as President of the Republic he has arrogated to himself undue powers, thus making himself a Dictator and governing the nation with troops which obey him personally. Therefore, all negotiations of a pecuniary nature which he may have drafted in order to raise funds for the continuation of a bloody civil war, for defense of a purely personal cause and [a cause] against the general will and against the Army are also declared void. Responsibility for similar violations by the minister or ministers who authorize them, although contrary to law, with their signatures is hereby declared.

Art. 7. International law as agreed to with foreign nations will be kept in the strictest possible way and the most faithful fulfillment of treaties which have been celebrated with them [will be observed.]

Art. 8. In consideration of the fact that the Army and its worthy generals secured with their blood the independence of the Fatherland, and while they do not see it free of enemies they are the only ones responsible for the success of the glorious enterprise; and that in order to free it from the great evils which threaten it through not having given it a constitution with the preferences which circumstances have demanded, it is indispensable to take the measures most suitable and conducive to that important end. The people, the nation, appeal to the Generals who today are issuing pronouncements against the tyranny of factions that they do not return the sword to the scabbard until they have succeeded in seeing all Mexicans reestablished in the full enjoyment of their rights.

God and Freedom.   (Signatures)

_____

El Siglo XIX, 14 October 1841.

* * * * *

PROCEEDINGS OF THE CITIZENS OF VERA CRUZ

11 September, 1841

After a lengthy essay on the parlous state of the Mexican union:

Art. 1. National representation will continue in a popularly elected council [junta] as the Supreme Court of Justice may designate as soon as the capital of the Republic sees itself free of the power that, violating the social pact, has taken upon itself by means of extraordinary prerogatives the exercise of the three [functions of government] Legislative, Executive, and Judicial.

Art. 2. The principal purpose of this junta will be first, to designate the citizen who by his recognized heroic services to the Fatherland may be worthy of its confidence to exercise on an interim basis the executive power. Second, to name immediately a committee composed of one person for each Department who may be a native or a resident of it [the Department] to serve as a council for the provisional Executive.The aforesaid citizens will be replaced by a deputy to be named by the departmental juntas as soon as they may enjoy complete freedom.

Art. 3. The provisional Executive will draft immediately a call for a new national representation, prescribing the fairest rules adaptable to the circumstances of the nation and taking into consideration [the regulations] that were established in the law which convoked the constituent Congress in 1823.

Art. 4. The power of the new national assembly will be as broad as may be necessary in order to constitute the nation under a popular representative republican system. The congress will concern itself with nothing beyond drafting a constitution, the call for the first constitutional Congress, and regulations for domestic affairs.

Art. 5. The provisional Executive will be responsible to the first constitutional Congress for all of his acts, especially for those which he may exercise in order to reestablish public order and peace, he declaring null and void from now on all that which may be contrary to religion, to independence, to individual guaranties, and for all that which constitutes a truly liberal government. Also, all the acts, rules and regulations which D. Anastasio Bustamante is enforcing or may enforce, or has been enforcing since the moment that, against the clear violation of his powers as President of the Republic, he assumed those powers which did not belong to him are hereby declared null and void. Likewise void are the acts since the date when he appropriated the financial resources in order to continue the bloody civil war while defending a purely personal cause and setting himself against the general will of the people. The responsibility for such transgressions will lie with the minister or ministers who, by their signatures, authorize them.

Art. 6. The provisional executive shall name a secretary of state besides the four already in existence who will be entitled "Minister of Interior Development" [Fomento] and his responsibilities will be to concern himself with all that relates to the development of the country: to see to it that his knowledge is up to date; that [he shall be up to date] in the drafting of a plan for liberal and proper education, in moral and public education, in primary schools, in the protection of industry, commerce, agriculture, and the development of mines, in the development of investment banking so that it may be useful and suitable for its establishment, in the reform and repair of public highways and secondary roads and in the opening of new roads, in the construction of railroads, of canals, and navigation of rivers, lakes, etc. in the collection of statistics, and in the general stability of the nation, in producing geographical charts; as well as proposing a standard of weights and measures. The Ministry will not raise costs [of government] because its job structure will be drawn from within the four existing secretaryships.

Art. 7. One of the primary obligations of the provisional executive power will be to be alert that justice is fully and promptly administered; that the national credit, both abroad and in the country itself, should be reestablished and secured in a solid and stable manner, and to procure absolute personal security on roads and in townships.

Art. 8. International rights with foreign nations shall be observed with utmost strictness and the most faithful fulfillment of treaties that have been signed shall be observed.

Art. 9. No person or corporation is to be persecuted, molested whether in law or outside it, for political opinions of whatever sort which may have been construed, without prejudice of third parties, until the promulgation of this Plan.

Art. 10. In consideration of the fact that the Army and its worthy generals contributed to and sealed the independence of the Fatherland, it is expected that while [the country] is not free of its enemies and of the serious evils which meance it because of not having had a constitution with the preferences which the circumstances demanded, that [the Army and Generals] should take the most energetic and suitable measures conducive to the success of the glorious future which this Plan proposes; and the Nation urges and exhorts the Generals who have pronounced today against the tyranny of the factions that they not lay down their arms until they have succeeded in seeing all Mexicans restored to the full exercise of their rights.

(Signatures)

El Siglo XIX, 14 October 1841

* * * * *

PLAN OF THE CONGRESS

Art. 1. The Supreme Conservative Power is urged to declare it the will of the nation that an extraordinary Congress of one Chamber with adequate powers should be convoked in order that it should make whatever changes it believes suitable in the political organization of the Nation, but retaining the form of a representative, popular Republic.

Art. 2. That the installation of the said extraordinary Congress should be authorized for January 1, 1842.

Art. 3. That the election of deputies should be done in accord with the laws now in effect, but omitting the exceptions established in the 7th article of the third constitutional law and that the elections should be set for the 15th of November next, with the Governors of the Departments vested with the authority to fix the dates of primary and secondary elections after previously consulting with the Departmental Councils [Juntas] where they are to meet. That in the Departments that by reason of distance elections cannot be held on the specified date, then they should be held on the date designated by the Governor and in agreement with the Departmental Council if it shall have met, and that these same Governors take care that the deputies so named shall immediately set out on the road to the capital in order that there should be a quorum for the installation of the Congress.

Art. 4. That the Executive Power be placed in the person or persons whom is judged suitable: that in the meantime the current President shall continue governing the Republic in company with the "Benemeritos of the Country" Nicolas Bravo and Don Antonio Lopez de Santa Anna, and that lacking some one or another of these individuals the Chamber of Deputies shall name the person or persons who should discharge these functions as alternates.

Art. 5. That the present Congress shall close its

sessions the day before the installation of the new Congress, and those who had been unseated as a result of the revolution shall be restored to their positions.

Art. 61 That there should be an absolute amnesty for all the political crimes which may have occurred since the 1st of August last until the date of the publication of this decree.

Presented by

Jose Maria Jimenez,
Minister of the Interior

V. Riva Palacio, <u>Mexico a traves de los siglos</u>, IV, 467, an Introduction and a conclusion is given in the text of the <u>Baletin Oficial,</u> no. 20, 15 September, 1841.

* * * * *

DECLARATION OF THE GARRISON AT PEROTE

13 September, 1841

At a gathering of the generals, the chief and the officers of the divisions of operations issued several paragraphs of explanations for their action, then declared:

Everything being well considered and moved by the sincerest desire to sacrifice themselves for the country, they have unanimously agreed to the following:

1st. To adopt the Plan proclaimed by the garrison of Jalisco and as amended in the Ciudadela of Mexico by His Excellency Sr. General D. Gabriel Valencia.

2nd. To respect and protect all the authorities who, by deserving public confidence, ought to continue in the exercise of their assigned offices.

3rd. To take no part in measures which have personal revenge as their object, nor to take part in measures designed to renew hatreds, because public policy and welfare require that [such things] should be forever forgotten.

4th. Not to lay down their arms until they see constitutional order reestablished as the nation may so order through its legitimate representatives.

5th. To conserve at all costs public peace and order, and to oppose whatever force which sets itself to impede the present pronouncement.

6th. And finally, to swear solemnly, as they do now swear on their word of honor to die in the undertaking if it should be necessary following the steps and obeying blindly the orders of His Excellency General Benemerito de la Patria D. Antonio Lopez de Santa Anna.

(Signatures)

El Siglo XIX, 14 October 1841.

* * * * *

DECLARATION OF THE GARRISON AND RESIDENTS OF
THE CAPITAL OF TAMAULIPAS

16 September, 1841

Under the leadership of General Francisco Vidal Fernandez this garrison at Tampico and concerned citizens at his home and "by an absolute majority" of votes cast unanimously agreed to the following articles:

1st. The citizens of the capital [Victoria] adhere to the Plan proclaimed in Guadalajara, Vera Cruz, and Tampico with this difference: that it disavows absolutely the conservative power and [declares] that the present general congress will exercise the intervention which as granted to him in the said Plan.

2nd. This latter [body] will be declared convoked and the call to the convocation will be in the same terms as that issued on June 27, 1823, equalizing the representation in the constituent Congress on the basis of three

367

representatives for each Department.

3rd. That the laws of November 26, 1839, and December 27the of the same year which imposed a tax on consumption is hereby repealed.

4th. That the tax rates for the maritime customs houses be reformed in such a manner as to encourage imports from foreign countries, and to abandon the unfair limitations on trade.

5th. That the present pattern of commissions be cancelled and another more just and reasonable be substituted.

6th. That the abolition of all internal customs houses be abolished, paying the same rates which are collected there as in the maritime customs houses.

7th. That the law which established the monopoly of tobacco be abolished.

8th. That laws which impose a personal contribution be reformed and that they be established on a more equitable and proporcionable basis.

9th. The emergency committee [junta] strongly and explicitly authorizes General D. Francisco Vital Fernandez so that by all possible means he should sustain the will of the people manifested in the present declaration and authorizes him to take all the measures which he judges necessary in support of the cause which has been invoked, and having concluded the purpose of the meeting all the individuals who composed the junta in Victoria, Tamaulipas, signed [the document].

(Signatures)

El Siglo XIX, 16th and 19th October 1841.

* * * * *

DECLARATION OF PEINOSA

September 26, 1841

The Honorable Town Council having met and with it the commandants, officers of the squadron of Defense, and citizens in the capitular reception, and presided over by the perfect of the party, the latter declared . . .

[There follows a survey of the precarious state of the Mexican nation, the equivalent of the traditional 'Considerandos']

Before presenting the Articles for discussion the Honorable President of the distinguished Council asked the privilege of the floor and gave a speech as follows: [Another speech.] The address of the Honorable President being concluded, they all discussed and approved the following articles:

Art. 1. The Town Council of this community, its squadron of Defense, and its citizenry announce their adherence to the Plan proclaimed in Guadalajara, Vera Cruz, and Matamoros but with this difference: that the Conservative Authority [Poder Conservador] and the right of intervention which is granted under the second section, and the present general congress exercising it are hereby repudiated.

Art. 2. The congress is declared ready to be summoned, and the terms of the call will be those laid down in the law of June 27, 1823, which provided for equal representation in the constituent Congress at three representatives for each Department.

Art. 3. The law which established the tax on tobacco is hereby annulled.

Art. 4. The abolition of internal customs houses is declared abolished.

Art. 5. The law imposing a personal tax is also repealed.

Art. 6. The Council, defenders, and citizenry solemnly protest that they will not support other political authorities in the Department which existed until the date of the Declaration [pronunciamento] of Guadalajara (August 8th) until under new laws new nominations, popularly supported, are verified.

Art. 7. The inhabitants of this Town swear that if, in order

369

to bring into effect the redeeming plan now proclaimed, the same as that of Art. 3 of this declaration, it should be necessary to take up arms, they will support it even to the shedding of blood.

They directed that certified copies should be made . . . The above agreement being concluded, the meeting was declared at an end, and as an evidence of their sincerity, they signed.

(Signatures)

El Siglo XIX, October 29, 1841.

* * * * *

PLAN OF TACUBAYA

28 September, 1841

Art 1. By the will of the nation the powers called supreme that the Constitution of 1836 established have ceased in their function; except the judicial, which shall limit its function to matters purely judicial, in accordance with the laws in force.

Art. Not knowing any other method to substitute the will of the departments than to appoint a junta composed of two deputies for each one, born in the same or citizens thereof and living in Mexico, who shall be elected by His Excellency the General-in-Chief of the Mexican army, with the object that these shall designate with entire liberty the person to whom shall be entrusted provisionally the Executive.

Art. 3. The person so designated shall immediately take charge of the function of the Executive, giving the oath in the presence of the junta itself to serve the nation well.

Art. 4. Within two months the provisional Executive shall request the summoning for a new Congress, which, amply authorized, shall be charged with constituting the nation as seems most convenient.

Art. 5. The extraordinary Congress shall meet within six months after issuance of the summons, and it shall not be able to concern itself with any other matter than that of forming the Constitution.

Art. 6. The provisional Executive shall account for its actions to the first Constitutional Congress.

Art. 7. The authority of the provisional Executive embraces all those [powers] necessary for the organization of all the branches of Public Administration.

Art. 8. Four ministers shall be appointed: one of Foreign and Domestic Relations, one of Public Education and Industry, one of Finance and one of War and Marine.

Art. 9. Each of the Departments shall appoint two individuals of his trust, for a council which shall pass judgment in all business affairs, for it to be consulted by the Executive.

Art. 10. While the council appointed by the Departments has not met a junta shall carry out its function, whose creation is established in the second basic proviso.

Art. 11. While a convenient organization of the Republic is being prepared, all the authorities of the Departments who have not and will not go counter to national opinion shall continue.

Art. 12. The General-in-Chief and all the generals and officers of the army pledge themselves by their sacred honor to forget forever the political conduct of the military or the non-military citizens which they may have observed in the present crisis, and not to consent to persecutions of any kind, because their object is the most sincere reconciliation of all Mexicans for the welfare of the country.

Art. 13. If, after the period of three days after the expiration of the armistice, these basic provisions are not adopted by His Excellency the General-in-Chief for the government troops, steps shall be taken without delay to insure its exact accomplishment; and we declare in the name of the nation which has so expressly manifested its sovereign will that they shall contribute to shedding Mexican blood uselessly, [blood] that shall bring sorrow on

371

their heads.

(Signed)

Antonio Lopez de Santa Anna
Gabried Valencia
Mariano Paredes y Arrillaga, and
others

V. Riva Palacio, <u>Mexico a traves de los siglos,</u>
IV, 469-470. The threat to those officers who do not
support this Plan [Item 13] is detailed somewhat more
vividly in the version given in C.M. Bustamante,
<u>Apuntes para la historia de Santa Anna</u>, 2-3: " . . .
and we declare in the name of the nation that has so
expressly manifested its sovereign will that the
General-in-Chief and the military officials who sign
below shall be responsible personally, and also all
the so-called authorities who either directly or
indirectly go contrary to this same will and who may
contribute to causing Mexican blood to be shed
uselessly, blood that shall bring sorrow on their own
heads." . . .

* * * * *

DECLARATION OF THE PEOPLE OF MEXICO
[CITY] FOR THE FEDERATION

30 September, 1841

In the city of Mexico on September 30, 1841, the
citizens who undersign held a meeting, requesting
that the prefect of the central area be pleased to
listen to the frank manifestation of their political
faith, so that when taken into consideration he
should allow them to help personally to assist in the
remedy of the evils that at present the Mexican
nation is enduring, and also in order to prevent
those that in the future might threaten the
independence of the country itself if the diverse
insurrections and anti-national plans which had been
forged in the Citadel by the enemies of the nation
should come to be realized. With common accord they
expressed themselves in the following terms:

372

That the commanders who sponsor the revolutions of the Citadel, far from inspiring confidence, on the contrary instill much suspicion.

That it having been manifested to be the overwhelming will of the nation that a popular representative federal system be adopted as the only one capable of saving it from ruin that threatens, they swear to sustain it an any risk, and for this purpose they request that the due fulfillment of the following be accomplished:

1st. the popular, representative, federal system and the Constitution of 1824 be re-established immediately.

2nd. The general congress shall meet immediately, likewise those of the particular States, and all the authorities as they existed in the year 1832.

3rd. The congresses of the States shall begin, and the general [congress] shall agree to the reforms that must be made in the Constitution of 1824.

4th. In consequence, the supreme executive power shall be carried out by His Excellency General Melchor Muzquiz, who in 1832 was the temporary president, because His Excellency General Bustamante has vowed not to occupy that office again in order to sustain his rights and to observe the laws.

Therewith this act was signed by the persons below:

(Signatures follow)

Castillo Negrete, Mexico en el siglo XIX, Vol. 21, 344-345.

* * * * *

PLAN (SO CALLED) OF THE SEMINARIO

1 October, 1841

1st. A popular, representative, federal system and the constitution of 1824 shall be established immediately.

2nd. For the discharge of the supreme executive power the person who was President of the Supreme Court of Justice at the time the federal system was abolished shall be called immediately in conformity with Article 9 of the federal constitution; or in his stead, the one before.

3rd. Immediately, and in conformity with the summons issued in 1823 on election, [the nation] shall proceed to elect the congress that should make the reforms stated in Article 3 of the pronouncement of September 30.

4th. The States shall call upon their federal authorities, in accordance with their respective constitutions.

5th. The President shall consult with his council of ministers in every case that the constitution demands.

6th. After the general congress is installed, the Chamber of Deputies shall appoint a temporary president while the rightful one is being elected constitutionally, voted by the States, as provided in the said constitution.

7th. In the States, when due to any accident this Plan in all its parts cannot be put into effect, the existing authorities shall put it into practice so far as possible, carrying on as best they can in agreement with the federal constitution and the particular one of each State.

(Signatures follow)

Lic. Juan B. Morales, et al.

J.M. Bocanegra, Memorias, II, 839.

* * * * *

AGREEMENT OF THE PRESA OF ESTANZUELA

6 October, 1841

Gathered at the Presa of the Estanzuela His Excellency Major-General Valentin Canalizo and Brigadier-General Benito Quijano, and the Brigadier-Generals Jose Maria Tornel and Jose Ignacio Gutierrez, the first commissioned by His Excellency Major-General, National Hero Anastasio Bustamente, General-in Chief of the troops situated in the city of Guadalupe Hidalgo, and the latter ones by His Excellency Major-General, National Hero Antonio Lopez de Santa Anna, General-in-Chief of the army of operations, with the object of discussing and agreeing to the terms that can be arrived at to put an end to the civil war, thus giving to the generous Mexican action the means that it needs to maintain its dignity and decorum among civilized nations, and the most sure means for sincere and cordial reconciliation of all its sons. After the showing of credentials, they agreed to the following articles.

1st. From this moment the intimate and cordial relations which must reign among all the members of the Mexican family are re-established; and neither now nor ever shall [Mexicans] be molested for their opinions expressed either in words or in writing and for their political actions, both the military citizens we well as the civilians. Their Excellencies the Generals-in-chief and the belligerent forces bind themselves that this forgetfulness shall be perpetual and sincere.

2nd. The acts of the administration of His Excellency General D. Anastasio Bustamente and of him who succeeded him temporarily from the first of August of the present year of whatever kind that they may be are to submitted to the first constitutional congress for approval, just as the actions of the provisional executive shall be submitted to the same [body] which will be installed in accord with the bases which the army of operations of the Very Excellent General D. Antonio Lopez de Santa Anna has adopted.

3rd. Their Excellencies the Generals-in-chief of both belligerent forces are bound to act as mediators with their worthy influence with the government that is established, so that the generals, commanders, and officers may be given their retirement or leaves when requested by them, and their requirement as pensioners for civilian employees on their request.

4th. The present agreement being ratified by their Excellencies the Generals-in-Chief of the belligerent forces, those [forces] situated in Guadalupe shall place themselves at the order of His Excellency General Antonio Lopez de Santa Anna, who shall give them the considerations which they deserve as soldiers of this part of the army which has contributed so much for the independence for the nation and whose arms and bravery can be so useful in any foreign war.

5th. The present agreement shall be ratified three hours after it has been signed by the commissioners of both parties.

(Signed by the parties named above)

J. M. Bocanegra, Memorias, II, 815-817; V. Rivas Palacio, Mexico a traves de los siglos, IV, 472, through some editorial error, omitted all of Article 2, save the opening phrase which named General Santa Anna rather than General Bustamante.

* * * * *

PLAN OF THE DEPARTMENTS

8 October, 1841

1st. An extraordinary Congress shall be summoned, freely elected and with an equal representation of each Department, with ample authority to occupy itself exclusively with the re-constitution of the Republic under the form of a popular representative government, which will be more in conformity to the opinion, interests, and welfare of the people.

2nd. The Executive Power of the nation shall be entrusted to a person appointed by the junta of commissioners summoned in Queretaro for this purpose by His Excellency General Mariano Paredes y Arrillaga, who at the time of appointing it shall outline the scope of its authority and the way [the junta] must act for the welfare of the nation. The said junta, due only to the urgency of the case and to avoid anarchy, shall represent the other Departments whose commissioners may not have been able to be present at the time of the appointment. These functions being concluded, the junta shall be dissolved.

3rd. The Executive Power, in agreement with a council that shall be composed of one individual appointed by each departmental junta with their respective governors, shall determine as soon as possible the bases for the convocation.

4th. Once gathered, the constituent Congress, in the same day of its installation shall elect the Executive who will administer the Republic while the new Constitution is being formed.

5th. The Executive shall be responsible for his actions before the first constitutional Congress.

6th. The extraordinary Congress stated in the first Article shall meet exactly in the Department of Guanajuato at the point designated by the Executive Power and shall issue the Constitution not later than within six months.

(Signed by representatives of the Departments)

C.M. Bustamante, Apuntes para la historia de Santa Anna, 2-3; V. Riva Palacio, Mexico a traves de los siglos, IV, 475; Also known as the "Exposition against the Plan of Tacubaya." Zamacois, Historia de Mexico, II, 240-241.

* * * * *

A PROJECTED CONSTITUTION FOR THE MEXICAN PEOPLE

26 October, 1841

(Presented anonymously by "a concerned Citizen.")

Introduction

Deeply affected by the miseries that have afflicted
our unfortunate nation, deserving a better fate, and
knowing that they all emanate not only by not
observing its fundamental laws but that on issuing
them the habits and respective circumstances from
every part of the country were not consulted, nor did
they endeavor to harmonize the eminently liberal
tendencies which the century advertises in the most
hidden corners of the world, I decided, in spite of
the smallness of my talents to draft a project of a
constitution which I timidly offer for the correction
of wise statement.

It is a difficult enterprise to give laws that will
organize any nation in the world, and much more
difficult for one like ours where the negative
principles are plentiful, where the most sordid
interests germinate, fermenting anti-social passions
and where the monster of discord dominates. Mexico
has passed through all the gradations of the
political scale, but not in the prudent, gradual
manner that insures the best results; rather by
violent jumps from the most barbarous and colonial
despotism nourished in the cradle of the Charleses
and the Phillipses up to the highest point of civil
freedom under the reflection of the great northern
lights of William Penn and George Washington; from
there it has suffered an indiscreet, badly calculated
retrocession. Could it, in the shade of much and so
different symbolic auspices of such strange tran-
sitions of so many contrary temperments--could it, I
repeat, be quiet and happy, liberal and illustrious,
prosperous, and tranquil? By no means. And when to
this we add the insidious artifices of the foreigner,
zealous in a venture whose appearance flatters us.
How could we have tasted the pleasures in a cruel

cup of the most lethal and deadly poison? So it is that neither the charter of 1824 in its totality nor that of 1836 could serve the country in a dignified manner.

In both there are happy births; but its integral union has brought forth a monster. What to do in this case? Choose the best from one and the other, accommodating them to ideas which have again stirred up the experiences and then try to uniform the whole, now with the doctrines of the best publicists, now with the customs of the nation that the former so much respect, so as to be able to say, although asking permission as did Solon, "If I have not given to my country the best laws, at least I have tried that they may be the most adaptable for its existence."

For this reason I wanted to point out among the forms of governments the system of a popular republic, not only because it is axiomatic in politics as because the first principle of knowledge of Decartes in metaphysics is that a large nation which resists monarchy because of the universal feelings of its sons cannot be governed in any other way, and not because the sad disappointments have confirmed this truth, but because the desire of the nation is no longer questionable on this point. On forming the local governments, on effecting the division of the nation's territory it was necessary to take into account besides the geographical position and the physical and moral resources also that which each section should possess in order to establish a whole equitably.

I have also wanted the people really to choose their representatives because this is just; and nothing that is just can fail to be suitable. Democracy has had in this constitution a latitude as extensive as simple, because that is how it should be where political liberty is the idol of their hearts and where the aristocracy is no more than a myth forged in the heads of some arrogant and fatuous people, for nobody has come out of a palace, nobody has a genealogical tree on golden parchment, nobody can

reasonably nourish ideas of another nobility, foreign
to wisdom and virtue.

I have tried to distinguish the latter; to it I have
attributed the highest points; but if I have
flattered amour-propre with pompous titles and vain
decorations, in substance, to gain respect and
esteem, following our old inherited habits and
customs, not for that have I put the terrible weapon
of the civil omnipotence in any hands nor given them
a preponderant influence. In a constitution everyone
fears for himself; everyone considers himself;
everyone has at hand the recourse of amendment;
nobody opens a breach to profane the sanctuary of the
laws. To say it once for all: moderation of articles,
because moderation in them must be a constitution:
respect and inviolable social and individual
guarantees: proceedings from the known to the
unknown: election of the best among both extremes, of
the best that the fathers of political policy
approve, matched, as well as possible, with
sensations and ideas that cannot be uprooted without
dangerous ulceration: obstacles and embarrassments to
the power for any abuse: satisfactions for the
people, giving the important place they merit:
remedies to correct without a crashing doing the
wrongs of this same constitution: remedies also to
cast out slowly but energetically the lapses that
deteriorate the Republic, that debase and disfigure
it: remedies, finally, to extirpate the serious
deformities of the old federation, namely, the native
spirit, that fussy fondness, peruile and contracted
to particular localities; no more love for virtue,
for abhorrence of vice. See what I have wanted so
intensely. It may be that I have not obtained it; but
"in magnia rebus tentasse sat est."

* * * * *

A POLITICAL CONSTITUTION OF THE MEXICAN REPUBLIC

26 October, 1841

IN THE NAME OF GOD ALMIGHTY, ONE AND TRIUNE, AUTHOR
AND SUPREME LEGISLATOR OF ALL SOCIEITES

Section I   Title I

Art. 1. The Mexican nation, zealous to preserve the

380

welfare joined to its sovereignty, declares: that is revises its previous constitutions, reducing them to this one.

Art. 2. The religion of the nation is Catholic, Apostolic and Roman. The tolerance of any other shall be sanctioned at the places that public convenience should require it, upon judgment of the authorities, and in the manner and time that shall be dealt with later.

Art. 3. The nation adopts for its form of government the system of a popular republic, according to the terms expressed in this constitution.

Art. 4. The territory of the Republic extends from the peninsula of Yucatan in the northern sea to upper California in the southern sea, with its adjacent islands in one and the other. For this reason it embraces the extension of all that formerly was called the Viceroyalty of New Spain, the captaincy-general of Yucatan, the part of Guatemala that by the will of its inhabitants wanted to join themselves to Mexico, the old commanderies of the Internal Provinces of the East and West, and their annexes to the total as delineated.

Art. 5. The Mexican Nation is divided into courts, departments, districts, territories, and cantons. A secondary constitutional law, following this order shall demarcate with all possible regularity the extension of its territories, taking into account the general statistics of the Republic, and taking as a base, besides the localities, population and resources, the moral aptitude above all. Meanwhile, the division of lands established up to now shall be in force.

<u>Title II</u>

Art. 6. The following are Mexicans: First: Those born in any part of the Republic. Second. The foreigners who resided in it before 1810 and have continued up to this date, without any subsequent conduct manifestly anti-patriotic. Third: Spaniards who

adhered to the Plan of Iguala and the treaties of Cordova, and who are comprised in the second part of the previous article. Fourth: Foreigners married to Mexicans, or who are of Mexican descent, according to the laws of the country.

Art. 7. The following are Mexican citizens: First: Those who, besides the requisites referred to in the previous article, may have obtained a letter of citizenship issued by the legislative power and registered by the first local political power with proper authority. Second: Those who with prior requisites live from some honest or useful occupation for society. Third: Those who have been distinguished in any action of a just war, qualified in this manner by a special decree of the legislative power; those who have been distinguished also by some scientific invention, some artistic perfection or sublime writings on any branch of politics, as long as they are thus esteemed in the departments and districts, and by the respective authorities of the capital to which the individual belongs. Any of these circumstances entitles him to merit a letter of citizenship, even without the other requisites expressed in the previous article.

Art. 8. The condition of Mexican citizenship is lost: First: For accepting or lending services to any other nation or foreign Prince. Second: For being a poisoner, an incendiary, a patricide, a forger, a murderer, for treachery, a sacrilegious thief, a slanderer, a traitor to the nation, or to constituted authorities, a smuggler, or a pirate. Third: For judicial sentence that has produced a judgment and for crimes which include a penalty of shame. Fourth: For the crime of housebreaking, arbitrary detention; and in general, for any attempt against the social or individual guarantees, sufficiently supported. Fifth: For fraudulent bankruptcy or theft in the public treasuries; for bribing, barratry; for cowardness proved in acts of military services, or in actions of national war; for apostasy of the religion of the country; for profession of the monastic state. Sixth: for being absent from the country without license of the government or exceeding that time granted.

Art. 9. The condition of Mexican citizenship is suspended: First: for still being under paternal care. Second: For not being able to read or write. Third: For a criminal case from the moment one is declared a formal prisoner until the sentence of acquittal. Fourth: For managing prohibited games. Fifth: For being a vagabond or Sixth: For the state of domestic servant; it being understood that these are to be those dedicated exclusively to persons from whom they receive a salary. Only the national congress is able to re-habilitate the one who has lost his rights of citizenship, except those cases expressed in paragraphs 2 and 5 of Article 8, in which only the legal prescription is valid for the said effect, and in the cases designated by the laws.

Art. 10. These are the obligations of all Mexicans: First: To rally to the defense of the nation with wealth and person when it is so demanded by decree of the national congress. Second: To enlist himself in the census of his respective municipality. Fourth: To contribute to the public treasury in the manner and with the quantity that the laws determine. Fifth: to give obedience, respect and help to that authority that demands it.

Art. 11. These are the rights of Mexican citizens: First: Not being sent to prison, except by the authority to whom the laws commit this action, but with a sufficient evidence to make him a suspicious criminal, and by virtue of an order issued in writing and signed by the proper authority. Second: Neither his house nor his papers and other personal effects may be violated except by the authorities to whom the law has conferred the said authority but with the requisite [documents] and for causes or crimes expressed in the same. Third: His property of any kind may not be occupied nor molested in its use, possession or benefit of it, except in urgent cases of known public necessity, as per the judgment of the respective supreme judicial power and the corresponding indemnification is to be paid at once.

Fourth: He cannot be prevented from moving his person, family or properties unless there is some cause or pending debt. Fifth: He cannot be punished or counter-charged merely for his political opinions, nor suffer any punishment whatsoever without being heard beforehand. Sixth: He cannot be detained for more that twelve hours by any political authority without being advised why he is considered to have trespassed the law, nor by the judicial authority for more than eighty days without having been declared a formal prinsoner. Seventh: He cannot be prevented nor have previously examined in any case whatsoever the publication of his political ideas by means of the press, under his own responsibility of the laws, decreed before 1835 or those that may be decreed henceforth. Eighth: To publicly accuse any official who has transgressed or broken the laws before the competent authority, being subject to the penalties that he deserves in case of slander or exaggeration. Ninth: To be able to enunciate any new law or decree or the derogation of any pre-existing disposition; and if any officer to whom is conceded the right of initiative should adopt it, it shall be taken immediately into consideration by the congress.

Title III

Art 12. National sovereignty is divided for its exercise into three active powers: legislative, executive, and judicial, which shall function in the court. Between these there shall exist the conservative or neutral power which is to maintain the equilibrium of the three. The place where these high powers shall function shall be denominated the court; and therein shall be established a frank administration similar to those of the territories.

Art. 13. The Departments shall be freely administered by three authorities in their internal administration which shall be called deliberative, governmental, and judicial. The deliberative body shall consist of not less than seven nor more than fifteen. With regards to the general [issues] and important [matters] involving another department, district, territory and region or in disagreement with the towns within its

boundaries challenging that decided by the main
authorities shall be subordinated to the high powers
of the Republic; so that the decrees and regulations
that are published shall be remitted at the same time
to the other localities and to the said powers; and
if those should be judged contrary to the union,
order, or prosperity of the nation or of one of their
localities, they shall not be in force in the whole
or a part may be disapproved, producing the crime of
lese-nation on the authority which does not respect
such dispositions. Second: The districts shall be
governed by three main authorities as in the
departments; the deliberative [body] shall be
composed of not less than five individuals nor more
than nine; the judicial [body] shall be that of the
nearest department that may be designated by the
supreme powers, only for the respective result. All
these districts as well as the departments shall
establish in their districts an administration by
means of prefects, similar to the political chiefs of
the territories. Third: Each of the territories shall
be governed by a political chief elected by the
supreme executive from the group of three persons
presented by the congress, to which election the
constitutional president shall not attend. These
shall have the authority designated for them and to
the deputations of the constitution of 1824 and shall
have besides three associates elected by the city
councils so that with [the political chiefs] they may
prepare all the initiatives, proposals, and
arrangements of the police. Fourth: The regions
shall be governed by the military, but in the part
that may have a population with some civilization the
military authority shall conduct itself as directed
by the political chiefs or prefects. Its election
shall be made by the president on nomination from a
ticket of three by the military court.

Section II   Title IV

Art. 14. The legislative power of the nation shall be
entrusted to two chambers, one of deputies and
another of senators. The former shall be apppointed
by electors chosen by the citizens, according to the

385

bases that a constitutional law shall fix; the latter shall be elected by the high powers of the nation: by the main authorities of the departments, districts and court, once the nomination of the prefects, sub-prefects, and municipal authorities have been heard, where such should exist.

Art. 15. The basis for the election of deputies shall be computed by one out of every hundred thousand people, and another reaching to more than two-thirds of one hundred thousand. The territory or region that should have this population shall nevertheless appoint one, while the distribution indicated in Article 5 is established. The senators shall be one for each department and district, another by the court, and another for each one of the high powers for the territories and regions. There shall be pointed also for each one of the chambers a number of substitutes equal to those officially elected. A secondary law shall regulate these dispositions, the requisites, the manner and the time of verifying them.

Art 16. To be elected it is required: First: To be a Mexican citizen in full exercise of his rights. Second: To be older than thirty years of age. Third: To have a presumption of legal suitability, qualified by an electoral junta which shall be able to appoint those to vacancies resulting from their exclusion. The elector of a locality cannot be a deputy or senator for the same place, if it is not a territory or a region.

Art 17. The following cannot be deputies: First: The president, his colleagues, the secretaries of office, the chancellor, nor the other persons of the administration. Second: The Most Worshipful Archbishops and Worshipful Bishops, the vicars and vicar-generals. Third: The priests. Fourth: The ministers and other diplomatic agents, the consuls, the employees of the Public Treasury and those of the government offices. Fifth: The canons and prebends. [The sixth point was omitted.] Seventh: The professional judges of law. Eighth: The permanent members of the City Councils. Ninth: The Governors. Tenth: The prefects. Eleventh: The sub-prefects.

Twelfth: The general attorneys, the magistrates and dependents of any tribunal. Thirteenth: Those who cannot be electors.

Art. 18. The following cannot be senators: Those embraced in the paragraphs--1st, 2nd, 3rd, 4th, 6th, 12th, and 13th of the previous article.

Art 19. The sessions of both chambers shall be daily, with exception only of a national holiday or a religious festival. On the other days the legislative sessions shall open at nine o'clock in the morning and shall end at two o'clock in the afternoon. The deputy or senator who should not observe this time-table during more than three days in every month without a justified cause shall suffer the discount of the third part of his respective allowance, and if he should repeat the offense, he shall also be registered in the newspapers as a transgressor of this article.

Art. 20. The deputies shall have the right of the initiative in all matters; the senators the right of revising the same.

Art 21. The chamber of deputies shall serve as grand jury in accusations against the President of the Republic, his colleagues, magistrates of the supreme court of justice, governors of the departments as well as districts, councillors, ministers near the other nations, consuls, diplomatic agents and general attorneys of the nation.

The dossier shall be ready before twenty days, and remitted to the chamber of senators for its revision which shall be ready within twelve hours. If the chamber of deputies should declare by a vote of two-thirds of its individuals present that there is cause to effect proceedings, the dossier shall pass on to the senators and there it will be sufficient to have one-half plus one of the total vote for the accused to be suspended and at the disposal of the competent tribunal. If the vote were less in the first chamber and if in the second there should be one-half, it shall be processed in the same terms, but in any other case all measures shall cease.

Art 22. In the making of the laws and in the parliamentary order of debates, while nothing is decreed, the dispositions stated in the federal code of 1824 and the internal rules of the congress which do not oppose this constitution shall prevail. Likewise shall prevail in questions concerning the organization of the chambers during the ordinary and extraordinary sessions matters which should be ventilated in one and the other, prerogatives of the members of both chambers, authority and powers of every kind not excepted in the present constitutional dispositions.

Art. 23. The third constitutional law of those of 1836 is declared in force while nothing else is decreed, as from Article 25 through 46, and those comprehended as from Article 51 through 57 as long as they are not contrary to the present provisions.

Art. 24. The term of the deputies and senators shall be that for two years for both, and the elections for all of its members shall be held on the same day.

Art. 25. Accusations against deputies and senators shall be disclosed first to the authorities who had a apart in their election; and if they declare by a majority that there is a cause for proceedings, the accused shall be suspended and at the disposal of the supreme court of justice. In any other case the accused shall be considered unconditionally [discharged], but in every case the dossier must be concluded before thirty days.

Art 26. The Congress cannot exercise other acts besides those contained in this constitution.

Art. 27. The senators shall be inviolable in their opinions in the debates, but responsible if they breach their internal rules of order and good faith in the matters they deal with.

Art. 28. The deputies shall be inviolable and responsible as stated in the previous article, with respect to the senators.

Art. 29. The senators and deputies shall enjoy a salary of three thousand pesos per annum, and shall be entitled to the courteous form of address as His Lordship, and the traveling expenses they shall receive shall be double their salary during the time that the government regulates traveling by land.

Art. 30. There shall be a legislator president, and he shall have the same qualifications as that for Supreme President.

Art. 31. The president legislator cannot be re-elected for this office until after two years have passed after having ceased in his function.

Art. 32. He who should be appointed president legislator shall fulfill this office with preference to any other.

Art. 33. The president legislator shall be nominated by the citizens of the area at the same time of the election of deputies. The nomination shall comprise a group of three persons in the same manner as for Supreme President; and the elections shall be effected in accordance with the order to be dictated for the districts, remitting the testimonies to the president of the judicial power.

Art. 34. The 6th of January next the testimonies shall be opened and read before the judicial power so that they may check them and be informed.

Art. 35. Then verified, the judicial power shall proceed to the certification and counting of the votes, and the one having the majority of the votes shall be the president legislator.

Art. 36. For the [contested?]cases that may occur at the elections, the same routine shall be observed as will be stated, consulting with the Supreme President as soon as he is accessible.

Art. 37. To deliberate in the cases comprehended in the three previous articles there must be present three-quarters of the membership at least of the judicial power.

Art. 38. The president legislator shall serve four years in the exercise of his office, beginning on the first of April. The first president shall serve two years.

Art. 39. If, for any reason, elections were not held nor published by April 1st in which the replacement should be verified or the elected one should not be ready to assume his office promptly, the previous one shall nevertheless cease on the same day; and in the meantime a president shall be appointed by the judicial power, [one] having the qualifications stated in Article 30 and choosing him in the place of the regularly elected one from among those who received an absolute majority in the last election and among the outgoing deputies of the vice-presidency of the chamber.

Art. 40. In case the president should be temporarily prevented [from assuming office] the process shall be observed as stated in the previous article; and if the impediment of the elected one should be prolonged, the election shall be repeated by the judicial power as indicated.

Art. 41. While the election or elections are being held as stated in the two previous articles, the president and vice-president of the legislative chamber shall occupy the office, no matter what period of the year of the said chamber; he shall be appointed monthly by the chamber according to its rules of order to take the place of the president in the discussions.

Art. 42. The day in which the president legislator begins to exercise his functions he shall take an oath before the executive power and the president and judicial secretaries, according to the routine to be dictated for the Supreme President.

Art. 43. The president legislator shall not be able to act beyond what is specifically granted in this constitution.

Art. 44. For the correction of errors in which the president legislator may be involved, a financial accounting shall be effected by the judicial power in the first month after he has left his office so that by virtue of the audit that in the same month shall be concluded and given to the public; and he may be ready to enter the council or else be declared ineligible for this service or any other important one for the nation; and consequently subject to the proper tribunal if he is considered to merit a greater penalty.

Art. 45. The honors of the president legislator shall be those of a Lieutenant General, and an address as His Highness, and his salary shall be twelve thousand pesos per annum.

Art. 46. The secretaries shall be two of the senator class and two of the deputies. They shall be respectively elected by the senators and deputies, as it is done today, holding their offices until their physical or moral incapacity, if their locality re-elects them.

Art. 47. The laws shall be drafted in the chamber of deputies by the initiative of the executive power, the judicial, the deputies, and the principal authorities of the departments, districts, and territories.

Art. 48. In the first three or four months of the year the chamber shall only occupy itself with the passage of new legislation, the repeal of others, and of amendments of this constitution, to perfect what concerns the better adherence to its basic principles.

Art. 49. In the remaining months of the year the chamber shall take into consideration and resolve the doubts on the modern laws, agreement of the old ones with these, and examine the regulations of police and of good administration as it relates to the courts, departments, districts, territories and regions.

Art. 50. The following are declared in effect as soon as the election is held and [are subject to the] exercise of the supreme executive power: Articles 1, 2, 3, 4, 5, of the 4th law of the constitution of the year 1836. Also declared in force are Articles 14, 15, 16, 17, 18 and 19 of the same law in all the points in accord with the present constitution.

Art. 51. The Supreme President of the nation shall assume his duties on the 1st of April and shall be replaced precisely on the same day every four years through a new constitutional election.

Art. 52. If for any reason the elections for President should not have been verified, or the person elected should not be ready promptly to exercise his office, the former president shall nevertheless cease on the same day and another shall be appointed by the chamber composed, as has been said, for the election of the duly elected one, choosing among the councillors of the election and among those who in the last group of three nominated by the local authorities had obtained one-third or more of the total number of votes.

Art. 53. If the President should be temporarily unable to serve, action shall be taken as provided in the previous article; and if the impediment of the holder or of his substitute should so happen when the deputies were not in session, the chamber of deputies and senators who may be present shall appoint a temporary president according to the terms expressed on this matter in the prior articles.

Art. 54. While the elections are being held as mentioned in the previous articles, the president of the judicial power, or this one failing, one of the legislative body shall assume the office of Supreme President; and in the extreme case that both holders be absent, they shall be succeeded in the order of seniority of the councillors of merit and eligibility, except the official president of the council.

Art. 55. In case of the inability of the Supreme President during all his period, the legislative power shall act as hitherto provided; it shall be arranged by the electoral power to proceed to the nomination of a Supreme President, according to the constitutional formulas.

Art. 56. The nomination in groups of three individuals for Supreme President shall be made by the local authorities; and as a consequence of perpetual impossibility of one not being elected to that office, it shall not prevent the ordinary nomination that must be made every four years on the first of August in order that the groups of three individuals be ready in the chamber of deputies for its action on the 1st of September.

Art. 57. The nomination shall be verified on persons who have attained and discharged the office of legislative and judicial president, councillors, secretaries of office, governors, political chiefs, commanders, visiting generals, and general attorneys;and in summary on all those indicated in Article No. 5 of the 4th Law of the constitutional law of 1836. The president newly elected every four years must be on the 1st of April at the place where the supreme powers of the nation may reside, and must take his oath before the Supreme President, with his councillors and ministers, being present also the legislative and judicial powers, to begin the fulfillment of his duties in the following manner:

"I, ..., appointed Supreme President of the Mexican Republic, swear by the name of God and the Holy Gospels, that I shall faithfully exercise the office which the Republic herself has confided to me and that I shall keep and see kept with exactness the constitution and general laws of the nation."

Art. 59. The persons who by accident may succeed to the Supreme Presidency shall be excused from taking the said oath because they have given it before.

Art. 60. The powers of the Supreme President are the following: First: To publish and see carried out the

laws and decrees as first representative of the
nation. Second: To issue regulations, decrees, and
orders for the best execution of the constitution and
the general laws. Third: To put into execution the
laws and decrees directed to preserve the integrity
of the nation, and to maintain its independence
abroad and its unity and freedom within. Fourth: To
pass on to the the legislative powers the proposals
or revisions of law that he believes are for the
general welfare. Fifth: Just for once only, within
ten working days, having once studied the report of
the ministers and taken the opinion of the council,
he can make the observations on the laws and decrees
that are passed to him by the legislative power,
suspend their publication until [the passage of] a
new resolution of the legislative body itself, except
in the cases exempted in this constitution. Sixth: To
appoint and remove freely the chancellor and the
employees of the chancery, whose regulations shall be
a matter of law. Seventh: In the scarcity of public
funds, to dictate, with the advice of the council,
the priorities that must be given to the expenditure
stated in the law. Eighth: To appoint the first chief
of every general office of the Treasury, of every
general commissariat, and to the chief of any
establishment important to the majority of the
nation; to the colonels and other superior officers
of the standing army, active militia and navy, to the
diplomatic envoys and consuls, by means of a report
of the respective minister, the opinion of council,
and the express conformity with the laws. Ninth: To
confirm all the appointments made by the other
personnel of the standing army, active militia and
navy, and of the offices of all the branches of the
nation, subject to what the law provides. Tenth: To
approve, with the opinion of the council, the
nominations which the judicial power may submit on
every judge of law, and on every district attorney of
the nation. Eleventh: To make decisions, with the
opinion of the council, on doubts and appeals on any
matter within the province of the ministers in strict
accord with the law. Twelfth: To dispose of the
standing armed forces of land and sea and the active
militia for the security of the internal and exterior
defense of the nation, based upon the prior report of

the ministers and the opinion of the council. Thirteenth: To dispose of the civil militia for the same purposes in the extension of their own localities up to the immediate neighboring ones, and also in agreement with the report of the ministers and opinion of council in all the extension of the departments, districts, courts, territories, or regions up to the respective neighboring ones, during the exact time that the standing and active force can relieve them. Fourteenth: To declare war in the name of the Mexican nation, celebrate agreements with the apostolic chair, promote the arrangement of discipline and patronage, direct diplomatic negotiations, and celebrate treaties of peace, friendship and alliance, truce, confederation, armed neutrality, commerce and any other matters with overseas, but all this after first seeing the report of the ministers, consulting the opinion of the council and the consent of the legislative and judicial power, or of one of these in what may be in full agreement with the council. Fifteenth: To grant patents of privatering in accordance with what the laws dispose by means of a report of the respective minister and the opinion of the council. Sixteenth: To receive ministers and other envoys of foreign powers in accord with the previous articles, as the case may require. Seventeenth: To summon the chamber for extraordinary sessions whenever he believes it suitable after Consultation with the ministers and council, or when the judicial power deems it necessary, by vote of two-thirds of its members. Eighteenth: To see that every officer and public employee, without any exception, fulfills his obligations correctly and promptly. Nineteenth: To suspend from their employments up to three months and to deprive them of half of their salaries during the same period for the officers and public employees of the nation who somehow do not fulfill their obligations; and in the cases where they may merit it, to prefer a charge by passing their dossier to the respective tribunal, excepting the senators, deputies and secretaries of the legislative power, with the president, ministers, district attorneys and secretaries of the judicial power, with the councillors and ministers of the executive, nor with the first deliberating authorities, governmental and judicial employees of the departments, districts, courts and territories.

Twentieth: To accuse, individually, having once heard the opinion of the council, all administrative authority, exempting the ones of the previous article, verifying the said accusation before the president of the legislative power, verifying the said power only through its secretary, that there is cause for suspension to be effected in the terms that shall be in entire agreement with the executive and to pass the dossier to the supreme judicial power so that if they find the suspension meriting a higher penalty the criminal being sentenced, he shall pass the case to the proper judge for the corresponding punishment. Twentifirst: To accuse individually any councillor, minister, senator, deputy or secretary of the legislative power, fiscal minister, or secretary of the judiciary, verifying the accusation before the legislative president if the accused are not from this said rank, otherwise it must be before the president of the judicial power, so that in any case the president or whoever it may fall upon may declare through the secretary if there may be cause for suspension and it be verified in the terms of complete agreement with the executive; then the dossier passes at once to the president who has not intervened in the suspension, so that together with him the corporation resolves the matter -- whether he merits a greater penalty [be assessed] and he declared a criminal, the cause may be referred to the judge concerned and the legal punishment be applied to [the delinquent]. Twentysecond: To grant the passage or hold up the [Church] council decrees, the pontifical bullas, apostolic briefs and rescripts, with advice to the legislative power if they contain general dispositions; hearing the council of the government and its ministers, if they should refer to private or governmental business; and to the judicial power, if they should have been issued on contentious matters. Twentythird: To grant retirements, leaves, and pensions in accord with the laws. Twentyfourth: To present [nominations] for all the bishops and dignitaries and ecclesiastic benefits in agreement with the council. Twentyfifth: To watch over the legality and exactness of the production of the coin currency. Twentysixth: To grant or deny, in accordance with the council, and in agreement with the laws, the pardons that may be requested on causes heard by the tribunals whose verdict may have caused the sentence and the supreme court of justice suspending the execution until the case is settled. This article does not grant the president the authority to free from the death penalty those who have lost the rights of citizenship in prison for crimes states in paragraph 2, Article 8 of the constitution. Twentyseventh: To make provisions relating to the conduct of good government of the nation, without intervening with the internal administration of the localities, without damaging the rights of Mexicans, without interfering in constitutional elections, without disturbing the free exercise of the employees in his branch, nor of the religion of the country. In summary, without taking on the assumption of other powers nor attempting to destroy in any respect any constitutional article.

Art. 61. In order to publish laws and decrees the Supreme President shall use the following formula. "The Supreme President of the Mexican Republic, let it be known: that the supreme government of the nation has sanctioned on (here the date is placed) the following agreement (here the text). Therefore, I order it to be published and circulated, so that, published and filed, it may be evident to the nation and have an exact fulfillment."

Art. 62. The restrictions on the authority of the Supreme President are the following: First: The President cannot command in person the forces of land and sea, nor under any motive whatever can he leave the territory of the Republic, not even away from the capital without previous knowledge of the legislative and judicial power, and when both have been notified according to the previous requisite, it shall be total cessation of the powers, prerogatives, honors and salary of president, because all those privileges will be passed on to the person who earlier shall be appointed to succeed him, as stated in this constitution. Second: the President shall not be able

to deprive anyone of his freedom, nor to impose upon
him any penalty whatsoever; but when it be demanded
for the welfare and security of the Republic, he may
order arrest, placing the persons within a period of
forty-eight hours at the disposal of the tribunal or
competent judge. Third: The President cannot occupy
the property of any private individual or
corporation, nor disturb him in his possession or use
of it; and if in some case it should be necessary for
some known reason of general necessity to take or to
use those properties, he cannot do so without the
report of the ministers, the opinion of the council,
acceptance of the legislative president can be
disregarded, when it is with the conformity of the
full council and always indemnifying the interested
party in accordance with the judgment of good and
expert men, elected for this purpose by the council
and government. Fourth: The Supreme President in
doubtful executive cases shall be held blameless in
his deliberations, binding himself to what a report
of the ministers and opinion of the council should
decide in agreement with the legislative and judicial
presidents. Fifth: The Supreme President, in short,
cannot exercise other acts than those detailed in
this constitution; any breach of it or of some
general law shall also bring with it the
responsibility of the minister or ministers who may
have authorized it with their signature. The
President shall only be personally responsible in the
case of having issued a formal decree for some
violation of the present code, making use of the
armed forces. Sixth: The Supreme President, during
his term of office, shall not be publicly slandered;
for if he should commit treason, as has been stated,
against the independence or internal freedom of the
nation, or should not comply with any part of this
constitution and the general laws, he can be accused
before the chamber of deputies, who, finding
undeniable evidence of the imputed crime, can pass
the matter and their conclusion to the senate for its
examination in secrecy in order to resolve whether or
not the President is required to give due explanation. In the affirmative, if so verified, and exactly
before twelve hours have passed, the minister or
ministers of state shall present themselves to

give it; and once received the legislature in the presence of the presidents of the judicial courts, shall decide upon his guilt or innocence in the matter and make a corresponding communication to the supreme court. In the latter case it shall be demanded of the Supreme President the correction deemed necessary if in the matter the constitutional laws are not compromised in a serious way, because if they are and the amendment not being verified in the time and manner demanded, both judicial and legislative powers agreeing once more in their deliberations, shall make public the occurrence, declaring the Supreme President in consequence suspended and questionable, and appointing as a contingent successor the individual of the council who may be designated.

TITLE VI

Art. 63. The honors of the Supreme President shall be those of Captain-General, and to be addressed as His Supreme Highness, a special uniform and a salary of twelve thousand pesos per annum, and the expenses of public festivities in the palace and functions of state being payable from the public treasury.

Art.64. When the President should temporarily cease in his functions, he shall receive one-third of his salary in cases of justified illness, without affecting the total salary that the one who substitutes for him shall receive.

TITLE VII

Art. 65. The government council shall consist of the retired presidents without impediments and fourteen directors of good moral standing, ten officials and four of honor.

The last retired President shall preside over the council and in his stead the other retired ones by order of seniority, and in place of them all should they be absent the councillor of greatest seniority. The President and five councillors shall form a corporation. For the branches of each ministry there shall be a special commission composed of not less than two councillors.

Art. 66. When one or more of the elected councillors should be absent, nominations shall be made by the ranking authorities of the localities, as stated, for the Supreme President.

Art. 67. The councillors shall be Mexicans by birth, grandsons of Mexicans of not less than forty years of age and highly educated.

Art. 68. When the affidavits have been received of the three-quarters parts who should vote, the legislative power may establish the qualification, as stated, for Supreme President: a list of names of the competent candidates shall be passed on to the judicial power; and the latter, before two days, shall return them, voting for those who are believed to have better aptitudes for councillors, and designating the order which is suitable for each one.

Art. 69. In consequence the legislative [branch] shall proceed to the counting of the votes and shall decide the election accordingly for Supreme President, it being understood that those nominated and recommended by the judicial power by the voting shall be considered with their respective majority of votes, even though they do not have it through nomination.

Art. 70. For the councillors to enter into office they must take an oath in the name of God and the Holy Scriptures to fulfill promptly and effectively the offices that by this constitution are entrusted to them.

Art. 71. In order that a councillor, whether by merit or election, to be separated from his office without being called by law to another office, he shall declare [his intention before] the chamber of deputies in accord with the official dossier which the Supreme President will pass on to him and from the opinion given by the judicial power.

Art. 72. To replace the elected councillors temporarily, even though they may be for temporary absence, they shall supply the salaries by drawing lots.

Art. 73. The powers of the councillors are as follows: First: To compile the disagreements, difficulties, and inconveniences that for the welfare and public prosperity they may find in this constitution and the general laws, contriving immediately the most sure and simple means for their correction.

Second: To make to the Supreme President the observations believed conducive to the best compliance with the constitution and laws. Third: To give their judgment on all other matters that even though they are not mentioned in this constitution the Supreme President may want to discuss. Fifth: To present to the Supreme President every year the compilations to which the first list of his powers refers in order that the chamber of deputies may take them into consideration in the ordinary sessions.

Art. 74. The councillors shall only be responsible when they should pass their judgment against what the law expresses, especially if it is constitutional; but the responsibility shall immediately fall on those who may offer their judgment. The councillors of merit shall have six thousand pesos as salary per year and be addressed as His Honorable Excellency; and the elected councillors shall have four thousand pesos as salary per annum, and the latter as well as the former shall be addressed as Excellency.

TITLE VIII

Art. 75. The secretary ministers shall be five: one of police, who shall attend to everything related to that field, agriculture, arts, mining, conservation of public worship and purity of the dogma; another of public Treasury, who shall attend to everything relative to active and passive credits of the nation, economy of its investments and matters related to commerce; another of justice who shall deal with everything concerning the administration of justice, be it civil, military, or ecclesiastic, and above all public education in general; another of war, whose object shall be to watch over the order, number, and service of the standing force, active, local navy and privatering; another for foreign relations, who shall deal with the treaties with foreign nations, of the notices and diplomatic negotiations that may occur; and in summary on all matters concerned with the good name and advantages of the nation with foreign [nations].

Art. 76. In order to be a minister of state it is necessary to be a Mexican by birth, a grandson of Mexicans, be older than forty years of age, to be known for integrity, education, activity and instruction on those matters relative to the better fulfillment in the fields of their office.

Art. 77. The ministers shall be nominated by the first authorities of the court, districts, departments, and territories and elected by the legislative, as stated for the councillors.

Art. 78. In order to assume their offices the ministers shall take an oath in the name of God and the Holy Scriptures to comply impartially, promptly and effectively with the offices with which they are entrusted under this constitution and to make positive efforts to see that their subordinates comply in the same manner.

Art. 79. On temporary absence of a minister because of illness duly confirmed, or by license granted by the Supreme President and supported by the opinion of the council, shall be the substitute, considering the report of all the first officers of all the branches which the ministers shall present every year.

Art. 80. In order that a minister may be separated from service without having been called by law to another position, the same process shall be followed as was done with respect to the councillors.

Art. 81. When a minister has been replaced perman- ently, the procedure shall be followed as stated in Article No. 78.

Art. 82. The oath shall be taken by the first officers of every branch when they occupy their offices, but they shall be exempted from taking it when they substitute for a minister who may be absent.

Art. 83. All the regulations and orders of the Supreme President must have the seal of office; the decrees shall bear his full signature as well. All the indicated depositions shall be authorized by the corresponding minister to whom the matter concerns; without said requisite they shall not be obeyed. Consequently, the secretary ministers shall be responsible for the actions of the Supreme President that are given for execution under their signatures when they are contrary to this constitution and general laws.

Art. 84. The appointments, dispatches, and other acts of the executive that are not stated in the authority of the Supreme President for his office shall be within the province of the ministers as long as they are in complete accord with the laws and regulations; in case of doubt they shall pass it on to the President for his decision, on hearing the council.

Art. 85. The ministers shall also make up the compilation stated in the first listing of Article No. 73, so that the President may pass it to the chamber.

Art. 86. The ministers shall draw up a regulation for the better distribution and trade of the business in his charge, so that the President with the opinion of the council may standardize it for the five ministers, and it shall have the same bases as follows: First: In each ministry there shall be for every branch of those in an office which may be sub-divided a first officer and the necessary subordinates. Second: The first officers shall be Mexican by birth, grandsons of Mexicans, thirty five years of age at least, and have seniority as good and continuous public service; they must also have the indispensable necessary education, activity, and honesty. The subordinates shall be Mexicans by birth, of good conduct and with proportional education. Third: The first officers shall be promoted by the minister and approved by the President after having consulted the opinion of the council; the subordinates shall be promoted by the first officer of the branch and approved by the minister after a consultation with the other first officers of the ministry. Fourth: All these officers shall enjoy retirement pension when they are worn out after twenty-four years of good services. Fifth: Every first officer shall take an oath as was pronounced by the ministers and on his responsibility he shall be obliged to give his opinion in a clear and concise manner, without ambiguities or evasions on the matters of the ministry that involve his conduct of office, quoting the laws and regulations pertinent to them. Sixth: When the minister makes a resolution in conformity with the opinion of the chief of the corresponding dispatch, if the resolution should seem illegal or absurd, it shall be the duty of the minister to correct it; but if it should have been done on the advice of the minister himself, the correction shall be the duty of the President, with the opinion of the council. Seventh: In order that the interested parties may deduce their rights according to what is stated in the previous article, the ministers, when writing the resolution, shall say, "In agreement with the chief of the branch"...if it be so.

Art. 87. The ministers shall have a salary and be accorded the treatment equal to that of Major-Generals.

Art. 88. The private office of the Supreme President shall consist of one chancellor as chief, appointed and freely removed by the President; with the understanding that the said chief shall be Mexican by birth and grandson of Mexicans, more than forty years of age and of recognized probity and education; his salary and address shall be those of the senators. His duties shall be to seal the official papers, orders or decrees which the President may send him; to read and to write the private matters which the he President may entrust to him; to take care of the receipt and remittance of both official and private correspondence of the government, and to supervise the routine sequence which the President observes in his office. His oath shall be, "To fulfill faithfully the written orders and to keep absolute secrecy." For the office work there shall be filing employees, clerks, and all the other persons necessary; and their creation and the total expenses shall be the responsibility of the legislative chambers.

SECTION IV   TITLE X

Art. 89. The judicial power of the nation shall retain the same faculties, authority and restrictions, the same structure and form that it has today, according to the fifth constitutional law of 1836 in all that does not go counter to the code of 1824, or with some article of the present [constitution]. Therefore, it shall not be attempted to change the personnel which comprise the said power, save in such cases and occasions as may be necessary.

Art. 90. The president of the supreme court shall be elected by the tribunal itself and whose term of office shall be the same as the legislative president; his honors and address shall be the same; the same his prerogatives and exemptions.

SECTION V   TITLE XI

Art. 91. The conservative power shall rest upon the three high powers, in the following manner: If the infringement, for example, were of the President, the legal authority or the citizen who has become aware of it, may resort either to the congress or to the supreme court of justice, stating in writing the infringement that he has noted. In this case, the three chambers shall meet and deliberate on the complaint; and if they agree by an absolute majority with the opinion of the complainant, the president of the court shall give notice to the legislative chambers with the original written evidence. If from the discussion of both chambers it should result in conformity with the court of justice, they shall immediately remit to the executive a signed indictment by the secretaries and presidents of both mentioned powers in advance of those where the written evidence originated in order that the executive may revoke immediately his sentence, but if any of the two powers should not deem the complaint to be well founded, it shall be understood legitimate to quash action on the complaint and no future procedure can take place on the matter. The same shall be the case when the complaint be on an action of the legislative or judicial power, because the other two powers shall be free to proceed in the same terms. Any disobedience of the said indictment shall make the way free for the two powers gathered together to discharge the persons who have concurred in the infringement and to proceed thereafter in accord with this constitution.

SECTION VI   TITLE XII

Art. 92. The court or capital of the Republic shall be situated before two years time in the most convenient and central part between Durango and Chihuahua; meanwhile they shall leave the capital of Mexico immediately and the supreme powers shall start locating themselves into he most convenient places that they may find in the direction of the said point. There also, of course, shall be located the main standing army, taking with it all the discharged employees and the retired military [pensioners] who want to be totally and punctually paid, all the vagrants of both sexes and those sentenced to prison.

Art. 93. The departments shall be reduced from the time being into seven, that are: Yucatan, Veracruz, Oajaca, Puebla, Mexico, Guanajuato and Jalisco. The districts shall also be for the time being fourteen, which are: Chiapas, Tabasco, Queretaro, Michoacan, San Luis Potosi, Zacatacas, Tamaulipas, Nuevo Leon, Coahuila and Texas, Sonora, Sinaloa, Durango and Chihuahua. The territories shall be: Tlaxcala, Colima, New Mexico, New California. The regions shall be: the peninsula of California, the Northwest frontier from the dividing line with the United

States by that route to the port of San Francisco inclusive with the missions which belong to it; and finally, that uninhabited part of Sinaloa, Sonora, Durango, Chichuhua, Coahuila and the part occupied by the heathen.

Art. 94. The congress shall lay out the boundaries of the divisions that exist and that there should be in the departments and districts, fixing their capitals according. The same demarcation shall be effected in the territories and regions; but to deliberate on all this a report shall be required of the supreme government when sufficiently instructed by a detailed statistical survey of all the Republic, which shall be begun at once and is to be made preferentially by the authorized officers, and which should be concluded within a period of three years.

Art. 95. The supreme government, notwithstanding that mentioned in the previous article, shall provisionally mark the regions with the object of facilitating the precise knowledge of the land for preparation of its statistics.

Art. 96. The political chiefs and general commanders of regions shall serve in their offices six years. In their absence due to illness or other accident, their immediate subordinates shall substitute for them; and if the absence should be prolonged, he who should be appointed as a result of a drawing from a proposed group of three shall retain it for the remaining time of the period if the executive should not have chosen any person before that time.

Art. 97. The political chiefs in their territories shall be the superior officials even in the field of the public treasury; but in the latter, only to see that the management of the employees is effected in accord with the laws and to correct the abuses while they give account of it to the court; they shall not be able to interfere with the judicial operations, because for these cases there shall be the necessary judges to be designated by the congress and they shall be appointed by the Supreme President on a proposal from the justice to be chosen from a group of three.

Art. 98. The general commanders of the regions shall be appointed in the same way, and for the same time as those of the political chiefs. They shall be the superior officers in all the fields of their territory, even in that of the public treasury, acting in civil matters as permitted to the political chiefs; and in the judicial field they shall act in the military way with the adviser or advisers whom the supreme court may propose and be approved by the supreme government. The said advisers shall not be removable save in the time and manner that the supreme court proposes and the congress may approve.

Art. 99. It is not required to be a resident for any of the aforementioned offices, but one must be Mexican by birth, of a suitably mature age, at least forty years old.

Art. 100. For the better organization of the territories and regions the superior chiefs shall make a report every year on what they believe most suitable for their prosperity, so that without any violent transition they can pass as quickly as possible to the rank of districts and departments.

Art. 101. Every two years the supreme government shall nominate the necessary voting inspectors, besides the additional ones which might be convenient, so that the good management of the government can be assured; and to require also in every second year of the renovation of the deputies that the chamber take into consideration the observations of the said visitor-inspectors which they shall present in their reports expressed in the previous article.

Art. 102. There shall be municipalities only in the regions and in the capitals of the departments and districts, as well as in the other capitals and locations whose population should so require according to the pre-existing laws; but in them there shall be included a fourth or third of permanent chapter members. In all the other towns there shall be justices of peace. Regarding the organization of the former, their authority, appointments and term of one and the other, that which was provided in the laws cited heretofore shall be observed as long as they are not in conflict with the present constitution.

Art. 103. These municipalities and the indicated justices of peace shall not be able to represent the people in cases not considered in the 6th law of the constitution of 1836, in the decree of March of 1837, and in what is expressed in the following article.

Art. 104. When the above mentioned municipal authorities shall know that their respective territories are involved in a case indicated in the 2nd article of this constitution, they shall send a reasoned presentation to the respective main government through the regular channels, and if it should appear that it is sufficiently supported, it is to be passed then with their respective report to the supreme government of the nation; and the latter shall send it on his initiative if he holds with the informers; but if he should not do so, the case shall nevertheless be submitted to the chamber of deputies, expanding the reasons of his opinions. They will take everything into consideration and shall consequently deliberate in the term of one year what they consider most likely to promote the glory and prosperity of the Republic.

SECTION VII   TITLE XIV

Art. 105. The attorney generals of the nation shall be two, appointed by the chamber of deputies, voting by states in the first ordinary session.

Art. 106. The attorney generals must be Mexicans by birth, grandsons of Mexicans, older than forty years, well-posted in the science of both rights, of recognized patriotism, good judgment, wisdom, and activity; eligible as stated and proposed in a group of three by the principal authorities of the departments, districts, regions and territories.

Art. 107. The day and manner of their election is determined by the Supreme President.

Art. 108. The following are the powers of the said attorneys: First: To see that all the tribunals are administered promptly, correctly, and with strict justice, becoming in the name of the nation public prosecutors of every judge or errant magistrate. In the same manner they shall proceed against the chiefs of the public treasury, clerks of the frontier guard posts and customs who may embezzle the wealth or fail in their duties or if they should exceed their own authority. Third: They shall listen to all complaints of citizens who consider themselves oppressed by the political, military or ecclesiastical authorities, by police agents, etc., so that if their claims are judged reasonable they will then support it with their accusation before the competent authority.

Art. 109. The general district attorneys shall be permanent in their offices; they shall have an assignment of eight thousand pesos per annum, and they will not be able to exercise any other office, employment, commission, or public or private dependence, except that of Supreme President. Their formal address shall be that of His Excellency; they may reside in any part of the Republic, although they have to travel in person throughout the country within a period of four years, repeating this every ten years; and they may be accused only before a tribunal in charge of judging the ministers of the supreme court of justice, once the declaration of the grand jury has been obtained.

Art. 110. Any corporation, the chief or prelate, the magistrate or judge who should disregard any accusation of one of the general district attorneys shall be dealt with as a criminal of high treason [lesa nacion].

SECTION VIII   TITLE XV

Art. 111. Neither the congress nor the government can remove to a higher court the dealings of the judicial affairs, and neither the latter nor the tribunals may

410

order terminated lawsuits to be re-opened.

Art. 112. They shall be considered as [terminated lawsuits] those which both parties have agreed by special grant or by voluntary acquiescence and proved to have been inactive for two years. Likewise they shall be considered as terminated law suits those that have ended in a court decision which shall be produced by two parallel judgments.

Art. 113. The manner of starting lawsuits shall be the same in all the Republic, and likewise the laws and order of the proceedings.

Art. 114. Only the military and the ecclesiastics are exempted from this regulation; it shall apply in their own affairs pertaining to their special rights [fueros] which shall be personal, and shall exist only the cases of their sort.

Art. 115. Neither the congress nor the government nor the tribunals shall be able to proscribe any person whatsoever, nor offer any reward of any kind, and much less grant it by actions repudiated by universal moral codes.

Art. 116. No criminal of one location shall get asylum from another; in fact, he shall be delivered at once to the authorities who may claim him.

Art. 117. The first authorities of the localities shall give preferential assistance to the deter-minations of the conservative power, placing at its disposal the local militia.

Art. 118. No one is born a slave in the Republic; neither shall the inhuman traffic be permitted; on the contrary, if someone should come [into the country] in such a degrading state, he shall be considered to be manumitted as soon as he arrives at any port of the nation.

Art. 119. No person who is condemned by law shall be obliged to work.

Art. 120. No person shall be judged except by the judges of his special privilege [fuero] nor suffer any penalty by the authority of an alien jurisdiction.

Art. 121. The general powers cannot interfere in the internal administration granted to the local authorities, nor can the latter determine any action whatsoever in conflict with the present constitution.

Art. 122. Any transgression of these [localities] shall produce public action, and the citizens shall have ready the resort with which they are granted in the present code.

Art. 123. The citizen declared in this way in conformity with the general laws shall be so considered in all the Republic; but he shall not be considered as such if he is lacking the special title which certifies it.

Art. 124. The presidents of the legislative and judicial power, without any exception whatever, shall, after the first month of their retirement, be investigated in a public hearing by the competent power on their good or bad fulfillment in their obligations of their office, so that by virtue of the judgment which during the same month shall be concluded and given to the public, he may be ready to move up to the council, or else be declared unfit for that service or for any other important work for the nation.

Art. 125. If the president or individuals who are designed for the fiscal audit should be excused in such a manner that it is not verified in the time and manner specified, they shall be stripped of their prerogatives and submitted to the common judges.

Art. 126. In case that the Supreme President together with the other existing, the opinion of the council being heard, they shall supply in the best possible manner the reinstatement of the retired person while by constitutional means it is being revised.

Art. 127. All the judges shall be sufficiently

competent for the fulfillment of their offices of the administration with which they are entrusted; and in the way that they shall firmly sustain their decisions they shall also be strictly supervised and punished by their superior officers.

Art. 128. All honest occupation is honorable in the Republic. Speculation, peculation, usury, extortion, and monoply shall be liable to public action, and [the guilty party] shall be deprived at once of the rights of citizenship. The proved prevarication of any officer shall suffer the same end, besides those stated in the laws of this branch.

Art. 129. Only the general congress shall resolve the doubts that may occur on the understanding of this constitution.

Art. 130. All public officers, before taking possession of their offices, shall swear to observe and see observed whatever relates to each and every one of the articles of this constitution under the strictest responsibility which will be made effective in each case.

Art. 131. No variation nor revision can be carried out in the present constitution without the majority of the nation having manifested their conformity through the official channels of the authorities of the departments, districts, regions, or territories with at least a two-third vote.

Art. 132. No taxation shall continue if it should be challenged by three-fourths parts of the departments, districts, regions, and territories.

Art. 133. The nation consecrates as perpetual and immutable bases of its existence: The religion and independence of the country, the division of the supreme powers and of the principal ones of the departments and districts, and in the same manner in the regions and territories, the political freedom of the press, the rights of the citizens, the responsibility of public employees.

Mexico: October 26, 1841.

POST SCRIPTUM

For many years this project has kept me awake, an idea which has been proving itself by subsequent events, for in the passage of time the wish to see it realized has fortified my will as an attempt to change the sad condition such as the one in which we have found ourselves. Nevertheless, I have been repressing that anxiety so as not to appear as a disturber of governmental order, as an imprudent novice, nor as an instigator of proselytism. However, a good patriot and a well-educated collaborator has caused these fears to vanish; and on considering first, that the government itself has urged [the public] through its official newspaper not once but many times to write about constitutional reforms, and second and principally, that now in these critical emergencies it will be service to distract attention, if it be possible, from the concern of the theatre of war to elucidate matters on which the happiness of the country is founded. Let us hope that it may be so! That the calm of cold reasoning succeed the tumultuous vortex of the masses; and to the ultimate reason of kings--cannons--we may add the first foundation of good laws: tranquil and thoughtful discussion!

Proyecto de Constitucion, Anon., circa 1841, New York Public Library.

* * * * *

PLAN OF THE GARRISON (1)

December, 1841

Art. 1. The Constitutent Congress is disavowed, having gone contrary to the will of the nation, because its fundamental laws have been as far removed from the exaggerations of the Constitution of 1824 as from the petty restrictions contained in that of 1836.

Art. 2. The Administration shall name a commission

---

(1) The garrison of San Luis Potosi, Puebla, Queretaro, Morelia, Zacatecas, Aguascalientes, and Jalisco adopted practically identical Plans.

414

[junta] of citizens, recognized for their wisdom, for their experience, patriotism, and services; that it shall consult with it on the terms in which a provisional Statute should be expressed that will assure the existence and the dignity of the nation, the prosperity of the Departments and the guarantees to which all Mexicans have a right. This statute shall be presented to the nation so that it may sanction it.

Art. 3. His Excellency Sr. Greatly-Deserving [Benemerito] of the Fatherland General-of-Division don Antonio Lopez de Santa Anna is again recognized as provisional President of the Republic and as a substitute His Excellency Deserving of the Fatherland [Benemerito] General of Division don Nicolas Bravo.

V. Riva Palacio, *Mexico a traves de los siglos,* IV, 492.

* * * * *

DECLARATION OF HEUJOTZINGO

13 December, 1842

Art. 1. The constituent Congress is disavowed in view of its projected Constitution which does not respect the sacronsanct religion of our fathers, because it permits the private exercise of any other, against the principles which ought to be followed in a truly Catholic country.

Art. 2. It enlarges the freedom of the press until it converts it into an Instrument of sedition beyond control; it repudiates the necessity, usefulness, and service of the Army which is composed of virtuous Mexicans; it places in danger the national independence, because at the same time that it establishes the civic militias--an inexhaustible source of evils and the most serious error contained in the Constitution of 1824--in the projected draft [of the Constitution] this [civic militia] is greatly extended; it prohibits the death penalty under the false pretext of philanthropy; and finally in each of its sections it systemizes anarchy.

> (Signed by representatives of the garrison).

V. Riva Palacio, Mexico a traves de los siglos, IV, 491-492.

* * * * *

PRONOUNCEMENT OF THE GARRISON OF MEXICO (CITY)

19 December, 1842

At five o'clock on Monday afternoon the pronouncement of the garrison of Mexico (City) was published by proclamation; it ended with the following articles:

Art. 1. Not being able in this crisis to leave the nation without hopes for an order of things that assure its liberty, its rights, the division of powers, the social guarantees and the prosperity of the Departments, the government shall name a committee [junta] composed of citizens distinguished for their learning and patriotism so that it may draft the bases, with the assistance of the ministry, that may serve to organize the nation, and that this government shall approve that it may govern [the nation].

Art. 2. The Committee shall be named as soon as possible, and it shall not be empowered to continue in the discharge of its task longer than six months, counting from this day.

Art. 3. Meanwhile the Bases agreed to in Tacubaya, in so far as they are not opposed to this decree, shall continue to govern [the country], and the council of the Departments shall continue functioning on the same basis that was planned for them.

Art. 4. Just as it will be the duty of the government

416

to prevent public peace being distributed (*) hereafter and going against this decree, he who signs below solemnly pledges to prevent Mexicans from being molested for their political conduct up to the present time.

(Signed) Nicolas Bravo, National
Palace Substitute President

(*) So long as Santa Anna does not change it, it shall not be changed.

Carlos Maria Bustamante, <u>Apuntes para la historia del gobierno del General D. Antonio Lopez de Santa Anna,</u> 96-97

* * * * *

DECLARATION OF THE ASSEMBLY OF JALISCO

6 November, 1844

[After a verbatim report of speeches by representatives...]

For the reasons thus expressed, the Departmental Assembly of Jalisco, in the use of the power committed to it in Article 53 of the Bases of Organization of the Republic, submits to the Honorable houses the present declaration of law as drafted in the following propositions:

Art. 1. The national congress will make effective the responsibility of the provisional government to which it submitted the 6th of the bases agreed to in Tacubaya and to which it swore and caused the nation to swear.

Art. 2. The Law of August 21st of this year by which extraordinary contributions were imposed is hereby repealed.

ARt. 3. Preferably the Congress will concern itself with reforming the constitutional articles which experience has shown to be contrary to the prosperity of the Departments.

Legislative Hall of the   (Signed by officials
Departmental Assembly.   of the Assembly)

[There is an identical resolution from Aquasc-
alientes.]

El Siglo XIX, November 17, 1844.

* * * * *

DECLARATION OF QUERETARO

20 December, 1844

On the 20th of December the officers of the Army met
in Queretaro and agreed to the articles of the
following Plan:

Art. 1. The Army reiterates its oaths of obedience to
the Organic Bases of the Republic.

Art. 2. In consequence the Army recognizes General
Don Antonio Lopez de Santa Anna as the constitutional
president.

Art. 3. The same Army repudiates the authorities who
are presiding in the capital of the Republic, and who
owe their existence to the seditious revolt of the
6th of the present month. Every act by whatever
authority that attacks the constitutional
prerogatives of His Excellency the legal occupant
will likewise be repud- iated by the Army.

Art. 4. The Army declares that it will not lay down
its arms until order is reestablished and until the
constitutional authority of the said Excellency Sr.
President, General of Division, and Well-Merited
[Benemerito] of the Fatherland don Antonio Lopez
deSanta Anna be respected and obeyed by all.

V. Riva Palacio, Mexico a traves de los siglos, IV,
533.

PLAN OF GENERAL RANGEL

7 June, 1845

Art. 1. From this moment the Constitution of 1824 is reestablished.

Art. 2. Temporarily the supreme executive power is deposited in the president of the Supreme Court of Justice and the two associates of which the mentioned constitution speaks.

These shall be named immediately by the Supreme Court of Justice, by the military [court], by the council of government, by the deputies and senators who opposed the ministry of Cuevas on the celebration of treaties with Texas, and also by the deputies who voted in favor of peaceful representations as did a multitude of citizens, asking for the reestablishment of the Federation.

Art. 3. Within three days the government shall issue a call for a convocation of an extraordinary congress.

Art. 4. This [Congress], without being prorogued, shall re-draft the constitution within four months, excepting only the form of government, the Catholic, Apostolic, and Roman religion, the privileges of the clergy and of the army to which they shall give an organization and a splendor that will serve as a stimulus hereafter for those who undertake the noble career of arms.

Art. 5. At its first session the congress shall elect an interim president who shall function as such until the constitutional one shall take possession.

Art. 6. On the day following the election of the general Congress the same electors shall elect the authorities of the States, who shall enter into the exercise of their functions in accordance with their particular constitutions.

Art. 7. The present authorities of the Departments shall be discharged if they do not support this Plan

419

and the commander [jefe] who may declare [for it] in their capitals shall organize their governments provisionally while subjecting themselves as far as possible to that provided in the constitutions of the States.

Art. 8. The government shall organize the national guard immediately, placing under arms that [part] which may be necessary to preserve public order and to reenforce the troops which may march into Texas, [troops] which ought to be provided with whatever may be necessary and to be paid punctually, because it is not fair that those who serve the nation, exposing their lives for it, should be as unattended by the government as has been so until this very day.

El Siglo XIX, 9 July 1845.

* * * * *

THE SALVADORAN PLAN

26 August, 1845

Art. 1. A congress shall be convoked in order to reorganize the nation according to its will and circumstances.

Art. 2. In order to keep the ignorant public from making a mistake, the deputies who are to be named for the purpose shall be elected by the Administration which will be discussed below.

Art. 3. The new constitution to be decreed shall not take effect until the war with Texas, with the United States, or with any other [country] that may present itself shall have ended; in the meantime depositing [the constitution] in a bronze chest with three locks whose keys the Administration which has already been mentioned shall keep held in custody; the commanding general of the land forces and the Grand Admiral of the Sea, newly created functionaries, shall name the new government.

420

Art. 4. This new government shall be composed of three persons chosen from among the most renowned of the military for their bravery and for undertaking and completing great enterprises.

Art. 5. This same Administration shall govern the nation with discretion and paternalisticaly in accord with its loyal knowledge and understanding until the war or wars previously mentioned have been concluded; and when the nation shall be enjoying a durable peace, the new constitution shall be set into effect.

Art. 6. Last article: Whatever person regardless of class or condition that he may be who in any way may oppose the new order of things either by word of mouth or by writing, or in any other way shall be held to be a criminal guilty of the crime of lesa nacion.

(Signed)   Jose   the Planner In the Cuidadela of San Hipolito.

El Monitor Constitucional, 9 September, 1845. Printed without comment. The anonymous signature causes one to wonder whether it was a serious Plan drafted by a journeyman from El Salvador, or if it was accepted as such in those days.

* * * * *

DECLARATION OF SAN LUIS

14 December, 1845

[A long, introductory paragraph of explanation and defense of a military revolt accompanies the Plan.]

The articles of this Pronouncement are as follows:

Art. 1. The army supports with its arms the protest which the nation makes against all the subsequent actions of the present Administration, and declares that as from today they shall be considered null and of no value.

Art. 2. Since neither the present congress nor the executive power are able to continue in their functions, they shall cease to exercise all of them.

Art. 3. Immediately after the army occupies the capital of the Republic, an _extraordinary_ Congress shall be summoned with ample powers to constitute the nation without any restriction whatsoever in these magnificent functions.

Art. 4. In the formation of this Congress the representation of all classes of society shall be combined.

Art. 5. As soon as it has been installed and begun to exercise its high offices, [the Congress] shall organize the Executive Power, and no other authority shall be able to exist, save by its sovereign sanction.

Art. 6. The same authorities that today are governing in the Departments shall continue personally until they are substituted for those that national representation provides.

Art. 7. The army shall appoint as its leader for this political movement His Excellency Major General Mariano Paredes y Arrillaga, who shall be invited immediately through a commission appointed by the members of this same junta, which remains together until his resolution is heard.

Art. 8. Another commission shall be appointed to invite His Excellency the Governor and the Assembly of this Department, so that he may adhere to these propositions.

Art. 9. The army protests in the most solemn manner that it does not intend nor shall intend in any case whatsoever to promote the leader whom it has chosen.

Art. 10. Likewise it also vows to punish severely in an exemplary manner all those who with arms should oppose the present Plan.

_____

Coleccion de las leyes fundamentales, (Mexico, 1856), 267-268; and M. Muro, Historia de San Luis, 345-346. El Siglo XIX, 26 Dec. 1845.

* * * * *

DECLARATION OF VERA CRUZ

23 December, 1845

[Note: The first ten articles are exactly the same as those of the Declaration of San Luis, dated 23 December 1845]. It continues as follows: All the commanders and officers being agreed, they furthermore agreed to the following articles:

Art. 1. We shall invite to second this Plan all the authorities of the Department, they doing so in this heroic city through a committee which shall present to the Most Excellent City Council the wishes of this garrison, because they preserve order and public tranquility by placing at their disposal the forces that are believed necessary to attain this sacred objective.

Art. 2. This action shall be communicated immediately to the garrison of Ulloa and to the general commander of the Navy.

Art. 3. Having refused to have General Jose Rincon assume the command, the invitation made to His Excellency General Ignacio Mora y Villamil shall be repeated so that he may receive it; and meanwhile General Jose Juan Landero shall exercise [this authority].

Art. 4. A respectful communication shall be sent to His Excellency General-in-Chief of the Army, Mariano Paredes y Arrillaga, placing this garrison at his orders and including the present declaration.

(Many signatures follow)

Castillo Negrete, <u>Mexico en el siglo XIX</u>, vol. 21,
437-439

* * * * *

THE GENERAL DECLARATION OF THE ARMY (1)

2 January, 1846

In Mexico City, the second of January, 1846, being
brought together in the general reception room of the
palace, the Generals of division, of brigade, and
brevet [generals] and the senior leaders of the army
corps present, convoked by His Excellency General-
in-chief D. Mariano Paredes y Arrillaga; His
Excellency opened the session with the following
discourse: SENORES: Being committed by the favor my
comrades-in-arms have bestowed upon me, adopting the
principles which I proclaimed as leader of the
reserve army on December 11, 1845, to save the nation
from the abyss of anarchy, from the disorder and
ignominy which it was about to fall into because of
the errors and stubborness of the people who
fulfilled the offices of the public administration,
on explaining my beliefs on the manner of ending the
present crisis, my feelings always in favor of
national freedom and of the guarantees of citizens, I
propose for deliberation of this honorable junta the
following propositions which I express, not so much
as of my own judgment but as it is understood to be
the opinion of the majority of the inhabitants of the
Republic, which I had to respect in San Luis Potosi
until hearing it and knowing it in the progress and

---

(1) The speech and the Declaration was republished
the following day under the heading "The Propositions
of General Mariano Paredes y Arrillaga."

march of events.

I solemnly vow to the _junta_ the complete freedom it enjoys and my submission to its prudent resolutions.

Art. 1. The citizens who exercise the legislative and executive powers have ceased the exercise of their functions because they have not responded to the wishes and demands of the nation, for not having sustained the dignity of its name, nor tried to secure the integrity of its territory in accord with the articles 1st and 2nd of the Plan of San Luis Potosi of December 14, 1845.

Art. 2. A commission [_junta_] of representatives of the Departments composed of two natives or residents of each one of them and appointed by the General-in-Chief of the Army shall elect immediately a person who shall discharge the office of the supreme executive power, while the extraordinary congress which is to constitute the nation shall meet in accord with Article 3 of the Plan published in San Luis Potosi on December 14, 1845.

Art. 3. The commission [junta] of representatives shall be dissolved as soon as it has elected the President and when it shall have received his oath to sustain the independence of the nation, the system of representative, popular, republican [government], and this administrative Plan of the Republic.

Art. 4. The authority of the interim president is that which the laws in force currently provide, and he shall be able to act beyond them only for the purpose of preparing the defense of national territory, conforming always to the guarantees established by the laws now in effect.

Art. 5. The ministers of the interim president are to be responsible for their actions to the first constitutional congress; moreover, these actions are not subject to review at any time.

Art. 6. Within eight days after having taken office the interim president shall issue the summons for the

convocation of an extraordinary congress which shall
meet within four months in the capital of the
Republic; and on issuing its constitution it shall
not touch nor alter the principles and guarantees
that [the Republic] has adopted for her internal
regime.

Art. 7. The present council shall be maintained, so
that the temporary president may consult with them on
all serious business of state.

Art. 8. Only the authorities of the Departments who
may oppose this Plan of regeneration of the Republic
shall cease their functions, and they shall be
replaced in conformity with the pertinent laws.

Art. 9. The judicial power shall discharge its
important powers in accord with the laws and without
any change whatever.

Art. 10. No one shall be persecuted for his previous
political opinions.

. . . .

Once concluded the reading of the above articles, His
Excellency General Jose Maria Tornel asked that two
secretaries be appointed from the members of the
junta, and His Excellency the president of the junta
appointed the Generals Pedro Amupia and Antonio Diaz
de Bonilla.

Immediately after they began to discuss the said
articles, some expressing themselves for and some
against, they were approved unanimously, with the
exception of the Generals Lino Jose Alcorta and Jose
Vicente Minon. With the vote this act was finished
and signed by His Excellency, the General-in-Chief of
the army who presided over the junta, and others.

Coleccion de las leyes fundamentales, 271-273.

* * * * *

426

PROPOSITIONS OF PAREDES (1)

2 January, 1846

Art. 1. The citizens who heretofore exercised legislative and executive powers have ceased as of now to perform their duties because they have not responded to the desires and the needs of the nation, because they have not sustained the dignity of its name, nor secured the integrity of its territory in accord with Articles I and II of the Plan of San Luis Potosi of December, 1845.

Art. 2. A commission [junta] of representatives of the departments to be composed of two natives or residents of each of them, appointed by the commanding General of the army, shall elect immediately a person who is to discharge the duties of the supreme executive power while the extraordinary congress which is to unite the nation shall be meeting as provided in Art. 3 of the Plan published in San Luis Potosi, the 14th of December, 1845.

Art. 3. The commission of representatives shall be dissolved as soon as the president shall have been elected and when it shall have received his oath to sustain the independence of the nation, the popular, representative, republican system, and this administrative Plan of the Republic.

Art. 4. The powers of the interim president are those provided in laws now in effect, and he shall be able to act beyond those laws only for the purpose of defending the national territory, always excepting the guarantees established by the laws now in effect.

Art. 5. The ministers of the interim president are to be responsible for his actions to the first constitutional congress; but these actions shall not be subject to review at any time.

Art. 6. Within eight days after having taken possession of his office the interim president shall issue the summons for the convocation of an

_____

(1) Sometimes called the Plan of Mexico.

427

extraordinary congress which within four months shall meet in the capital of the Republic, and on issuing its constitution it shall not touch nor alter the principles or guarantees which the nation has adopted for its domestic administration.

Art. 7. The present council shall be maintained, so that the interim president may confer with it in all serious matters of State.

Art. 8. Only the departmental authorities who oppose this Plan for regeneration of the Republic shall surrender their functions, and they shall be replaced in conformity with the laws of their region.

Art. 9. The judicial power shall discharge its important powers in accord with the law and without any change whatever.

Art. 10. No one shall be persecuted for his previous political opinions.

> Gen. Mariano Paredes y Arrillaga to his military staff.
>
> "The above articles were approved unanimously, excepting two generals."

Zamacois, Historia de Mexico, XII, 405-406.

* * * * *

PLAN DE MEXICO

3 January, 1846

By General Mariano Paredes y Arrillaga

I. The citizens who are exercising the legislative and executive powers have ceased to discharge their duties because they have not met the desires and the needs of the nation, because they have not sustained the dignity of its name, nor secured the integrity of its territory according to Articles I and II of the Plan of San Luis Potosi of December, 1845.

II. A Committee of representatives of the Departments, composed of two natives or residents of each one of them and named by the Commanding General of the Army will elect immediately the person who is to discharge the supreme executive power while a special congress that will constitute the nation shall meet, in accordance with Article III of the Plan published in San Luis Potosi on December 14, 1845.

III. The Committee of representatives shall dissolve as soon as the President shall have been elected, and he has taken the oath to defend the independence of the nation, the popular, representative, republican system and [to support] this administrative plan of the Republic.

IV. The powers of the interim President are [those] of the laws now in effect, and he may function beyond them only for the purpose of preparing for the defense of the national territory, always excepting the guarantees established by the existing laws.

V. The ministers of the interim President are responsible for his acts to the first constitutional Congress, but these acts are not subject to review at any time.

VI. Within one week after the interim President has assumed his duties, he shall issue a call for the convocation of an extraordinary congress that shall meet within four months in the capital of the Republic and on issuing its constitution it shall not touch nor alter the principles and guarantees that [the Constitution] has adopted for its interior administration.

VII. The present council will be retained in order that the interim President may consult with it in all important affairs of State.

VIII. Only those Departments which oppose this Plan for the regeneration of the Republic will cease to discharge their responsibilities, and they will be replaced according to the laws which created them.

IX. The judicial power will discharge its important powers in accord with the law, and without any change whatever.

X. No person whall be persecuted for prior political opinions.

Text found without signatures.
Zamacois, Historia de Mexico, XII, 405-406.

* * * * *

PLAN OF REGENERATION (1)

20 May, 1846

The Garrison of the City of Guadalajara, capital of the Department of Jalisco, moved by the very urgent necessity of responding at once to the grave danger in which the republic finds itself, and considering that . . . (seven 'considerandos' follow) we hereby come to proclaim the following Plan of True and Genuine Regeneration of the Republic:

Art. 1. The garrison of the City of Guadalajara repudiates the edict issued the 27th of January last by the said interim President and his ministers as totally offensive to the sovereignty of the nation, and decreed with the apparent object of making it appear that [the nation] was calling upon a monarchy with a foreign price to govern it.

Art. II. In the place of a congress called by the aforesaid decree another composed of representatives named freely and by popular consent will meet according to the electoral laws established for nominations to the said body in [the Constitution] of 1824. This said congress will be charged with the establishment of a republic, adopting whatever form of government that it deems suitable, only excluding that of a monarchy which the nation detests; and with

---

(1) Also called Declaration of Guadalajara
430

submitting it to the general will, clearly explaining all matters relative to the question of Texas and the other frontier Departments.

Art. III. Within four months after the liberating forces have occupied the capital of the Republic, the Congress referred to in the previous article shall meet. The General-in-Chief shall have as his obligation the issuance of the call according to the terms indicated, and he shall take care that the elections are to be held with the greatest possible freedom.

Art. IV. The existence of the Army is guaranteed, it being treated as befits a deserving military class of a free poeple.

Art. V. Any person who may try to prevent the meeting of the said Congress is hereby declared a traitor to the nation; so also is any person who may obstruct the liberty of its members, or who may dissolve or suspend its sessions, or who seeks to oppose the Constitution which it may adopt; so also any who [violates] the laws expedited in accord with this Plan.

Art. VI. Since his Excellency, Gen. Antonio Lopez de Santa Anna had the glory of founding the Republic, and whatever may have been his errors, he has been its strongest support in spite of European politics and of the instigations of some perverse Mexicans; and he has opposed the North American usurpation. [Therefore] the garrison of Jalisco proclaims the Said Excellency and General as the leader in the great undertaking which this Plan envisions.

Art. VII. The question which now involves Texas and North America being so vital to the Republic, hereby is allocated a fourth part of the income of the Departments in order to conduct the war which so deeply involves the national honor. The said fourth part will be remitted directly to the Army of the North.

Art. VIII. Since one ought to give every preference to the internal administration, and since the Governor who has presided to the present time has not been able to carry out his functions because he is not an adherent of the Plan, the Senor and Licenciado Juan Nepomuceno Cumplido will be called to discharge the First Magistry of the Department, it being agreeable to the majority of said Department.

Art. IX. During the present crisis the Governor shall exercise his own discretion in the discharge of his duties without, thereby, attacking individual guarantees.

Art. X. He will be guided according to the spirit and tenor of the above Plan of political regeneration, and he shall observe all laws which, not being in conflict with republican institutions, are considered in effect and in accord with this Plan.

In Guadalajara, 20 May 1846
Jose Maria Yanez, Commanding General.
Other signatures follow

Coleccion de los leyes fundamentales, 277-279

* * * * *

THE DECLARATION OF THE GARRISON OF VERA CRUZ (1)

31 July, 1846

In the heroic city of Vera Cruz, the Generals, leaders, and officials of the Garrison subscribed hereunto met in the quarters of the 8th Regiment for the purpose of considering the calamitious state into which the Republic has arrived, and to search for the most suitable remedy for rescuing it and putting it on the high road to prosperity.

---

(1) Plan of Regeneration

432

The principle cause of the said discord that exists is, in their opinion, the lack of a fundamental code drafted freely by the nation which has clearly indicated its destation of monarchy, also [the lack of] an administration which may be the result of public opinion and not that of contests between factions.

[Also they believe] that the present administration is lacking in legality, and that it has discharged its mission in an oppressive manner, and is dictating an unpopular assembly which tends toward monarchy and while in this detestable plot it has paid no attention to defense of the national territory and has abandoned at the frontier that part of the army charged with defending it. Furthermore, [those present] believed that the Republic is marching to its ruin and that it is more necessary now than ever before to work assiduously to tighten the bonds of union which have been loosened by our misfortunes, and by foregoing all our opinions. They agreed to support the Plan proclaimed by the people and the garrison of Guadalajara on 20th of May last down through Article 5, with the following additions:

Art. 1. All prisoners of those exiled for political reasons from 1821 to the present date may return to the Republic, and they are hereby invited to cooperate in the defense of the present Plan.

Art. 2. In reference to the circumstances of the war in which the Republic is now engaged with the United States of the North, it is the obligation of the coming Congress to resolve the question, and all Mexican to obey its resolutions.

Art. 3. All those within or without the Department who have taken up arms against the present order of things are invited to support this Plan which only has for its purpose the public good. The same invitation is advanced to all the political and military authorities of all the Departments.

Art. 4. Since His Excellency General D. Antonio Lopez de Santa Anna had the glory of founding the Republic, and whatever may have been his errors since, he always has given the firmest support to public liberties and to the security of the national domain.

The Garrison proclaims the said Excellency and General the leader in the great design to which this Plan is dedicated.

Herewith the Act was concluded, and all present signed at 12 o'clock noon, the 31st of July, 1846.

(Signed) Jose Juan Landero et al

Text from Castello Negrete, <u>Mexico en el siglo XIX</u>, vol 21, p. 456.

* * * * *

THE PROPOSAL OF NICOLAS BRAVO

3 August, 1846

Don Nicolas Bravo initiated the following bill, and introduced it to the special Congress:

Art. 1. The Special Congress, in fulfillment of its mission, declares that the Organic Bases, explicitly santioned by the nation as decreed in December, 1845, are the political constitution of the Republic.

Art. 2. [The nation] will proceed to the election of all those constitutional entities which are due to begin to function January 1, 1847, in accord with the election laws of December 10, 1841 and of July 8, 1845.

Art. 3. The Government will function in terms of these particular Bases and the laws in effect, it being furthermore authorized, A) To assure the domestic peace of the Republic pardons and amnesties for political crimes committed since December, 1845, and thereafter are granted, the Special Congress to use this authority in the time and form which it deems convenient. B) To draft colonization regulations for the benefit of the people, of agriculture, and the arts. C) To establish security patrols in the settled areas and country roads, [the said patrols] to have as their sole duty the arrest of evil-doers, and of bringing them to trial and swift and summary punishment.

Art. 4. As soon as this decree is expedited, the present Special Congress will stand in recess and it will meet again only when convened by the Government if the occasion should arise for the legislative body to have to use the powers mentioned in Parts IX and XI of Article 66 of the Organic Bases.

V. Riva Palacio, Mexico a traves de los siglos, IV, 569

* * * * *

THE PLAN OF GENERAL SALAS

4 August, 1846

The citizens and the garrison of the _____, convinced of the very urgent necessity to respond at once to the very grave danger in which the Republic finds itself, and Whereas . . . ('Considerandos... follow) We have met to proclaim and hereby do proclaim the following Plan of genuine regeneration of the Republic:

Art. 1. Instead of the existing Congress another composed of representatives named by the people according to the electoral laws which governed the nominations of 1824. This Congress will be charged with constituting a nation and adopting the form which it judges conforms to the national will, as well as all that relative to the war with the United States and the question of Texas and the other frontier departments. The monarchial form of government is to be excluded from consideration since the nation evidently detests it.

Art. 2. All Mexicans who are faithful to their country, including those outside it, are called to lend their services in the present national movement. To this end His Excellency and General Benemerito of the Fatherland, Don Antonio Lopez de Santa Anna is especially invited. He is recognized immediately as Commander-in-Chief of all forces involved and of those determined to fight so that the nation may recover its rights, assure its liberties, and govern itself.

Art. 3. In the meantime a sovereign Congress will gather and decree whatever may be suitable for the war. It will be the explicit responsibility of the Executive to decree whatever measures may be urgent and necessary for sustaining with decorum the national banner, and to fulfill this sacred duty without loss of even a single moment.

Art. 4. Four months after the liberating forces have occupied the capital of the Republic, the Congress mentioned in the first Article shall meet. The Commander-in-Chief will have the responsibility of issuing the call for the convocation in the terms indicated and to take care that the elections are held with the greatest possible freedom.

Art. 5. The existence of the Army is guaranteed; it is hereby assured that it will be provided for and protected as is due the well-merited military class of a free poeple.

Art. 6. Whoever tries to delay the meeting of the said Congress is declared a traitor to the nation; so also any who opposes it, who may place obstacles to the freedom of its members by dissolving or suspending its sessions or pretending to oppose the constitution which it may establish, or by opposing the laws expedited in accord with this Plan.

                    (Signed) Gen. Mariano Salas
A draft as circulated by General Salas.

V. Riva Palacio, Mexico a traves de los siglos, IV, 570-571

* * * * *

DECLARATION OF JALAPA

20 August, 1846

In the City of Jalapa, on the 20th day of August, in the year one thousand eight hundred and forty six, the Illustrious Town Council being met under the Presidency of the interim Senor Prefect of the District D. Jose Maria Grajales y Espino ... and having called the attention of the resident citizens to the declaration which the Very Excellent Senor General, Well-Deserving [Benemerito] of the Nation Citizen Antonio Lopez de Santa Anna has issued from Vera Cruz the sixteenth of the current month; and it being indubitable that the wishes of this Leader are those of all Mexicans as has been demonstrated by various uprisings that have taken place in the greater part of the Departments and through lamentable error have destroyed the Federation Pact that was given to the nation freely and spontaneously in 1824; and at the same time desirous that these wishes should be attended to in an effective way, it is requested that through the Corporation a determination be made of a suitable response in terms of the common interest for so laudable a purpose.

[There follows a speech by the leader of a concerned citizens committee, and then eight declarations of "Whereas..." which conclude with the following points:]

Art. 1. That it is the wish of [the Corporation] that the national assembly which meets in the Capital of the Republic by virtue of call for Convocation issued by the Leader vested with the Supreme Executive Power instead of occupying itself with constituting the Nation shall be authorized to resolve all matters relative to the Public Administration which affects the general interests, and of the competence of the Legislative Power; working in subordination to those supreme resolutions [shall be] the interim Executive Power which shall be vested in His Excellency Senor Well-Merited of the Nation, General D. Antonio Lopez de Santa Anna as leader of the Mexican People who shall work wholly in accord with the Constitution of 1824.

Art. 2. That the war being unjustly declared against Mexico by the United States of the North, this [war] shall be continued with vigor by the hero of Vera Cruz until he shall have gained a complete triumph over the arms of that nation or until that nation shall sue for peace which will be done only in an honorable way.

Art. 3. That since the Higher Authorities of the Governing and Legislative Department, convinced of the illegality of their nominations because it was born out of the arbitrary legislative decree of March 13th, the latter had made a proposition in the session of the 10th of the current month that they should be relieved by person to be named popularly, and since this cannot take effect because the call for a Convocation issued by the Supreme Government in its Article 73 indicates the method and time of verifying it, and since the Department ought not to remain without a Director in the meantime, an interim Governor shall be named whose election shall be made by all the Town Council heads of the Party, forming lists of three [ternas] that shall be printed afterwards in the Zempoalteca and dispatching them to this Corporation as soon as possible so that the person emerging with the most votes after verifi - cation in a public count is declared nominated, notifying him in order that he should take over the reins of government, and he guiding his decisions according to the provisions of the Federal Code of 1824, which will be in effect in the Department until [the Code] which is to govern thereafter may be issued by the said Sovereign Assembly.

Art. 4. That until the nomination of the repre- sentative of the interim Leader of the Department, the person whom this Corporation may name, shall assume this charge as of today who shall be notified immediately, and likewise the Authorities of the Department, the Superior [Authorities] of the Nation, and General Citizen Antonio Lopez de Santa Anna, and there shall be sent to them a copy of this Plan and they shall be urged that for their part to contribute

to its success by some opinions always directed to
the good and the prosperity of the Nation itself.

Art. 5. To all the Municipal Authorities of the
Department a copy of this disposition will be sent
and they will be urged to support the present
declaration on their own account and to communicate
the same to the Military of the Department.

Being taken into consideration and again discussed
without vote by the aforesaid commission of
residents, the above articles suffered some slight
alterations and were unanimously approved.

In consequence Sr. Ahumada was named to propose the
individuals whom this Body should name for the
purpose of naming a Governor referred to in Article
4, and he immediately nominated the following ...
[Details of the Departmental election follow, also a
resolution to congratulate General Santa Anna.]

Signed by members of the
Ayuntamiento

Original circular, Beinicke Library, Yale University.

* * * * *

PLAN FOR THE RESTORATION OF THE FEDERAL SYSTEM (1)

22 August, 1846

The Minister of Foreign Affairs, Administration and
Policy. His Excellency the Commander-in-Chief in the
exercise of Supreme Executive Power has dispatched to
me the following decree:

Jose Mariano Salas, brigadier general of the
republican liberating army and exercising the Supreme
Executive Power, To All and Sundry: Be It Known, That
in consideration of the state in which the Republic
finds itself, I have seen fit to decree the following:

---

(1) Plan of Salas

Art. 1. Until the new Constitution is published, that of 1824 shall be in effect in all matters not related to the execution of the plan proclaimed in the Cuidadela of his capital the 4th of the present month, (1) and as they uniquely difficult position of the Republic permits.

Art. 2. It not being compatable with the fundamental code, the existence of departmental assemblies and the present council of Government will forthwith cease in the exercise of their functions.

Art. 3. The governors now in office shall continue, notwithstanding, entitling themselves "of the States," with the exercise of all those powers which their respective constitutions vest in them.

Art. 4. The governors of the new Departments which lack their own constitution shall gague the discharge of duties according to the norm of the state nearest to them.

Art. 5. Since the functionaries referred to in the articles directly above do not have a legal title, it is hereby declared that they owe their existence to the political movement that is going to regenerate the nation, and consequently whenever the interests of the above coincide, the Commander-in-Chief charged with general Executive Power shall be able to replace them.

THEREFORE, I order that the same be printed, published, and circulated, in order that it may be duly enforced.

(Signed) Jose Mariano de Salas

I communicate to you for your information and consequent action.
God and Liberty. Mexico. August 22, 1840
Jose Maria Ortiz Monasterio

V. Riva Palacio, <u>Mexico a traves de los siglos</u>, IV, 576

* * * * *

PLAN SALVADOR of Religion, Independence
and Liberty of the Mexican Republic

11 February, 1847

"Published by a patriot into whose hands it fell
by accident, with the hope that the supreme congress,
the supreme government and the nation should be
disillusioned and should see what are the evils, what
are the liberty killing plans with which the infamous
moderates and the fanatical religionists seek to
establish a foreign monarchy."

[After a very lengthy survey of the iniquities of
both parties over the years since Independence, the
anonymous patriot concludes:]

Get rid of the congress with its majority either
useless or harmful; send home the humiliated and
shameful _puros_, if they are really capable of
understanding these sentiments. Those worthy
representatives who, with their heroic conduct have
so well deserved the consideration of the nation
await elections for the two Chambers, and in them or
thorough their legislation they may continue lending
their important services--establish a provisional
government in accord with the constitution now in
effect; let it proceed to the nomination of senators,
deputies, a president and vice-president of the
republic; keep General Santa Anna as commanding
general of the Army of the North, if, as is quite
likely, and in line with his principles, he should
adhere to this plan which in substance His Excellency
initiated on his arrival in Vera Cruz--that is, let
the judicious honorable centralists sacrifice their
opinions and submit themselves to the majority;
forget forever the name of monarchists; let us all be
moderate federalists; let us hold popular elections
that are conducted with freedom by all citizens and
without pretending that any political party should
prevail.

Thus and only thus, shall we have order and
peace: a truly national government shall be
organized; the war shall be ended with the triumph of

our arms and through an honorable treaty; the States with their share, the clergy with a considerable portion of its income, the rich landowners, the miners, merchants and farmers, the workman, the middle class, and even the poorest segment of society shall all contribute in order that the essentials may not be wanting, and the nation will escape the death that threatens it.

To this end it would be suitable if some of the more near-by legislatures would initiate or the present congress should adopt the plan as indicated that for greater clarity is drafted in the following articles.

1st. The emergency congress which has been labeled 'constituents' shall cease, and the political con- stititution of the United States of Mexico as decreed on October 4, 1824 be therewith re-established.

2nd. Neither General D. Antonio Lopez de Santa Anna nor D. Valentin Gomez Farias shall be recognized as president or as vice-president.

3rd. The decrees relative to the occupation of the property of the Dead Hand shall have no effect, nor shall the decree that authorized the government to expropriate on an emergancy basis five million pesos.

4th. The other acts of the congress as well as those of the provisional government of General Sales remain subject to revision by the constitutional congress, while in the meantime observing everything that may not be contrary to the constitution.

5th. Elections for deputies, senators, president and vice-president for the republic shall be held on the days designated by the provisional administration.

6th. This [administration] shall be entrusted to the president of the supreme court of justice in accord with the provision of the constitution in its articles 97 and 98.

7th. The lack of a governing council shall be provided for by a supplemental one to be composed of other such individuals as today may be in the states of the federation, and they shall be designated by the supreme court of justice the following day after this plan shall have taken effect, and these persons must be natives or residents of the States that they may represent and have the other requirements that the constitution stipulates in order to be a senator.

8th. The provisional council shall be installed the third day after its nomination and immediately it shall elect the two colleagues who are to join with the president of the supreme court in the exercise of the supreme executive power. Its authority shall be those which the constitution grants to the council of government and furthermore it shall extend or deny its approval to the bills or decrees which the administration may present as very urgent and necessary only in the areas of war and treasury.

9th. The president with the two colleagues shall convoke immediately a constitutional congress, determing the days for election in accord with that which was established in article five within no more than four months in order that the two chambers should be installed and the constitution be observed.

10th. General D. Antonio Lopez de Santa Anna shall continue as commander-in-chief of the army of the north, subject to the orders of the administration which shall provide to him all necessary assistance for the war.

11th. The army shall be treated with all the preference which its great importance requires, for all the great services that it has performed and will perform for the conservation of our nationality, independence, religion and liberty.

12th. If the unexpected should occur and some legislature should oppose this plan, it shall be replaced by proceeding to hold new elections totally

443

in accord with the constitution of the State.

---

* * * * *

PRONOUNCEMENT OF OAXACA*

15 February, 1847

After a brief series of "Considerandos", the Pronouncement concludes . . . .

In order to pay attention to the irresistable torrent of public opinion The Undersigned declare the imperious necessity of agreeing to the following articles:

Art. 1. The federal, republican form of government will be strictly in conformity with the general constitution and that of the State, while the Congress of the Union does not reform the fundamental charter of the nation.

Art. 2. The personnel of the present State administration is unworthy of public confidence and on its own expressed free will the executive, legislative, and judicial authorities should cease their functions, save the Senor vice-Governor Don Juaquin de Guergue, who will take the reins of government immediately, and he will be guided in all his actions by the particular constitution [of the State].

Art. 3. The right of representation which the Deputies of this State hold to the sovereign national congress is illegal because they have acted contrary to the will of those they represented by supporting and sanctioning needlessly the decree of January 11th of the current year which attacks the immunities and guarantees of the Catholic Church, Apostolic and

---

* The following day this Declaration was labeled a "Plan" by the participants.

444

Roman, and as a consequence their authority is revoked.

Art. 4. The law relative to the occupation of church properties will not be enforced in this State, nor will it be permitted that they should be touched by force. In case of contributions to support the just war against the United States of the North, a due and just portion on the basis of equality will be guaranteed.

Art. 5. On the third day after the installation of the new executive authority of the State an order to observe the call for elections will be given, as issued lately on the 6th of August of the year just past, so that within the terms which it specifies the representatives of the State and that of the congress of the nation may be restored.

Art. 6. As of now four individuals who enjoy the confidence of the Undersigned shall form the Executive Authority until the new congress shall meet, and this governing council shall have the attributes which the State constitution designates.

Art. 7. The council of government on the same day shall respond to its free election by a majority of votes, and likewise the Honorable Court of Justice in acordance with the constitution of the State will be installed at the same ceremony.

Art. 8. The judges of the first instance and other public functionaries will continue discharging their duties temporarily until the newly named authorities shall make suitable arrangements.

Art. 9. An invitiation will be issued through a committee to the Benemerito Commanding General Juan Diaz that he place himself at the head of the forces which have thus pronounced [their support], it being understood that his seniority [in the armed forces] remain, and that he be authorized to modify or to add to this plan, excepting the essence of the federal system and the Catholic religion and the immunities of the Church.

(Signatures: military)

El Monitor Republicano, February 22, 1847.

* * * * *

DECLARATION OF OAXACA

22 February, 1847

In the capital of the free and sovereign State of Oaxaca on the 16th day of the month of February, 1847, being met in the alameda of Guadalupe, we, the undersigned, as General Commandant of the State on the one hand, and as leader [jefe] of the forces which have "pronounced" on the other: Considering the sad consequences which continuation of the civil war would produce, that the purpose of the Pronouncement verified at the Fort of Santo Domingo has not been in any way either to disavow the supreme government nor to product a secession of the State, but, rather, to remedy the ills which this very State was suffering economically in its administration, and that the guarantees granted by the general constitution [of the Nation] and that of the State in particular be respected, and that [the State] contribute toward the indispensable costs of the war of the North, but in an equitable and just manner. We are met together and we protest in a most solemn manner for ourselves and in the name of both belligerent forces that we will support each one of the articles of the Plan proclaimed on the 15th of the current month in the Fort of Santo Domingo of this city with the following modifications and additions:

First: Articles 3 and 9 are eliminated.

Second: In the place of Art. 4 the following is

446

substituted: In the State of Oaxaca the effects of the Law of January 11th last on the occupation of properties of the Church [manos muertas] are suspended; and it is left to the legislature of this State to decide upon a suitable policy on the matter by reconciling constitutional principles and those of justice with the circumstances of this same State with the urgent necessities of the general government of the North.

Third: In the place of Art. 8 the following is substituted: The judges of the first instance and the other public functionaries with the exception of the governor of the capital who will immediately be replaced according to law by the person charged with executive authority, will continue in their work on an interim basis until new persons may be named as is convenient.

Fourth: The National Guard corps now in the State are to remain at the disposition of the executive authority of the said State in accord with the laws of its creation. For this particular occasion the troops are at liberty to belong to any body of troops which they may choose.

Fifth: Colonel Juan Diaz will continue as the commanding officer of the State as he has served until now.

Sixth: Employment is guaranteed to all the commanders [jefes], officers, and troops of both belligerent forces. [Also guaranteed] is the liberty and consideration to those who do not like to give adherence to the present Plan, nor may any person be molested for the attitude which he may have had in respect to the present pronouncement, nor shall anyone in the State be persecuted solely for his political opinions.

(Signed)

Juan Diaz

El Monitor Republicano. February 22, 1847.

* * * * *

PLAN OF THE RESTORERS

27 February, 1847

The bases of the Plan for the Restoration of true federative principles, as proclaimed by the Garrison and National Guard of this capital:

Art. 1. The general Legislative and Executive agencies shall cease the exercise of their functions because they have lost the confidence of the nation.

Art. 2. This cessation implies no change whatever in the validity of the Constitution of 4 October 1824 which the nation has adopted, nor in the organization of the States or the continuation of their present powers. But if, though it is not to be expected, some legislature should oppose this Plan, it shall be re-constituted by the calling of new elections, all according to the Constitution of the State.

Art. 3. In the meantime and while the legislatures of the States are proceeding to the election of a President and vice-President of the Republic, the general executive power will be exercized by the president of the Supreme Court of Justice in conformity with the aforesaid Constitution in Articles 97 and 98.

Art. 4. The Council of Government being lacking, it will be filled by a supplementary one, composed of other such persons as are now in the States of the Federation, and they will be named the day following the adoption of this Plan and by the Supreme Court of Justice. [Such persons] must be residents of the State which they represent and have the other requirements which the Constitution sets for a senator.

Art. 5. The provisional council will be installed the third day after being named, and immediately it will choose the two colleagues who will join with the President of the Supreme Court of Justice for the exercise of the Supreme Executive Power. Its assumption of power will be that which the

448

Constitution grants to the Council of Government, and furthermore it shall indicate its approval or disapproval of bills which the Administration shall present as urgent or necessary only in the branches of War and Treasury.

Art. 6. Within two weeks of the establishment of a government in conformity with this Plan, it will proceed to designate those who are to take part in the election of deputies to the general Congress in accordance with the call of December, 1841, or to this Plan.

Art. 7. One week after the election of deputies to the general Congress, the legislatures of the States shall proceed to elect senators in conformity with the Constitution of 1824.

Art. 8. The installation of both Houses will be observed two months after the elections; and on the day following their election the general Congress will designate the day on which the legislatures will proceed to the election of the President and vice-President of the Republic as well as the day when these functionaries will assume their duties; and it will try to make the periods indicated as short as possible.

Art. 9. The general Congress preferably will concern itself with reforming the federal Constitution. The reforms can be made at any time, and in the laws which may be drafted in reference to this material, all the aforesaid provisions in respect to the formation of the common laws will be observed without any greater difference than that in voting for reforms; namely a two-thirds majority of both Houses shall be required. The Executive shall not be empowered to voice an opinion about any reform.

Art. 10. During the constitutional interim the Executive who is empowered by Art. 3 of this Plan will have all necessary faculties for waging to an end the present war, and all other matters shall be carried out according to the Constitution and the laws in force.

Art. 11. Until the Houses have been installed and until the legislatures have chosen a President and vice-President, the interim Executive shall have no other powers or allocations than those granted by the Constitution of 1824 to the holder of that post.

Art. 12. None of the decrees relative to the occupation of the property of Dead Hands shall go into effect, nor that which authorized the government to take over a special assessment of 5,000,000 pesos.

Art. 13. The Benemerito of the fatherland, General of Division Antonio Lopez de Santa Anna is recognized as Commander-in-Chief of the Mexican Army and as interim President of the Republic.

(Signed)

Matias de la Pena Barragan
Commanding General

V. Riva Palacio, Mexico a traves de los siglos, IV, 633.

* * * * *

PLAN OF FATHER JARAUTA(1)

1 June, 1848

Mexicans: The work which inequity and treason commenced in 1845 has just been consumated. More than half the Republic was sold to the enemy invader for a trifling sum; the rest of our territory will remain occupied by these very North American soldiers, now converted into guards for the traitor, Pena, in order to perpetuate the most atrocious crime that the centuries have seen. * * * *[And finally...]

The undersigned are few in number, but we are resolved to persevere in sustaining those cherished interests. We invite you to follow our example in

---

(1) Sometimes called the "Plan of the Garrison of Lagos."

pushing the fight against the traitorous government
by raising the flag of insurrection: to insurrection
Spain, Mexico, and other nations appealed in order to
sustain their independence, and they succeeded. Let
us do the same today, as we proclaim the following
articles:

Art. 1. Let us disavow the present administration for
having betrayed the nation.

Art. 2. Let the State, in consequence, resume their
sovereignty.

Art. 3. The above [States] will agree on some method
of replacing the overturned government.

Art. 4. Their Excellencies the Governors of the
States will designate the person or persons to
command the troops which may be within their
boundaries.

Art. 5. The units of the regular Army which may
adhere to this Plan will be, according to military
regulation, at the command of the chief or ranking
general of those who support it.

(Signed)

Caledonio Domeco de Jarauta
et al.

V. Riva Palacio, Mexico a traves de los siglos, IV,
712.

* * * * *

PLAN OF GENERAL PAREDES

1 June, 1848

MEXICANS: The work of inequity and of treason
which they commenced in 1845 has now been consumated:
more than half the republic was sold to the enemy
invader for a pitiful sum: the rest of our country
will be occupied by these same North American
soldiers who are converted into a guard for the
traitor, Pena, in order to support the most atrocious
crime witnessed by the centuries.

451

The years past remind us of Count Julian handing over his country for a personal resentment; but this horrible deed bears no comparision with that of Pena: that miserable creature, blind with cholera, let the Moors enter Spain, jeopardizing himself personally, but this latest person in order to return to the easy life, to the conveniences of Mexico [City] and to keep himself in power, sells his country without the least risk, after having disarmed the nation, extinguished its public spirit and persuaded it that his outrage is a public good, that his disgrace is an honor, and that the State, humiliated as we now see it, prostrate at the foot of its enemy is in a brilliant situation and is to enjoy an encouraging future.

And will it be possible, Mexicans, that you will suffer such an affront quietly and impassively? Will you look upon your brothers in California, New Mexico, and Chihuahua with indifference? Will you thus regard those brave men who have battled constantly as your vanguard in order to support the religion, the customs, and the nationality of Mexico? No, no, a thousand times no!

We the undersigned are few in number but we are resolved to perish in support of such cherished interests; we invite all of you to follow our example and bring arms to bear against the traitorous government, to raise the flag of insurrection. To it Spain appealed, so did Mexico and other nations in order to gain independence, and they won it. Let us do the same thing now, by proclaiming the following articles:

1. The present administration is repudiated for having betrayed the nation.

2. Consequently, let the State resume their sovereignty.

3. These States shall agree upon methods to be used in replacing the present decrepit government.

4. The present Most Excellent Senores, the Governors of the States, shall designate the person or persons who are to command the forces that may be in them.

5. The forces of the standing army who may adhere to this plan shall remain, in conformity with General Regulations at the orders of the commander or General of highest rank of those who support this plan.

(Signed)

(Signatures follow)

El Siglo Diez y Nueve, June 19, 1848.

* * * * *

DECLARATION OF THE PRONOUNCEMENT OF GUANAJUATO(1)

17 June, 1848

In the city of Guanajuato, Capital of the State of the same name, on the 17th day of the month of June, 1848, [the undersigned] met in one of the reception rooms of the State Palace under the presiding official [presidencia] Lieutenant-Colonel Nicolas Flores, he being the outstanding one of those composing the group; and thereafter Colonel D. Jesus Corrion was named as secretary. An official notice was received for the Excellency General D. Mariano Paredes y Arrillage, giving the details of a political plan which he did not present in person in order to allow the committee free discussion. This same having been done, the said Plan was adopted unanimously after vote by the leaders who are listed below.

[After a paragraph of "Considerandos"]: They have agreed on the aim of assuring independence [of the country] and thus proclaim and intend to support to the end the following Plan:

(1) Also referred to as "The Plan of General Paredes."

453

Art. 1. Immediately a meeting of a national convention is to be called; it is to be composed of two deputies popularly elected from each State and the Federal District; one from each Territory.

Art. 2. This national convention, which is to meet within five months after this Plan has been adopted by the whole Republic, will be charged with examining and determining what it judges advisable relative to the treaties of peace celebrated with the United States and to determine the responsibility of those who may have agreed to the celebration [of the treaty] according to that [standard] established under the laws of the Republic.

Art. 3. In the meantime a national convention will be convoked; the Executive Authority of the Union will be deposited in the hands of three or five individuals who will elect a committee [junta] to be composed of one deputy named for this one body only--one for each State, District, and Territory of the federation.

Art. 4. This Executive Power shall be vested with the special authority for providing the resources of the people, munitions, and other items which it may consider necessary in order to organize forces capable of carrying to a successful conclusion the resolutions of the convention and to remove the obstacles which may present themselves, so that the true will of the nation may be revealed in reference to the serious matters upon which it might wish to consult [the nation].

Art. 5. While the Executive Authority, which Art. 3 of this present Plan mentions, is being organized the leader named to the pact by the majority of the legislatures will be able to use the faculties previous mentioned above.

Art. 6. The legal privileges [fueros] and the property of the honorable clergy will be strictly protected, and likewise the Army will be taken care of as is fitting for the defenders of a free people.

(Signatures follow)

El Monitor Republicano, June 24, 1848.

* * * * *

PLAN SALVADOR

8 September, 1849

Art. 1. The present administration is repudiated by reason of ineptitude and incapacity.

Art. 2. The Benemerito General of Division Don Antonio Lopez de Santa Anna is named supreme dictator of the Republic.

Art. 3. The Right Illustrious Bishop of Michoacan Don Juan de Portugal is named adjutant supreme dictator.

Art. 4. The Senor General-of-Division Don Mariano Paredes y Arrillaga is named Commander-in-Chief of the Army.

Art. 5. All military personnel that is found in active service or has been retired by the present administration and does not present itself for service under my command or else to some worthy leader who supports this plan within the ordered time of one month will be discharged from his position, and furthermore shall lose his share for the expenses of the war without any appeal whatever.

Art. 6. There shall be no other religion except that of the Catholic, Roman, and Apostolic, nor will the worship of any other sect be permitted, providing that the ministers of the holy Church shall be respected and supported.

Art. 7. The full weight of the law shall fall upon any individual quite regardless of rank that he may hold who directly or indirectly shall lend assistance to the prsent adminsistration in order to thwart this plan.

Art. 8. All the authorities, civil as well as military, who do not support this plan shall suffer the penalties decribed in Article 5.

Art. 9. Any foreigner who lends any assistance to support this plan will be recognized as a good Mexican and furthermore shall enjoy the corresponding guarantees. On the other hand if he shall lend aid to the government he will be held as a traitor to the nation and shall suffer without appeal the penalties appertaining thereunto.

                                   Rufino Rodriguez, Sec.
Ciudad Victoria

El Siglo Diez y Nueve, September 17, 1849.

                    * * * * *

                 REVOLUTIONARY PLAN

                                          8 October, 1849

In the town of Cocula the undersigned being met, and considering that [here follows a long accusatory paragraph] we have agreed, and we resolve to declare ourselves publicly and to sustain with arms in hand the following articles:

Art. 1. The present government is repudiated because it has responded badly to the confidence of the nation, and as soon as it is overthrown the will of the nation shall decide what shall be the political system under which it seems that it can best be governed.

Art. 2. The demands for the surveying of the boundaries of lands that have been pending or which may be agitated hereafter shall be determined governmentally in order to remove all basis of complaint from the towns, and these shall be protected, thereby assuring their civilization and advancement in order to improve their present situation and for this purpose from the date of the promulgation of this Plan all the taxes, assessments, and impositions which they endure today shall no longer be reported.

Art. 3. The property now belonging either to private persons or to corporations shall be respected as inviolable.

Art. 4. The forces that are to be collected to defend the ideas which these articles above express shall be called "The Regenerating Army of the Mexican Republic," and it proclaims as its commander-in-chief His Excellency General of Division and Well-merited of the Fatherland D. Antonio Lopez de Santa Anna.

Cocula.   Signatures follow

El Siglo XIX, 19 October 1849.

* * * * *

PLAN OF GREGORIO MELENDEZ

November, 1850

It appears that in Juchitan the famous Gregorio Melendez has declared again for the following Plan:

1st. The chief of each section shall sustain the form of government that presently governs the destiny of the Republic to the last drop of blood.

2nd. The authorities of the State of Oaxaca are disavowed while they refuse to name an administration which secures the happiness of the people.

457

3rd. All dry-land customs houses in the State are suppressed in order to promote in this way trade and [the prosperity] of the towns.

4th. Since it is not fair that the military [personnel] of the Army who have contributed such important services to the nation should be discharged from the service, their restitution [to their posts] is asked.

5th. That all the individuals who, on this occasion, give their services to bring about this Plan shall be recompensed in due time.

6th. That the majority of the States not accepting the nomination that was attempted on behalf of the person of Sr. Minister Arista for president of the Mexican Republic, he is repudiated if the nomination should become effective on account of the scandalous intrigue that has been made in this Department in order to name him.

7th. That those who are opposed to the prosecution of this Plan shall be punished by the commander of this section.

El Universal, 28 November, 1850.

* * * * *

PLAN OF ELIGIO ORTIZ

19 July, 1851

Art. 1. The illustrious and Well-merited a [Benemerito] General don Antonio Lopez de Santa Anna shall be called to rule the nation as supreme dictator, while a new general congress is convoked.

Art. 2. The call for the said Congress shall be made within six months at the latest after His Excellency shall have received the authority of supreme dictator, and his election shall be in accordance with that of the present congress.

458

Art. 3. Until His Excellency Sr. General don Antonio Lopez de Santa Anna enters upon the exercise of the functions of supreme dictator, the Excellency Sr. General Nicolas Bravo shall rule the Republic with equal authority.

Art. 4. The Treaties of Guadalupe celebrated between the plenipotentiaries fo the Mexican Republic and those of the United States of North America on the ___ day of ___ [sic] 1848 are hereby annulled.

Art. 5. The goods and properties of the regular and secular clergy shall be respected as heretofore. All the functionaries of the present adminsitration are held to the strictest responsibility, which will be demanded in due form by the Congress which is mentioned in the first article.

[The author had been imprisoned, but during a change of the guard he and two others escaped. He left behind in the possession of the governor the above Plan.]

V. Riva Palacio, Mexico a traves de los siglos, IV, 757.

* * * * *

PLAN OF GENERAL CANALES

3 September, 1851

The undersigned, all citizens of the City of Guerrero of the State of Tamaulipas, are convinced that they have not been accorded attention by the national representation concerning the repeated petitions which they have made to that sovereignty through the respective channels relative to the raising of prohibitions, the lowering of tariffs and the protection in order that the continual depredations of the Indians, no longer endurable, may be repaired; likewise the oppression on which they are based by virtue of the restrictions that, united

459

with the hostilities of the Indians [barbaros] is the complete destruction not only of the town of those now speaking but also of the whole frontier, they have decided to support by force of arms the content of the following articles:

Art. 1. The permanent troops shall be sent out of the territory of the State because they are pernicious, oppressive, and useless.

Art. 2. The citizen is inviolable in the enjoyment of his rights and properties and in the exercise of his opinions; the judicial power shall be sustained in the free exercise of its duties, and no assistance shall be taken by the liberal forces without being paid for.

Art. 3. In order to guarantee the rights and sovereignty of the States, the reform of the federal constitution, reserving to the States all the authority and possessions not expressly granted to the general government.

Art. 4. The national representation, at least in the Senate, shall be equal, or by States and elected popularly, abolishing the authority of the executive to name senators.

Art. 5. The abolition of the raising of prohibitions and the loweering of import duties on foreign goods is demanded, and not surpassing those on which when imposed amount to more than 40% above appraisal.

Art. 6. Excessive penalties applied upon contraband shall be abolished; those who declare the crime disproportionate shall be fined, even to the loss of the items without further responsibility, and from these products there is formed a fund for the exclusive and sacred object of making war on the savages.

Art. 7. The introduction of supplies will be permitted on the frontier of the Rio Bravo [Rio Grande] free of import duties for a period of five years.

Art. 8. A frontier customs house shall be established at the village of Reynosa for foreign trade.

Art. 9. The towns allied under this Plan are subject to the authority of their respective States which support this plan.

Art. 10. This movement is eminently national and liberal; as a consequence the States and towns which adopt it will be supported by the liberating forces.

Art. 11. A part of the aforesaid forces shall be destined to wage war permanently against the barbarous Indians until complete pacification in the frontier States.

Art. 12. The towns will not lay down their arms while all that contained in the preceding eleven articles is not granted. If the general government persists in denying the armed petition of this frontier that contains all the necessities of any nation, the States that adopt this plan, casting aside all idea of schism or of annexation, will be able to organize a provisional government.

And in order that this plan might have the necessary publicity, this meeting has agreed to direct it to the illustrious town council, the corporate body of this city, leaving to its consideration and deliberation the method that is chosen to promulgate it.

(Signature)

Campo en la Loba.

El Siglo Diez y Nueve, October 12, 1851.

* * * * *

PLAN OF THE PRONOUNCEMENT ADVANCED IN
SAN NICOLAS DE LOS RANCHOS

16 December, 1851

Rather lengthy "Considerandos" precede the terms of the Plan. And then in the name of God the All

461

Powerful, supreme author of societies, to whose most wise dispositions we are subject, and under whose protection we place ourselves.

Art. 1. The Mexican nation is and shall remain free, independent and sovereign master of itself: its religion Catholic, Apostolic and Roman, without infusion of any other sect regardless of what it may be.

Art. 2. The nation adopts for its system of government the organic bases proclaimed, recognized, and sworn to in the year 1843, retroactive to the situation prevailing until August 2, 1846, having as a consequennce to reestablish as soon as possible the same authorities that were functioning in that era.

Art. 3. As soon as the Administration may be established, it shall concern itself as a first priority with the convocation of an extraordinary congress to be composed of two individuals from each Department and one from each territory; that as a constituent body it will make reforms which the present circumstances demand and that experience shows to be necessary.

Art. 4. All the notable and influential men of all sorts without exception and wherever they may be found are invited so that they may take the part due them to save the independence and nationality of the republic so nearly threatened by death.

Art. 5. The worthy [benemerita] military class that so carelessly and imprudently has been released or suspended and prior to a recognition and evaluation of its services will be attended to and considered for its due recompense. The national guard is invited also.

Art. 6. The lives, property and the persons of all classes are guaranteed, as individuals or corporation.

Art. 7. The introduction of alien goods is prohibited in all ports of entry of the Mexican republic; the items that are cultivated or manufactured in the nation under the pain of becoming liable under the law of _____and the violator will be condemned in accord with the law in this matter.

Art. 8. There shall be established in Mexico a general junta for the classification of all sorts of arts, agriculture, and sciences with the worthy object of protecting and rewarding the industry of the country, and with the passage of five years the Mexican people can occupy a distinguished place among the artists of Europe.

Art. 9. All existing Treasury obligations as of today will be recognized as well as those issued hereinafter, whatever their origin may be, provided that they represent licit contracts without any legal impediment.

Art. 10. There shall be a general amnesty for all crimes that do not involve third parties except those of betrayal and treason of the country, that will be punished with all the vigor of the laws, providing the drafting of proper cause of action. The administration shall determine in which court they may be tried.

Art. 11. This Plan being eminently national, any person who presents formal opposition to it will be treated as a traitor.

(Signed) Felix Lopez Sastre
(Other signatures follow)

_____

El Siglo Diez y Nueve, Jan. 7, 1852.

* * * * *

PRONOUNCEMENT OF ORIZABA

2 January, 1852

Several long paragraphs of justification precede the following Articles:

Art. 1. The plan proclaimed in the cities of Guadalajara and Santa Anna de Tamaulipas is seconded, along with the clarifications which the following articles establish:

Art. 2. In conformity with Article I manifested in the Act advanced in Guadalajara on October 20, 1852, the Mexican republic shall continue being administered through the popular, representative federal system.

Art. 3. Since General D. Mariano Arista ought to surrender the exercise of executive power because of having become unworthy of the confidence of the people, the general congress shall elect the person who is to succeed him, according to the terms provided in Articles 96 and 97 of the constitution of 1824.

Art. 4. If for whatever reason the general congress should cease to exist, the supreme executive authority shall be vested in the president of the supreme court of justice, and in two individuals who shall elect by an absolute plurality of votes the governing council in accordance with that which Article 97, previously cited, provides.

Art. 5. The new executive authority shall expedite a new election law upon the basis of [the law] of Dec. 10, 1841, outlining the authority that is conferred upon the representatives of the people to act as provided in the constitution of 1824 and in the reforming measure of 1847 to do those things which experience has demonstrated to be absolutely necessary in order to avoid those commercial barriers that today interfere between one State and another, and in order to provide that the union of these [States] may result in power and authority, and not in weakness and isolation as has happened until now through the faulty interpretation that has been given to the sovereignty or independence of the States.

Art. 6. The executive authority shall be used immediately to organize a treasury system sufficient to cover public expenses, and for this purpose a consultive junta composed of persons of probity and competence in this important matter of public administration shall be established; it giving the congress an account of the provisions which it may dictate for the purpose but without prejudice for putting them into effect immediately.

464

Art. 7. The president of the republic who while by reason of circumstances may find hemself invested with absolute power, shall not be empowered to attack either the person or property of the inhabitants of the republic nor to exercise the powers committed to the judicial authority.

And these articles being approved unanimously and without discussion, it was ordered to present the testimony of the present agreement to the commander of the garrison of this city, those present signing along with the secretary who agrees.

(Signatures follow)

El Siglo Diez y Nueve, January 20, 1853

* * * * *

PLAN OF BLANCARTE

26 July, 1852

In the City of Guadalajara, capital of the free and sovereign State of Jalisco, the forces commanded by Sr. D. Jose Maria Blancarte and the people without exception of class came together.

[There follow six paragraphs of justification for the meeting, and then:]

Art. 1. As of this day the State of Jalisco returns to the constitutional order from which the publication of decree #135 had separated it.

Art. 2. As a consequence, it repudiates the present administration for not being an emanation of law, for having established itself against the legitimate expression of the people, and for having conspired in its acts against our present form of government.

465

Art. 3. While the interim government of the State is being organized in accordance with its constitution, the [Commander] Lic. Gregorio Davila is named provisional governor, who having offered to keep and cause to be kept the general Constitution of the nation and the particular one of the State, and the present Plan is, as of now, in the exercise of power.

Art. 4. The provisional governor shall issue within two months an official summons for the meeting of an extraordinary congress.

Art. 5. This [congress] shall proceed to reform the fundamental charter of the state and it should conclude its labors within six months, and it can concern itself during this time with the measures that may be considered necessary in the branch of the Treasury.

Art. 6. All the laws and dispositions that, in the opinion of the provisional governor are contrary to our Constitution are without effect; he is to guide all his administrative actions in accord with [the Constitution] wherever it may be possible and as the present state of irregular circumstances makes possible.

(Signed)

Jose Maria Blancarte
and others

V. Riva Palacio, Mexico a traves de los siglos, IV, 780-781.

* * * * *

THE SECOND PLAN OF BLANCARTE

13 September, 1852

After several 'Considerandos' which justify the issuance of the Plan, the document continues:

Realizing that the nation is on the verge of losing its independeence, and using the same rights which our fathers used in 1821 in the City of Iguala, the sovereign State of Jalisco proclaims and promises it support to the following:

Art. 1. That the Mexican nation is one and indivisible and that the States of the federation are free and sovereign in all matters relative to their internal administration, and in conformity with the provisions contained in the general Constitution of the Republic.

Art. 2. Public officials who have lost or no longer deserve the confidence of the people shall by will of the nation cease the exercise of their duties.

Art. 3. It being well known what is the public opinion in regard to those persons in Jalisco who exercise executive and legislative power, hereby is ratified the Plan proclaimed July 26, 1852, and its terms are made to extend in its impact to the persons and effects of those who discharge executive functions of the Union because their continuance [in office] is contrary to the will of the nation.

Art. 4. The Houses of the general Congress will come together in order to name an interim President who will discharge the function of the deposed [predecessor] until such time as the States shall designate the method and form under which the provisional government is to be created, as indicated in the following article.

Art. 5. There will be organized an Executive Power deposited in one person and invested with all the facilities which may not be contrary to the Federal Constitution and whose exercise will have for its purpose the reestablishment of order and justice in the Republic as well as to secure federal institutions.

Art. 6. The governments of the States which support this Plan are hereby granted whatever power that may be necessary to reorganize themselves for the purpose of attending immediately to the defense of the frontier states which have been devastated by savages, and for the regeneration of the Republic.

Art. 7. The situation of the Republic demanding the adoption of extraordinary measures, any state which supports this Plan will promulgate and will declare at once to be in effect the Law of 21 April 1847 as passed by the constituent Congress.

Art. 8. The nation invites General Antonio Lopez de Santa Anna to return to the territory of the Republic in order to join in the task of sustaining the federal system, and the reestablishment of order and peace.

Art. 9. Every corporate body or individual which opposes the present Plan or gives aid to those agencies which disowns it are responsible with their persons and goods and will be treated as enemies of the independence and unity of the Republic.

Art. 10. The units of the National Guard of the States will recognize only the present commander of troops, Jose Maria Blancarte.

Art. 11. His Excellency the provisional governor, Lic. Gregorio Davila, will be urged, fully aware of the reasons which animate the undersigned, to adhere to the present act and to continue in the forefront of the destiny of the State, which today, as never before, needs his judgment and patriotism.

(Signed)

Jose Marie Blancarte

V. Riva Palacio, Mexico a traves de los siglos, IV, 782-783

* * * * *

PRONOUNCEMENT OF GUADALAJARA

13 September, 1852

[Six brief paragraphs precede the concluding justification:]

Realizing that the nation is on the verge of losing its independence, and using those same rights which our fathers used in 1821 in the city of Iguala, the sovereign State of Jalisco proclaims and solemnly promises to support the following:

Art. 1. That the Mexican nation is one and indivisible and that the States of the Federation are free and sovereign in all matters relative to their interior regimen, in conformity with the disposition contained in the general constitution of the republic.

Art. 2. By the will of the nation the public authorities that have lost the confidence of the nation or are now underserving of its confidence to hereby cease to function.

Art. 3. It now being well known what is the public opinion in respect to the persons who are exercising the legislative and executive powers in Jalisco, the Plan proclaimed the 26th of July, 1852, is hereby ratified and is declared ample in references to the person who is discharging the executive power of the Union, for the will of the nation opposes his remaining in office.

Art. 4. The Houses of the General Congress shall meet in order to name an interim President who shall discharge the functions of the one displaced, until the States may designate the method and form under which the provisional government is to be created, and in accordance with the following article.

Art. 5. There shall be organized an executive power entrusted to one person who shall be vested with all the authority that does not oppose the Federal constitution, and whose duty shall be to reestablish order and justice in the republic, as well as to secure federal institutions.

Art. 6. The governments of the States which may endorse this plan shall have full authority that may be necessary to be reorganized for the purpose of attending immediately to the defense of the frontier States devastated by the savages and in order to make effective the regeneration of the republic.

Art. 7. The situation of the Republic demanding the adoption of extraordinary measures, every State that may second this plan shall therewith promulgate and shall declare in effect the law of April 21, 1847, as passed by the constituent congress.

Art. 8. The nation invites General Antonio L. de Santa Anna to return to the territory of the republic in order that he may cooperate with sustaining the federal system and the reestablishment of order and peace.

Art. 9. Any corporate body or individual who may oppose the present plan or who may lend aid to those authorities whom it disavows are responsible along with their persons and properties, and will be treated as enemies of independence and unity of the republic.

Art. 10. The units of the National Guard only recognize as leader the present commandant C. Jose Maria Blancarte.

Art. 11. His Excellency the provisional Governor, Lic. Gregorio Davila shall be notified in order that he may know the reasons that animate those who subscribe, who adhere to the present act, and who continue to command the destiny of the State that now more than ever needs his understanding and patriotism.

(Many military
signatures follow)

El Siglo Diez y Nueve, September 21, 1852.

* * * * *

PLAN OF THE GARRISON OF JALISCO

20 October, 1852

In the city of Guadalajara, 20th of October, 1852, having met in the Hospital for the Poor, being a sheltered place which is outside the fortified district, the men who have signed below and inspired solely and exclusively by the most intense desire of securing the peace of the State which is menaced at this very moment by all the horrors of civil war, point out that this step will lead to general quiet in the Republic. Taxes will be collected scrupulously by Sr. Lazaro J. Gallardo and that these important ends will succeed in making the forces of the City and the State stronger, the State Administration may order some modificiations to the Plan very recently proclaimed in the capital the 13th of September.(1) Whereas . . . (a relatively brief paragraph of justification follows) Moved by these concepts, the undersigned agreed to forward to the Honorable General Jose Maria Yanez the principles that, in their opinion, are the expression of the general will; and being drafted in due form are as follows:

Art. 1. The Mexican nation is one and indivisible and is constituted under a popular, representative federal system.

Art. 2. All public authorities who have or may hereafter lose the confidence of the people shall cease the exercise of their functions.

Art. 3. While an interim President is being named, an Executive Power to be vested in one person shall be organized. [This official] shall reestablish order and justice in the Republic, confirm its institutions, guarantee its independence, and promptly attend to the security of the frontier States.

---

(1) The second Plan of Blancarte

Art. 4. When the national forces which advance the reform shall occupy the capital, the General-in-Chief shall within thirty days convoke an emergency congress which shall be composed of two Deputies from each State, these to be named according to the law which served to elect the congress of 1842.

Art. 5. This congress, being met, shall proceed 1) to the election of an interim President whose term shall last for the remainder of the constitutional four-year period. 2) It will concern itself with those reforms to the constitution which will give general respectability to the Administration, and power compatable with the sovereignty and independence of the States, and adequate for domestic administration. 3) It shall create and organize a National Treasury. 4) It shall reestablish domestic and foreign trade by means of moderate tax rates which shall rationalize that branch and put an end to contraband which victimizes honest trade. 5) On the State frontiers a system of defense will be devised against the savages. 6) Elections will be arranged in such a way as to modify the covetousness that has been the source of so many evils to the Republic. [The Congress] will devise a general scheme of economic administration in order that the people may be freed of some [inter] state taxes. 8) The army, today destroyed, will positively be reorganized as well as some other class of militia which will serve as a reserve, and [it will] disband the hateful part of the National Guard that is made to occupy garrisons in the towns and for whom special contributions are made, these contributions being very heavy for the unfortunate citizens. 9) It will pass a Law of Amnesty for all political offenses. This Congress will last for a year at the most.

Art. 6. Until the Treasury system is arranged, the States will contribute half of their tax income, except those which suffer invasions of savages.

Art. 7. In order that the people may begin to feel the improvement of a positive reform, the head of tax and the National Guard levy shall cease.

Art. 8. The government of the states which support this Plan have the power which may be necessary to organize under these principles in order to attend immediately to the defenses of the frontier states which have been devastated by savages and in order to carry into effect the regeneration of the Republic.

Art. 9. The situation of the Republic demanding the adoption of extraordinary measures, every State which supports this Plan will publicize it at once and will declare in effect the law of April 26th, 1847, as expedited by the Constituent Congress.

Art. 10. Every corporate body or individual which shall reject this Plan or who lends aid to the forces which reject it are responsible with their persons and goods and will be treated as enemies of the independence and unity of the Republic.

Art. 11. In regard to the eminent services that His Excellency Sr. D. Antonio Lopez de Santa Anna has devoted to the country in all periods, these make him worthy of national gratitude, and since in all major conflicts of the Republic he has always been the first who has presented himself to save it, and since His Excellency has voluntarily left Mexican territory, as soon as the Administration is organized as indicated in Art. 3 of this Plan, the provisional Executive shall invite the said General to return to the Republic whenever he deems it convenient.

Art. 12. The troops of Jalisco, in order to support his Plan, name as its General the distinguished citizen of the State of Guanajuato, General Jose L. Uraga, who while maintaining the most strict order and discipline, will function with all the power of a general on campaign.

Art. 13. The executive authority of the free and sovereign State of Jalisco will continue to reside in the person of the commanding General Jose Maria Yanez who will dictate the provisions which may be necessary for the purpose of organizing the State powers, as has been detailed in Art. 8 of this Plan.

Art. 14. Since the purpose of the individuals who sign this present arrangement is to avoid the shedding of blood with which the capital is threatened and to conciliate as far as possible the minds of individuals divided by political interests, the persons who were occupying [posts] in the State administration on the 26th of July of the current

473

year will be able to return without molestation to live peaceably in their homes equally with all other citizens.(2)

(Signed)

Lazaro J. Gallardo _et_ _al_.

_____

(2) This Plan is identical with that of the Plan of Hospicio and of even date.

Colleccion de las leyes fundamentales, 300-303.

* * * * *

PLAN OF HOSPICIO*

20 October, 1852

Art. 1. The Mexican nation is one and indivisible and constituted under the Federal system; it is popular and representative.

Art. 2. All public officials who are underserving or have lost public confidence shall hereby cease the exercise of all their functions.

Art. 3. While an interim President is being named, an Executive Power vested in one person shall be organized. He shall reestablish order and justice in the Republic, stabalize institutions, guarantee independence, and at once attend to the security of frontier States.

Art. 4. When the national forces which support this reform shall occupy the capital, the General-in-Chief within twenty days shall convoke a special congress which shall be composed of two deputies from each State, these to be named according to the law which served to elect the Congress of 1842.

Art. 5. This Congress, being convened, shall proceed 1) To the election of an interim President who will

_____

(*) Also called Plan of Guadalajara

hold office the remainder of the four year, constitutional term. 2) It shall concern itself with Constitutional reforms which will give to the Administration general responsibility and power compatable with the sovereignty and independence of the States in domestic affairs. 3) It will create and organize a National Treasury. 4) It will readjust domestic and foreign trade by means of moderate tariffs which justify this branch, and abolish contraband which victimizes honest trade. 5) It will systematize the defense of the frontier against the invasions of the barbarous [Indians]. 6) It will arrange elections in such a way as to bridle undue ambition which has been the origin of so many evils for the Republic. 7) It shall draft a general project for an economical administration so that the people may be free of certain duties. 8) Positively it shall reorganize the Army, at the present time destroyed, and [it shall reorganize] another class of militia which shall serve as a Reserve, abolishing the hateful duties of the National Guard which is required to fill garrisons in the towns, and for which service special and very heavy taxes on those unfortunate localities are collected.

9) A law of Amnesty shall be passed for all political offenses. This Congress shall sit for a year at the longest.

Art. 6. In the meantime a Treasury system shall be arranged whereby the States will contribute half of their income, except those which suffer incursions of the wild Indians.

Art. 7. In order that the people may commence to feel the benefit of a positive reform, the head tax and special national guard assessments shall stop.

Art. 8. The governments of the States which may support this Plan are hereby given all authority which may be necessary in order to organize themselves under these provisions, so that they may immediately attend to the defenses of the frontier States which have been devastated by the savages, and in order to carry into effect the regeneration of the Republic.

Art. 9. Since the situation of the Republic demands the adoption of extraordinary measures, every State which supports this Plan will forthwith promulgate and declare in effect the law of 20 April, 1847 as passed by the constituent Congress.

Art. 10. Every corporate body or individual which opposes the present Plan or who lends aid to the powers which oppose it are responsible in their persons and possessions and will be treated as enemies of the independence and unity of the Republic.

Art. 11. In consideration of the eminent services which his Excellency General Antonio Lopez de Santa Anna has afforded the country on all occasions and which makes him deserving of national gratitude, and whereas in the great battles of the Republic he has always been the first to press forward to save it, and whereas he has voluntarily left Mexican territory, as soon as the Government has been organized according to Art. 3 of this Plan, the provisional executive will invite the said General to return to the Republic whenever he deems it convenient.

Art. 12. In order to support this Plan, the forces of Jalisco will name as its General the distinguished citizen of the state of Guanajuato, General Jose Lopez Uraga, who, while maintaining the strictest order and discipline, will act with all the authority of a general on campaign.

Art. 13. The Executive [Power] of the free and sovereign State of Jalisco will remain vested in the person of the General and citizen Jose Maria Yanez who will set forth the provisions that may be necessary for organizing the powers of the State, as is foreseen in Art. 8 of this Plan.

Art. 14. Since the purpose of the individuals who support this Plan is to avoid the shedding of blood with which the capital is threatened and to conciliate wherever possible the opinions, divided by political interests, those persons who were occupying the administration of the State on July 26th of the current year will be able to return, without anyone molesting them, to live peacefully in their homes along with all other citizens.

(Signed)

Lic. Lazaro J. Gallardo

Gamboa, <u>Leyes y constitucions de Mexico</u>, 484-489.

* * * * *

NEW PLAN OF GUADALAJARA

21 October, 1852

Two paragraphs of justification, and then:

Art. 1. The Mexican nation is one and indivisible, and is constituted under a popular representative and federal system.

Art. 2. All public authorities who have lost or may now be losing public confidence shall cease in the exercise of their official duties.

Art. 3. There shall be organized an executive authority to be vested in one person who shall until an interim president has been named reestablish order and justice in the republic: he shall refinance the institutions [of government], guarantee independence, and immediately assure the security of the frontier States.

Art. 4. After the national forces that are supporting this reform shall have occupied the capital, the commander-in-Chief shall, within thirty days, convoke an extraordinary congress to be composed of two deputies from each State, who are to be named according to the law that served to elect the congress of the year 1842.

477

Art. 5. This congress having assembled, it shall proceed:

a. To the election of an interim president who shall preside for what remains of the constitutional quadrennium.

b. It shall concern itself with the reforms of the constitution that may give the general government respectability, authority reconcilable with the sovereignty and independence of the States in their internal administration.

c. It shall create and organize the treasury of the nation.

d. It shall administer interior and exterior commerce by means of moderate tariffs that may establish this branch on a sound basis and may put an end to the contraband that victimizes legal trade.

e. It shall systemize the defense of the frontier States against the invasions of the barbarians [Indians].

f. It shall regulate elections in such a way that it will invalidate dilenttante candidates [aspirantismo] that has been the source of so many misfortunes in the republic.

g. It shall establish a general headquarters for an economic council in order that the towns may free themselves of some taxes (gabelas).

h. It shall absolutely reorganize the army, today destroyed, and with some other kind of militia that may serve as a reserve get rid of the hated part of the national guard that has been used to supply garrisons in the towns and for which they have collected special contributions that have been very serious for those unfortunate places.

i. It shall issue a law of amnesty for all political crimes. This congress shall last a year at the most.

Art. 6. While the treasury system is being arranged the States shall contribute one half of their income, except those that suffer the incursions of the uncivilized Indians [barbaros].

Art. 7. In order that the towns may commence to feel the benefits of a positive reform, the poll taxes and the exception of the national guard shall cease.

Art. 8. The administration of the States that may support this plan have full authority as may be necessary to organize themselves under this plan for the purpose of attending to the defense of the frontier States devastated by the savages, and in order to carry into effect the regeneration of the republic.

Art. 9. The situation of the republic requiring the adoption of extraordinary measures, every State which may support the present plan shall promulgate immediately and declare in effect the law of April 26, 1847, as issued by the constituent congress.

Art. 10. Every corporate body or individual who may oppose this plan or who may provide support to those bodies which it disavows are responsible with their persons and property as enemies of the independence and unity of the republic.

Art. 11. In consideration of the eminent services that the Most Excellent Senior General Don Antonio Lopez de Santa Anna has devoted to the country in all epochs, they make him worthy of national gratitude, for in the great conflicts of the republic he has ever been the first to give of himself to save it, and for which he has voluntarily departed from Mexican territory; as soon as the administration about which Art. 3 of this plan speaks shall have been organized, the provisional executive shall invite the aforesaid general to return to the republic when he may deem it convenient.

Art. 12. The forces of Jalisco, in order to support this plan, name as its general the distinguished citizen of Guanajuato, General Jose Lopez Uraga, who, while preserving the most strict order and discipline shall operate with all the authority of a general on campaign.

Art. 13. The executive of the free and sovereign State of Jalisco shall continue to be vested in the person of citizen-general the distinguished citizen of Guanajuato, General Jose Lopez Uraga, who, while preserving the most strict order and discipline shall operate with all the authority of a general on campaign.

Art. 14. Since the purpose of the individuals who form the present agreement is to avoid the effusion of blood with which the capital is treatened and is to reconcile in so far as possible the minds divided by political interests, the persons who were occupying the administration of the State on July 26th of the current year shall be able to return without being molested to live peacefully in their homes as all other citizens [may do].

Many signatures follow.

El Siglo Diez y Nueve, October 28, 1852.

* * * * *

ADDITIONS TO THE PLAN OF JALISCO
OF 20TH OF OCTOBER

13 November, 1852

Art. 1. The present constitutional period that ends the year 1853 being concluded, the new congress that may be elected for the period due to begin in 1854 shall be convoked under the title of "extraordinary."

Art. 2. The congress thus convoked extraordinary shall concern itself with the following points of first priority:

a. To make the necessary reforms to the general constitution of the republic, considering the necessities and exigences of the nation.

480

b. To create an equitable financial system, sufficient to cover the budgets of the civil service list and the other ordinary expenses of general administration in normal times.

c. To draft a law adequate for determining the manner of underwriting any other extraordinary expenses in exceptional times or circumstances.

d. To determine the size of the permanent armed forces and the method of forming it, both in time of peace as well as in time of war.

e. To expedite a broad and protective colonization law, allowing for methods of saving the republic.

Art. 3. All distinguised and influential men of all social segments without exception are invited to take their due share in order to save the independence and national entity of the republic, now so threatened by death.

Art. 4. The wholly deserving military group that has been unjustly and unwisely released and suspended from service is invited, and with prior recognition and evalutation of services will be given attention and consideration for due recompense, and the national guard is likewise invited.

Art. 5. All current Treasury liabilities as of today will be recognized, as well as those which may be issued, whatever their origin, provided that they proceed from legal contracts and are without stain.

Art. 6. The sales tax [alcabala] in the State of Vera Cruz is abolished.

Art. 7. This plan being eminently national, whoever presents formal opposition will be treated as a traitor.

(Signed)

J. C. Rebolledo
and the forces under his command.

El Siglo Diez y Nueve, November 20, 1852.

* * * * *

481

REVISIONS TO THE PLAN OF HOSPICIO

29 November, 1852

"In Tamualipas the revolution triumphed after the fall of the City of Victoria and as a consequence D. Ramon Prieto was elevated to the governorship. ...The Commanding Officer, Colonel Casanova, led the pronouncement of Tampico, adopting the Plan of Jalisco when it had been modified by the Junta of Hospicio. Casanova made some variations to the said Plan in respect to the method of electing the provisional President and of convoking the Congress. Below are the articles taken precisely from the Act of 29th of November. ..."

Art. 2 (1) The third and fourth articles of the said Plan (that of the 20th of October) are revised in the following terms: The governors of the States, in agreement with the respective military authorities shall each name two representatives in order that they might meet and proceed to the election of the person who is to be charged provisionally with the supreme executive power. -- To those States who are unable to send their representatives under the terms of the General-in-Chief of the forces which have pronounced [against the Government] they will be represented by persons residing in the capital of the Republic and deserving through their honor and capacity the confidence of the nation to name the General-in-Chief.

---

(1) Article I was unchanged.

Art. 3. As soon as the 'pronounced' forces have
entered [the Capital of the Republic] the one charged
with executive duties shall call a popular
representative assembly which shall name the
president of the Republic; this shall take place
within thirty days after having made their entrance
into the capital.

Art. 4. It shall be one of the designated duties of
the assembly to expedite a judicious and thorough law
of amnesty for all political crimes, and in the
judgment of the same body shall rest the censure of
those who, being able to cause a new disturbance in
the counry, it may be necessary to restrain them
whenever it may judge suitable, the extent of the
disposition which Article 9 of the Plan of
Guadalajara asks for.

The introduction and text of the proposed revisions
are found in Juan Suarez Navarro, El General Santa
Anna burlandose de la Nacion, (1856), 123-125.

* * * * *

A PROPOSAL SUBMITTED TO THE CHAMBER OF DEPUTIES

19 January, 1853

A long paragraph dedicated to the proposition
that "the first object of the attention [of the
Chamber of Deputies] is to discover the true origin,
the pace, and the depth of the violence which
agitates the Republic in order to evaluate its
character, attack its impetus, and to be able to
predict a less violent development."

Art. 1. A convention is to be convoked that will be
composed of representatives of all the States and to
be elected in the number and in the form and under
the rules established in the decree of 10 December,
1841.

Art. 2. This conventin ought to be held in the capital of the Federation by the 15th of June of this year and for this purpose there shall take place in all points in the Republic the nomination of primary electors the first Sunday of next April, [nomination] of the secondaries the second Sunday of the same month and [nominations] of deputies the second Sunday of May next.

Art. 3. On the first active day of the sessions of the convention the present administration shall give an account of the use it may have made of the authorization which was granted by the law of the 11th of January of this year.

Art. 4. The national convention cannot last more than a year, and its duties shall be to revise the present consitution, conserving the form of a republican, representative, popular federal government, to name within the first three days of its session the interim President who shall govern the Republic while the new constitution is being issued, and the duly elected one who is to enter the office is being elected and as the Constitution may provide, and to exercise the other faculties which the two general chambers have today.

Art. 5. The governors of the States who now exist in some of them by virtue of the revolution shall be responsible for calling together in the shortest time possible their respective legislatures, and these shall concern themselves immediately with setting the time that they are to continue and to return their States to the constitutional order in accord with their particular laws.

(Signed)

J. M. Arroyo

Archivo Mexicano, I, (1853)

*   *   *   *   *

PLAN OF ARROYO ZARCO

4 February, 1853

In the hacienda of Arroyo Zarco on the fourth day of February, 1853, the following generals, Commanding General of the National Army which supports the Plan of Regeneration adopted in Jalisco the 20th of October of last year, (1) Jose L. Uraga, and the General of Division Robles met for the purpose of celebrating pact which would end the crisis in which the Republic now finds itself.

Senor Uraga, in his character of Commander-in-Chief and being recognized by all the forces which have 'pronounced' and be the States which have supported the political movement, and Senor Robles as General of his Division authorized for this pact by the second of the resolutions adopted in Celaya the 31st of January last and who support the said Act.

They proceeded to examine all the additions made to the Plan of Jalisco and [to consider] the several manifestations of public opinion, and they discovered that the opinion of the majority of the States was in accord with the following points:

1st. That one national government should be recognized in the Republic with discretional and all-embracing powers in the legislative and executive branches. 2nd. That this government should have sufficient time to plan a good administration throughout all the Republic. 3rd. For this purpose the date of the convocation of a constituent congress should be set by the administration itself, and [the Generals] will accept its judgment for the time for convoking a constitutent Congress. 4th. That this time limit may be sufficient, the country being tranquil and genuine public opinion having been investigated, the said congress should be able to complete its assignment. 5th. That in the call for the Congress it be expressly stated that the Congress is not called for any other duty than for the sole and exclusive duty of giving a constitution to the

(1) See the Plan of Hospico

country, and that it is without legislative power in any other area. On presenting the constitution, IT DOES NOT HAVE any other specified and admissable duty with which to concern itself other than the frame of government which it may establish, provided that it be republican, representative, and popular. 6th. That the provisionary government shall cease when the new, reformed constitution which is due to be established may appear, and that its acts and decrees shall have the substance which the emanations of a sovereign authority enjoy. They can be modified or cancelled in the manner and form which the former may modified or cancelled. [The Generals] agreed upon the following Plan:

Art. 1. The majority of the States having indicated their purpose of establishing an extraordinary Power which, dominating the situation, will satisfy the national desire to bring an end to anarchy and that political institutions should be reformed, [this Power] shall procede within five days after the [national] capital has adhered to the pact to elect a person who shall exercise the authority of a provisional government while the new constitutional order is being established.

Art. 2. An executive committee [junta] composed of two persons from each State, District, or Territory of the Federation and one person from each class of the following: the secular clergy, the Army, the Magistracy, the Landowners, the Miners, the Merchants and Industrialists shall be formed. [This Committee] will designate the person who is to discharge the executive power of the nation under the title of Interim-President.

Art. 3. Since the Commander-in-Chief will not be able to extend further the date for the nomination of an interim President, he will name the members of the aforesaid Junta). [He] shall take care that the election falls to persons known for their antecedents and services to the nation, and if it be possible natives of the State which they represent.

Art. 4. The Junta being installed, it will proceed

486

immediately by secret vote to the election of an interim President and it shall notify the one elected, summoning him to receive the oath on the following day. He shall present himself before the junta and before God and the Nations. [This one] shall promise faithfully to discharge that which is committed to him according to the dictates of his conscience without any other consideration than the good and well-being of the nation. After this act he will receive charge which he currently exercises, and he will be installed as provisioal government shall exercise its power optionally without any restriction, and [shall use] all the faculties which may be necessary for the good of the nation.

Art. 6. The Government will create a council which it will direct as it sees fit, and its authority will be merely consultative, in order to render its opinion in all those cases, matters of business and affairs which it seems suitable.

Art. 7. Having determined that there is order in the whole Republic, and within the space of one year of the term of the installed government, it shall send out a summons for a convocation in conformity with which are to be named the deputies to extraordinary congress which shall freely reform institutions, save only the basis of a republican system, at once representative and popular, and under the recognition that it cannot legislate on any other matter except that of its mission which is restricted to producing a reformed Constitution.

Art. 8. The Judicial Power shall enjoy the same independence that it has so far enjoyed and will exercise its functions in accord with pre-existing laws.

The pact being ended, they agree to go personally to the capital of the Republic to present [this Plan] to His Excellency Juan B. Cevallos who is exercising the power there, so that being accepted by His Excellency and by his subordinates, as is to be expected from one of his known patriotism, an end was brought to the present crisis, and again peace and order appeared. [The Generals subscribed below] signed the pact as testimony of its validity in reference to the points expressed.

(Signed)

Jose L. Uraga

Manuel Robles Pezuela

J. Suarez y Navarro, Santa-Anna burlandose de la Nacion, 132-135. This same text, with slight variations is found in the newspaper Siglo XIX, 22 March, 1853.

* * * * *

PACT OF FEBRUARY 6, 1853

6 February, 1953

Art. 1. The Plan proclaimed in Guadalajara the 20th of October, 1852 (1), is hereby endorsed in all its provisions, along with the amplifications which follow.

Art. 2. Satisfying, as is due and in accord with the demands of the very serious and exceptional situation in which the Republic now finds itself, and in order to meet the clamor of public opinion which desires that domestic tranquility be secured at once, it is hereby declared: THAT the Executive Power which may be chosen shall conform to the terms of this Pact; that it will have, until the promulgation of the new political Constitution which is to be drafted, all necessary faculties for reestablishing the social order, promoting public administration, forming a national Treasury, and expediting the attributes of the judicial process; and it shall make all suitable reforms without limiting its independence.

Art. 3. As soon as public peace has been reestablished and when, in the opinion of the executive it

---

(1) Plan of Guadalajara

is practical to hold public elections, the Government shall summon a national Convention which is referred to in the previous article will have full power to constitute the Nation under a popular, representative, republican form of government; and it being concerned exclusively with this purpose, the Executive Power shall not be empowered in any way to suspend or retard its functions.

Art. 5. The legislatures of the States, and where there are no such, or they have not been reconstituted, the presiding Governors, acting with their Cabinets, and in the District and the Territories the governors or political leaders [jefes politicos], shall proceed within two days after receiving this Pact to the election of a President of the Republic. In the meantime and by the vote of all the reestablished authorities the Executive [Power] is to be lodged in the President of the Supreme Court of Justice Juan B. Ceballos, who shall on the 17th of March next officially open the envelopes which will contain the votes of the States, Districts, and Territories; and he shall declare the person who shall have been nominated. As soon as this person shall have presented himself at the Capital (or immediately if he should be there) he shall take the oath before the Supreme Court of Justice according to the following terms: "Do you swear before God to defend the Independence and integrity of the Mexican territory and to promote the well-being and prosperity of the Nation according to the prinicples adopted in the Plan of Jalisco and the Pact celebrated the 6th of last February in the Capital by the united agencies of government? If you will do this, may God reward you; and if not may He and the Nation punish you." This action being completed, the person so named shall assume his duties.

Art. 6. The election referred to in the previous Article will be held without excluding Mexican citizens who may not be residing in the national domain. In order to be elected, it will be sufficient to receive a simple majority of the votes cast, and in case of a tie the united Generals of Divisions shall choose from among the persons who may have obtained the same number of votes.

Art. 7. Allowing for the disposition of the new Constitution and in order to expedite the progress of public administration, there shall be established a Council of State to be composed of twenty-one persons known for their wisdom and patriotism, named and organized by the Executive Power two weeks after the latter has been installed.

Art. 8. In case of a declaration of war against the Republic, and that [the Executive] shall have to repel it, or in case it may be necessary to make an urgent treaty with foreign powers, the Administration will act in accord with the Council of State.

Art. 9. As soon as the provisional government referred to in this Plan shall have been installed, it will fulfill the precept contained in Art. 11 of the Plan of Jalisco that solemnly names His Excellency Antonio Lopez de Santa Anna as "Benemerito" of the Fatherland."

Art. 10. A general amnesty for all crimes purely political in nature is granted; and it is declared that for occupation of public office, for promotion or whatever other benefit one shall not allege as merit that he served the cause of the revolution, nor will it be a disqualification that he opposed it, for the government ought to employ without distinction men of all parties who have probity, intelligence, and patriotism.

Art. 11. The leaders [jefes] who ratify this Pact promise to remain united in order to make possible its fulfillment.

Art. 12. The Secretaries of Office will be responsible for their acts to the first constitutional Congress.

(No signatures attached)

Gamboa, Leyes y constituciones de Mexico, 489.
V. Riva Palacio, Mexico a traves de los siglos, IV, 802.

* * * * *

BASES FOR PROMOTING THE PLAN OF JALISCO

6 February, 1853

Art. 1. Within five days after occupying the capital the General-in-Chief shall name a Junta of outstanding persons to be composed of two individuals from each class, and one from each State and territory.

Art. 2. Each junta, before five days, shall nominate [and send] to the interim president of the republic: 1) a council of government, 2) shall indicate its number, and 3) shall indicate the salary that shall ensue.

Art. 3. The president shall take possession at once, receiving the government from the hands of the presiding (president). He shall swear before God and the nation to defend the independence and integrity of the territory; to submit himself to these principles and in consequence to instigate all the reforms necessary, and to eliminate all the abuses that to this day are precipitating us into ruin.

Art. 4. The president-elect has all the authority [for the task] except to reform our foreign relations, draft treaties, declare war, and grant privileges that effect the nation itself, all of which he can do only after a hearing before the junta of distinguished persons.

Art. 5. The said junta shall present within six months a convocation that shall bring together an extraordinary congress fully authorized to give a constitution to the country.

Art. 6. This congress shall last for one year and shall be occupied with its commission, and, as it may indicate, a constitutional election for president and for the [legislative] chamber, and of the governors of the States in order to enter at the same time into the constitutional circle.

Art. 7. Until then the States shall remain suspended

by their governors and a council of government.

Art. 8. Half the income of the States shall be its assessment for the general government, except for the frontiers attacked by the barbarous Indians, all of whose income shall be employed in its defense, at most for whatever may be necessary for its security.

Art. 9. Any citizen who may be named for the discharge of a public position shall accept it, and if he should refuse he shall suffer a fine from one to ten thousand pesos.

General Jose Lopez Uraga.

El Siglo Diez y Nueve, March 22, 1853.

* * * * *

EXPOSITION OF THE PROGRESSIVE DEMOCRATIC PARTY

April, 1853

A simultaneous listing and commentary) "We have read with great attention this pamphlet and we are pleased to observe that the political principles which the progressive party supports are, in their major points, entirely in accord with the exposition which we presented to General Santa Anna in our article of [April] 4th." -- El Siglo Diez y Nueve.

The exposition which concerns us declares that the revolution was liberal and that it advanced the conservation of the representative system, and it wished:

1. The convocation of a popular congress. "We are in agreement with this and a large number of our articles in these days have been devoted to defending "universal suffrage."

2. Reform of the army in such a way that it may have morality, discipline, and instruction, and that it may defend the frontiers. "More than once we have supported the same idea."

492

3. Reorganization of the national guard. "We are entirely in agreement with this point."

4. The prompt colonization of the country, going from the center to the circumference and providing the colonizers with liberal legislation. "We believe that besides promoting foreign immigration colonies should be formed with Mexicans in order to lessen the numbers of the very poor [proletarios] and to increase the number of small property owners.

5. To lift the prohibitions and to lower the duties. "This important conquest of the revolution had merited the most exclusive attention of our paper and we have added that it is indispensable to suppress the direction of industry. These are the ideas that we found in the exposition. In addition it recommends the diffusion of primary instruction, the improvement of secondary teaching, the protection of agriculture and mining, and all the major materials, and finally the conservation of freedom of the press and the ending of the tobacco monopoly."

El Siglo Diez y Nueve, April 23, 1853.

* * * * *

BASIS FOR ADMINISTRATION OF THE REPUBLIC UNTIL THE PROMULGATION OF THE CONSTITUTION

22 April, 1853

Art. 1. For the dispatch of business there shall be five secretaries of State with the following titles: 1) Foreign Affairs, 2) Domestic Affairs, Justice, Church Relations and Public Instruction, 3) Development [Fomento], Colonization, Industry and Commerce, 4) War and Navy, 5) Treasury.

Art. 2. There shall be a suitable distribution of business between these secretaries for the most prompt dispatch of business among them.

Art. 3. The subjects which shall concern the new Minister of Development [Fomento], Colonization,

Industry and Commerce are the following: Formation of general statistics of industry, agriculture, mining and mercantile affairs, following up each year the movement that may be taken in these areas.

Colonization.

Measures conducive to the development of all industrial and mercantile branches in all areas.

The issuance of patents and concessions.

Public expositions of products of farming, mining and the textile industries.

Roads, canals, and all the avenues of communications of the Republic.

The drainage of Mexico [City] and all the works related to the same.

All the public works both useful and decorative that may be done with public funds.

Art. 4. As a consequence of the creation of this ministry, the direction of industry and colonization and all the individual management programs of the diverse branches that embrace the scope of the said ministry are hereby abolished. The employees of this office [of government] will be considered according to their merits.

Art. 5. With the purpose that there should be the necessary regularity in the dispatch of business, all those matters that concern some general issue, that may cause injury to the Treasury, or in its importance may require the consideration of the Administration, the ministers, in committee, will confer upon the basis of a written report to be provided by the ministers of the individual branches [of government], and the decision of the committee being adopted by the president, the responsibility for its execution shall lie with the respective ministry to whom it was assigned.

Art. 6. To this end a record of agreements of the

committee of ministers shall be prepared and kept by the senior official of the Ministry of Relations, and another individual record [shall be] kept in each ministry in which will be noted the items assigned to that department.

Art. 7. The sites of the secretaries of customs, of the general accounting office, of the general Treasury and other offices as well as the current regulations now in effect will be surveyed in order to make such changes and improvements as appear appropriate.

Art. 8. An exact national budget will be adopted; it shall be examined by the ministers in committee, and it shall serve as the standard for all expenditures, and nothing shall be spent unless it is provided for in the budget, or else is decreed with the usual formalities.

Art. 9. In order that the national interests may be expeditiously handled in disputed areas that may be presented to them or are already pending or may arise in the future, and in order to promote whatever is advantageous for the public Treasury, and to provide necessary information on points of law when the need arises in the other branches [of administration], a national finance minister [procurador general de la nacion] shall be named with a salary of 4,000 pesos, honors and decorations as a minister of the Supreme Court of Justice in which and in all the superior tribunals he will be received as a party for the nation, and in the inferior courts likewise when the respective ministry so desires it, and he will issue all the legal reports which may be requested for the government. He shall be removable at the will of the government, and he shall receive instructions for his proceedings from the respective ministries.

Art. 10. Suitable measures will be dictated so that at the earliest possible moment the civil, criminal, and commercial codes and procedures shall be drafted and published, as well as all others which may be convenient for the improvement of the administration of justice.

Art. 11. All the dispositions and measures which have been dictated by individuals who exercised the Executive power since the dissolution will be taken into consideration in order to determine what most comports with the best service for the nation.

SECOND SECTION
Council of State

Art. 1. Proceeding to the establishment of the council of State, twenty-one persons who are to compose it will be named and these will be endowed with the qualities necessary for the discharge of such a high responsibility.

Art. 2. This body will be divided into five sections corresponding to each one of the secretaries of State, which will transact for themselves the judgments that are asked of them in their respective branches, as a private council when they have to discuss in council those points which in the judgment of the government require it on account of their gravity and importance, or being one of those cases where the government has to proceed in agreement with the council.

Art. 3. Besides the twenty-one who are to compose the council, ten others are to be named who may replace the former in event of absences or illnesses, in order that the body may always have the required number. The government will provide for vacancies which may occur.

Art. 4. The president and vice-president of the Council, as well as those of the sections, will be named by the president of the Republic, and also the secretary who will be outside that body. The council shall hold its sessions in the salon allotted to the senate.

THIRD SECTION

Domestic Government

Art. 1. In order to exercise the wide powers which the nation has granted to me for the reorganization of all branches of public administration, all legislatures or other authorities which discharge legislative functions in the States and territories will stand in recess.

Art. 2. There shall be drafted and published a regulation on the manner in which the governors are to exercise their functions until the publication of the consitution.

Art. 3. The districts, cities and towns which have been separated from the states or departments to which they belong and those that have been constituted under a new political form shall return to their former entity and demarcation until the government, taking into consideration the reasons which they may allege for their separation, and provided that [their action] comports with the well being of the Republic, shall decide. The previous partition of Aguascalientes is excepted from the above.

Art. 4. For the defense of the districts invaded by the wild tribes, for the security of the roads and the hamlets and in order that the inhabitants may enjoy the social guarantees in an effective manner, necessary measures will be taken to prevent disorders and to punish evildoers.

Art. 5. The four secretaries of office shall sign this decree and shall communicate it to those whose duty it may be to issue orders suitable for the execution of all the above in these Bases, according to the branch [of government] to which they may belong.

Therefore, I order it to be printed, published, and circulated and let it be given due fulfillment.

Issued from the National   Antonio Lopez de Santa Anna
Palace   and ministers.

Felipe Tena Ramirez, Leyes fundamentales de Mexico,
1808-1967, 482-484.

* * * * *

RESOLUTION OF GUADALAJARA

17 November, 1853

First: It is hereby declared that there not being
enough time in the remaining part of the year as
provided for in the pact of last February 6th for the
complete organization of all branches of the national
administration, the date is hereby extended as may be
necessary according to the judgment of His
Excellency, the President of the Republic, General
Antonio Lopez de Santa Anna.

Second: To that end His Excellency the President
shall remain invested with the full powers which he
has exercised until the present time.

Third: In order to provide for death or other
impediment which might impede the distinguished
present head of the Nation physically or mentally, he
shall take care to name the person worthy to replce
him, and the nomination made and sealed, it will be
deposited in the Ministry of Relations under suitable
formalities and securities.

Fourth: In reference to the many and distinguished
merits and relevant services of the said Excellency
the President, it is hereby proclaimed in spite of
the resistance, which he previously manifested with
the use of military power, that only he shall be
designated Captain General of the Republic with
honors and perquisites appertaining to the rank, in
accord with the decree of 11 April of the present
year, with the indicated modification.

Fifth: A copy of this declaration shall be sent to
the aforesaid Excellency the President of the

498

Republic through the agency of a special commission of the Department in order to congratulate him for this spontaneous action of the people for his understanding, and in order to beg him to accept it as a due reward and a just hommage for his honorable, constant, and distinguished services in behalf of the Fatherland.

J. M. Gamboa, Leyes y constituciones de Mexico durante el siglo XIX, 507-508.

* * * * *

DECLARATION OF SANTA MARIA ZOQUIZOQUIPAN

14 December, 1853

In the town of Santa Maria Zoquizoquipan of the district of Meztitlan, on the 14th day of December, 1853, with all principal residents gathered in the most public area and joined by the officials of adjacent areas, under the presidency of His Honor Judge Manuel Najera, who ordered the reading of the Act which was declared in Guadalajara the 17th of November of the present year. With its main point explained, he asked that [the citizens] should express with full freedom and frankness their opinion of the present administration. They replied as in once voice and supported the said Act in all its provisions. Furthermore, reminded that for a government to make a nation happy it must combine as necessary elements firm authority, unity of control, and strong patriotism, and next, that these three qualities are better combined in a constitutional empire than in any other, [the citizens] declared that making use of the right of invitation to other towns, they invited all to proclaim the establishment in the nation of a constitutional imperial government. And then it being clear that the Mexican who has united [in his person] since independence the most authority, firmness of will, and the most patriotism is His Excellency General D. Antonio Lopez de Santa Anna, and in exercise of the said right and that of the offer to His Excellency, they proclaimed him Emperor of the Mexican Nation, and their declaration was summarized in the following articles:

Art. 1. The town of Zoquizoquipan adopts unreservedly the Act given at Guadalajara the 17th of November of the present year.

Art. 2. Making use of the right of invitation to the other towns of the nation, it desires the establishment of a constitutional Empire to be proclaimed.

Art. 3. Using the right of proclamation and of [public] offering, the town declares as Emperor of the Mexican nation the illustrious Don Antonio Lopez de Santa Anna, General of Division, Benemerito of the Fatherland, Grand Master of the distinguished Order of Guadalupe, Knight of the Grand Cross of the distinguished Order of Charles III, and President of the Mexican Republic.

With this resolution the Act was finished.

(Signatures follow)

V. Riva Palacio, Mexico a traves de los siglos, IV, 823.

* * * * *

PLAN OF AYUTLA

1 March, 1854

The political leaders, officers, and individual members of the troops undersigned, being called together by Colonel Florencio Real, in the town of Ayutla, district of Ometepec, of the Department of Guerrero:

WHEREAS: 1) The permanence of D. Antonio Lopez de Santa Anna in power is a constant threat to the liberties of the people in-as-much as with the greatest scandal and under his administration individual guarantees that are respected even in the lease civilized countries have been trampled under foot.

2) Mexicans, so zealous of their liberty, find themselves in imminent danger of being subjugated by an absolute power exercised by a man to whom both generously and deplorably they entrusted the destinies of the Fatherland.

3) Very far from responding to so honorable a challenge, he has come to oppress and to vex the people, burdening them with onerous taxation without consideration for the general poverty, and he has employed the produce [of taxation] in superfluous expenses, and in building a fortune, as in another era [was done by] various favorites.

4) The Plan proclaimed in Jalisco, which opened the gates of the Republic to him has been falsified in spirit and purpose by going contrary to the torrent of public opinion which was suffocated by aribtrary restriction of the press.

5) He has defaulted the solemn obligation which he contracted with the nation on setting foot on native soil when he offered to forget personal resentments, and [promised] that he would never commit himself to any one party.

6) Although he was obligated to conserve the integrity of the territory of the Republic, he has sold a considerable part of it and has sacrificed our brothers on the frontier of the North who, henceforth, will be foreigners in their own country and to be dispossessed afterwards as happened to the Californios.

7) The nation cannot continue any longer without establishing itself as a stable and durable [institution] and cannot depend for its existence upon the capricious will of a single man.

8) Republican institutions are the only ones that are suitable to the country, to the absolute exclusion of any other form of government.

9) And finally, remembering that national independence finds itself threatened under a situation not
less dangerous, through the notorious efforts of the
dominant party led by General Santa Anna, and using
the same rights which our fathers used in 1821 in
order to win liberty, those undersigned proclaim and
promise to support to Death itself, if it should be
necessary the following Plan:

1st. Antonio Lopez de Santa Anna and the rest of the
functionaries who, like him, have misplaced the
confidence of the people, or all those opposed to
this Plan shall cease the exercise of public office.

2nd. When this Plan shall have been adopted by the
majority of the nation, the ranking General of those
who sustain it will call a representative for each
State and Territory in order that, being met in the
place deemed convenient they shall elect an interim
President of the Republic, and shall serve as an
executive committee during the brief period of his
term.

3rd. The interim President will be vested immediately
with ample authority for attending to the security
and independence of the national territory, and [for
conducting] the other branches of public administration.

4th. In the States in which this political Plan may
be supported, the ranking commander of the forces
which have adhered to it and associated with seven
recommended persons which he will choose, will agree
upon and promulgate within a month after having met
the provisional Statute which is to govern in their
respective State or Territory. An indispensable base
for each Statute [shall be] that the nation is and
always will be one, indivisible, and independent.

5th. Within two weeks after having assumed his duties
the interim President shall summon a special
congress, in conformity with the basis of the law
which was issued with the same purpose in the year
1841. The Congress shall occupy itself exclusively
with constituting a nation under the form of a

republican government, representative, popular, and shall reexamine the acts of the provisional executive as mentioned in Article 2.

6th. Since the Army must be the support of order and of the social guarantees, the interim government will take care to conserve it and to attend to its needs as is due this noble institution. [The interim government] will also protect the freedom of domestic and foreign trade, and shall issue within the shortest possible time the customs duties which shall prevail; and immediately the maritime rates published under the administration of Senor Cevallos shall prevail.

7th. Immediately the laws in effect on lotteries and passports, and the tax imposed on the people under the name of a "poll tax" shall cease to be valid.

8th. All who are opposed to the present Plan or who lend direct aid to the officials whom it no longer acknowledges will be treated as an enemy of the independence of the nation.

9th. Their Excellencies Generals D. Nicolas Bravo, D. Juan Alvarez, and D. Tomas Moreno are invited to place themselves at the forefront of the liberating forces which accept this Plan; and that [these men] support and carry into effect the administrative reforms which are set forth in it, [it being understood] that they are authorized to make such modifications as they consider convenient for the good of the nation.

Ayutla, 1 March, 1854.   (Signatures follow)

Zamacois, Historia de Mexico, XIII, 873-879.

Estatuto organico provisional (Pueblo, 1856)

Portilla, Historia de la revolucion de Mexico contra Santa Anna, Appendix, xv-xxvi.

* * * * *

THE REVISED PLAN OF AYUTLA

11 March, 1854

In the city of Acapulco, on the 11th day of March, 1854, met in the Fort of San Diego, by invitation of Colonel D. Rafael Solis, the political leaders, officers, individuals from the permanent troops, the national guard and the registered naval personnel, and he reported: THAT he had received from the principal commandant of Costa Chica, Colonel D. Florencio Villarreal, a courteous note in which he urged him to support, along with the garrison, the political Plan which had been proclaimed in Ayutla. This Plan he then read. When this was finished, he explained that although his convictions were in agreement with the principles in that Plan, and that if it should come to be realized it would promptly bring the nation out of the state of slavery and depression into which by degrees the arbitrary and despotic power of His Excellency General Antonio Lopez de Santa Anna had reduced it. Nevertheless, he wished to consult the opinion of his companions-in-arms so as to rectify his own ideas and to proceed with more assurance in a business so important and which to such a great degree affected the dearest interests of the Fatherland. After had made this simple statement, those present unanimously expressed themselves as in agreement with him. At the same time they judged it an opportunity, since by a happy accident Colonel D. Ignacio Comonfort was in the port, a man who had given so many and such good sevice to the South, should be invited to the meeting also so that in case he should adhere to whatever the emergency committee [junta] should resolve, he could take command of the city and could put himself at the forefront of his troops. A committee was dispatched to instruct him of the events above, the charge being given to the commander of batallion D. Ignacio Perez Vargas, Captain D. Genaro Villagran, and to another of equal rank, D. Jose Marin, who immediately went to fulfill their mission. Within a half-hour they returned and reported that in reply Senor Comonfort had indicated that if it were agreed that in the opinion of the garrison of this city that the Fatherland required from him the sacrifice of taking

an active part in the political events which were
going to be initiated, he would do it gladly in
fulfillment of the sacred duty which every citizen
has of postponing his untroubled days and his private
interests [in favor of] the well-being and happiness
of his compatriots. However, in his judgment, the
Plan which they were trying to support needed some
slight changes so as to show the nation with total
clarity that those of its good sons who were putting
themselves forward on this occasion as the first to
vindicate their rights so scandalously trampled under
foot did not have even the most remote idea of
imposing conditions on the sovereign will of the
country. [They desired] reestablishment through force
of arms of the federal system or restoration of
things to the same state in which they were found
when the Plan of Jalisco was proclaimed. [Certainly]
everything relative to the form in which the nation
was ultimately to be constituted ought to be subject
to the congress which will be called for this
purpose, and this should be explicitly stated at
once. In view of those reasons which won the approval
of the men present, it was unanimously voted to
proclaim and indeed was proclaimed the Plan of
Ayutla, but revised in the following terms.

WHEREAS: The continuing of his Excellency General
Antonio Lopez de Santa Anna in power is a constant
threat to the independence and the liberty of the
nation because under his admistration a part of the
territory of the Republic has been needlessly sold,
and individual guarantees which are respected even in
the least civilized peoples have been trampled under
foot. AND the Mexican, so zealous of his sovereignty,
has been traitorously dispoiled of it and enslaved by
absolute power, despotic and capricious, which he has
indefinitely vested in himself, the man whom the
nation with such generosity and confidence called
from exile in order to entrust its destiny to him.

AND very far from responding to such an honorable
challenge, he has occupied himself only in oppression
and vexing the people, levying upon them onerous
contributions without consideration for their general
poverty, and employing the product [of the levies] as

he has done on other occassions in superfluous
expenses and in making scandalous fortunes for his
favorites.

AND the Plan proclaimed in Jalisco, which opened the
doors of the Republic have been falsified in its
spirit and purpose with obvious disdain of public
opinion whose voice was suffocated beforehand by
means of hateful and tyrannical restrictions imposed
upon the press.

AND he has defaulted on the solemn promise that on
stepping on native soil he contracted with the
nation--to forget personal resentments and not to
become a member of any of those political parties
which unfortunately divide the nation.

AND this [nation] cannot continue any longer without
establishing itself in a stable and enduring way, nor
can it continue depending for its political existence
and its future upon the capricious will of a single
man.

AND liberal institutions are the only ones which suit
the country to the absolute exclusion of any others
whatever; and these find themselves in imminent danger of being lost beneath the present administration
whose tendencies are to the establishment of a
ridiculous monarchy; and contrary to our character
and customs he has indicated in a clear and indisputable way with the creation of orders, of treatment
and privileges which are openly opposed to republican
equality.

AND FINALLY, considering that the independence and
freedom of the nation are found threatened also
beneath another aspect no less dangerous through the
notorious efforts of the dominant party which today
directs the policy of General Santa Anna, we, the
undersigned, using the same rights which our fathers
used to win these two inestimable benefits, proclaim
and protest that we will persist to death if it be
necessary to sustain the following:

PLAN

1st. His Excellency General Antonio Lopez de Santa Anna and the other functionaries who, like him, have been unworthy of the confidence of the people, or all those who are opposed to the present Plan shall cease exercising public authority.

2nd. When this Plan shall have been adopted by the majority of the nation, the commanding general of the forces which support it will call a representative for each department and territory of those which exist today, as well as for the district of the capital, in order that, united in the place that is deemed best, they may elect an interim President of the Republic, and [this group] shall serve him as an [advisory] council during the short period of his term.

3rd. The interim President, without other restriction than that of respecting inviolably individual guarantees will be forthwith invested with ample facilities for reforming all the branches of public administration in order to attend to the security and independence of the nation and in order to promote whatever may be conducive to its prosperity, growth, and progress.

4th. In the Departments and Territories in which this political Plan may be supported, the principal political leader of the forces which shall proclaim it, associated with five persons well known for their integrity whom he, himself, shall elect, will agree upon and promulgate within the month after they have met the provisional Statute which must govern in their respective department or territory. Serving as an indispensable base [will be the fact that] the nation is and will always be one, separate, indivisible, and independent.

5th. Within two weeks after having commenced to exercise his duties, the interim President will convoke an extraordinary congress, conforming to the bases of the law which was expedited with the same object on December 10, 1841. [This congress] shall occupy itself exclusively with constituing the nation beneath the republican, popular, representtative form of a Republic, and of revising the acts of the present government, as well as with those pertaining to the provisional executive which is spoken of in Art. 2. This constituent congress must meet within four months after the summons for the convocation has been issued.

6th. Since the Army ought to be the defender of independence and the support of order, the interim government will take care to maintain it and attend to it with whatever this noble institution may demand.

7th. Commerce being one of the sources of public income and one of the most powerful elements for the advancement of civilized nations, the provisional government shall occupy itself at once in providing all the liberties and franchises which are necessary for its prosperity. To this end it will immediately expedite the publication of tax rates for the maritime and for the frontier tariffs which must be observed. In the meantime that which was promulgated during the administration of Senor Cavallos shall prevail, unless the new one which is to substitute for it should be based upon a system less liberal.

8th. The provisions of law now in effect in relation to lotteries, passports, head taxes, consumer legislation, and all laws which have been issued which conflict with the republican system shall cease at once.

9th. All those who oppose the principles which are drafted here will be treated as enemies of national independence. Their Excellencies Generals D. Nicolas Bravo, D. Juan Alvarez, and D. Tomas Moreno, if they should adopt these measures, are invited to place themselves at the head of the liberating forces which proclaim [these terms], until they shall have gained complete realization.

10th. If the majority of the nation should judge it convenient that some modifications should be made in this Plan, the undersigned declare themselves at all times to be respectful of its sovereign will.

It was furthermore agreed before the meeting was adjourned that copies of this Plan should be sent to their Excellencies General Don Juan Alvarez, D. Nicolas Bravo, and D. Tomas Moreno for the points expressed in No. 9; that another copy should be sent to Colonel Don Florencio Villarreal, commandant of Costa Chica, asking him to be so kind as to adopt it with the reforms which it contains; that [a copy] be circulated to all their Excellencies the Governors and commanding Generals of the Republic, inviting them to support it; that it be circulated equally to the civil authorities of this District with the same purpose; that it be dispatched to Colonel Ignacio Comonfort so that he might be pleased to sign it, and also indicating to him that from this moment he is recognized as the governor of the fortress and principal commandant of the demarcation; and finally that the present act be distributed for due record.

(Signatures follow)

Zamacois, Historia de Mexico, XIII, 879-886.

* * * * *

PLAN OF ACAPULCO

11 March, 1854

In the city of Acapulco, on the 11th of March, 1854, the leaders, the officers and members of the permanent troop personnel, and members of the National Guard met at the Fortress of San Diego upon invitation of Colonel Rafael Solis, and the under-signed declared [here begins a justification for the meeting and thereafter a list of "Considerandos." The meeting concluded by proclaiming and promising to sustain until death, if necessary, the following Plan]

1. His Excellency General D. Antonio Lopez de Santa Anna shall cease his exercise of public power, likewise all those other fuctionaries who have proved themselves unworthy of the confidence of the people,

or who are opposed to this Plan.

2. When it shall have been adopted by the majority of the nation, the ranking General of the forces which shall sustain the Plan will convoke an assembly which shall consist of one representative for each Department or Territory of those presently in existence, and for the capital District so that having met as soon as possible in the place deemed most suitable they will elect an interim President of the Republic and they shall serve as an advisory council during the brief period of their authorized service.

3) The interim President, without any restriction save that of respecting as inviolable individual guarantees will be invested immediately with ample powers to reform all branches of public administration in order to watch after the security and independence of the nation, and to promote whatever may be conducive to its prosperity, growth, and progress.

4) In the Departments or Territories where this political Plan may be supported, the ranking general of the forces which proclaim it, associated with five knowledgeable persons which he, himself, shall appoint, will accept and promulgate within a month after having met, the provisional Statute that is to apply in their respective Department or Territory, and serving as the indispensable basis of each statute will be the fact that the nation is and always will be one, indivisible, and independent.

5. Within fifteen days after having entered into the exercise of his duties the interim President shall summon an extraordinary congress in conformity with the basis of the law that was passed for the same purpose on December 10, 1841. [This Congress] shall occupy itself with cosntituting a nation under the form of a representative and popular Republic, and with revising the acts of the present government as well as those of the provisional executive which is mentioned in the second article. This constituent congress shall meet within three months after the

issuance of the call for meeting.

6. The Army being the defender of independence and the support of public order, the temporary government must see that it is preserved and attended to as this noble institution deserves.

7. Since trade is one of the sources of public wealth and one of the most powerful elements in the advancement of civilized nations, the privisonal Administration will concern itself immediately to provide for it all the rights and franchises which may be necessary for its prosperity. To this end it will dispatch immediately the scale of customs duties for ports of entry and for the frontiers that are to be observed, and in the meantime the scale promulgated during the administration of Senor Ceballos shall prevail, nor shall the system to be substituted for it be based upon a scale less liberal.

8) Immediately all laws governing lotteries, passports, per capita taxes, and excise taxes shall no longer be in effect, nor shall any others be passed which may be contrary to the republican system.

9) Those who oppose the principles herein drafted will be treated as enemies of national independence, and the following: Generals Nicolas Bravo, Juan Alvarez, and Tomas Moreno are here and now invited to adopt [these provisions] and to place themselves at the forefront of the Liberating Forces which proclaim them and to remain there until they have been fully realized.

10) If the majority of the nation should judge it suitable that some modifications should be made in this Plan, the undersigned profess that always they accept its sovereign will.

Before ending the meeting it was agreed to send copies of this Plan to the Generals above named, etc...

(Signed)
Ignacio Comonfort and others.

Estatuto organico Provisional, (Puebla, 1856), 10-12.

* * * * *

PLAN OF THE DECLARATION OF MEXICO

(No date: circa March 1854)

Yesterday afternoon a vast multitude of citizens from all classes of society assembled in the Alameda for the purpose of signing the resolution which had been posted there, a resolution supporting the provisions of the Plan of Ayutla, in the State of Guerrero. Their Plan is the following:

1. Don Antonio Lopez de Santa Anna shall cease the exercise of public power, and the other funtionaries who, like him, have been unworthy of the confidence of the people or who are opposed to this Plan.

2. When [this Plan] has been adopted by a majority of the nation, the ranking General of the forces supporting the Plan shall call for a representative from each State and Territory in order that, having met in a place deemed suitable, they shall elect an interim President of the Republic and they shall serve as an advisory Council during the short term of his office.

3. The Interim President shall at once be invested with ample authority for attending to [domestic] security and national independence and to the other branches of public administration.

4. In those states where this political Plan may be supported, the ranking officer of the troops who adhere to it, aided by seven persons of good repute whom he shall name, will draft and promulgate within a month after having had them meet, the provisional Statute which shall prevail in their respective State or Territory. It is presumed as an indispensable part of each Statute that the Nation is and shall always remain one, separate, indivisible, and independent.

5. Fifteen days after having assumed his duties the imterim President shall convoke an extraordinary Congress, according to the legal requirements as were issued for the same purpose in the year 1841. [The Congress] shall occupy itself exclusively with the

task of constituting a nation in the form of a popular, representative republic and of revising the decrees of the provisional Executive about which Article 2 speaks.

6. Since the Army must be the support of order and of the guarantees of Society, the Interim Government shall take care to keep it, to pay attention to it, as is fitting for the demands of this noble institution; likewise it shall protect free trade, both domestic and foreign and [the Government] shall dispatch as soon as possible the customs regulations which must to be observed, and in the meantime the customs regulations published under the administration of Sr. Cevallos shall be observed.

7. Immediately the authority of laws now in effect on lotteries and passports shall cease; so likewise those forced taxes imposed on the towns under the guise of a poll tax.

8. Anyone who is opposed to the present Plan or who lends direct or indirect assistance to the forces which are hereby disavowed will be treated as an enemy of national independence.

9. The Honorable Senores General D. Nicolas Bravo, Don Juan Alvarez, and Don Tomas Moreno are invited to put themselves in front of the liberating forces which proclaim this Plan and that they support and carry into effect the administrative reforms which are indicated therein; however, they are authorized to make any modifications which they consider for the good of the nation.

(No signatures)

* * * * * * *

This action being concluded, the crown trooped to the National Palace and carried [this Plan] there for approval by those charged with supreme authority and they were received with the pealing of bells in the Cathedral and in the principal churches of this capital.

Translated from a Broadside.

* * * * *

PLANS OF THE GARRISON OF MEXICO CITY

13 August, 1855

In the City of Mexico, the 13th of August, 1855, the Generals undersigned having been called by his Excellency General of Division Romulo Diaz de la Vega, Commanding General and governor of the District of Mexico, His Excellency gave notice that he had received two telegraphic notices which were in all respects official, in which the commanding officer of War and His Excellency General D. Antonio Lopez de Santa Anna had announced his departure from supreme command of the Republic. Also, that the military corps which form the garrison of this Capital not having been able to meet the Executive Power named by the decree of the current month, they published an act through which they recognized the necessity of adopting the Plan formulated at Ayutla the 1st of March 1854, since it is clear that in it are designated the principles and guarantees which the nation desires for the provisional organization of a national government which guarantees a future well-being. Also, considering the resignation which His Excellency General Santa Anna made of the Executive Power, [the corps] inquired whether the Generals who were present were adopting the declarations of this garrison, and they made equally clear the imperious necessity of reestablishing at once public confidence and causing the evils of war to cease as well as [ending] the uncertainty in respect to the guarantees and the rights of all citizens.

After a discussion among the Generals present the suitability of accepting the Plan indicated providing an end of the present crisis as well as accepting that one formulated by the garrison, they decided unanimously upon the following articles:

Whereas: The Plan of Ayutla is the choice of the nation;

Whereas: some of the articles are no longer pertinent because they are in fact consumated in the revolution at the capital;

Whereas: by his retirement His Excellency General Santa Anna has terminated his administration, the expressed Plan was adopted in the following terms:

1st. The Plan of Ayutla having been adopted by the majority of the nation, the commanding General recognized in this capital will proceed immediately to summon a special committee [junta] composed of two individuals from each Department, including the District.

2nd. This Committee will meet immediately after its nomination and will proceed to elect in a single act by an absolute majority of votes the President of the Republic.

3rd. The Committee will serve as a council to the interim President during the short period of his office.

4th. The interim President will immediately be invested with ample powers for attending to the security and independence of the national territory and for the other branches of public administration.

5th. Within two weeks after having assumed his duties of office the interim President will convoke a special congress in conformity to the law which was drafted for that purpose in the year 1841. [This congress] will concern itself exclusively within the stipulated term of six months with organizing the nation under the representative popular form of a republic and of revising the acts of the provisional Executive.

6th. The Army must be the support of order and of social guarantees, [as such] the interim government will be careful to conserve it and attend to whatever this noble institution may demand as well as to protect the freedom of domestic and foreign trade, and shall expedite in the shortest possible time the custom rates which should be observed.

7th. Immediately the law in effect in relation to lotteries, passports, and the tax imposed upon the people under the name of "poll tax" shall cease to be observed.

(Signatures follow)

Archivo Mexicano, 18-20.

* * * * *

DECLARATION OF JALAPA

15 August, 1855

WHEREAS: General Antonio Lopez de Santa Anna has abandoned the power which those who concurred in the Pact of Arroyo-Zarco on 6 February 1853 conferred upon him; AND the Nation has found itself completely abandoned and if [the situation] were regarded with indifference would terminate in a real division; AND the Nation generally adopted the movement of Guadalajara when it was reformed, declaring as a national necessity the reform of the Constitution of 1824; AND this public vote was that which was falsified in the pact of the above mentioned Arroyo-Zarco; AND the parenthesis which was then opened on the 8th of August of this year was terminated, it is incumbent upon the Nation and upon each one of its towns to renew the desires and votes which they indicated at the beginning of 1853. The Authorities and residents of the City which undersign hereby adhere to the articles of the Plan of Ayutla, re-enacted in the following terms and with the following additions:

Art. 1. The ranking General of the forces which sustain this Plan will summon a representative from each State or Territory in order that being met in the place esteemed suitable they shall elect a President of the Republic and shall serve as his Council during the short period of his term.

2nd. The interim President will immediately be invested with full powers for attending to the security and independence of the national territory, and for the other branches of public administration.

Art. 3. The political leaders of the States which are elected will govern them with a Council composed of five individuals named by these same leaders and they will agree upon and promulgate within a month after having met the provisional organic law which is to go into effect in their respective State or Territory while the Nation is being definitively constituted.

Art. 4. Within two weeks after having entered into his term the interim President will summon an extraordinary Congress in accord with the basis of the electoral law which was expedited with this same purpose in the year 1841. [The congress] will occupy itself exclusively with reforming the Constitution of 1824 in accord with public need and in revising the acts of the provisional Executive as indicated in Article. 2.

Art. 5. Since the Army must be the support of independence, of order and of the social guarantees, the interim Government will take care to conserve it and to attend to it as this noble institution demands.

Additional Articles:

1st. The undersigned Citizens proclaim as interim Governor of the State Sr. D. Jose M. Pasquel, and propose him for election by the other towns of this same State.

2nd. The Towns of the State to whom this Act is dispatched will, through the illustrious Council of this City, be so kind as to direct to the Secretary of the Superior Tribunal of Justice in a sealed envelope their respective votes for Governor of the State so that a count of them can be made by this same body along with the Illustrious Council of this City, and the one elected will take possession on the 16th of September next, having taken the oath to observe this Plan before the President of the said

Superior Tribunal of Justice.

3rd. Operating under this Plan, no innovation of any kind shall be made in the branches of Justice and Treasury. The functionaries and employees in these said branches in everything concerning public service shall reach an understanding with the political leaders in those Departments (today Districts) while the elected Governor is assuming his office. These latter functionaries shall be responsible for their acts before this said Governor so that in his case he can be responsible for whatever accrues.

4th. Interim political authority of the Department, or the present District, is entrusted to Sr. D. Antonio M. Priani, and General D. Carlos Oronoz will continue in command of the armed forces. The Town Council will in cases of necessity name a substitute for the former [individual].

5th. The Sres. D. Bernardo Sayago and D. Joaquin Llera are commissioned to present this Plan and to support it before the Government established in Mexico [City].

Manuel B. Trens, Historia de Vera Cruz, V. 102-103.

* * * * *

PLAN OF TOLIMAN

2 December, 1855

Colonels Antonio Montes Velasquez, Prefect and Military Commandant of the District of Toliman, and Tomas Mejia, Commandant and Prefect of the District of Jalpan, to their fellow citizens.

Fellow Citizens

Today we leave our hearthstone and family in order to answer the call of our Fatherland, which is the first duty of every citizen. Today, as always, we take up arms without aspirations or ambition, and by God's help we will conclude our mission and will return as

518

always to our homes and our private tasks in order to devote ourselves to the subsistence of our families.

[There follows a vivid defense of their actions as private citizens, a defense which includes the major points to be covered in the Plan to follow. The paragraphs which follow express the indignation of the Colonels with greater ardor and more skillful rhetoric than one generally finds]. And then:
Fellow Citizens, we have adopted the Plan below which is the most national, the most adequate in these critical times. We will support it without equivocation and, with the aid of God, it will rebuild our Fatherland.

1. In order that all despotism over the people should cease and in order that law and not the caprice of an Administration such as now guides its destiny, there will be recognized provisionally a government freely and spontaneously based upon the Constitution of 1824 with all the reforms which have been authorized under it thereafter.

2. The present Governors of the States, (or, if they are opposed, then the ranking officer of the forces which have "pronounced" for it) will, on taking possession of the Capital, issue the order or decree for the election of governmental administration in accord with their individual constitutions. These councils [juntas], while naming the Governor, will choose five individuals to serve as an advisory Council for their resolutions.

3. The Governor of each State or the Political leader [jefe politico] of the Territory, in accordance with its constitution, will elect an individual in order that within five days at the latest of the entrance of the army into the Capital of the Republic, they shall meet there under the leadership of the General-in-Chief, serving as the depository of Executive Power, and they will procede to expedite the decree for the election of an interim President who will hold power while the Nation is being constituted.

519

4. This same junta will continue as the advisory body for the Executive who, within a month, shall issue the call for an election of a Constituent Congress which will convene within three months after the said call.

5. The problems that may arise in the development of this Plan whose principal object is that the Republic should be constituted in accord with its desires for growth and happiness and that a fundamental law should be drafted that would stabalize its interests will be solved by the holder of the Supreme Executive Power in agreement with his Council.

6. The State of Iturbide, forming a part of the Mexican Confederation, will be considered an independent state, and will be composed of the Districts which have solicited its.

7. Those who directly or indirectly oppose the development and completion of this Plan will be judged traitors to the Nation and to the establishment of all public order.

8. The armed forces which have declared [in favor of the Plan] will recognize the Honorable Sr. General, Don Jose Lopez Uraga who will carry forward to completion without compromise or change the completion of this Plan.

(Signatures)
Jose Antonio
Montes Velasquez
Tomas Mejia

Genaro Garcia, <u>Documentos ineditos</u>, vol, 31, 85-91.

* * * * *

THE DEFINITIVELY REGENERATIVE PLAN
proclaimed in the Llano del Rodeo

December, 1855

Whereas in the long period of thirty-five years since
our happy political emancipation the good people of
Mexico have gained nothing more than seeing ourselves
alternatively and incessantly oppressed by revolutions which have regularly occurred through violation of the Plan of Iguala and the Treaty of
Cordoba. It was public faith in these documents that
brought about the independence of the fatherland and
then was introduced, contrary to our habits and
genius, the federal republic, the most unfortunate
choice that one could or has been able to present in
the history of the world; likewise the centralists no
less violent and consequently impossible, and finally
a dictatorship the most infamous and hateful that
this nation has ever endured.

[Then follow five "Considerandos", with the following
conclusion.] We have decided to adopt and to propose
to the heroic Mexican nation the definitively regenerative Plan for its political and social future as
found in the articles which follow:

1) The Mexican nation is and will be independent and
sovereign and it will for the third time again assume
the heroic designation of The Empire of Anahuac.

2) Its religion is and will remain Catholic,
Apostolic, and Roman without public tolerance of any
other.

3) Its form of government will be an hereditary,
constitutional monarchy, according to the habits and
customs and necessities of the country according to
the judgment of its representatives.

4) The nation herewith proclaims as its Emperor Sr.
D. Augustin de Iturbide the Elder; and in case he
does not accept [the nation] does then proclaim in

521

the same category Senor D. Antonio de Haro Tamariz;
and in the event that the latter does not accept, he
shall be Emperor whom the Cortes called for the
purpose shall elect.

5. Immediately after the present political movement
shall have been consummated a supreme provisional
legislative junta will be formed--to be composed of
two representatives from each department or territory
of those that at the present time make up the nation.
These individuals will be named by the
Commander-in-Chief of the present Plan, he consulting
with four individuals who will enjoy his confidence
and approval. The said junta, prior to its formal
inauguration, will procede immediately to name a
regency composed of three persons who will be
charged, provisionally, with the administration of
the Empire to expedite in agreement with the Regency
the corresponding convocation of the deputies who are
to form the Constitution or the Fundamental Law of
the Empire within six months after the convocation.
Meanwhile they are to see that the present Plan in
all its ramifications is fulfilled.

6) The same provisional legislative junta, in
agreement with the Regency, will require the Emperor
proclaimed by the said Body, to present himself to
the agency immediately to take the required oath. In
the event that neither of the two persons heretofore
named shall be declared Emperor, the first congress
in the constituent Cortes shall by a plurality of
votes choose the one who seems the best and most
fitted to establish definitively the Empire, and
shall give his oath as prescribed.

7. From this day henceforth it is unalterably
established that all Mexicans either by birth or
adoption, according to laws passed on this matter,
are citizens of the Empire with the right to
employments and public positions according to their
merits and moral qualities without distinction
whatsoever of race or of the classes that make up the
nation.

8. The persons and property of all the inhabitants of the Empire, whether citizens or not, will be inviolably respected and protected by this Plan and by the Administration that through it is established to handle domestic affairs.

9. The secular and regular clergy as well as the Army will enjoy its provileges and exemptions in accordance with the laws that were in effect on July 31, 1855, and with others which may be passed thereafter.

10. The supreme provisional legislative junta, as well as the Cortes, in its turn, will be responsible for the regulation and improvement of all branches of public administration and that all public employees, civil and military be continued and respected in their particular positions according to their merits, and only those who express openly and notoriously their disapproval of this Plan and the form of government established under it will be removed.

11. The Army which proclaims [this Plan] and which adheres to it until the consumation of its complete triumph is now and hereafter shall be called The Regenerator, and shall immediately take under its protection a) the conservation of the Catholic religion, Apostolic and Roman; b) the independence of the Empire under the form of government already proclaimed: c) the preservation of all the social guarantees; d) the preservation of military discipline in all respects; and e) the faithful observance of the interim legislation until the Empire is definitively established.

12. The courts and judges in their respective branches of government as well as the administration of justice that is entrusted to them will continue to perform [their duties] according to the organization and the laws in effect on July 31, 1855, unless the Supreme Junta, with the concurrance of the Regency, shall authorize other measures.

13. Immediately amnesty and absolute oblivion for all political offenses is granted without exception, save for the rights of third persons who may be prejudiced by this act and who may be able to validate the claim legally before a competent judicial authority.

14. It is hereby recommended to the first congress assembled as a Cortes that it shall declare that if the first emperor who accepts this high and august position shall be a bachelor that he shall contract a marriage with a Mexican woman directly sprung from the orignal, indigenous race, and whose selection shall be by an absolute plurality of votes, and this duty shall be vested in the aforesaid first congress assembled in a constituent Cortes.

15. In the meantime until this body can meet and draft an Imperial constitution, the responsibility is assigned to the Regency or the Emperor, if he is installed, with the prior consent of the supreme provisional legislative junta, to give to this present Plan the requisite interpretation and development both in its spirit and its literal meaning.

[The original draft of this Plan was found in the home of Sr. D. Antonio Haro y Tamariz.]

Zamocois, Historia de Mexico, vol. 13, 851-858.

* * * * *

PLAN OF ZACAPOAXTLA   (1)

19 December, 1855

We, the undersigned, having met in committee [junta] and having taken into consideration

1. That the revolution initiated against the Administration was eminently national and for that reason ought to be carried to its conclusion in terms of the general interest of the Nation.

---

(1) Sometimes called "Plan of Antonio Haro".

2. That the principal causes of the revolution were the lack of guarantees for the citizens, the most rigorous exclusivism in administration, and the unfairness in the distribution of national income.

3. That the present Administration has these same vices because the same lack of guarantees exists, the same exclusivism in administration and an even greater unfairness in allocating the national income.

4. That the nomination of the current President is not the expression of the national will.

5. That if the present Administration is permitted to continue any longer, one cannot expect any other result than the continuation of anarchy, of the most terrible disorder, of division of the Republic, and of the secession of some of the states.

6. That within a very short time such results will bring about the ruin of the Republic and its national existence.

We declare that

1. The aim of the revolution has been falsified so that it redounds to the benefit of private individuals and with injury to the general public.

2. The present Administration is hereby repudiated.

3. The Organic Bases as sworn to in June, 1843, are now proclaimed, and by the same token they will come into effect immediately throughout the Republic.

4. Until Congress can meet, in fulfillment of the said Bases a provisional President will be named and be fully empowered to govern.

5. The person who may be named as leader in order to executive effectively the present Plan, assisted by a Council of persons known for their morality, talent, and patriotism and who, likewise, represent the interests of all classes and section, without distinction as to parties, shall proceed to the election of a provisonal President.

6. The first Congress which may meet by virtue of the provisions of the Organic Bases is to be fully empowerd to revise the said Bases and to insert into them the reforms which will assure the progress of the Republic and fortify its independence and national existence.

7. The individuals who comprise the present Administration shall give an account for their deeds before the first Congress which will meet according to this present Plan.

Zacapoaxtla, Dec. 19, 1855   (Signatures)

Genaro Garcia, <u>Documentos</u> <u>ineditas</u>, vol. 31, 149-150.

* * * * *

PLAN OF D. JESUS CARMONA

4 January, 1856

Considering the state of anarchy in which most unfortunately our unhappy country finds itself, through the diverse parties in which it is divided and through the many aspirations to positions of high rank, and considering also that the persons that today have been installed in those posts do not merit public confidence, infringing upon the most sacred duties, they trample under foot the just; they abuse the sacred, and they do not provide guarantees because they forget and they repudiate their own judgments with the same criminality of leading us to the loss of our beloved and sacred religion and of our dear and costly independence. We have agreed to cleave to and to support the following plan:

Art. 1. The Catholic religion, Apostolic and Roman, will be supported and respected with all its forces and its resources.

Art. 2. Equally all the other forces of the military, of public officers, and of all foreigners will be supported.

Art. 3. The general with the greatest seniority within the republic will be the one who rules the destiny of the country until he may be in control of the whole country and until the constitutional congress may have designated who it is that is to command [the army].

Art. 4. As soon as this general shall occupy the post of the first interim magistrate of the republic, he shall order a convocation in order that the said constitutional congress may be formed. It shall be composed of all classes in society except those persons whose opinions are recorded in favor of the pernicious federal system, as immoral as irreligious, as exaggerated as impracticable; and empowering him who may be elected president to annul by virtue of this article the nomination that might come for deputy upon such persons as are indicated above.

Art. 5. In this congress the number that is to represent each one of all the classes [in society] that are to form it shall be equal, nor shall the total number of members be greater than has been the custom in the central governments.

Art. 6. On the month of its installation congress shall name the president of the republic, and within six months it shall issue a constitution that is more suitable to the nation.

Art. 7. All the congress as well as the executive shall serve for seven years so that being the authors of the republic they may carry it forward and overcome all the difficulties thay may present themselves.

Art. 8. If there should be any doubt or question concerning the seniority of the general who as an interim should designate the executive, the supreme court of justice shall be the only one who can decide who shall be the senior [officer].

Art. 9. The professional judges are to retire in all these points in which the present plan my be seconded, until the interim president or the congress may decide that they may exercise their functions again, and the justices of peace and the conciliators that were named by the past administration are to remain in power.

Art. 10. The army shall be reestablished and reformed according to the decision of the first magistrate; but it shall be great enough in number to defend the nationality and the integrity of Mexican government.

Art. 11. While the congress determines the income which the treasury may count upon, the sales taxes [alcabalas] that have substituted for the taxes shall remain in effect.

(Signed)

_____

El Siglo Diez y Nueve, January 21, 1856.

* * * * *

DECREE OF THE STATE OF JALISCO

10 February, 1856

Santos Degollado, Governor and Commanding General of the State of Jalisco, to the inhabitants of the same, Know Ye:

1. Notwithstanding the private conviction which the present Governor entertains concerning the reactionaries, enemies of public tranquility, they will not be able to overpower the principles proclaimed in the Plan of Ayutla, for this is the standard of national thought against whose power the rash attempts of disturbers of public order will not prevail. This present government persuaded that one of its dearest duties which the Organic Statute imposes upon it is to prevent by every means the attempts at overthrow that have taken place in some

points in the Republic in the name of the State of Jalisco, I have seen it to make the following declarations:

1. Since the State adopted for its regeneration the principles proclaimed in the Plan of Ayutla, it has turned to the exercise of all its powers and rights in domestic order with full authority, thereupon gaining in the use of its sovereignty its own authority to celebrate with the other Mexican -states the pact of alliance which is not convenient for securing union, peace, and public liberties.

2. In consequence the State of Jalisco condemns as subversive and unlawful those reactionary movements led by Uraga and Haro y Tamariz and any others which attack public order. [The State] disavows henceforth all authority which eminates from such movements, and reassuming in such event its sovereignty, it protests that it will not return to a union with Mexico or with any other state which separates from order while this [order] is not reestablished.

3. The State recognizes and supports, as is proper, the supreme national government as well as that of sovereign Congress which is to be formed as a result of the will of the nation explained in compliance with the law issued in Cuernavaca on the 16th of October of the year just ended.

4. The State, in the event that the supreme powers judge it convenient, offers to them any spot in its territory where they may wish to locate, and the government of the same will dictate whatever provisions it judges adequate for the purpose of assuring the free exercise of the functions for the [supreme powers of the nation].

5. The State of Jalisco invites the other Mexican States to a formal coalition under the standard of union, liberty, integrity of the national territory, inviolibility of the principle of democratice popular government, independence of the state among them-selves for internal administration, and reciprocal exchange of assistance and resources as necessity

may require.

6. The pact of alliance may be consumated and will be fulfilled by means of a representative for each State of those admitted and will be established in a place which the [states] may mutually agree upon. The powers of those states will be those considered necessary to effectuate, develop, and consolidate the principles which were outlined in the previous declaration.

In order that [this Decree] should come to the attention of all citizens, I order that it be printed, published, and circulated to all to whom it may concern.

Santos Degollado,
Governor
Pedro Ogazon, Sec.

V. Riva Palacio, <u>Mexico a traves de los siglos</u>, V. 110.

* * * * *

PLAN OF ZULOAGA   (1)

16 December, 1857

1st. From this date, henceforth the Constitution of 1857 shall cease to rule.

2nd. The vote of the people freely given in favor of His Excellency the President, D. Ignacio Comonfort, is to be respected; he will continue to be invested with the supreme command with all the powers necessary for reestablishing peace, promoting the welfare of the national and directing the various branches of public administration.

3rd. Three months after the states have adopted the Plan the person charged with the executive power shall call an extraordinary Congress whose only mission shall be to draft a Constitution which shall be in harmony with the will of the nation and to promote the true interests of the people.

---

(1) Also called the Plan of Tacubaya

The said Constitution will be submitted to the vote of the residents of the Republic before its promulgation.

4th. If it should be sanctioned by this referendum, the Constitution shall be publicized, and the Congress shall issue a decree of the election of a constitutional president of the Republic; but if it should not be approved by a majority of the residents of the Republic; it shall be redrafted so as to bring it into conformity with the will of the majority.

5th. During the time required for the labor of redrafting the Constitution, the President shall name a council composed of a representative and an alternate from each state. This council shall have the authority which a special law shall designate.

6th. All the authorities who do not declare in favor of this Plan shall be discharged.

> (Signed) Felix Zuloaga, and officers of his brigade.

Arrangoiz, Francisco de Paula, <u>Mexico desde 1810 hasta 1867,</u> 430.

* * * * *

PLAN OF AYOTLA (1)

23 December, 1857

(Modified after agreement with Echeagaray)

Quite lengthy "Considerandos" precede the terms given below:

Art. 1. The Government established in Mexico as a consequence of the Plan of Tacubaya is disavowed.

(1) (Proclaimed by the battalion of Celaya Quartered in the Covent of San Augustine).

Art. 2. A Council [junta] of the people will meet in this capital. It will be composed of persons from all parts of the Republic and from the various classes of society, [persons] of recognized patriotism, refinement, and probity without distinction of political parties. [This Council] representing the nation, will proceed to establish a provisional administration and to name the person who is to exercise supreme power and to fix the bases which he is to abide by and to determine the method and form which is to be presented to the nation in order that it may be constituted freely.

Art. 3. The aforesaid Council will be convoked in the shortest time possible by a commission composed of the first political authorities of this capital who may adopt this Plan [The council] will be composed of one person named by the General of the Division of the East and the other by the [commander] of the garrison; [the Council] will finish its work within five days, counting from its installation, and to this end it shall hasten the legal proceedings and without more discussion than necessary in order to establish propositions and suggestions.

Art. 4. Once these provisional bases, whatever they may be, have been adopted, the person named to exercise the supreme power will take the oath corresponding to his office before the same Council which will then dissolve itself, thus leaving a provisional government established.

Art. 5. The Esteemed D. Manuel Robles Pezuela will be invited to take command of the forces which garrison this capital until the establishment of the provisional government.

V. Riva Palacio, Mexico a traves de los siglos, V, 340-341.

* * * * *

A NATIONAL APPEAL FROM THE STATE OF JALISCO

23 December, 1857

After a brief list of "Considerandos"...

1. The State of Jalisco invites [the other States] of the Union to join with it in opposition to the pro - nouncement which General Zuloaga issued in Tacubaya the 17th of the current month.

2. In order for this coalition to go into effect the [state] government will name commissioners to the neighboring states with instructions which it will delineate afterward, and once an agreement is reached, then it will be circulated to the other [states] in terms which also will be stated.

3. The instructions to which the previous articles refer are as follows:

I. To indicate to their Excellencies the Governors the firm resolution which is found in the Legislature of this State, in its Administration and in the people of Jalisco as well as the Parrodi Division to sustain at all costs and by all possible means the political instructions drafted in the Constitution of Febuary 5th of the current year for the reason that it was the legitimate expression of the wish of the majority of the Mexican people, as well as because its Art. 127 frankly opens the door for reforms without the necessity of appealing to mobs.

II. To invite confidentially the Legislatures to give wide authorizations to their Administrations in terms of the prior instruction.

III. To invite also their Excellencies the Governors to place under the orders of the Commander [jefe] of the State of Jalisco for the purpose of organizing an expedition against the revolutionaries of Mexico the following forces: Zacatecas and Guanajuato, one thousand infantry each, four hundred horses, one hundred artillerymen, and four or six pieces of field guns with adequate munitions, and to support this force during the time that it remains on campaign outside its State; San Luis Potosi and Michoacan each in terms indicated above, eight hundred infantry, three hundred horses, and fifty artillerymen with two or three field guns; Colima three hundred infantry, Aguascalientes and Queretero, each one in terms referred to about five hundred infantry, two hundred horses, and twenty-five artillerymen with two or three field pieces.

IV. The State of Jalisco will supply two thousand men with all branches of the service along with fourteen field pieces. This force, united with the contingents designated in the prior paragraph will form the Federal Army, and the other States with the rest of their forces and constituents for war will provide for their interior defense by fortifying, in case it may be necessary, the capital [cities] and the more defensible points.

V. Once the coalition proposed to the State is agreed upon, then the Administrative government of the States will be prohibited from having individual communication with the revolutionary elements concerning the points at issue.

VI. The States which may enter the coalition will invite those of Tamaulipas, Nuevo Leon, Chihuahua, Durango, Sonora, Sinaloa, and the Territory of Lower California to incorporate themselves in it and [to join] against all the enemies of public order and democratic institutions. Also, they will invite [the states of] Guerrero, Mexico, Puebla, Oaxaca, Vera Cruz, Chiapas, Tabasco, Taxcala, and Yucatan to form another caolition for the purpose of resisting with every hostile means the revolutionary government of Mexico, and to reach an agreement on the commander who shall direct its military operations, because the command of armies, in order for it to be successful, requires absolute unity of action.

VII. The [State] Governments who may form the first coalition will recommend to that of Tamaulipas that it direct its armed forces against the City [Plaza]

of Tampico in case it may second or it is feared that
it may second the absurd Plan of Tacubaya, in order
to lay siege or to prevent the entry of money as well
as to blockade the export of goods, until the said
City shall surrender.

Manual Cambre, La guerra de Tres Anos en el Estado de
Jalisco, 1822.

* * * * *

PLAN OF ECHEAGARAY

20 December, 1858

After a very long justification:

Art. 1. As soon as the division supporting his
present Plan shall occupy the capital for the
Republic there shall meet [a national assembly] to be
composed of three deputies named from each department
in conformity with the electoral law which will be
expedited immediately under the guarantee that it
shall be voted upon by all citizens and without
exception of classes or persons.

Art. 2. The mission of the national assembly is to
give a constitution to the country without other
restrictions that those which the assembly itself may
impose, because the purpose is to leave to this body
the widest liberty of action and time to formulate it.

Art. 3. Six months after the formulation of the
Constitution it will be submitted to a public vote
and it shall come into effect only if it obtains a
majority of those balloting. The provisional
government shall regulate the distribution of [the
constitution].

Art. 4. The leaders of the contending parties will be
urged to support the present Plan on the basis that
their ranks will be respected and that all the past
will be forgotten.

Art. 5. In the meantime the constitution will come
into effect and the Commanding General will assume
supreme power and undertake whatever may be necessary
to maintain the independence of the country from the

exterior and peace in the interior of the Republic.

(Signed) Miguel Maria
de Echeagaray

Signed in the headquarters in Ayotla, December 20, 1858

_____

V. Riva Palacios, <u>Mexico a traves de los siglos,</u> V, 339.

* * * * *

PLAN OF SANTOS DEGOLLADO

21 September, 1860

Extract from a letter which General Santos Degollado sent to George W. Matthews, British Charge d'Affairs, in which he proposed a Plan designed to terminate the civil war in the Republic. After reminders of the domestic conflict which had devastated Mexico for three years and which showed no signs of ending in a victory for either side, he concluded, "I am ready to propose to my Government and to my comrades-in-arms the following bases or considerations for pacification of the country."

1st. That there be installed a committee composed of the members of the Diplomatic Corps resident in Mexico including His Excellency the Minister of the United States and of a representative named by each Government, declaring solemnly what are the bases of the constitution of the Mexican government:

First. National representation in a Congress freely elected.

Second. Religious liberty.

Third. The Supremacy of the civil power.

Fourth. The nationalization of the so-called property of the clergy.

Fifth. The principles contained in the laws of the reform.

2nd. A provisional body [junta] which is referred to in the previous article shall name a provisional President of the Republic, who will be recognized by all, and this person shall function from the day of his nomination until that time when the Congress of the Union shall meet.

3rd. The Congress ought to be convoked immediately in accord with the latest electoral law, and it shall be installed precisely three months after publication of the call for convocation.

4th. The first act of the Congress shall be the nomination of an interim President of the Mexican Republic, and the declaration that the items contained in Article I are to be the bases of the constitution of the country.

5th. The Congress shall freely decree the Mexican constitution precisely at the end of three months, counting from the day of its installation.

Such is my proposition. My determination, in case none of the above is accepted by the two parties, is to retire completely from the political scene of my country. ..."

(Signed)

[Santos] Degollado

Genaro Garcia, Documentos ineditos o muy raros, XI, p.130-133.

* * * * *

PLAN OF CORDOBA

19 April, 1862

General Antonio Taboada issued a declaration against the government of the Capital in the following articles:

Art. 1. The authority of the man bearing the title of the President of the Republic, D. Benito Juarez, is repudiated.

Art. 2. The Honorable Sr. General Don Juan Nepomuceno Almonte is recognized as the supreme leader [of the Nation] and of the forces which may accept this Plan.

Art. 3. The above named Excellency and General is hereby fully empowered to use an agreement with the commanders of the allied forces that presently are found in the Republic in order to convoke a national assembly which, taking into consideration the deplorable situation in which the country finds itself, will declare the form of government that may be most suitable to establish in the country in order to cut the root of anarchy and to bring to Mexicans the peace and order which they have desired for so long and for the purpose of replacing the enormous losses which they have suffered during the civil war which for so many years has laid waste the entire Republic.

Art. 4. The Honorable General D. Juan Nepomuceno Almonte will be apprised of this action, and at the same time it will also be made very clear to him the firm faith which those undersigned entertain that on so solemn occasion he will not refuse his services to the Fatherland which now as never before stands in need of them.

(Signatures)

Gen. Antonio Taboada
and others

The following day this Plan
was endorsed in Orizaba also,
and again re-issued in Cordoba
29 April, 1862.

Manuel B. Trens, <u>Historia de Vera Cruz</u>, V. 361; Arrengoiz, Francisco de Paula, Mexico desde 1810 hasta 1864, 513.

* * * * *

A PROVISIONAL PLAN FOR THE ADMINISTRATION OF
GOVERNMENT UNDER EMPEROR MAXIMILIAN

16 June, 1863

The Franco-Mexican troops remained in their positions from Vera Cruz to Orizaba until the relief of General Lorenzo by General Forey, who arrived from France with more troops. A part of these, under orders of General Bazaine, advanced upon Jalapa,

539

covering this new line as far as Perote. At the beginning of 1863 the division of Bazaine left this line in order to join the mass of the expeditionary forces which then commenced to advance on Puebla.

The siege of that plaza commenced in the middle of March. The Juarista army under the command of General Commonfort who was coming to the aid of Puebla, was defeated a short distance from there on the 8th of May. The city was occupied on the 17th of that month by General Forey.

The allied troops commenced to advance on Mexico [City] from which Juarez had fled on the afternoon of May 31st.

The expeditionary troops made their solemn entrance into the capital on June 10th.

On the 16th General Forey issued the following decree relative to the formation of a provisional government.

The General of Division, Senator, Commanding
General of the Expeditionary force
in Mexico

Considering that it is urgent to organize the public powers that are to replace the Intervention in the direction of affairs in Mexico:

According to the report of the minister of the Emperor, I have seen fit to decree the following:

Art. 1. According to the presentation of the minister of the Emperor, a special decree will designate thirty-five Mexican citizens who will form a superior council [junta] of government.

Art. 2. This Superior Council shall meet in the place designated two days after the publication of the decree which nominates them.

Art. 3. The session of installation shall be presided over by the oldest person among them, and assisted by the two youngest of them who shall serve as secretaries.

Art. 4. The Superior Council shall proceed at the first session to the nomination of a president and of his two secretaries. The election shall not be valid until the elected candidates shall have obtained a majority plus one of the votes.

Art. 5. The installation of the dignitaries shall take place at the same session.

Art. 6. The Council shall proceed immediately to the nomination of three Mexican citizens who shall be vested with the Executive Power, and of two Alternates for these high duties. The election shall not be valid until the candidates shall have obtained a half plus one of the votes.

Art. 7. As soon as they have been elected the members of the Executive Power shall assume direction of Mexican affairs.

Art. 8. The Superior Council shall set the honoraria which ought to be given to the members of the prov - isional government.

Art. 9. [The Council] shall be divided into several sections in order to deliberate on pertinent ques - tions of the various ministries.

    A general assembly shall be convoked by its president in order to consider the more important business whenever the Executive Power may ask it.

Concerning the Assembly of Notables

Art. 10. In order to form the Assembly of Notables, the Superior Council shall be joined by two hundred and fifteen members elected from among Mexican citizens without distinction to rank or class.

Art. 11. In order to belong to the Assembly of Notables it shall be necessary to be older than twenty-five years of age nor disqualified by any

541

political or civil charge.

Art. 12. The meetings of the Assembly of Notables shall be carried into effect immediately after the formation of this body.

Art. 13. The first session shall be destined for the election and two secretaries, persons who will be installed immediately by the provisional committee [mesa] to be composed of the oldest member and the youngest members.

Art. 14. The Assembly of Notables shall concern itself, first of all, with the form of the definitive government of Mexico. The vote on this question must receive at least two-thirds of the ballots cast.

Art. 15. In case that this two-thirds majority is not obtained after three days of balloting, the Executive Power shall dissolve the Assembly of Notables and the Superior Council shall proceed without delay to the formation of a new assembly.

Art. 16. Members of the preceding assembly shall be eligible for re-election.

Art. 17. The Assembly of Notables shall concern itself, after having determined the definitive form of government, with questions which may be presented to it by decree of the Executive Power.

The first period of sessions shall be for five days; it may be prorogued by the Executive Power.

General Dispositions Common to All Deliberative Bodies

Art. 18, The secretaries of the Superior Council and of its various sections as well as those of the Assembly of Notables shall draw up the minutes of the sessions; they shall sign with the presidents the resolutions voted by these corporations and which will be transmitted to the Executive Power.

Art. 19. The sessions of the Superior Council and its sections as well as the Assembly of Notables shall not be public. The official acts will be permitted to be published in the newspapers provided that they are transmitted by the secretaries with the authori - zation of the respective presidents.

Art. 20. Members of the Superior Council and of the Assembly of Notables shall not receive any honorarium.

Of the Executive Power

Art. 21. The members of the Executive Power shall be divided into six ministries; they shall each name the clerks for all their particular offices.

Art. 22. The Executive Power shall receive so that it may promulgate both the decrees and the resolutions of the Assembly of Notables.

It shall have the absolute right of veto over these resolutions.

The bills prepared by the Superior Council shall be forwarded for their passage to the Assembly of Notables.

Art. 23. The functions of the Executive Power shall cease from the moment of the installation of the definitive government proclaimed by the Assembly of Notables.

Art. 24. The minister of the Emperor is vested with the execution of the present decree which he shall insert into the Bulletin of the official acts of the Intervention, and they shall be posted at the corners of the capital.

(Signed)

Issued from Mexico [City].   Forey

Anon, Advenimiento de Maximiliano y Carlotta, (Mexico, 1864), 20-22.

* * * * *

ASSEMBLY OF NOTABLES; Report of its Commission

10 July, 1863

[After a lengthy survey of Mexican misfortunes since Independence the report concluded the following propositions:]

1st. The Mexican nation adopts as its form of government a conservative monarchy, hereditary, and with a Catholic prince.

2nd. The sovereign shall take the title of Emperor of Mexico.

3rd. The imperial crown of Mexico shall be offered to His Royal Highness Prince Ferdinand Maximillian, Archduke of Austria, for himself and his descendants.

4th. In the event of and through circumstances now impossible to foresee the Archduke Ferdinand Maximilian should not come to take possession of the throne that is offered to him, the Mexican nation refers the matter to the benevolence of His Majesty Napoleon III, emperor of the French, in order that he may name another Catholic prince.

Arrangoiz, Francisco de Paula, Mexico desde 1810 hasta 1867, 542-543.

* * * * *

DECLARATION CONCERNING THE DEFINITIVE FORM OF GOVERNMENT TO BE ADOPTED IN MEXICO

10 July, 1863

"The judgment relative to the form of government which, in order to be established definitively, is suitable for adoption in Mexico; presented by a special commission in the session of July 8, 1863. It was named by the Assembly of Notables being met in fulfillment of the decree of June 16th last."

[After some thirty pages of justification of its position, the Commission concluded below.]

544

Summarizing, then, briefly all that expressed above, the Commission judges it to have been demonstrated fully and satisfactorily:

1st. That the republican system, whether under the federal system or under that with a more centralized power, has been during the many years that it was tried a rich well-spring for all the evils that have afflicted our country, and that neither good sense nor political judgment permit us to hope that they may be remedied without extripating at the root the only cause that has produced them.

2nd. That only the institution of Monarchy is adaptable for Mexico, especially in the present circumstances because, combining in it order with liberty and force with strictest equity, it almost always overpowers anarchy, and it holds in check demagoguery which is essentially immoral and disorganizing.

3rd. That in order to establish the throne it is not possible to choose a sovereign from the sons of the country (which, on the other hand, is not lacking men of eminent merit) because those principal qualities which constitute a king are those that cannot be improvised, and it is simply not given to a plain individual in his private life to possess such traits, and even less if without other antecedents they are based only upon the public vote.

4th and finally: That among the princes known for their illustrious and sublime lineage no less for his personal gifts is the Archduke Ferdinand Maximillian of Austria on whom the vote of the nation should fall in order that he should guide its destiny, because his is one of those off-springs of royal stock particularly distinguished for its virtues, extensive knowledge, keen intelligence, and a special gift for government.

Therefore, the Commission submits for final resolution of this honorable Assembly the propositions that follow:

1) The Mexican nation adopts as its form of government that of a conservative [moderado] Monarchy, hereditary, with a Catholic prince.

2) The sovereign shall assume the title of Emperor of Mexico.

3) The imperial crown of Mexico is offered to His August Imperial and Royal Prince Ferdinand Maximillian, Archduke of Austria for himself and his descendants.

4) In the event of and through circumstances impossible to foresee, the Archduke Ferdinand Maximilian should not come to accept the throne that is offered to him, the Mexican nation submits to the benevolence of His Majesty Napoleon III, Emperor of the French, in order that he may name another Catholic prince.(1)

Mexico [City]   Signed by five members of
                                 the Commissions

10 July, 1863.

---

(1) An identical resolution was passed by the Assembly of Notables on the same day.

Anon. Advenimiento de Maximiliano y Carlota, 62-63.

* * * * *

PLAN OF GENERAL COBOS

7 November, 1863

On the seventh of November, 1863, the undersigned met in the city of Matamoros to consider the situation in which the country finds itself. [There follows a catalogue of national problems and three paragraphs of "Considerandos..."]

WE PROCLAIM

Art. 1. The Constitution of 1857 and the Administration which emanates from it hereby ceases to be in effect.

Art. 2. We proclaim the Honorable Sr. General Don Jose Maria Cobos as commander of the forces which may be raised to support this Plan and the one who will draft the measures necessary in order to publicize its adoption in the rest of the Republic.

Art. 3. The towns, on adopting the Plan, will send to the said commander confirmation of their respective declarations.

Art. 4. The said Senor General-in-Chief will convoke immediately a meeting in the town of Matamoros in order that by its own vote it should form an executive committee [junta] composed of five individuals of wisdom and discretion in order that this [junta] should propose without delay a plan which would have as its object the establishment of a provisional government that would have direction of public administration and provide the necessary means for the defense of our venerated independence.

Art. 5. In the meantime the collection of income due to the Treasury will be deposited in secure custody, and there will be withdrawn only those sums which the costs of war require, and those of administration; likewise there will be set aside a portion for foreign affairs.

[Here ends the Plan of Cobos. He was arrested while composing the Plan and promptly executed.]

Zamacois, Historia de Mexico, 16: 1059-1061.

* * * * *

A POST-MORTEM PLAN: "ABDICATION" OF
EMPEROR MAXIMILIAN

20 March, 1867

Considering that if our death should occur the government of the Empire would be acephalous in the absence of its legitimate regent, our august wife, the Empress Carlota;

Considering that if this great evil should occur and in order to provide on our part for the good of the Mexican nation even after our day, it is indispensable to leave an established government which will be recognized as the center of union for the said nation;

Considering that meanwhile the latter by means of a congress freely convoked and met does not declare the form in which it will continue to be constituted, the present form, which is the Monarchy, exists, and for the same We being lacking, the administration ought to be deposited in a regency; WE DECLARE

Art. 1. The regents of the Empire, We being lacking on account of death: don Teodosio Lares, don Jose M. Lacunza, and General don Leonardo Marquez.

Art. 2. The Regency shall convoke the congress, which is to constitute the nation definitively as soon as the war has been brought to an end either through armed force or by armistice; then the free and legitimate meeting of the constituent body may take place.

Art. 4. With the act of the installation of the Congress the Regency shall cease; with this act the authority which We confer through this decree will be terminated.

Our minister of Public instruction and Religious Services is charged with the duty of making this decree known, and equally for the Regents which we leave nominated.

(Signed)

Maximilian

V. Riva Palacio, <u>Mexico a traves de los siglos</u>, V. 850-851.

* * * * *

PLAN OF LA NORIA

11 November, 1871

To the Mexican People:

[There follows a survey of unfortunate events in the Mexican experience since 1857 and a vigorous pro - testation of patriotism on the part of General Diaz during that time.]

We will fight, then, for the cause of the People and the People shall be the only judge of its victory. "The Constitutution of 1857 and a free elections" will be our motto; and "Less government and more freedom" our program.

A convention of three representatives from each State, popularly elected, will draft the program of constitutional reconstruction, and it will name a constitutional president of the Republic who for no motive whatever will be the present trustees of the war. The delegates, who will be patriots of crystal-clear honor, will bring to the consideration of the convention their ideas and the aspirations of their respective states, and they will know how to formulate with loyalty and to support with under - standing the truly national necessities. I will permit myself to echo those which have been pointed out to me as the greatest [needs], but [I list them] without any pretense of completeness nor through any desire to impose them as preconceived resolutions, and protesting that from here on I will ·accept without reservation or any reserve the decisions of the convention.

THAT the election of the President be direct and personal and that no citizen who, in the year pre - ceding may have exercised for a single day authority or whose responsibility extended throughout the whole republic shall be eligible for election.

THAT the Congress of the Union shall be able to exercise electoral functions only in purely economic matters, and in no case for designation of high public officials.

THAT the nomination of secretaries of the cabinet and of any other employee or functionary who enjoys a salary or any emolument of more than 3,000 pesos annually shall be subject to the approval of the Congress.

THAT the Union guarantee to the town councils the authority and suitable resources as indispensable for their freedom and independence.

THAT all inhabitants of the Republic should be guaranteed a trial by a jury of the people who will declare and judge the culpability of those accused; that [the juries shall do this] in such a way that judicial officals will be granted only the authroity of applying the penalty which pre-existing laws have designated.

THAT the hateful sales tax [alcabala] be abol - ished and the statutes of customs houses, both maritime and at the frontier be reformed to accord with constitutional precepts and the diverse nec - essities of our coasts and frontiers.

The Convention will take into account these matters and shall promote all that which may be conducive to the re-establishment of the principles of earlier days, to the establishment of instit - utions, and the general welfare of the inhabitants of the Republic.

I do not admit to illegitimate ambitions nor do I wish to respond to the deep hatreds planted by the audacity of the administration. The national insurrection which will restrain its power to violate the Law and to outrage morality must inspire one with noble and patriotic sentiments of dignity and justice.

The lovers of the Constitution and of free elections are sufficiently strong and numerous in the country of Herrera, Gomez Farias, and Ocampo to accept the struggle against the usurpers of popular suffrage.

Let the patriots, sincere constitutionalists, men of responsibility, lend their presence to the cause of free elections, and the country will save their dearest interests. Let public officials, recognize that their powers are limited, and honorably return to the voting public the trust of their confidence in legal periods and strict observance of the Constitution will be the real guarantee of peace. That no citizen impose himself and perpetuate himself in the exercise of power, and this will be the last revolution.

(Signed)

Porfirio Diaz

Archivo del General Porfirio Diaz, 10: 43 48.

* * * * *

REVISED PLAN OF LA NORIA

3 April, 1872

Considering that the civil war which has broken out throughout the Republic is decimating the towns and with the purpose of bringing the present fighting to a successful conclusion, I have decided in agree - ment with the advice of my best friends to modify the Plan proclaimed at La Noria in the following terms:

I. To fight for the cause of the people: It alone will be the master of our triumphs; the Constitution of 1857 and free elections--such will be our flag; less government and more freedom--such will be our program.

II. The President of the Supreme Court of Justice from this day will commence to fulfill his functions, following in all points the present Plan, and taking as a guide the representative, popular system.

III. A Convention of three representatives for each State, elected by the people and approved by the

President of the Supreme Court of Justice will issue the call for elections of a President of the Republic and of Deputies to the Congress of the Union; [it should also concern itself with] drafting the program of constitutional reconstruction.

IV. The delegates who will be patriots of unstained probity will bring to the inner council of the Convention the ideas and aspirations of their respective States and they will know how to formulate with loyalty and to press with energy the truly national needs.

V. The election of the President will be direct and personal, and he who has won the plurality of votes will be declared elected.

VI. That the Congress of the Union shall be able to exercise electoral functions only in purely economic questions, and in no case for the designation of high public officials.

VII. That the nomination of ministers and of any employee or funtionary whose emoluments are greater than 3,000 pesos per year shall be subject to the approval of the Congress.

VIII. That the Union guarantee to the Town Councils the rights and suitable resources as indispensable elements for their freedom and independence.

IX. That there be guaranteed to all inhabitants of the Republic a trial by jurors, named by the people; that they declare his guilt and qualify the degree of guilt of those accused in such a way that judicial officials shall have no other duty than that of applying the penalty which the existing laws may designate.

X. That the hateful sales Tax [alcabala] be abolished and that the statutes of the maritime and frontier customs regulations be reformed in accord with constitutional precepts and the diverse necessities of our coasts and frontiers.

XI. The Convention will take into account these questions and shall promote all that which may be conducive to the re-establishment of the principles of earlier days, to the consolidation of institutions, and the general welfare of all the inhabitants of the Republic.

I do not admit to illegitimate ambitions nor do I wish to revive the deep hatreds planted by the excesses of the administration.

The national insurrection which is to take the first step toward law and outraged morality ought to inspire noble sentiments of dignity and justice.

The lovers of the Constitution and of free elections are too strong and too numerous in the Fatherland of Herrera, of Gomez Farias and of Ocampo to accept the fight against the dealers who trade off popular suffrage.

Let the patriots, the sincere constitutionalist, men of responsibility, lend their presence to the cause of free elections and the country will have their dearest interests.

Let public officials recognize that their powers are limited; let them honorably return to the people the trust of their confidence in the legal terms of service and strict observance of the Constitution will be the real guarantee of peace.

Let no citizen impose himself or perpetuate himself in the exercise of power and this revolution will be the last.

* * * * * * * * *

Send a copy of this Plan to the Generals in order that they may be fully acquainted with its contents. [The names follow.]

(Signed)

Ameca, April 3, 1872.   Porfirio Diaz.

Ciro B. Ceballos, Aurora y ocaso, I, 261-263.

* * * * *

PROGRAM OF THE PROGRESSIVE REPUBLICAN PARTY

in support of the candidacy of C. Sebastian

Lerdo de Tejada for the Presidency. 1872-1876.

[After a hopeful discussion of the state of the Mexican Union, the Party presented the following:]

From these simple observations is derived the central idea in which our program is cast and which can be reduced to the following formula:

Keep the public trust and guarantee the political institutions under which the nation is constituted.

Here, in our opinion, are the principle demands of the present situation in order to obtain this great achievement:

1. Mexico will not renew its relations with foreign powers except on prudent and long-range bases. Our treaties and agreements must be expressed in the most precise language possible and must contain in them the beginning of their reform or modification.

2. The independence and sovereignty of the states will be profoundly respected, with the general government abstaining from all intervention in their internal problems.

3. To initiate the necessary measures in order that the reorganization and replacement of the Army shall be in accord with the spirit of democratic institutions and public necessity.

4. Respect for individual guarantees as granted by the constitution and punishing with all the vigor of the law any authorities who may violate them.

5. Unlimited support of free public schools, especially at the primary level, and to try to extend it wherever possible to the indigenous race, which has been viewed so far with criminal indifference.

6. To make individual security effective by means of a well-organized police which pursues evil-doers effectively.

7. Guarantee the inviolable right to property against all invasion of power, this right being considered as the foundation of social order.

8. Organization of the public Treasury so that expenditures is equal to receipts, and introduction of a prudent economy in the costs [of administration] by reducing the number of employees to those absolutely necessary and by exercising the strictest oversight over those charged with the management of national funds and by making effective their responsibility for any discrepancies which may occur.

9. To arrange a preference on a fair basis for the amortization of the public debt and to protect the development of all types of credit institutions in order to mobilize the wealth of the country and to fund the national credit.

10. The government ought not to be an entrepreneur: in consequence, public works will be auctioned to private companies, and so arranging it that it should be on terms most favorable to the general interest and with the greatest economy possible for the Treasury.

11. To stimulate especially immigration and the best materials, and to offer to business firms that may be formed for this purpose all franking privileges con - sistent with public interest.

12. To arrange matters so that democracy and sovereignty of the people shall be truly practiced through the following measures: Strict observance of the law; respect and support to established legal authorities; acceptance to be freely given to the vote of the majority; condemnation of all activity that tends to disturb public order, to subvert institutions or to overthrow functionaries duly

constituted by law; total condemnation of all maneuvers that set out to falsify the popular will, whether it proceeds from [legal] authorities or from parties, and application of the full force of the law to offenders.

13. To introduce the most strict moral code in all branches of public administration, by demanding of employees honesty, competence adequate to the dis - charge of their tasks.

14. To initiate measures conducive to the freedom of municipal government.

15. By means of a reform of our financial system to expedite freedom of trade.

16. To give special attention to the frontier states and to the Yucatan peninsula and to promote [measures] which will hasten the end of the race war [guerras de castas] and that against the savage Indians, especially by means of colonization.

17. Not to fail in a single point the faithful fulfillment of the Constitution and laws of the Reform, looking always at individual cases that present themselves for the most practical and most rational application and that which most conforms with the spirit [of the Constitution] and the welfare of the people.

V. Riva Palacio. Historia de la administracion de lerdo de Tejada, 215-219.

* * * * *

556

LIBERATING PLAN OF MANUEL LOZADA (1)

17 January, 1873

Proclaimed in the town of San Luis and
no specific date given in the text.

Art. 1. We, the people of the Sierra de Alicia, a
place always designated as the center of the union of
Nayarit and known as the seventh canton of Tepic,
State of Jalisco, have met with the sole purpose of
deliberation and we are moved by the most sound
intentions of avoiding the unjust war which the
government has declared against us, and by the desire
to continue as in years past busy with our honorable
employment as the general countryside is a witness
thereof. After many sessions and our points of view
having been made perfectly clear, no other course has
remained open to us, to our sorrow, than to accept
the war, as unjust as infamous, which has been
declared against us. The sister communities of
Nayarit have taken the initiative and the unpatriotic
and unbending personnel of the said Government must
assume before God and the whole world the incalculable consequences [of consequent hostilities]. In
virtue whereof we shall make use of our means of
waging war and of all available forces at our
disposal, and as we proceed to thrust ourselves into
full-fledged deeds, it is with the consciousness that
we are acting in terms of true righteousness and with
faith in the triumph of our cause. Furthermore, we
are confident that all classes of society which
consider with good judgment and imparciality the
principles which we support will lend us their moral
and physical support. We assure them that the corrupt
civil employees will be discharged from their
position, those persons who for so long have had no
other income than that of public funds, the major
part of it coming from the proletariat. These
officials, along with those who have encouraged their
profigate conduct have demonstrated that in the days
of trial for the salvation of the country that

---

(1) Also called "Plan Libertador de Nagarit".

557

are the first to ignore danger and to put to the sword the class of the said people. In a like manner there will be avoided all abuses in the admini – stration of justice that are so common through the increasing number of wandering, shyster lawyers of bad law. Therfore we the people, awakening from their lethargy, arise en masse, arms in hand in order that from the strong shock which the nation must exper – ience may result the happy success of the great principle of regeneration. The people of Nayarit are proud to accept the war in circumstances that no armed forces attracts the attention of the Govern – ment. The many and generous invitations which the principal leaders of various revolutions have made to us ought not to be forgotten, but these invitations which we as lovers of peace did not accept. For reasons given above, doubly honorable and meritorious, will be the triumph of our cause.

Art. 2. The armed forces which support this cause will be called The Mexican Army of Populist Restoration, and C. Manuel Lozada is recognized as the Commanding General; or in his absence, him whom he may name and shall grant to him therewith extra – ordinary war powers and financial authority. When the period of his trusteeship shall have been concluded, he will give a full account of his actions.

Art. 3. Let full knowledge of this Plan be presented to the Congress of the Union and let them understand the unjustifiable procedure against this integral part of the country, particularly when subjects relative to the difficulties mentioned heretofore even now are found pending in the Chamber of Congress. The people in general are within their rights in repelling an [armed] force when a Government such as the present one conducts itself in terms so unworthy of a presumably civilized nation. Therefore, we proceed in terms expressed above while holding to the great principle that "The People are governed by the People."

Art. 4. The individual or individuals, whatever may be their category or nationality, who offer pro –

tection of any sort to the enemy will be considered
hostile to the People and will be punished as
circumstances may demand.

Art. 5. It is hereby prohibited for Mexicans to leave
for foreign parts during the duration of the current
war, except with a passport signed by the Commanding
General of the insurrection.

Art. 6. Once the triumph of the present Plan is
secured, the First Chief [principal caudillo] of the
insurrection will issue a call to the Town Councils
[ayuntamientos] in order that by their conduct as
representatives of the People and in the most
spontaneous manner and by direct election each State
of the Mexican Confederation may name three repre -
sentatives who will meet in a place designated by the
said Chief for the purpose of determining the form of
popular representative government that ought to be
provided for the Nation, whether it be that of a
Republic, an Empire, or a Kingdom, provided that what
is considered is the true greatness [of the nation]
and enduring peace.

Art. 7. While the Nation is being reconstructed it
will be governed by municipal councils which the
people will designate by direct election. The said
Towns or municipal corporations shall enjoy the right
of absolute independence and sovereignty in the areas
of administration of government and in financing, yet
recognizing the capital of a province, district, or a
municipality as superior to a town council [ayun -
tamiento].

Art. 8. Since one of the principal purposes of this
movement is to guarantee the rights of the People,
for this reason the forces that with arms in hand who
shall sustain this Plan will not receive more
supplies than those with which can be provided, or
which we shall take from the enemy.

Art. 9. Let it be known to the employees of the
Federation to whom it may concern as well as to the
merchants, both Mexican and Foreign, that after the
promulgation of this Plan all liquidation or trans-

action of any sort in the customs houses of any port of entry, either maritime or inland, is totally prohibited and quite invalid. Other federal offices shall also make the most scrupulous accounting, the Commanding General being empowered to name those who shall substitute for them provisionally. The employee or merchant who shall fail to observe this provision will be punished as the circumstances may require.

Art. 10. In order to expedite activity and the improvement of commerce, all inland custom houses are hereby abolished and widest powers are granted to the town councils of the capitals of the canton, district or portion thereof or to municipalities in order to supply themselves with the resources necessary for the operation of the State, as representatives of the People.

Art. 11. Once the success of this uprising is assured, the public debt in general will be amortized both to foreign creditors and to [Mexican] nationals with utmost care.

Art. 12. In order that the nation at large may know its rights and in order that they may not fail in their efforts, the Town Councils [ayuntamientos] are authorized to establish public instruction, both for youth and for those who may need it. It is understood that this principle will be the salvation from the evil condition in which we find ourselves.

Art. 13. The Press being one of the civilizing agencies of the People, it shall retain its right of freedom provided that its productions promote progress and morality of the People themselves, and [publishers] are sternly prohibited from occupying themselves with offensive publications against both deliberating parties without having sufficient justification. The slightest failure in this matter will be duly punished.

Art. 14. For the greater progress of the country and of commerce in general, ports of the latitude and of

560

deposit along the coast will be designated by the authority of the Commanding General of this in - surrection who shall consider himself empowered to act.

Art. 15. The Forces of Populist Restoration guarantee the lives and interests and the conservation and protection of material improvements such as railroad telegraph lines, etc., etc.

Art. 16. Let the Present Plan be brought to the knowledge of foreign governments, and indicate to them the positive desire to renew the most cordial relations of friendship and trade; the Commanding General heretofore cited being authorized to name on an interim basis the diplomatic representatives to those nations.

(Signatures follow)

Silvano Barba Gonzalez, La lucha por la tierra, p.-208-212; also Ciro B. Ceballos, Aurora y Ocaso, 853-pp.

* * * * *

REVOLUTIONARY PLAN (1)

2 March, 1875

[After a two-page justification for another Plan, the author presented the following points:]

Art. 1. The President of the Repulbic, Don Sebastian Lerdo de Tejada, and all functionaries and those employed under him are hereby disavowed.

Art. 2. Also by reason of its complete illegality the

---

(1) This Plan was published anonymously, but gene- rally it was supposed to have been written by General Sostenes Rocha, nor did he deny the attribution.

so-called Supreme Court of Justice and the so-called Seventh Constitutional Congress are repudiated.

Art. 3. All the State Administrations which adhere to the present Plan will be recognized as such until the complete triumph of the revolution.

Art. 4. In a state in which the Governor does not accept this Plan, then the military commander who may proclaim this Plan, shall take the first steps of a permanent nature in the capital of the State and shall be recognized as the governor.

Art. 5. The Leader [caudillo], the General-in-Chief of the Army of the Regeneration, on occupying the Capital of the Republic, will issue a call for election of a President of the Republic, but on no account shall it fall upon the Commander [jefe] who is exercising authority at the time of the election, and for President or Justice of the Supreme Court of Justice.

Art. 6. Until the day on which the popularly chosen President-elect shall take charge of the adminis-tration, the General-in-Chief of the Army will retain the powers of War and command of the Republic, under the title of Depository of Executive Power.

Art. 7. The States will be reorganized while observing in them the same terms marked for the reorganization of the Republic, it being within the authority of the Depository of Executive Power to dictate all the measures which he may deem necessary to assure the fulfillment of the promises of this Plan.

Art. 8. The Depository of Executive Power is fully authorized [to determine] the responsibility of Don Sebastian Lerdo de Tejada and his accomplices, and to apply to them fitting punishment in order to make [this Plan] effective in the most positive way.

Art. 9. Once this Plan has triumphed in whatever State of the Republic, by that very act the hated imposition of the sales tax [alcabala] will be abolished, and the commander who may occupy that State shall be personally responsible for the fulfillment of this article.

Art. 10. The Eighth Congress having met, it having the character of a constituent body, its first task will be constitutional reform that will guarantee municipal independence, and a law for the political organization of the Federal District and of the Territory of Lower California.

Freedom and Regeneration.

Ciro B. Ceballos, Aurora y ocaso, 8750-877.

* * * * *

REVOLUTIONARY PLAN OF NUEVO UTRECHO

3 March, 1875

[After one paragraph of introductory Con - siderandos, the Undersigned called upon Mexicans as Christians and citizens to support the following:]

1st. The Constitution of the United Mexican States, sanctioned on the 5th of February, 1857, its reforms and additions, its laws, regulations, as well as all those [measures] which would have emanated from that code shall cease being observed herewith.

2nd. Senor Licenciado D. Sabastian Lerdo de Tejada and all the other functionaries, legislative, political, and judicial, who, against the express will of the people today form the personnel for the Administration of the Mexican Republic, shall hereby cease the exercise of public office.

3rd. Once this Plan has been adopted by the majority of the nation, it will proceed to name an Interim President of the Republic.

The election shall be by a council [junta] of representatives called together by the commander in-chief of the forces which sustain this Plan in a place considered most suitable in the opinion of the said Commander.

4th. The Interim President immediately shall be invested with ample powers in all branches of public administration; but he shall be strictly obligated to respect the Catholic religion, individual guarantees, to attend to the security and independence of the Nation, and to provide whatever may be conducive to its prosperity and greatness.

5th. As soon as the Interim President has assumed the exercise of his office, he shall name without delay a plenipotentiary near to the Holy See and be invested with the powers necessary to negotiate a CONCORDAT which, soothing the conscience, will adjust the effect of the acquisitions of ecclesiastical property by virtue of the so-called Laws of the Reform.

6th. Within two months after having entered into the exercise of his duties as Interim President, [this person] shall convoke an extraordinary Congress which shall occupy itself solely with constituting a Nation under the form of a Popular Representative Republic and with revising the acts of the present Congress as well as those of the Provisional Executive who is mentioned in Article 3.

7th. The Constitution shall recognize the Catholic Church, Apostolic and Roman, as the religion of the State, and shall grant to it all the rights and all the liberties inherent in its nature and indispensable for its high and noble mission on earth as well as for the maintenance of charity and harmony which always ought to reign between the spiritual and temporal powers without sacrifice of independence by the respective parties.

8th. The Commander of the forces in each State which sustains this Plan will call together a committee [junta] formed by representatives of the municipalities so that they may elect an Interim Governor, and this latter person shall exercise the powers necessary to organize public administration in his respective territory.

9th. Immediately there shall cease all observance of the so-called "curfew laws", the regulations of the National Guard, and the head tax and personal taxes which are in effect in some States. The General Administration and the private persons therein during the Interim period will reduce the roster of em - ployees to those strictly necessary for good public service, and they will moderate the taxes and contributions, taking into account for this [purpose] the many urgent demands of the Administration and the state of poverty which the present prodigal Govern - ment now ruling the destiny has left the People.

10th. All those who oppose this Plan will be treated as enemies of the People and of National Indepen - endence; and the Army officers who support [the People] will be recognized in the rank at the time of their acceptance they occupy on the military roster.

11th. This Plan will be modified if the majority of the Nation judges it advisable.

(Two signatures)

Ciro B. Ceballos, *Aurora y ocaso*, 878-879.

* * * * *

PLAN OF TUXTEPEC

10 January, 1876

Art. 1. The Constitution of 1857, the acts of the Reform promulgated on September 25, 1873, and the law of December 14, 1876 are the supreme laws of the Republic.

Art. 2. The law of No-Reelection of the President of the Republic and of Governors of the States will have the same character of a supreme law.

Art. 3. Don Sebastian Lerdo de Tejada is repudiated as President of the Republic, and likewise all the functionaries and those employed by him, as well as all those named in the elections of July last year.

Art. 4. All the governors of all the States who adhere to this Plan will be recognized as such. Where this does not take place, he whom the commander of the armed forces may name will be recognized temp - orarily as governor.

Art. 5. Elections will be held for the Supreme Powers of the Union within two months after the occupation of the capital of the Republic and without the necessity of a new call [for elections]. The elections shall be held in accord with the laws of February 12, 1857, and of October 23, 1872, the primaries [to be held] the first Sunday following the two months after occupying the capital, and the final elections on the third Sunday.

Art. 6. Until the elections are held the Executive Power will be vested in the citizen who obtains a majority of the votes of the Governors of the States, and he will have no other attributes than merely administrative functions.

Art. 7. The Eighth Constitutional Congress having met, its first task will be the consitutional reform referred to in Article 2, that which guarantees the indepdendence of municipalities and gives political organization to the Federal District and to the Territory of Lower California.

Art. 8. All those who directly or indirectly cooperated in sustaining the Administration of Don Sebastian Lerdo de Tejada will be held personally and pecuniarily responsible, and the penalties will become effective from the moment that the guilty ones or their interests are found in possession of what - ever force belongs to the regenerative army.

Art. 9. The Generals, Commanders [jefes], and off - icers who in due course second this Plan will be recognized in their assignments, ranks, and decorations.

Art. 10. The Commanding General, Porfirio Diaz, will be recognized as the General-in-Chief of the regenerative army.

Art. 11. On a fitting occasion recognition will be made of a General of the line of the East, to which we belong, whose commander shall enjoy extraordinary powers in Treasury and War.

Art. 12. For no reason whatever may one enter into a treaty with the enemy, under penalty of death to any who should do it.

Issued in the village of Ojitian
    District of Tuxtepec.   Colonel-in-Chief
                                      H. Sarmiento and
                                      other signatures.

Archivo del General Porfirio Diaz, XII:99-100.

* * * * *

PLAN OF TUXTEPEC, revised at Palo Blanco (1)

21 March, 1876

Art. 1. The Constitution of 1857, the Act of the Reforms promulgated 25 September, 1872, and the Law of 1874 are the supreme laws of the land.

Art. 2. Also having the character of the supreme law is that of No-Re-election of the President of the Republic and of governors of the states until this principle can be elevated to the rank of a constitutional reform by the legal means established in the Constitution.

---

(1) Sometimes called the "Plan of Palo Blanco." The only revisions were in the Considerandos and were insignificant.

Art. 3. Don Sebastian Lerdo de Tejada is disavowed as President of the Republic, and also [repudiated] are the functionaries and those employed by him, as well as those nominated in the elections of 1875.

Art. 4. All the Governors of the States who adhere to this Plan will be recognized as such. Wherever this does not occur he whom the Commander of the Armed Forces may name will be recognized temporarily as Governor.

Art. 5. Elections for the Supreme Powers of the Union will be held within two months after the Capital of the Republic has been occupied, in the terms of the call which the Chief Executive shall make one month after the day that the occupation shall have taken place and in accord with the electoral laws of 12 February, 1857 and 23 October, 1872. A month after the final elections have been verified, Congress shall meet and shall occupy itself in fulfilling the prescriptions of Art. 51 of the first of the said laws so that immediately the constitutional President of the Republic shall begin the exercise of his office, and the Supreme Court of Justice shall be installed.

Art. 6. The Executive Power, without any other claim of authority than that of administration, will be deposited until elections can be held in the Presidency of the Supreme Court of Justice now sitting, or in the magistrate who may discharge his functions, always provided that the one or the other accepts this Plan in all its provisions and shall make known his acceptance in the Press within one month counted from the day that this Plan is pub - lished in the periodicals of the Capital. Silence or refusal of the one who presides over the Supreme Court will thereby invest the commander of the armed forces with the character of Chief Executive.

Art. 7. The 8th Constitutional Congress having met, its first tasks will be the constitutional reform which is mentioned in the second article [of this

Plan], that which guarantees independence to muni -
cipalities, and the law which will provide a poli -
tical organization to the Federal District and to the
Territory of Lower California.

Art. 8. The generals, commanders [jefes] and officers
who in due course support this present Plan will be
recognized in their assignments, ranks, and decor -
ations.

Campo de Palo Blanco.

[Signed] Porfirio Diaz

Archive del General Porfirio Diaz, XII, 96-99.

* * * * *

PLAN OF SALAMANCA (1)

28 October, 1876

[After a dissertation extending over five pages,
the undersigned concluded by saying:]

The Executive presents [the points] as briefly as
possible in the form of issues for whose passage he
will constantly agitate. The general catalogue is as
follows:

A constitutional reform prohibiting re-election
of the President of the Republic for the period
immediately following that in which he has exercised
the power of office.

Complete freedom in the next elections with the
express renunciation of my own candidacy and that of
the ministers who form the cabinet, and the total
suppression of all official candidacy.

Immediate raising of the State of Siege in States
subject to this measure as contrary to the Constit -
ution.

Appeal to the patriotism of the revolutionary

---

(1) Sometimes called "The Program of the Government
of the Interim Constitutional President."

leaders [jefes] that their claims do not exceed constitutional limits.

Reorganization of Congress with deputies and senators faithful to their duties and united with alternates for those who have proved delinquent.

Balancing of Income with that of Expenses through economies which may be made in the branches of Administration, Treasury and Development [Fomento], and especially that of War.

Immediate reestablishment of the National Guard in order without danger to make an arrangement with the Army and to anticipate defense of institutions.

Profound respect for individual guarantees which are recognized as the rights of Mankind, and not to consent to the violation of any of them.

Particular inviolability of the Press as a sec - urity for the others, and suppression of subsidized publications.

Reform of the Law of Asylum [amparo] in the sense that immediately there should be opened an appeal for responsibility against the Authority which may have violated any individual guarantee whatever.

Obedience to judicial decisions linked with the complete independence of the judiciary.

Constant respect for the sovereignty of the States in all matters concerning their interior adminis - tration.

Unceasing promotion of Public Instruction, especially in the primary area in its well-defined areas of being free and obligatory.

Development of the best materials especially those relative to construction of railroads in order to transport abroad more easily the fruits of our agriculture and of our industry; in order to revive foreign and domestic trade, and to obtain good income from our maritime customs.

Establishment of a good system of colonization on the basis of essential peace, freedom of religious practices, assurance of individual guarantees, and practical advantages for the colonists.

Faithful observance of treaties now in effect in relation to the nations with whom we have them; and a favorable attitude toward accepting the advances of those who wish to renew relations interrupted through no fault of ours, or to formalize them for the first time.

Total allegiance to the dignity of the nation in respect to appeals designed to re-validate concess - ions which have lapsed.

Immediate and total organization of the Federal District in conformity with the Constitution.

Easements to be granted to the Drainage Works and to the construction of drainage canals in the Valle of Mexico while the Legislature and the Executive shall function as a body with local powers for the District.

Construction of a Mexican Penitentiary which will facilitate the abolition of the death penalty and put an end to the horrible conditions in which the prisons of the City and of Belem find themselves so long as the Powers of the Union shall be those of local [officials] within the District.

* * * * * * * * *

Such is in summary the system of government which I will observe during the short period of my pro - visional administration.

The respective ministries will immediately work with zeal in the development of the parts of the program which relate to their areas. If the idea is

good in its over-all concept, I shall smooth the road
of my successors. If it should be defective, they
will know how to correct the defects from which it
suffers. As far as I am concerned, on leaving a post
for which I have never aspired and to which I have
come in the fulfillment of an ineluctable duty, I
shall carry the satisfaction of having done all that
which was in my power in order to merit the esteem of
the Mexican People.

(Signed)

J. M. Iglesias

Ciro B. Ceballos, Aurora y ocaso, 960 - 961.

* * * * *

PLAN OF SINALOA

25 November, 1876

We the Undersigned:

CONSIDERING: That the legal period of Don Sebastian
Lerdo de Tejada as president of the Republic has come
to its end because although the so-called Congress of
the Union has declared the said citizen re-elected
for the next quadrenium, and the said declarations,
from any point of view, illegal because in the public
conscience there was no election.

CONSIDERING: That the said Congress, convinced that
retaining the present President in power is incomp -
atible with all constitutional order, has again
invested him with extraordinary authority and has
suspended all the guarantees which the Constitution
of 1857, which has cost the Mexican people so much
blood, grants to mankind and to the citizen.

CONSIDERING: That the President of the Supreme Court
of Justice has protested against the usurpation of
Don Lerdo de Tejada and thus respecting the nation

572

will which does not wish to suffer any longer the oppression and tyranny of the present executive.

AND CONSIDERING finally: That it is a duty of all Mexicans to unite to combat dictatorship which is desired to be imposed on the Nation and to save the democratic institutions acquired at such cost: We have agreed upon the following political plan which we promise to defend at the cost of our lives if it should be necessary.

1. We support the Plan of Tuxtepec and Palo Blanco and in consequence we disavow as a depository of Executive Power the Citizen Sebastian Lerdo de Tejada and all the authorities and employees acting under his authorization.

2. General Porfirio Diaz is recognized as the depository of the powers of war and as commanding General of the Constitutionalist Army; and the Licenciado Jose Maria Iglesias [is recognized] as Vice-President.

3. Colonel Jesus Ramirez reassumes political and military control of the State, and who, as soon as the districts of the State may be occupied by the Constitutionalist forces, shall convoke a council [junta] of commanders in order to name a person who should be put in charge of the Government of the State while its constitutional reorganization may proceed.

(Signed)

"Constitution of '57 and   Jesus Ramirez
No Re-election"

Archivo del General Porfirio Diaz, XV, 171.

* * * * *

REVOLUTIONARY PLAN de GARZA

September, 1891

In the trail of Carmen Ibanez before the U.S.

Commissioner the Plan Revolucionario de Garza was
offered in order to show that such a thing as a
revolutionary movement existed at one time on the
Mexican border. Judge McLeary objected to the
testimony on the ground that the translation was not
written in ink. Commissioner Price sustained the
objection. The document is one of the most
interesting pieces of revolutionary literature that
has so far been brought to light in connection with
the Garza affair. (1) (It) is headed

"REVOLUTIONARY PLAN"

The revolutionary plan is conceived and published
with the only purpose of uprooting the tyranny and
despotism of General Porfirio Diaz and restoring the
constitution of 1857. The undersigned Mexican
citizens in full enjoyment of our rights and making
use of the laws conceived by us for our government
and the pursuit of happiness, considering, first that
the people have at all times the right to revoke the
charge of their sovereignty when the executive con -
verts himself into a tyrant and uses his power for
his personal advantage, assert the following reasons
as causes for their action:

FIRST--That General Porfirio Diaz and his cabinet
pervert their power for private advancement, holding
as law the caprices of their will to the end of
satisfying their illegitimate ambition or private
vengeance, and they exceed in cruelty the most
ferocious beasts in order to gratify their avarice
and other distorted passions.

SECOND--That to arrive at that state of affairs
they have demoralized the nation with a system of
subordination, assassinating some and prostituting
others, making them in their company steal and sack
the national treasury, having the people under the
most horrible yoke, suppressing their principal
rights: to wit, the rights of personal security,
individual liberty and the right of property.

---

(1) Comment from the DAILY EXPRESS.

THIRD--That General Porfirio Diaz in his ambition to acquire riches has compromised the future of the nation by thefts, such as the recognizing of the English and Spanish debts, the settlement of the interior debts, contraction of the German and other loans that are at present being negotiated.

FOURTH--That the integrity of the nation is so imminently in danger that in the United States a member has proposed to congress that the American Union utilize its extra funds in the purchase of Lower California, (the same as if they were treating of the purchase of a wild oceanic island) and adducing in support of his proposition the reason that in his opinion Mexico is at present governed by another General Santa Ana [sic].

FIFTH--That this shameful condition has the probabilities of being prolonged to the extent of the life of this autocrat who styles himself president, for his audacity and cynicism have reached the extreme of imposing indefinite re-election after having advocated the principle of no re-election.

SIXTH--And lastly that civil obedience has its limits because the people on being deprived partly of their will and strength to constitute social powers are not compelled to sacrifice completely those rights: that is to say, they do not absolutely abdicate their will and strength only in so much as it is exacted by the good, the prosperity and the security of their co-associates, by reason of all of which we have agreed in proclaiming and sustaining the following

REVOLUTIONARY PLAN

for casting from power General Porfirio Diaz and re-establishing in the country the constitution of 1857.

Article 1. We do not recognize General Porfirio Diaz as president of the Mexican United States, and on being captured he shall be tried as a traitor to the country, to the constitution that he swore to defend, and to the plan of Tuxtepec, which elevated him to power.

Article 2. We equally do not recognize the secretaries of state and government who shall be tried and punished according to the charges which may result to them.

Article 3. The military chiefs or civil authorities of whatever category they may be that should take up arms against this plan shall be held as traitors to the country and punished as such.

Article 4. From and after the publication and circulation of this plan the nation is declared in a state of war, and for its proper execution the Mexican people are convoked to arms.

Article 5. With the same purpose the co-operation of the independent press is solicited.

Article 6. The armed body of men shall be named "Constitution Army". Its watchword shall be 1857 and National Integrity.

Article 7. The frontier writer, Don Catarino E. Garza, is named as chief of the Constitutional army of the north; and Don Francisco Ruiz Sandoval supreme director of the war who shall use the title of General-in-chief of the Constitutional army and supreme director of the war.

Article 8. On taking possession of the capital of the republic the supreme chief director of war shall convoke the country to elections for a constitutional convention which shall be convened in Mexico within four months, counted from the occupation of the country.

Article 9. This constitutional convention will proceed to revise the constitution of 1857, adding or reforming what it may deem proper, but always in accord with the mind of the delegates and in conformity to a liberal federal system.

Article 10. In the constitutional provision spoken of in the foregoing article, the following constitutional principles shall be elevated to precepts:

First--Absolute prohibition of re-election of public functionaries in the country.

Second--Absolute prohibition of election to the presidency of the Mexican United States of any chief or revolutionary officer immediately after triumph, he being qualified only after a presidential term.

Third--To give full liberty to all political parties; forever suppressing that political assassination known by the name of the fugitive law.

Fourth--To remove every obstacle from commerce and industry.

Fifth--To give sovereignty to the states and indep - endence to municipalities.

Sixth--To base all additions or reforms on Democratic principles.

Article 11. The revolution triumphant and the government constituted, all vacant lands shall be distributed among the Mexicans who will agree to cultivate them.

Article 12. The government and other authorities who from now will recognize the present plan shall be retained in their posts provided they fully show that they have behaved themselves honorably during the trying period of Tuxtepec; otherwise they shall be tried by their obedience and respect to the aforesaid plan used as mitigating circumstances; likewise all the military who shall adhere to it shall be recognized in their grades and declarations.

Constitution of 1857 and national integrity!

Free suffrage and no re-election.

On the margin of the Rio Bravo in the state of Tamaulipas, September, 1891.

Signatures: Julian Flores, Santos Cadena, Marcario
Rios, Alejandro Zuinones, C. Garcia Elizondo, Sixto
Longorio, Eustorgio Ramon, Ramon Vasquez, Marcos
Sandoval, Benito Barrientos. Following are more than
a thousand signers.

The San Antonio DAILY EXPRESS

* * * * *

PROGRAM OF THE LIBERAL PARTY

1 July, 1906

An extremely long exposition of protest and
indignation precedes the text of the program which is
given below.

Constitutional Reforms

1. Reduction of the Presidential term to four years.

2. Suppression of the re-election for the President
and for the governors of the States. Those func -
tionaries can be re-elected only after two terms have
intervened since they have been in office.

3. Disqualification of the Vice-President to dis -
charge legislative functions or any other office of
popular election and authorization to the said
official in order to fulfill a charge conferred by
the Executive.

4. Suppression of obligatory military service and
establishment of the National Guard. Those who devote
their services to the standing Army will do it freely
and voluntarily. The military organization will be
revised in order to get rid of that which is con -
sidered oppressive or humiliating to the dignity of
man, and the income of those who are in the National
Militia will be increased.

5. To reform and redraft constitutional Articles 6
and 7, suppressing the restrictions which private
life and public peace impose on the freedom of speech

578

and of press, and declaring in this sense that only lack of truth which entails pain, blackmail, and viola - tions of law relative to moral issues will be punished.

6. Abolition of the death penalty except for traitors to the Fatherland.

7. To make heavier the responsibility of public servants, and imposing severe penalties for the delinquents.

8. Restore the territory of Quintana Roo to Yucatan.

9. Suppression of military tribunals in time of peace.

Improvement and promotion of instruction

10. Multiplication of primary schools on such a scale that those educational institutions which were closed because they belonged to the clergy may be advantag - eously replaced.

11. Obligation to impart a totally lay instruction in all schools of the Republic, be they Government or private institutions, is declared the responsibility of the Directors [of the said schools], even if they do not approve of this precept.

12. To declare instruction until the age of fourteen obligatory, the Government having the duty to provide protection in whatever way possible to poor children who by reason of poverty would lose the benefits of instruction.

13. To pay good salaries to teachers of primary instruction.

14. To make obligatory throughout all the schools of the Republic the teaching of arts and trades, and military instruction and to pay especial attention to civic instruction which now receives so little attention.

Foreigners

15. To prescribe that foreigners by the very act of acquiring real estate lose their original nationality and become Mexican citizens.

16. To prohibit Chinese immigration.

Restrictions on abuses of the Catholic Clergy

17. Church buildings [templos] are considered as places of business and are, therefore, obliged to keep financial records and to pay the corresponding taxes.

18. Nationalization, according to law, of the real estate which the Clergy holds through dummy figureheads.

19. To increase the penalties which the Laws of the Reform provide; for infraction of the same.

20. Suppression of schools run by the Clergy.

Capital and Labor

21. To set a maximum of eight hours of labor and a minimum salary in the following ratio: one peso for the country in general where the average equals this stated amount, and more than one peso for those regions where the cost of living is more expensive and in those where this salary will not be sufficient to rescue the worker from his poverty.

22. Regulation of domestic service and of work in the home.

23. To adopt such measures that for piece work the bosses do not abuse the application of maximum time and minimum pay.

24. To prohibit absolutely the employment of children under the age of fourteen.

25. To require that the owners of mines, factories, and workshops etc. to maintain the best conditions of hygiene on their properties, and to keep the

dangerous areas in conditions which will give safety to the lives of the operatives.

26. To oblige the bosses or rural owners to provide hygienic quarters to laborers when the nature of the work of the latter requires that they receive lodging from the said bosses or owners.

27. To require the bosses to pay indemnity for accidents on the job.

28. To declare null and void the present debts which rural day laborers owe to the masters.

29. To adopt measures by which the landowners do not abuse the co-partners [in a ranch or farm].

30. To oblige the owners of land and houses to indemnify the renters of their property for the necessary improvements which they may leave behind them.

31. To prohibit the owners, under severe penalty, from paying the workers in any other form than that of cash [dinero efectivo]; to prohibit and to punish any who may impose fines on the laborers, or who gives them a reduction in the day's work, or who holds back pay for more than a week, or who refuses immediate payment to anyone leaving his work for what he has already done; to suppress all private ranch stores.

32. To require that all enterprises or businesses to hire among their employees or workers no more than a minority of foreigners. Not to permit in any event that in work of the same sort that they should pay less to the Mexican than to the foreigner in the same establishment, or that the Mexican should be paid in any other form than that of the foreigners.

33. To make obligatory one day's rest in seven.

Lands

34. The owners of land are required to make pro-ductive all the land which they may possess.

Whatever land area the owner leaves unproductive the
State will re-possess and will use it according to
the following articles.

35. To Mexican residents living abroad and who make
application the government will re-patriate them,
paying the cost of their trip and will give them land
for cultivating.

36. The State will give land to whoever solicits it
without any other condition than to devote [the land]
to agricultural production, and not to sell it. The
maximum area which the State may grant to one person
will be established.

37. In order that this benefit may be available not
only to those who have the basic means for cultivation of the land, but also to the poor who lack
these elementary necessities, the State shall create
and promote a Farm Bank which will make loans to poor
farmers at low rates of interest and provide for
repayment in installments.

Taxes

38. Abolition of the tax on moral capital and of the
head tax, and it is recommended that the Government
study the best means for diminishing the Stamp tax
and, if it be possible, its complete abolition.

39. Elimination of all taxes against capital amounts
less than one hundred pesos, excepting from this
privilege all church buildings and other businesses
which are considered undesirable and which ought not
to have the right to the guarantees accorded to
useful enterprises.

40. To tax usury, articles of luxury, vices, and to
lighten taxes on articles of basic necessity. Not to
permit the rich to make agreements with the govern -
ment in order to pay a less amount than the law
imposes on them.

General Points

41. To make the right of injunction [amparo] pract - ical by simplifying the procedures.

42. Restitution of Free Zone.

43. To establish civil equality between the children of the same father, thus abolishing the differences which the present law sets up between the legitimate and the illegitimate.

44. To establish, when possible, penitentiary plantations for rehabilitation in place of the prisons and penitentiaries in which delinquents endure their punishment.

45. Suppression of the political bosses [jefes politicos].

46. Reorganization of the municipalities which have been suppressed, and strengthening of municipal power.

47. Means for suppressing or restricting usury, poverty, and the high price of the basic necessities.

48. Protection of the indigenous race.

49. To establish ties of union with the Latin Amer - ican countries.

50. On the triumph of the Liberal Party the property of the functionaries who were enriched under the present Dictatorship will be confiscated, and what - ever sum may be produced will be applied to the ful - fillment of the Land Charge--especially to offer restitution to the Yaquis, the Mayas, and other trives, whose lands were despoiled--or to the service of amortization of the national Debt.

51. The first National Congress to function after the fall of the Dictorship will annul all the amendments made to our Constitution by the Government of Porfirio Diaz; it will amend our Magna Carta wherever necessary in order to put this Program into effect; it will draft legislation that may be necessary for the same purpose; it will regularize the articles of

583

the Constitution and the other laws which may require
it, and it will study all those questions which it
considers of interest to the Country whether or not
they may have been enunciated in this Plan, and it
will strengthen the points contained here, especially
in relation to Work and Land.

Special Proviso

52. The Organizing Committee [Junta] of the Liberal
Party is hereby directed to address the foreign
governments as soon as possible and to make clear to
them in the name of the Party that the Mexican People
do not wish more debts piled up against the Country
and, therefore, that it will not recognize any debt
which, under any form or pretext which the
Dictatorship has brought upon the Nation, either
through contracting debts or else by recognizing
after long delay past obligations which have no legal
value.

Reform, Freedom, Justice.
St. Louis, Missouri   Ricardo Flores Magon

            (Other signatures)

Silva Herzog, La revolucion Mexicana, I, 96-101.

F. Barrera Fuentes, Historia de la revolucion
Mexicana: la etapa precursoria.

Felipe Tena, Leyes fundamentales de Mexico,
1910-1967, 728-732.

* * * * *

PLATFORM OF THE ANTI-REELECTIONIST PARTY
Adopted at the National Convention of April, 1910.

First: To re-establish the rule of the Constitution
of 1857, making effective the obligations and rights
that it precribes, such as the independence of the
authorities of the Federation and the responsibi -
lities of civil servants.

Second: To secure the reform of the Constitution, establishing the principle of no re-election of the President and Vice-President of the Republic. To secure the same reform in the constitutions of the states by which Governors are seleted, and to make effective the stipulation of residence in the dis - trict, territory, or state, for the election of deputies and senators.

Third: To secure the reform of the electoral law, in order to achieve the effectiveness of the suffrage. To increase the authority and freedom of the municipal governments and to secure the elimination of the _Jefaturas_ and _Prefecturas Politicas_.

Fourth: To regulate article seven of the federal constitution, to make effective the freedom of the press.

Fifth: To improve and develop public instruction and break the bonds that restrain academic freedom.

Sixth: To improve the material, intellectual, and moral conditions of the worker, creating factory schools, securing the passage of laws for pensions or indemnification for labor accidents, and combating alcoholism and gambling. To have equal solicitude for the indigenous people in general, especially the Maya and the Yaqui Indians, repatriating those despoiled and founding agricultural cultrual colonies on national lands, or those that can be acquired for that purpose. To accelerate the employment of Mexican railroad personnel at all levels, putting into law the special educational schools that will be necessary.

Seventh: To favor the development of public wealth; to assess taxes equitably, to abolish the system of inequities and to combat monopolies and privileges; and above all, to take care that the public funds are invested in the commonwealth of the Nation.

Eight: To foster large, and especially small, agriculture and irrigation, to which will be assigned a portion of the public funds. Regarding mining, industry, and commerce, they will be conceded all the franchises that will assure their development and prosperity.

Ninth: To study and to put into practice the most efficient methods to improve the army so that it be better able to accomplish the high duty that it is charged with: that of guarding the institutions and defending the honor and integrity of the Republic. Military instruction will be made obligatory as one of the principal means.

Tenth: To tighten the good relations with foreign countries, especially with those of Latin America, and prudently to direct the policy of the government to obtain a union of the Central American Nations.

Mexico, April 26, 1910.   Francisco I. Madero

                              Francisco Vazquez Gomez

From Roque Estrada, La revolucion, 220-222.

Reprinted from Insurgent Governor, Abraham Gonzalez and the Mexican Revolution in Chihuahua, by William H. Beezley, by permission of University of Nebraska Press. Copyright (C) 1973 by the University of Nebraska Press.

Also Barrera Fuentes, Historia de la revolucion: La etapa precursora (Mex. 1955)

* * * * *

REVOLUTIONARY PLAN OF DZELKOOP (1)

                              10 May, 1910

After a reasonably short list of "Considerandos", the final one declares "Whereas, from what has been said the time has come to make a powerful effort to save the country, and the People ought to make the supreme effort in order to end the torment that consumes them and threatens to destroy them com -

---

(1) While issued to secure immediate overthrow of state administration, success of the Plan presumed a national military victory.

586

pletely. We have agreed to the present Plan which is the true expression, the true advantage, and the only salvation of the People and of the State [Yucatan].

Art. 1. The present government of Enrique Munoz Aristegui is hereby repudiated as illegal by virtue of the fact that it has not been sanctioned by the sovereign people.

Art. 2. A governing Committee [Junta] is to be named, and is to be composed of seven individuals of re - cognized capacity, love of order and unquestioned patriotism in order to save the state from the ruin which threatens it through the imperious and despotic attitude of our bureaucratic enemies.

Art. 3. From this Committee will be named two individuals from the Capital, one from the Division of the East, another from the Division from the South, another from the Division of the Coast, and two from the so-called Territory of Quintana Roo, which we believe in all justice belongs to us. All these individuals, with the extraordinary powers granted under this Plan will govern the State within a month or earlier, if it should be possible, under the system which now prevails.

Art. 4. The components of the Committee will be named by the leader of the Revolution, in agreement with the other officials who may accompany them, in the place considered most convenient.

Art. 5. The Committee will declare, preferentially, the most urgent measures for making individual freedom effective so that in this way the abuses will cease and so will others as circumstances warrant, with the Administration taking care to keep public credit inviolate and respecting the obligations of just creditors of the State and arranging in the best way possible the best means of satisfying them, excepting the creditors who contract with the present government to defeat this Plan or [are considered] favorable to it in Public Opinion.

Art. 6. Both civilian and military employees who oppose the progress of this Plan will be discharged from their posts and will be held responsible for damages which may result through their obstinacy.

Art. 7. All persons who are proved to be spies in order to block this Plan will be shot, and for this act it will not be necessary to form a Council of War.

Art. 8. All informers and traitors who may be discovered among us will be tried before a Council of War with all vigor and obvious resolution.

Art. 9. The leaders [caudillos] of this Revolution are Cols. Maximiliano R. Bonilla and Jose Cristano Chi, to whom are granted the necessary powers for saving the State and bringing about the rule of public opinion.

Art. 10. Let copies be sent to other towns within the State so that they may support this Plan in the same terms.

Issued in the town of Dzelkoop. (Signatures follow)

F. Barrera Fuentes, Historia de la revolucion Mexicana: la etapa precursora, 293-295.

* * * * *

PLAN OF SAN LUIS POTOSI

5 October, 1910

After a long condemnation of the Diaz regime, Madero concluded his list of inequities by declaring:

I have designated Sunday, the 20th of next November, from six o'clock in the afternoon and thereafter in all the towns of the Republic, that [the people] should arise in arms under the following Plan:

1st. The elections for President and Vice-President of the Republic, for magistrates of the Supreme Court

of the Nation, for deputies and senators as celebrated in June and July of the current year are
declared null.

2nd. The present Administration of General Diaz is
repudiated, as well as all the officials whose power
ought to spring from the will of the People, because
besides not having been elected by the People they
have lost whatever title they could have had of
legality, committing and assisting with all the
elements which the People put at their disposition
for the defense of their interests the most
scandalous electoral fraud ever registered in Mexican
history.

3rd. In order to avoid in so far as possible the
disturbances inherent in any revolutionary movement,
all laws promulgated by the present administration
and the regulations appertaining thereto are declared
in effect while intending in due course to revise
constitutionally and by constitutional means those
which require reform, while excepting those laws
which obviously are not found contrary to the
principles proclaimed in this Plan. Likewise a survey
of the laws, decisions of the Courts and decrees
which may have authorized the accounts and management
of funds of all the agencies of the Porfirista Administration in all brances; because when the Revolution
shall triumph the formation of investigative comm -
issions will begin in order to determine the
responsibilities which the functionaries of the
Federation of the State and of the Municipalities may
have incurred. In any case the engagements contracted
by the Porfirista Administration with foreign
governments and corporations before the 20th of the
coming month will be respected.

Through the abuse of the Law of Public Lands
numerous small proprietors, the majority of them
indigenous Indians, have been despoiled of their
lands through agreement with the Secretary of
Development [fomento] or through decisions of the
courts of the Republic. It being no more than justice

to the former owners of the land of which they have
been robbed in so arbitrary a fashion that such
dispositions and decisions are declared subject to
revision, and it will be required of those who
acquired [the lands] in so immoral a manner, or of
their heirs, that they restore them to the original
owners to whom they shall also pay indemnities for
the damages suffered. Only in case that these lands
have been passed to third persons before the
promulgation of this Plan, the former owners will
receive indemnity from those for whose benefit the
spoilation was accomplished.

4th. In addition to the Constitution and the laws now
in force, the principle of NO RE-ELECTION of the
President and Vice-President of the Republic, of
governors of the States and of presidents of municipalities is declared the Supreme Law of the
Republic until the respective constitutional reforms
can be effected.

5th. I assume the position of provisional President
of the United Mexican States with the necessary
powers to make war on the usurper government of
General Diaz. As soon as the capital of the Republic
and more than half of the states of the Federation
are in possession of the forces of the People, the
provisional President shall issue a call for special
general elections for the month thereafter and he
will deliver the power to the President who may have
been elected as soon as the results of the election
have been determined.

6th. The provisional President, before surrendering
power, shall give an account to the Congress of the
Union of the use he has made of the powers which the
present Plan confers upon him.

7th. On the 20th of November after six o'clock and
thereafter all citizens of the Republic will take up
arms in order to throw out of office the authorities
who are presently in office. The people who may be
deprived of means of communication shall so act after

sunset.

8th. When authorities offer armed resistance, they will be required by force of arms to respect the popular will, but in this case the laws of war will be rigorously observed; their attention is called to [the prohibitions against] the shooting of prisoners. Also, attention is called in respect to the duty of every Mexican to respect foreigners in regard to their persons and their property.

9th. The authorities who offer resistance to the realization of this Plan will be sent to prison in order that they may be tried by the courts of the Republic when the revolution shall have ended. As soon as each city or town recovers its freedom the chief military commander will be recognized as the legitimate provisional authority with the power to delegate this function to some other designated person who will be confirmed in his office or removed by the Provisional Government. One of the principal measures of the Provisional Government will be to set at liberty all political prisoners.

10th. The nomination of a Provisional Governor of each State which has been occupied by the forces of the Revolution will be made by the provisional President. This Governor will have the strict obligation of calling elections for a constitutional Governor for the State as soon as possible in the opinion of the provisional President. Excepted from this requirment are the States which within two years from this date have had democratic campaigns to change the Government, because in these [elections] he who was the candidate of the people will be considered the provisional governor, provided he actively adheres to this Plan. In case the provisional President has not made a nomination or that the nomination has not arrived to its destined place, or that the grantee does not accept for whatever circumstances, then the Governor will be designated by a vote of the military leaders

who are operating in the territory of the respective
State, provided that his nomination be ratified by
the provisional President as soon as possible.

11th. The new officers will use all the funds which
are found in all the public offices for the ordinary
expenses of administration; for the costs of the war
they will collect loans, either voluntary or forced.
These latter only with citizens or national institutions. A careful account shall be made of these
loans, and receipts in due form will be given to
those concerned so that with the triumph of the
Revolution that which was borrowed may be returned.

Transitory provisions

A. The commanders of the volunteer forces will take
the rank which corresponds to the number of troops
under their command. In cases of volunteer forces and
regular military units, the highest ranking officer
shall take command, but in case that both commanders
have the same rank, the command will pass to the
professional military officer. Civilian military
officers will enjoy the benefit of their military
rank while the war continues, and once ended those
nominated at the request of interested parties will
be reviewed by the Secretary of War who will confirm
some in their rank or reject them according to their
merits.

B. All commanders, civilian as well as military, will
see that their troops observe the strictest discipline because they will be responsible before the
provisional Government for the excesses which the
troops under their command may commit unless they can
explain that it was not possible to control the
soldiers, and that they had imposed on the culprits
due punishment. The most severe penalties will be
applied to the soldiers who sack a town or who kill
defenseless prisoners.

C. If the forces and the authorities who support

General Diaz shoot their prisoners of war, not for that [reason] or in retaliation will the same be done with those who fall into our power; but, on the other hand, the civilian authorities and military officers in the sevice of General Diaz will be shot within twenty-four hours and after a summary trial if, once the Revolution has broken out, they have ordered in any form or have transmitted an order, or have shot any of our soldiers. Not even the highest function - aries will be exempt from this penalty; the only exception will be General Diaz and his ministers to whom, in case they have ordered the said executions or have permitted it, the same penalty will be applied to them, but after having been judged by the courts of the Republic when the Revolution has ended. In the event that General Diaz orders that the laws of war should be respected and that prisoners who should fall into his hands will be humanely treated, his life will be spared, but in any event he will have to answer before the courts about how he has managed the wealth of the nation and how he has fulfilled the law.

D. Since it is an indispensable requisite in the laws of warfare that belligerent troops should wear some uniforms or distinctive mark, and since it would be difficult to uniform the numerous forces of the people who are going to take part in the struggle, a three-colored ribbon worn on the hat or tied around the arm will be adopted as the distinctive [identi-fication] of the liberating forces, whether they be volunteers or of the regular military establishment.

FELLOW CITIZENS: If I call upon you to take up arms and to overthrow the Government of General Diaz, it is not only for the crimes which he has committed during the latest election, but also to save the country from the dark future which awaits it under the dictatorship and under the Administration of the nefarious scientific oligarchy which without scruple and so rapidly are absorbing and destroying the national resources, and if we permit them to continue in power in a very short time they will have completed their work: they will have sucked up all its riches and have left it in utmost misery; they will have caused the bankruptcy of the Fatherland, so that weak, impoverished, and shackled, it will find itself helpless to defend its frontiers, its honor, and its institutions.

As for myself, I have a tranquil conscience and no one can accuse me of promoting a Revolution for personal advantage because it is common knowledge that I did everything possible to arrive at a peace - ful arrangement and I was ready to announce my candidacy provided that General Diaz would have permitted the Nation to designate who should be the Vice-President of the Republic. But dominated by incomprehensible pride and by an unheard of haughtiness, he was deaf to the voice of the Fatherland, and he preferred to precipitate it into a Revolution rather than concede the least point, rather than return to the people an atom of their rights, rather than fulfilling, even though it should be in the last years of his life, the promises which he made at La Noria and Tuxtepec.

He himself justified the present Revolution when he said, "Let no citizen impose himself and perpet - uate himself in the exercise of power and this will be the last revolution."

If the interests of the Fatherland had weighed more in the mind of General Diaz than the sordid interests of himself and of his counsellors, this Revolution would have been avoided by making some concessions to the people, but he has not done so. So much the better!--the change will be more rapid, more radical, because the Mexican people, instead of cry - ing like a coward, will accept the challenge like a brave man, and while General Diaz pretends to help himself by use of brute force to impose an ignominous yoke, the people will take recourse to this same force in order to shake off that yoke and to toss this dismal man from power and to reconquer its freedom.

San Luis Potosi.   Francisco I. Madero

Effective suffrage to Re-election

Silva Herzog, La revolucion Mexicana, I, 133-142.

* * * * *

SOCIO-POLITICAL PLAN

18 March, 1911

Proclaimed by the States of Guerrero, Michoacan, Tlaxcala, Campeche, Puebla, and the Federal District.

After three paragraphs of Considerandos the representatives of the States concluded, "We proclaim the following Plan and invite all our fellow citizens to adopt it in order to agree thus on the necessities of the nation and on an epoch of regeneration and reform."

I. The President and Vice-President of the Republic are repudiated, along with the senators and deputies, as well as all the rest of the employees who are elected by popular vote, on account of the omissions, frauds, and pressures which took place in the previous elections.

II. General Diaz with his ministers, Miguel Macedo who fills the position of subsecretary of Government, the members of the united commissions which voted for the suspension of guarantees, the judges who, having under their charge the trials of the so-called political criminals, have violated the Law by obeying a countersign, a slogan, or they have withheld a sentence of justice, Traitors to the cause and all the commanders of the Army are outlaws: they will be judged according to the dispositions that they have taken in respect to the revolutionaries.

III. Senor Francisco I. Madero is recognized as provisional President and supreme leader [jefe] of the Revolution.

IV. The Constitution of 1857, the Free Vote, and No Re-election are proclaimed as the supreme law.

V. The Press Law will be reformed in a clear and precise way so as to determine those cases where a person may justly complain of defamation, as well as determining those cases also in which it is a criminal offense to disturb public order by paying attention to the causes and the reasons of the act so as to punish the guilty party in due fashion if the disturbance really constitutes a crime.

VI. The suppressed municipalities will be reorganized.

VII. Centralization of education is abolished forthwith, and established in its place is a federation of the same.

VIII. The indigenous race will be protected in every sense of the word, promoting thus by every means its dignity and its prosperity.

IX. All the property which has been usurped by the present Administration in order to give it to favorites will be returned to its former owners.

X. The daily wage of all workers of both sexes will be increase, both in the countryside as well as in the city, in relation to the return on capital, for which purpose commissions of competent persons for each case will be named, and these will decide in view of the data the necessities for each situation.

XI. The hours of labor will not be less than eight nor exceed nine.

XII. Foreign enterprises established in the Republic will employ on their jobs at least half Mexican nationals, both in subordinate positions as well as in superior posts, with the same salaries, considerations, and perogatives which [the foreign firms] grant to their compatriots.

XIII. As soon as circumstances permit, the value of urban property will be revised in order to establish an equality in rentals, and so avoiding [a situatin where] the poor pay a higher rent relative to the capital invested than these properties represent. Thus it is intended to secure subsequently jobs for construction of sanitary and comfortable housing with long-term mortgages for the working classes.

XIV. All property owners who have more land than they can or they wish to cultivate are obliged to surrender these untilled lands to those who ask for

596

them. The owners, for their part, have the right to expect a return of 6% annually corresponding to the money value of the land.

XV. All monopolies of whatever class are hereby abolished.

Free vote and no reelection   (Signed)

Sierra de Guerrero   Representatives
                                     of the States.

Silva Herzog, La revolucion Mexicana, I, 143-166.

* * * * *

REVOLUTIONARY PLAN OF CABORCA

10 April, 1911

Fellow Patriots:

The undersigned Mexican citizens in the exercise of our rights, declare: That the suffering and the misery of the Mexican people through bad administration which they have had to endure for thirty years; that the injustice with which the present despots treat them has reached such a point that they have deprived them of the means of livelihood, reducing them to the level of outcasts. Therefore, desiring to look for the means of freeing our dear Fatherland from so distressing a condition, and having used the means which the laws provide for achieving it and never did we get our complaints heard and our desires respected by those charged with this duty, we have had to appeal to the last resort -force of arms in order to free us from a condition so disasterous since we do not have secure even the right to live.

In such a case we declare:

First: We repudiate the present Government because its members were not named in conformity with our law.

Second: We accept the Plan of San Luis Potosi dated 5 October, 1910 in all its parts.

Third: We sustain the principle of Effective Suffrage, No Reelection.

Fourth: We will fight for the principles of strict justice and of liberty, and we will not exercise against our conquered enemies any act of vengeance, because our action is only that of defending our - selves against our executioners.

Issued at Caborca.   (Signatures)
_____

    Gonzalez Ramirez, <u>Planes politicos, y otros documentos</u> 50-51.

* * * * *

PROGRAM AND BASES: POPULAR EVOLUTIONIST PARTY

5 June, 1911

The concluding sentence of the <u>Considerandos</u> reads, "The only way to block the personal Government here - after, and by the same token, to create and sustain a regimen of national Government is by adopting the following

"PLAN"

1st. Respect for the political and administrative sovereignty of the States through the free election of its authorities and the reorganization of its local militias or national guards.

2nd. Constitution of a Federal Legislative Power, really and completely independent of the Executive Power, also by means of the free election of its [legislative] assemblies.

3rd. Real and effective independence of the Judicial Power, a thing which can be secured by abandoning its elective origin, and through the permanence of magistrates and judges [on the bench], accompanied by an effective law on their responsibilities.

598

4th. Diffusion in all classes, especially in the indigenous race, of rudimentary education which shall consist of instruction in the Spanish language, of reading and writing, and of the primary arithmetical functions. Also some orientation in a practical sense of their activity in industry, farming, and in trade.

5th. Development of sentiments and concepts of patriotism in a form which brings assurance of social cooperation instead of promoting the germs of social dissolution and of anarchy in the country. The adoption of real and effective, although gradual, obligatory military service will be one of the most characteristic methods of promoting these sentiments and notions of patriotism.

6th. Absolute suppresion of personal taxes, whatever the name or appearance may be given to it, since it is completely innocuous in its base and cruel in its compulsory proceedings.

7th. Reform of the laws governing ownership of land, including the right to use of water, for the purpose of demanding more than technical perfection of the title, [such as] the practical and juridicial importance of immemorial possession, with which indigenous [i.e. Indian] property will be approved and whose unfamiliarity [with the law] has given rise to so many public disturbances.

In order to carry on to an end this double political and social program, it is not sufficient that it should be adopted or agreed to by the person who assumes the Presidency of the Republic; this would mean that its success would have to depend for its success upon one personality.

It is necessary that the whole program be adopted by the Nation or by a very considerable group of citizens who are lovers of the country, and that this group should organize in a political party which will operate systematically under its own discipline.

What we propose, then, is to publicize the political and social bases before mentioned, to recruit

followers for these bases, to organize them into a
Party and to work in the next elections, so that the
local Authorities of the States and the Federal
Congress should be composed of men belonging to the
Party who would assume the obligation of supporting
their platform until they had made it triumphant.

The Party which is to be constituted, conse -
quently, does not have for its object the nomination
of a particular person for President or Vice -
President of the Republic; it does not have as its
purpose the opposition to the nomination of this or
that person as a candidate; it is not devoted to
special interests nor to personal ambitions.

In its [political] clubs all citizens who accept
its platform can be affiliated, provided that they
are honorable. For the present the Party will work in
the election of Deputies and Senators, and in the
elections of Governors and Legislatures of the State,
and it will have as its purpose to voice its policy,
a policy eminently national, by means of the
Authorities thus consituted.

In a word, it will be the realization of this
ideal: the government of a Nation by a Nation,
embodied not only in the President of the Republic
but in the Legislative Body and in the Legislative
and Executive Authorities of the States.

Jorge Vera Estanol

Original print, New York Public Library; Jorge Vera
Estanol, Historia de la Revolucion Mexicana; 228-229.

* * * * *

PLAN OF TEXCOCO

23 August, 1911

1. The Federal Government over which Lic. don

600

Francisco Leon de la Barra presides is hereby repu - diated. Equally, the governments of the States, and the Federal Districts which presently function are disavowed, and throughout the whole Republic the constitutional order is suspended in the functioning of the Legislative Authorities and the Federal Exec- utive and the local administrations of the States until by the complete domination of the revolutionary forces effective peace in all the Republic is made really and truly effective, and one can be assured without danger of some upset the advance of the reforms contained in the revolutionary laws which form an integral part of this Plan.

2nd. The undersigned will assume the functions of the Legislative and Executive Powers, which are hereby suspended until constitutional order is reestablished in the country.

3rd. The Undersigned will assume the functions which are abrogated until a special Council is formed--one to be composed of the following persons: Lic. don Emilio Vazquez Gomez, Ing. don Manuel Bonilla, Gen. don Pazcual Orozco, Gen. don Emiliano Zapata, Gen. don Camerino Mendoza, Gen. don Rafael Tapia, and Sr. don Paulino Martinez--the first three persons mentioned before to form a government until it is possible to return to a constitutional order.

4th. In case the undersigned should die, the first commander [jefe] with superior command who proclaims it shall take the leadership of the movement; and if the Council should be constituted and one of its members should die, the two remaining will freely elect the third, and if all three should die, then the person whom the revolutionaries acting in obedience to this Plan shall accept will assume the power.

5th. Pursuant to this Plan the leaders of the Liberating Army and who have superior commands and who adhere to the Plan in its entirety will be assigned as military commanders of the State, the Federal Districts, and the Territories; by the same token the Commander-in-Chief will assume his position, and if he does not do it at once, the person next in line below him, or the one thereafter through the respective ranks, and so successively until [the leadership] falls upon some person, and this one will accept it without hesitation.

6th. The military commanders will dissolve immediately the Legislative and Executive authorities of the entities under their command, but they shall exercise no legislative function whatever, this [authority] for all legislative action in the Republic being reserved for the undersigned himself and for the Council when this Plan comes into effect.

7th. The military commanders of the States will proceed immediately to the execution of the laws which form an integral part of this revolutinary Plan.

8th. The undersigned assumes the responsibility for the actions of the Nation in its relations with foreign countries; the revolution from this day henceforth will be responsible for the lives and interests of foreigners within the Nation, and it will act through the operation of military court - martial to punish all acts of destruction which may be committed.

9th. All general and local laws as expedited until now are declared in effect, with the exception of those which are to determine the personnel of the Legislative and Executive Authorities of the Fed - eration and of the States which are functioning; and all the aforementioned laws as well as those which have called for elections for the renovation of the said Authorities are also annulled.

10th. By virtue of this Plan all the complementary dispositions of the essentials which it contains for the constitution of the Council are declared in operation, so that this same Council may provide the necessities of the Government of the Republic.

Issued at Texcoco.   Andres Molina Enriquez

Gonzalez Ramirez, Planes politicos y otros documentos, 71-72.

* * * * *

PLAN OF BERNARDO REYES

16 November, 1911

The revised Plan is as follows:

1st. The so-called elections in the month of October of the present year for President and Vice-President of the Republic are declared null, for in reality they were conducted through the impositions and persecutions of only one political faction and not by the Nation.

2nd. All existing authorities who do not second this Plan are repudiated herewith.

3rd. All current laws and respective regulations now in force which do not conflict with this Revolu - tionary Plan remain in effect under the concept that in due course they will be revised in conformity with constitutional prescriptions--those which are demand- ed in order to harmonize the legislation of the Republic with the ideas which are proclaimed. The provisions and laws approving verified expenses in the previous Administration and of the Interim Government which followed it are also nullified and to be subjected to suitable review according to the revision and comprobation of accounts which will be verified at the triumph of the Revolution. In any case the obligations contracted with foreign governments or companies until that date will be respected.

4th. Especially subject to revision and in a position to be annulled are all agreements, dispositions, decrees, and sentences referring to alienation of land declared public domain and which previously were owned [privately], and likewise the verified owners are due proper restitutions.

5th. Besides the Constitution, treaties, and Federal Laws, the principle of No Reelection of the Pres - ident, Vice-President, Governors of the States and Presidents of Municipalities is declared the Supreme Law of the Republic.

6th. By means of laws and whatever regulations it may be necessary to expedite, the elections of the Republic will be truly free and effective.

7th. The Undersigned assumes the character of Prov - isional President of the Republic with authority to wage war against the bastard power existing in the same until victory is achieved, after which, con - sulting with the leaders who have joined in the struggle, they will name an Interim President who will summon the people to an election of all auth- orities.

8th. When the Congress which has resulted from these elections has met, the Undersigned, in his character as Chief of the Revolution and Interim President will give an account of his actions.

9th. In the States where the higher authorities accept this Plan, they will continue their admin - istration, limited by the action of the military chief of the highest rank who occupies each of the respective territories, and in the places where the existing authorities oppose resistance to the real - ization of this Plan, or where they may prove in any way hostile, the superior commander shall take both political and military command. When officers of equal category meet, those who are career soldiers shall assume command, and in equality of all cir - cumstance, then the one of greater seniority and rank.

10th. The Interim President and the State authorties who may call the elections cannot be elected.

11th. The military commander who, according to the second article may have taken military and political command of a State, will name whomsoever is to substitute for him on having to leave the territory on account of the exigencies of war.

12th. All the political and military authorities who combine to bring the triumph of the Revolution have the right to present a detailed bill for the sums that were used for their expenses, and reimbursement coming from the Public Treasury or from any other source. They shall keep an account of all items of value which they collect and fairly evaluate what they may receive in arms, horses, fodder, food supplies, and other effects and always they shall issue to interested parties receipts which, when the costs of the Revolution are being verified, shall bear an interest rate of one percent monthly rate over the sums voluntarily secured.

13th. The leaders who may organize forces and are not men with military career nor may not be in a place where they may find command officers who can confirm their rank or intending to issue it to them will assume the rank that corresponds to the number of men and according to the units which they present. The commanders, officers, and those arising from the Revolution will enjoy their respective ranks which will be ratified according to their services by the Secretary of that branch [of the armed services]. In every case a certificate will be issued to comm - anders, officers and enlisted men who have served the cause for their own satisfaciton. In order to be perfectly fair, it might be preferred to draw up a list of personnel of the Administration.

14th. Every military or other authority in operations who adhere to the present Plan will have the respon - sibility and within their jurisdiction to make every effort to maintain order in the towns and discipline in the troops.

15th. The distinctive insignia of the revolutionary troops which will form the Army, to be called the Constitutionalist, shall consist of a red ribbon on the hat or on the left arm.

16th. After its triumph the Revolution offers a revision of the Stamp Law and the moderation of all classes of taxes, and to inititate it in a constit - utional form, and to support it, the reestablishment of the Free Zone along the whole northern frontier of the Republic.

Plan of San Luis revised and   (Signed)

issued at Soledad, Tamaulipas.   Bernardo Reyes

Gonzalez   Ramirez,   Planes   politicos   y   otros
documentos. 65-67.

* * * * *

PLAN OF AYALA

28 November, 1911

We, the Undersigned, organized as a Revolutionary
body [Junta] in order to support and bring to
realization the Revolutionary promises made the 10th
of November last, declare solemnly before the
civilized world which judges us and before the Nation
to which we belong and which we love the propositions
which we have formulated in order to bring an end to
tyranny which oppresses us and to redeem the Father -
land from the dictatorship which oppresses us. [These
propositions] are set forth in the following Plan.

Art. 1. [This Article beginning "Taking into
consideration..." embodies the Considerandos of the
traditional Plan and in strenuous language states the
reasons for repudiation of the Francisco I. Madero
regime. The positive proposals of the Plan are set
forth in successive Articles.]

Art. 2. Commandante Francisco I. Madero is repudiated
as chief of the Revolution as well as President of
the Republic for reasons heretofore expressed and
which have brought about the overthrow of this
functionary.

Art. 3. The Eminent Commander General Pascual Orozco,
second in command of the Leader Francisco I. Madero
is recognized as Chief of the Revolution; and in case
he may not be able to accept this delicate post, then
Commandante Emiliano Zapata will be recognized as
Chief of the Revolution.

606

Art. 4. The Revolutionary Committee [Junta] of the State of Morelos declares to the Nation under formal protestation: THAT it accepts as it own the Plan of San Luis Potosi with the additions expressed below, for the benefit of oppressed towns, and it makes itself defender of the principles which it will defend either to victory or death.

Art. 5. The Revolutionary Committee of the State of Morelos does not accept either the transactions or political compromises which did not lead to the overthrow of the dictatorial forces of Porfirio Diaz and Don Francisco I. Madero, because the Nation is tired of deceitful men and traitors who make promises as liberators, but on gaining power forget them and set themselves up as tyrants.

Art. 6. As an additional part of the Plan which we support, we make the following declaration: THAT the lands, mountains, and waters and all landed properties which the big landowners [hacendados], that fancy politicians [cientificos)] or the pol - itical hacks [caciques] under shadow of tyranny and of venal justice usurped will be turned over at once to the towns or to the citizens who have proper titles to these properties, [property] of which they have been dispoiled through the bad faith of our oppressors, these [citizens and towns] maintaining by all means, arms in hand, this said possession, and the usurpers who may consider that they have equal rights with them may present their case before special tribunals which will be established on the triumph of the Revolution.

Art. 7. By virtue of the fact that the immense majority of the towns and Mexican Citizens are no longer owners of the soil which they set foot upon, suffering the horrors of poverty without being able to improve their social condition in the least, neither by turning to industry nor to agriculture, for both lands, mountains and waters are monopolized by a restricted number of people. For this reason one-third of these monopolies will be expropriated by prior indemnification to the powerful owners in order that the towns and the citizens of Mexico may obtain

public lands [ejidos], new lands, rural property for
towns, and fields for sowing or for cultivation, and
in all ways may improve that which was lacking for
the prosperity and well-being of all Mexicans.

Art. 8. The big landowners, fancy politicians, or
party hacks who directly or indirectly may oppose
this present Plan shall have their property nationalized and two-thirds of what belongs to them will be
destined for war indemnities, pensions to widows and
orphans of the victims who succumbed in the fight for
the present Plan.

Art. 9. In order to execute the proceedings in
respect to the properties hertofore mentioned, the
laws of disentailment will be applied as is conven -
ient. However, normally the example put into effect
by the immortal Juarez against ecclesiastical
property ought to serve as an example; exemplary
punishment was served up to despots and conservatives
who in all ages have pretended to impose on us the
ignominious yoke of oppression and reaction.

Art. 10. The insurgent Military Commanders of the
Republic who rose up with arms in hand at the call of
Don Francisco I. Madero in order to defend the Plan
of San Luis Potosi and who now are opposing this
present Plan with armed force will be judged as
traitors to the cause which they we defending and to
the Fatherland since, in the present situation, many
of them through accomodation of tyrants, for a hand -
ful of money or through bribery or subornation are
spilling the blood of their brothers who are calling
out for the fulfillment of the promises made to the
nation by Don Francisco I. Madero.

Art. 11. All the costs of war will be covered in
accord with that prescribed in Art. IX of the Plan of
San Luis Potosi, and all the proceedings employed by
the Revolution which we support will be in conformity
with the identical instructions which the Plan itself
provides.

Art. 12. Once the Revolution which we have brought to
the point of realization has triumphed, a Committee

[Junta] of the principal revolutionary leaders [jefes] of the various states will name or designate an interim President of the Republic who will call for elections in order to form a new Congress of the Union, and this [body] then will call for elections for the organization of the other federal branches.

Art. 13. The principal revolutionary chiefs in each State in committee will designate the provisional governor of the State to which they belong, and this functionary, thus elevated, shall call for elections for the designated organization of the public auth - orities with the object of avoiding the countersigns which ornament the unhappy of the towns, such as the well-known countersign of Ambrosio Figueroa in the State of Morelos and others which brought us to the beginning of the bloody conflicts supported by the caprice of the Dictator Madero and of the circle of fancy politicans and landowners who have suggested it.

Art. 14. If President Madero and the other dictator - rial elements of the present and former regime desire to avoid the terrible misfortunes which afflict the Fatherland, let them immediately renounce the offices which they now hold, and with their act they will somewhat close the great wounds which they have opened in the breast of the Fatherland, for if they do not do this then on their heads will flow the blood poured out by our brothers.

Art. 15. Mexicans: Remember that the cunning and bad faith of a man is spilling blood in a scandalous way through being incompetent to govern. Remember that his system of government is shackling the Fatherland, and shackling with brute force of bayonets our institutions. And so as we now raise our arms in order to lift [the Fatherland] to power, we turn our weapons against him for having defaulted in his obligations to the Mexican people and of having betrayed the Mexican Revolution. We are not followers of a person; we are partisans for principle and not of men.

Mexican People: Support with arms in hand this

Plan and you will promote the prosperity and well-being of the Fatherland.

Ayala, November 28, 1911.   (Signed)

Emiliano Zapata and others.

Jorge Vera Estanol, Historia de la Revolucion Mexicana, 253-256.

* * * * *

PLAN OF SANTA ROSA

2 February, 1912

We, the Undersigned, commit ourselves to realize by means of arms the definitive triumph of the Plan of San Luis Potosi, betrayed by "scientific modernism." We add to the said Plan the following articles:

1st. The slogan on our flag is LAND AND JUSTICE.

2nd. On grounds of prior public need, through legal formalities expropriation of Public Land will be decreed, excepting the land occupied by urban prop - erty, [the land] with buildings constructed which they generally call 'hacienda shells,' factories, farms, and lands owned by railroads. The Government will remain the exclusive owner forever of the prop - erties and it will rent them only to those who apply for them and in amounts which they can cultivate personally and with members of their family. Also, grazing lands will be rented to private individuals, providing that their disposition corresponds with the purposes of equity which the prior clause seeks [to provide].

3rd. The code of civil proceedings and penalties will be revised in order to make possible rapid distrib - ution of justice.

4th. The electoral law will punish with prison and fine those Town Councils which do not distribute the tickets for elections with reasonable dispatch or may in some way cheat on the right of suffrage; and [it] will punish with prison those citizens who with tricks evade the vote.

5th. The States shall have their own militias and the Federation will not be able to command these forces unless their respective Executives solicit them in accord with prior agreement with the local Legis - latures. The Legislative Houses of the Union will determine the places where forts or emcampment sites of the Federal Army will be established.

6th. Hereafter the Federation will not receive the tax known under the title of "The Federal 20%" unless the States will devote it to the increase of educa - tion of the indigenous race; this tax will be called "the 20% Indian education fund."

7th. The Secretaries of State of the President of the Republic will be named by him, and will be respon - sible, both personally and financially before the Law.

8th. All public functionaries will be responsible, both personally and financially before the law.

9th. Criminal action against delinquent officials is imprescriptible.

10th. Only in case of manifest disturbance of public peace will extraordinary powers be granted to Execu - tives.

LAND AND JUSTICE

(Signatures)

_____

Manuel Gonzalez Ramirez, Planes politicos y otros documentos; 66-67.

* * * * *

611

PLAN OROZQUISTA

25 March, 1912

After a long and exceeding bitter denunciation of Francisco I. Madero and his whole administration, Pascual Orozco concluded:

Because of these facts, as heralds of national dignity, and with arms in hand and representing the revolutionary junta, we declare before the nation that:

1. The initiator of the Revolution, Francisco I. Madero, falsified and violated the Plan de San Luis Potosi.

2. Francisco I. Madero made the Revolution with the money of American Millionaires and with the indirect or covert assistance of the government of the United States. This is shown even in Madero's own declara - tions.

3. Francisco I. Madero, used Americans and other foreign nationals in his lines to assassinate Mexicans.

4. Francisco I. Madero, together with other members of his family, robbed the nation on the pretext of raising an armed force during the elections which carried him and Jose Maria Pino Suarez to the presidency and vice-presidency of the Republic.

6. Francisco I. Madero imposed interim governors by armed force and sanctions fraudulent elections in violation of the sovereignty of the states. (1)

7. Francisco I. Madero contracted for and received FOURTEEN MILLION dollars from Wall Street within two days after assuming power on the pretext of expanding the services of the National Railroad Lines (some - thing that was not of great urgency). The true object of this loan was to pay debts contracted [by Madero]

---

(1) None of the copies of the Plan Orozquista that Prof. Meyer found contained an Article 5. He supposes that probably the original was incorrectly numbered.

through two attorneys of the Water, Pierce Oil Company of the United States during the Revolution. Earlier Madero had named these two attorneys advisers of the National Railraod Lines.

8. Francisco I. Madero, in a manner prejudicial and humiliating to the nation, placed the destiny of the Fatherland in the hands of the American government by means of contemptable complacency and promises that encumbered our nationality and integrity.

9. Because of the above-mentioned indiscretions and crimes, Francisco I. Madero and his accomplices are declared traitors to the Fatherland and outside the law.

10. Because both fraud and armed force intervened in the elections of October, 1911, the election for the presidency and vice-presidency are considered null and void. As a consequence Francisco I. Madero is not recognized as president nor Jose Maria Pino Suarez as vice-president.

11. In honor of the principles of equity--and so as not to injure various interests--loans contracted with foreigners up to the date of this pronouncement will be recognized; however, it is solemnly declared that after the date of this proclamation no loan, concession, or contract made with foreigners residing in or out of the country will be recognized, even though it may be the cause of a great conflict.

12. The revolution does not recognize, and declares null and void, all concessions and contracts made by the usurping government with members of the Madero family or with blood relatives or relatives through marriage and with the so-called ministers of this cabinet. And in order to recover the capital gains made by these concessions they will be confiscated and adjudicated, one-half going to the denouncer and the other half to the orphans and widows of the victims of the revolution.

13. In order to avoid disturbances in the civil administration of towns and cities, the revolution

recognizes all present authorities as long as they adhere to the revolution and recognize its prin - ciples. If they refuse, they will be considered rebels against the fatherland and accomplices of the usurping and disloyal government; as such they will be punished with the full rigor of the law.

14. The congress of the union and the local legislatures are recognized as legitimate, as are the judicial powers of the entire Republic. They must, however, recognize the revolution, withdraw recog - nition of Madero, and pledge their concurrence with the principles proclaimed in this manifesto.

15. This being a revolution of principles, in the interest of democracy and national sovereignty, personalism is absent. As a consequence there is no provisional president nor candidate for the Pres - idency. The revolution recognizes as operative only the legislative and judicial branches of government. As stipulated in the previous article, the executive branch is considered acephalous.

16. The revolution declares the constitutional reform which established the vice-presidency of the Republic abolished and places in force the constitutional precept which invests the president of the senate as a substitute for the executive; but since at the present time there is no legislative president of the senate, since the so-called vice-president Pino Suarez was acting in that capacity, this constit - utional arrangement will be temporarily suspended until a legal regime begins to function regularly at the triumph of the revolution.

17. By virtue of the previous [article], and in agreement with the principles of the most pure form of democracy, when the revolution triumphs it will declare as interim president of the United Mexican States, the citizen designated in an election of the following type: all of the generals, chiefs, and officers of the National Revolutionary Army and civilian members of the army which occupy the capital of the Republic, will elect a junta, composed of fifteen individuals; this junta--by secret ballot

--will designate the person who will occupy the first magistracy as interim president, or, it will determine if it should establish a government junta of three members following the Swiss system, which would function temporarily as the executive; neither the interim president in the first instance, nor any member of the government junta in the second will be eligible for election as constitutional President in the following elections.

18. The interim period will last one year, beginning on the date that [the revolution] takes possession of [Mexico City.]. This will be sufficient time for complete pacification of the nation so that the people may freely exercise the right of suffrage.

19. The revolution considers the elections for deputies and senators held during the administration of the usurping government illegal because it considers those elections as the spurious fruit of a government of traitors. It therefore declares that at the moment of triumph it will recognize the present members of both chambers as legitimate representat - ives of the people only until the end of the interim government. At that time their terms will be prologued and new elections will be held simul - taneously with those for the executive. In this way the performance of the new government will be uniform and will emanate totally from the will of the people as expressed freely in the voting. This will be the case if the legislators have adhered to the revolu- tion in accordance with Article 14. [If they do not adhere to Article 14] the revolution will dissolve the chambers and the executive will assume legis - lative powers during the interim period.

20. The armed elements of the revolution, upon its triumph, will remain intact under the command of their own chiefs. These armies will remain in the areas in which they have been operating in order to serve as a guarantee for the aspirations of the revolution and for the sovereignty and rights of each of the states to which they belong. Their mission is not to support the ambitions of a single man, who arbitrarily alters the destiny of the fatherland, but rather to defend and contribute to the effectiveness

of the suffrage and the sovereignty of each one of
the entities of the federation in agreement with the
general interest of national unity (not subordinating
one to another but harmoniously consolidating them).
It is necessary that these forces support the
legitimate desires of the people. With this support
the interim government will be able to carry out the
promises of the revolution.

21. The militarization of the country is unconstitutional and contrary to democratic principles; therefore Madero's despotic law of obligatory military
service (which takes sons away from widows and
fathers from infants to support the ambitions of a
despot) is abolished. Citizens are not obliged to
serve their country in a foreign war, but under the
[principles] laid down in the constitution. In such a
manner the glorious federal army will continue
standing up as the guarantor of sovereignty and
national dignity as well as a defender of institutions, but it will be filled with volunteers who are
well paid and well fed. Its standing size in time of
peace will not exceed 28,000 men in the three arms.

22. All of the states of the federation will comply
with the obligation imposed upon them by the constitution of organizing and maintaining a national guard.
This guard will be formed by the revolutionary forces
of each state. So that the guard will not be burden -
some on the treasury, the states will maintain in
active service only that number indispensable to an
[efficient] veteran corps.

23. The instruction of the national guard will be
conducted by the federation so that it will be
uniform and efficient. Recruiting and organization
will be determined by the respective organic laws
[the state constitutions].

24. The remaining revolutionary forces, after the
formation of the veteran corps of the national guard,
will be gradually discharged after the president,
having been freely elected by the people, takes

office.

25. The presidential term of Senor General Don Porfirio Diaz will be declared terminated at the end of the interim presidency. As a consequence, the President elected by the people will begin a new term which will last six years in accordance with the law.

26. In a like manner the remaining federal functionaries, after the popular election, will be restored to the terms provided by law.

27. The executive will not be given extraordinary powers to legislate in any branch of public administration for any cause or motive, imperative as they may seem, except in the field of war so that he can mobilize and direct the army and the national guard in the case of a foreign invasion.

28. The revolution will make effective the indep - endence and autonomy of the town councils so that they can legislate and administer their taxes and other funds.

29. The duties of the _jefes_ _politicos_ throughout the entire Republic are eliminated. These duties will be performed by the municipal presidents.

30. In order to improve the federal system of the Republic, the territories of Tepic and Baja California will be incorporated as states of the federation. The opinion of the inhabitants will first be consulted. Their economic resources will be studied so that their estimated debits will not be encumbered in any harmful manner.

31. The territory of Quintana Roo will be reincorporated with the state of Yucatan from which it was separated for reasons which no longer exist.

32. In order to prevent the reduction of government control over the National Railways, the government will not, for any motive, alienate the stock which it already possesses. On the contrary, in order to acc - elerate complete nationalization of the lines in an effective manner, it will create an annual fund in

the budget for the purpose of purchasing a greater number of shares in that corporation.

33. In a like manner, in order to make the nation - alization of personnel effective, the government will encourage the practical and technical advancement of Mexican personnel and will demand that the company make substitution of Mexican personnel and will demand that the company make substitution of Mexican for foreign employees. Taking ability into consid - eration, Mexicans will be paid the same wages as foreigners.

34. In order to improve and raise the conditions of the working class the following measures will be adopted:

a) The company stores, with their systems of notebooks and charge accounts, are abolished.

b) The wages of workers will be paid totally in effective money.

c) Working hours will be reduced to a maximum of ten hours for those who work by the day and twelve hours for those who do piece work.

d) Children under ten will not be permitted to work in factories and those between ten and sixteen will only work a maximum of six hours a day.

e) [The government] will try to raise the daily wage of workers, harmonizing the interests of capital and labor, so that it does not cause an economic conflict which would obstruct the industrial progress of the country.

f) [The governmental] will demand that the owners of factories provide hygenic working conditions which guarantee the health of the workers.

35. Because the agrarian problem in the Republic demands the most careful and violent solution, the revolution guarantees that it will gradually proceed

to resolve that problem according to the following principles:

a) The property of persons who have lived peacefully on the land for over twenty years will be recognized.

b) Revalidation and improvement of all legal titles will be made.

c) Lands seized by despoilment will be returned.

d) Uncultivated and nationalized land throughout the Republic will be redistributed.

e) All of the land which the large land owners do not regularly keep under cultivation will be expropriated in the public interest after being appraised. The land thus expropriated will be partititoned to improve intensive agriculture.

f) In order not to burden the state treasuries, nor use up the reserves of the national treasury, and in order not to increase the national debt by contracting foreign loans, the government will float a special agricultural bond in order to pay for the expropriated land. The holders of the bonds will be paid four percent interest annually until their amortization. This will occur every ten years. The proceeds from the redistributed lands will form a special fund earmarked for the amortization.

g) A regulatory organic law will be dictated on this subject.

36. The official Register in the Federal District, the territories, and the states of the federation will be reorganized in an efficient manner so that an equitable leveling of taxes can be made. These will be graduated with the intervention of consulting boards for each branch or source of tax. The system of annual fees of contributors will be completely eliminated because this system is harmful, improper, and constitutes a monopoly or privilege prohibited by the constitution.

37. Freedom of the press and of thought in all its forms will be made operative without restrictions other than those imposed by Article 7 of the Constitution [of 1857] before it was reformed.

The present revolutionary plan duly satisfies national needs and aspirations. We are confident that the public will respond to our call.

The parties which go to the peaceful electoral fight with a previously designated candidate exercise a democratic right.

The revolutionary parties which, with antic - ipation of triumph, hoist a personalist banner do no more than ruin the country and enslave the people. In advance they place enormous power into the hands of a single individual. They factionalize the revolution and reinforce the strength of a single individual who can convert himself later into their executioner.

It is for this reason that this program does not proclaim any provisonal president, but merely expresses the manner in which a citizen or governing junta will be chosen to exercise the executive power of the Republic during an interim period. In this way [the revolution] guarantees compliance with and realization of national desires.

FELLOW CITIZENS: We call all patriots to our ranks; we call those who have holy faith and who dare to offer their lives for the happiness of the country; and we call all those who have abstained from participating in the fight. For the salvation of the country and national dignity there should be no distinctions between parties in this moment of common danger. In democratic countries [parties] should only fight before the election turns and not on the fields of battle.

SOLDIERS OF THE REPUBLIC: Your sacred mission is to guard the institutions of the nation and not to serve and sustain a man who criminally deceives it, robs it, floods it with anarchy, turns it over to the foreigner, impoverished and manacled.

We don't call you to insult your duties or loyalty because we do not exhort you to violate laws or overthrow constitutions but to withdraw recog - nition of the government of an ominous man who is carrying the country to ruin and slavery.

Your heroism and discipline in the last contest won you the admiration of the world!

If the chivalrous spirit in your souls evokes scruples about having to shoot fellow Mexicans, we ask that you bear in mind that this is a true fight of emancipation. Remember Colonel Morelos and the other victims who sacrificed their lives in a fratricidal war. You will be judged by the sublime Ninos Martires, who sacrificed themselves for our honor and our liberty.

Chihuahua Headquarters,   Gen. Pascual Orozco, Jr.
March 25, 1912   and others

[Sometimes called the Plan of the Empacadora
because it was signed in a cotton warehouse
of ginned, bailed cotton.]

Reprinted from Mexican Rebel: Pascual Orozco and the Mexican Revolution, 1910-1915, 138-146, Michael C. Meyer, by permission of University of Nebraska Press. Copyright (c) 1967 by the University of Nebraska Press..

* * * * *

PLAN OF FELIX [DIAZ]

16 October, 1912

Mexicans: In moments of supreme anguish for the Fatherland I come to raise my voice in order to ask for the assistance of all men of good will who are desirous of contributing to the rebirth among us of an era of peace and concord.

It is not possible to endure in silence any longer the great evils which the ominous administration that arose out of the revolutionary movement has caused and continues to be causing.

Removing the mask of democracy and altruism which he used so vilely to deceive the people and degrading it into an armed movement, he now cynically and without any right shows his true face since another was the soul of the Revolution. He proclaimed himself leader of [the Revolution] and in a moment of national frenzy elevated himself as its favorite. His true face is that of a being avid for riches for himself and for his very numerous family. [He is] without any gift for governmental administration, cruel and sanguinary like any weak and pusilanimous person, and it causes one to wonder about the state of his reason on seeing the unconscious way that he discharges the responsibility of the high post which he occupies.

Fire, loot, and slaughter with the arms which the present Government avails itself, not to defend itself against agressions, but to silence the voices of its own former partisans who cry out to it, "Fulfill your promises!" And slaughter, loot, and fire is the retaliation of deceivers, those who in the height of their madness, through the impatience of their complaints have no choice but to die fighting with arms in their hands in order not to perish hunted like wild savages on the ashes of their demolished homes, and the bodies of their sisters, children, wives, and mothers sacrificed uselessly and ignominously. Let it be known to all so that there can be no room for doubt: the present Revolution is nothing more tha a provoked insubordination demanded by the most cruel abuse of authority, by that which ignores not only property [rights], but also honor and life itself ... that which absolves even the terrible military laws.

It is necessary, then, in order that the life of the Republic should be as prosperous as it deserves to make a supreme effort to destroy the evil at its origin and to snatch power from the inept and bloody hands which abuse it.

For such a noble purpose I am going to gamble my life and that of the brave men who have gathered around me. If we die it will be with the satisfaction of having tried [to promote] the good of the country; if triumph favors us, the Provisional Government which we will institute will bring into it persons of recognized probity, intelligence, and prestige with - out distinction on the basis of political affiliation or beliefs; and that Government will work tirelessly to realize the idea written on the banner of the rebellion which it has hoisted, "Impose Peace through Justice."

As soon as the country has turned to peace, elections will be called and will be respected and the popular mandate will be sustained on a base desired by all aspirants and now vilely mocked--free suffrage and no reelection--and we promnise that the crucl joke of false elections like the last fraud - ulent one that covered the vacant Vice-Presidential position will not be repeated, it being of no legal value.

Noble Army to which since my youth I have had the honor to belong and from which I just suffered the pain of separating myself as an energetic protest that criminals taken from the steps of the scaffold, adventurous foreigners, or even relatives of the commander should be our equals or even our superiors; My Comrades, especially you my brothers, the sons of the glorious Military College, discipline has its limits as I clearly expressed to the supreme military authorities who were governing the country on August 2, 1908, in a discourse which I gave on that date at the closing of the meetings of our Association. Discipline, I repeat, has as its limit the supreme good of the Fatherland, and the arms which the Nation has delivered to you the present Government has transformed into the headsman's axe in order to impose its tyranny. I call to you to unite with us in order to perform an act of justice.

Good sons of the present Revolution, let us come together in order that our action may be more effective. Thus I offer my name along with my life, which, I promise you, will always travel the road of patriotism and honor.

All Mexicans: Lend me your moral and material means for the task of assuring the peace which I undertake with war. I do not present myself before you with the promises of impossibly good ends to be attained, nor do I resort to tricks in order to surprise your good faith as the men of the prior revolution did in a most infamous manner. I only promise you peace; I will only work for and fight for peace, and when this has become a fact, for the elimination of those who provoked war in order to benefit from the storehouses of the public Treasury between the rivers of blood of their compatriots. You will see how all the material goods will come for your benefit and within the reign of justice; all the practices of liberty will come of themselves like the natural fruit of order at work within a serene and impartial justice for all.

Let our motto be that which here I seal with my signature:

PEACE AND JUSTICE

(Signed)

Felix Diaz

Gonzalez Ramirez, Planes politicos, 129–131.

* * * * *

PLAN OF THE HACIENDA OF GUADALUPE

March 26, 1913

After a vigorous declaration to the nation on the illegalities of the administration of Victoriano Huerta, a very long list of officers of the Constitutionalist army commanded by Venustiano Carranza concluded, "The undersigned Commanders and officers in command of the Constitutionalist forces have agreed upon and we will support with arms the following

PLAN

1st. General Victoriano Huerta as President of the Republic is repudiated.

2nd. The Legislative and Judical Authorities are also repudiated.

3rd. Also the Governments of the States which still recognize the Federal Authorities of the present Administration thirty days after publication of this Plan are repudiated.

4th. For the organization of the Army charged with bringing our aims to fulfillment we name as First Commander Venustiano Carranza, Constitutional Governor of Coahuila.

5th. When the Constitutionalist Army shall have occupied the City of Mexico, it will commission as Interim President Citizen Venustiano Carranza or the one who may have come into command in his stead.

6th. The Interim President of the Republic will call for general elections as soon as peace has been secured, and will deliver his Authority to whoever may be elected.

7th. The citizen who acts as First Commander [Jefe] of the Constitutionalist Army in the States whose Administrations have recognized that of Huerta will assume the task of the Provisional Governor, and will call local elections after the citizens who had been elected to discharge the high Authority of the Federation have taken possession of their posts, as the previous article provides. (1)

(Signatures)

_____

(1) A document signed by Venustiano Carranza on March 26, 1913, reads in part, "I accept, in all its parts, the Plan of Guadalupe which was presented to me by the Constitutionalist Commanders and officers of this State on the 26th of March of the current year in the hacienda of Guadalupe."

Gonzalez Ramirez, Planes politicos, 137-138.

* * * * *

MODIFICATIONS OF THE PLAN OF GUADALUPE

1 April, 1913

Art. 1. The Federal Executive Power is hereby repudiated, regardless of who may be heading it, since the resignations of Francisco I. Madero, Jose Maria Pino Suarez, and Pedro Lascurain.

Art. 2. Also repudiated are the Legislative and Judicial Authorities of the Federation, unless within the space of ___ days, counting from this date, they have not aided the present armed movement which has as its purpose the restoration of the rule of the Constitution.

Art. 3. The Executives of the States will be disavowed if within ___ days after the date of this Plan they should still be recognizing the Federal Executive authority, present or that which may succeed it, as transmitted by usurpation. Immediately all the governors and members of the Legislatures who have been imposed by the illegitimate Administration of General Victoriano Huerta are repudiated.

Art. 4. For the organization of the army charged with bringing to fulfillment the aims of the constit - utionalist movement, I assume the character of First chief of the same, which will be known as the CONS-TITUTIONALIST ARMY in my capacity of legitimate Governor of the State of Coahuila. I count on the agreement of all the leaders [jefes] who have supported the movement of constitutional restoration.

Art. 5. When the Constitutionalist Army shall have occupied Mexico City, I shall take charge on an interim basis of the Executive Authority of the Federation as the First Chief which I am of the Constitutionalist Army, or he shall occupy it who, in case of my absence, shall substitute for me in command, provided that cannot be accomplished according to the Constitution.

Art. 6. The Interim President of the Republic will call for the election of the President, and

Vice-President as soon as peace has been secured throughout the country, and he will deliver the executive authority to the citizens who have thus been elected.

Art. 7. The Executives of the States who, in spite of the provisions of Article 3 of this Plan have not repudiated the usurping Executive Authority, will be occupied by the military commanders from among those who may have been operating in the State under consideration, or else by civilians identified with the constitutional movement. [These officials] shall call for local elections immediately after the functionaries who were elected for the discharge of these high powers of the Federation have assumed their posts, according to the prior Article.

Art. 8. A period of ___ days, counting from this date, is granted to the commanders and officers of the National Army who have supported the rebellion of General Huerta for them to return to the path of legality by placing themselves under the orders of the Constitutionalist First Cheif. Those who after the lapse of time here indicated do not support the legality of the restorative movement of the constitutional order will be tried by a Council of War.

Art. 9. Individuals of the enlisted Federal troops in the armed services are declared at complete liberty, and they may enlist in the Constitutionalist Army if they so desire.

Transitory Article: On account of the pressure which the usurpating government of General Huerta has exerted over the Federal Legislative Branch and of the connivance of some of them with him, [they] are herewith disavowed and all their acts are deemed totally illegal; likewise all contracts and decisions which may emanate from the said government of usurpation, counting from February 13, 1913.(1)

(Signed)

Roque Gonzalez Garza

---

(1) A letter to Victoriano Carranza:

To this letter you will find a copy of the modification to the Plan of Guadalupe made by me. I hope with good reason that you will take them into consideration and if you find them reasonable they will deserve your well-reasoned and authoritative attention. etc.

San Antonio, Texas.   (Signed)

Roque Gonzalez Garza.

* * * * *

PLAN OF PARACUARO

21 April, 1913

After a vigorous Considerando which condemned the administration of General Victoriano Huerta and approved of the resistance of Carranza, the paragraph concluded, "For the reasons expressed above the Revolutionary Committee [Junta] which was constituted by those Undersigned is to operate under the following conditions:"

First: The Undersigned are solemnly committed on their word of honor to keep the reserves due at this time, to work with all zeal for the reunion of the elements favorable to the ends that are being pursued and, if the circumstances precipitate, to reunite under the initiative of any of the members of the Committee which have been able to unite in order to determine what ought to be done and to reach prior agreement on who ought to assume command, with the understanding that a designation of a Supreme Commander for the movement will be made, in respect to the Undersigned, in terms of discipline for the

628

best success of the enterprise, because we all consider ourselves equally as initiators.

Second: The mission of the Undersigned will be limited to promoting the triumph of the just cause being pursued, which consists in the overthrow of President Victoriano Huerta and not to admit any other authority whatsoever which arises from his administration, and which will reestablish legally the authority constituted under the conditions which the Senores Carranza and Maytorena expressed fully in the agreement with the principal leaders who support the movement.

Third: The Undersigned will respect the Governor of Michoacan, Doctor Miguel Silva, because we are convinced that his election was popular, and that he possesses the gifts necessary to make the State prosper under his administration, provided that the central [authority] does not exert any pressure, a thing which we would oppose energetically with arms since we have them in hand, and we repudiate the Government of Huerta as illegal.

Fourth: The Revolutionary Committee lacking the financial and military resources to wage war for the purposes stated, it will resort to forced loans, to confiscation of amunition, horses, and any other element necessary to the ends being pursued, by prior agreement with the Committee; but in no case will there be sacking of property nor will assassinations or other outrages which may disgrace the cause be permitted, because the end we pursue is entirely patriotic, and after getting rid of the outside elements which members of the Committee cannot support, the Committee shall be limited strictly to those items indispensable for supporting the Committee and its forces.

Fifth: Once the cause has triumphed, we will not ask the government to confer legally any military rank or honor since our recompense later will be that of having been useful to our Fatherland and to return to our homes ready to resume the tasks which produce for us the sustenance of our families.

Sixth: Since the incidents of the struggle which we are going to undertake may deprive us of the existence of some of our members of this Committee, and since we all have large families, we solemnly promise each other that all the survivors will lend financial and moral support, or in any other nec - essary form, to the parents, brothers, widows, or children of those who unfortunately succumb in the fight for the well-being of the Fatherland.

Seventh: Except in case of greater force, the members of the Committee agree that on the 5th of May next in this heroic town to give the call for rebellion with the elements which they have been able to gather, but with the understanding that the revelation of these plans or any other unforeseen circumstance may oblige all or any one of the members to act in a way which best may promote the common interests, provided that [such actions] be not against the ends which we seek.

Those who attended the present Committee [Junta], after having heard the reading of this declaration, ratified the above and signed accordingly.

(Signatures)

Village of Paracuraro, Morelos

Gonzalez Ramirez, Planes politicos, 203-205.

* * * * *

AMENDMENTS TO THE PLAN OF AYALA

30 May, 1913

First: The first article of this Plan is revised in terms expressed below;

Art. 1. Officially the concepts contained in this article as regards the usurper of public power, General Victoriano Huerta, is applicable. His presence in the Presidency of the Republic accentuates each day and more and more his character so at odds with all that signifies law, justice, and that which is right and moral until his reputation has sunk lower than Madero. In consequence the revolution will continue until it accomplishes the overthrow of the false leader. The demands of the national public well-being demands it and are entirely in accord with the principles given in this Plan--principles which the revolution itself is determined to sustain with the same firmness and magnamimity which it has done until the present time and based upon the confidence which the supreme national will inspires.

Second: The third Article of this Plan is revised in the following terms:

Art. 3. General Pascual Orozco is declared unworthy of the honor which had been conferred upon him by the elements of the Revolution of the South and Center. Because of his knowledge of and compromises with the illicit and ominous, and false government of Huerta he has dropped in the esteem of his fellow citizens until he has reached the level of a social zero, that is, without any social significance, as a traitor to the principles to which he swore [allegiance].

In consequence, General Emiliano Zapata is recognized as the leader of the Revolution as condensed in those principles of this Plan.

                                    Emiliano Zapata and
Revolutionary Camp in Morelos

                                    other signatures.

Gonzalez Ramirez, Planes politicos, 84.

* * * * *

PACT OF TORREON

4 July, 1914

In the City of Torreon, State of Coahuila, a large delegation of officers and civilians associated with the Divsion of the North met in a large room over the Bank of Coahuila and debated the role of the Army and the progress of the Revolution. Ultimately

the delegates of the Division of the North proposed
the following reforms to the Plan of Guadalupe:

That the Plan of Guadalupe in its 6th and 7th
clauses be revised as follows:

6th. The Interim President of the Republic will call
for general elections as soon as the triumph of the
Revolution has been assured, and he will surrender
his authority to the citizen who may be elected.

7th. In the same way the ranking military commander
in each State where the administration of Huerta was
recognized will call for local elections as soon as
the Revolution shall triumph.

The same delegation agreed that the following
should be added to the said Plan:

8th. No Constitutionalist Commander shall stand for
election as a candidate for President or Vice –
President of the Republic in the elections referred
to in the prior Article.

9th. Without prejudice to the call for elections to
which Art. 6 refers, on the triumph of the election,
a Convention will meet and there will be formulated
the program which the Administration-Elect is to
follow.

"In this Convention representatives will be
elected on the ratio of one for each thousand men."

When the former proviso as well as various points
of a constitutional, military, and political nature
were advanced by the Delegates, and after having
arrived at an agreement, they declared as follows:

"When the First Chief of the Constitutionalist
Army shall take possession in conformity with the
Plan of Guadalupe of the post of Interim President of
the Republic, he shall convoke a Convention which
will have for its object to discuss and to fix the
date on which elections will be held, the program
which the functionaries who may be elected ought to
put into practice, as well as other topics of general
interest. The Convention will be composed of

632

delegates of the Constitutionalist Army on the ratio of one delegate for each thousand men under arms. Each delegate to the convention will verify his position by means of a credential which will be countersigned by the Commander of the respective Division."

[An afternoon session was devoted to discussion of a political disagreement in the State of Sonora, and the First Chief was asked to intervene for the sake of harmony among the Revolutionaries. On the following day the delegates of the Division of the North asked the Assembly to be so kind as to approve the proviso which is as follows:]

7th. The nomination and removal of employees of the Federal Administration in the States controlled by the Constitutionalist forces lies exclusively with in the province of the First Chief, and he shall assign their jurisdictions and authority.

"The Divisions of the North and the Northeast, understanding that the present [conflict] is a struggle of the disinherited against the powerful, pledge themselves to fight until the ex-Federal Army completely disappears and the Constitutionalist Army shall take its place; to promote the democratic regime in our country; to punish and subdue the Roman Catholic clergy which ostensibly allied itself with Huerta, and to emancipate economically the prole - tariat by making an equitable distribution of lands and by promoting the well-being of the workers."

When offered for discussion, the Delegates of the North accepted the proposition in principle, and with additions and the following corrections it was approved in the following terms:

8th. "The prsent conflict being a struggle of the disinherited against the abuses of the powerful, and understanding that the causes of the misfortunes which afflict the country emanate form a prae - torianism, from a plutocracy and from the clergy, the Divisions of the North and Northeast solemnly pledge themselves to fight until the ex-Federal Army

shall disappear completely; to implant in our nation
a democratic regime; to promote the well-being of the
workers; to emancipate economically the rural workers
by making an equitable distribution of lands, or by
other means which tend toward the resolution of the
agrarian problem, and to admonish, punish, and to
demand the proper responsibilities of the members of
the Roman Catholic clergy who both materially and
intellectually have aided the usurper, Victoriano
Huerta."

With the above [approved], the delegates of the
Division of the North concluded the meeting, since
they had unanimously approved the provisions in the
present resolution which was prepared in quadrup-
licate, and they duly signed along with the Secre -
taries.

(Signatures)

Gonzalez Ramirez, Planes politicos, 152-156.

* * * * *

ADDITIONS TO THE PLAN OF GUADALUPE

12 December, 1914

After extensive Considerandos related to the
progress of the Revolution, General Venustiano
Carranza, speaking in the name of the commanders of
the Constitutionalist Army, the Governors of the
States, and the laborers in the Cause, felt it
suitable to decree the following:

Art. 1. The Plan of Guadalupe of 26 march 1913
continues in effect until the complete triumph of the
Revolution, and, therefore, the Commander Venustiano
Carranza will continue in his role as First Chief of
the Constitutional Revolution and as the one vested
with the Executive Power of the Nation until the
enemy has been conquered and peace established.

Art. 2. The First Chief of the Revolution vested with
Executive Power will expedite and put into effect

634

during the struggle all the laws, dispositions and measures designed to give satisfaction to the eco - nomic, social, and political necessities, thus acc - omplishing the reforms which public opinion demands as indispensable for establishing the regime which may guarantee the equality of Mexicans among them - selves; [for promoting] agrarian laws which will favor the formation of small property by dissolving the big landholdings [latifundios] and restoring to the people the lands of which they were unjustly deprived; [for drafting] fiscal laws designed to secure an equitable system of taxation on real estate; [to design] legislation to improve the con - dition of the rural peasant, of the laborer, of the miner, and of the working classes in general; [to secure] establishment of municipal liberty as a constitutional institution; [to provide] bases for a new system of organization of an Independent Judicial Branch, both in the Federation and in the States; [to order] revision of the laws relative to marriage and the civil state of persons; [to declare] dispositions which will guarantee the strict fulfillment of the laws of the Reform, revision of the Civil, Criminal, and the Commercial codes; reforms of judicial pro - cedure with the aim of expediting and making effec - tive the administration of justice, revision of laws relative to the exploitation of mines, oil, water, timber, and the natural resources of the country, and to prevent this being done in the future; [to institute] reforms which may guarantee the faithful application of the Constitution of the Republic, and in general to provide laws which may be deemed necessary in order to assure to the inhabitants of the country the full and effective enjoyment of their rights and of equality before the law.

Art. 3. In order to be able to continue the struggle and in order to be able to bring to accomplishment the work of the reforms which are referred to in the preceding Article, the Chief of the Revolution is expressly authorized to convoke and to organize the Constitutionalist Army and to direct the operations of the campaign; [he is authorized] to name governors and military commanders of States and to remove them

635

freely; he is also to make expropriations on grounds of public welfare which may be necessary for division of lands, the funding of towns, and other public services; [he is authorized] to contract loans and to issue notes on the National Treasury with indication of the properties which will guarantee them; he may also name and freely remove federal employees as well as those of the civil administration of the States and define the qualification of each one of them, and to make directly or through the Chiefs which he may authorize the requisitions of lands, buildings, arms, horses, vehicles, provisions, and other necessities of war; and to establish military decorations and to decree recompense for services devoted to the Revolution.

Art. 4. On the triumph of the Revolution and with the Supreme Command reinstalled in the City of Mexico and after elections to the Town Councils [Ayuntamientos] in the majority of the States have been completed, the First Chief of the Revolution, as the one vested with Executive Authority, will call for elections for the Congress of the Union and will set the date and the manner in which the elections are to be held.

Art. 5. The Congress of the Union being installed, the First Chief of the Revolution will render an account of the use he has made of the powers which have for the present been invested in him, and especially he will submit to it the reforms expedited and placed into effect during the struggle so that Congress may ratify them conditionally or completely, and so that he may raise to the level of constitutional issues those which are of that character, before constitutional order may be reestablished.

Art. 6. The Congress of the Union will expedite the corresponding calls for the election of the President of the Republic, and once this has been done, the First Chief of the Nation will hand over to the person elected the Executive Authority of the Nation.

Art. 7. In case of the total absence of the present Chief of the Revolution and while the Generals and

Governors are proceeding to elect another who is to substitute for him, the Commanding General of the Army Corps will temporarily discharge the First Chief's office from the place wherever the Revolutionary Government may be when the First Chief may be found absent.

Constitution and Reform

(Signed)

Venustiano Carranza,
Adolfo de la Huerta
Chief of Staff.

Silva Herzog, La revolucion Mexicana, II, 160-168.

* * * * *

PLAN OF FELIX DIAZ

23 February, 1916

The Undersigned, met in the encampment of Tierra Colorado, State of Vera Cruz, on the 23rd of February 1916, decided to undertake an armed movement in the Republic, in conjunction with those other groups which have been initiated already in various parts of the country. [We will] work for the reestablishment of order, the reorganization of our authorities and institutions under the legal norms which were in effect on the 10th of October, 1913, the date when General Huerta dissolved the Congress of the Union which was legally elected by the people. Protesting their determination to fight to the end, advancing the salvation of the country as the sole object by means of the cessation of anarchy, the re-installation of public authorities, the re-establishment of our institutions and improvement of our working classes, they agreed upon the following:

First: The Army to which is entrusted the task referred to in the preceding paragraph is hereby designated The National Reorganizing Army.

Second: Citizen Felix Diaz is named General-in-Chief of the said Army.

Third: There are conferred upon the said Chief for the duration of the campaign for the reaffirmation of institutions and reestablishment of peace extra - ordinary and ample powers in the branches of War, Finance and Administration.

Fourth: The National Reorganizing Army will aid and cause to be fulfilled all the decrees issued by the General-in-Chief in the use of the powers which this act confers upon him.

Fifth: It is declared that from the 10th of October, 1913, General Victoriano Huerta, on dissolving the Congress of the Union and interrupting the constitutional order, became a usurper of public functions. In respect to functionaries who may have contracted responsiblities for acts which have a direct connection with that act, they are subject to what the Law and the Courts define in that matter.

Sixth: All acts and contracts executed by the Citizen Victoriano Huerta after October 10th, 1913, and all decrees, laws, and dispositions of general observance issued by the so-called Congress of the Union which substituted for the 26th Legislature of the Congress of the Union are repudiated. All private interests created in good faith under the shadow of such acts, contracts, and laws will be respected in so far as they do not conflict with public interest.

Seventh: All the acts and contracts of the gangs and groups which under diverse persons have usurped the functions which the Law reserves for functionaries elected by the people are declared null and of no effect and are incapable of being revalidated. Essentially and originally national sovereignty stems from those elected by the people and from them must emanate all public authority if it is to be legitimate. As a consequence, all verifiable acts through whom they derived the authority of which they were said to be invested whether of military rank or nomination arising from gangs or groups alluded to or

638

simply by force which they have been able to exert in order to support the usurpation are declared null also.

Eighth: The towns and communities of indigenous people who feel that they have been robbed of their property, whose use or ownership legally belonged to them, once order has been reestablished, will be able to reclaim the plunder before competent Courts, even when the authors of [the seizure] find themselves supported by decisions which may have executive authority. Immediately an exception to the Stamp Tax and of every other effort made by the towns to recover their property will be granted, and the Courts will give preferential attention to these reclamations and will substantiate them as rapidly as possible.

Ninth: Considering that the desire to own land is a legitimate manifestation of the desire to progress by means of work, and that the subdivision of rural property and its improved use will increase public wealth and, therefore, the good of all social classes, the program of reorganization will embrace very largely the problem of the division of lands. For this purpose, as soon as order has been re - established, a commission will be created to study each and all of the formulas proposed to satisfy such aspirations, and it will accept forthwith as firm and secures bases for the solution which will be adopted as follows:

a) There will be returned to the towns all the village lands [ejidos] and lands set aside for common use of which they may have been unjustly deprived; and to all those towns which are lacking them, lands will be given in such a way as to satisfy their necessities. For this purpose they will be acquired through the nation and following the procedure which the law requires for expropriations for reasons of public welfare in those cases in which the present owners prove that their rights are based on some quite legal title; but otherwise proceedings will be begun as the law provides for cases of dispossession.

b) All national lands and all underdeveloped properties not restricted by private ownership will be set aside principally for the formation of ag - ricultural colonies whose lots will be distributed by preference among those individuals who, as enlisted troops, have given their services for order by fighting in the ranks of the National Reorganizing Army.

c) The Government of the Union will expropriate through legal proceedings against the large landowners that part or parts of the estates or haciendas which may be necessary in each region to meet the demand for requested lands by the working classes, in accord with the special law which will regulate this matter.

d) Laws for facilitating and protecting contracts of partnerships and joint operations will be prescribed. Fiscal legislation will be drafted which, taxing the big landholding in direct relation to its size and reducing the taxes on small property, will favor the subdivision of haciendas, thus placing the poor farmer in a more favorable position than the great landholder so far as taxes on rural property are concerned.

e) The allotment of water and of irrigation works necessary for village lands and agricultural colonies constitute works of preferential national interest, and the Government which will be established is solemnly obligated to secure its prompt execution.

Tenth: The legal rural entities and the ejidos which the people still own cannot be divided unless it be with the consent of those people themselves as expressed in the manner which the law will provide on matters related to the subject.

Eleventh: All confiscations which have been made are declared entirely null as well as those which are being made in violation of the constitution provision which declares that the penalty of confiscation is forever abolished. All persons who through any title whatever should acquire confiscated lands whether in

ownership or by leasing, in possession or by virtue
of grant of free use, or under any other type [of
title] are obligated to return all property, moveable
or immovable, to their legitimate owners whenever the
latter shall reclaim them, without prejudice to the
deforciants [detentadores] who are subject to the
responsibilities for which, according to the laws,
they may have incurred.

Twelfth: The adjudication of moveable or immovable
property by public auction or by any other method,
when they may have originated through lack of payment
of impositions or taxes, of monthly payments, money
or capital given in satisfaction of lapsed payment
which were guaranteed by mortgage or loan will be
void, provided that the facts have been verified
within the last three years or that it be verified in
the future until order be established, if it suffices
to prove by the damaged parties that the lack of
payment was due to the absence of the owner, the
necessity of remaining hidden, or the impossibility
of a representative appearing in court and that all
this was acknowledged as the cause for the necessity
of eluding political persecutions.

Thirteenth: No property, neither public nor private,
through authority or some person may be occupied
without the full consent of the owners. As for the
public [property] the consent ought to be expressed
by the public functionary who represents the entity
to which the property legally belongs. An exception
to this rule will be the occupation of property
demanded by the operations of war, but such occupation will always be transistory and without forgetting in any event the nature or ownership and its
rights, and among the latter that of being indemnified for the damage which may be caused.

Fourteenth: No agricultural negotiation, commercial
or industrial, may be subjected to an intervention if
it is not through the order of a competent Judge.

Fifteenth: The inhabitants of the Republic will enjoy
full religious liberty. All religions and religious
sevices [cultos], without any distinction, shall have

the free exercise which the Constitution of 1857 and the Laws of the Reform grant to them.

Sixteenth: Immediately the various towns may be occupied by the National Reorganizing Army, the local authorities and the Courts will be installed in them so that public administration may recover its normal function. On establishing the Provisional Government in the capital of the Republic, the Supreme Court of Justice of the Nation and subordinate Courts will be installed--also on a provisional basis. Then the Mexican People will be called to elect the Legis - lative Branch after a Law of Amnesty has been issued; [this law] given the circumstances which prevail, will facilitate the union of all Mexicans and bring to an end an era of hate and vengeance. The Congress of the Union, elected by the people, will convoke elections for the other Branches.

Seventeenth: The Administration to be established will recognize all contracts and concessions given by prior legitimate governments to citizens or to either Mexican or foreign business provided that they are in accord with the principles of Law.

Nineteenth: The motto of the National Reorganizing Army as well as the partisans and citizens who are cooperating in the national reorganization pledge themselves not to support candidates in the elections which are brought about with the purpose of install- ing the Federal Authorities whom the People will finally elect if these candidates do not accept the principles of this Act as they may apply hereafter. And all those who were present affirmed that it was necessary to demand that all those who wished to incorporate themselves into the National Reorganizing Army should pledge adhesion to this Act.

FELLOW CITIZENS: Now you know the propositions which will carry us to victory or death: the moment has come to appeal to arms in order to reconquer the liberties which they have snatched from us without pity, even the liberty of conscience which is the base and support of the others, in order to rebuild our homes so basely leveled, in order to assure our

children of the right to live like civilized beings
on their own land, to erase by means of work and the
peaceful exercise of our own rights the shameful
things which make us blush, to expel forever the
hatred and the desires for vengeance which has
transformed the great Mexican family into a group of
bloody fratricides, and finally to punish those who
pretend to deprive us of our Fatherland.

Accompany me to the struggle although in it we
may have to sacrifice our lives which are as nothing
if we lose them in order to save the life of the
Republic which, bled white and in agony, is about to
expire.

(Signed)

Felix Diaz

M. Gonzalez Ramirez, Planes politicos, 223-227.

* * * * *

PROGRAM OF POLITICAL-SOCIAL REFORMS OF THE
REVOLUTION

18 April, 1916

The Revolution proposes to realize the following
reforms:

Art. 1. To destroy big landholding [latifundismo] and
to create small property holdings, and to provide to
every Mexican who solicits it a piece of land sufficient to meet his needs and those of his family, with
the understanding that preference will be given to
the rural peasants.

Art. 2. To return to the village the common lands
[ejidos] and the water of which they have been
despoiled, and to give to other towns who do not have
them or at least not sufficient lands for their needs.

Art. 3. To promote agriculture, funding Farm Banks
which will provide capital for the cultivation of

small holdings, and investing in irrigation works, the planting of forests, in communication routes, and all the sums necessary for any other kind of works for the improvement of farming to the end that our soil produce the riches that it is capable of.

Art. 4. To promote the establishment of regional agricultural schools and experiment stations for the teaching and application of the best methods of cultivation.

Art. 5. To authorize the Federal Government to expropriate real estate on the basis of the value presently declared to the Tax Collector by the respective owners, and once the agrarian reform is consumated, to adopt as a basis of expropriation the taxable value which is found in the latest declara - tion which the interested parties have made. In both cases popular action is granted to denounce the properties badly evaluated

The Problem of Labor

Art. 6. To prevent the misery and the future exhaustion of the workers by means of timely social and economic reforms such as the following: a moralizing education, laws covering accidents while at work and pensions for retirement, regulation of hours of work, provisions which guarantee sanitation and safety in workshops, factories, and mines, and in general through legislation to make less cruel the exploitation of the proletariat.

Art. 7. To recognize the unions and workers' societies as juridial persons so that businessmen, capitalists, and bosses would have to treat with strong and well organized unions of workers and not with the isolated and defenseless operative.

Art. 8. To give guarantees to workers, recognizing the right to strike and the right to boycott.

Art. 9. To suppress the company stores [tiendas de raya], the system of vouchers for the payment for a day's work in all the negotiations of the Republic.

Art. 10. To protect natural children and women who may have been the victims of masculine seduction by means of laws which will grant to them wide rights and will sanction investigation of paternity.

Art. 11. To favor the emancipation of workmen by means of a judicious divorce law which will cement the conjugal union on the basis of mutual esteem and love, and not on the meanness of social prejudice.

Art. 12. To attend to the prodigious needs of education and lay instruction which make themselves felt in our midst, and to this end to realize the following reforms:

I. To establish with Federal funds elementary shcools throughout the Republic where, today, the benefits of education have not reached, without prejudice to the States and Municipalities which continue with those [benefits] for those who depend on them.

II. To demand that the institutions of primary instruction devote more time to physical education, to manual training, and to practical instruction.

III. To finance normal schools in each State or regions where they may be needed.

IV. To elevate the remuneration and the esteem of the teaching profession.

Art. 13. To emancipate the National University.

Art. 14. To give preference in higher education to the teaching of manual arts and industrial applications of science over the study and promotion of the so-called liberal professions.

Art. 15. To promote reforms which the common rights demand so urgently in accord with the social and economic necessities of the country; to modify the legal codes in this sense, and to suppress all cumbersome technicalities in order to make expeditious and efficient the administration of justice, so as to avoid assisting the litigants of bad faith.

Art. 16. To establish special proceedings which may permit the artisans, workmen and employees rapid and efficient collection of the value of their work.

Art. 17. To avoid the creation of every sort of monopoly; to destroy those in existence, and to revise the laws and concessions which protect them.

Art. 18. To reform legislation dealing with corporations in order to prevent the abuses of the boards of directors [juntas directivas] and to protect the rights of minority stockholders.

Art. 19. To reform the legislation according to the following principles: To favor mining and oil exploration; to promote the establishment of a bank to finance mining; to prevent the monopolization of vast areas; to grant liberal and meaningful rights to discoverers of metalbearing deposits; to grant to the State proportional participation in the gross production in the two industries mentioned; to declare as lapsed pertinent conscessions in case of suspension or possible reduction of work for more than a certain time without justifiable cause, the same also in cases of waste of the said riches or for the violation of laws which protect the life and health of the workers or nearby inhabitants.

Art. 20. To revise the laws, concessions, and railroad rates; to abolish the rate differentials on matters of transport and to guarantee [indemnity] to the public in case of accidents.

Art. 21. To declare as available for expropriation by reason of public utility the lands necessary for the passage of oil pipelines, canals for irrigation, and all forms of communication destined to the service of agriculture and the oil and mining industries.

Art. 22. To require of the foreign companies who may wish to do business in Mexico to fulfill the following requirements:

I. To establish in the Republic executive agencies [junta directivas] sufficiently competent to authorize the declaration of dividends, to present information to stockholders, and to exhibit all types

646

of books and documents.

II. To comply with the rule, until today unobserved, of being submitted to the jurisdiction of Mexican courts which will be the only ones competent to pass judgment on lawsuits which originate in reference to the interests based here, and, likewise, on the judicial demands which may be presented against the companies.

Art. 23. To revise the import taxes, the stamp taxes, and the other federal imposts, so as to produce better bases for taxation; to destroy the present exemptions and privileges in favor of the big capitalists, and to lower the protective tariffs gradually without injuring the interests of national industry.

Art. 24. To exempt all items of prime necessity from any type of indirect taxation.

Art. 25. To exempt artisans and small-shop merchants from any sort of taxation as well as farms of negligible value.

Art. 26. To abolish the so-called personal or the poll tax and other similar imposts.

Art. 27. To abolish the system of equalization both in the Federation and in the States.

Art. 28. To establish a progressive tax on inheritances, legacies, and gifts.

Art. 29. To tax the operations of loans now contracted, whether they have or do not have a mortgage guarantee, with a tax which will fall exclusively upon the creditors and which these latter persons will pay on receiving the tax on their loan.

Art. 30. To tax with heavy duties the sale of processed tobacco and alcoholic drinks, and to establish prohibitions against the latter when their manufacture is made with items of prime necessity.

Art. 31. To establish a real estate and fiscal census throughout the whole Republic.

Political Reforms

Art. 32. To establish effectively the independence of municipalities, by providing wide freedom of action for them so as to permit them to attend efficiently to communal interests and so may preserve them from attacks and control by local and federal administrations.

Art. 33. To adopt the parliamentarian form of Government for the Republic.

Art. 34. To abolish the Vice-Presidency of the Republic and the Political Chieftancies [Jefaturas Politicas].

Art. 35. To abolish the Senate, a conservative and aristocratic institution par excellence.

Art. 36. To reorganize the Judicial Branch on new bases in order to obtain independence, competence, and responsibility of its functionaries and to make effective also the responsibilities which other public agents who are paid in the fulfillment of their duties may incur.

Art. 37. To initiate the system of direct voting both in Federal as well as in local elections and to reform the electoral laws of the Federation and of the States so as to prevent the falsification of the vote of citizens who can neither read nor write.

Art. 38. To punish the enemies of the revolutionary cause by means of confiscation of their property and in acordance with just procedures.

Transistory Articles

First: The naming of governors which has been made or which hereafter will be made by the local committees [juntas] of the States shall be submitted for validation to the ratification of the Sovereign Revol-

648

utionary Convention.

The following will serve to deny ratification:

I. If the nominee has not committed himself to total agreement to Article 13 of the Plan of Ayala.

II. If the candidate is lacking in prior revolu - tionary credentials.

Second: The governors will be subject to removal by the convention, the prior process being in due form, when they violate the Plan of Ayala or the present Program of Reforms, or when they may commit serious crimes against the common good; a when they shall tolerate or allow to go unpunished the abuses which their subordinates may commit, or give shelter to the reactionary elements in the recesses of the Govern - ment.

Third: Only those leaders [jefes] who had taken up the cause of the revolution before the fall of Victoriano Huerta shall have the right to take part in the local elections.

REFORM, LIBERTY, JUSTICE, and LAW	(Signed) Jenaro Amezcua representing General
Jojutla, State of Morelos	Eufemio Zapata, and others.

Gonzalez Ramirez, Planes politicos, 123-127.

* * * * *

A DECREE REVISING CERTAIN ARTICLES OF THE
PLAN OF GUADALUPE

14 September, 1916

Venustiano Carranza, First Chief of the Constitutionalis Army and vested with Executive Power of the Republic, in the use of those powers which I find myself vested, and

649

CONSIDERING [herewith follows a very long explanation of the developments within the Mexican revolutionary experience, developments which require revisions of the previously amended Plan of Guadalupe]

For reasons given above I have felt it suitable to decree the following: Art. 1. Articles 4, 5, 6 of the Decree of 12 December, 1914, issued in the H. Vera Cruz are revised in the following terms:

Article 4: The Constitutionalist cause having triumphed and elections for Town Councils [Ayuntamientos] are being held throughout the Republic, the First Chief of the Constitutionalist Army, vested with the Executive Authority of the Nation, will call for elections for a Constituent Congress and shall set the date and the manner in which they shall be conducted, and the place where the Congress is to meet.

In order to form the Constituent Congress the Federal District and each State and Territory shall name a proprietary deputy and an alternate for each 60,000 inhabitants or a fraction which may exceed 20,000, based upon the general census of 1910. The population of any State or Territory which may be less than the figure which has been set in this general declaration shall elect one proprietary deputy and an alternate nevertheless.

In order to be elected a Deputy to the Constituent Congress, the same requisites demanded for the Constitution of 1857 will be necessary in order to be sent as a Deputy to the Congress of the Union; but besides those individuals who would have had the impediments which the said document stipulated, those who may have aided with arms or served as public employees in the governments or factions hostile to the Constitutionalist cause cannot be elected.

Art. 5. The Constituent Congress being installed, the First Chief of the Constitutionalist Army, Vested with the Executive Authority of the Union, will present to it the draft of a revised Constitution in order that it should be discussed, approved, or modified, with the understanding that in the said draft the declared reforms and those which may have been issued until the meeting of the Constituent Congress will be included.

Art. 6. The Constituent Congress may not concern itself with any other subject than that indicated in the prior Article; it ought to discharge its commission in a period of time not to exceed two months, and on concluding its task it will issue the Constitution so that the Chief of the Executive Branch, in conformity with it, may call for elections of general authorities throughout the Republic. Its labors terminated, the Constituent Congress will dissolve.

The elections for the Federal Authority verified and the General Congress installed, the First Chief of the Constitutionalist Army, Vested with the Executive Authority of the Nation, will present a report on the state of public administration, and having made the declaration of the person elected for President, he will deliver to the elected one the Executive Authority of the Nation.

Art. 2. This decree will be published by solemn edict throughout the whole Republic.

CONSTITUTION AND REFORMS

(Signed)

Venustiano Carranzo

Gonzalez Ramirez, Planes politicos, 197-202.

* * * * *

PLAN OF MILPA ALTA

The Revised Plan of Ayala in Milpa Alta

6 August, 1919

We, the Undersigned, former revolutionaries of the South, proclaim to the Mexican people the following Revolutionary Plan.

First: The Political Constitution of 1857 is declared in effect along with the reforms which in this situation are made in accord with those provisions which it, itself, provides.

Second. The properties of which they may have been despoiled during past administrations are restored or repossessed to the persons or civil communities, with the understanding that only those who possess their legal titles should enter into possession of their property immediately, and the despoilers will be at liberty to plead the rights which they may allege before the respective courts.

Third: Expropriation is declared by reason of public utility through indemnification, this being the form which agrees with the Administration for all the lands in the Republic with the exception of those properties which do not exceed fifty hectares in the States that are lacking in land, and one hundred hectars in which there is an abundance of land.

Fourth: The division of the expropriated lands is ordered in lots or parcels which will be assigned to the laborers and to the C.C. who intend to devote themselves to agriculture.

Fifth: The size of the lots or parcels will be such that they will satisfy the necessities of one family.

Sixth: The assignment of property into lots or parcels of land will be free to those who take up arms in order to defend this Plan, and to the widows and orphans of those who have succumbed in the fight defending the division of land, and the lots will be

652

sold to pay for them in thirty years in the form of payments or in annual mortgages to persons who were not a part of the armed conflict.

Seventh: The lots or parcels of land which are being cultivated will revert to the Treasury at so much al millar for the year of contribution for the land which the Government shall indicate, and it will levy an extra charge of 75 millar for parcels which fail to be cultivated.

Eighth: The lots or parcels of land which the Government shall allot may not be rented, encumbered, nor sold before fifty years have elapsed since the date of its adjudication.

Ninth: Outside colonization will be given preference as a basis for establishing a colony, but are to be formed by settlers of the race most advanced in agriculture, for each ten villages of aborigines, and that settlement referred to is embraced within the boundary laid out for the mentioned settlements so that the aborigine laborers by this method would improve the system of cultivating their lands.

Tenth: The waters used and suitable for irrigation of lands of the Republic are declared available through regular indemnification for the waters belonging to private individuals.

Eleventh: To the lots or parcels of property of those who take up arms in defense of this Plan, or the widows and orphans of those who have succumbed in the struggle for the division of land, grants of water will be gratis, but to the persons who are not embraced in the armed struggle the allocation of water will be sold to them so that they can pay in the form of installments or in annual assessments in a period of twenty, thirty, or forty years the cost of the irrigation works which the Government will bring to completion.

Twelfth: [We declare] that the Government which may emanate from the Revolution by means which it judges most advantageous for the country will establish a

National Farm Bank so that it may be concerned only and exclusively with assisting the small land owners to obtain credit.

Thirteenth: [We declare] that improvement of [the condition of] the worker should be searched for and carried out in an effective way, for which laws will be established which will offer guarantees to the worker as well as the landowner and that the laws should prove equitable for both parties.

Fourteenth: [We declare] that with the triumph of the Revolution the principal revolutionary leaders of the Republic will meet to designate a provisional President of the Nation and the Provisional Magistrates of the Supreme Court of Justice of the country.

Fifteenth: The Governors of the States will be designated by the Provisional President of the Republic.

Sixteenth: The Provisional President of the Republic and the Provisional Governors of the States will, within the first three months of their admin - istration, issue calls for elections for Deputies and Senators to the Congress of the Union and the local congresses of the States respectively.

Seventeenth: Within the first three months after being in office the Congress of the Union, and at the initiative of the C. Provisional President of the Republic, the former shall make the reforms to the Constitution of 1857 in order to embrace within it the principles which the Revolution proclaims.

Eighteenth: Six months after the Provisional President of the Republic and the Provisional Governors of the States have assumed their duties, the latter shall immediately call for elections within the four months without possibility of prorogation from the date of the call for election of the Constitutional President of the Republic and Constitutional Governors of the States and the election of other public officials who may be needful.

Nineteenth: We who subscribe to the present Plan promise under oath to fight to victory or death for the ideals of the said Plan.

Effective Distribution of Land or Death

(Signatures)

M. Gonzalez Ramirez, Planes politicos, 90-92.

* * * * *

PLAN OF AGUA PRIETA

23 April, 1920

After four paragraphs of Considerandos the sponsors of the Plan continue:

The Organic Plan of the Movement for Recovery of Democracy and Law

Art. 1. Citizen Venustiano Carranza shall cease to exercise the Executive Authority of the Federation.

Art. 2. The public officials whose investitures takes its origin in the latest election of Local officials as verified in the States of Guanajuato, San Luis Potosi, Queretaro, Nuevo Leon, and Tamaulipas are repudiated.

Art. 3. Likewise repudiated are the legal advisers of the Council of Mexico City as they were elected in accordance with the latest elections which were celebrated in the said capital.

Art. 4. Commandant Jose Santos Godinez is recognized as the Constitutional Governor of the State of Nayarit.

Art. 5. Likewise all the other legitimate authorities of the Federation and of the States are recognized. The Liberal Constitutional Army will support the said authorities provided that they do not show themselves hostile to the present movement.

Art. 6. The Political Constitution of the 5th of February, 1917, is expressly recognized as the Fundamental Law of the Republic.

Art. 7. All the generals, leaders, [jefes], officers, and soldiers who may support this Plan will constitute the Liberal Constitutional Army. The present Constitutional Governor of Sonora, Commandant Adolfo de la Huerta, will exercise on an interim basis the authority of Supreme Chief of the Army with all the facilities necessary for the political and administrative organization of this movement.

Art. 8. Each one of the Constitutional Governors of the States which recognize and adhere to this Plan within the space of thirty days counting from its promulgation will name a duly authorized repre - sentative for the purpose that when the said dele - gates have met within sixty days from the date of the issuance of this Plan and at a place to be designated by the Interim Supreme Chief they may procede directly to name by a majority of votes the Supreme Chief of the Liberal Constitutional Army.

Art. 9. If, by virtue of the circumstances originating in the campaign, a majority of the Committee [junta] of Delegates of the Constitutional Governors to which the previous article refers may not meet on the date specified, then the present Constitutional Governor of the State of Sonora, C. Adolfo de la Huerta, will become officially the Supreme Chief of the Liberal Constitutionalist Army.

Art. 10. As soon as the present Plan shall be adopted by the majority of the Nation and the City of Mexico is occupied by the Liberal Constitutionalist Army, procedures will be initiated to name a Provisional President of the Republic in the manner indicated in the following articles.

Art. 11. If the Movement should be successful before the term of the present period of the Federal Congress, the Chief of the Liberal Constitutionalist Army will call the Congress of the Union into extraordinary session in a place where it is possible to meet and the members of both houses will elect the Provisional President in conformity with the Constitution now in effect.

Art. 12. If the event foreseen by Art. 10 should occur after the termination of the constitutional period of the present Houses, the Supreme Chief of the Liberal Constitutional Army will assume the Provisional Presidency of the Republic.

Art. 13. The Provisional President will issue a call for election of the Executive and Legislative officials of the Federation immediately after taking possession of his office.

Art. 14. The Supreme Chief of the Liberal Constitutionalist Army will name provisional governors of the States of Guanajuato, San Luis Potosi, Queretaro, Nuevo Leon, and Tamaulipas, and also [governors] of those [states] which do not have Constitutional Governors; and also [he shall name] all those other Federative Entities whose ranking officials may oppose or repudiate this movement.

Art. 15. With the triumph of this Plan secure, the Provisional President shall authorize the Provisional Governors to call for elections immediately of Local Authorities in conformity with respective Laws.

Art. 16. The Liberal Constitutionalist Army will be administered according to the General Ordinance and Military Law presently in force in the Republic.

Art. 17. The Supreme Chief of the Liberal Constitutionalist Army and all the civil and military authorities who may support this Plan will require guarantees from nationals and foreigners, and they will protect especially the development of industry and commerce, and all businesses.

Effective Suffrage   No Re-election

(Signed)

General of Division P. Elias Calles
and other Generals of Brigades.

M. Gonzalez Ramirez, Planes politicos, 251-256
Antonio G. Rivera, La revolucion en Sonora, 525-526.

* * * * *

REVOLUTIONARY MANIFESTO OF DON ADOLFO
DE LA HUERTA

7 December, 1923

After a general condemnation of the adminis -
tration of President Obregon for various high-handed
actions, Adolfo de la Huerta concluded:

In the face of such evils which it is necessary
to bring to an end, and having been nominated by the
great majority of the nation as a candidate for the
Presidency of the Republic, I would be lacking the
fundamental duty of a citizen if I did not respond to
the national outrage which has resolved not to
support a Government which goes against our
Constitutional principles. For this reason, and
accepting provisionally as an honor the leadership of
the liberating movement which the patriotic soldiers
have initiated and supported as representatives of
the people, I therefore issue the present Manifesto,
thus letting the Nation understand the basic
postulates to which it will be subject.

I. Absolute respect for the life and liberty and the
property of all habitants, nationals, and foreigners.

2. Immediate enforcement of Art. 123 of the Federal
Constitution so as to delineate equitably the
prerogatives of the workers and the obligations of

the owners.

3. For the resolution of the most intense national problem--land and justice for all--[I shall promote] establishing and organizing the small farm property for anyone who truly wishes to cultivate the soil, breaking up of the big farm holdings in strict obedience to the spirit of the constitutional Art. 27 with the Government mediating actively, efficiently and fairly between the big landowners and those getting land, [mediating] the endowment of ejidos for those towns which as yet have not left the communal state and only until the development of those communities and by petition they may wish to enter the system of private property. Indemnification by reason of expropriation for ejidal endowment will be determined by means of the formation of a property census for the purpose of paying in accord with the fiscal value and with equity. For payment in cash for these indemnifications a loan of fifty million pesos will be made which in substance was already settled when the undersigned on his authority served as Secretary of Treasury and Public Credit. In order to refinance the small proprietors there will be established throughout the country institutions for farm credit so as to facilitate the cultivation of land and increase produciton. The bonds of the farm debt originating from the partition of the latifundia and the constitution of the small property owner will be floated in the domestic and foreign market with the direct intervention of the Federal Government so as to make possible the payment of the indemnifi - cation in cash.

4. We will be absolutely irrevocable in respect to the suffrage which today for the third time has been violated in the course of the last ten years in order to guarantee the sovereignty of the people forever.

5. Constitutional reform in order to establish the effective abolition of the death penalty, save that a traitor ought to suffer it in a war with a foreign power.

6. Granting of suffrage to women, duly registered and

she being educated to the discharge of communal
duties.

7. Intensification not only of [book] instruction,
but of education in a practical form.

With these postulates and through the basic
principles expressed, the repudiation of the
Executive Power of the Union is reiterated; also
repudiated are the State Governors and repre -
sentatives to the Congress of the Union who may have
supported or do not support the burdensome and
unlawful labor of the President of the Republic.
Equally to be repudiated are those other function -
aries of popular election, direct or indirect, who
within fifteen days do not indicate their adherence
to the present movement.

(Signed)

Adolfo de la Huerta

Issued in Vera Cruz.

Gonzalez Ramirez, Planes politicos, 266-269.

* * * * *

PLAN OF EL VELADERO

26 May, 1926

After a survey of Mexican history since the
conquest, a survey which stressed the suppression of
the Indian race, the Undersigned continued....

The cause which I defend, like all those that
have been drafted by the free nations of the world in
order to achieve progress and civilization, will come
to constitute the happiness of our native Land;
therefore look at and reflect upon the sound
principles on which its hopes are based.

1) The Fundamental Charter promulgated at Queretaro
on the 5th of February, 1917, is recognized.

2) Fron now to eternity we repudiate the 13th proviso of the Plan of Iguala of 1821, for through it the Spaniards assured to themselves the property that they were managing was to be stripped from the Mexican nation by force; therefore they had no legitimate right to possess it.

3) General expulsion of Spaniards and nationalization of property which they hold as a compensation for the plunder visited upon the nation by virtue of the 13th clause of the said Plan.

4) The return of Spaniards to the Mexican nation will not be permitted until fifteen years after the nationalization of the property vested in the nation, even when they may return under the protection of another flag.

5) All public or private documentation through which title to real estate or businesses that may have been recorded in the Public Registry of Property and Trade prior to the date of May 6th, 1926, in the name of Spaniards will be null and void. Whether Mexican or foreigner, he shall be dispossessed of it. Furthermore, all scribes and notaries, judges, or whomsoever may verify title of this nature will be punished as criminals guilty of high treason against the Fatherland; so likewise those employees and directors of the migration offices who permit the entrance of Spaniards who may leave the national domain after the 6th of May, 1926, and then return nationalized in any other country.

6) Title to the properties restored to the nation will pass to the free municipality for its management as a source of our life, be they urban properties, factories, or any kind of industries which Spaniards own in the Mexican nation, and their usufruct will be destined only and exclusively to the promotion of public education and of national agriculture.

7) The property restored to the nation which may consist of rural estates will immediately be turned over to those towns, parties, settlements, or groups who, lacking property, may apply according to the

procedure of the Decree of January 6, 1915. The delivery or possession shall be verified by the military leaders of the present movement which will be legal and recognized as such by the governments of the nation. This charge includes the big landowners of the country.

8) In conformity with that provided for in Title One, Section One of the General Constitution of the Republic, the lives and the property of nationals and foreigners NOT Spaniards will be protected and respected.

9) The interests of non-Spanish foreigners which during the course of the war may be damaged by reason of force shall be paid immediately by the Government from the property which has reverted to the nation.

10) The States of the Republic which adhere to or support the Liberating Movement of the Mexican Economic Recuperation will recognize as the directing body that [unit] established in the State of Guerrero in accordance with the present Plan.

11) Those disabled while campaigning [in support of this Plan] will be liberally compensated and assisted; the parents, widows, and the children of those who succumb during the struggle will be pensioned and protected until their death by all the governments of the nation.

12) This Plan totally redrafts the manifesto of Linares, N(uevo) L(aredo) issued to the Mexican nation on the 16th of September, 1922, by the citizens Richard and Robert D. Fernandez and F. Batista. Separate appeals are made to the country peasants, to the National Army, and to foreign nations.

                              (Signed)

El Veladero,   Amadeo S. Vidales,
District of Tavares   First Chief,

Municipio of Acapulco,   Mexican Economic
Guerrero.   Regeneration.

M. Gonzalez Ramirez, Planes politicos, 270-278.

* * * * *

PLAN OF VASCONCELOS

10 December, 1926

[After a sharp indictment of the Calles political complex for its denial of freedom of the ballot, for its fraudulent procedures, and for its "dictatorship without decency, without honor," Vasconcelos concluded with the following:]

Considering, then, that it is necessary to demand of the people that it carry forward the effort that is implied in the vote, I address myself to all my fellow citizens, and I ask their firm support for the following resolutions:

I. It is declared that in the Republic there is for the present no authority more legitimate than Licenciado Jose Vasconcelos, elected by the people in the primaries of 17th of November, 1929, for the Presidency of the Republic. As a consequence there will be punishment for all authorities, including members of the Army, who continue giving support to the Administration which has betrayed the purpose for which it was created.

II. The undersigned President-Elect will present his protest according to law before the first freely named Town Council in the Republic which is able to receive it, and then he will proceed to organize a legitimate Administration.

III. Hereby repudiated are all the de facto auth - orities, both those of the States and the Muni - cipalities who, for thirty years have been bleeding the country, raiding the public Treasury and creating ruin and confusion of the Fatherland, and have endeavored to scoff at the public vote in the latest presidential election.

IV. The citizen in each and every one of the States who may take command of the forces which will expel the incumbents of public office shall take charge of the local Government on an interim basis, and will proceed to organize it in accord with the laws then in force, with the proviso that his governmental acts shall receive the ratification of the legitimate President of the Republic so that he may conform with his authority, but even so he will not lose his character as a provisional officer.

V. In each Municipality the people shall freely name those citizens who are to take charge of Municipal Administration.

The President-Elect now procedes to a foreign land, but he will return to the country to assume direct control as soon as there may be a group of armed free men who may be able to make him be respected.

Let the above be circulated and fulfilled.

(Signed)

Given in Guaymas,   J. Vasconcelos

State of Sonora.

M. Gonzalez Lopez, Planes politicos, 316-319.

* * * * *

MANIFESTO OF GENERAL ENRIQUE GOROSTIETA

as issued from the glorious region of Los Altos

28 October, 1928

(The text circulated surreptitiously in Mexico City)

After an extensive justification for the revolt against the Plutarco Calles administration, and after many calumies circulated by the Government, General Gorostieta has declared the following:

1) Having been named by genuine national repre - sentation, I [Enrique Gorostieta] assume the post of Chieftan of the Liberating Movement.

664

2) The Liberating Movement, in both its civil and military order, is subject henceforth to the following principles:

3) The repudiation which the Liberators declared against all the usurping powers both of the Federation and of the States is hereby confirmed.

4) The establishment of the Constitution of 1857 WITHOUT the Laws of the Reform is hereby declared; but to be incorporated into its precepts and therefore revising the said articles are the modifications which the national referendum of 1926 demanded, supporting the petition drafted by the illustrious Mexican prelates under the date of 6th of September of that year and also the amplifications contained in the "Catholic Memorial" as presented to the Houses [of Government] on the 3rd of September, 1928.

5) The Constitution may be reformed by the process established in Art. 127 of the same, and by "plebicite" or "referendum" in order that all citizens, armed or not, should be able to make known their desires, and thus the Mexican people might have at last a Constitution truly their own, [one] born out of their desires and traditions and which corresponds to the needs of the people.

6) In cases where use is made of the "plebicite" or "referendum", adult women shall have the obligation to vote.

7) Whatever measures that have been issued up to the present date and which have as their purpose the recognition of the right of the working man to form unions, to gain his rights, to defend them and to better his condition shall be recognized, provided that they be fair. The application of these said measures shall be effective for all those in whose behalf they were issued and not for the benefit of favorites.

8) In reference to ejidal allotments, the Liberating Government will establish commissions that will reach

agreements between the residents of the ejidos and the owners, and it will adopt adequate procedures for indemnification that should be paid to the latter in order to be effective and fair. Furthermore, the distribution of rural properties will be continued for the common good, but in a just and equitable manner and with prior indemnification; in this way it will be possible to make property available to the greatest number.

9) Our liberating forces constitute the "National Guard," a name that will be used hereafter, and the slogan of the "National Guard" shall be "God, Fatherland, and Liberty."

10) The civil leader of the Liberating Movement will be named by the Directive Committee of the National Defense League of Religious Liberty after prior consultation to determine the feelings of the National Guard, and in the meantime the Military Commander will recognize as leader the person who may be named by agreement between the Directive Committee and the Military Commander.

11) The Military Commander shall have all necessary authority in the areas of Treasury and War.

12) This Plan may not be modified save by common agreement between the Directive Committee of the National Defense League of Religious Liberty and the Military Commander.

13) Once named Civilian Leader by the Directive Committee of the National Defense League of Religious Liberty, the Military Commander shall retain all the authorities which appertain to his office and he shall recognize in the latter body the Supreme Authority of the Liberating Movement.

14) On capturing the Capital of the Republic and reestablishing order in the nation, political reconstruction of the same shall proceed in conformity with the precepts of the Constitution of 1857.

[The Plan concludes with exhortations to "Liberators, true Revolutionaries, old soldiers, and companions in the struggle." Also, "Viva Christ the King! Viva the Virgin of Guadalupe! and Death to Bad Government!"]

Gonzalez Ramirez, Planes politicos, 280-287.

* * * * *

PLAN OF HERMOSILLO

3 March, 1929

[After a three-page essay on the inadequacies of the Calles Administration, after condemning it for the outrage to public conscience, and after concluding with a total repudiation of provisional President, Emilio Portes Gil, the Army officers, undersigned, led by Generals Francisco R. Manzo, Fausto Topete, Roberto Cruz, Eduardo C. Garcia, who were indignant at the assassination of former President Obregon, issued the following terms:]

1) The Provisional Presidency of the United Mexican States, now vested in Emilio Portes Gil, is hereby repudiated.

2) All those who occupy the posts of deputies and senators of the Congress of the union and who either directly or indirectly combat or oppose the present movement shall cease the discharge of their offices.

3) Members of the Supreme Court of the Nation who combat and oppose either directly or indirectly the present movement shall surrender their duties on the said Tribunal.

4) The governors, deputies, and magistrates of the individual Federative agencies who, in either a direct or indirect manner combat or prove hostile to this movement shall cease the discharge of the duties embraced in their investiture.

5) If on the triumph of this Plan there should be in

the Federal [Legislative] Houses a majority of its members who may have recognized and sanctioned this movement, this [majority] shall proceed in due course to the designation of a new Provisional President in the form as prescribed in the terms of the Constitution of the Republic.

6) In the event that at the triumph of this movement it should not be possible to compose the General Congress legally, the leader of the movement shall call for an extraordinary election of Deputies and Senators as soon as possible and shall dictate all the measures pertinent to the complete and prompt reestablishment of the constitutional regime in the country.

7) In the event that the Supreme Court of Justice of the Nation should have been dissolved, the Provisional President who may designate the Congress shall oversee the integration of the said Tribunal in due course and with due legality.

8) If, with the triumph of this movement the authority of some of the Federal entities should disappear through having fought against the present Plan or have been opposed to it, local Congresses, or in their place the Senate of the Republic, shall decree the reintegration of the same in due course and legally.

9) In case the Federal Congress should not be reestablished legally at the triumph of this Plan, it shall be the inherent duty of the Chief Executive of the Union to do so.

10) During the time of fighting and provided that a constitutional regime has not been reestablished in the country, it shall be the responsibility of the commanding officer of this movement to form by appointment a provisional Administration for the dispatch and administration of public affairs of the country.

11) The leader of this movement is authorized to make appointments of provisional governors and chiefs of

operations which he may consider federal [in scope] until a constitutional regime may be established.

12) Also the leader of this movement is authorized to decree all measures which he may consider necessary in order to safeguard the national interest.

13) The organized forces which recognize and support the present Plan and those which may expressly adhere to this Plan during the period of struggle and who subordinate themselves to the same will make up the Reforming Army of the Revolution.

14) The Commanding General of Division, General Jose Gonzalo Escobar, is recognized as the supreme Commander of this movement and of the Reforming Army of the Revolution.

15) The leader of the movement and commanding officer of the Revolution shall have all the powers necessary to direct the military campaign in the country and to decree all those measures of a military nature which may secure the triumph of the movement and the interests of the Nation. On inviting the Mexican People to support this armed protest as the only form of amputating the prophetic evils which overwhelm our country, we do it in the conviction that all hope of national betterment has been exhausted as long as Elias Calles, without any rights whatsoever, continues to pilot the ship of State with those perverse purposes that have always constituted his normal conduct, and preferring as we do to shed blood rather than permit this bungling man to abuse in so open a manner the civil liberties which the Great Revolution has won and so discourage foot-draggers and traitors. After the infamous assassination of General Alvaro Obregon when the Fatherland was inundated with a black surge of an uncertain future, an act for which Elias Calles has been considered either directly or indirectly responsible, after the premeditated declarations given out even before the miserable deed, in which he declared that he would leave the country free to enter wholly into the "Institutinal Regime," free of the system of self - serving provincial chieftains--declarations ridi-

culed as the finest example of cynicism, after the insolent action of this dreadful man, who, without running any risk whatever, was managing the shabby structure of imposition politics such as the slaughter of brothers in the States of Jalisco, Colima, and Michoacan only because they claimed the sacred right based upon liberty of conscience, after the obvious incapacity of Lawyer Emilio Portes Gil to shake off the disgraceful influence of the man who continues to be responsible for the fact that the soil of the Fatherland is stained again with the purple blood of all the liberties, after he has made the State of Sonora hostile with his brutal autonomy, after having the clear conviction that the finger of Plutarco Elias Calles has guided the course of the daggers which wounded his protector, Alvaro Obregon, Flores, Gil, Villa, Serrano, and recently General Samaniego, there remains no other meaningful course other than to say to our people, "To Arms! The defense of national liberties demands from us a new effort." Now let us exterminate the power of the reactionaries; it is necessary now to exterminate the traitors of the Revolution and of Liberty.

Down with the domination of Plutarco Elias Calles.

Down With Imposition.

We want to constitute a society free to think, to believe, to work according to the provisions of our laws which have been won at so great sacrifices.

(Signatures of the Military)

M. Gonzalez Ramirez, Planes politicos,. 295-300.

* * * * *

MANIFESTO OF COLONEL HERNANDEZ NETRO

15 May, 1938

After four pages of violent condemnation of the Cardenas Administration for its various and total inadequacies, the Governor of the State of San Luis

Potosi concluded:

For all the prior considerations and others that could be brought for his discredit, we echo the popular clamor for putting an end to the sufferings of the people, that will register the opinion of all sectors which call for piety and justice before the barbarous Administration of the sectarian group of Cardenas. The 35th Local Legislature of the Free and Sovereign State of San Luis Potosi

DECREES THE FOLLOWING:

Art. 1. The Free and Sovereign Government of San Luis Potosi reassumes its Soveriegnty and repudiates the Central Administration presided over by General Lazaro Cardenas because, with his Administration, he has interfered with the faithful observance of the General Constitution of the Mexican Republic.

Art. 2. The repudiation to which the prior article refers shall last until the complete reestablishment of constitutional order.

Art. 3. The Free and Sovereign Government of San Luis Potosi reassumes its historical responsibility immediately and abrogates completely any national representation, and as a consequence declares that it represents the Legitimate Institutions.

Art. 4. The present Legal movement will have as its faithful standard the exact observance of the General Constitution of the Republic.

Art. 5. The present movement of defense of the exact fulfillment and observance of the General Constitution of the Republic will be achieved by force of arms if necessary.

Art. 6. The Army which with arms in hand defends the present Legal movement which may be set forth in this Statute will be named The Mexican Constitutional Army.

Art. 7. General of Division Saturnino Cedillo will be named Commander-in-Chief of the Mexican

Constitutional Army which will guarantee the armed development of the present movement which will cause observance of the Constitution to prevail.

Art. 8. A space of thirty days from the date of the issuance of this decree is designated as the time in which the other legislatures, governors of States, and the Congress of the Union may recognize the Legal movement for faithful observance of the Constitution, and it declares to be Traitors to the Fatherland those who do not support it, and they stand thereby exposed by such circumstances to corresponding sanctions for opposing a movement of constitutional revindication which guarantees the veritable existence of our free Fatherland.

Art. 9. On the triumph of the movement the Local Legislature of the Free and Soveriegn State of San Luis Potosi and the other Legislatures which may have supported this legal movement shall be charged with designating a substitute President who shall finish the term of Lazaro Cardenas and shall call for elections for the succeeding legal period.

Art. 10. Contributions which may be paid to the anti-Constitutional regime presided over by Lazaro Cardenas will not be recognized after the promulgation of the present Decree.

Art. 11. The Commander-in-Chief of the Mexican Constitutional Army is authorized to dispose of such funds as may be found in public offices of the towns that are being incorporated into the Legal movement, and in case these funds may not be sufficient for the expenses of the war, the said Commander-in-Chief is authorized to contract loans, either voluntary or forced. With the triumph of the movement restitution to the value of such loans will be made, but a receipt or corresponding document must be offered to cover these loans.

Transitory Provisions

a) All the Leaders and Offices of the Army who may support the legal movement will be promoted one grade immediately higher. The perquisites for the Army will be augmented in the following manner: Soldiers, two pesos per day and a twenty-five percent increase over the present scale from Corporal to General of Division, quite apart from the assignments and bonuses made for unhealthy climates and other reasons that may be necessary.

b) The medal to be awarded with the decoration "Favorite Son of the Fatherland" will be created, and will be granted without exception to all Mexicans who may take an active part in this movement for the revindication of constitutional order.

c) The slogan CONSTITUTION, JUSTICE, AND LAW is adopted.

The Executive of the State understands the above and will cause it to be published, circulated, and obeyed. Given in the Hall of Sessions of the Hon - orable Congress of the State.

Therefore, I order the present Decree to be executed and fulfilled, and that all authorities shall cause it to be kept and observed and to this effect it is printed, published, and circulated for all to whom it may concern.

(Signed)

Secretary-General of Government

_____

M. Gonzalez Ramirez, Planes politicos, 323-325.

* * * * *

PLAN OF THE ALMAZANISTAS

22 September, 1940

The Substitute Constitutional President, General Hector F. Lopez, to his fellow citizens:

On establishing in this place, temporarily, the seat of Executive Power of the Federation of which I find myself invested by agreement with the legitimate Congress of the United Mexican States and substitu - ting for the functionary who did not know how to honor the solemn oath which he made to keep and cause the Constitution to be kept, my first act is to inform my fellow citizens and the inhabitants of all the nation of the norms and principles which will guide the operations of the Substitute President.

The government over which I preside arose from the most genuine and indisputable expression of the will of the people. In order to fulfill their mandate, it is indispensable to guide the nation along a truly liberal path, advanced and progressive, from which it has departed. My brief role will be directed, absolutely, in making this mandate of the people effective--[a mandate] which usurpers pre - tended to supplant.

Without any compromise whatever with reaction - aries, domestic or foreign, whatever may be the pretext with which the totalitarian triumvirate of Hitler-Stalin-Mussolini may stamp them, I will take care to raise the standard of living of all Mexicans, of all Mexicans without distinction, both spirit - ually, morally, and materially, and at the same time giving special attention to the helpless. These latter ones have been the most exploited and oppressed by a policy which, with sarcastic cruelty, proclaims that they are the objects of its special concern in order to achieve the goal of a republic of the proletariat.

Our program, in both the political and social [area] will continue being the Constitution of 1917.

Sincerely democratic, and as an old soldier of Madero, the administration over which I preside will guard with zeal and devotion the rights and liberties of Mankind, and of our democratic institutions--all immently menaced by the agents of the totalitarian triumvirate whom we will sweep from our Fatherland without any compassion or condescending exceptions, since they ought to be resisted tenaciously, inflexibly by free men of the whole world.

674

Within the framework and for the ends here expressed I will make use of all the powers which the Honorable Congress of the Union has conferred upon me in the departments of Government, Treasury, and National Defense, and within a few days I shall name the Secretaries of the Cabinet.

The reality of Mexico, troubling and difficult, living at the threshold of the most intense hunger--a direct product of a government of unprepared persons, imitators of totalitarian efforts--cannot nor ought not to serve to cover up or justify electoral fraud, the most obvious and cynical falsification of the sovereignty of the people. On the contrary, to tolerate usurpation of public power and with it the continuation of the only party (a totalitarian party) and the "six-year plans" (Communist plans) which have determined that troubling reality would be to work for the consummation of national disaster.

Those who today rebel against the Government are not the only ones who have sought to cover themselves with the sacred mantle of the Fatherland. All the usurpers of Mexico allege that over and above the defense of democratic institutions is the Fatherland which they dare to personify.

After forcing the mind of the child and of young people into the hard mold of Marxist Communism, of attacking the inviolability of conscience and the moral unity of the family; besides exercising an illegal despotism and of extending from first one place to another persecution and political assass - ination in order to impose a successor, when the land of our elders and of our children is turned into an international dumping ground and is attracting and receiving the political and social outcasts, the troublesome agents of foreign government; after all this unpatriotic labor [the Administration] has the audacity, the nerve to occupy the venerable stage of Father Hidalgo in order to ask the union of all Mexicans, [to ask] appeasement which would be nothing less than complicity in usurpation, the cowardly renunciation of Democracy.

Such a union and such appeasement cannot exist because they do not exist in the world [of Mexicans]. If Democracy is truly the bond and the standard of Liberty which the Western Hemisphere has raised on high, if the union of the American Republics, reiterated in the Conference in Havana is to preserve Christian civilization in them in order to defend our families, our homes, our corporal and spiritual liberty, all that which enobles and dignifies the human being and to defend it for the free determination of the popular will, then our first duty is and shall be to defend and to preseve the democratic institutions of Mexico, presently ignored and outraged.

In order to overcome the international totalitarian threat with the banner of Democracy, it is indispensable that each American Republic should attain an internal victory with the abnegation and the bravery of its sons who are guided by this same banner.

In order that Mexico should be an active and effective member in the defense of Democracy in the Americas and not a disturbing element for the straw man dummy of foreign dictators, it is imperative--[a decision] which cannot be postponed--that all Mexicans restore the power of national sovereignty which "resides essentially in the people," and as was manifested in the elections of the 7th of last July. It is necessary for us to install the Legislative and Executive branches with full powers of their office, as the people themselves indicated. The union of Democracy in the Americas would be a myth without the existence of Democracy in each one of the Republics.

Our present mission is to defend and reintegrate Democracy in Mexico, and if, in order to defend it "the calamity of a fratricidal war" should happen, those at fault will not be those whom we represent and those whom we support as legally elected to public office, but those who attack them and who ignore the sovereignty of the people.

In order to fulfill this high civic duty I issue

676

a call to the Mexican people, to all men and women who are resolved to be free to make their rights as citizens be respected, so that with the means which everyone has within his reach he may block the consumation of electoral fraud and of usurpation by adding his efforts to those of this Government. I trust that each and everyone will fulfill his duty and I can assure [them all] that at the end of our sacrifices and self-denial which will be accompanied by the understanding of all democratic people, liberty, order, and social justice shall reign.

                              (Signed)
Yautepec, Morelia.

                    Hector F. Lopez,

                    Substitute Constitutional

                    President of the Republic.

M. Gonzalez Ramirez, Planes politicos, 326-328.

* * * * *

And now after all these years, after all the Plans there is nothing more to say. They are Mexico's unique contribution to the science of politics, and, as the lawyers say, "Res ipsa loquitur."

* * * * *

THE POLITICAL PLANS OF MEXICO

681

684

685